W9-CIJ-365

*The Charlton
Standard Catalogue of*

ROYAL
DOULTON
BESWICK
FIGURINES

Fifth Edition

By
Jean Dale

Introduction
by
Louise Irvine

W. K. Cross
Publisher

The Charlton Press

Birmingham, Michigan ●Toronto, Ontario

COPYRIGHT AND TRADEMARK NOTICE

Copyright © 1996 Charlton International Inc. All Rights Reserved

Photographs © Charlton International Inc. 1996

No part of this publication, except the HN and M Numbering Systems, may be reproduced, stored in a retrieval system, or transmitted in any form by or by any means, electronic, mechanical, photocopying, recording, or otherwise, without the prior written permission of the copyright owner.

No copyright material may be used without written permission in each instance from Charlton International Inc. Permission is hereby given for brief excerpts to be used in newspapers, magazines, periodicals and bulletins, other than in the advertising of items for sale, providing the source of the material so used is acknowledged in each instance.

The terms Charlton, Charlton's, The Charlton Press and abbreviations thereof are trademarks of Charlton International Inc. and shall not be used without written consent from Charlton International Inc.

The words Royal Doulton are a registered trade mark of Royal Doulton (UK) Limited and are used herein to express items of collector interest.

While every care has been taken to ensure accuracy in the compilation of the data in this catalogue, the publisher cannot accept responsibility for typographical errors.

DISCLAIMER

Products listed or shown were manufactured by Royal Doulton (UK) Limited. This book has been produced independently and neither the author nor the publisher has any connection whatsoever with either Royal Doulton (UK) Limited or the Royal Doulton International Collectors Club. Royal Doulton is a registered trade mark and is used in this book with the permission of Royal Doulton (UK) Limited. Any opinions expressed are those of the author and not necessarily endorsed by Royal Doulton (UK) Limited.

Canadian Cataloguing in Publication Data

The National Library of Canada has catalogued this
publication as follows:
Charlton standard catalogue of Royal Doulton figurines (1991)
    The Charlton standard catalogue of Royal Doulton
figurines
Biennial.
2nd ed. (1991) —
Title varies slightly.
Issued 1981 as a monograph, with no set frequency,
under the same title.
ISSN 0228-6947
ISBN 0-88968-161-9 (5th ed.)
1. Royal Doulton figurines - Catalogs.   I. Title: Royal Doulton figurines

NK4660.C54   38.8'2'0294   C91-031034-3

Printed in Canada
in the Province of Quebec

The Charlton Press

Editorial Office
2010 Yonge Street
Toronto, Ontario M4S 1Z9
Telephone: (416) 488-4653 Fax: (416) 488-4656
Telephone: (800) 442-6042 Fax: (800) 442-1542

EDITORIAL

Editor	Jean Dale
Editorial Assistant	Nicola Leedham
Editorial Assistant	Davina Rowan

SPECIAL THANKS

The publisher would like to thank Louise Irvine for writing the introduction to *The Charlton Standard Catalogue of Royal Doulton Beswick Figurines*, and for her research in connection with the Doulton Lambeth and Vellum sections added to the fifth edition. Louise Irvine is an independent writer and lecturer on Royal Doulton's history and products.

Thanks also to Royal Doulton plc for supplying information and photographs, and to Pamela Smith, Manageress, of the Royal Doulton Shop, Stoke-on-Trent.

Thanks also to the Powerhouse Museum, Sydney, Australia for providing the photograph of Diana from their collection.

Also we would like to thank Harvey May for his contribution of the original Beswick figure research which was a foundation for future Beswick listings.

CONTRIBUTORS

The following contributors graciously supplied photographs, price lists, data and other invaluable information for the fifth edition for which we offer a profound thank you:

DEALERS

Gavin Attenbury, Lawleys, London, England; **George and Nora Bagnall**, Precious Memories, Winsloe, P.E.I.; **Arnie and Judi Berger,** Yesterday's South, Miami, Florida; **Laura Campbell**, Site of the Green, Dundas, Ontario; **Charles and Joann Dombeck,** Plantation, Florida; **Arnold and Margaret Krever**, Marnalea Antiques, Campbellville, Ontario; **Glynnis Moyter**, Fingal's Cave, London, England; **Ed Pascoe**, Pascoe and Company, Miami, Florida; **Jamie Pole**, Seaway China, Marine City, MI; **Tom Power**, The Collector, London, England; **Eugene Truitt**, Tru-Find Collectables, Richmond, Virginia; **Bea and John Vitkovics**, Parma, Ohio; **Princess and Barry Weiss**, Yesterday's, New City, N.Y.; **Paul Williams**, Great Britain Collectables, Toronto, Ontario; **Stan Worrey**, Colonial House Antiques and Gifts, Berea, Ohio.

COLLECTORS

John and Diana Callow, London, England; **Frank Eck**, Ohio; **Dr. Stanley Jones,** Newcastle upon Tyne, England; **William L. Peck,** Seattle, Washington; **H. Rothberg, Marilyn and Peter Sweet,** Bolton, England; **Bob Tschantz**, Berea, Ohio; **Lucy Weizer**, Florida; **D. Wertzberger**

A SPECIAL NOTE TO COLLECTORS

We welcome and would appreciate any comments or suggestions in regard to *The Charlton Standard Catalogue of Royal Doulton Beswick Figurines* that you might have. If you would like to participate in pricing or supplying new data, such as information on unlisted figures or varieties, please call Jean Dale at (416) 488-4653.

CONTENTS

THE LISTINGS

On the pages that follow, Royal Doulton figurines are listed, illustrated, described and cross-referenced in numerical order by HN and M numbers. Their names immediately follow their numbers.

When two or more figures have the same name - but different physical modelling characteristics - they are listed as **Style One**, **Style Two** and so on after their names. Such figures will also have different HN numbers.

When known, the figurine's modeller or **Designer** is listed next.

What then follows is the figure's **Height**, given in inches and centimeters.

The actual **Colour** (or colours) of the figure is listed next.

The date (or dates) when the figure was **Issued** then follows.

The HN numbers of all **Varieties** are then listed. Only colour differences, other minor decorative alterations and slight changes in size due to firing constitute varieties. Different physical modelling characteristics constitute different styles, dictating different HN numbers and so are not called varieties.

If the figure is part of a **Series**, that series name is given next.

The final listing gives the **Price**, the current market value of the figure described. The price appears in U.S. funds, then Canadian dollars and then pounds sterling.

Although the publisher has made every attempt to obtain and photograph all figurines and their varieties, several pieces, naturally, have not come into the publisher's possession. In a number of cases, then, photographs of some figures have been used to represent unobtainable varieties of that particular piece. The reader is cautioned, then, that photographs are to be used for design characteristics only. The more specific details of a figurine (i.e. colourway) should be determined from the actual information printed below the specific figure.

A WORD ON PRICING

The purpose of this catalogue is to give readers the most accurate, up-to-date retail prices for Royal Doulton figurines in the United States, Canada and the United Kingdom.

To accomplish this, The Charlton Press continues to access an international pricing panel of Royal Doulton experts who submit prices based on both dealer and collector retail price activity as well as current auction results in the U.S., Canadian and UK markets. These market figures are carefully averaged to reflect accurate valuations for the Doulton figurines listed herein in each of these three markets.

Please be aware that prices given in a particular currency are for figurines in that particular country. The prices published herein have not been calculated using exchange rates - they have been determined solely by their supply and demand within the country in question.

A necessary word of caution. No pricing catalogue can be, or should be, a fixed price list. This catalogue, therefore, should be considered as a guide only - showing the most current retail prices (based on market demand within a particular region) for the various figurines.

Current figurines, however, are priced differently in this catalogue. Such pieces are priced according to the manufacturer's suggested retail price in each of the three market regions. For example, **Gardening Time** (HN 3401) has been priced at $250 in the U.S., $330 in Canada and £99.95 in the UK as this is how it is priced by the three Doulton divisions themselves. It should be noted, however, it is likely dealer discounting from these prices will occur.

The prices published herein are for figures in mint condition. Collectors are cautioned that a repaired or restored piece may be worth as little as 50 percent of the value of the same figurine in mint condition. The collector interested strictly in investment potential will avoid damaged figurines.

Doulton has produced the HN series of figurines for over 80 years. Over this period, changes in trademarks (or backstamps as they are often called) and other base markings have naturally occurred. Earlier examples of figurines manufactured basically unchanged over the years will become available. The **Old Balloon Seller** for example, was issued from 1929 to the present. Older examples of such figures may have unique markings on their bases. These markings often dictate an earlier date of manufacture. Prices in this catalogue are for figurines without regard to any special marks on their bases - such as hand-written script titles and HN numbers, designer's signatures or the phrase "Potted by Doulton & Co." These older (and often harder to find) markings are illustrated and discussed in detail on page 22 under "A Guide to Backstamps and Dating."

In this regard, of the figurines that have enjoyed long production periods, the advanced collector will naturally prefer older examples of the same model. Such figures are not marked with their year of production, but the knowledgeable collector will recognize older pieces by their unique marks and their special workmanship that can include careful and subtle painting, delicate flesh tones and more detailed modeling that can be seen in individual flower bouquets, balloon clusters and so on.

Rarity, age and artistry are the characteristics that most often make the value of one figurine greater than another. It is generally thought that many of the early discontinued figures were produced in quantities of less than 2,000. Usually, figures manufactured more recently have been made in quantities greater than this. However, it is a Royal Doulton business practice to limit production by systematically discontinuing figures at the same time as they introduce new ones. According to the latest published lists, over 300 different Royal Doulton figurine versions are currently in production.

A further word on pricing. As mentioned elsewhere, this is a catalogue giving prices for figurines in the currency of a particular market (Canadian dollars for the Canadian market; U.S. dollars for the American market; and Sterling for the UK market). The bulk of the prices given herein are not determined by currency exchange calculations but by actual market activity in the market concerned.

An exception, however, occurs in the case of current figurines and very recent limited editions issued in only one of the three markets. Since such items are priced by Doulton only in the country of sale.

Additionally, collectors must remember that all relevant information must be known to make a proper valuation. When comparing auction prices to catalogue prices, collectors and dealers must remember two important points.

First, to compare "apples and apples," be sure that auction prices realized for figures include a buyer's premium if one is due. Prices realized for figures in auction catalogues may not include these additional costs. Secondly, if a figure is restored or repaired, this fact may not be noted or explained in the listings and as a result, its price will not be reflective of that same piece in mint condition. Please beware of repairs and restorations and the effect they may have on values.

INSURING YOUR FIGURINES

As with any other of your valuables, making certain your figurines are protected is a very important concern. It is paramount that you display or store any porcelain items in a secure place - preferably one safely away from traffic in the home.

Your figurines are most often covered under your basic homeowner's policy and there are generally three kinds of such policies - standard, broad and comprehensive. Each has its own specific deductible and terms.

Under a general policy, your figurines are considered 'contents' and are covered for all of the perils covered under the contractual terms of your policy (fire, theft, water damage and so on).

However, since figurines are extremely delicate, breakage is treated differently by most insurance companies. There is usually an extra premium attached to insure figures against accidental breakage by or carelessness of the owner. This is sometimes referred to as a 'fine arts' rider.

You are advised to contact your insurance professional to get all the answers.

In order to help you protect yourself, it is critical that you take inventory of your figurines and have colour photographs taken of all your pieces. This is the surest method of clearly establishing, for the police and your insurance company, the items lost or destroyed. It is also the easiest way to establish their replacement value in the event of a tragedy.

HN AND M NUMBER SEQUENCING

In an effort to help readers understand the numbering rationale of Royal Doulton, we have included a chart on the following page outlining the sequencing of all existing HN and M series numbers. It shows the existing gaps in numbering when HN and M numbers have been used for items not listed in this catalogue (animals, birds, wall masks, bookends, napkin rings and so on). It also contains additional notes.

In the text of this catalogue, an asterisk (*) in the lower left corner of a listing indicates that one or more of the following HN or M numbers was either not issued or used for a piece other than a figurine. A black square (■) in a listing indicates there is additional information to be found in the chart below.

The black and white photographs in this publication identify figurines in shape and overall design only. Colours, patterns and glazes may differ within individual figurines.

MISCELLANEOUS AND UNISSUED HN NUMBERS

An asterisk (*) in the lower left corner of a listing signifies that one or more of the following HN or M numbers was not issued. It can also denote items produced but not included in this catalogue (animals, birds, wall masks, bookends, napkin rings, etc.). A square (■) in the lower left corner of a listing signifies further information.

HN 100 -299
Animal and Bird Figures
HN 360 - Not Issued
Page 70 - Note: HN 423, 423A - E; Due to the size of these figures the HN number is not recorded on the base. However the model number is incised and thus this style can be identified by the model number.

HN Number	Model Number
423	291
423A	295
423B	296
423C	299
423D	300
423E	301

HN 452 - Not Issued
Page 84 - Note: HN 529 to 541 and 544, 545 and 546 were discontinued in 1932 as HN numbers and renumbered as M numbers.

HN 574 - Not Issued
HN 602 - Not Issued
HN 607 - Not Issued
HN 737 - Not Issued
HN 800 - 1200
Animal and Bird Figures
HN 1239 - 1241 - Bird Figures
HN 1381 - 1386 - Not Issued
HN 1403 - Not Issued
HN 1415 - Not Issued
HN 1477 - Not Issued
HN 1590 - 1597 - Wall Masks
HN 1601 - 1603 - Wall Masks
HN 1608 - 1609 - Wall Masks
HN 1611 - 1614 - Wall Masks
HN 1615 - 1616 - Bookends
HN 1623 - 1625 - Bookends
HN 1630 - Wall Mask
HN 1658 - 1661 - Wall Masks
HN 1671 - 1676 - Wall Masks
HN 1733 - Wall Mask
HN 1781 - 1786 - Wall Masks

HN 1787 - 1790 - Not Issued
HN 1816 - 1817 - Wall Masks
HN 1823 - 1824 - Wall Masks
HN 2083 - Not Issued
HN2124 - Not Issued
HN 2155 - Not Issued
HN 2164 - Not Issued
HN 2182 - Not Issued
HN 2187 - 2190 - Not Issued
HN 2194 - 2195 - Not Issued
HN 2197 - 2201 - Not Issued
HN 2232 - Not Issued
HN 2285 - 2286 - Not Issued
HN 2288 - 2303 - Not Issued
HN 2350 - 2351 - Not Issued
HN 2353 - 2355 - Not Issued
HN 2357 - 2358 - Not Issued
HN 2360 - Not Issued
HN 2363 - 2367 - Not Issued
HN 2402 - 2407 - Not Issued
HN 2409 - Not Issued
HN 2411 - 2416 - Not Issued
HN 2447 - 2454 - Not Issued
HN 2456 - 2459 - Not Issued
HN 2462 - Not Issued
HN 2464 - Not Issued
HN 2486 - Not Issued
HN 2488 - 2491 - Not Issued
HN 2493 - Not Issued
HN 2495 - 2498 - Not Issued
HN 2495 - 2498 - Not Issued
HN 2500 - 2501 - Animal Figures
HN 2503 - 2519 - Animal Figures
HN 2522 - 2541 - Animal Figures
HN 2548 - 2553 - Bird Figures
HN 2556 - 2670 - Animal and bird figures
HN 2672 - 2676 - Not Issued
HN 2681 - 2862 - Not Issued
HN 2684 - 2692 - Not Issued
HN 2730 - Not Issued
HN 2785 - 2787 - Not Issued
HN 2812 - 2813 - Not Issued
HN 2817 - Not Issued
HN 2819 - 2823 - Not Issued

HN 2847 - 2850 - Not Issued
HN 2852 - 2854 - Not Issued
HN 2869 - Not Issued
HN 2893 - Not Issued
HN 2904 - 2905 - Not Issued
HN 2947 - 2951 - Not Issued
HN 2973 - Not Issued
HN 2982 - 2987 - Not Issued
HN 3022 - 3023 - Not Issued
HN 3062 - 3065 - Not Issued
HN 3081 - Not Issued
HN 3101 - 3104 - Not Issued
HN 3131 - Not Issued
HN 3146 - 3154 - Not Issued
HN 3158 - Not Issued
HN 3193 - 3194 - Not Issued
HN 3224 - 3227 - Not Issued
HN 3237 - 3243 - Not Issued
HN 3352 - Not Issued
HN 3385 - 3387 - Not Issued
HN 3463 - 3469 - Not Issued
HN 3500 - 3599 - Not Issued
HN 3614 - 3616 - Not Issued
HN 3619 - Not Issued
HN 3666 - 3673 - Not Issued
HN 3711 - 3717 - Not Issued
HN 3734 - Not Issued
HN 3736 - 3739 - Not Issued
HN 3745 - 3747 - Not Issued
HN 3749 - Not Issued
HN 3753 - Not Issued
HN 3771 - 3779 - Not Issued
HN 3781 - 3784 - Not Issued
HN 3787 - 3789 - Not Issued
HN 3815 - 3819 - Not Issued
HN 3823 - 3824 - Not Issued
HN 3827 - 3829 - Not Issued
HN 3836 - 3850 - Not Issued
HN 3858 - 3889 - Not Issued
HN 3891 - 3919 - Not Issued
Page 351 - Note: M 41-56 were originally issued 1922-1932 as HN 529-541, 544, 545 and 546.
M 57 - 62 - Napkin Rings
M 63 - Not Issued

INTRODUCTION
By Louise Irvine

THE HISTORY OF ROYAL DOULTON FIGURES

The history of Royal Doulton dates back to 1815 when John Doulton became involved in a little pottery in Lambeth on the banks of the River Thames in London. Trading as Doulton and Watts, they made general stonewares, such as ink wells and ginger beer bottles for daily use. When John's son, Henry, joined the firm in 1835 the business expanded rapidly producing chemical and industrial ceramics. The young entrepreneur also set up a new factory supplying drainpipes to service major cities around the world. The success of this sanitary ware business eventually enabled Henry Doulton to pursue more artistic interests and in 1867 he employed a young sculptor, George Tinworth, to establish an art pottery studio in Lambeth. Tinworth's monumental sculptures and decorative vases quickly focused public attention on this new venture and more artists were recruited until, by the mid 1880s, there were over 300 young men and women producing vases, figures and other ornaments for the Victorian home.

George Tinworth's Boy With Vase

During his long career at the Lambeth studio, Tinworth modelled a wide range of figures, mainly of chubby children at play and animals in human situations. The medium he used is known as salt glaze stoneware, a high-fired clay body, literally glazed with salt. Tinworth's colleague John Broad also used this material as well as terracotta to produce royal portraits, military figures and female studies in classical style. He was a very versatile artist and his figures could range from six inches for the mantlepiece to six feet in height for the garden. He also introduced some fashionable ladies modelled in white bisque porcelain, as did fellow artist Mark Marshall.

The last modeller of note to join the Lambeth studio was Leslie Harradine who contributed a variety of stoneware figure subjects in the early 1900s, some of which were slip-cast in small editions. During the 1920s several of his Lambeth figures, including his Dickens characters, were reproduced in the famous HN collection at Doulton's other factory in Burslem, Stoke-on-Trent.

Henry Doulton invested in the Nile Street pottery at Burslem in 1877 in order to manufacture tableware and ornamental ware at the centre of the British ceramic industry. Charles Noke, an experienced modeller from the Worcester factory, was recruited in 1889 to model exhibition vases but within a few years he had also produced a range of figures. These Vellum figures, as they are now known, are very different in style from the examples sold in china shops today. They are much larger than contemporary models, some nearly 20 inches tall, and they are much less colourful. Most have an ivory body with tinted and gilded decoration by the leading studio artists and they bear a strong resemblance to the figures produced at Worcester.

Noke's first figure, introduced in 1892, was an extraordinary double-sided model depicting Mephistopheles and Marguerite from Faust, as played by the great Victorian acting duo, Henry Irving and Ellen Terry. The theatre, and these actors in particular, inspired many of Noke's early studies and his interest in the stage continued throughout his career. A selection of the early Vellum figures was shown at the Chicago exhibition of 1893 but they do not seem to have captured the public imagination, perhaps because they were very expensive. Despite their disappointing reception, Charles Noke continued to add occasional figures to the collection and by 1900 he had produced 21 free-standing figures and 4 wall-mounted models. Only a very limited number of each design was ever produced making them extremely hard to find today and until recently they were not well documented. However, serious collectors are gradually recognizing the desirability of these distinctive models.

In the opening years of the 20th century, Charles Noke was preoccupied with the development of other Doulton ranges and no new figures were produced. He did, however, experiment with smaller sizes and brighter colours for his existing designs to widen their appeal. For example, his early study of a **Jester** was given a suit of motley colours and it eventually became one of the most popular figures in the collection.

Noke was convinced that a revival of the 18th century Staffordshire figure tradition was desirable and

Ellen Terry as Queen Catharine, Henry Irving as Wolsey

feasible at the Doulton studio but he was aware that he could not achieve his goal alone. Accordingly, in 1909, he began to invite well-known independent sculptors to submit designs that they thought would be suitable for reproducing as small scale ceramic figures. By 1912 he had accumulated the nucleus of a collection and he decided to launch the new range during King George and Queen Mary's visit to the factory in 1913. The Queen was very impressed with the figures, particularly a study of a little child in a nightgown by Charles Vyse. Apparently she exclaimed "isn't he a darling" and the figure was later named **Darling** in her honour and given the first number in the collection, HN1. The 'HN' refers to Harry Nixon who was in charge of the new figure painting department, which comprised three artists in the early years. The HN numbering system is still used today and the company has issued over 3,000 numbers although they are not all new models: some are assigned to colourways of existing figures and some to animal subjects.

Between the Royal visit and the end of the decade, 80 figures were introduced and their relative popularity is recorded in some surviving production statistics for the years 1913-17. During this period 680 figures were produced, an average of 3 a week, and **Darling** (HN1) was by far the most popular with 148 sold, compared with 51 orders for the **Crinoline** (HN8) the first 'fair lady' figure, which was modelled by George Lambert, an Australian artist working in England. Doulton's first 'street vendor' figure **Madonna of the Square** (HN10), by London sculptor Phoebe Stabler, sold 35 in the first three years whilst there were 40 orders for **A Spook** (HN50) by the talented in-house artist Harry Tittensor. Less than a dozen copies of some subjects were produced making these amongst the rarest figures to buy today.

According to the records there were only 7 orders for Noke's **Pedlar Wolf** (HN7) in these early years, which explains why it is particularly elusive today along with his other bizarre subjects **Boy on a Crocodile** (HN373) and **Child on a Crab** (HN32).

Noke continued to draw upon the ideas and talents of other artists, most significantly Leslie Harradine who had worked for Doulton's factory in Lambeth from 1902-12. He left to farm with his brother in Saskatchewan, Canada, but the First World War interrupted their new life and, after fighting in Europe, Harradine eventually returned to England. When Noke heard of his return he endeavoured to persuade him to work in the Potteries but Harradine valued his new found independence too much and agreed instead to work on a freelance basis, first from his studio in Kent and then from the Channel Islands. His first figure **The Princess** (HN391) was introduced in 1920 along with **Contentment** (HN395), which was purchased by Queen Mary at the British Industries Fair that year.

For more than 30 years, Harradine sent at least one model a month to Stoke, sometimes two or three, and they ranged from stylish ladies dressed in the latest fashions, such as **The Sunshine Girl** (HN1344) or **Scotties** (HN1281), to penetrating studies of Dickens'characters. Some of his figures from the 1920s are still being made today, for example **The Old Balloon Seller** (HN1315) of 1929. Such was the demand for Harradine's figures that the painting department was expanded to 10 artists by 1927, many of whom were transferred from painting bone china vases and dessert services following a slump in that market. Thus some of Doulton's most talented artists, including the bird painter Harry Allen and the game painter Charles Hart, introduced their considerable expertise to the decoration of Doulton figures. Many alternative colourways were produced during this decade and most involved several firings to achieve the subtle shaded effects. By the end of the decade nearly 200 new figures had been introduced, most of them the work of Leslie Harradine.

Harradine also dominated the output of the 1930s and in 1937 he introduced his most popular figure ever **Top of the Hill** (HN1833). Many of his most successful pretty ladies were also introduced in a miniature size between 1932 and 1939, enabling collectors with limited display space to enjoy a wide range of his work. Some of the miniatures figures were mounted on ash-trays, calendars and book-ends so that they could be useful as well as decorative whilst the larger ladies were incorporated in electric lamps with complimentary shades.

Harradine's 1930s lady figures, for example **Aileen** (HN1645) and **Rhythm** (HN1903), reflect the sophisticated elegance of the period with glamorous evening gowns, as worn in the Hollywood movies by Greta Garbo and others. Gone were the boyish fashions of the 1920s with their short tube-like dresses and cropped hairstyles. As the decade progressed, more famous porcelain artists joined the figure decorating department, notably the flower painter Percy Curnock, so that by 1939 there were 27 painters at work on the collection. The influence of these master painters can be seen most clearly in the faces of the 1930s fair ladies which have much more expression than the earlier models. Instead of the dark 'button' eyes of the 1920s, the iris and pupil are clearly delineated and the lips are brightly painted in one of the fashionable lipstick shades. This more detailed approach to face painting began around 1934 and can be used as a guide to dating figures..

The Second World War limited the production of figures as luxury goods could only be made for export and, in addition, many of the experienced artists joined the armed forces. It was a time of assessment and appraisal and many of the early figures were discontinued between 1941 and 1949. Charles Noke retired in 1941 but Peggy Davies, who had been engaged as an assistant modeller before the war, decided to set up her own studio and produce figures on a contract basis for Royal Doulton. Her first, in 1946, was **Christmas Morn** (HN1992) and this was followed by **Minuet** (HN2019), a delightful study of a dancer in Regency costume. Peggy was fascinated with fashion and history and enjoyed all the research necessary to produce realistic, accurate figures. One of her most successful early collections portrayed eight illustrious ladies from English history and these are very sought after today.

From the mid 1950s Peggy worked with the new art director Jo Ledger and produced several figures in a contemporary style, mostly teenagers with pony tails and flat pumps. Her most significant piece from this era was the **Marriage of Art and Industry** (HN2261), which was designed for the Brussels exhibition of 1958. Only 12 copies of this prestigious figure were made and they were not on public sale. Peggy rapidly proved her diversity as an artist producing historical characters, fair ladies, ballerinas and other dancers, child studies and later prestige collections. More and more she dominated the collection as Harradine prepared for retirement, contributing his last figure **Dimity** (HN2169) in 1956.

A new talent, Mary Nicoll, appeared on the scene in the mid 1950s. Her father had been illustrating books for the company and he effected an introduction. It soon became apparent that this young artist had tremendous potential as a character figure modeller. In 1955 she began to contribute a wide range of nautical personalities, street entertainers and historical characters, which she modelled in her Devon studio and sent to Stoke on a regular basis. During the 1950s and 60s nearly all the figures were produced by Mary Nicoll and Peggy Davies. Although Peggy was primarily concentrating on crinoline ladies at this time, she also undertook some ambitious large scale subjects, including the **Matador and Bull** (HN2324), the **Indian Brave** (HN2376) and the **Palio** (HN2428) all of which raised the potential of the ceramic medium to its limits, so intricate and complex were her designs.

Peggy continued this prestige work in the 1970s with several extremely popular limited edition collections. **The Lady Musicians, Femmes Fatales** and **Dancers of the World**, were produced under the

supervision of the new Director of Sculpture, Eric Griffiths. He had joined the company in 1972 and his early training as a portrait painter soon became evident in his choice of famous subjects for the figures collection. Good examples are the actor Laurence Olivier and various members of the British Royal family. Eric Griffiths preferred working on a larger scale than the average 8 inch tall Doulton figure and in 1974 he introduced a collection of figures, around 12 inches tall, entitled **Haute Ensemble**. He also advocated the use of a matt finish, believing that a shiny glaze obscured some of the finer points of detail and several of Mary Nicoll's character studies were issued in the matt style.

Mary Nicoll's matt figures The Judge and Parisian

Sadly, Mary died in 1974, but the character figure range was continued by Bill Harper, a versatile modeller with considerable experience in the ceramic industry. He has been responsible for such perennial favourites as the **Punch and Judy Man** (HN2765) and **Thanks Doc** (HN2731), which is essentially a self portrait. Amongst the other sculptors who worked for the collection during the 1970s were Robert Jefferson, Douglas Tootle, Peter Gee, Alan Maslankowski and Robert Tabbenor. Most of these artists still work for the company today.

Not surprisingly after some 90 years of figure production Royal Doulton had a 'huge' collector following and in 1978 the first book to document the HN range, **Royal Doulton Figures**, was written by Desmond Eyles and Richard Dennis. Prior to this reference work there had been no concept of rarity on the secondary market and all the figures had sold in the region of $75 - $100. Now it was apparent that some figures were more desirable that others, depending on how attractive they were and how long they had been in production. Some models had not been found in time for illustration in the first edition of the book and the hunt was on for these elusive pieces, with prices escalating accordingly. A second edition was published in 1989, including many of the rare commissions as well as all the new models produced during the 1980s.

In response to the new collecting boom of the 1980s, Royal Doulton introduced many new series of figures appealing to different tastes and budgets. Several featured children, such as **Characters from Childrens' Literature** and **Childhood Days**. For those interested in royalty and history there were portraits of the current Royal family as well as historical **Queens of the Realm** and for collectors of the crinoline ladies there was the modestly priced **Vanity Fair** range of figures that were very simply decorated. A new contemporary look was achieved in 1981 with the **Images** range of stylised, symbolic sculptures in black basalt or white bone china. In 1987 the **Reflections** range of attenuated figures in fashionable pastel shades was launched.

To keep collectors abreast of all these new developments a Collectors Club was established in 1980 and many figures were commissioned exclusively for members, notably **Prized Possessions** (HN2942) by Robert Tabbenor. This piece features a lady collector consulting the figures book with her latest acquisition by her side. Another popular club commission was **Sleepy Darling** (HN2953) by Pauline Parsons, inspired by Doulton's first figure in the HN collection. Like most of the members' exclusives, it was only made for a six month period. Pauline Parsons has produced other models for the Club and is now one of the foremost modellers of the 'fair lady' figures following Peggy's retirement in 1984. Eric Griffiths also retired at the end of 1990 and a new era has begun with the appointment of Amanda Dixon, Doulton's first female art director. It will be interesting to see what the future holds under this new direction as Royal Doulton enters its second century of figure production.

BUILDING A COLLECTION

Since the 1890s, more that 2,000 figures have been added to the range and these are now avidly collected in many parts of the world. It would be virtually impossible to acquire them all, even if space and budget allowed, but there is plenty of scope to build interesting collections, based on artist, period, style or theme.

COLLECTING LAMBETH FIGURES

Royal Doulton's famous HN series is known and appreciated all over the world, but few collectors are aware of the other types of Royal Doulton figures made at their Lambeth factory in London. They are quite different in appearance from their Burslem counterparts, being made of salt glaze stoneware or terracotta, and they are scarce in the market place as they were produced in very limited numbers.

George Tinworth's Merry Musicians

George Tinworth, Doulton's first resident sculptor, often included human figures in practical items, such as candlesticks, menu holders and spill vases, but in the 1890s he produced an extensive collection of free-standing figures featuring boys playing musical instruments. These **Merry Musicians** have been recorded playing about 40 different instruments. They stand around 5 inches high and are executed in a plain brown stoneware body, although some have white faces. Occasionally, Tinworth produced other figurative subjects, such as the teatime group, **Scandal**, and a portrait of his favourite Dickens character, **Mr. Pickwick**, but these seem to have been unique pieces. A notable exception is the terracotta figure of a jester that he made for the Art Union of London in an edition of 12, around 1900.

One of the most versatile figure modellers at the Lambeth factory was **John Broad**, who was equally at home producing small studies with the aid of a magnifying glass and huge monumental commissions that required scaffolding. He particularly enjoyed working in terracotta and one of his first small-scale figures in this medium was a study of a **Thrower** in 1883. Later terracotta figures by Broad include a devotional statuette of **Our Lady** and a study of **Pomona**, the classical goddess of fruit.

Broad also modelled some delightful studies of classical maidens in salt glaze stoneware, and these were reproduced in limited numbers before and after the First World War, as denoted by their X pattern numbers. The different numbers for **Atalanta** (X7910 and X8707) and the **Bather** (X7912 and X8706) denote different types of stoneware, either plain brown or fully coloured (also known as Doultonware).

John Broad's The Bather in coloured
Doultonware and brown stoneware

Important national events in the early 1900s, such as the Boer War, Nelson's Centenary, the death of Queen Victoria and the coronation of her son, inspired Broad to produce a number of commemorative figures, including handsome terracotta portraits of **King Edward** and **Queen Alexandra**, a faience figure of **Nelson** and imposing salt glaze stoneware studies of **Queen Victoria** and the **Boer War Soldier**.

During the First World War, Doulton developed a hard paste porcelain body for making laboratory ware, and John Broad used this new medium, with either a biscuit or glost finish, for some delicate figures of pretty ladies. His porcelain figures, particularly the portraits of the American actress **Doris Keane**, were a major influence on the HN collection in Burslem, as indeed were the pretty lady figures by **Mark Marshall**. Although Marshall is best known for his art nouveau style vases, adorned with grotesque dragons and reptiles, he dabbled occasionally in figurative sculpture, producing fashionable ladies in white glazed stoneware, accented in blue. His **Crinoline** of 1910 is almost identical to the figure of the same name (HN13) introduced a few years later in Burslem.

Marshall, Broad and Tinworth all helped train the young **Leslie Harradine** when he joined the Lambeth studio in 1902. Unlike his mentors, Harradine's special interest was modelling ornamental figures and animals and he disliked having to design vases for reproduction. Broad's **Boer War** soldier inspired him to produce a group of contemporary soldiers in salt glaze stoneware, including a **British Tommy**, a **French Legionaire**, a **North African Spahi** and a **Cossack**, whilst Marshall's pretty ladies prompted elegant figures such as **Polly Peachum**.

Most importantly, Tinworth's enthusiasm for *The Pickwick Papers* led Harradine to discover all the colourful characters created by Charles Dickens, and he modelled a selection of stoneware figures in time for the centenary of Dickens's birth in 1912. These were made of slip cast stoneware on square bases and were available in brown, buff or coloured Doultonware. Harradine also modelled different versions of the Dickens characters in rich brown stoneware, and these were reproduced in the HN collection (HN553-558) in 1923. He also modelled a set of miniature Dickens figures as prototypes for the HN collection and these were introduced in 1922.

Harradine's Stoneware Fat Boy converted into a
coloured figure for the HN series (HN55)

Harradine spent little time in London after he completed his apprenticeship, preferring to work in his country studio in Hertfordshire, where he produced some powerful studies of farm workers, notably **The Harvester**, **The Peat Cutter** and **The Reaper**. This last character was available in three different effects, plain brown stoneware, coloured Doultonware and brighter 'toby' colours. European peasants were also favourite subjects, and he modelled a very striking group of two Brittany peasants gossiping, a mother with her baby and some Dutch characters.

Several of Harradine's models were reproduced in white slip cast stoneware, sometimes with blue detailing, and these were allocated H pattern numbers along with his animal models and vase designs. They remained in production long after Harradine had left Doulton to emigrate to Canada. After serving in the First World War, Harradine returned to the UK and worked on a freelance basis for Charles Noke, the art director of the Burslem studio, where he became better known as the star modeller of the HN collection.

Harradine's stoneware prototype of Sydney Carton

Harradine's departure from London virtually marked the end of purely ornamental figures at the Lambeth studio. Harry Simeon did some sterling work reviving the Staffordshire toby jug tradition, and little stoneware figures of Toby Philpotts and related characters were incorporated in match stands and ashtrays during the mid 1920s. At the same time, he also included models of a pixie and Pan playing his pipes in a range of bibelots or trinket trays.

Occasionally freelance artists contributed designs for reproduction at the Lambeth studio, but these are even harder to find than the work of the resident modellers. Around 1912, the successful sculptor Stanley Nicholson Babb contributed a figure of a **Lute Player**, which was issued in salt glaze stoneware in a small edition. Twenty years later, Richard Garbe, a professor at the Royal College of Art, produced several designs in conjunction with the Lambeth studio, including a salt glaze stoneware figure of a **Sea Sprite**, which was based on a bronze original.

Another twenty years elapsed before figures were made again at Lambeth, this time by Helen Walters, who worked at the studio between 1953 and 1956. Two of her salt glaze stoneware figures were exhibited at the Royal Academy, and her study of **Demeter** was purchased by Stoke City Art Gallery. It was probably the last figure model to be fired in the Lambeth kilns, as the factory closed down in 1956, thus ending another remarkable chapter in the story of Royal Doulton figures.

COLLECTING VELLUM FIGURES

In the 1890s, some twenty years before the HN collection was launched, Charles Noke was experimenting with a very different style of Doulton figures. Known as the Vellum figures, because of

their parchment colour, they are very similar to the work he was doing at the Worcester factory in the 1880s.

Usually the Vellum figures are tinted with soft sheens of pink and green, but occasionally bolder on-glaze colours are used, such as scarlet or black. Gold highlights were often added and sometimes intricate printed patterns of flowers. Each figure is slightly different, thanks to the varied talents of the prestige artists who worked in Robert Allen's decorating studio. Generally the Vellum figures are much larger than the HN models, ranging from 10 to 20 inches in height, and they were made in very small editions.

In the past, collectors tended to overlook these early Noke designs as they do not come onto the market very often and information was scarce. However, there has been a new awareness of the Vellum models ever since they were catalogued in the classic reference book, *Royal Doulton Figures*. Their pioneering status is now fully recognised, and connoisseurs around the world appreciate the quality of Noke's early modelling and the decorative skills of Robert Allen's artists.

Most of the themes explored in the Vellum figure range preoccupied Noke throughout his modelling career. There are jesters, pierrots and other entertainers from the Victorian stage. His admiration for the acting talents of Henry Irving and Ellen Terry led to several models of them in famous roles, including **Shylock** and **Portia** from *The Merchant of Venice*, **Mephistopheles** and **Marguerite** from *Faust* and **Cardinal Wolsey** and **Queen Catharine** from *Henry VIII*. This last pair seems to have been the most popular, as they turn up most frequently today.

Velllum figures of Shylock and Portia

It would appear that **The Devil** was also based on Henry Irving's role in *Faust*, but so far this figure is only known from the pattern books. New discoveries are still being made in the Vellum range, notably an imposing figure of Lily Langtry as **Cleopatra**, which was not recorded in the Doulton archives. More recently **The Moorish Minstrel** has come to light as part of a candlestick.

Many of the Vellum figures also served practical purposes, either being incorporated into light fittings or flower holders. **The Lady Jester**, **The Sorceress** and **The Geisha** were all made with flat backs for wall

Vellum wall mounts of The Lady Jester and Sorceress

Vellum figure of The Moorish Minstral

mounting as vases, whilst **The Witch** was a wall mounted electric light, with the bulb at the end of her broomstick!

Charles Noke showed his first Vellum figures at the Chicago exhibition of 1893, but the reception was luke-warm. Perhaps the colouring was too bland for the taste of the times and they were very expensive. Noke continued to exhibit the figures in Paris (1900), St. Louis (1904) and Christchurch (1906), and it is likely that they continued to be made in small numbers until work on the HN collection began in 1909.

Some of the most successful Vellum models were later reissued in brighter colours as HN figures, notably **The Jester, Jack Point, Cardinal Wolsey** and **Queen Catharine**. Other Vellum designs can also be found with on-glaze enamel colours, even though they were never assigned HN numbers, for example, **The Kneeling Jester** and **The Witch**.

In all, 21 free-standing Vellum figures have been recorded in a variety of colourways, plus four wall mounted pieces. Perhaps there are even more models waiting to be discovered. Forming a complete collection would be a challenging but rewarding experience if patience and purse strings allow.

COLLECTING THE HN SERIES BY ARTIST

New collectors quickly gravitate towards a particular style of figure and often discover that they favour the work of a specific artist. In the early years the artist was acknowledged on the base of the figures and collectors could appreciate the diverse modelling skills of artists such as Charles Noke, Harry Tittensor and others. After a gap of many years, this practice was revived in 1984 when the artist's facsimile signature was incorporated into the backstamp, making identification as easy as it had been previously.

The work of each Doulton artist has a distinctive quality, even though their figures might be classified with many others as 'fair ladies' or 'character studies'. An experienced eye can quickly spot the difference between a Peggy Davies crinoline lady and one by Leslie Harradine. Similarly Mary Nicoll's nautical figures are quite distinct from Bill Harper's. Each of these artists has a wide following and the scope for collecting their work is often vast and varied, particularly in the case of Peggy Davies, who produced about 250 figures in her 40 year career with Royal Doulton.

COLLECTING BY PERIOD

It has been said of Royal Doulton figures that they are a reflection of the times in which they are made. Certainly, with many of the subjects it is possible to attribute them to a particular period, based on costume, fabric designs and hair styles. The bright young things of the 1920s, such as **Lido Lady** (HN1200) and **Angela** (HN1204) with their negligees and lounging pyjamas, are amongst the most appealing of these period figures but collections can also be formed from other decades. The glamorous style of the 1930s, inspired by the Hollywood stars, is represented in figures such as **Gloria** (HN1488) and **Clothilde** (HN1598) whilst the teenage trends of the 1950s can be seen in **Faraway** (HN2133) and **Sweet Sixteen** (HN2231).

For the fashion conscious, it is possible to create a cat-walk of costumes through the ages from the Medieval period to the 20th century. Some collectors focus exclusively on 18th century style costumes, as worn by **Antoinette** (HN1850) and **Kate Hardcastle** (HN1861), which were notable for their wide hooped skirts adorned with ribbons, bows and ruffles of lace. Others prefer Victorian dresses with their flounced skirts and frothy petticoats, represented by such pieces as **Spring Morning** (HN1922) and **Chloe** (HN1470). Whether it be hats (from wimples to poke bonnets), or fluttering fans, even ladies' fashionable accessories have inspired collections.

COLLECTING BY SUBJECT

Child Studies

Darling, the first figure in the HN collection, was so successful that it was soon followed by many more child studies. Consequently, there is plenty of scope to form a delightful collection, whether it includes the sort of children who were 'seen but not heard' in Victorian times, like **Monica** (HN1467) or **Lily** (HN1798), or the mischievous kids of today like **Pillow Fight** (HN2270) and **Lights Out** (HN2262). There are many popular series inspired by childhood, including Leslie Harradine's **Nursery Rhymes** figures and the recently introduced **Age of Innocence** series. Many of the latest child studies incorporate animals and the special relationship young children enjoy with their pets would be an interesting theme

Nursey Rhyme Figures

to explore with both new and discontinued figures. As well as puppies and kittens, Doulton children also play with teddies, dolls and other toys. It would be fun to track down a representative collection, although there will be competition from serious Teddy Bear collectors. **Sleepyhead** (HN2114), cuddling her teddy, would be a very exciting discovery whilst **Nanny** (HN2221), mending her charge's teddy, is more readily available.

Fair Ladies

There are more fair ladies than any other type of Doulton figure so it is a good idea to specialize at an early stage. Collecting by artist has already been discussed and, as well as the great names of the past, such as Leslie Harradine and Peggy Davies, there are many talented modellers to look for today. Recently Pauline Parsons has portrayed many famous **Queens of the Realm** and Peter Gee has been inspired by the famous paintings of **Gainsborough** and **Reynolds** ladies. The latest recruits to the studio are Nada Pedley and Valerie Annand who have given us romantic interpretations of Victorian and Edwardian fashions.

Faced with this wide choice, a popular approach is to collect by colour, choosing only shades which harmonize with the furnishings of particular rooms. For example, ladies dressed in pastel shades might be suitable for a bedroom whilst richer colours might be more appropriate for the lounge or dining room. Displays could be changed to match the seasons, with all the ladies dressed in yellow and green featured in the spring and all the red outfits at Christmas time. There are many Doulton figures which celebrate the festive season, including **Noelle** (HN2179) with her ermine trimmed cloak and muff and **Santa Claus** himself (HN2725).

Figures can also be used effectively as table centres, whatever the season, or as feature displays with flower arrangements. Some of the figures are even portrayed arranging bowls of tiny hand-made flowers, whilst others carry baskets of blooms, lavish bouquets or a single red rose, so a fair ladies collection could be 'all a blooming'.

Swirling voluminous gowns have inspired many collections of dancing ladies, most of them the work of Peggy Davies who excelled at conveying movement in the folds of the fabric. Peggy's talent in this area can be seen in **Ninette** (HN2379) and **Elaine** (HN2791). **Minuet** (HN2019), one of her earliest figures (HN2019) was inspired by the stately minuet and over the years she added **Polka** (HN2156) **First Waltz** (HN2862) and the flamboyant **Gypsy Dance** (HN2230). She also studied many national dances and costumes for her **Dancers of the World** collection.

Many collectors are influenced by the names of the figures, whether it be the sentiment conveyed or the name of a loved one. In some cases it has been possible to put together a 'family' of figures representing children, grandchildren, and so on. 'Fair ladies', of course, can form part of much wider theme collections of the types suggested below.

Character Figures

As with the fair ladies there is a huge choice of character figures from all walks of life and most collectors look for a particular artist or theme. Art director Charles Noke specialized in character modelling and many of his personal interests can be seen in his range, including literature, history and the theatre. Leslie Harradine, renowned for his beautiful lady figures, was equally at home with characters, contributing country folk, such as **Lambing Time** (HN1890), and colourful street vendors selling balloons, silks and ribbons or fruit and flowers. One such example is **The Orange Seller** (HN1325).

Mary Nicoll dominated the character collection from the mid 1950s to the 1970s and she also launched the nautical figures, which are so popular with sea lovers today. She also developed a collection of figures featuring traditional crafts and professions, for example **The Clockmaker** (HN2279) and **The Judge** (HN2443) and she celebrated the twilight years

StreetVendors

in her studies of Old Dears, notably **Family Album** (HN2321) and **Teatime** (HN2255). All these successful sub-collections have been continued in recent years by Bill Harper, who has also recently expanded the London collection of characters with **The Lifeguard** (HN2781) and **The Guardsman** (HN2784). Former Art Director Eric Griffiths portrayed many members of the British Royal family before his retirement in 1991 and he was also responsible for the **Soldiers of the Revolution** collection of military figures.

Younger modellers are also making their mark. Robert Tabbenor is producing some fine sporting characters, such as **Teeing Off** (HN3276) and Alan Maslankowski has excelled with his limited edition

historical subjects, notably **Christopher Columbus** (HN3392).

Any one of these themes can form the basis of a fascinating collection, which can become even more rewarding by researching the characters behind the figures.

The World of Entertainment

Collecting Royal Doulton figures can literally be an 'entertaining' hobby as many of the stars of stage and screen have been portrayed by Doulton modellers. From the pierrots of pantomime and sea side concerts, to the great Shakespearean roles played by Henry Irving and Ellen Terry, many of the earliest figures reflect Charles Noke's fascination with the theatre. A taste for the exotic is particularly evident in his work, stemming from the fashionable oriental flavour of many operas, musicals and ballets of the time. Examples are the **Mandarin** (HN84) and the Eastern **Cobbler** (HN542).

An interesting collection could include famous stage personalities of the past, such as the American actress **Doris Keane** (HN90), and more recent stars from the silver screen such as **Groucho Marx** (HN2777) and **Charlie Chaplin** (HN2771). As well as these classic clowns of the cinema, there are also lots of circus clowns by Mary Nicoll and Bill Harper to collect. Their ancestors of mirth, the court jesters, have also been popular characters in the figures collection since the earliest days, notably **Jack Point** (HN85) and **The Wandering Minstrel** (HN1224) from Gilbert and Sullivan's famous operettas.

The ballet has been a fertile source of inspiration for Doulton modellers from the great **Pavlova** (HN487) in her most famous role as 'The Dying Swan' to aspiring young dancers practising in frilly tutus, such as **Little Ballerina** (HN3395). Like many young girls, Peggy Davies had ambitions to be a ballerina and as a result she contributed many delightful studies of dancers, including **Coppelia** (HN2115) and **Giselle** (HN2140).

Music lovers can seek out figures playing instruments, whether they be an elegant orchestra of **Lady Musicians** or a precocious violinist such as **The Young Master** (HN2872). Even street performers, such as **The Organ Grinder** (HN2173) and **The Punch and Judy Man** (HN2765), could be included in this colourful revue of the world of entertainment.

Literature

Book lovers will enjoy all of the characters from literature that have been portrayed in the figure collection over the years. Classical myths, Eastern romances, European folklore and English classics have all provided inspiration for individual figures and series. Art Director Charles Noke was a great admirer of Shakespeare and he modelled the great bard himself for the Vellum range, as well as several of his characters. The novels of Charles Dickens were an even greater influence and there are several sets of his famous characters, including the very collectable miniatures. Children's books have also been a fertile source of ideas and, as well as the obvious collection of **Characters from Children's Literature**, there have been figures based on nursery rhymes, Kate Greenaway's picture books and Victorian classics, such as 'Treasure Island'. The figure of this name depicts a young boy poring over the pages of Stevenson's great adventure yarn and pages from the book can be enjoyed with the aid of a magnifying glass. There are many other 'readers' in the figures range, including several others with legible books and this has become a particularly popular collecting theme. A representative display might include the scholarly **Professor** (HN2281) with his nose in a book, **The Wizard** (HN2877) who is consulting his book of spells, or some of the daydreaming fair ladies who rest closed books on their laps.

History

The figures collection is like a historical pageant with famous people from all ages commemorated in clay. It is to be expected that an English company would pay homage to British national heroes and heroines such as **Florence Nightingale** (HN3144) and more recently **Winston Churchill** (HN3057), but there are also many historical personalities from other countries. It would be possible for patriotic Americans to form a 'Stars and Stripes' collection, which might include the **Soldiers of the Revolution** or the **Characters from Williamsburg** series. Canadians can look for the unusual Mountie busts of **R.C.M.P.1973** (HN2547) and **R.C.M.P.1873** (HN2555) or the portrait figure of **Sir John A. MacDonald** (HN2860).

Those interested in military history could seek out the rare First World War soldiers, **Digger** (HN3221-2) and **Blighty** (HN323) or the **Drummer Boy** (HN2679) from the Napoleonic Wars whilst naval historians could add **Captain Cook** (HN2889) or **The Captain** (HN2260) to a general seafaring collection.

The current British royal family has proved to be a popular collection in recent years and many of the Queen's illustrious ancestors have also been portrayed as Doulton figures. **Henry VIII** (HN370, 1792 & 3350) and **King Charles I** (HN404) are good examples. As well as the reigning monarchs, there have also been portraits of their consorts, courtiers and even one of their courtesans, **Nell Gwynne** (HN1882)!

COLLECTING BY SIZE

For collectors with limited display space miniature figures are particularly appealing. The M series was launched in 1932 but there had been miniature figures in the HN range before that, notably the tiny Dickens characters which were re-numbered in line with all the new introductions. By 1949, there were 24 Dickens characters in the M series and they continued in production with minor alterations until 1981-3.

The majority of the miniature fair ladies were scaled down versions of existing figures by Leslie Harradine. Although only 3 to 4 inches tall, the detailing of the costumes and accessories is exceptional, with tiny flower baskets 3/4 inch across and parasols less than an inch long. As in the standard range of the 1930s, there was also a wide range of colourways and **Polly Peachum** has been found in at least 15 different costumes. Unfortunately, rising labour costs led to the withdrawal of the miniature ladies by 1949 and, as many had only been made for about 10 years, they are very elusive for today's collector. Consequently, their prices do not match their diminutive size and they can cost as much, or more, than their standard size counterparts.

Miniature figures were revived in 1988 when the Royal Doulton International Collectors Club commissioned a tiny version of the ever popular **Top o' the Hill** (HN2126). More fair ladies followed in quick succession, with special rich colourways produced exclusively for Michael Doulton's signature collection. All have been allocated HN numbers and are reduced versions of popular figures in the current range. A selection of miniature character figures was introduced in 1989 but these were not well received. Several were quickly withdrawn so they will no doubt become hard to find in the future.

Also easily accommodated in a small display area are the figures of young girls dressed in fashions of the past. These range in size from 4 to 6 inches tall and some, such as **Dinky Do** (HN1678) and **Monica** (HN1467) were in continuous production for over 50 years testifying to the appeal of this scale and subject matter.

Today, the average Doulton fair lady stands around 8 inches tall, whilst seated subjects in proportion measure around 6 inches. Limited editions and character figures tend to be a little larger, averaging 9 inches for standing subjects. Eric Griffiths, the former director of Sculpture, favoured larger scale figures, particularly for character portraits, as he believed a better likeness could be achieved. Consequently his figure of **Lord Olivier as Richard III** (HN2881) is above average size. He also introduced the **Haute Ensemble** series of tall, slender ladies and the attenuated **Images** and **Reflections** series.

In the past, there was much more variety of scale in the collection and figures of more than 12 inches in height were not unusual. **The Welsh Girl** (HN39) and **Lady With Shawl** (HN447) are good examples. Some large scale figures from the past now form the **Prestige** collection and **Princess Badoura** (HN2081), at 20 inches in height, is the largest in the range.

COLLECTING BY SERIES

Numerous collectors subscribe to Royal Doulton's established series of figures, many of which are limited editions. In these cases the company has already chosen all the characters to fit a specific theme and has defined the limits of the collection so there are fewer decisions required than with the more general themes already discussed. This method also allows collectors to budget for forthcoming annual introductions in the more expensive limited edition series.

Some of the recently discontinued series are becoming increasingly difficult to find and it could take some time to find all 18 of the **Kate Greenaway** figures or all 24 **Dickens** miniatures. There always seems to be one or two figures in a series which are rarer than the others and prices rise accordingly. For example, **Tom Bombadil** (HN2924) is a particularly elusive model in the now desirable **Tolkien** series. Occasionally complete series come up for sale but for some collectors that spoils the fun of the chase.

Limited Edition Series

Age of Chivalry
Age of Innocence
Charleston
Children of the Blitz
Dancers of the World
Disney Princess Collection
Edwardian String Quartet
Elegance
Entertainers
Fabled Beauties
Flowers of Love
Gainsborough Ladies
Gentle Arts
Great Lovers
King Henry VIII's Wives
Lady Musicians
Les Femmes Fatales
Les Saisons
Movie Comedians
Myths and Maidens
National Society for the Prevention
    of Cruelty to Children Centenary (NSPCC)
Queens of the Realm
Reynolds Ladies
Royal Family
Shakespearian Ladies
Ships Figureheads
Six Wives of Henry VIII
Soldiers of the Revolution
Stuart Kings
Sweet and Twenties
Tudor Roses
Victorian and Edwardian Actresses

Other Series

Beggar's Opera
Character Sculptures (Resin)
Characters from Children's Literature
Charleston
Childhood Days
Clowns
Dickens Characters
Doulton Collectors Roadshow Events
Elegance Collection
Enchantment
Flowers of Love
Figure of the Month, Child

Figure of the Year
Flambé
Flower of the Month
Four Seasons
Gilbert and Sullivan
Haute Ensemble
Holy Family
Images
Kate Greenaway
Ladies of the British Isles
Ladies of Covent Garden
Lady Doulton
Little Cherubs
Michael Doulton Exclusives
Michael Doulton Signature Collection
Middle Earth
Miniatures
    Character Studies
    Ladies
Nursery Rhymes
Period Figures in English History
Reflections
Royal Doulton International Collectors
    Club Exclusives
Sea Characters
Seasons
Sentiments
Special Occasions
Sweet and Twenties
Vanity Fair
    Children
    Ladies
Wildflower of the Month
Williamsburg

COLLECTING BESWICK FIGURES

The John Beswick factory has been part of the Royal Doulton group since 1969, and they are best known today for their naturalistic studies of animals. However, ever since the company was founded in 1894, they have offered a range of decorative figures. Initially these were mantlepiece ornaments of the traditional Staffordshire type, and a dozen assorted figures cost as little as 4 shillings and 6 pence. Production continued until the 1930s, but unfortunately the Beswick models are not marked so it is difficult to distinguish their designs from the many thousands of Staffordshire figures produced by rival potteries.

Tablewares, tea services, toilet sets, vases and flower pots were also staple products in the early years and ensured the firm's prosperity through the upheaval of the First World War and the Great Depression. By the mid 1930s, the focus at Beswick had changed from practical pottery to novelty wares decorated with art glazes developed by Jim Hayward, the decorating manager. Freelance modellers were commissioned to produce figures and animals for the new look range, and a Miss Greaves contributed 12 figures, mostly of children, that attracted favourable comment from the *Pottery Gazette*.

In 1939, Arthur Gredington, a graduate of the Royal College of Art, was recruited as the first resident modeller, and this versatile artist made a remarkable contribution to the success of the firm. By the time he retired in 1968, he had produced nearly 400 models, including wild animals, farm breeds, race horses and championship dogs. He also modelled comical character animals, initiating the famous Beatrix Potter collection and figures of cartoon stars, such as **Snow White and the Seven Dwarfs** from Disney's classic.

Gredington's first major figure project at the Beswick factory was only made possible by the outbreak of war with Germany. He was asked to copy a collection of 12 figures designed by a Franciscan nun, Maria Innocentia Hummel, which were produced at the Goebel Porcelain factory in Germany. The hostilities negated any copyright claims, and the Beswick management obviously thought that they could do brisk business with these cute figures during the war years. Today these

Happiness by Beswick (l) and Hummel (r)

Hummel look-alikes are as desirable as the originals - if not more so.

The war also inspired a few patriotic figures, notably a portrait of Winston Churchill, inscribed 'We shall not flinch nor fail.' In a lighter vein, Gredington modelled a group of four fairies, which are hard to find today, and figures of a clown and a jester. His postwar figures are usually wearing contemporary dress and so have a nostalgic period feel, for example, the **Butcher Boy**, **Hiker** and **Sportsman**. It was perhaps his **Scotsman**, in kilt and tammy, that inspired his assistant Jan Granoska to produce a range of figures in national costume.

Miss Granoska came from eastern Europe and trained as a modeller at the Beswick factory between

1951 and 1954. In just a few years, she produced some of the company's finest figures. Her interpretation of Disney's famous cartoon characters, such as **Peter Pan** and **Pinocchio**, has drawn high praise from collectors past and present. Equally popular are her national characters who demonstrate their country's dances or interact with farm animals, for example, the **Swedish Girl** cradling a cockerel and the **Italian Girl** struggling with a goat that is eating her hat!

Incorporating animals into figure groups allowed Beswick to demonstrate its prowess in this field. Arthur Gredington was able to combine his talent for portraying horses with his interest in figure modelling in a series of 15 equestrian studies, beginning with a **Rearing Horseman** in 1940 and ending in 1966 with a portrait of the racehorse **Arkle** with Pat Taffe up. When Gredington retired, Albert Hallam kept the tradition going with models such as **Nijinksy**, with Lester Piggott up, and the **Highwayman**, whilst Graham Tongue has continued to the present with the **Blues and Royals on Horseback**.

Beswick's equestrian figures are now all very sought after, whether it be Gredington's imposing **Knight in Armour**, the highly stylized clowns on horseback designed by Colin Melbourne in the 1950s or the comical Thelwell series of young riders on their shaggy ponies, taken from the successful book, Angels on Horseback, in the 1980s.

Humour has always been an important ingredient in the Beswick range, and several of the figure groups raise a smile, notably Albert Hallam's **Bedtime Chorus** and Harry Sales' **Road Gang** from the 1960s. For the most part, Beswick artists steered away from the traditional crinoline lady figures that were the speciality of the Doulton factory, but there are a few rare exceptions, including the **Lady in Ballgown**, which was only produced for a year. Instead they have concentrated on cute and appealing characters, such as the doll-like children drawn by Joan Walsh Anglund for her book, A Friend is Someone Who Likes You, or the **Little Lovables** clowns, created by Amanda Hughes Lubeck to express popular greetings and sentiments.

In the past Beswick Figures were overshadowed by Royal Doulton's famous HN range, but thanks to Harvey May's research for the first Beswick Collectors Handbook, which was published in 1987, and the subsequent formation of the Beswick Collectors Circle, they now have their own dedicated collector following.

MAKING DOULTON FIGURES

There are many people involved in the creation of each Royal Doulton figure, beginning with the artist who works with modelling clay to transform an image in his head, or on paper, into a three dimensional sculpture.

When the original model is complete it is taken to the mould maker, whose years of experience enable him to cut up the figure into separate parts so that a master mould, known as a block, can be produced.

Complex figures are divided into many parts and a plaster of Paris mould is made from the original head, torso, arms, skirts and so on. Working moulds are made as required and care is taken to ensure that they are replaced regularly during production so that the crisp detail of the original is maintained.

Liquid clay, known as slip, is gently poured into each mould by the caster and once the body has set to the required thickness the excess slip is poured out. At this stage the parts of the figure are carefully removed from the mould and, as the clay is still very fragile, they are pieced together using slip as an adhesive.

Before the complete figure has been thoroughly dried, the seams are sponged away in a process known as fettling. The piece is then ready for its first firing. It is removed from the kiln, having shrunk to its 'biscuit' state and then, if it is a character figure, it is ready for painting. Painting takes place at this stage because pieces are coloured under-glaze to give the more rugged effect expected of these subjects.

Fair lady figures in their biscuit state are dipped into a vat of glaze and fired again before decorating begins. The dresses and accessories are painted with on-glaze colours and to achieve the rich colour effects, like the deep red, several applications of colour are needed. Each layer requires a separate firing. When the costume decoration is complete, the faces of the fair ladies are painted by the most experienced artists and a final firing ensures that the colours are permanently sealed under the glaze.

Bodies And Glazes

The fair lady figures are made from bone china which is a traditionally British body, composed of China clay, Cornish stone and bone ash. Most character figures are made from English Porcelain, a whiter coloured body formerly known as English Translucent China, which was pioneered by Royal Doulton chemists in 1959. Before the invention of English Porcelain, many Doulton figures were produced in an earthenware body, which is fired to a lower temperature than china and is more porous. There are slight differences in size between figures made of earthenware and those made of porcelain and colours often look different on the two bodies.

Most Royal Doulton figures have a brilliant glossy glaze. In the early 1970s, however, some matt figures were produced and this matt finish was also used for limited edition subjects as it enhanced the intricate modelling and gave a distinctive effect. A matt glazed black basalt body has been used more recently in the **Images** range of modern style sculptures.

There is obviously much more to a Royal Doulton figure than first meets the eye and collectors can enjoy watching the creative process during a tour of the Royal Doulton factory. For opening times and tour bookings contact: The Tours Organizer, Royal Doulton, Nile Street, Burslem, Stoke-on-Trent ST6 2AJ.

Care And Repair

A Royal Doulton figure collection can be enjoyed indefinitely as long as care is taken when handling and cleaning. When dusting in situ, a soft cosmetic brush or photographic lens brush is useful for getting into tight corners, particularly hand-modelled floral bouquets and baskets. When necessary, glazed figures should be washed in luke-warm water, using a mild liquid detergent, then rinsed thoroughly and dried naturally or buffed gently with a soft cloth. It is important that water does not get inside the figure so the hole in the bottom should be blocked up beforehand, perhaps with a cork or a rubber bung. Care should be taken not to knock figures against the tap or against each other as this may cause chips or imperceptible cracks in the glaze which could open up at a later date.

If the worst does happen, a professional restorer should be consulted as they can work 'miracles' with damaged figures. Whether it be a small chip or a shattered body, pieces can be mended so that the repair is invisible to all but the most experienced eye. It follows that when buying figures on the secondary market, it is advisable to check for restorations. The head, the arms and any projecting accessories are the most vulnerable parts, so look at these areas carefully in a good light. Repaired cracks can sometimes be detected by looking inside the figure through the hole in the bottom. There are special ultraviolet lamps which highlight some types of restoration but these are not widely used, except by professionals. Restored figures should be priced less than perfect examples, according to the amount of damage and the quality of the repair. Always enquire about the condition of a piece when buying, as a reputable dealer will stand by any guarantees they give regarding restorations.

Current And Discontinued Figures

Figures which are produced at the Royal Doulton factories today are generally referred to as 'current' whilst models which are no longer made are variously described as 'withdrawn', 'retired' or 'discontinued'. A current figure might have been in the range for a long time and one or two have been in continuous production for over fifty years, for example **The Old Balloon Seller**. Because this figure is still generally available today, a 1930s version is unlikely to be worth more than the current model, even though it is older and probably differs slightly in appearance, due to changes in body and paint formulations over the years. It is worth remembering, however, that originally it would have been purchased for just a few pounds or dollars.

Figures are discontinued on an annual basis in order to make way for new introductions. There is a limit to the number of models the factory can produce, or the retailer can display, so eventually some have to go. In some cases the choice is easy as it is apparent that all the collectors who want a particular model have already purchased it and world-wide sales are decreasing. Occasionally figures disappear after only a couple of years in the range and these short-lived models often become very desirable on the secondary market.

The number of figures withdrawn each year varies enormously. Sometimes it is less than 12 a year and other times, after a major reassessment of the range, there might be 50 or so. The first withdrawals took place during the Second World War and it is unlikely that more than 2,000 of each of the early models were produced. This is less than many limited editions, so it is not surprising that these pieces are amongst the most desirable figures on the secondary market today. Older figures with short production runs are obviously less likely to appear in the market-place than those that were made for many years. However, this alone does not affect the price, which will probably also be governed by aesthetic considerations and market awareness.

In 1990, the company introduced a system of marking the bases of retiring figures 'last year of issue' but this practice ceased in 1993.

Limited Editions, Prestige Figures and Special Editions

In 1933, discerning customers were offered a range of specially commissioned figures by Richard Garbe RA, a distinguished sculptor of the day. Inspired by his sculptures in other media, the new figures were larger than most others in the HN collection and many were embellished with gold. In order to emphasise their prestige status, it was announced that only a limited number of each model would be produced and the edition size was marked on the base. The editions ranged from 25 to 150 pieces and took several years to sell out. Not surprisingly, they are now very desirable on the secondary market. At the same time, Charles Noke introduced a limited edition figure of King Henry VIII, which is more typical of Doulton's later limited editions in terms of subject matter, scale and decoration.

During the 1950s, some of the largest and most impressive figures in the range were revamped to form the basis of a Prestige collection. Three of these subjects were originally modelled by Charles Noke, **The Moor** (HN2082), **Jack Point** (HN2080), and **King Charles** (HN2084), and the first two are still produced today, although in very limited quantities to special order. The most expensive prestige figure of all, **Princess Badoura** (HN2081), was introduced in 1952. The painting and gilding on this figure take about eight weeks to complete, hence the high cost. Repeated kiln firings and complex model assembly also add to the expense of producing prestige pieces, as with the spectacular **Matador and Bull** (HN2324), which was modelled by Peggy Davies in 1964. Two more of Peggy's ambitious large scale sculptures were produced in limited editions of 500 each, **The Indian Brave** (HN2376) produced in 1967 and **The Palio** (HN2428) of 1971. However, she is better known today for her limited edition collections of **Lady Musicians** (1970 - 76) and **Dancers of the World** (1977 - 82). These highly detailed and richly decorated models were each limited to 750 pieces and were introduced at the rate of one or two each year,

complete with presentation boxes and certificates of authenticity. This has become the pattern for most of the company's limited editions today, although edition sizes have grown to reflect increased demand.

Special occasions have also inspired limited editions and there are portrait figures celebrating Royal weddings, birthdays and coronation anniversaries. Expo'92 in Seville, for example prompted a limited edition colourway of **Mantilla** (HN3192) and a special edition of **Discovery** (HN3428), a reduced version of the symbolic sculpture in the British Pavilion. This piece was offered exclusively to members of the Royal Doulton International Collectors Club. The opportunity to purchase limited editions and special editions of figures is one of the benefits of joining the Club. Generally speaking, **special** editions are limited by the offer period, which in the case of the early Doulton Club commissions was six months. The term is also used more widely to describe special products commissioned by independent companies which are not individually numbered on their bases nor accompanied by a certificate of authenticity.

For the collector looking for something extra special, Royal Doulton limited and special editions are in great demand today and popular subjects are often quickly oversubscribed. It is important, therefore, to respond quickly to the announcements for new releases. Discontinued limited editions command premium prices in the secondary market, particularly if they are sold with their original literature and packaging and the first of a collection of six or twelve figures is usually the hardest to find.

Colourways and Variations

From the earliest days of the figures collection, some of the most popular models have been produced in alternative colourways. The first fair lady figure, **The Crinoline**, was originally offered in a plain lilac dress or with a floral design. Each colourway was assigned a different HN number to distinguish the decorative treatment. Charles Noke's study of **A Jester** has been available in 12 different coloured suits as well as in Parian and Vellum finishes. Noke also experimented with different glaze effects on figures, including a lustrous red flambé, a mottled blue green Titanian, a glittering gold and a dark brown to simulate bronze. These were produced only in very limited numbers and were not given HN references.

During the 1920s, when more master painters joined the figure painting department, colour effects and patterns became more ambitious. The lady figures were dressed in all of the fashionable fabrics of the day with floral designs, polka dots, stripes, diapers and checks painted by hand. It was unusual to have a lady figure in just one colourway and in the case of **Victorian Lady**, there was a choice of 15 varied designs.

After the Second World War the collection was rationalized and alternative colourways became less common. However, the idea was revived during the 1980s, initially for special occasions such as Michael

Doulton tours. A new colourway of **Wistful** (HN2472) was devised exclusively for his personal appearances in 1985. Since then, five figures have been given a new look for this purpose. Colourways have also been commissioned by independent retailers and in some cases the name has been changed as well as the colours. For example, a variation of **Adrienne** (HN2304) was commissioned to promote Joan's Gift Shop in Scotland and was renamed **Joan** (HN3217).

Alternative colourways now appear regularly in the general range, sometimes with a new name, and it is not just fair ladies which ring the changes. Character figures have also been given a fresh new look from time to time. **The Lobster Man**, for instance, is available with two different coloured sweaters (HN2317 and HN2323).

During the 1970s, former Art Director Eric Griffiths experimented with matt glazes but these were not a commercial success and most of the models were quickly withdrawn. An exception is **The Judge** (HN2443) which was changed from a matt to a glossy finish because it was so popular.

From time to time alterations have been made to models after they have been introduced, usually to decrease the risk of damage during production or in transit. In early models of **The Carpet Seller** (HN1464) for example, the character's hand is outstretched, whereas in later models the fingers are clasped around the carpet, making them less vulnerable to breakage. The figure of **Masque** (HN2554) also had to be modified as the long metal handle of the mask was easily broken. It was removed and the hand was remodelled. Eagle eyed collectors will also notice that early models of **Autumn Breezes** (HN1911) have two feet peeping out from under the dress whilst later models have only one.

There are some keen collectors who enjoy tracking down the different model and colour variations but the majority take advantage of the wide choice of shades and patterns to co-ordinate a new purchase with an existing display.

The Carpet Seller Hand Open and Hand Closed

A GUIDE TO BACKSTAMPS AND DATING

There is a wealth of information on the base of a Royal Doulton figure and some of it will help date the piece.

Most prominent is the Royal Doulton factory mark which has featured a lion standing on a crown ever since the company was awarded the Royal Warrant in 1901. Before this honour was bestowed, the mark comprised a different style of crown and the words 'Doulton Burslem England.' This early mark is found on most of the Vellum figures modelled by Charles Noke in the 1890s.

The Royal Doulton lion and crown mark has been altered slightly over the years and this can help date the figure to a specific era. Collectors should note that the words 'Made in England' were added around 1920 so figures without this reference are usually very early models.

1902-1922
Printed or Impressed　　**1922-1927**
Printed

1927-1932
Printed or Impressed　　**1932**
Present

Often on miniature figures there was not enough room for the standard factory mark and so either part of it was used or just the words 'Doulton England.' Between 1932 and 1949 miniature figures were given M pattern numbers but earlier and later models have HN numbers.

Miniature
from 'M' Series　　**Miniature**
from 'HN' Series

Some early figures have an impressed date on the base which gives the month, year and sometimes the day, when the mould was made (not when a particular finished piece was produced). For example, 12-10-23 represents October 12th, 1923. This practice ceased during the 1930s.

Printed numeral
'1' stands for 1928, '2' for 1929, etc.

The precise year of manufacture, however, can be determined if the figure has a date code on the right side of the lion and crown symbol. A printed number 1 was used in 1928, when this dating system began. This system continued to number 27 in 1954. The year of manufacture can be easily calculated by adding the number on the figure to 1927. For example, a figure with the number 13 on it indicates that it was manufactured in 1940 (13+1927). Between 1990 and 1993 new introductions were marked 'first year of issue' and planned withdrawals 'final year of issue,' which makes precise dating possible again for some figures.

Registration numbers, when they are present, indicate when the design was first registered, which could be up to a year before the figure was put into production. After the Second World War, it was usual to have several registration numbers which protected the design in Royal Doulton's main export markets but this has not been required since the early 1980s. Copyright dates have also been incorporated into the backstamp since the 1940s.

RᵈN° 791566

Registered Mark

H.N.2041.
COPR.1948.
DOULTON & CO. LIMITED.
RᵈN° 855287.
RᵈN° 26360.
RᵈN° 5772.
RᵈN° 133/48.

**Registered Mark with
Copyright Date**

HN 2871
ⓒ ROYAL DOULTON
TABLEWARE LTD 1979

Copyright Mark

Usually the design is copyrighted at least a year before production begins so, as with registration numbers, the copyright date does not necessarily indicate the year of introduction.

The HN number is particularly important as this catalogue and other reference works are designed to follow the HN sequence. Until the 1950s the HN number was written on the base by the painter so very occasionally it has been omitted. It is now incorporated in the printed backstamp along with the figure's name and copyright information. The initials stand for Harry Nixon who devised the colour schemes for the figures and recorded all the painting instructions in the pattern books. Each new decorative treatment was given an HN number, not necessarily in chronological order, and so a popular model such as **Victorian Lady** has several different numbers. Pattern number HN 1 was allocated to the figure **Darling** because of Queen Mary's interest, although it was not the first figure to be modelled.

Figures also have a model number impressed in the base but this does not normally concern collectors unless there are no other details recorded, which is sometimes the case with prototypes. Model numbers can be authenticated by referring to the shape books held in Royal Doulton's archive in Stoke-on-Trent.

Until around 1930 the figure's name was written by hand on the base and the modeller's name was sometimes included. This practice lapsed in the general range for over 50 years but was revived in 1984 when the modeller's facsimile signature was incorporated in the backstamp.

Figure's name styles

Modeller's Signature

The painters responsible for the decoration of the figures usually initial their work on the base and in recent years the individual craftsmanship of the piece has been further emphasised by the addition of the words "Hand made and hand decorated".

Backstamps on limited edition pieces have added information about the edition size and, decorative typefaces and motifs inspired by the subject are now often incorporated into the design. Special commissions, including new models, colourways and pre-releases, frequently have backstamps with details of the event being commemorated. Backstamps may also include the customer who has commissioned the piece. For example, all of the annual figures produced exclusively for Michael Doulton's tours have a special backstamp.

Although 'seconds' figures are not sold by Royal Doulton to the public, slightly faulty models can be bought by company employees at special sales and so they occasionally come on to the secondary market. They are now clearly marked with either a scored line through the backstamp or a drilled hole defacing the centre of the lion and crown symbol.

WHERE TO BUY

Discontinued Royal Doulton figures can be found in antique shops, markets and fairs as well as auction houses. Specialist dealers in Royal Doulton figures attend many of the venues and events below.

UNITED KINGDOM

Auction Houses

Phillips
101 New Bond Street
London W1

Christie's South Kensington
85 Old Brompton Road
London SW5

Bonhams
Montpelier Street
London SW7

Sotheby's
Summer's Place
Billingshurst, West Sussex

Louis Taylor
Percy Street
Hanley, Stoke-on-Trent

Peter Wilson
Victoria Gallery
Market Street
Nantwich, Cheshire

Antique Fairs

UK Doulton Collectors Fair
The Queensway Hall
Civic Centre
Dunstable, Bedfordshire

Annual Royal Doulton Show
Trentham Gardens
Stoke-on-Trent

Doulton and Beswick Collectors Fair
National Motorcycle Museum
Meriden, Birmingham

Antique Markets

Portobello Road Market
London W11
Saturday only

New Caledonian Market
Bermondsey Square
London SE1
Friday morning

Alfie's Antique Market
13-25 Church Street
London NW8
Tuesday - Saturday

Camden Passage Market
(off Upper Street)
London N1
Wednesday and Saturday

Potteries Antique Centre Ltd.
271 Waterloo Road
Cobridge, Stoke-on-Trent,
Staffordshire ST6 3HR
Seven days a week

USA

Auction Houses

Phillips New York
406 East 79th Street
New York, NY 10021

Antique Fairs

Florida Doulton Convention
Guest Quarters Suite Hotel
Cypress Creek
555 NW 62nd Street
Fort Lauderdale, Florida 33309

Doulton Show
Sheraton Poste House
Cherry Hill, New Jersey

Strongsville Pottery and Porcelain Show
Holiday Inn
Strongsville, Ohio

CANADA

Auction Houses

Ritchies
288 King Street East
Toronto, Ontario, M5A 1K4

Antique Shows

Canadian Doulton and Beswick Show and Sale
The Toronto Hilton Hotel
5875 Airport Road
Mississauga, Ontario

Antique Markets

Harbourfront Antique Market
390 Queen's Quay West
Toronto, Ontario
(Tuesday - Sunday)

PLACES TO VISIT

Royal Doulton Factory Tour
and Visitors Centre
Nile Street
Burslem, Stoke-on-Trent
For opening times and tour information telephone
(01782) 744766

John Beswick Factory Tour
Gold Street
Longton, Stoke-on-Trent
ST3 2JP
For opening times and tour information telephone
(01782) 292292

CLUBS AND SOCIETIES

The Royal Doulton International Collectors Club was founded in 1980 to provide an information service on all aspects of the company's products, past and present. The Club's magazine 'Gallery' is published four times a year and local branches also publish newsletters. There are also several regional groups in the USA, which meet for lectures and other events and some publish newsletters. Contact the USA branch for further information.

Headquarters and UK Branch

Royal Doulton
Minton House
London Road
Stoke-on-Trent, ST4 7QD

Australian Branch

Royal Doulton Australia Pty Ltd.
17-23 Merriwa Street, Gordon,
Australia NSW 2072

Canadian Branch

Royal Doulton Canada Inc.
850 Progress Avenue
Scarborough, Ontario, M1H 3C4

New Zealand Branch

Royal Doulton
P.O. Box 2059
Auckland, New Zealand

USA Branch

Royal Doulton USA Inc.
P.O. Box 1815
Somerset, New Jersey 08873

FURTHER READING

Figures, Animals and Character Jugs

Royal Doulton Figures by Desmond Eyles, Richard Dennis and Louise Irvine
The Charlton Standard Catalogue of Royal Doulton Animals by Jean Dale
The Charlton Standard Catalogue of Royal Doulton Jugs by Jean Dale
The Character Jug Collectors Handbook by Kevin Pearson
Collecting Character and Toby Jugs by Jocelyn Lukins
Collecting Doulton Animals by Jocelyn Lukins
The Doulton Figure Collectors Handbook by Kevin Pearson

General

Discovering Royal Doulton by Michael Doulton
The Doulton Story by Paul Atterbury and Louise Irvine
Royal Doulton Series Wares by Louise Irvine (Vols 1-4)
The Charlton Price Guide to Royal Doulton Beswick Storybook Figures by Jean Dale
The Charlton Standard Catalogue of Beswick Animals by J & D Callow and P & M Sweet
Royal Doulton Bunnykins Figures by Louise Irvine
Bunnykins Collectors Book by Louise Irvine
Beatrix Potter Figures edited by Louise Irvine
Limited Edition Loving Cups and Jugs by Louise Irvine and Richard Dennis
Doulton for the Collector by Jocelyn Lukins
Doulton Kingsware Flasks by Jocelyn Lukins
Doulton Burslem Advertising Wares by Jocelyn Lukins
Doulton Lambeth Advertising Wares by Jocelyn Lukins
The Doulton Lambeth Wares by Desmond Eyles
The Doulton Burslem Wares by Desmond Eyles
Hannah Barlow by Peter Rose
George Tinworth by Peter Rose
Sir Henry Doulton Biography by Edmund Gosse
Phillips Collectors Guide by Catharine Braithwaite
Royal Doulton by Jennifer Quérée
Collecting Doulton Magazine edited by Doug Pinchin, published by Francis Joseph

DOULTON LAMBETH

GEORGE TINWORTH
LAMBETH FIGURES

Boy Cricketer

Designer: George Tinworth
Height: 5", 13 cm
Colour: 1. Coloured Doultonware
2. Brown Siliconware
Issued: c.1890

Description	U.S. $	Can. $	U.K. £
1. Coloured Doultonware	1,200.00	1,200.00	500.00
2. Brown Siliconware	1,200.00	1,200.00	500.00

Boy Jester

Designer: George Tinworth
Height: 5", 13 cm
Colour: Brown stoneware
Issued: c.1890

Description	U.S. $	Can. $	U.K. £
Brown stoneware	1,500.00	1,500.00	500.00

Boy with Melon

Designer: George Tinworth
Height: 3 1/2", 9cm
Colour: Brown stoneware
Issued: c.1890

Description	U.S. $	Can. $	U.K. £
Brown Stoneware	1,500.00	1,500.00	500.00

Boy with Vase

Designer: George Tinworth
Height: Unknown
Colour: Coloured Doultonware
Issued: c.1890

Description	U.S. $	Can. $	U.K. £
Coloured Doultonware	1,800.00	1,800.00	650.00

Drunken Husband

Designer:	George Tinworth		
Height:	5 1/4", 12 cm		
Colour:	Coloured Doultonware		
Issued:	1881		

Description	U.S. $	Can. $	U.K.
Coloured Doultonware	1,500.00	1,500.00	500.00

Five Miles to London

Designer:	George Tinworth		
Height:	9", 23 cm		
Colour:	Coloured Doultonware		
Issued:	c.1885		

Description	U.S. $	Can. $	U.K.
Coloured Doultonware	3,000.00	3,000.00	1,250.00

Photograph not
available
at press time

Girl with Tambourine

Designer:	George Tinworth		
Height:	9", 23 cm		
Colour:	Coloured Doultonware		
Issued:	c.1885		

Description	U.S. $	Can. $	U.K.
Coloured Doultonware	3,500.00	3,500.00	1,500.00

Jester

Designer:	George Tinworth		
Height:	12 1/2", 31.5 cm		
Colour:	Terracotta		
Issued:	1900		
	Produced for the Art Union in an edition of 12		

Description	U.S. $	Can. $	U.K.
Terracotta	6,500.00	6,500.00	2,500.00

The Merry Musicians

The exact number of Merry Musicians is not recorded but there are probably around a hundred different figures, playing at least forty different instruments, some of which are listed here on the following page. The figures can be found with endless variations of poses, expressions, hats and instruments, many of which are very obscure. The Musicians were produced from the 1890s until the early 1900s in small numbers. Around 1910 a set was produced with white faces for the Australian agent, John Shorter. Many of the Musicians have Tinworth's monogram although some were produced entirely by assistants.

BAGPIPES

BOTUTO

CONCERTINA

LUTE

ORGAN

PIANO

PICCOLO

SCOTTISH BAGPIPES

SCOTTISH BAGPIPES

VIOLIN

A List of Recorded Merry Musicians to Date

Bagpipes	Harp	Positive Organ
Banjo	Horn	Rebec
Barrel Drum	Hurdy Gurdy	Saxophone
Bass Clarinet	Kettle Drum	Sousaphone
Bells	Lute	Scottish Bagpipes
Botuto	Lyre	Spiral Horn
Carillon	Mandolin	Tambourine
Cello	Marimba	Trombone
Cittern	Military Bass Type	Trumpet
Concertina	Drum	Tuba
Conductor	Military Side Drum	Tympanum
Cornet	One Man Band	Ukulele
Cymbals	Organ	Viola
Flageolet	Organistrum	Violin
Flute	Piano	Whistle
French Horn	Piccolo	

Pricing: The Merry Musicians can only be priced by an indicating range, within the group will be rare figures, so that any demand for a scarce or rare musician could easily double or triple the price.

U.S.: $1,000.00 - 1,500.00   Can.: $1,000.00 - 1,500.00   U.K.: £500.00 - 750.00

Note: We would appreciate any new information, and/or photographs, of the Merry Musicians. Please refer to our editorial office address in the front of the catalogue as to where to send the information.

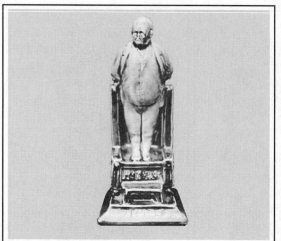

Mr. Pickwick

Designer:	George Tinworth
Height:	5",, 12.5 cm
Colour:	Coloured Doultonware
Issued:	c.1895

Description	U.S. $	Can. $	U.K.
Coloured Doultonware	.	Rare	

Scandal

Designer:	George Tinworth
Height:	6 1/4", 16 cm
Colour:	Coloured Doultonware
Issued:	1891

Description	U.S. $	Can. $	U.K.
Coloured Doultonware	3,500.00	3,500.00	1,500.00

Photograph not
available
at press time

Young Carpenter

Designer:	George Tinworth
Height:	5 1/4", 13.0 cm
Colour:	Brown stoneware
Issued:	c.1892

Description	U.S. $	Can. $	U.S.£
Coloured Doultonware		Rare	

JOHN BROAD
LAMBETH FIGURES

Atalanta (Headband)

Designer: John Broad
Height: 9", 23 cm
Colour: 1. X7910, Brown stoneware
        2. X8707, Coloured Doultonware
Issued: 1. 1912
        2. 1928

Description	U.S. $	Can. $	U.K. £
Brown Stoneware	2,000.00	3,000.00	1,250.00
Coloured Doultonware	2,000.00	3,000.00	1,250.00

Photograph not
available
at press time

Atalanta (Flowers)

Designer: John Broad
Height: 9", 23 cm
Colour: 1. X7910, Brown stoneware
        2. X8707, Coloured Doultonware
Issued: 1. 1912
        2. 1928

Description	U.S. $	Can. $	U.K. £
Brown Stoneware		Rare	
Coloured Doultonware		Rare	

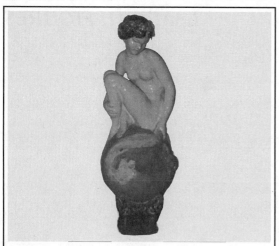

Bather

Designer: John Broad
Height: 13 1/2", 34 cm
Colour: 1. X7912, Brown stoneware
        2. X8706, Coloured Doultonware
Issued: 1. 1912
        2. 1928

Description	U.S. $	Can. $	U.K. £
1. Brown stoneware	3,000.00	3,000.00	1,250.00
2. Coloured Doultonware	3,000.00	3,000.00	1,250.00

Boer War Soldier

Designer: John Broad
Height: 12 1/2", 32 cm
Colour: Brown stoneware
Issued: 1901
Series: Soldiers

Description	U.S. $	Can. $	U.K. £
Brown stoneware	3,000.00	3,000.00	1,250.00

Diana

Designer:	John Broad
Height:	11 1/2", 29.7 cm
Colour:	Terracotta
Issued:	c. 1880

Description	U.S. $	Can. $	U.K. £
Terracotta	3,000.00	3,000.00	1,250.00

Doris Keane
(also called The Minuet)

Designer:	John Broad
Height:	9", 23 cm
Colour:	White glost porcelain
Issued:	c.1918

Description	U.S. $	Can. $	U.K. £
White glost	1,300.00	1,300.00	450.00

Doris Keane
(also called Romance)

Designer:	John Broad
Height:	8 3/4", 22.5 cm
Colour:	White biscuit porcelain
Issued:	c.1918

Description	U.S. $	Can. $	U.K. £
White biscuit	1,400.00	1,400.00	500.00

Girl Holding Vase

Designer:	John Broad
Height:	13 1/4", 33 cm
Colour:	X8708, Coloured Doultonware
Issued:	1928

Description	U.S. $	Can. $	U.K. £
Coloured Doultonware	2,200.00	2,200.00	900.00

King Edward VII

Designer: John Broad
Height: 16 3/4", 42 cm
Colour: Terracotta
Issued: 1901

Description	U.S. $	Can. $	U.K. £
Terracotta		Rare	

Lady in Elizabethan Dress

Designer: John Broad
Height: 8", 20.5 cm
Colour: White biscuit porcelain
Issued: c.1918

Description	U.S. $	Can. $	U.K. £
White biscuit	1,500.00	1,500.00	650.00

Lady with Dog

Designer: John Broad
Height: 7 1/2", 19 cm
Colour: White biscuit porcelain
Issued: c.1918

Description	U.S. $	Can. $	U.K. £
White biscuit		Rare	

Lady with Muff

Designer: John Broad
Height: 7 1/4", 18.5 cm
Colour: White biscuit porcelain
Issued: c.1918

Description	U.S. $	Can. $	U.K. £
White biscuit	1,200.00	1,200.00	500.00

Lady with Rose

Designer: John Broad
Height: 8", 20.5 cm
Colour: White biscuit porcelain
Issued: c.1918

Description	U.S. $	Can. $	U.K. £
White biscuit	1,200.00	1,200.00	500.00

Lady with Tall Hat

Designer: John Broad
Height: 8", 20.5 cm
Colour: White biscuit porcelain
Issued: c.1918

Description	U.S. $	Can. $	U.K. £
White biscuit	1,200.00	1,200.00	500.00

Madame Pompadour

Designer: John Broad
Height: 8 1/2", 21.5 cm
Colour: 1. White biscuit porcelain
2. X8754, Coloured Doultonware
Issued: c.1918

Description	U.S. $	Can. $	U.K. £
White biscuit	1,350.00	1,350.00	450.00
Coloured Doultonware	1,350.00	1,350.00	450.00

Photograph not
available
at press time

Nelson

Designer: John Broad
Height: 8", 20.5 cm
Colour: 1. X6426, Brown stoneware
Issued: 2. 1905 Green faience

Description	U.S. $	Can. $	U.K. £
Brown stoneware	600.00	600.00	275.00
Green faience	600.00	600.00	275.00

Our Lady

Designer: John Broad
Height: Unknown
Colour: Terracotta
Issued: c.1910

Description	U.S. $	Can. $	U.K. £
Terracotta		Extremely Rare	

Pomona

Designer: John Broad
Height: 14", 35 cm
Colour: X7911, Terracotta
Issued: 1912

Description	U.S. $	Can. $	U.K. £
Terracotta	3,000.00	3,000.00	1,250.00

Photograph not
available
at press time

Queen Alexandra

Designer: John Broad
Height: 16 1/2", 42 cm
Colour: Terracotta
Issued: 1901

Description	U.S. $	Can. $	U.K. £
Terracotta	3,500.00	3,500.00	1,500.00

Queen Victoria

Designer: John Broad
Height: 11 3/4", 29.75 cm
Colour: Brown salt glaze stoneware
Issued: 1901

Description	U.S. $	Can. $	U.K. £
Brown salt glaze	4,000.00	4,000.00	1,500.00

Thrower

Designer: John Broad
Height: 7", 18 cm
Colour: 1. Terracotta
          2. Brown stoneware
Issued: 1883

Description	U.S. $	Can. $	U.K. £
Brown Stoneware		Rare	
Terracotta		Rare	

Note: This figure was also issued as a 27" model.

MARK MARSHALL
LAMBETH FIGURES

Bear Stripper

Designer: Mark Marshall
Height: 5 1/2", 14 cm
Colour: White stoneware
Issued: c.1910

Description	U.S. $	Can. $	U.K. £
White stoneware		Rare	

Crinoline (as HN13)

Designer: Mark Marshall
Height: 7", 18 cm
Colour: Matt white stoneware with blue details
Issued: 1910

Description	U.S. $	Can. $	U.K. £
Matt white stoneware		Rare	

18th Century Figure with Fan

Designer: Mark Marshall
Height: 8", 20.5 cm
Colour: Matt white stoneware with blue details
Issued: c.1890

Description	U.S. $	Can. $	U.K. £
Matt white stoneware		Rare	

Old Woman Figure

Designer: Mark Marshall
Height: 9 1/2", 24.3 cm
Colour: Unknown
Issued: c.1900

Description	U.S. $	Can. $	U.K. £
		Extremely Rare	

LESLIE HARRADINE
LAMBETH FIGURES

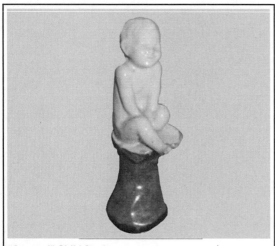

"Amused" Child Study

Model No.:	H48
Designer:	Leslie Harradine
Height:	6", 15.5 cm
Colour:	Slip cast buff stoneware on either a green base or a blue base
Issued:	c.1912

Description	U.S. $	Can. $	U.K. £
1. Slip cast		Rare	

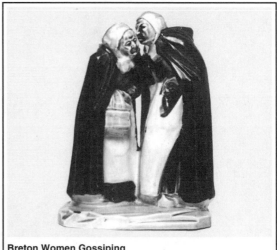

Breton Women Gossiping

Model No.:	H64
Designer:	Leslie Harradine
Height:	10", 25.5cm
Colour:	Black and white stoneware
Issued:	c.1912

Description	U.S. $	Can. $	U.K. £
Black/white stoneware		Rare	

British Soldier

Model No.:	Unknown
Designer:	Leslie Harradine
Height:	9 1/2", 24 cm
Colour:	Brown stoneware
Issued:	1910
Series:	Soldiers

Description	U.S. $	Can. $	U.K. £
Brown stoneware	700.00	700.00	295.00

Cossack

Model No.:	H78
Designer:	Leslie Harradine
Height:	9 1/2", 24 cm
Colour:	Brown stoneware
Issued:	c.1910
Series:	Soldiers

Description	U.S. $	Can. $	U.K. £
Brown stoneware	700.00	700.00	295.00

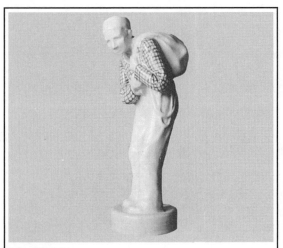

Dutch Man
also called "The Toiler"

Model No.:	H10
Designer:	Leslie Harradine
Height:	8 1/2", 21.5 cm
Colour:	White slip cast stoneware with blue detailing
Issued:	1912

Description	U.S. $	Can. $	U.K. £
White slip cast stoneware	850.00	850.00	325.00

Dutch Woman

Model No.:	H3 (X7728)
Designer:	Leslie Harradine
Height:	7 3/4", 19.5 cm
Colour:	White slip cast stoneware with blue detailing
Issued:	1912

Description	U.S. $	Can. $	U.K. £
White slip cast stoneware	850.00	850.00	325.00

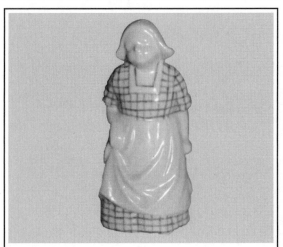

Dutch Woman

Model No.:	H9
Designer:	Leslie Harradine
Height:	4 1/2", 11.5 cm
Colour:	White slip cast stoneware with blue or green detailing
Issued:	1912

Description	U.S. $	Can. $	U.K. £
White slip cast stoneware	850.00	850.00	325.00

French Legionnaire

Model No.:	H72
Designer:	Leslie Harradine
Height:	9 1/2", 24 cm
Colour:	Brown stoneware
Issued:	c.1910
Series:	Soldiers

Description	U.S. $	Can. $	U.K. £
Brown stoneware	750.00	750.00	350.00

Harvester (with Scythe)

Model No.:	H66			
Designer:	Leslie Harradine			
Height:	7", 18 cm			
Colour:	Brown stoneware			
Issued:	c.1910			

Description	U.S. $	Can. $	U.K. £
Brown stoneware	650.00	650.00	295.00

Hunched Figure on Pedestal

Model No.:	H45
Designer:	Leslie Harradine
Height:	Unknown
Colour:	White slip cast stoneware on brown base
Issued:	c.1910

Description	U.S. $	Can. $	U.K. £
White slip cast stoneware	650.00	650.00	325.00

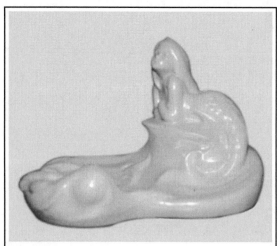

Mermaids

Model No.:	H29
Designer:	Leslie Harradine
Height:	7", 18 cm
Colour:	White slip cast stoneware
Issued:	1912

Description	U.S. $	Can. $	U.K. £
White slip cast stoneware		Rare	

Mother and Child Standing

Model No.:	H24
Designer:	Leslie Harradine
Height:	8 3/4", 23 cm
Colour:	1. Brown stoneware
	2. White slip cast stoneware
Issued:	1912

Description	U.S. $	Can. $	U.K. £
Brown stoneware		Rare	
White slip cast stoneware		Rare	

Motherhood

Model No.	H4 (X7729)
Designer:	Leslie Harradine
Height:	5", 12.5 cm
Colour:	White slip cast stoneware
Issued:	1912

Description	U.S. $	Can. $	U.K. £
White slip cast stoneware		Rare	

North African Spahi

Model No.:	Unknown
Designer:	Leslie Harradine
Height:	9 1/2", 24 cm
Colour:	Brown stoneware
Issued:	c.1910
Series:	Soldiers

Description	U.S. $	Can. $	U.K. £
Brown stoneware	800.00	800.00	350.00

Peasant Girl

Model No.:	H8
Designer:	Leslie Harradine
Height:	8", 21 cm
Colour:	White slip cast stoneware
Issued:	1912

Description	U.S. $	Can. $	U.K. £
White slip cast stoneware	750.00	750.00	250.00

Peat Cutter

Model No.:	Unknown
Designer:	Leslie Harradine
Height:	7", 18 cm
Colour:	Brown stoneware
Issued:	c.1912

Description	U.S. $	Can. $	U.K. £
Brown stoneware	700.00	700.00	300.00

Reaper

Model No.:	H68
Designer:	Leslie Harradine
Height:	7 1/2", 19 cm
Colour:	1. (X8666), Brown stoneware
	2. Coloured Doultonware and toby colours
Issued:	1. c.1912; 2. 1927

Description	U.S. $	Can. $	U.K. £
1. Brown stoneware	700.00	700.00	300.00
2.. Coloured Doultonware	700.00	700.00	300.00

Soldier

Model No.:	H78
Designer:	Leslie Harradine
Height:	9 1/2", 24 cm
Colour:	Brown stoneware
Issued:	1910
Series:	Soldiers

Description	U.S. $	Can. $	U.K. £
Brown stoneware	850.00	850.00	350.00

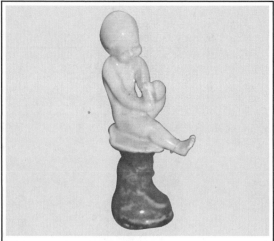

"This Little Pig" Child Study

Model No.:	H49
Designer:	Leslie Harradine
Height:	5", 13 cm
Colour:	Slip cast buff and brown stoneware
Issued:	c.1912

Description	U.S. $	Can. $	U.K. £
Slip cast buff stoneware		Rare	

Worker (with Bucket)

Model No.:	Unknown
Designer:	Leslie Harradine
Height:	7", 18 cm
Colour:	Brown stoneware
Issued:	c.1912

Description	U.S. $	Can. $	U.K. £
Brown stoneware		Rare	

LESLIE HARRADINE
LAMBETH DICKENS FIGURES

Mr. Micawber

Model No.:	H20
Designer:	Leslie Harradine
Height:	9 1/4", 24 cm
Colour:	1. Brown
	2. buff slip cast stoneware
	3. Coloured Doultonware
Issued:	1912
U.S.:	**$1,100.00**
Can.:	**$1,100.00**
Ster.:	**£ 295.00**

Mr. Pickwick

Model No.:	H19
Designer:	Leslie Harradine
Height:	8 3/4", 22cm
Colour:	Brown or buff slip cast
	stoneware
Issued:	1912
U.S.:	**$1,100.00**
Can.:	**$1,100.00**
Ster.:	**£ 295.00**

Mr. Squeers

Model No.:	Unknown
Designer:	Leslie Harradine
Height:	9 1/4", 23.5 cm
Colour:	Brown or buff slip cast
	stoneware
Issued:	1912
U.S.:	**$1,200.00**
Can.:	**$1,200.00**
Ster.:	**£ 350.00**

Pecksniff

Model No.:	H21
Designer:	Leslie Harradine
Height:	9", 23 cm
Colour:	Brown or buff slip cast
	stoneware
Issued:	1912
U.S.:	**$1,100.00**
Can.:	**$1,100.00**
Ster.:	**£ 295.00**

Sairey Gamp

Model No.:	Unknown
Designer:	Leslie Harradine
Height:	7 1/2", 20 cm
Colour:	Brown or buff slip cast
	stoneware
Issued:	1912
U.S.:	**$1,300.00**
Can.:	**$1,300.00**
Ster.:	**£ 395.00**

Sam Weller

Model No.:	H23
Designer:	Leslie Harradine
Height:	9 1/2", 24.5 cm
Colour:	Brown or buff slip cast
	stoneware
Issued:	1912
U.S.:	**$1,100.00**
Can.:	**$1,100.00**
Ster.:	**£ 295.00**

CHARLES NOKE
VELLUM FIGURES

Beefeater Toasting the Queen

Designer: Charles Noke
Height: 12 3/4", 32.5 cm
Colour: 1. Ivory with pink and blue tints
2. Scarlet
Issued: 1899

Description	U.S. $	Can. $	U.K. £
1. Ivory/pink/blue	6,000.00	6,000.00	2,500.00
2. Scarlet	6,000.00	6,000.00	2,500.00

Cleopatra

Designer: Charles Noke
Height: 12", 30.5 cm
Colour: Ivory with pink and green tints
Issued: c.1892

Description	U.S. $	Can. $	U.K. £
Ivory/pink/green	8,000.00	8,000.00	2,750.00

Photograph not
available
at press time

Columbus

Designer: Charles Noke
Height: 20", 51 cm
Colour: 1. Ivory
2. Parian
3. Gold printed pattern
Issued: 1893

Description	U.S. $	Can. $	U.K. £
1. Ivory		Rare	
2. Parian		Rare	
3. Gold printed pattern		Rare	

Devil

Designer: Charles Noke
Height: Unknown
Colour: 1. Ivory with pink and green tints
2. Scarlet and gold
Issued: 1893

Description	U.S. $	Can. $	U.K. £
1. Ivory/pink/green		Rare	
2. Scarlet and gold		Rare	

Photograph not
available
at press time

Diana

Designer:	Charles Noke
	Height: 11 1/2", 29.5 cm
Colour:	1. Ivory with pink and green tints
	2. Printed flowers
	3. Printed scroll pattern
Issued:	1893

Description	U.S. $	Can. $	U.K. £
1. Ivory/pink/green	5,000.00	5,000.00	2,000.00
2. Printed flowers	5,000.00	5,000.00	2,000.00
3. Printed scroll pattern	5,000.00	5,000.00	2,000.00

Ellen Terry as Queen Catharine

Designer:	Charles Noke
Height:	12 1/2", 31 cm
Colour:	1. Ivory
	2. Ivory with green and gold tints
Issued:	1893

Description	U.S. $	Can. $	U.K. £
1. Ivory	3,000.00	3,500.00	1,250.00
2. Ivory/green/gold	3,000.00	3,500.00	1,250.00

Note: Also known in 9" size

Henry Irving as Cardinal Wolsey

Designer:	Charles Noke
Height:	13", 33 cm
Colour:	1. Ivory
	2. Ivory with green and pink sheen
Issued:	1899

Description	U.S. $	Can. $	U.K. £
1. Ivory	3,500.00	3,500.00	1,250.00
2. Ivory/green/pink	3,500.00	3,500.00	1,250.00

Note: Also known in 9 1/4" size

Photograph not
available
at press time

Jack Point

Designer:	Charles Noke
Height:	16", 40.5 cm
Colour:	Ivory
Issued:	1893

Description	U.S. $	Can. $	U.K. £
Ivory		Rare	

Jester

Designer: Charles Noke
Height: 9 1/2", 23.5 cm
Colour: 1. Ivory
2. Parian
3. Ivory with pink and green tints
Issued: 1892

Description	U.S. $	Can. $	U.K. £
1. Ivory	3,500.00	3,500.00	1,500.00
2. Parian	3,500.00	3,500.00	1,500.00
3. Ivory/pink/green	3,500.00	3,500.00	1,500.00

Jester (Kneeling)

Designer: Charles Noke
Height: 4 1/2", 11.5 cm
Colour: Scarlet with gold
Issued: c.1900

Description	U.S. $	Can. $	U.K. £
Scarlet/gold	6,000.00	6,000.00	6,000.00

Mephistopheles and Marguerite

Designer: Charles Noke
Height: 12 1/2", 32 cm
Colour: 1. Ivory
2. Ivory with pink and green tints;
3. Scarlet
4. Scarlet and gold
5. Purple and gold
6. Deep blue with printed dragon design
Issued: 1891

Description	U.S. $	Can. $	U.K. £
1. Ivory	3,750.00	3,750.00	1,500.00
2. Ivory/pink/green	3,750.00	3,750.00	1,500.00
3. Scarlet	3,750.00	3,750.00	1,500.00
4. Scarlet/gold	3,750.00	3,750.00	1,500.00
5. Purple/gold	3,750.00	3,750.00	1,500.00
6. Blue/dragon design	3,750.00	3,750.00	1,500.00

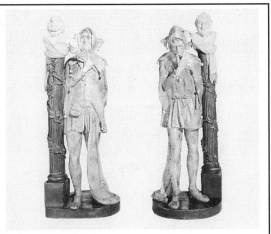

Mirth and Melancholy

Designer: Charles Noke
Height: 16", 40.5 cm
Colour: 1. Ivory
        2. Ivory with pink and green tint
        3. Gold printed pattern
Issued: 1892

Description	U.S. $	Can. $	U.K. £
1. Ivory		Rare	
2. Ivory/pink/green		Rare	
3. Gold printed pattern		Rare	

Moorish Minstrel

Designer: Charles Noke
Height: Unknown
Colour: 1. Ivory with green and pink tints
        2. Ivory with green and pink tints, white and gold flowers
        3. Blue and grey; scarlet and blue
Issued: 1892

Description	U.S. $	Can. $	U.K. £
1. Ivory/green/pink	3,000.00	3,000.00	1,000.00
2. Ivory/green/pink/white/gold	3,000.00	3,000.00	1,000.00
3. Blue/grey/scarlet/blue	3,000.00	3,000.00	1,000.00

Oh! Law

Designer: Charles Noke
Height: 8 1/2", 21.5 cm
Colour: 1. Ivory
        2. Gold printed pattern
        3. Ivory with green and pink tints
Issued: 1893

Description	U.S. $	Can. $	U.K. £
1. Ivory	3,500.00	3,500.00	1,250.00
2. Gold printed pattern	3,500.00	3,500.00	1,250.00
3. Ivory/green/pink	3,500.00	3,500.00	1,250.00

Pierrot

Designer: Charles Noke
Height: 6 1/2", 16.5 cm
Colour: 1. Ivory with black details
        2. Ivory with green and gold details
Issued: 1899

Description	U.S. $	Can. $	U.K. £
1. Ivory/black	3,750.00	3,750.00	1,500.00
2. Ivory/green/gold	3,750.00	3,750.00	1,500.00

Portia

Designer: Charles Noke
Height: 16 3/4", 42.5 cm
Colour: 1. Ivory
        2. Green and pink with flowers
        3. Green and pink with scrolls and flowers
Issued: 1893

Description	U.S. $	Can. $	U.K. £
1. Ivory	6,500.00	6,500.00	2.250.00
2. Green/pink/flowers	6,500.00	6,500.00	2.250.00
3. Green/pink/scrolls/flowers	6,500.00	6,500.00	2.250.00

Photograph not
available
at press time

St. Mark's Birds

Designer: Charles Noke
Height: 17 1/2", 44 cm
Colour: 1. Ivory with pink tints
        2. Printed flowers
        3. Ivory and gold
Issued: 1892

Description	U.S. $	Can. $	U.K. £
1. Ivory/pink		Rare	
2. Printed flowers		Rare	
3. Ivory/gold		Rare	

Photograph not
available
at press time

Sentimental Pierrot

Designer: Charles Noke
Height: 6", 15 cm
Colour: 1. Ivory with pink and green tints
        2. Ivory
Issued: 1899

Description	U.S. $	Can. $	U.K. £
1. Ivory/pink/green	3,750.00	3,750.00	1,250.00
2. Ivory	3,750.00	3,750.00	1,250.00

Shakespeare

Designer: Charles Noke
Height: 12 1/2", 31 cm
Colour: Ivory
Issued: c.1899

Description	U.S. $	Can. $	U.K. £
Ivory	5,000.00	5,000.00	2,000.00

Shylock

Designer: Charles Noke
Height: 16", 40.5 cm
Colour: 1. Ivory
        2. Brown with gold printed pattern
Issued: 1893

Description	U.S. $	Can. $	U.K. £
1. Ivory	6,500.00	6,500.00	2,250.00
2. Brown/gold printed pattern	6,500.00	6,500.00	2,250.00

Water Carrier

Designer: Charles Noke
Height: 20 3/4", 52 cm
Colour: Ivory with pink and green tints
Issued: 1893

Description	U.S. $	Can. $	U.K. £
Ivory/pink/green		Rare	

CHARLES NOKE
WALL POCKETS AND LIGHTS

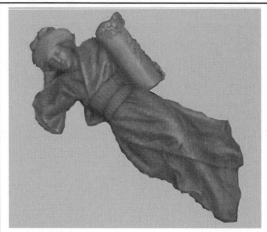

Geisha Wall Pocket

Designer:	Charles Noke
Height:	9 1/4", 23.5 cm
Colour:	1. Ivory
	2. Ivory with pink tints
	3. Gold printed pattern
Issued:	1893

Description	U.S. $	Can. $	U.K. £
1. Ivory	3,000.00	3,000.00	1,000.00
2. Ivory/pink	3,000.00	3,000.00	1,000.00
3. Gold printed pattern	3,000.00	3,000.00	1,000.00

Lady Jester Wall Pocket

Designer:	Charles Noke
Height:	9 3/4", 24.5 cm
Colour:	1. Ivory with green and pink tints
	2. Printed floral pattern
Issued:	1892

Description	U.S. $	Can. $	U.K. £
1. Ivory/green/pink	3,750.00	3,750.00	1,250.00
2. Printed floral pattern	3,750.00	3,750.00	1,250.00

Sorceress Wall Pocket

Designer:	Charles Noke
Height:	10 3/4", 27.5 cm
Colour:	1. Ivory
	2. Green tint with white floral pattern
Issued:	1892

Description	U.S. $	Can. $	U.K. £
1. Ivory	3,500.00	3,500.00	1,250.00
2. Green/white floral pattern	3,500.00	3,500.00	1,250.00

The Witch Wall Light

Designer:	Charles Noke
Height:	Unknown
Colour:	Green and scarlet with gold floral pattern
Issued:	1897

Description	U.S. $	Can. $	U.K. £
Green/scarlet/gold		Extremely Rare	

HN SERIES

HN 1
Darling
Style One
Designer: C. Vyse
Height: 7 3/4", 19.5 cm
Issued: 1913-1928
Colour: Light grey
Varieties: HN 1319, 1371, 1372

U.S.:	**$2,750.00**
Can.:	**$2,750.00**
Ster.:	**£1,350.00**

HN 2
Elizabeth Fry
Designer: C. Vyse
Height: 17", 43.2 cm
Issued: 1913-1936
Colour: Light blue,
                 green base
Varieties: HN 2A

U.S.:	**$7,000.00**
Can.:	**$6,000.00**
Ster.:	**£2,500.00**

HN 2A
Elizabeth Fry
Designer: C. Vyse
Height: 17", 43.2 cm
Issued: 1913-1936
Colour: Light blue,
                 blue base
Varieties: HN 2

U.S.:	**$7,000.00**
Can.:	**$6,000.00**
Ster.:	**£2,500.00**

HN 3
Milking Time
Designer: P. Stabler
Height: 6 1/2", 16.5 cm
Colour: Blue dress,
                 white apron
Issued: 1913-1938
Varieties: HN 306

U.S.:	**Only**
Can.:	**three**
Ster.:	**known**

HN 4
Picardy Peasant (woman)
Designer: P. Stabler
Height: 9 1/4", 23.5 cm
Colour: Blue and white
Issued: 1913-1938
Varieties: HN 5, 17A, 351, 513

U.S.:	**$3,100.00**
Can.:	**$3,250.00**
Ster.:	**£1,500.00**

HN 5
Picardy Peasant (woman)
Designer: P. Stabler
Height: 9 1/2", 24.0 cm
Colour: Grey
Issued: 1913-1938
Varieties: HN 4, 17A, 351, 513

U.S.:	**Extremely rare**
Can.:	
Ster.:	

HN 6
Dunce
Designer: C.J. Noke
Height: 10 1/2", 26.7 cm
Colour: Light blue
Issued: 1913-1936
Varieties: HN 310, 357

U.S.:	**Only**
Can.:	**three**
Ster.:	**known**

HN 7
Pedlar Wolf
Designer: C.J. Noke
Height: 5 1/2", 14.0 cm
Colour: Blue and black
Issued: 1913-1938

U.S.:	**Only**
Can.:	**two**
Ster.:	**known**

HN 8
The Crinoline
Designer: G. Lambert
Height: 6 1/4", 15.8 cm
Colour: Lavender
Issued: 1913-1938
Varieties: HN 9, 9A, 21, 21A,
413, 566, 628

U.S.: **$2,800.00**
Can.: **$3,000.00**
Ster.: **£1,350.00**

HN 9
The Crinoline
Designer: G. Lambert
Height: 6 1/4", 15.8 cm
Colour: Light green,
flowers on skirt
Issued: 1913-1938
Varieties: HN 8, 9A, 21, 21A,
413, 566, 628

U.S.: **$2,800.00**
Can.: **$3,000.00**
Ster.: **£1,350.00**

HN 9A
The Crinoline
Designer: G. Lambert
Height: 6 1/4", 15.8 cm
Colour: Light green,
no flowers
Issued: 1913-1938
Varieties: HN 8, 9, 21, 21A,
413, 566, 628

U.S.: **Extremely rare**
Can.:
Ster.:

HN 10
Madonna of the Square
Designer: P. Stabler
Height: 7", 17.8 cm
Colour: Lavender
Issued: 1913-1936
Varieties: HN 10A, 11, 14,
27, 326, 573, 576,
594, 613, 764,
1968, 1969, 2034

U.S.: **$2,300.00**
Can.: **$2,000.00**
Ster.: **£ 650.00**

HN 10A
Madonna of the Square
Designer: P. Stabler
Height: 7", 17.8 cm
Colour: Green and blue
Issued: 1913-1936
Varieties: HN 10, 11, 14, 27,
326, 573, 576, 594,
613, 764, 1968,
1969, 2034

U.S.: **Extremely rare**
Can.:
Ster.:

HN 11
Madonna of the Square
Designer: P. Stabler
Height: 7", 17.8 cm
Colour: Grey
Issued: 1913-1936
Varieties: HN 10, 10A, 14, 27,
326, 573, 576, 594,
613, 764, 1968,
1969, 2034

U.S.: **Extremely rare**
Can.:
Ster.:

HN 12
Baby
Designer: C.J. Noke
Height: 4 3/4", 12.0 cm
Colour: Pale pink
Issued: 1913-1938

U.S.: **Only**
Can.: **two**
Ster.: **known**

HN 13
Picardy Peasant (man)
Designer: P. Stabler
Height: 9", 22.9 cm
Colour: Blue costume
with white cap
Issued: 1913-1938
Varieties: HN 17, 19

U.S.: **Extremely rare**
Can.:
Ster.:

HN 14
Madonna of the Square
Designer: P. Stabler
Height: 7", 17.8 cm
Colour: Blue
Issued: 1913-1936
Varieties: HN 10, 10A, 11, 27, 326, 573, 576, 594, 613, 764, 1968, 1969, 2034

U.S.: **$2,300.00**
Can.: **$2,000.00**
Ster.: **£ 750.00**

HN 15
The Sleepy Scholar
Designer: W. White
Height: 6 3/4", 17.2 cm
Colour: Blue
Issued: 1913-1938
Varieties: HN 16, 29

U.S.: **$6,750.00**
Can.: **$6,750.00**
Ster.: **£2,250.00**

HN 16
The Sleepy Scholar
Designer: W. White
Height: 6 3/4", 17.2 cm
Colour: Green
Issued: 1913-1938
Varieties: HN 15, 29

U.S.: **$6,750.00**
Can.: **$6,750.00**
Ster.: **£2,250.00**

HN 17
Picardy Peasant (man)
Designer: P. Stabler
Height: 9 1/2", 24.0 cm
Colour: Green
Issued: 1913-1938
Varieties: HN 13, 19,

U.S.: **Extremely rare**
Can.:
Ster.:

HN 17A
Picardy Peasant (woman)
Designer: P. Stabler
Height: 9 1/2", 24.0 cm
Colour: Green
Issued: 1913-1938
Varieties: HN 4, 5, 351, 513

U.S.: **Extremely rare**
Can.:
Ster.:

HN 18
Pussy
Designer: F.C. Stone
Height: 7 3/4", 19.7 cm
Colour: Light blue
Issued: 1913-1938
Varieties: HN 325, 507; also called "The Black Cat"

U.S.: **Only**
Can.: **five**
Ster.: **known**

HN 19
Picardy Peasant (man)
Designer: P. Stabler
Height: 9 1/2", 24.0 cm
Colour: Green
Issued: 1913-1938
Varieties: HN 13, 17

U.S.: **Extremely rare**
Can.:
Ster.:

HN 20
The Coquette
Designer: W. White
Height: 9 1/4", 23.5 cm
Colour: Blue
Issued: 1913-1938
Varieties: HN 20A, 37

U.S.: **$4,500.00**
Can.: **$4,500.00**
Ster.: **£2,250.00**

HN 20A
The Coquette
Designer: W. White
Height: 9 1/4", 23.5 cm
Colour: Green
Issued: 1913-1938
Varieties: HN 20, 37

U.S.:	**$4,500.00**
Can.:	**$4,500.00**
Ster.:	**£2,250.00**

HN 21
The Crinoline
Designer: G. Lambert
Height: 6 1/4", 15.8 cm
Colour: Yellow with
rosebuds
Issued: 1913-1938
Varieties: HN 8, 9, 9A, 21A,
413, 566, 628

U.S.:	**$3,000.00**
Can.:	**$3,000.00**
Ster.:	**£1,350.00**

HN 21A
The Crinoline
Designer: G. Lambert
Height: 6 1/4", 15.8 cm
Colour: Yellow, no
rosebuds
Issued: 1913-1938
Varieties: HN 8, 9, 9A, 21,
413, 566, 628

U.S.:	**Extremely rare**
Can.:	
Ster.:	

HN 22
The Lavender Woman
Designer: P. Stabler
Height: 8 1/4", 21.0 cm
Colour: Light blue
Issued: 1913-1936
Varieties: HN 23, 23A,
342, 569, 744

U.S.:	**$6,000.00**
Can.:	**$5,000.00**
Ster.:	**£2,000.00**

HN 23
The Lavender Woman
Designer: P. Stabler
Height: 8 1/4", 21.0 cm
Colour: Green
Issued: 1913-1936
Varieties: HN 22, 23A, 342,
569, 744

U.S.:	**Extremely rare**
Can.:	
Ster.:	

HN 23A
The Lavender Woman
Designer: P. Stabler
Height: 8 1/4", 21.0 cm
Colour: Blue and green
Issued: 1913-1936
Varieties: HN 22, 23, 342,
569, 744

U.S.:	**Extremely rare**
Can.:	
Ster.:	

HN 24
Sleep
Designer: P. Stabler
Height: 8 1/4", 21.0 cm
Colour: Light green
Issued: 1913-1936
Varieties: HN 24A, 25, 25A,
424, 692, 710

U.S.:	**$2,750.00**
Can.:	**$2,750.00**
Ster.:	**£1,000.00**

HN 24A
Sleep
Designer: P. Stabler
Height: 8 1/4", 21.0 cm
Colour: Dark blue
Issued: 1913-1936
Varieties: HN 24, 25, 25A,
424, 692, 710

U.S.:	**$2,750.00**
Can.:	**$2,750.00**
Ster.:	**£1,000.00**

HN 25
Sleep
Designer: P. Stabler
Height: 8 1/4", 21.0 cm
Colour: Dark green
Issued: 1913-1936
Varieties: HN 24, 24A, 25A,
424, 692, 710

U.S.: **$2,750.00**
Can.: **$2,750.00**
Ster.: **£1,000.00**

HN 25A
Sleep
Designer: P. Stabler
Height: 8 1/4", 21.0 cm
Colour: Dark Green
Issued: 1913-1936
Varieties: HN 24, 24A, 25,
424, 692, 710

U.S.: **Extremely rare**
Can.:
Ster.:

HN 26
The Diligent Scholar
Designer: W. White
Height: 7", 17.8 cm
 Colour: Mottled brown
and green
Issued: 1913-1936
Varieties: Also called "The
Attentive Scholar"

U.S.: **$6,750.00**
Can.: **$6,750.00**
Ster.: **£2,250.00**

HN 27
Madonna of the Square
Designer: P. Stabler
Height: 7", 17.8 cm
Colour: Blue
Issued: 1913-1936
Varieties: HN 10, 10A, 11,
14, 326, 573, 576,
594, 613, 764,
1968, 1969, 2034

U.S.: **Extremely rare**
Can.:
Ster.:

HN 28
Motherhood
Style One
Designer: P. Stabler
Height: 8", 20.3 cm
Colour: Light blue
Issued: 1913-1936
Varieties: HN 30, 303

U.S.: **$6,000.00**
Can.: **$6,000.00**
Ster.: **£2,500.00**

HN 29
The Sleepy Scholar
Designer: W. White
Height: 6 3/4", 17.2 cm
Colour: Brown
Issued: 1913-1938
Varieties: HN 15, 16

U.S.: **$6,750.00**
Can.: **$6,750.00**
Ster.: **£2,250.00**

HN 30
Motherhood
Style One
Designer: P. Stabler
Height: 8", 20.3 cm
Colour: White, blue
and yellow
Issued: 1913-1936
Varieties: HN 28, 303

U.S.: **None**
Can.: **known**
Ster.: **to exist**

Photograph
Not
Available

HN 31
The Return of Persephone
Designer: C. Vyse
Height: 16", 40.6 cm
Colour: Grey and
grey-blue
Issued: 1913-1938

U.S.: **Only**
Can.: **one**
Ster.: **known**

HN 32
Child on Crab
Designer: C.J. Noke
Height: 5 1/4", 13.3 cm
Colour: Pale blue, green and brown
Issued: 1913-1938
Varieties: Also known in flambé

U.S.:	**$6,000.00**
Can.:	**$6,000.00**
Ster.:	**£2,250.00**

HN 33
An Arab
Designer: C.J. Noke
Height: 16 1/2", 41.9 cm
Colour: Dark blue, green
Issued: 1913-1938
Varieties: HN 343, 378; also called "The Moor" HN 1308, 1366, 1425, 1657, 2082, 3642

U.S.:	**$3,700.00**
Can.:	**$3,500.00**
Ster.:	**£1,450.00**

HN 34
A Moorish Minstrel
Designer: C.J. Noke
Height: 13 1/2", 34.3 cm
Colour: Deep purple
Issued: 1913-1938
Varieties: HN 364, 415, 797

U.S.:	**$4,000.00**
Can.:	**$4,000.00**
Ster.:	**£2,000.00**

Derived from Burslem figure produced in 1890s

HN 35
Charley's Aunt
Style One
Designer: A. Toft
Height: 7", 17.8 cm
Colour: Black and white
Issued: 1913-1936
Varieties: HN 640

U.S.:	**$1,250.00**
Can.:	**$1,250.00**
Ster.:	**£ 450.00**

HN 36
The Sentimental Pierrot
Designer: C.J. Noke
Height: 5 1/2", 14.0 cm
Colour: Grey
Issued: 1914-1936
Varieties: HN 307

U.S.:	**$6,000.00**
Can.:	**$6,000.00**
Ster.:	**£2,500.00**

HN 37
The Coquette
Designer: W. White
Height: 9 1/4", 23.5 cm
Colour: Green flowered dress
Issued: 1914-1938
Varieties: HN 20, 20A

U.S.:	**$6,000.00**
Can.:	**$6,000.00**
Ster.:	**£2,500.00**

HN 38
The Carpet Vendor
Style One
Designer: C.J. Noke
Height: 5 1/2", 14.0 cm
Colour: Blue, yellow and green
Issued: 1914-1936
Varieties: HN 76, 350; also known in flambé

U.S.:	**Extremely rare**
Can.:	
Ster.:	

Photograph
Not
Available

HN 38A
The Carpet Vendor
Style Two
Designer: C.J. Noke
Height: 6 1/4", 15.9 cm
Colour: Blue and yellow, patterned long carpet
Issued: 1914-1936
Varieties: HN 348

U.S.:	**Extremely rare**
Can.:	
Ster.:	

HN 39
Myfanwy Jones
Designer: E.W. Light
Height: 12", 30.5 cm
Colour: Red, black, purple
Issued: 1914-1936
Varieties: HN 92, 456, 514,
516, 519, 520, 660,
668, 669, 701, 792;
"The Welsh Girl"

U.S.: $6,000.00
Can.: $5,500.00
Ster.: £2,500.00

HN 40
A Lady of the
Elizabethan Period
Style One
Designer: E.W. Light
Height: 9 1/2", 24.1 cm
Colour: Orange and brown
with pattern
Issued: 1914-1938
Varieties: HN 40A, 73, 411;
"Elizabethan Lady"

U.S.: **Extremely rare**
Can.:
Ster.:

HN 40A
A Lady of the
Elizabethan Period
Style One
Designer: E.W. Light
Height: 9 1/2", 24.1 cm
Colour: Orange and brown
Issued: 1914-1938
Varieties: HN 40, 73, 411;
"Elizabethan Lady"

U.S.: **Extremely rare**
Can.:
Ster.:

HN 41
A Lady of the
Georgian Period
Designer: E.W. Light
Height: 10 1/4", 26.0 cm
Colour: Gold and blue
Issued: 1914-1936
Varieties: HN 331, 444,
690, 702

U.S.: $3,500.00
Can.: $3,500.00
Ster.: £1,500.00

HN 42
Robert Burns
Style One
Designer: E.W. Light
Height: 14", 35.5 cm
Colour: Brown, green
and yellow
Issued: 1914-1938

U.S.: **Only**
Can.: **one**
Ster.: **known**

HN 43
A Woman of the
Time of Henry VI
Designer: E.W. Light
Height: 9 1/4", 23.5 cm
Green and yellow
Issued: 1914-1938

U.S.: **Only**
Can.: **three**
Ster.: **known**

HN 44
A Lilac Shawl
Designer: C.J. Noke
Height: 8 3/4", 22.2 cm
Colour: Cream and blue
Issued: 1915-1938
Varieties: HN 44A; "In Grand-
ma's Days" HN 339,
340, 388, 442;
"The Poke Bonnet"
HN 362, 612, 765

U.S.: $2,750.00
Can.: $2,750.00
Ster.: £1,200.00

HN 44A
A Lilac Shawl
Designer: C.J. Noke
Height: 8 3/4", 22.2 cm
Colour: White and lilac
Issued: 1915-1938
Varieties: HN 44; "In Grand-
ma's Days" HN 339,
340, 388, 442;
"The Poke Bonnet"
HN 362, 612, 765

U.S.: $2,750.00
Can.: $2,750.00
Ster.: £1,200.00

HN 45
A Jester
Style One
Designer: C.J. Noke
Height: 9 1/2", 24.1 cm
                  Black and white
Issued: 1915-1938
Varieties: HN 71, 71A, 320,
                  367, 412, 426, 446,
                  552, 616, 627,
                  1295, 1702, 2016

U.S.: $5,000.00
Can.: $5,000.00
Ster.:   £1,750.00

HN 45A
A Jester
Style Two
Designer: C.J. Noke
Height: 10 1/4", 26.0 cm
                  Green and white
Issued: 1915-1938
Varieties: HN 45B, 55,
                  308, 630, 1333

U.S.: $7,500.00
Can.: $7,500.00
Ster.:   £1,750.00

HN 45B
A Jester
Style Two
Designer: C.J. Noke
Height: 10 1/4", 26.0 cm
Colour: Red and white
Issued: 1915-1938
Varieties: HN 45A, 55, 308,
                  630, 1333; Also
                  known in black
                  and white

U.S.: $7,500.00
Can.: $7,500.00
Ster.:   £1,750.00

HN 46
The Gainsborough Hat
Designer: H. Tittensor
Height: 8 3/4", 22.2 cm
Colour: Lavender
Issued: 1915-1936
Varieties: HN 46A, 47,
                  329, 352, 383,
                  453, 675, 705

U.S.: $3,500.00
Can.: $3,500.00
Ster.:   £1,750.00

HN 46A
The Gainsborough Hat
Designer: H. Tittensor
Height: 8 3/4", 22.2 cm
Colour: Lavender with
                  black collar
Issued: 1915-1936
Varieties: HN 46, 47,
                  329, 352, 383,
                  453, 675, 705

U.S.:   None
Can.:   known
Ster.:   to exist

HN 47
The Gainsborough Hat
Designer: H. Tittensor
Height: 8 3/4", 22.2 cm
Colour: Green
Issued: 1915-1936
Varieties: HN 46, 46A,
                  329, 352, 383,
                  453, 675, 705

U.S.: $4,500.00
Can.: $4,500.00
Ster.:   £2,000.00

HN 48
Lady of the Fan
Designer: E.W. Light
Height: 9 1/2", 24.1 cm
Colour: Lavender
Issued: 1916-1936
Varieties: HN 52, 53, 53A,
                  335, 509

U.S.:   None
Can.:   known
Ster.:   to exist

HN 48A
Lady with Rose
Designer: E.W. Light
Height: 9 1/2", 24.1 cm
Colour: Cream and orange
Issued: 1916-1936
Varieties: HN 52A, 68,
                  304, 336, 515,
                  517, 584, 624

U.S.: $3,750.00
Can.: $3,750.00
Ster.:   £1,500.00

HN 49
Under the Gooseberry
Bush
Designer: C.J. Noke
Height: 3 1/2", 8.9 cm
Colour: Green and brown
Issued: 1916-1938
U.S.: **$3,500.00**
Can.: **$3,500.00**
Ster.: **£1,500.00**

HN 50
A Spook
Style One
Designer: H. Tittensor
Height: 7", 17.8 cm
Colour: Green robe,
black cap
Issued: 1916-1936
Varieties: HN 51, 51A, 51B,
58, 512, 625; Also
known in flambé
U.S.: **$3,750.00**
Can.: **$3,750.00**
Ster.: **£1,450.00**

HN 51
A Spook
Style One
Designer: H. Tittensor
Height: 7", 17.8 cm
Colour: Green robe, red cap
Issued: 1916-1936
Varieties: HN 50, 51A, 51B,
58, 512, 625; Also
known in flambé
U.S.: **$3,750.00**
Can.: **$3,750.00**
Ster.: **£1,450.00**

HN 51A
A Spook
Style One
Designer: H. Tittensor
Height: 7", 17.8 cm
Colour: Green robe,
black cap
Issued: 1916-1936
Varieties: HN 50, 51, 51B,
58, 512, 625; Also
known in flambé
U.S.: **$4,000.00**
Can.: **$4,000.00**
Ster.: **£1,500.00**

HN 51B
A Spook
Designer: H. Tittensor
Height: 7", 17.8 cm
Colour: Blue robe, red cap
Issued: 1916-1936
Varieties: HN 50, 51, 51A,
58, 512, 625; Also
known in flambé
U.S.: **None**
Can.: **known**
Ster.: **to exist**

HN 52
Lady of the Fan
Designer: E.W. Light
Height: 9 1/2", 24.1 cm
Colour: Green
Issued: 1916-1936
Varieties: HN 48, 53, 53A,
335, 509
U.S.: **$4,500.00**
Can.: **$4,500.00**
Ster.: **£1,850.00**

HN 52A
Lady with Rose
Designer: E.W. Light
Height: 9 1/2", 24.1 cm
Colour: Yellow
Issued: 1916-1936
Varieties: HN 48A, 68,
304, 336, 515,
517, 584, 624
U.S.: **None**
Can.: **known**
Ster.: **to exist**

HN 53
Lady of the Fan
Designer: E.W. Light
Height: 9 1/2", 24.1 cm
Colour: Dark purple
Issued: 1916-1936
Varieties: HN 48, 52, 53A,
335, 509
U.S.: **$4,500.00**
Can.: **$4,500.00**
Ster.: **£2,000.00**

HN 53A
Lady of the Fan
Designer: E.W. Light
Height: 9", 22.9 cm
Colour: Green
Issued: 1916-1936
Varieties: HN 48, 52, 53, 335, 509

U.S.: **None**
Can.: **known**
Ster.: **to exist**

HN 54
The Ermine Muff
Designer: C.J. Noke
Height: 8 1/2", 21.6 cm
Colour: Grey coat, pale green dress
Issued: 1916-1938
Varieties: HN 332, 671; also called "Lady With Ermine Muff" and "Lady Ermine"

U.S.: **$3,500.00**
Can.: **$3,500.00**
Ster.: **£1,500.00**

HN 55
A Jester
Style Two
Designer: C.J. Noke
Height: 10 1/4", 26.0 cm
Colour: Black and lavender
Issued: 1916-1938
Varieties: HN 45A, 45B, 308, 630, 1333

U.S.: **$7,500.00**
Can.: **$7,500.00**
Ster.: **£1,750.00**

HN 56
The Land of Nod
Designer: H. Tittensor
Height: 9 1/2", 24.1 cm
Colour: Ivory, green candlestick
Issued: 1916-1938
Varieties: HN 56A, 56B

U.S.: **$6,000.00**
Can.: **$6,000.00**
Ster.: **£2,000.00**

The owl was produced as animal figure HN 169

HN 56A
The Land of Nod
Designer: H. Tittensor
Height: 9 1/2", 24.1 cm
Colour: Light grey, green candlestick
Issued: 1916-1938
Varieties: HN 56, 56B

U.S.: **$6,000.00**
Can.: **$6,000.00**
Ster.: **£2,000.00**

HN 56B
The Land of Nod
Designer: H. Tittensor
Height: 9 1/2", 24.1 cm
Colour: Light grey, red candlestick
Issued: 1916-1938
Varieties: HN 56, 56A

U.S.: **$6,000.00**
Can.: **$6,000.00**
Ster.: **£2,000.00**

HN 57
The Curtsey
Designer: E.W. Light
Height: 11", 27.9 cm
Colour: Orange
Issued: 1916-1936
Varieties: HN 57B, 66A, 327, 334, 363, 371, 518, 547, 629, 670

U.S.: **None**
Can.: **known**
Ster.: **to exist**

HN 57A
The Flounced Skirt
Designer: E.W. Light
Height: 9 3/4", 24.7 cm
Colour: Orange
Issued: 1916-1938
Varieties: HN 66, 77, 78, 333; also called "The Bow"

U.S.: **None**
Can.: **known**
Ster.: **to exist**

HN 57B
The Curtsey
Designer: E.W. Light
Height: 11", 27.9 cm
Colour: Lavender
Issued: 1916-1936
Varieties: HN 57, 66A, 327,
334, 363, 371, 518,
547, 629, 670

U.S.: **$3,500.00**
Can.: **$3,500.00**
Ster.: **£1,500.00**

HN 58
A Spook
Style One
Designer: H. Tittensor
Height: 7", 17.8 cm
Colour: Unknown
Issued: 1916-1936
Varieties: HN 50, 51, 51A,
51B, 512, 625; Also
known in flambé

U.S.: **None**
Can.: **known**
Ster.: **to exist**

HN 59
Upon Her Cheeks She
Wept
Designer: L. Perugini
Height: 9", 22.8 cm
Colour: Grey dress
Issued: 1916-1938
Varieties: HN 511, 522

U.S.: **$5,000.00**
Can.: **$5,000.00**
Ster.: **£1,750.00**

HN 60
Shy Anne
Designer: L. Perugini
Height: 7 3/4", 19.7 cm
Colour: Blue dress with
flowers, blue bow
in hair
Issued: 1916-1936
Varieties: HN 64, 65, 568

U.S.: **Extremely rare**
Can.:
Ster.:

HN 61
Katharine
Designer: C.J. Noke
Height: 5 3/4", 14.6 cm
Colour: Green
Issued: 1916-1938
Varieties: HN 74, 341,
471, 615, 793

U.S.: **$3,500.00**
Can.: **$3,500.00**
Ster.: **£1,500.00**

HN 62
A Child's Grace
Designer: L. Perugini
Height: 6 3/4", 17.2 cm
Colour: Green and black
coat with yellow dress
Issued: 1916-1938
Varieties: HN 62A, 510

U.S.: **Only**
Can.: **two**
Ster.: **known**

HN 62A
A Child's Grace
Designer: L. Perugini
Height: 6 3/4", 17.2 cm
Colour: Green coat,
yellow dress
Issued: 1916-1938
Varieties: HN 62, 510

U.S.: **Extremely rare**
Can.:
Ster.:

HN 63
The Little Land
Designer: H. Tittensor
Height: 7 1/2", 19.1 cm
Colour: Green and yellow
Issued: 1916-1936
Varieties: HN 67

U.S.: **Extremely rare**
Can.:
Ster.:

HN 64
Shy Anne
Designer: L. Perugini
Height: 7 3/4", 19.7 cm
Colour: Pale blue, white
bow in hair
Issued: 1916-1936
Varieties: HN 60, 65, 568

U.S.: **$5,000.00**
Can.: **$5,000.00**
Ster.: **£2,250.00**

HN 65
Shy Anne
Designer: L. Perugini
Height: 7 3/4", 19.7 cm
Colour: Pale blue, dark
blue stripe around
hem of skirt, white
bow in hair
Issued: 1916-1936
Varieties: HN 60, 64, 568

U.S.: **$5,000.00**
Can.: **$5,000.00**
Ster.: **£2,250.00**

HN 66
The Flounced Skirt
Designer: E.W. Light
Height: 9 3/4", 24.7 cm
Colour: Lavender
Issued: 1916-1938
Varieties: HN 57A, 77, 78, 333;
also called "The Bow"

U.S.: **$3,500.00**
Can.: **$3,500.00**
Ster.: **£1,500.00**

HN 66A
The Curtsey
Designer: E.W. Light
Height: 11", 27.9 cm
Colour: Lavender
Issued: 1916-1936
Varieties: HN 57, 57B, 327,
334, 363, 371,
518, 547, 629, 670

U.S.: **$3,500.00**
Can.: **$3,500.00**
Ster.: **£1,400.00**

HN 67
The Little Land
Designer: H. Tittensor
Height: 7 1/2", 19.1 cm
Colour: Lilac and yellow
Issued: 1916-1936
Varieties: HN 63

U.S.: **$5,000.00**
Can.: **$5,000.00**
Ster.: **£2,500.00**

HN 68
Lady With Rose
Designer: E.W. Light
Height: 9 1/2", 24.1 cm
Colour: Green and yellow
Issued: 1916-1936
Varieties: HN 48A, 52A,
304, 336, 515,
517, 584, 624

U.S.: **$3,750.00**
Can.: **$3,750.00**
Ster.: **£1,450.00**

HN 69
Pretty Lady
Designer: H. Tittensor
Height: 9 1/2", 24.1 cm
Colour: Blue dress
with flowers
Issued: 1916-1938
Varieties: HN 70, 302, 330,
361, 384, 565,
700, 763, 783

U.S.: **None**
Can.: **known**
Ster.: **to exist**

HN 70
Pretty Lady
Designer: H. Tittensor
Height: 9 1/2", 24.1 cm
Colour: Grey
Issued: 1916-1938
Varieties: HN 69, 302, 330,
361, 384, 565,
700, 763, 783

U.S.: **$2,200.00**
Can.: **$2,500.00**
Ster.: **£1,250.00**

HN 71
A Jester
Style One
Designer: C.J. Noke
Height: 9", 22.9 cm
Colour: Light green checks
Issued: 1917-1938
Varieties: HN 45, 71A, 320,
367, 412, 426, 446,
552, 616, 627,
1295,1702, 2016

U.S.: **$5,000.00**
Can.: **$5,000.00**
Ster.: **£1,750.00**

HN 71A
A Jester
Style One
Designer: C.J. Noke
Height: 91/2", 24.1 cm
Colour: Dark green checks
Issued: 1917-1938
Varieties: HN 45, 71, 320,
367, 412, 426, 446,
552, 616, 627,
1295, 1702, 2016

U.S.: **$5,500.00**
Can.: **$5,500.00**
Ster.: **£1,750.00**

HN 72
An Orange Vendor
Designer: C.J. Noke
Height: 6 1/4". 15.9 cm
Colour: Green, white
and orange
Issued: 1917-1938
Varieties: HN 508, 521, 1966

U.S.: **$1,500.00**
Can.: **$1,500.00**
Ster.: **£ 750.00**

HN 73
A Lady of the
Elizabethan Period
Style One
Designer: E.W. Light
Height: 9 1/2", 24.1 cm
Colour: Dark turquoise
Issued: 1917-1938
Varieties: HN 40, 40A, 411;
also called
"Elizabethan Lady"

U.S.: **Extremely rare**
Can.:
Ster.:

HN 74
Katharine
Designer: C.J. Noke
Height: 5 3/4", 14.6 cm
Colour: Light blue dress
with green spots
Issued: 1917-1938
Varieties: HN 61, 341, 471,
615, 793

U.S.: **None**
Can.: **known**
Ster.: **to exist**

HN 75
Blue Beard
(With Plume on Turban)
Style One
Designer: E.W. Light
Height: 11", 27.9 cm
Colour: Light blue
Issued: 1917-1936
Varieties: HN 410

U.S.: **$8,000.00**
Can.: **$8,000.00**
Ster.: **£3,500.00**

HN 76
The Carpet Vendor
Style One
Designer: C.J. Noke
Height: 5 1/2", 14.0 cm
Colour: Blue and orange
Issued: 1917-1936
Varieties: HN 38, 350; also
known in flambé

U.S.: **$5,000.00**
Can.: **$4,000.00**
Ster.: **£1,500.00**

HN 77
The Flounced Skirt
Designer: E.W. Light
Height: 9 3/4", 24.7 cm
Colour: Yellow dress
with black trim
Issued: 1917-1938
Varieties: HN 57A, 66, 78,
333; also called
"The Bow"

U.S.: **$3,500.00**
Can.: **$3,500.00**
Ster.: **£1,250.00**

HN 78
The Flounced Skirt
Designer: E.W. Light
Height: 9 3/4", 24.7 cm
Colour: Yellow dress
with flowers
Issued: 1917-1938
Varieties: HN 57A, 66, 77,
333; also called
"The Bow"

U.S.: $4,200.00
Can.: $3,750.00
Ster.: £1,250.00

HN 79
Shylock
Designer: C.J. Noke
Height: Unknown
Colour: Multi-coloured
robe, yellow
sleeves
Issued: 1917-1938
Varieties: HN 317; Also known
with Titanian glaze

U.S.: Only
Can.: one
Ster.: known

HN 80
Fisherwomen
Designer: C.J. Noke
Height: 11 3/4", 29.8 cm
Colour: Lavender,
pink and green
Issued: 1917-1938
Varieties: HN 349, 359, 631;
"Waiting For The
Boats" and "Looking
For The Boats"

U.S.: None
Can.: known
Ster.: to exist

HN 81
A Shepherd
Style One
Designer: C.J. Noke
Height: 13 1/4", 33.6 cm
Colour: Brown
Issued: 1918-1938
Varieties: HN 617, 632

U.S.: **Extremely rare**
Can.:
Ster.:

Earthenware

HN 82
Lady with an Ermine Muff
Designer: E.W. Light
Height: 6 3/4", 17.2 cm
Colour: Grey and cream
grey hat
Issued: 1918-1938
Varieties: Also called
"Making a Call"
and "Afternoon Call"

U.S.: $5,000.00
Can.: $5,000.00
Ster.: £2,000.00

HN 83
The Lady Anne
Designer: E.W. Light
Height: 9 1/2", 24.0 cm
Colour: Yellow
Issued: 1918-1938
Varieties: HN 87, 93

U.S.: $6,000.00
Can.: $6,000.00
Ster.: £2,250.00

HN 84
A Mandarin
Style One
Designer: C.J. Noke
Height: 10 1/4", 26.0 cm
Colour: Mauve and green
Issued: 1918-1936
Varieties: HN 316, 318, 382,
611, 746, 787, 791;
"Chinese Mandarin"
and "The Mikado"

U.S.: None
Can.: known
Ster.: to exist

HN 85
Jack Point
Designer: C.J. Noke
Height: 16 1/4", 41.2 cm
Colour: Red checks,
green base
Issued: 1918-1938
Varieties: HN 91, 99, 2080,
3920

U.S.: None
Can.: known
Ster.: to exist

HN 86
Out For a Walk
Designer: E.W. Light
Height: 10", 25.4 cm
Colour: Grey, white
and black
Issued: 1918-1936
Varieties: HN 443, 748
U.S.:   **$5,500.00**
Can.:   **$5,500.00**
Ster.:   **£2,000.00**

HN 87
The Lady Anne
Designer: E.W. Light
Height: 9 1/2", 24.0 cm
Colour: Green
Issued: 1918-1938
Varieties: HN 83, 93
U.S.:   **$6,000.00**
Can.:   **$6,000.00**
Ster.:   **£2,250.00**

HN 88
Spooks
Designer: C.J. Noke
Height: 7 1/4", 18.4 cm
Colour: Green robes,
black caps
Issued: 1918-1936
Varieties: HN 89, 372; also
called "Double Spook"
U.S.:   **$5,500.00**
Can.:   **$5,500.00**
Ster.:   **£2,500.00**

HN 89
Spooks
Designer: C.J. Noke
Height: 7 1/4", 18.4 cm
Colour: Green robes,
red caps
Issued: 1918-1936
Varieties: HN 88, 372; also
called "Double Spook"
U.S.:   **$5,500.00**
Can.:   **$5,500.00**
Ster.:   **£2,500.00**

HN 90
Doris Keene as Cavallini
Style One
Designer: C.J. Noke
Height: 11", 27.9 cm
Colour: Dark green
Issued: 1918-1936
Varieties: HN 467
U.S.:   **$3,000.00**
Can.:   **$3,000.00**
Ster.:   **£1,500.00**

HN 91
Jack Point
Designer: C.J. Noke
Height: 16 1/4", 41.2 cm
Colour: Green and black
checked suit
Issued: 1918-1938
Varieties: HN 85, 99, 2080
U.S.:   **$6,000.00**
Can.:   **$6,000.00**
Ster.:   **£2,000.00**

HN 92
Myfanwy Jones
Designer: E.W. Light
Height: 12", 30.5 cm
Colour: White
Issued: 1918-1936
Varieties: HN 39, 456, 514,
516, 519, 520, 660
668, 669, 701, 792;
also called
"The Welsh Girl"
U.S.:   **Only**
Can.:   **two**
Ster.:   **known**

HN 93
The Lady Anne
Designer: E.W. Light
Height: 9 1/2", 24.0 cm
Colour: Blue
Issued: 1918-1938
Varieties: HN 83, 87
U.S.:   **$6,000.00**
Can.:   **$6,000.00**
Ster.:   **£2,250.00**

HN 94
The Young Knight
Designer: C.J. Noke
Height: 9 1/2", 24.1 cm
Colour: Purple, green
and black
Issued: 1918-1936

U.S.:	**Extremely**
Can.:	**rare**
Ster.:	**only one known**

HN 95
Europa and the Bull
Style One
Designer: E.W. Light
Height: 9 3/4", 24.7 cm
Colour: Lavender with
browns
Issued: 1918-1936

U.S.:	**$7,500.00**
Can.:	**$7,500.00**
Ster.:	**£3,500.00**

HN 96
Doris Keene as Cavallini
Style Two
Designer: C.J. Noke
Height: 10 3/4", 27.8 cm
Colour: Black and white
Issued: 1918-1936
Varieties: HN 345; also
called "Romance"

U.S.:	**$3,750.00**
Can.:	**$3,500.00**
Ster.:	**£1,500.00**

HN 97
The Mermaid
Designer: H. Tittensor
Height: 7", 17.8 cm
Colour: Green and cream
Issued: 1918-1936
Varieties: HN 300

U.S.:	**$1,500.00**
Can.:	**$1,500.00**
Ster.:	**£ 450.00**

HN 98
Guy Fawkes
Style One
Designer: C.J. Noke
Height: 10 1/2". 26.7 cm
Colour: Red cloak, black
hat and robes
Issued: 1918-1949
Varieties: HN 347, 445; Also
known in Sung

U.S.:	**$2,500.00**
Can.:	**$2,500.00**
Ster.:	**£1,250.00**

HN 99
Jack Point
Designer: C.J. Noke
Height: 16 1/4", 41.2 cm
Colour: Purple and green
Issued 1918-1938
Varieties: HN 85, 91, 2080,
3920

U.S.:	**$4,000.00**
Can.:	**$4,000.00**
Ster.:	**£1,750.00**

HN 300
The Mermaid
Designer: H. Tittensor
Height: 7", 17.8 cm
Colour: Green and cream,
red berries in hair
Issued: 1918-1936
Varieties: HN 97

U.S.:	**Only**
Can.:	**two**
Ster.:	**known**

HN 301
Moorish Piper Minstrel
Designer: C.J. Noke
Height: 13 1/2", 34.3 cm
Colour: Purple
Issued: 1918-1938
Varieties: HN 328, 416

U.S.:	**$3,600.00**
Can.:	**$3,600.00**
Ster.:	**£1,500.00**

HN 302
Pretty Lady
Designer: H. Tittensor
Height: 9 1/2", 24.1 cm
Colour: Green and lavender dress
Issued: 1918-1938
Varieties: HN 69, 70, 330, 361, 384, 565, 700, 763, 783

U.S.:	**$2,200.00**
Can.:	**$2,200.00**
Ster.:	**£1,250.00**

HN 303
Motherhood
Style One
Designer: P. Stabler
Height: 8", 20.3 cm
Colour: White dress with black
Issued: 1918-1936
Varieties: HN 28, 30

U.S.:	**None**
Can.:	**known**
Ster.:	**to exist**

HN 304
Lady with Rose
Designer: E.W. Light
Height: 9 1/2", 24.1 cm
Colour: Patterned lavender dress
Issued: 1918-1936
Varieties: HN 48A, 52A, 68, 336, 515, 517, 584, 624

U.S.:	**None**
Can.:	**known**
Ster.:	**to exist**

HN 305
A Scribe
Designer: C.J. Noke
Height: 6", 15.2 cm
Colour: Green, blue and orange
Issued: 1918-1936
Varieties: HN 324, 1235

U.S.:	**$2,500.00**
Can.:	**$2,250.00**
Ster.:	**£ 850.00**

HN 306
Milking Time
Designer: P. Stabler
Height: 6 1/2", 16.5 cm
Colour: Light blue dress with black
Issued: 1913-1938
Varieties: HN 3

U.S.:	**Extremely rare**
Can.:	
Ster.:	

HN 307
The Sentimental Pierrot
Designer: C.J. Noke
Height: 5 1/2", 14.0 cm
Colour: Black, white
Issued: 1918-1936
Varieties: HN 36

U.S.:	**$6,000.00**
Can.:	**$5,500.00**
Ster.:	**£2,500.00**

HN 308
A Jester
Style Two
Designer: C.J. Noke
Height: 10 1/4", 26.0 cm
Colour: Black and lavender
Issued: 1918-1938
Varieties: HN 45A, 45B, 55, 630, 1333

U.S.:	**None**
Can.:	**known**
Ster.:	**to exist**

HN 309
An Elizabethan Lady
Style Two
Designer: E.W. Light
Height: 9 1/2", 24.1 cm
Colour: Dark green-blue, green and black
Issued: 1918-1938
Varieties: Also called "A Lady of the Elizabethan Period"

U.S.:	**$5,500.00**
Can.:	**$5,500.00**
Ster.:	**£2,000.00**

HN 310
Dunce
Designer: C.J. Noke
Height: 10 1/2", 26.7 cm
Colour: Black and white
with green base
Issued: 1918-1936
Varieties: HN 6, 357

U.S.: **None**
Can.: **known**
Ster.: **to exist**

Photograph
Not
Available

HN 311
Dancing Figure
Designer: Unknown
Height: 17 3/4", 45.0 cm
Colour: Pink
Issued: 1918-1938

U.S.: **Only**
Can.: **one**
Ster.: **known**

HN 312
Spring
Style One
Designer: Unknown
Height: 7 1/2". 19.1 cm
Colour: Yellow
Issued: 1918-1938
Varieties: HN 472
Series: The Seasons
(Series One)

U.S.: **$2,000.00**
Can.: **$2,000.00**
Ster.: **£ 950.00**

HN 313
Summer
Style One
Designer: Unknown
Height: 7 1/2". 19.1 cm
Colour: Pale green
Issued: 1918-1938
Varieties: HN 473
Series: The Seasons
(Series One)

U.S.: **$2,000.00**
Can.: **$2,000.00**
Ster.: **£ 950.00**

HN 314
Autumn
Style One
Designer: Unknown
Height: 7 1/2", 19.1 cm
Colour: Lavender
Issued: 1918-1938
Varieties: HN 474
Series: The Seasons
(Series One)

U.S.: **$2,000.00**
Can.: **$2,000.00**
Ster.: **£ 950.00**

HN 315
Winter
Style One
Designer: Unknown
Height: 7 1/2". 19.1 cm
Colour: Pale green
Issued: 1918-1938
Varieties: HN 475
Series: The Seasons
(Series One)

U.S.: **$2,000.00**
Can.: **$2,000.00**
Ster.: **£ 950.00**

HN 316
A Mandarin
Style One
Designer: C.J. Noke
Height: 10 1/4", 26.0 cm
Colour: Black and yellow
Issued: 1918-1936
Varieties: HN 84, 318, 382,
611, 746, 787, 791:
"Chinese Mandarin"
and "The Mikado"

U.S.: **$7,500.00**
Can.: **$7,500.00**
Ster.: **£3,000.00**

HN 317
Shylock
Designer: C.J. Noke
Height: Unknown
Colour: Brown and
green
Issued: 1918-1938
Varieties: HN 79; Also known
with Titanian glaze

U.S.: **Extremely rare**
Can.:
Ster.:

HN 318
A Mandarin
Style One
Designer: C.J. Noke
Height: 10 1/4", 26.0 cm
Colour: Gold
Issued: 1918-1936
Varieties: HN 84, 316, 382,
611, 746, 787, 791;
"Chinese Mandarin"
and "The Mikado"

U.S.: $7,500.00
Can.: $7,500.00
Ster.: £3,500.00

HN 319
A Gnome
Designer: H. Tittensor
Height: 6 1/4", 15.9 cm
Colour: Light blue
Issued: 1918-1938
Varieties: HN 380, 381

U.S.: **Extremely rare**
Can.:
Ster.:

HN 320
A Jester
Style One
Designer: C.J. Noke
Height: 10", 25.4 cm
Colour: Green and black
Issued: 1918-1938
Varieties: HN 45, 71, 71A,
367, 412, 426, 446,
552, 616, 627,
1295, 1702, 2016

U.S.: $5,500.00
Can.: $5,500.00
Ster.: £1,750.00

HN 321
Digger (New Zealand)
Designer: E.W. Light
Height: 11 1/4", 28.5 cm
Colour: Mottled green
Issued: 1918-1938

U.S.: $2,750.00
Can.: $2,750.00
Ster.: £1,250.00

HN 322
Digger(Australian)
Designer: E.W. Light
Height: 11 1/4", 28.5 cm
Colour: Brown
Issued: 1918-1938
Varieties: HN 353

U.S.: $2,750.00
Can.: $2,750.00
Ster.: £1,250.00

HN 323
Blighty
Designer: E.W. Light
Height: 11 1/4", 28.5 cm
Colour: Green
Issued: 1918-1938
Varieties: Khaki version

U.S.: $2,500.00
Can.: $2,500.00
Ster.: £1,450.00

HN 324
A Scribe
Designer: C.J. Noke
Height: 6", 15.2 cm
Colour: Brown, green
and orange
Issued: 1918-1938
Varieties: HN 305, 1235

U.S.: $2,500.00
Can.: $2,250.00
Ster.: £ 850.00

HN 325
Pussy
Designer: F.C. Stone
Height: 7 1/2", 19.1 cm
Colour: White patterned
dress with black
Issued: 1918-1938
Varieties: HN 18, 507; also
called "The Black Cat"

U.S.: **Only**
Can.: **one**
Ster.: **known**

HN 326
Madonna of the Square
Designer: P. Stabler
Height: 7", 17.8 cm
Colour: Grey
Issued: 1918-1936
Varieties: HN 10, 10A, 11,
14, 27, 573, 576,
594, 613, 764,
1968, 1969, 2034

U.S.: $2,800.00
Can.: $2,600.00
Ster.: £ 850.00

HN 327
The Curtsey
Designer: E.W. Light
Height: 11", 27.9 cm
Colour: Blue
Issued: 1918-1936
Varieties: HN 57, 57B, 66A,
334, 363, 371,
518, 547, 629 670

U.S.: $3,500.00
Can.: $3,500.00
Ster.: £1,250.00

HN 328
Moorish Piper Minstrel
Designer: C.J. Noke
Height: 13 1/2", 34.3 cm
Colour: Green and
brown stripes
Issued: 1918-1938
Varieties: HN 301, 416

U.S.: **None**
Can.: **known**
Ster.: **to exist**

HN 329
The Gainsborough Hat
Designer: H. Tittensor
Height: 8 3/4", 22.2 cm
Colour: Patterned
blue dress
Issued: 1918-1936
Varieties: HN 46, 46A,
47, 352, 383,
453, 675, 705

U.S.: **None**
Can.: **known**
Ster.: **to exist**

HN 330
Pretty Lady
Designer: H. Tittensor
Height: 9 1/2", 24.1 cm
Colour: Patterned
blue dress
Issued: 1918-1938
Varieties: HN 69, 70, 302,
361, 384, 565,
700, 763, 783

U.S.: **None**
Can.: **known**
Ster.: **to exist**

HN 331
A Lady of the
Georgian Period
Designer: E.W. Light
Height: 10 1/4", 26.0 cm
Colour: Mottled green
overskirt, yellow
underskirt
Issued: 1918-1936
Varieties: HN 41, 444, 690, 702

U.S.: $3,700.00
Can.: $3,500.00
Ster.: £1,450.00

HN 332
The Ermine Muff
Designer: C.J. Noke
Height: 8 1/2", 21.6 cm
Colour: Red coat, green
and yellow skirt
Issued: 1918-1938
Varieties: HN 54, 671; also
called "Lady with
Ermine Muff" and
"Lady Ermine"

U.S.: **Only**
Can.: **one**
Ster.: **known**

HN 333
The Flounced Skirt
Designer: E.W. Light
Height: 9 3/4", 24.7 cm
Colour: Mottled green
and blue
Issued: 1918-1938
Varieties: HN 57A, 66, 77, 78;
also called "The Bow"

U.S.: $3,500.00
Can.: $3,500.00
Ster.: £1,250.00

HN 334
The Curtsey
Designer: E.W. Light
Height: 11", 27.9 cm
Colour: Purple
Issued: 1918-1936
Varieties: HN 57, 57B, 66A,
327, 363, 371, 518,
547, 629, 670
U.S.: $3,500.00
Can.: $3,500.00
Ster.: £1,250.00

HN 335
Lady of the Fan
Designer: E.W. Light
Height: 9 1/2", 24.1 cm
Colour: Blue
Issued: 1919-1936
Varieties: HN 48, 52, 53,
53A, 509
U.S.: $4,500.00
Can.: $4,500.00
Ster.: £1,750.00

HN 336
Lady with Rose
Designer: E.W. Light
Height: 9 1/2", 24.1 cm
Colour: Multi-coloured
Issued: 1919-1936
Varieties: HN 48A, 52A,
68, 304, 515,
517, 584, 624
U.S.: None
Can.: known
Ster.: to exist

HN 337
The Parson's Daughter
Designer: H. Tittensor
Height: 10", 25.4 cm
Colour: Lavender dress
with brown flowers
Issued: 1919-1938
Varieties: HN 338, 441,
564, 790, 1242,
1356, 2018
U.S.: $2,200.00
Can.: $2,200.00
Ster.: £ 900.00

HN 338
The Parson's Daughter
Designer: H. Tittensor
Height: 10", 25.4 cm
Colour: Green and red
Issued: 1919-1938
Varieties: HN 337, 441,
564, 790, 1242,
1356, 2018
U.S.: $2,800.00
Can.: $2,200.00
Ster.: £ 750.00

HN 339
In Grandma's Days
Designer: C.J. Noke
Height: 8 3/4", 22.2 cm
Colour: Green and yellow
Issued: 1919-1938
Varieties: HN 340, 388, 442;
"The Poke Bonnet"
HN 362, 612, 765;
"A Lilac Shawl"
HN 44, 44A
U.S.: $3,500.00
Can.: $3,500.00
Ster.: £1,450.00

HN 340
In Grandma's Days
Designer: C.J. Noke
Height: 8 3/4", 22.2 cm
Colour: Yellow and lavender
Issued: 1919-1938
Varieties: HN 339, 388, 442;
"The Poke Bonnet"
HN 362, 612, 765;
"A Lilac Shawl"
HN 44, 44A
U.S.: $3,500.00
Can.: $3,500.00
Ster.: £1,450.00

HN 341
Katharine
Designer: C.J. Noke
Height: 5 3/4", 14.6 cm
Colour: Red
Issued: 1919-1938
Varieties: HN 61, 74, 471,
615, 793
U.S.: $3,500.00
Can.: $3,500.00
Ster.: £1,250.00

HN 342
The Lavender Woman
Designer: P. Stabler
Height: 8 1/4", 21.0 cm
Colour: Multi-coloured dress,
               lavender shawl
Issued: 1919-1938
Varieties: HN 22, 23, 23A,
               569, 744
U.S.:   **$6,000.00**
Can.:   **$5,000.00**
Ster.:   **£2,000.00**

HN 343
An Arab
Designer: C.J. Noke
Height: 16 1/2", 41.9 cm
Colour: Yellow and purple
Issued: 1919-1938
Varieties: HN 33, 378; "The
               Moor" HN 1308,
               1366, 1425, 1657,
               2082, 3642
U.S.:   **None**
Can.:   **known**
Ster.:   **to exist**

HN 344
Henry Irving as
Cardinal Wolsey
Designer: C.J. Noke
Height: 13 1/4", 33.7 cm
Colour: Red
Issued: 1919-1949
U.S.:   **$5,000.00**
Can.:   **$4,000.00**
Ster.:   **£1,750.00**

HN 345
Doris Keene as Cavallini
Style Two
Designer: C.J. Noke
Height: 10 1/2", 26.6 cm
Colour: Black and white,
               dark collar and
               striped muff
Issued: 1919-1949
Varieties: HN 96
U.S.:   **$5,000.00**
Can.:   **$4,000.00**
Ster.:   **£1,500.00**

Photograph
Not
Available

HN 346
tony Weller
Style One
 Designer: C.J. Noke
Height: 10 1/2", 26.7 cm
Colour: Green, blue
               and brown
Issued: 1919-1938
Varieties: HN 368, 684
U.S.:   **None**
Can.:   **known**
Ster.:   **to exist**

HN 347
Guy Fawkes
Style One
Designer: C.J. Noke
Height: 10 1/2", 26.7 cm
Colour: Brown cloak
Issued: 1919-1938
Varieties: HN 98, 445; Also
               known in Sung
U.S.:   **Extremely**
Can.:   **rare**
Ster.:

HN 348
The Carpet Vendor
Style Two
Designer: C.J. Noke
Height: 6 1/4", 15.9 cm
Colour: Turquoise, long
               carpet
Issued: 1919-1936
Varieties: HN 38A
U.S.:   **None**
Can.:   **known**
Ster.:   **to exist**

HN 349
Fisherwomen
Designer: C.J. Noke
Height: 11 3/4", 29.8 cm
Colour: Lavender, yellow
               and green
Issued: 1919-1938
Varieties: HN 80, 359, 631;
               "Waiting For The
               Boats" and "Looking
               For The Boats"
U.S.:   **None**
Can.:   **known**
Ster.:   **to exist**

HN 350
The Carpet Vendor
Style One
Designer: C.J. Noke
Height: 5 1/2", 14.0 cm
Colour: Blue and
mottled green
Issued: 1919-1936
Varieties: HN 38, 76; Also
known in flambé
U.S.: **$5,000.00**
Can.: **$4,000.00**
Ster.: **£1,450.00**

HN 351
Picardy Peasant (woman)
Designer: P. Stabler
Height: 9 1/2", 24.0 cm
Colour: Blue striped skirt,
spotted hat
Issued: 1919-1938
Varieties: HN 4, 5, 17A, 513
U.S.: **$3,500.00**
Can.: **$3,000.00**
Ster.: **£1,250.00**

HN 352
The Gainsborough Hat
Designer: H. Tittensor
Height: 8 3/4", 22.2 cm
Colour: Yellow dress,
purple hat
Issued: 1919-1936
Varieties: HN 46, 46A, 47, 329,
383, 453, 675, 705
U.S.: **None**
Can.: **known**
Ster.: **to exist**

HN 353
Digger (Australian)
Designer: E.W. Light
Height: 11 1/4", 28.5 cm
Colour: Brown
Issued: 1919-1938
Varieties: HN 322
U.S.: **Extremely rare**
Can.:
Ster.:

HN 354
A Geisha
Style One
Designer: H. Tittensor
Height: 10 3/4", 27.3 cm
Colour: Yellow, pink and blue
Issued: 1919-1938
Varieties: HN 376, 376A,
387, 634, 741,
779, 1321, 1322;
"Japanese Lady"
U.S.: **$8,500.00**
Can.: **$8,500.00**
Ster.: **£2,500.00**

HN 355
Dolly
Style One
Designer: C.J. Noke
Height: 7 1/4", 18.4 cm
Colour: Blue
Issued: 1919-1938
U.S.: **$5,000.00**
Can.: **$5,000.00**
Ster.: **£2,000.00**

HN 356
Sir Thomas Lovell
Designer: C.J. Noke
Height: 7 3/4", 19.7 cm
Colour: Brown and green
Issued: 1919-1936
U.S.: **$6,000.00**
Can.: **$5,000.00**
Ster.: **£2,250.00**

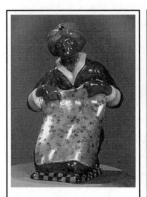

HN 357
Dunce
Designer: C.J. Noke
Height: 10 1/2", 26.7 cm
Colour: Light brown
Issued: 1919-1936
Varieties: HN 6, 310
U.S.: **Extremely rare**
Can.:
Ster.:

HN 358
An Old King
Designer: C.J. Noke
Height: 9 3/4", 24.7 cm
Colour: Green and purple
Issued: 1919-1938
Varieties: HN 623, 1801, 2134

U.S.: **None**
Can.: **known**
Ster.: **to exist**

HN 359
Fisherwomen
Designer: C.J. Noke
Height: 11 3/4", 29.8 cm
Colour: Lavender, red
and green
Issued: 1919-1938
Varieties: HN 80, 349, 631;
"Waiting For The
Boats" or "Looking
For The Boats"

U.S.: **Extremely rare**
Can.:
Ster.: *

HN 361
Pretty Lady
Designer: H. Tittensor
Height: 9 1/2", 24.1 cm
Colour: Turquoise
Issued: 1919-1938
Varieties: HN 69, 70, 302,
330, 384, 565,
700, 763, 783

U.S.: **$2,500.00**
Can.: **$2,500.00**
Ster.: **£1,250.00**

HN 362
The Poke Bonnet
Designer: C.J. Noke
Height: 8 3/4", 22.2 cm
Colour: Green, yellow, red
Issued: 1919-1938
Varieties: HN 612, 765; "In
Grandma's Days"
HN 339, 340, 388,
442; "A Lilac Shawl"
HN 44, 44A

U.S.: **$3,500.00**
Can.: **$3,500.00**
Ster.: **£1,250.00**

HN 363
The Curtsey
Designer: E.W. Light
Height: 11", 27.9 cm
Colour: Lavender
and peach
Issued: 1919-1936
Varieties: HN 57, 57B, 66A,
327, 334, 371, 518,
547, 629, 670

U.S.: **None**
Can.: **known**
Ster.: **to exist**

HN 364
A Moorish Minstrel
Designer: C.J. Noke
Height: 13 1/2", 34.3 cm
Colour: Blue, green
and orange
Issued: 1920-1938
Varieties: HN 34, 415, 797

U.S.: **$3,750.00**
Can.: **$4,000.00**
Ster.: **£1,750.00**

Photograph
Not
Available

HN 365
Double Jester
Designer: C.J. Noke
Height: Unknown
Colour: Brown, green
and purple
Issued: 1920-1938

U.S.: **Only**
Can.: **one**
Ster.: **known**

HN 366
A Mandarin
Style Two
Designer: C.J. Noke
Height: 8 1/4", 21.0 cm
Colour: Yellow and blue
Issued: 1920-1938
Varieties: HN 455, 641

U.S.: **Only**
Can.: **one**
Ster.: **known**

HN 367
A Jester
Style One
Designer: C.J. Noke
Height: 10", 25.4 cm
Colour: Green and red
Issued: 1920-1938
Varieties: HN 45, 71, 71A,
320, 412, 426, 446,
552, 616, 627,
1295, 1702, 2016

U.S.: **$6,000.00**
Can.: **$6,000.00**
Ster.: **£1,750.00**

HN 368
Tony Weller
Style One
Designer: C.J. Noke
Height: 10 1/2", 26.7 cm
Colour: Green and brown
Issued: 1920-1938
Varieties: HN 346, 684

U.S.: **$3,500.00**
Can.: **$2,700.00**
Ster.: **£1,250.00**

Photograph
Not
Available

HN 369
Cavalier
Style One
Designer: Unknown
Height: Unknown
Colour: Turquoise
Issued: 1920-1936

U.S.: **None**
Can.: **known**
Ster.: **to exist**

Photograph
Not
Available

HN 370
Henry VIII
Style One
Designer: C.J. Noke
Height: Unknown
Colour: Brown,green
and purple
Issued: 1920-1938
Varieties: HN 673

U.S.: **Only**
Can.: **one**
Ster.: **known**

HN 371
The Curtsey
Designer: E.W. Light
Height: 11", 27.9 gm
Colour: Yellow
Issued: 1920-1936
Varieties: HN 57, 57B, 66A,
327, 334, 363, 518,
547, 629, 670

U.S.: **None**
Can.: **known**
Ster.: **to exist**

HN 372
Spooks
Designer: C.J. Noke
Height: 7 1/4", 18.4 cm
Colour: Brown
Issued: 1920-1936
Varieties: HN 88, 89;
also called
"Double Spook"

U.S.: **$5,500.00**
Can.: **$5,500.00**
Ster.: **£2,250.00**

HN 373
Boy on Crocodile
Designer: C.J. Noke
Height: 5", 12.7 cm;
Length: 14 1/2", 36.8 cm
Colour: Green-brown
Issued: 1920-1936
Varieties: Also known in
flambé

U.S.: **Only**
Can.: **two**
Ster.: **known**

NOTES ON PRICING

The prices on the secondary market for Royal Doulton Figures, particularly the early HN Numbers, have risen considerably over the years. As values rise, the condition and quality of these figurines take on an increasingly important role.

The prices listed in *The Charlton Standard Catalogue of Royal Doulton Beswick Figurines* are for figures in mint condition.

Naturally, repaired or restored figures, no matter how professionally done, will sell at a substantial discount.

On Condition: For figures to command catalogue prices they must be in mint condition. This simply means that a figure will not have paint chips, scratches, hairline cracks, crazing or blemishes. Any of which will remove from the mint category figure.

On Quality: Some figures can be better moulded, assembled or painted than others. High quality figures will command catalogue prices. Low quality figures will not.

If the quality or condition of the figures is below the standard for mint, look for that figure to be priced at a percentage of the catalogue prices.

HN 374
Lady and Blackamoor
Style One
Designer: H. Tittensor
Height: Unknown
Colour: Blue and green
Issued: 1920-1936
Varieties: HN 375, 377, 470

U.S.:	Only
Can.:	one
Ster.:	known

HN 375
Lady and Blackamoor
Style Two
Designer: H. Tittensor
Height: Unknown
Colour: Purple and yellow
Issued: 1920-1936
Varieties: HN 374, 377, 470

U.S.:	Only
Can.:	one
Ster.:	known

HN 376
A Geisha
Style One
Designer: H. Tittensor
Height: 10 3/4", 27.3 cm
Colour: Lilac and yellow
Issued: 1920-1936
Varieties: HN 354, 376A, 387, 634, 741, 779, 1321, 1322; "The Japanese Lady"

U.S.:	$8,500.00
Can:	$8,500.00
Ster.:	£2,500.00

HN 376A
A Geisha
Style One
Designer: H. Tittensor
Height: 10 3/4", 27.3 cm
Colour: Blue
Issued: 1920-1936
Varieties: HN 354, 376, 387, 634, 741, 779, 1321, 1322; "The Japanese Lady"

U.S.:	$8,500.00
Can:	$8,500.00
Ster.:	£2,500.00

HN 377
Lady and Blackamoor
Style Two
Designer: H. Tittensor
Height: Unknown
Colour: Pink and green
Issued: 1920-1936
Varieties: HN 375, 470

U.S.:	None
Can.:	known
Ster.:	to exist

HN 378
An Arab
Designer: C.J. Noke
Height: 16 1/2", 41.9 cm
Colour: Green, brown and yellow
Issued: 1920-1938
Varieties: HN 33, 343; also called "The Moor" HN 1308, 1366, 1425, 1657, 2082, 3642

U.S.:	$4,500.00
Can:	$3,500.00
Ster.:	£1,400.00

HN 379
Ellen Terry as
Queen Catharine
Designer: C.J. Noke
Height: 12 1/2", 31.7 cm
Colour: Purple and blue
Issued: 1920-1949

U.S.:	$5,000.00
Can.:	$4,000.00
Ster.:	£1,500.00

HN 380
A Gnome
Designer: H. Tittensor
Height: 6 1/4", 15.9 cm
Colour: Purple
Issued: 1920-1938
Varieties: HN 319, 381

U.S.:	None
Can.:	known
Ster.:	to exist

HN 381
A Gnome
Designer: H. Tittensor
Height: 6 1/4", 15.9 cm
Colour: Green
Issued: 1920-1938
Varieties: HN 319, 380

U.S.:	**Only**
Can.:	**one**
Ster.:	**known**

HN 382
A Mandarin
Style One
Designer: C.J. Noke
Height: 10 1/4", 26.0 cm
Colour: Green
Issued: 1920-1936
Varieties: HN 84, 316, 318,
611, 746, 787, 791;
"Chinese Mandarin"
and "The Mikado"

U.S.:	**$7,500.00**
Can.:	**$7,500.00**
Ster.:	**£3,000.00**

HN 383
The Gainsborough Hat
Designer: H. Tittensor
Height: 8 3/4", 22.2 cm
Colour: Green stripes
Issued: 1920-1936
Varieties: HN 46, 46A, 47, 329,
352, 453, 675, 705

U.S.:	**None**
Can.:	**known**
Ster.:	**to exist**

HN 384
Pretty Lady
Designer: H. Tittensor
Height: 9 1/2", 24.1 cm
Colour: Red
Issued: 1920-1938
Varieties: HN 69, 70, 302,
330, 361, 565,
700, 763, 783

U.S.:	**$2,500.00**
Can.:	**$2,500.00**
Ster.:	**£1,250.00**

HN 385
St. George
Style One
Designer: S. Thorogood
Height: 16", 40.6 cm
Colour: Grey, purple
and gold
Issued: 1920-1938
Varieties: HN 386, 1800, 2067

U.S.:	**$6,500.00**
Can.:	**$4,500.00**
Ster.:	**£2,000.00**

HN 386
St. George
Style One
Designer: S. Thorogood
Height: 16", 40.6 cm
Colour: Blue and white
Issued: 1920-1938
Varieties: HN 385, 1800, 2067

U.S.:	**$6,500.00**
Can.:	**$4,500.00**
Ster.:	**£2,000.00**

HN 387
A Geisha
Style One
Designer: H. Tittensor
Height: 10 3/4", 27.3 cm
Colour: Blue and yellow
Issued: 1920-1936
Varieties: HN 354, 376,
376A, 634, 741,
779, 1321, 1322;
"Japanese Lady"

U.S.:	**$8,500.00**
Can.:	**$8,500.00**
Ster.:	**£2,500.00**

HN 388
In Grandma's Days
Designer: C.J. Noke
Height: 8 3/4", 22.2 cm
Colour: Blue
Issued: 1920-1938
Varieties: HN 339, 340, 442;
"The Poke Bonnet"
HN 362, 612, 765;
"A Lilac Shawl"
HN 44, 44A

U.S.:	**None**
Can.:	**known**
Ster.:	**to exist**

HN 389
Dolly
Style Two
Designer: H. Tittensor
Height: 11", 27.9 cm
Colour: Pink dress, blond hair
Issued: 1920-1938
Varieties: HN 390; also called "The Little Mother," HN 469

U.S.:	**Only**
Can.:	**two**
Ster.:	**known**

HN 390
Dolly
Style Two
Designer: H. Tittensor
Height: 11", 27.9 cm
Colour: Pink dress, brown hair
Issued: 1920-1938
Varieties: HN 389; also called "The Little Mother," HN 469

U.S.:	**Only**
Can.:	**one**
Ster.:	**known**

HN 391
The Princess
Designer: L. Harradine
Height: 9 1/4", 23.5 cm
Colour: Green and purple
Issued: 1920-1936
Varieties: HN 392, 420, 430, 431, 633

U.S.:	**Only**
Can.:	**one**
Ster.:	**known**

HN 392
The Princess
Designer: L. Harradine
Height: 9 1/4", 23.5 cm
Colour: Multi-coloured
Issued: 1920-1936
Varieties: HN 391, 420, 430, 431, 633

U.S.:	**Only**
Can.:	**one**
Ster.:	**known**

Photograph
Not
Available

Photograph
Not
Available

HN 393
The Necklace
Designer: G. Lambert
Height: 9", 22.9 cm
Colour: Yellow, green and purple
Issued: 1920-1936
Varieties: HN 394

U.S.:	**Only**
Can.:	**one**
Ster.:	**known**

HN 394
The Necklace
Designer: G. Lambert
Height: 9", 22.9 cm
Colour: Green and yellow
Issued: 1920-1936
Varieties: HN 393

U.S.:	**Extremely rare**
Can.:	
Ster.:	

HN 395
Contentment
Designer: L. Harradine
Height: 7 1/4", 18.4 cm
Colour: Yellow and lilac
Issued: 1920-1938
Varieties: HN 396, 421, 468, 572, 685, 686, 1323

U.S.:	**$3,000.00**
Can.:	**$3,000.00**
Ster.:	**£1,250.00**

HN 396
Contentment
Designer: L. Harradine
Height: 7 1/4", 18.4 cm
Colour: Blue, yellow and pink
Issued: 1920-1938
Varieties: HN 395, 421, 468, 572, 685, 686, 1323

U.S.:	**$3,000.00**
Can.:	**$3,000.00**
Ster.:	**£1,350.00**

HN 397
Puff and Powder
Designer: L. Harradine
Height: 6 1/2", 16.5 cm
Colour: Yellow skirt, brown bodice
Issued: 1920-1936
Varieties: HN 398, 400, 432, 433

U.S.:	**$5,000.00**
Can.:	**$5,000.00**
Ster.:	**£1,800.00**

HN 398
Puff and Powder
Designer: L. Harradine
Height: 6 1/2", 16.5 cm
Colour: Lavender
Issued: 1920-1936
Varieties: HN 397, 400, 432, 433

U.S.:	**None**
Can.:	**known**
Ster.:	**to exist**

HN 399
Japanese Fan
Designer: H. Tittensor
Height: 4 3/4", 12.1 cm
Colour: Dark blue and yellow
Issued: 1920-1936
Varieties: HN 405, 439, 440; also known in flambé

U.S.:	**$4,750.00**
Can.:	**$4,750.00**
Ster.:	**£1,750.00**

HN 400
Puff and Powder
Designer: L. Harradine
Height: 6 1/2", 16.5 cm
Colour: Green, blue and yellow
Issued: 1920-1936
Varieties: HN 397, 398, 432, 433

U.S.:	**None**
Can.:	**known**
Ster.:	**to exist**

Photograph
Not
Available

HN 401
Marie
Style One
Designer: L. Harradine
Height: 7", 17.8 cm
Colour: Pink, cream and blue
Issued: 1920-1938
Varieties: HN 434, 502, 504, 505, 506

U.S.:	**Extremely rare**
Can.:	
Ster.:	

Photograph
Not
Available

HN 402
Betty
Style One
Designer: L. Harradine
Height: 7 1/2", 19.1 cm
Colour: Pink and black
Issued: 1920-1938
Varieties: HN 403, 435, 438, 477, 478

U.S.:	**Extremely rare**
Can.:	
Ster.:	

Photograph
Not
Available

HN 403
Betty
Style One
Designer: L. Harradine
Height: 7 1/2" 19.1 cm
Colour: Green, blue and yellow
Issued: 1920-1938
Varieties: HN 402, 435, 438, 477, 478

U.S.:	**Extremely rare**
Can.:	
Ster.:	

HN 404
King Charles
Designer: C.J. Noke and H. Tittensor
Height: 16 3/4", 42.5 cm
Colour: Black, pink base
Issued: 1920-1951
Varieties: HN 2084, 3459

U.S.:	**$4,500.00**
Can.:	**$3,500.00**
Ster.:	**£1,500.00**

HN 405
Japanese Fan
Designer: H. Tittensor
Height: 5", 12.7 cm
Colour: Light yellow
Issued: 1920-1936
Varieties: HN 399, 439, 440;
Also known in flambé

U.S.:	**None**
Can.:	**known**
Ster.:	**to exist**

HN 406
The Bouquet
Designer: G. Lambert
Height: 9", 22.9 cm
Colour: Yellow and blue
Issued: 1920-1936
Varieties: HN 414, 422, 428,
429, 567, 794; also
called "The Nosegay"

U.S.:	**$5,000.00**
Can.:	**$4,000.00**
Ster.:	**£1,500.00**

HN 407
Omar Khayyam
and the Beloved
Designer: C.J. Noke
Height: 10", 25.4 cm
Colour: Unknown
Issued: 1920-1936
Varieties: HN 419, 459, 598

U.S.:	**Only**
Can.:	**one**
Ster.:	**known**

HN 408
Omar Khayyam
Style One
Designer: C.J. Noke
Height: 6", 15.2 cm
Colour: Blue, green
and brown
Issued: 1920-1938
Varieties: HN 409

U.S.:	**Only**
Can.:	**one**
Ster.:	**known**

HN 409
Omar Khayyam
Style One
Designer: C.J. Noke
Height: 6", 15.2 cm
Colour: Black and yellow
Issued: 1920-1938
Varieties: HN 408

U.S.:	**Only**
Can.:	**one**
Ster.:	**known**

HN 410
Blue Beard
(Without plume on turban)
Style One
Designer: E.W. Light
Height: 11", 27.9 cm
Colour: Green and blue
Issued: 1920-1936
Varieties: HN 75

U.S.:	**$8,500.00**
Can.:	**$8,500.00**
Ster.:	**£3,500.00**

HN 411
A Lady of the Elizabethan
Period
Style One
Designer: E.W. Light
Height: 9 3/4", 24.7 cm
Colour: Purple
Issued: 1920-1938
Varieties: HN 40, 40A, 73;
"Elizabethan Lady"

U.S.:	**$4,250.00**
Can.:	**$4,250.00**
Ster.:	**£1,500.00**

HN 412
A Jester
Style One
Designer: C.J. Noke
Height: 10", 25.4 cm
Colour: Green and red
Issued: 1920-1938
Varieties: HN 45, 71, 71A,
320, 367, 426,
446, 552, 616, 627,
1295, 1702, 2016

U.S.:	**Extremely rare**
Can.:	
Ster.:	

HN 413
The Crinoline
Designer: G. Lambert
Height: 6 1/4", 15.8 cm
Colour: Light blue
            and lemon
Issued: 1920-1938
Varieties: HN 8, 9, 9A, 21,
            21A, 566, 628

U.S.:   **$3,200.00**
Can.:   **$3,000.00**
Ster.:   **£1,350.00**

HN 414
The Bouquet
Designer: G. Lambert
Height: 9", 22.9 cm
Colour: Pink and yellow
Issued: 1920-1936
Varieties: HN 406, 422, 428,
            429, 567, 794; also
            called "The Nosegay"

U.S.:   **None**
Can.:   **known**
Ster.:   **to exist**

HN 415
A Moorish Minstrel
Designer: C.J. Noke
Height: 13 1/2", 34.3 cm
Colour: Green and yellow
Issued: 1920-1938
Varieties: HN 34, 364, 797

U.S.:   **$4,000.00**
Can.:   **$4,000.00**
Ster.:   **£2,000.00**

HN 416
Moorish Piper Minstrel
Designer: C.J. Noke
Height: 13 1/2", 34.3 cm
Colour: Green and yellow
            stripes
Issued: 1920-1938
Varieties: HN 301, 328

U.S.:   **None**
Can.:   **known**
Ster.:   **to exist**

HN 417
One of the Forty
Style One
Designer: H. Tittensor
Height: 8 1/4", 21.0 cm
Colour: Green and blue
Issued: 1920-1936
Varieties: HN 490, 495, 501,
            528, 648, 677,
            1351, 1352

U.S.:   **None**
Can.:   **known**
Ster.:   **to exist**

HN 418
One of the Forty
Style Two
Designer: H. Tittensor
Height: 7 1/4", 18.4 cm
Colour: Striped green
            robes
Issued: 1920-1936
Varieties: HN 494, 498, 647,
            666, 704, 1353

U.S.:   **None**
Can.:   **known**
Ster.:   **to exist**

HN 419
Omar Khayyam
and the Beloved
Designer: C.J. Noke
Height: 10", 25.4 cm
Colour: Green and blue
Issued: 1920-1936
Varieties: HN 407, 459, 598

U.S.:   **Only**
Can.:   **two**
Ster.:   **known**

HN 420
The Princess
Designer: L. Harradine
Height: 9 1/4", 23.5 cm
Colour: Pink and green
            striped skirt,
            blue cape
Issued: 1920-1936
Varieties: HN 391, 392,
            430, 431, 633

U.S.:   **Only**
Can.:   **one**
Ster.:   **known**

HN 421
Contentment
Designer: L. Harradine
Height: 7 1/4", 18.4 cm
Colour: Light green
Issued: 1920-1938
Varieties: HN 395, 396,
 468, 572, 685,
 686, 1323
U.S.: **$3,200.00**
Can.: **$3,200.00**
Ster.: **£1,250.00**

HN 422
The Bouquet
Designer: G. Lambert
Height: 9", 22.9 cm
Colour: Yellow and pink
Issued: 1920-1936
Varieties: HN 406, 414, 428,
 429, 567, 794; also
 called "The Nosegay"
U.S.: **None**
Can.: **known**
Ster.: **to exist**

HN 423
One of the Forty
Style Three
Designer: H. Tittensor
Height: 3", 7.6 cm
Colour: Varied
Issued: 1921-1936
U.S.: **$1,200.00**
Can.: **$1,200.00**
Ster.: **£ 550.00**

Photograph
Not
Available

HN 423A
One of the Forty
Style Four
Designer: H. Tittensor
Height: Unknown
Colour: Varied
Issued: 1921-1936
U.S.: **$1,200.00**
Can.: **$1,200.00**
Ster.: **£ 550.00**

HN 423B
One of the Forty
Style Five
Designer: H. Tittensor
Height: 2 3/4", 6.9 cm
Colour: Varied
Issued: 1921-1936
U.S.: **$1,200.00**
Can.: **$1,200.00**
Ster.: **£ 550.00**

HN 423C
One of the Forty
Style Six
Designer: H. Tittensor
Height: 2 3/4", 6.9 cm
Colour: Varied
Issued: 1921-1936
U.S.: **$1,200.00**
Can.: **$1,200.00**
Ster.: **£ 550.00**

HN 423D
One of the Forty
Style Seven
Designer: H. Tittensor
Height: 2 3/4", 6.9 cm
Colour: Varied
Issued: 1921-1936
U.S.: **$1,200.00**
Can.: **$1,200.00**
Ster.: **£ 550.00**

Photograph
Not
Available

HN 423E
One of the Forty
Style Eight
Designer: H. Tittensor
Height: Unknown
Colour: Varied
Issued: 1921-1936
U.S.: **Extremely rare**
Can.:
Ster.:

HN 424
Sleep
Designer: P. Stabler
Height: 6", 15.2 cm
Colour: Blue
Issued: 1921-1936
Varieties: HN 24, 24A, 25, 25A, 692, 710

U.S.:	**$2,750.00**
Can.:	**$2,500.00**
Ster.:	**£1,000.00**

HN 425
The Goosegirl
Style One
Designer: L. Harradine
Height: 8", 20.3 cm
Colour: Blue
Issued: 1921-1936
Varieties: HN 436, 437, 448, 559, 560

U.S.:	**None**
Can.:	**known**
Ster.:	**to exist**

HN 426
A Jester
Style One
Designer: C.J. Noke
Height: 10", 25.4 cm
Colour: Pink and black
Issued: 1921-1938
Varieties: HN 45, 71, 71A, 320, 367, 412, 446, 552, 616, 627, 1295, 1702, 2016

U.S.	**$6,500.00**
Can.:	**$6,500.00**
Ster.:	**£1,750.00**

Photograph
Not
Available

HN 427
One of the Forty
Style Nine
Designer: H. Tittensor
Height: Unknown
Colour: Green
Issued: 1921-1936

U.S.:	**Extremely rare**
Can.:	
Ster.:	

HN 428
The Bouquet
Designer: G. Lambert
Height: 9", 22.9 cm
Colour: Blue and green
Issued: 1921-1936
Varieties: HN 406, 414, 422, 429, 567, 794; also called "The Nosegay"

U.S.:	**$5,000.00**
Can.:	**$5,000.00**
Ster.:	**£1,500.00**

HN 429
The Bouquet
Designer: G. Lambert
Height: 9", 22.9 cm
Colour: Green and red
Issued: 1921-1936
Varieties: HN 406, 414, 422, 428, 567, 794; also called "The Nosegay"

U.S.:	**$5,000.00**
Can.:	**$5,000.00**
Ster.:	**£1,500.00**

HN 430
The Princess
Designer: L. Harradine
Height: 9 1/4", 23.5 cm
Colour: Green
Issued: 1921-1936
Varieties: HN 391, 392, 420, 431, 633

U.S.:	**Only**
Can.:	**one**
Ster.:	**known**

HN 431
The Princess
Designer: L. Harradine
Height: 9 1/4", 23.5 cm
Colour: Yellow and white
Issued: 1921-1936
Varieties: HN 391, 392, 420, 430, 633

U.S.:	**Only**
Can.:	**one**
Ster.:	**known**

HN 432
Puff and Powder
Designer: L. Harradine
Height: 6 1/2" 16.5 cm
Colour: Lavender and
orange
Issued: 1921-1936
Varieties: HN 397, 398,
400, 433

U.S.:	**None**
Can.:	**known**
Ster.:	**to exist**

HN 433
Puff and Powder
Designer: L. Harradine
Height: 6 1/2", 16.5 cm
Colour: Lilac and green
Issued: 1921-1936
Varieties: HN 397, 398,
400, 432

U.S.:	**$5,000.00**
Can.:	**$5,000.00**
Ster.:	**£1,750.00**

HN 434
Marie
Style One
Designer: L. Harradine
Height: 7", 17.8 cm
Colour: Yellow and orange
Issued: 1921-1938
Varieties: HN 401, 502,
504, 505, 506

U.S.:	**None**
Can.:	**known**
Ster.:	**to exist**

Photograph
Not
Available

HN 435
Betty
Style One
Designer: L. Harradine
Height: 7 1/2", 19.1 cm
Colour: Blue and yellow
Issued: 1921-1938
Varieties: HN 402, 403,
438, 477, 478

U.S.:	**None**
Can.:	**known**
Ster.:	**to exist**

HN 436
The Goosegirl
Style One
Designer: L. Harradine
Height: 8", 20.3 cm
Colour: Green and blue
Issued: 1921-1936
Varieties: HN 425, 437,
448, 559, 560

U.S.:	**$6,000.00**
Can.:	**$6,000.00**
Ster.:	**£2,250.00**

HN 437
The Goosegirl
Style One
Designer: L. Harradine
Height: 8", 20.3 cm
Colour: Brown and blue
Issued: 1921-1936
Varieties: HN 425, 436,
148, 559, 560

U.S.:	**$6,000.00**
Can.:	**$6,000.00**
Ster.:	**£2,250.00**

Photograph
Not
Available

HN 438
Betty
Style One
Designer: L. Harradine
Height: 7 1/2", 19.1 cm
Colour: Blue and cream
Issued: 1921-1938
Varieties: HN 402, 403,
435, 477, 478

U.S.:	**Only**
Can.:	**one**
Ster.:	**known**

HN 439
Japanese Fan
Designer: H. Tittensor
Height: 4 3/4", 12.1 cm
Colour: Blue with
green spots
Issued: 1921-1936
Varieties: HN 399, 405, 440;
Also known in flambé

U.S.:	**None**
Can.:	**known**
Ster.:	**to exist**

HN 440
Japanese Fan
Designer: H. Tittensor
Height: 4 3/4", 12.1 cm
Colour: Cream and orange
Issued: 1921-1936
Varieties: HN 399, 405, 439;
Also known in flambé
U.S.: $5,500.00
Can.: $5,500.00
Ster.: £1,800.00

HN 441
The Parson's Daughter
Designer: H. Tittensor
Height: 10", 25.4 cm
Colour: Yellow and orange
Issued: 1921-1938
Varieties: HN 337, 338,
564, 790, 1242,
1356, 2018
U.S.: $2,200.00
Can.: $2,200.00
Ster.: £ 900.00

HN 442
In Grandma's Days
Designer: C.J. Noke
Height: 8 3/4", 22.2 cm
Colour: White and green
Issued: 1921-1938
Varieties: HN 339, 340, 388;
"The Poke Bonnet"
HN 362, 612, 765;
"A Lilac Shawl"
HN 44, 44A
U.S: None
Can.: known
Ster.: to exist

HN 443
Out For a Walk
Designer: E.W. Light
Height: 10", 25.4 cm
Colour: Brown check
Issued: 1921-1936
Varieties: HN 86, 748
U.S.: None
Can.: known
Ster.: to exist

HN 444
A Lady of the
Georgian Period
Designer: E.W. Light
Height: 10 1/4", 26.0 cm
Colour: Blue-green
spotted dress
Issued: 1921-1936
Varieties: HN 41, 331,
690, 702
U.S.: None
Can.: known
Ster.: to exist

HN 445
Guy Fawkes
Style One
Designer: C.J. Noke
Height: 10 1/2", 26.7 cm
Colour: Green cloak
Issued: 1921-1938
Varieties: HN 98, 347; Also
known in Sung
U.S.: Extremely rare
Can.:
Ster.:

HN 446
A Jester
Style One
Designer: C.J. Noke
Height: 10", 25.4 cm
Colour: Black, green, blue
Issued: 1921-1938
Varieties: HN 45, 71, 71A,
320, 367, 412, 426,
552, 616, 627,
1295, 1702, 2016
U.S: $7,500.00
Can.: $7,500.00
Ster.: £1,750.00

HN 447
Lady with Shawl
Designer: L. Harradine
Height: 13 1/4", 33.7 cm
Colour: Green and cream
striped dress
Issued: 1921-1936
Varieties: HN 458, 626,
678, 679
U.S.: $5,500.00
Can.: $5,500.00
Ster.: £1,750.00

HN 448
The Goosegirl
Style One
Designer: L. Harradine
Height: 8", 20.3 cm
Colour: Blue
Issued: 1921-1936
Varieties: HN 425, 436,
437, 559, 560

U.S.:	None
Can.:	known
Ster.:	to exist

HN 449
Fruit Gathering
Designer: L. Harradine
Height: 7 3/4", 19.7 cm
Colour: Blue
Issued: 1921-1936
Varieties: HN 476, 503, 561,
562, 706, 707

U.S.:	None
Can.:	known
Ster.:	to exist

Photograph
Not
Available

HN 450
Chu Chin Chow
Style One
Designer: C.J. Noke
Height: 6 1/2", 16.5 cm
Colour: Red coat and
green cap
Issued: 1921-1936
Varieties: HN 460, 461

U.S.:	Extremely rare
Can.:	
Ster.:	

Photograph
Not
Available

HN 451
An Old Man
Designer: Unknown
Height: Unknown
Colour: Green, red
and blue
Issued: 1921-1938

U.S.:	Only
Can.:	One
Ster.:	known

*

HN 453
The Gainsborough Hat
Designer: H. Tittensor
Height: 8 3/4", 22.2 cm
Colour: Red, blue and green
Issued: 1921-1936
Varieties: HN 46, 46A, 47,
329, 352, 383,
675, 705

U.S.:	None
Can.:	known
Ster.:	to exist

HN 454
The Smiling Buddha
Designer: C.J. Noke
Height: 6 1/4", 15.9 cm
Colour: Green-blue
Issued: 1921-1936
Varieties: Also known in
flambé and Sung

U.S.:	$5,000.00
Can.:	$5,000.00
Ster.:	£2,000.00

HN 455
A Mandarin
Style Two
Designer: C.J. Noke
Height: 8 1/4", 21.0 cm
Colour: Green
Issued: 1921-1938
Varieties: HN 366, 641

U.S.:	None
Can.:	known
Ster.:	to exist

HN 456
Myfanwy Jones
Designer: E.W. Light
Height: 12", 30.5 cm
Colour: Green and brown
Issued: 1921-1936
Varieties: HN 39, 92, 514, 516,
519, 520, 660, 668,
669, 701, 792; also
called "The Welsh Girl"

U.S:	$6,000.00
Can.:	$6,000.00
Ster.:	£2,500.00

Photograph
Not
Available

HN 457
Crouching Nude
Designer: Unknown
Height: 5 1/2", 14.0 cm
Colour: Cream, green base
Issued: 1921-1936

U.S.: **$4,200.00**
Can.: **$3,750.00**
Ster.: **£1,500.00**

HN 458
Lady with Shawl
Designer: L. Harradine
Height: 13 1/4", 33.7 cm
Colour: Pink
Issued: 1921-1936
Varieties: HN 447, 626, 678, 679

U.S.: **None**
Can.: **known**
Ster.: **to exist**

HN 459
Omar Khayyam
and the Beloved
Designer: C.J. Noke
Height: 10", 25.4 cm
Colour: Multi-coloured
Issued: 1921-1936
Varieties: HN 407, 419, 598

U.S.: **Extremely rare**
Can.:
Ster.:

HN 460
Chu Chow Chin
Style One
Designer: C.J. Noke
Height: 6 1/2", 16.5 cm
Colour: Blue and green
Issued: 1921-1936
Varieties: HN 450, 461

U.S.: **Only**
Can.: **one**
Ster.: **known**

Photograph
Not
Available

HN 461
Chu Chow Chin
Style One
Designer: C.J. Noke
Height: 6 1/2", 16.5 cm
Colour: Red
Issued: 1921-1936
Varieties: HN 450, 460

U.S.: **Only**
Can.: **one**
Ster.: **known**

HN 462
Motherhood
Style Two
Designer: Unknown
Height: 9 1/4", 23.5 cm
Colour: Green and white
Issued: 1921-1938
Varieties: HN 570, 703, 743

U.S.: **$7,000.00**
Can.: **$6,500.00**
Ster.: **£3,000.00**

HN 463
Polly Peachum
Style One
Designer: L. Harradine
Height: 6 1/4", 15.9 cm
Colour: Pale blue
Issued: 1921-1949
Varieties: HN 465, 550, 589, 614, 680, 693
Series: Beggar's Opera

U.S.: **$1,200.00**
Can.: **$1,200.00**
Ster.: **£ 500.00**

HN 464
Captain MacHeath
Designer: L. Harradine
Height: 7", 17.8 cm
Colour: Red, yellow and black
Issued: 1921-1949
Varieties: HN 590, 1256
Series: Beggar's Opera

U.S.: **$1,250.00**
Can.: **$1,250.00**
Ster.: **£ 550.00**

HN 465
Polly Peachum
Style One
Designer: L. Harradine
Height: 6 1/4", 15.9 cm
Colour: Red
Issued: 1921-1949
Varieties: HN 463, 550, 589,
614, 680, 693
Series: Beggar's Opera
U.S.: **$1,000.00**
Can.: **$1,100.00**
Ster.: **£ 500.00**

HN 466
Tulips
Designer: Unknown
Height: 9 1/2", 24.1 cm
Colour: Green
Issued: 1921-1936
Varieties: HN 488, 672,
747, 1334
U.S.: **None**
Can.: **known**
Ster.: **to exist**

HN 467
Doris Keene as Cavallini
Style One
Designer: C.J. Noke
Height: 11", 27.9 cm
Colour: Dark green with
gold jewellery
Issued: 1921-1936
Varieties: HN 90
U.S.: **Extremely rare**
Can.:
Ster.:

HN 468
Contentment
Designer: L. Harradine
Height: 7 1/4", 18.4 cm
Colour: Green spotted dress
Issued: 1921-1938
Varieties: HN 395, 396, 421,
572, 685, 686, 1323
U.S.: **$3,500.00**
Can.: **$3,500.00**
Ster.: **£1,250.00**

HN 469
Dolly
Style Two
Designer: H. Tittensor
Height: 11", 27.9 cm
Colour: White
Issued: 1921-1938
Varieties: Also called "The
Little Mother"
HN 389, 390
U.S.: **Only**
Can.: **one**
Ster.: **known**

Photograph
Not
Available

HN 470
Lady and Blackamoor
Style Two
Designer: H. Tittensor
Height: Unknown
Colour: Green and lavender
Issued: 1921-1936
Varieties: HN 374, 375, 377
U.S.: **None**
Can.: **known**
Ster.: **to exist**

HN 471
Katharine
Designer: C.J. Noke
Height: 5 3/4", 14.6 cm
Colour: Patterned green
dress
Issued: 1921-1938
Varieties: HN 61, 74, 341,
615, 793
U.S.: **$3,500.00**
Can.: **$3,500.00**
Ster.: **£1,500.00**

HN 472
Spring
Style One
Designer: Unknown
Colour: Patterned
lavender robe
Height: 7 1/2", 19.1 cm
Issued: 1921-1938
Varieties: HN 312
Series: The Seasons
(Series One)
U.S: **$3,000.00**
Can.: **$3,000.00**
Ster.: **£1,100.00**

HN 473
Summer
Style One
Designer: Unknown
Height: 7 1/2", 19.1 cm
Colour: Patterned light
                   green robes
Issued: 1921-1938
Varieties: HN 313
Series: The Seasons
                   (Series One)

U.S.:   None
Can.:   known
Ster.:   to exist

HN 474
Autumn
Style One
Designer: Unknown
Height: 7 1/2", 19.1 cm
Colour: Patterned pink robes
Issued: 1921-1938
Varieties: HN 314
Series: The Seasons
                   (Series One)

U.S.:   None
Can.:   known
Ster.:   to exist

HN 475
Winter
Style One
Designer: Unknown
Height: 7 1/2", 19.1 cm
Colour: Patterned pale
                   green robes
Issued: 1921-1938
Varieties: HN 315
Series: The Seasons
                   (Series One)

U.S.:   None
Can.:   known
Ster.:   to exist

HN 476
Fruit Gathering
Designer: L. Harradine
Height: 8", 20.3 cm
Colour: Lavender and yellow
Issued: 1921-1936
Varieties: HN 449, 503, 561,
                   562, 706, 707

U.S.: $4,000.00
Can.: $4,000.00
Ster.:   £1,450.00

Photograph
Not
Available

HN 477
Betty
Style One
Designer: L. Harradine
Height: 7 1/2", 19.1 cm
Colour: Green
Issued: 1921-1938
Varieties: HN 402, 403,
                   435, 438, 478

U.S.:   Only
Can.:   one
Ster.:   known

Photograph
Not
Available

HN 478
Betty
Style One
Designer: L. Harradine
Height: 7 1/2", 19.1 cm
Colour: White
Issued: 1921-1938
Varieties: HN 402, 403,
                   435, 438, 477

U.S.:   Extremely rare
Can.:
Ster.:

HN 479
The Balloon Seller
Designer: L. Harradine
Height: 9", 22.9 cm
Colour: Dark blue and
                   lavender
Issued: 1921-1938
Varieties: HN 486, 548, 583,
                   697; also called "The
                   Balloon Woman"

U.S.: $4,000.00
Can.: $4,000.00
Ster.:   £1,250.00

HN 480
One of the Forty
Style Ten
Designer: H. Tittensor
Height: 7", 17.8 cm
Colour: Brown, yellow
                   and blue
Issued: 1921-1938
Varieties: HN 493, 497, 499,
                   664, 714

U.S.:   Extremely rare
Can.:
Ster.:

HN 481
One of the Forty
Style Eleven
Designer: H. Tittensor
Height: Unknown
Colour: Dark colour
Issued: 1921-1936
Varieties: HN 483, 491, 646,
667, 712, 1336,
1350; Also known
in flambé

U.S.:	None
Can.:	known
Ster.:	to exist

HN 482
One of the Forty
Style Twelve
Designer: H. Tittensor
Height: 6", 15.2 cm
Colour: White
Issued: 1921-1938
Varieties: HN 484, 492,
645, 663, 713

U.S.:	None
Can.:	known
Ster.:	to exist

HN 483
One of the Forty
Style Eleven
Designer: H. Tittensor
Height: Unknown
Colour: Brown and green
Issued: 1921-1938
Varieties: HN 481, 491, 646,
667, 712, 1336, 1350;
Flambé

U.S.:	None
Can.:	known
Ster.:	to exist

HN 484
One of the Forty
Style Twelve
Designer: H. Tittensor
Height: 6", 15.2 cm
Colour: Green
Issued: 1921-1938
Varieties: HN 482, 492,
645, 663, 713

U.S.:	None
Can.:	known
Ster.:	to exist

HN 485
Lucy Lockett
Style One
Designer: L. Harradine
Height: 6", 15.2 cm
Colour: Green
Issued: 1921-1949
Series: Beggar's Opera

U.S.:	$2,000.00
Can.:	$2,000.00
Ster.:	£ 900.00

HN 486
The Balloon Seller
Designer: L. Harradine
Height: 9", 22.9 cm
Colour: Blue dress, no hat
Issued: 1921-1938
Varieties: HN 479, 548, 583,
697; also called
"The Balloon Woman"

U.S.:	None
Can.:	known
Ster.:	to exist

HN 487
Pavlova
Designer: C.J. Noke
Height: 4 1/4", 10.8 cm
Colour: White, black base
Issued: 1921-1938
Varieties: HN 676; also
called "Swan Song"

U.S.:	Only
Can.:	two
Ster.:	known

HN 488
Tulips
Designer: Unknown
Height: 9 1/2", 24.1 cm
Colour: Cream
Issued: 1921-1936
Varieties: HN 466, 672,
747, 1334

U.S.:	None
Can.:	known
Ster.:	to exist

HN 489
Polly Peachum
Style Two
Designer: L. Harradine
Height: 4 1/4", 10.8 cm
Colour: turquoise
Issued: 1921-1938
Varieties: HN 549, 620,
694, 734
Series: Beggar's Opera

U.S.:	$1,000.00
Can.:	$1,000.00
Ster.:	£ 400.00

HN 490
One of the Forty
Style One
Dsigner: H. Tittensor
Height: 8 1/4", 21.0 cm
Colour: Blue and brown
Issued: 1921-1938
Varieties: HN 417, 495, 501,
528, 648, 677,
1351, 1352

U.S.:	None
Can.:	known
Ster.:	to exist

HN 491
One of the Forty
Style Eleven
Designer: H. Tittensor
Height: Unknown
Colour: Green and white
Issued: 1921-1936
Varieties: HN 481, 483, 646,
667, 712, 1336, 1350;
Flambé

U.S.:	None
Can.:	known
Ster.:	to exist

Photograph
Not
Available

HN 492
One of the Forty
Style Twelve
Designer: H. Tittensor
Height: 6", 15.2 cm
Colour: Yellow and white
Issued: 1921-1938
Varieties: HN 482, 484, 645,
663, 713; Flambé

U.S.:	None
Can.:	known
Ster.:	to exist

HN 493
One of the Forty
Style Ten
Designer: H. Tittensor
Height: 6 3/4", 17.1 cm
Colour: Blue and black
Issued: 1921-1938
Varieties: HN 480, 497,
499, 664, 714

U.S.:	None
Can.:	known
Ster.:	to exist

HN 494
One of the Forty
Style Two
Designer: H. Tittensor
Height: 7 1/4", 18.4 cm
Colour: Cream and blue
Issued: 921-1936
Varieties: HN 418, 498, 647,
666, 704, 1353

U.S.:	None
Can.:	known
Ster.:	to exist

HN 495
One of the Forty
Style One
Designer: H. Tittensor
Height: 8 1/4", 21.0 cm
Colour: Brown and blue
Issued: 1921-1938
Varieties: HN 417, 490,
501, 528, 648,
677, 1351, 1352

U.S.:	None
Can.:	known
Ster.:	to exist

Photograph
Not
Available

HN 496
One of the Forty
Style Thirteen
Designer: H. Tittensor
Height: 7 3/4", 19.6 cm
Colour: Orange and
yellow checks
Issued: 1921-1938
Varieties: HN 500, 649,
665, 1354

U.S.:	None
Can.:	known
Ster.:	to exist

Photograph
Not
Available

HN 497
One of the Forty
Style Ten
Designer: H. Tittensor
Height: 6 3/4", 17.1 cm
Colour: Brown and green
Issued: 1921-1938
Varieties: HN 480, 493
499, 664, 714

U.S. **Extremely rare**
Can.
Ster.:

HN 498
One of the Forty
Style Two
Designer: H. Tittensor
Height: 7 1/4", 18.4 cm
Colour: Dark colours
Issued: 1921-1936
Varieties: HN 418, 494, 647,
666, 704, 1353

U.S.: **None**
Can.: **known**
Ster.: **to exist**

HN 499
One of the Forty
Style Ten
Designer: H. Tittensor
Height: 6 3/4", 17.1 cm
Colour: Cream and green
Issued: 1921-1938
Varieties: HN 480, 493,
497, 664, 714

U.S.: **None**
Can.: **known**
Ster.: **to exist**

HN 500
One of the Forty
Style Thirteen
Designer: H. Tittensor
Height: 7 3/4", 19.6 cm
Colour: Orange checks
and red turban
Issued: 1921-1938
Varieties: HN 496, 649,
665, 1354

U.S.: **None**
Can.: **known**
Ster.: **to exist**

HN 501
One of the Forty
Style One
Designer: H Tittensor
Height: 8 1/4", 21.0 cm
Colour: Green stripes
Issued: 1921-1938
Varieties: HN 417, 490, 495,
528, 648, 677, 1351,
1352

U.S.: **None**
Can.: **known**
Ster.: **to exist**

HN 502
Marie
Style One
Designer: L. Harradine
Height: 7", 17.8 cm
Colour: White, red and blue
Issued: 1921-1938
Varieties: HN 401, 434,
504, 505, 506

U.S.: **None**
Can.: **known**
Ster.: **to exist**

HN 503
Fruit Gathering
Designer: L. Harradine
Height: 7 3/4", 19.7 cm
Colour: Brown and blue
Issued: 1921-1936
Varieties: HN 449, 476, 561,
562, 706, 707

U.S.: **$4,000.00**
Can.: **$4,000.00**
Ster.: **£1,250.00**

HN 504
Marie
Style One
Designer: L. Harradine
Height: 7", 17.8 cm
Colour: Green, blue and red
Issued: 1921-1938
Varieties: HN 401, 434,
502, 505, 506

U.S.: **None**
Can.: **known**
Ster.: **to exist**

HN 505
Marie
Style One
Designer: L. Harradine
Height: 7", 17.8 cm
Colour: Blue, green
and lavender
Issued: 1921-1938
Varieties: HN 401, 434,
502, 504, 506

U.S.: **None**
Can.: **known**
Ster.: **to exist**

HN 506
Marie
Style One
Designer: L. Harradine
Height: 7", 17.8 cm
Colour: Blue, green
and lavender
Issued: 1921-1938
Varieties: HN 401, 434,
502, 504, 505

U.S.: **None**
Can.: **known**
Ster.: **to exist**

HN 507
Pussy
Designer: F.C. Stone
Height: 7 1/2", 19.1 cm
Colour: Spotted blue dress
Issued: 1921-1938
Varieties: HN 18, 325;
also called
"The Black Cat"

U.S.: **None**
Can.: **known**
Ster.: **to exist**

HN 508
An Orange Vendor
Designer: C.J. Noke
Height: 6 1/4", 15.9 cm
Colour: Red, cream and
orange
Issued: 1921-1938
Varieties: HN 72, 521, 1966

U.S.: **$2,500.00**
Can.: **$2,000.00**
Ster.: **£ 950.00**

HN 509
Lady of the Fan
Designer: E.W. Light
Height: 9 1/2", 24.1 cm
Colour: Green and lavender
Issued: 1921-1936
Varieties: HN 48, 52,
53, 53A, 335

U.S.: **None**
Can.: **known**
Ster.: **to exist**

HN 510
A Child's Grace
Designer: L. Perugini
Height: 6 3/4", 17.2 cm
Colour: Green and yellow
Issued: 1921-1938
Varieties: HN 62, 62A

U.S.: **None**
Can.: **known**
Ster.: **to exist**

HN 511
Upon Her Cheeks She Wept
Designer: L. Perugini
Height: 9", 22.8 cm
Colour: Lavender
Issued: 1921-1938
Varieties: HN 59, 522

U.S.: **None**
Can.: **known**
Ster.: **to exist**

HN 512
A Spook
Style Two
Designer: H. Tittensor
Height: 7", 17.8 cm
Colour: Purple
Issued: 1921-1936
Varieties: HN 50, 51, 51A
51B, 58, 625; Also
known in flambé

U.S.: **Extremely rare**
Can.:
Ster.:

HN 513
Picardy Peasant (woman)
Designer: P. Stabler
Height: 9 1/2", 24.0 cm
Colour: Blue
Issued: 1921-1938
Varieties: HN 4, 5, 17A, 351
  U.S.: **None**
  Can.: **known**
  Ster.: **to exist**

HN 514
Myfanwy Jones
Designer: E.W. Light
Height: 12", 30.5 cm
Colour: Green and red
Issued: 1921-1936
Varieties: HN 39, 92, 456, 516,
  519, 520, 660, 668,
  669, 701, 792; also
  called "The Welsh Girl"
  U.S.: **None**
  Can.: **known**
  Ster.: **to exist**

HN 515
Lady with Rose
Designer: E.W. Light
Height: 9 1/2", 24.1 cm
Colour: Lavender, green
Issued: 1921-1936
Varieties: HN 48A, 52A,
  68, 304, 336,
  517, 584, 624
  U.S.: **None**
  Can.: **known**
  Ster.: **to exist**

HN 516
Myfanwy Jones
Designer: E.W. Light
Height: 12", 30.5 cm
Colour: Black and lavender
Issued: 1921-1936
Varieties: HN 39, 92, 456, 514,
  519, 520, 660, 668,
  669, 701, 792; also
  called "The Welsh Girl"
  U.S.: **None**
  Can.: **known**
  Ster.: **to exist**

HN 517
Lady with Rose
Designer: E.W. Light
Height: 9 1/2", 24.1 cm
Colour: Lavender with
  orange spots
Issued: 1921-1936
Varieties: HN 48A, 52A,
  68, 304, 336,
  515, 584, 624
  U.S.: **None**
  Can.: **known**
  Ster.: **to exist**

HN 518
The Curtsey
Designer: E.W. Light
Height: 11", 27.9 cm
Colour: Lavender
Issued: 1921-1936
Varieties: HN 57, 57B, 66A,
  327, 334, 363, 371,
  547, 629, 670
  U.S.: **None**
  Can.: **known**
  Ster.: **to exist**

HN 519
Myfanwy Jones
Designer: E.W. Light
Height: 12", 30.5 cm
Colour: Blue and lavender
Issued: 1921-1936
Varieties: HN 39, 92, 456, 514,
  516, 520, 660, 668,
  669, 701, 792; also
  called "The Welsh Girl"
  U.S.: **None**
  Can.: **known**
  Ster.: **to exist**

HN 520
Myfanwy Jones
Designer: E.W. Light
Height: 12", 30.5 cm
Colour: Black and lavender
Issued: 1921-1936
Varieties: HN 39, 92, 456, 514,
  516, 519, 660, 668,
  669, 701, 792; also
  called "The Welsh Girl"
  U.S.: **None**
  Can.: **known**
  Ster.: **to exist**

HN 521
An Orange Vendor
Designer: C.J. Noke
Height: 6 1/4", 15.9 cm
Colour: Pale blue, black
                   and purple
Issued: 1921-1938
Varieties: HN 72, 508, 1966

U.S.:   **None**
Can.:   **known**
Ster.:   **to exist**

HN 522
Upon Her Cheeks She Wept
Designer: L. Perugini
Height: 9", 22.8 cm
Colour: Lavender
Issued: 1921-1938
Varieties: HN 59, 511

U.S.:   **None**
Can.:   **known**
Ster.:   **to exist**

HN 523
Sentinel
Designer: Unknown
Height: 17 1/2", 44.4 cm
Colour: Red, blue
                   and black
Issued: 1921-1938

U.S.:   **Only**
Can.:   **two**
Ster.:   **known**

HN 524
Lucy Lockett
Style Two
Designer: L. Harradine
Height: 6", 15.2 cm
Colour: Orange
Issued: 1921-1949
Varieties: Earthenware
                   and China
Series: Beggar's Opera

U.S.:   **$1,100.00**
Can.:   **$1,100.00**
Ster.:   **£   450.00**

HN 525
The Flower Seller's
Children
Designer: L. Harradine
Height: 8 1/4", 21.0 cm
Colour: Green and blue
Issued: 1921-1949
Varieties: HN 551, 1206,
                   1342, 1406

U.S.:   **None**
Can.:   **known**
Ster.:   **to exist**

HN 526
The Beggar
Style One
Designer: L. Harradine
Height: 6 1/2", 16.5 cm
Colour: Green and blue
Issued: 1921-1949
Varieties: HN 591
Series: Beggar's Opera

U.S.:   **$750.00**
Can.:   **$750.00**
Ster.:   **£450.00**

HN 527
The Highwayman
Designer: L. Harradine
Height: 6 1/2", 16.5 cm
Colour: Green and red
Issued: 1921-1949
Varieties: HN 592, 1257
Series: Beggar's Opera

U.S.:   **$1,100.00**
Can.:   **$1,100.00**
Ster.:   **£   450.00**

HN 528
One of the Forty
Style One
 Designer: H. Tittensor
Height: 8 1/4", 21.0 cm
Colour: Brown
Issued: 1921-1938
Varieties: HN 417, 490,
                   495, 501, 648,
                   677, 1351, 1352

U.S.:   **None**
Can.:   **known**
Ster.:   **to exist**

HN 529
Mr. Pickwick
Style One
Designer: L. Harradine
Height: 3 3/4", 9.5 cm
Colour: Black and tan
Issued: 1922-1932
Varieties: M41
Series: Dickens (Series One)

U.S.: **$150.00**
Can.: **$125.00**
Ster.: £ 45.00

■

HN 530
Fat Boy
Style One
Designer: L. Harradine
Height: 3 1/2", 8.9 cm
Colour: Blue and white
Issued: 1922-1932
Varieties: M44
Series: Dickens (Series One)

U.S.: **$150.00**
Can.: **$125.00**
Ster.: £ 45.00

HN 531
Sam Weller
Designer: L. Harradine
Height: 4", 10.1 cm
Colour: Yellow and brown
Issued: 1922-1932
Varieties: M48
Series: Dickens (Series One)

U.S.: **$145.00**
Can.: **$125.00**
Ster.: £ 45.00

HN 532
Mr. Micawber
Style One
Designer: L. Harradine
Height: 3 1/2", 8.9 cm
Colour: Tan and black
Issued: 1922-1932
Varieties: M42
Series: Dickens (Series One)

U.S.: **$145.00**
Can.: **$125.00**
Ster.: £ 45.00

HN 533
Sairey Gamp
Style One
Designer: L. Harradine
Height: 4", 10.1 cm
Colour: Light and
dark green
Issued: 1922-1932
Varieties: M46
Series: Dickens (Series One)

U.S.: **$165.00**
Can.: **$125.00**
Ster.: £ 45.00

HN 534
Fagin
Style one
Designer: L. Harradine
Height: 4", 10.1 cm
Colour: Dark brown
Issued: 1922-1932
Varieties: M49
Series: Dickens (Series One)

U.S.: **$160.00**
Can.: **$125.00**
Ster.: £ 45.00

HN 535
Pecksniff
Style One
Designer: L. Harradine
Height: 3 3/4", 9.5 cm
Colour: Brown
Issued: 1922-1932
Varieties: M43
Series: Dickens (Series One)

U.S.: **$150.00**
Can.: **$125.00**
Ster.: £ 45.00

HN 536
Stiggins
Designer: L. Harradine
Height: 3 3/4", 9.5 cm
Colour: Black
Issued: 1922-1932
Varieties: M50
Series: Dickens (Series One)

U.S.: **$150.00**
Can.: **$125.00**
Ster.: £ 45.00

HN 537
Bill Sykes
Designer: L. Harradine
Height: 3 3/4", 9.5 cm
Colour: Black and brown
Issued: 1922-1932
Varieties: M54
Series: Dickens (Series One)

U.S.: $150.00
Can.: $125.00
Ster.: £ 45.00

HN 538
Buz Fuz
Designer: L. Harradine
Height: 3 3/4", 9.5 cm
Colour: Black and brown
Issued: 1922-1932
Varieties: M53
Series: Dickens (Series One)

U.S.: $165.00
Can.: $125.00
Ster.: £ 45.00

HN 539
Tiny Tim
Designer: L. Harradine
Height: 3 1/2", 8.9 cm
Colour: Black, brown
       and blue
Issued: 1922-1932
Varieties: M56
Series: Dickens (Series One)

U.S.: $150.00
Can.: $125.00
Ster.: £ 45.00

HN 540
Little Nell
Designer: L. Harradine
Height: 4", 10.1 cm
Colour: Pink
Issued: 1922-1932
Varieties: M51
Series: Dickens (Series One)

U.S.: $165.00
Can.: $125.00
Ster.: £ 45.00

HN 541
Alfred Jingle
Designer: L. Harradine
Height: 3 3/4", 9.5 cm
Colour: Brown and black
Issued: 1922-1932
Varieties: M52
Series: Dickens (Series One)

U.S.: $150.00
Can.: $125.00
Ster.: £ 45.00

HN 542
The Cobbler
Style One
Designer: C.J. Noke
Height: 7 1/2", 19.1 cm
Colour: Green and brown
Issued: 1922-1939
Varieties: HN 543, 682

U.S.: $1,600.00
Can.: $1,500.00
Ster.: £ 650.00

HN 543
The Cobbler
Style One
Designer: C.J. Noke
Height: 7 1/2", 19.1 cm
Colour: Green and brown
Issued: 1922-1938
Varieties: HN 542, 682

U.S.: Only
Can.: two
Ster.: known

HN 544
Tony Weller
Style Two
Designer: L. Harradine
Height: 3 1/2", 8.9 cm
Colour: Green and yellow
Issued: 1922-1932
Varieties: M47
Series: Dickens (Series One)

U.S.: $150.00
Can.: $125.00
Ster.: £ 45.00

HN 545
Uriah Heep
Style One
Designer: L. Harradine
Height: 4", 10.1 cm
Colour: Black
Issued: 1922-1932
Varieties: M45
Series: Dickens (Series One)

U.S.: **$150.00**
Can.: **$125.00**
Ster.: **£ 45.00**

HN 546
Artful Dodger
Designer: L. Harradine
Height: 3 3/4", 9.5 cm
Colour: Black and brown
Issued: 1922-1932
Varieties: M55
Series: Dickens (Series One)

U.S.: **$150.00**
Can.: **$125.00**
Ster.: **£ 45.00**

HN 547
The Curtsey
Designer: E.W. Light
Height: 11", 27.9 cm
Colour: Blue, green
and yellow
Issued: 1922-1936
Varieties: HN 57, 57B, 66A,
327, 334, 363, 371,
518, 629, 670

U.S.: **Extremely rare**
Can.:
Ster.:

HN 548
The Balloon Seller
Designer: L. Harradine
Height: 9", 22.9 cm
Colour: Blue and black
Issued: 1922-1938
Varieties: HN 479, 486, 583,
697; also called
"The Balloon Woman"

U.S.: **Extremely rare**
Can.:
Ster.:

HN 549
Polly Peachum
Style Two
Designer: L. Harradine
Height: 4 1/4", 10.8 cm
Colour: Rose pink
Issued: 1922-1949
Varieties: HN 489, 620,
694, 734
Series: Beggar's Opera

U.S.: **$850.00**
Can.: **$650.00**
Ster.: **£325.00**

HN 550
Polly Peachum
Style One
Designer: L. Harradine
Height: 6 1/2", 16/5 cm
Colour: rose pink
Issued: 1922-1949
Varieties: HN 463, 465, 589,
614, 680, 693
Series: Beggar's Opera

U.S.: **$1,000.00**
Can.: **$1,000.00**
Ster.: **£ 400.00**

HN 551
The Flower Seller's
Children
Designer: L. Harradine
Height: 8 1/4", 21.0 cm
Colour: Blue, orange
and yellow
Issued: 1922-1949
Varieties: HN 525, 1206,
1342, 1406

U.S.: **None**
Can.: **known**
Ster.: **to exist**

HN 552
A Jester
Style One
Designer: C.J. Noke
Height: 10", 25.4 cm
Colour: Black and red
Issued: 1922-1938
Varieties: HN 45, 71, 71A,
320, 367, 412, 426,
446, 616, 627, 1295,
1702, 2016

U.S.: **$6,500.00**
Can.: **$6,500.00**
Ster.: **£1,750.00**

HN 553
Pecksniff
Style Two
Designer: L. Harradine
Height: 7", 17.8 cm
Colour: Black and brown
Issued: 1923-1939
Varieties: HN 1891
Series: Dickens (Series Two)

U.S.: $700.00
Can.: $700.00
Ster.: £350.00

HN 554
Uriah Heep
Style Two
Designer: L. Harradine
Height: 7 1/4", 18.4 cm
Colour: Black
Issued: 1923-1939
Varieties: HN 1892
Series: Dickens (Series Two)

U.S.: $700.00
Can.: $700.00
Ster.: £350.00

HN 555
Fat Boy
Style Two
Designer: L. Harradine
Height: 7", 17.8 cm
Colour: Blue and cream
Issued: 1923-1939
Varieties: HN 1893
Series: Dickens (Series Two)

U.S.: $750.00
Can.: $750.00
Ster.: £350.00

HN 556
Mr. Pickwick
Style Two
Designer: L. Harradine
Height: 7", 17.8 cm
Colour: Blue, yellow and tan
Issued: 1923-1939
Varieties: HN 1894
Series: Dickens (Series Two)

U.S.: $700.00
Can.: $700.00
Ster.: £350.00

HN 557
Mr. Micawber
Style Two
Designer: L. Harradine
Height: 7", 17.8 cm
Colour: Brown, black and tan
Issued: 1923-1939
Varieties: HN 1895
Series: Dickens (Series Two)

U.S.: $700.00
Can.: $700.00
Ster.: £350.00

HN 558
Sairey Gamp
Style Two
Designer: L. Harradine
Height: 7", 17.8 cm
Colour: Black
Issued: 1923-1939
Varieties: HN1896
Series: Dickens (Series Two)

U.S.: $850.00
Can.: $850.00
Ster.: £395.00

HN 559
The Goosegirl
Style One
Designer: L. Harradine
Height: 8", 20.3 cm
Colour: Pink
Issued: 1923-1936
Varieties: HN 425, 436,
437, 448, 560

U.S.: $6,000.00
Can.: $6,000.00
Ster.: £2,250.00

Earthenware

NOTE ON PRICING

Prices are given for three separate and distinct market areas.

Prices are given in the currency of each of these different trading areas.

Prices are not exchange rate calculations but are based on supply and demand in that market.

Prices listed are guidelines to the most current retail values but actual selling prices may vary slightly.

Prices for current figurines are taken from the Royal Doulton suggested retail lists.

Extremely rare figurines have widely fluctuating retail values and their prices must therefore be determined between buyer and seller.

Figurines where there are only one or two known are possibly best priced in an auction environment.

Prices given are for figurines in mint condition.

HN 560
The Goosegirl
Style One
Designer: L. Harradine
Height: 8", 20.3 cm
Colour: . Pink and white
Issued: 1923-1936
Varieties: HN 425, 436,
             437, 448, 559

U.S.:   **Extremely rare**
Can.:
Ster.:

HN 561
Fruit Gathering
Designer: L. Harradine
Height: 7 3/4", 19.7 cm
Colour: Green, white
             and pink
Issued: 1923-1936
Varieties: HN 449, 476, 503,
             562, 706, 707

U.S.:   **None**
Can.:   **known**
Ster.:   **to exist**

HN 562
Fruit Gathering
Designer: L. Harradine
Height: 7 3/4", 19.7 cm
Colour: Pink, white
             and green
Issued: 1923-1936
Varieties: HN 449, 476, 503,
             561, 706, 707

U.S.:   **$4,000.00**
Can.:   **$4,000.00**
Ster.:   **£1,400.00**

HN 563
Man in Tudor Costume
Designer: Unknown
Height: 3 3/4", 9.5 cm
Colour: Orange striped
             tunic, black cloak
Issued: 1923-1938

U.S.:   **$4,800.00**
Can.:   **$4,800.00**
Ster.:   **£2,250.00**

HN 564
The Parson's Daughter
Designer: H. Tittensor
Height: 9 1/2", 24.1 cm
Colour: Red, yellow
             and green
Issued: 1923-1949
Varieties: HN 337, 338, 441,
             790, 1242, 1356, 2018

U.S.:   **$575.00**
Can.:   **$575.00**
Ster.:   **£275.00**

HN 565
Pretty Lady
Designer: H. Tittensor
Height: 10", 25.4 cm
Colour: Yellow and green
Issued: 1923-1938
Varieties: HN 69, 70, 302,
             330, 361, 384, 700,
             763, 783; appears in
             two colours, yellow
             and orange

U.S.:   **$2,500.00**
Can.:   **$2,250.00**
Ster.:   **£ 950.00**

HN 566
The Crinoline
Designer: G. Lambert
Height: 6 1/4", 15.8 cm
Colour: Cream and green
Issued: 1923-1938
Varieties: HN 8, 9, 9A, 21,
             21A, 413, 628

U.S.:   **$3,300.00**
Can.:   **$3,300.00**
Ster.:   **£1,350.00**

HN 567
The Bouquet
Designer: G. Lambert
Height: 9 1/2", 24.1 cm
Colour: Pink dress, beige
             patterned shawl
Issued: 1923-1936
Varieties: HN 406, 414, 422,
             428, 429, 794; also
             called "The Nosegay"

U.S.:   **$4,000.00**
Can.:   **$4,000.00**
Ster.:   **£1,250.00**

HN 568
Shy Anne
Designer: L. Perugini
Height: 7 1/2", 19.1 cm
Colour: Green dress
with black spots
Issued: 1923-1936
Varieties: HN 60, 64, 65

U.S.: $4,500.00
Can.: $4,500.00
Ster.: £2,000.00

Earthenware and China

HN 569
The Lavender Woman
Designer: P. Stabler
Height: 8 1/4", 21.0 cm
Colour: Lavender
Issued: 1924-1936
Varieties: HN 22, 23, 23A,
342, 744

U.S.: $6,000.00
Can.: $6,000.00
Ster.: £2,000.00

HN 570
Motherhood
Style Two
Designer: Unknown
Height: 9 1/4", 23.5 cm
Colour: Pink and green
Issued: 1923-1938
Varieties: HN 462, 703, 743

U.S.: $7,000.00
Can.: $6,500.00
Ster.: £2,750.00

HN 571
Falstaff
Style One
Designer: C.J. Noke
Height: 7", 17.8 cm
Colour: Brown and green
Issued: 1923-1938
Varieties: HN 575, 608, 609,
619, 638, 1216, 1606

U.S.: $2,500.00
Can.: $2,250.00
Ster.: £ 900.00

HN 572
Contentment
Designer: L. Harradine
Height: 7 1/4", 18.4 cm
Colour: Cream and orange
Issued: 1923-1938
Varieties: HN 395, 396, 421,
468, 685, 686, 1323

U.S.: $3,000.00
Can.: $3,000.00
Ster.: £ 800.00

HN 573
Madonna of the Square
Designer: P. Stabler
Height: 7", 17.8 cm
Colour: Orange
Issued: 1923-1936
Varieties: HN 10, 10A, 11, 14,
27, 326, 576, 594,
613, 764, 1968, 1969,
2034

U.S.: None
Can.: known
Ster.: to exist

*

HN 575
Falstaff
Style One
Designer: C.J. Noke
Height: 7", 17.8 cm
Colour: Brown and yellow
Issued: 1923-1938
Varieties: HN 571, 608, 609,
619, 638, 1216, 1606

U.S.: $2,500.00
Can.: $2,250.00
Ster.: £ 900.00

HN 576
Madonna of the Square
Designer: P. Stabler
Height: 7", 17.8 cm
Colour: Green and black
Issued: 1923-1936
Varieties: HN 10, 10A, 11, 14,
27, 326, 573, 594,
613, 764, 1968, 1969,
2034

U.S.: $2,700.00
Can.: $2,800.00
Ster.: £ 950.00

HN 577
The Chelsea Pair (woman)
Designer: L. Harradine
Height: 6", 15.2 cm
Colour: White dress
with blue flowers
Issued: 1923-1938
Varieties: HN 578

U.S.: $1,250.00
Can.: $1,250.00
Ster.: £ 450.00

HN 578
The Chelsea Pair (woman)
Designer: L. Harradine
Height: 6", 15.2 cm
Colour: White dress with
yellow flowers
Issued: 1923-1938
Varieties: HN 577

U.S.: $1,500.00
Can.: $1,500.00
Ster.: £ 450.00

HN 579
The Chelsea Pair (man)
Designer: L. Harradine
Height: 6", 15.2 cm
Colour: Red and black,
yellow flowers
Issued: 1923-1938
Varieties: HN 580

U.S.: $1,250.00
Can.: $1,250.00
Ster.: £ 450.00

HN 580
The Chelsea Pair (man)
Designer: L. Harradine
Height: 6", 15.2 cm
Colour: Red and black,
blue flowers
Issued: 1923-1938
Varieties: HN 579

U.S.: $1,500.00
Can.: $1,500.00
Ster.: £ 450.00

HN 581
The Perfect Pair
Designer: L. Harradine
Height: 6 3/4", 17.2 cm
Colour: Pink and red
Issued: 1923-1938

U.S.: $1,600.00
Can.: $1,400.00
Ster.: £ 600.00

HN 582
Grossmith's 'Tsang Ihang'
Perfume of Thibet
Designer: Unknown
Height: 11 1/2", 29.2 cm
Colour: Yellow, black
and blue
Issued: 1923-Unknown

U.S.: $1,200.00
Can.: $1,200.00
Ster.: £ 550.00

Earthenware

HN 583
The Balloon Seller
Designer: L. Harradine
Height: 9", 22.9 cm
Colour: Green and cream
Issued: 1923-1949
Varieties: HN 479, 486, 548,
697; also called "The
Balloon Woman"

U.S.: $1,200.00
Can.: $1,200.00
Ster.: £ 400.00

HN 584
Lady with Rose
Designer: E.W. Light
Height: 9 1/2", 24.1 cm
Colour: Green and pink
Issued: 1923-1936
Varieties: HN 48A, 52A,
68, 304, 336,
515, 517, 624

U.S.: None
Can.: known
Ster.: to exist

HN 585
Harlequinade
Designer: L. Harradine
Height: 6 1/2", 16.5 cm
Colour: Purple, black
           and green
Issued: 1923-1940
Varieties: HN 635, 711, 780
U.S.:   **$2,200.00**
Can.:   **$2,200.00**
Ster.:   **£ 750.00**

HN 586
Boy with Turban
Designer: L. Harradine
Height: 3 3/4", 9.5 cm
Colour: Blue and green
Issued: 1923-1936
Varieties: HN 587, 661,
           662, 1210, 1212,
           1213, 1214, 1225
U.S.:   **$1,100.00**
Can.:   **$1,250.00**
Ster.:   **£ 600.00**

HN 587
Boy with Turban
Designer: L. Harradine
Height: 3 3/4", 9.5 cm
Colour: Green, red
           and blue
Issued: 1923-1936
Varieties: HN 586, 661, 662,
           1210, 1212, 1213,
           1214, 1225
U.S.:   **$1,100.00**
Can.:   **$1,250.00**
Ster.:   **£ 600.00**

HN 588
Spring
Style Two
Designer: Unknown
Height: 6 1/4". 15.9 cm
Colour: Yellow
Issued: 1923-1938
U.S.:   **Extremely rare**
Can.:
Ster.:

HN 589
Polly Peachum
Style One
Designer: L. Harradine
Height: 6 1/2", 16.5 cm
Colour: Pink and yellow
Issued: 1924-1949
Varieties: HN 463, 465, 550,
           614, 680, 693
Series: Beggar's Opera
U.S.:   **Extremely rare**
Can.:
Ster.:

HN 590
Captain MacHeath
Designer: L. Harradine
Height: 7", 17.8 cm
Colour: Red, black
           and yellow
Issued: 1924-1949
Varieties: HN 464, 1256
Series: Beggar's Opera
U.S.:   **$1,500.00**
Can.:   **$1,500.00**
Ster.   **£ 450.00**

HN 591
The Beggar
Style One
Designer: L. Harradine
Height: 6 3/4", 17.2 cm
Colour: Green and blue
Issued: 1924-1949
Varieties: HN 526
Series: Beggar's Opera
U.S.:   **$1,300.00**
Can.:   **$1,200.00**
Ster.:   **£ 450.00**

Earthenware

HN 592
The Highwayman
Designer: L. Harradine
Height: 6 1/2", 16.5 cm
Colour: Green and red
Issued: 1924-1949
Varieties: HN 527, 1257
Series: Beggar's Opera
U.S.:   **$1,400.00**
Can.:   **$1,400.00**
Ster.:   **£ 500.00**

HN 593
Nude on Rock
Designer: Unknown
Height: 6 3/4", 17.1 cm
Colour: Blue
Issued: 1924-1938

U.S.:	**Only**
Can.:	**one**
Ster.:	**known**

HN 594
Madonna of the Square
Designer: P. Stabler
Height: 7", 17.8 cm
Colour: Green and brown
Issued: 1924-1936
Varieties: HN 10, 10A, 11,
14, 27, 326, 573,
576, 613, 764,
1968, 1969, 2034

U.S.:	**None**
Can.:	**known**
Ster.:	**to exist**

HN 595
Grief
Designer: C.J. Noke
Height: 1 3/4", 4.5 cm
Colour: Blue
Issued: 1924-1938

U.S.:	**Only**
Can.:	**three**
Ster.:	**known**

Photograph
Not
Available

HN 596
Despair
Designer: C.J. Noke
Height: 4 3/4", 9.5 cm
Colour: Mottled blue
Issued: Unknown
Varieties: Also known in flambé

U.S.:	**Only**
Can.:	**one**
Ster.:	**known**

HN 597
The Bather
Style One
Designer: L. Harradine
Height: 7 3/4", 19.7 cm
Colour: Grey
Issued: 1924-1938
Varieties: HN 687, 781,
782, 1238, 1708

U.S.:	**$3,500.00**
Can.:	**$3,500.00**
Ster.:	**£1,250.00**

HN 598
Omar Khayyam
and the Beloved
Designer: C.J. Noke
Height: 10", 25.4 cm
Colour: Green, pink
and blue
Issued: 1924-1936
Varieties: HN 407, 419, 459

U.S.:	**None**
Can.:	**known**
Ster.:	**to exist**

HN 599
Masquerade (man)
Style One
Designer: L. Harradine
Height: 6 3/4", 17.2 cm
Colour: Red
Issued: 1924-1936
Varieties: HN 636, 683

U.S.:	**$1,400.00**
Can.:	**$1,400.00**
Ster.:	**£ 500.00**

HN 600
Masquerade (woman)
Style One
Designer: L. Harradine
Height: 6 3/4", 17.2 cm
Colour: Pink
Issued: 1924-1949
Varieties: HN 637, 674

U.S.:	**$1,400.00**
Can.:	**$1,400.00**
Ster.:	**£ 500.00**

Royal Doulton News

Marine City, MI, 1996

Thousands of Figures in Stock

Store Specializes in Discontinued Figurines

As well as thousands of Discontinued Figures, Discontinued Character Jugs, Seaway China also features Bunnykins, Beatrix Potter and the Snowman Collection

Odd Characters in Figurine Book

In a book filled with thousands of fine Royal Doulton Figurines...just look at these little characters. Just a reminder that Seaway China, which **specializes** in **discontinued figurines** and Character Jugs, can help with most Royal Doulton Bunnykins and Beatrix Potter Character figures.

Seaway is known for its ability to find that special figurine to enhance your collection.

We always welcome calls from Royal Doulton collectors looking for special figurines and character jugs. There is never any obligation.

Call Seaway China in Marine City, Michigan at **1-800-968-2424**.

Just Released

Fourth and Final Royal Doulton Santa Tiny Jug

Seaway China has just received the fourth and final in their set of four Santa Tiny Character Jugs. The 1996 version is Santa Tiny with a Teddy Bear Handle. It is limited to only 2500 pcs. and retails for $65. US.

The Character Jug is available now by calling **1-800-968-2424**.

32 Page Colour Catalogue
from *Seaway China Company*

Now Available

Order your copy today.....

To obtain your personal copy of our colour catalogue featuring new and discontinued Royal Doulton Figures - send **$3.00 US**, cheque or money order along with your name and address to:

Seaway China Company

135 Broadway
Marine City, MI
USA 48039-1607
1-800-968-2424

HN 601
A Mandarin
Style Three
Designer: C.J. Noke
Height: 10", 25.4 cm
Colour: Red
Issued: 1924-1938
U.S.: **$7,500.00**
Can.: **$7,500.00**
Ster.: **£2,500.00**

*

HN 603A
A Child Study
Style One
Designer: L. Harradine
Height: 4 3/4", 12.0 cm
Colour: White, primroses
around base
Issued: 1924-1938
Varieties: HN 603B, 1441; also
known in flambé
U.S.: **$950.00**
Can.: **$750.00**
Ster.: **£250.00**

HN 603B
A Child Study
Style One
Designer: L. Harradine
Height: 4 3/4", 12.0 cm
Colour: White, kingcups
around base
Issued: 1924-1938
Varieties: HN 603A, 1441
U.S.: **$950.00**
Can.: **$750.00**
Ster.: **£250.00**

HN 604A
A Child Study
Style Two
Designer: L. Harradine
Height: 5 1/2", 14.0 cm
Colour: White, primroses
around base
Issued: 1924-1938
Varieties: HN 604B, 1442, 1443
U.S.: **$950.00**
Can.: **$750.00**
Ster.: **£250.00**

HN 604B
A Child Study
Style Two
Designer: L. Harradine
Height: 5 1/2", 14.0 cm
Colour: White, kingcups
around base
Issued: 1924-1938
Varieties: HN 604A, 1442, 1443
U.S.: **$950.00**
Can.: **$750.00**
Ster.: **£250.00**

HN 605A
A Child Study
Style Three
Designer: L. Harradine
Height: Unknown
Colour: White, primroses
around base
Issued: 1924-1938
Varieties: HN 605B
U.S.: **$950.00**
Can.: **$750.00**
Ster.: **£250.00**

HN 605B
A Child Study
Style Three
Designer: L. Harradine
Height: Unknown
Colour: White, kingcups
around base
Issued: 1924-1938
Varieties: HN 605A
U.S.: **$950.00**
Can.: **$750.00**
Ster.: **£250.00**

HN 606A
Female Study
Designer: L. Harradine
Height: 5", 12.7 cm
Colour: White, primroses
around base
Issued: 1924-1936
Varieties: HN 606B; also
known in flambé
U.S.: **$950.00**
Can.: **$750.00**
Ster.: **£225.00**

HN 606B
Female Study
Designer: L. Harradine
Height: 5", 12.7 cm
Colour: White, kingcups
around base
Issued: 1924-1936
Varieties: HN 606A; Also
known in flambé

U.S.: **$950.00**
Can.: **$750.00**
Ster.: **£225.00**

*

HN 608
Falstaff
Style One
Designer: C.J. Noke
Height: 7", 17.8 cm
Colour: Red
Issued: 1924-1938
Varieties: HN 571, 575, 609,
619, 638, 1216, 1606

U.S.: **None**
Can.: **known**
Ster.: **to exist**

HN 609
Falstaff
Style One
Designer: C.J. Noke
Height: 7", 17.8 cm
Colour: Green
Issued: 1924-1938
Varieties: HN 571, 575, 608,
619, 638, 1216, 1606

U.S.: **None**
Can.: **known**
Ster.: **to exist**

HN 610
Henry Lytton as Jack Point
Designer: C.J. Noke
Height: 6 1/2", 16.5 cm
Colour: Blue, black
and brown
Issued: 1924-1949

U.S.: **$1,350.00**
Can.: **$1,200.00**
Ster.: **£ 475.00**

HN 611
A Mandarin
Style One
Designer: C.J. Noke
Height: 10 1/4", 26.0 cm
Colour: Gold and yellow
Issued: 1924-1936
Varieties: HN 84, 316, 318,
382, 746, 787, 791;
"Chinese Mandarin"
and "The Mikado"

U.S.: **$7,500.00**
Can.: **$7,500.00**
Ster.: **£3,000.00**

HN 612
The Poke Bonnet
Designer: C.J. Noke
Height: 9 1/2", 24.1 cm
Colour: Yellow and green
Issued: 1924-1938
Varieties: HN 362, 765; "A
Lilac Shawl" HN 44,
44A; "In Grandma's
Days" HN 339, 340,
388, 442

U.S.: **$3,200.00**
Can.: **$3,200.00**
Ster.: **£1,250.00**

HN 613
Madonna of the Square
Designer: P. Stabler
Height: 7", 17.8 cm
Colour: Pink and orange
Issued: 1924-1936
Varieties: HN 10, 10A, 11,
14, 27, 326, 573,
576, 594, 764,
1968, 1969, 2034

U.S.: **$2,500.00**
Can.: **$2,500.00**
Ster.: **£ 850.00**

HN 614
Polly Peachum
Style One
Designer: L. Harradine
Height: 6 1/2", 16.5 cm
Colour: Pale pink and blue
Issued: 1924-1949
Varieties: HN 463, 465, 550,
589, 680, 693
Series: Beggar's Opera

U.S.: **$1,250.00**
Can.: **$1,250.00**
Ster.: **£ 500.00**

HN 615
Katharine
Designer: C.J. Noke
Height: 5 3/4", 14.6 cm
Colour: Red with green spots
Issued: 1924-1938
Varieties: HN 61, 74, 341,
471, 793

U.S.: **$3,500.00**
Can.: **$3,500.00**
Ster.: **£1,400.00**

HN 616
A Jester
Style One
Designer: C.J. Noke
Height: 10", 25.4 cm
Colour: Black and white
Issued: 1924-1938
Varieties: HN 45, 71, 71A,
320, 367, 412,
426, 446, 552, 627,
1295, 1702, 2016

U.S.: **None**
Can.: **known**
Ster.: **to exist**

HN 617
A Shepherd
Style One
Designer: C.J. Noke
Height: 13 1/4", 33.6cm
Colour: Dark blue
Issued: 1924-1938
Varieties: HN 81, 632

U.S.: **Extremely rare**
Can.:
Ster.:

China

HN 618
Falstaff
Style Two
Designer: C.J. Noke
Height: 7", 17.8 cm
Colour: Black, red and green
Issued: 1924-1938
Varieties: HN 2054

U.S.: **Extremely rare**
Can.:
Ster.:

HN 619
Falstaff
Style One
Designer: C.J. Noke
Height: 7", 17.8 cm
Colour: Brown, green
and yellow
Issued: 1924-1938
Varieties: HN 571, 575, 608,
609, 638, 1216, 1606

U.S.: **Extremely rare**
Can.:
Ster.:

HN 620
Polly Peachum
Style Two
Designer: L. Harradine
Height: 4 1/4", 10.8 cm
Colour: Pink
Issued: 1924-1938
Varieties: HN 489, 549,
694, 734
Series: Beggar's Opera

U.S.: **$1,000.00**
Can.: **$1,000.00**
Ster.: **£ 350.00**

HN 621
Pan on Rock
Designer: Unknown
Height: 5 1/4", 13.3 cm
Colour: Cream, green base
Issued: 1924-1936
Varieties: HN 622

U.S.: **Extremely rare**
Can.:
Ster.:

HN 622
Pan on Rock
Designer: Unknown
Height: 5 1/4", 13.3 cm
Colour: Cream, black base
Issued: 1924-1938
Varieties: HN 621

U.S.: **Extremely rare**
Can.:
Ster.:

HN 623
An Old King
Designer: C.J. Noke
Height: 9 3/4", 24.7 cm
Colour: Grey, red
and green
Issued: 1924-1938
Varieties: HN 358, 1801, 2134
U.S.: **None**
Can.: **known**
Ster.: **to exist**

HN 624
Lady with Rose
Designer: E.W Light
Height: 9 1/2", 24.1 cm
Colour: Turquoise
Issued: 1924-1936
Varieties: HN 48A, 52A,
68, 304, 336,
515, 517, 584
U.S.: **None**
Can.: **known**
Ster.: **to exist**

HN 625
A Spook
Style One
Designer: H. Tittensor
Height: 7", 17.8 cm
Colour: Yellow
Issued: 1924-1936
Varieties: HN 50, 51, 51A,
51B, 58, 512; Also
known in flambé
U.S.: **$3,750.00**
Can.: **$3,750.00**
Ster.: **£1,500.00**

HN 626
Lady with Shawl
Designer: L. Harradine
Height: 13 1/4", 33.6 cm
Colour: Yellow and white
Issued: 1924-1936
Varieties: HN 447, 458,
678, 679
U.S.: **None**
Can.: **known**
Ster.: **to exist**

HN 627
A Jester
Style One
Designer: C.J. Noke
Height: 10", 25.4 cm
Colour: Brown checks
Issued: 1924-1938
Varieties: HN 45, 71, 71A,
320, 367, 412, 426,
446, 552, 616,
1295, 1702, 2016
U.S.: **$6,500.00**
Can.: **$6,500.00**
Ster.: **£1,750.00**

HN 628
The Crinoline
Designer: G. Lambert
Height: 6 1/4", 15.8 cm
Colour: Yellow and blue
Issued: 1924-1938
Varieties: HN 8, 9, 9A, 21,
21A, 413, 566
U.S.: **None**
Can.: **known**
Ster.: **to exist**

HN 629
The Curtsey
Designer: E.W. Light
Height: 11", 27.9 cm
Colour: Green and black
Issued: 1924-1936
Varieties: HN 57, 57B, 66A,
327, 334, 363, 371,
518, 547, 670
U.S.: **None**
Can.: **known**
Ster.: **to exist**

HN 630
A Jester
Style Two
Designer: C.J. Noke
Height: 10 1/4", 26.0 cm
Colour: Brown
Issued: 1924-1938
Varieties: HN 45A, 45B,
55, 308, 1333
U.S.: **$7,500.00**
Can.: **$7,500.00**
Ster.: **£1,750.00**

HN 631
Fisherwomen
Designer: C.J. Noke
Height: 11 3/4", 29.8 cm
Colour: Mauve and green
Issued: 1924-1938
Varieties: HN 80, 349, 359;
"Waiting For The
Boats" or "Looking
For The Boats"

U.S.: **Extremely rare**
Can.:
Ster.:

HN 632
A Shepherd
Style One
Designer: C.J. Noke
Height: 13 1/4", 33.6 cm
Colour: Blue and white
Issued: 1924-1938
Varieties: HN 81, 617

U.S.: **None**
Can.: **known**
Ster.: **to exist**

China

HN 633
The Princess
Designer: L. Harradine
Height: 9 1/4", 23.5 cm
Colour: Black and white
Issued: 1924-1936
Varieties: HN 391, 392,
420, 430, 431

U.S.: **None**
Can.: **known**
Ster.: **to exist**

HN 634
A Geisha
Style One
Designer: H. Tittensor
Height: 10 3/4", 27.3 cm
Colour: Black and white
Issued: 1924-1936
Varieties: HN 354, 376, 376A,
387, 741, 779, 1321,
1322; "The Japanese
Lady"

U.S.: **$8,500.00**
Can.: **$8,500.00**
Ster.: **£2,500.00**

HN 635
Harlequinade
Designer: L. Harradine
Height: 6 1/2", 16.5 cm
Colour: Gold
Issued: 1924-1940
Varieties: HN 585, 711, 780

U.S.: **$2,200.00**
Can.: **$2,200.00**
Ster.: **£ 550.00**

HN 636
Masquerade (man)
Style One
Designer: L. Harradine
Height: 6 3/4", 17.2 cm
Colour: Gold
Issued: 1924-1936
Varieties: HN 599, 683

U.S.: **$1,400.00**
Can.: **$1,400.00**
Ster.: **£ 550.00**

HN 637
Masquerade (woman)
Style One
Designer: L. Harradine
Height: 6 3/4", 17.2 cm
Colour: Gold
Issued: 1924-1938
Varieties: HN 600, 674

U.S.: **$1,300.00**
Can.: **$1,150.00**
Ster.: **£ 550.00**

HN 638
Falstaff
Style One
Designer: C.J. Noke
Height: 7", 17.8 cm
Colour: Red and cream
Issued: 1924-1938
Varieties: HN 571, 575, 608,
609, 619, 1216, 1606

U.S.: **$2,500.00**
Can.: **$2,500.00**
Ster.: **£1,000.00**

HN 639
Elsie Maynard
Style One
Designer: C.J. Noke
Height: 7", 17.8 cm
Colour: Mauve and pink
Issued: 1924-1949
U.S.: **$1,500.00**
Can.: **$1,500.00**
Ster.: £ 525.00

HN 640
Charley's Aunt
Style One
Designer: A. Taft
Height: 7", 17.8 cm
Colour: Green and lavender
Issued: 1924-1936
Varieties: HN 35
U.S.: **$2,500.00**
Can.: **$2,500.00**
Ster.: £1,000.00

HN 641
A Mandarin
Style Two
Designer: C.J. Noke
Height: 8 1/4", 21.0 cm
Colour: Yellow and blue
Issued: 1924-1938
Varieties: HN 366, 455
U.S.: **Only**
Can.: **one**
Ster.: **known**

HN 642
Pierrette
Style One
Designer: L. Harradine
Height: 7 1/4", 18.4 cm
Colour: Red
Issued: 1924-1938
Varieties: HN 643, 644, 691, 721, 731, 732, 784
U.S.: **Extremely rare**
Can.:
Ster.:

HN 643
Pierrette
Style One
Designer: L. Harradine
Height: 7 1/4", 18.4 cm
Colour: Red, black
and white
Issued: 1924-1938
Varieties: HN 642, 644, 691, 721, 731, 732, 784
U.S.: **$3,500.00**
Can.: **$3,000.00**
Ster.: £1,250.00

HN 644
Pierrette
Style One
Designer: L. Harradine
Height: 7 1/4", 18.4 cm
Colour: White and black
Issued: 1924-1938
Varieties: HN 642, 643, 691, 721, 731, 732, 784
U.S.: **$2,300.00**
Can.: **$2,300.00**
Ster.: £1,000.00

Photograph
Not
Available

HN 645
One of the Forty
Style Twelve
Designer: H. Tittensor
Height: 6", 15.2 cm
Colour: Blue, black
and white
Issued: 1924-1938
Varieties: HN 482, 484, 492, 663, 713
U.S.: **None**
Can.: **known**
Ster.: **to exist**

HN 646
One of the Forty
Style Eleven
Designer: H. Tittensor
Height: Unknown
Colour: Cream, blue
and black
Issued: 1924-1936
Varieties: HN 481, 483, 491, 667, 712, 1336, 1350;
Also known in flambé
U.S.: **Extremely rare**
Can.:
Ster.:

HN 647
One of the Forty
Style Two
Designer: H. Tittensor
Height: 7 1/4", 18.4 cm
Colour: Blue, black and white
Issued: 1924-1936
Varieties: HN 418, 494, 498, 666, 704, 1353

U.S.: **None**
Can.: **known**
Ster.: **to exist**

HN 648
One of the Forty
Style One
Designer: H. Tittensor
Height: 8 1/4", 21.0 cm
Colour: Blue, black and white
Issued: 1924-1938
Varieties: HN 417, 490, 495, 501, 528, 677, 1351, 1352

U.S.: **None**
Can.: **known**
Ster.: **to exist**

Photograph Not Available

HN 649
One of the Forty
Style Thirteen
Designer: H. Tittensor
Height: 7 3/4", 19.7 cm
Colour: Blue, black and white
Issued: 1924-1938
Varieties: HN 496, 500, 665, 1354

U.S.: **None**
Can.: **known**
Ster.: **to exist**

HN 650
Crinoline Lady
Designer: Unknown
Height: 3", 7.6 cm
Colour: Green and white
Issued: 1924-1938
Varieties: HN 651, 652, 653, 654, 655

U.S.: **$2,500.00**
Can.: **$2,500.00**
Ster.: **£1,000.00**

HN 651
Crinoline Lady
Designer: Unknown
Height: 3", 7.6 cm
Colour: Orange and white
Issued: 1924-1938
Varieties: HN 650, 652, 653, 654, 655

U.S.: **$2,500.00**
Can.: **$2,500.00**
Ster.: **£1,000.00**

HN 652
Crinoline Lady
Designer: Unknown
Height: 3", 7.6 cm
Colour: Purple
Issued: 1924-1938
Varieties: HN 650, 651, 653, 654, 655

U.S.: **$2,500.00**
Can.: **$2,500.00**
Ster.: **£1,000.00**

HN 653
Crinoline Lady
Designer: Unknown
Height: 3", 7.6 cm
Colour: Black and white
Issued: 1924-1938
Varieties: HN 650, 651, 652, 654, 655

U.S.: **$2,500.00**
Can.: **$2,500.00**
Ster.: **£1,000.00**

HN 654
Crinoline Lady
Designer: Unknown
Height: 3", 7.6 cm
Colour: Red and purple
Issued: 1924-1938
Varieties: HN 650, 651, 652, 653, 655

U.S.: **$2,500.00**
Can.: **$2,500.00**
Ster.: **£1,000.00**

HN 655
Crinoline Lady
Designer: Unknown
Height: 3", 7.6 cm
Colour: Blue and black
Issued: 1924-1938
Varieties: HN 650, 651, 652, 653, 654

U.S.: $2,500.00
Can.: $2,500.00
Ster.: £1,000.00

HN 656
The Mask
Designer: L. Harradine
Height: 6 3/4", 17.2 cm
Colour: Blue and purple
Issued: 1924-1938
Varieties: HN 657, 729, 733, 785, 1271

U.S.: $4,000.00
Can.: $4,000.00
Ster.: £1,500.00

HN 657
The Mask
Designer: L. Harradine
Height: 6 3/4", 17.2 cm
Colour: Black and white
Issued: 1924-1938
Varieties: HN 656, 729, 733, 785, 1271

U.S.: $4,000.00
Can.: $4,000.00
Ster.: £1,500.00

HN 658
Mam'selle
Designer: L. Harradine
Height: 7", 17.8 cm
Colour: Black and white
Issued: 1924-1938
Varieties: HN 659, 724, 786

U.S.: $4,000.00
Can.: $4,000.00
Ster.: £1,250.00

HN 659
Mam'selle
Designer: L. Harradine
Height: 7", 17.8 cm
Colour: Dark blue
Issued: 1924-1938
Varieties: HN 658, 724, 786

U.S.: $4,000.00
Can.: $4,000.00
Ster.: £1,250.00

HN 660
Myfanwy Jones
Designer: E.W. Light
Height: 12", 30.5 cm
Colour: White and blue
Issued: 1924-1936
Varieties: HN 39, 92, 456, 514, 516, 519, 520, 668, 669, 701, 792; also called "The Welsh Girl"

U.S.: Extremely rare
Can.:
Ster.:

HN 661
Boy with Turban
Designer: L. Harradine
Height: 3 3/4", 9.5 cm
Colour: Blue
Issued: 1924-1936
Varieties: HN 586, 587, 662, 1210, 1212, 1213, 1214, 1225

U.S.: $1,100.00
Can.: $1,250.00
Ster.: £ 650.00

HN 662
Boy with Turban
Designer: L. Harradine
Height: 3 3/4", 9.5 cm
Colour: Black and white
Issued: 1924-1936
Varieties: HN 586, 587, 661, 1210, 1212, 1213, 1214, 1225

U.S.: $1,100.00
Can.: $1,250.00
Ster.: £ 650.00

HN 663
One of the Forty
Style Twelve
Designer: H. Tittensor
Height: 6", 15.2 cm
Colour: Yellow
Issued: 1924-1938
Varieties: HN 482, 484,
492, 645, 713,

U.S.: **Extremely rare**
Can.:
Ster.:

HN 664
One of the Forty
Style Ten
Designer: H. Tittensor
Height: 7 3/4", 19.7 cm
Colour: Yellow, green
and black
Issued: 1924-1938
Varieties: HN 480, 493,
497, 499, 714

U.S.: **Extremely rare**
Can.:
Ster.:

HN 665
One of the Forty
Style Thirteen
Designer: H. Tittensor
Height: 7 3/4", 19.7 cm
Colour: Yellow
Issued: 1924-1938
Varieties: HN 496, 500,
649, 1354

U.S.: **Extremely rare**
Can.:
Ster.:

HN 666
One of the Forty
Style Two
Designer: H. Tittensor
Height: 7 1/4", 18.4 cm
Colour: Yellow
Issued: 1924-1936
Varieties: HN 418, 494, 498,
647, 704, 1353

U.S.: **Extremely rare**
Can.:
Ster.:

HN 667
One of the Forty
Style Eleven
Designer: H. Tittensor
Height: Unknown
Colour: Yellow and black
Issued: 1924-1936
Varieties: HN 481, 483, 491,
646, 712, 1336, 1350;
Also known in flambé

U.S.: **Extremely rare**
Can.:
Ster.:

HN 668
Myfanwy Jones
Designer: E.W. Light
Height: 12", 30.5cm
Colour: Yellow and pink
Issued: 1924-1936
Varieties: HN 39, 92, 456,
514, 516, 519, 520,
660, 669, 701, 792;
also called "The
Welsh Girl"

U.S.: **$6,500.00**
Can.: **$5,500.00**
Ster.: **£2,250.00**

HN 669
Myfanwy Jones
Designer: E.W. Light
Height: 8 1/2", 21.5cm
Colour: Yellow and green
Issued: 1924-1936
Varieties: HN 39, 92, 456,
514, 516, 519, 520,
660, 668, 701, 792;
also called "The
Welsh Girl"

U.S.: **$6,500.00**
Can.: **$5,500.00**
Ster.: **£2,000.00**

HN 670
The Curtsey
Designer: E.W. Light
Height: 11", 27.9 cm
Colour: Pink and yellow
Issued: 1924-1936
Varieties: HN 57, 57B, 66A,
327, 334, 363, 371,
518, 547, 629

U.S.: **$3,500.00**
Can.: **$3,500.00**
Ster.: **£1,250.00**

HN 671
The Ermine Muff
Designer: C.J. Noke
Height: 8 1/2", 21.6 cm
Colour: Green and yellow
Issued: 1924-1938
Varieties: HN 54, 332; also
called "Lady with
the Ermine Muff"
and "Lady Ermine"

U.S.: None
Can.: known
Ster.: to exist

HN 672
Tulips
Designer: Unknown
Height: 9 1/2", 24.1 cm
Colour: Green and blue
Issued: 1924-1936
Varieties: HN 466, 488,
747, 1334

U.S.: $4,700.00
Can.: $4,000.00
Ster.: £1,500.00

Earthenware

Photograph
Not
Available

HN 673
Henry VIII
Style One
Designer: C.J. Noke
Height: Unknown
Colour: Brown and lavender
Issued: 1924-1938
Varieties: HN 370

U.S.: None
Can.: known
Ster.: to exist

HN 674
Masquerade (woman)
Style One
Designer: L. Harradine
Height: 6 3/4", 17.2 cm
Colour: Orange and yellow
Issued: 1924-1938
Varieties: HN 600, 637

U.S.: $1,400.00
Can.: $1,450.00
Ster.: £ 650.00

HN 675
The Gainsborough Hat
Designer: H. Tittensor
Height: 8 3/4", 22.2 cm
Colour: Cream
Issued: 1924-1936
Varieties: HN 46, 46A, 47, 329,
352, 383, 453, 705

U.S.: $3,750.00
Can.: $3,750.00
Ster.: £1,350.00

HN 676
Pavlova
Designer: C.J. Noke
Height: 4 1/4", 10.8 cm
Colour: White and blue
tutu, black base
Issued: 1924-1938
Varieties: HN 487; also called
"Swan Song"

U.S.: Extremely rare
Can.:
Ster.:

HN 677
One of the Forty
Style One
Designer: H. Tittensor
Height: 8 1/4", 21.0 cm
Colour: Orange, yellow
and red
Issued: 1924-1938
Varieties: HN 417, 490, 495,
501, 528, 648, 1351,
1352

U.S.: Extremely rare
Can.:
Ster.:

HN 678
Lady with Shawl
Designer: L. Harradine
Height: 13 1/4", 33.7 cm
Colour: Black, yellow
and white
Issued: 1924-1936
Varieties: HN 447, 458, 626,
679

U.S.: $7,500.00
Can.: $7,500.00
Ster.: £2,250.00

HN 679
Lady with Shawl
Designer: L. Harradine
Height: 13 1/4", 33.7 cm
Colour: Black, yellow,
blue and white
Issued: 1924-1936
Varieties: HN 447, 458, 626,
678
U.S.: None
Can.: known
Ster.: to exist

HN 680
Polly Peachum
Style One
Designer: L. Harradine
Height: 6 1/2", 16.5 cm
Colour: White
Issued: 1924-1949
Varieties: HN 463, 465, 550,
589, 614, 693
Series: Beggar's Opera
U.S.: None
Can.: known
Ster.: to exist

HN 681
The Cobbler
Style Two
Designer: C.J. Noke
Height: 8 1/2", 21.6 cm
Colour: Green and red
Issued: 1924-1938
Varieties: HN 1251, 1283
U.S.: None
Can.: known
Ster.: to exist

HN 682
The Cobbler
Style One
Designer: C.J. Noke
Height: 7 1/2", 19.1 cm
Colour: Red and green
Issued: 1924-1938
Varieties: HN 542, 543
U.S.: None
Can.: known
Ster.: to exist

HN 683
Masquerade (man)
Style One
Designer: L. Harradine
Height: 7 1/4", 18.4 cm
Colour: Green
Issued: 1924-1936
Varieties: HN 599, 636
U.S.: $1,400.00
Can.: $1,400.00
Ster.: £ 550.00

Earthenware

HN 684
Tony Weller
Style One
Designer: C.J. Noke
Height: 10 1/4". 26.0 cm
Colour: Green and brown
Issued: 1924-1938
Varieties: HN 346, 368
U.S.: $2,500.00
Can.: $2,500.00
Ster.: £1,000.00

HN 685
Contentment
Designer: L. Harradine
Height: 7 1/4", 18.4 cm
Colour: Black and white
Issued: 1924-1938
Varieties: HN 395, 396, 421,
468, 572, 686, 1323
U.S.: None
Can.: known
Ster.: to exist

HN 686
Contentment
Designer: L. Harradine
Height: 7 1/4", 18.4 cm
Colour: Black and white
Issued: 1924-1938
Varieties: HN 395, 396, 421,
468, 572, 685, 1323
U.S.: None
Can.: known
Ster.: to exist

HN 687
The Bather
Style One
Designer: L. Harradine
Height: 7 3/4", 19.7 cm
Colour: Blue
Issued: 1924-1949
Varieties: HN 597, 781, 782,
1238, 1708
U.S.: $1,500.00
Can.: $1,500.00
Ster.: £ 750.00

HN 688
A Yeoman of the Guard
Designer: L. Harradine
Height: 5 3/4", 14.6 cm
Colour: Red, gold
and brown
Issued: 1924-1938
Varieties: HN 2122
U.S.: $1,750.00
Can.: $1,750.00
Ster.: £ 800.00

HN 689
A Chelsea Pensioner
Designer: L. Harradine
Height: 5 3/4", 14.6 cm
Colour: Red
Issued: 1924-1938
U.S.: $2,400.00
Can.: $2,400.00
Ster.: £ 800.00

Also produced as a miniature
figurine, but without "M" number

HN 690
A Lady of the Georgian
Period
Designer: E.W. Light
Height: 10 1/4", 26.0 cm
Colour: Pink, white and
yellow over dress
Issued: 1925-1936
Varieties: HN 41, 331, 444, 702
U.S.: None
Can.: known
Ster.: to exist

HN 691
Pierrette
Style One
Designer: L. Harradine
Height: 7 1/4", 18.4 cm
Colour: Gold
Issued: 1925-1938
Varieties: HN 642, 643, 644,
721, 731, 732, 784
U.S.: $3,000.00
Can.: $3,000.00
Ster.: £1,250.00

HN 692
Sleep
Designer: P. Stabler
Height: 6", 15.2 cm
Colour: Gold
Issued: 1925-1936
Varieties: HN 24, 24A, 25, 25A,
424, 710
U.S.: $3,000.00
Can.: $3,000.00
Ster.: £1,250.00

HN 693
Polly Peachum
Style One
Designer: L. Harradine
Height: 6 1/2", 16.5 cm
Colour: Pink and green
Issued: 1925-1949
Varieties: HN 463, 465, 550,
589, 614, 680
Series: Beggar's Opera
U.S.: $1,250.00
Can.: $1,250.00
Ster.: £ 450.00

HN 694
Polly Peachum
Style Two
Designer: L. Harradine
Height: 4 1/4", 10.8 cm
Colour: Pink and green
Issued: 1925-1949
Varieties: HN 489, 549, 620, 734
Series: Beggar's Opera
U.S.: $1,600.00
Can.: $1,500.00
Ster.: £ 550.00

HN 695
Lucy Lockett
Style Three
Designer: L. Harradine
Height: 6", 15.2 cm
Colour: Orange
Issued: 1925-1949
Varieties: HN 696
Series: Beggar's Opera

U.S.:	**$1,250.00**
Can.:	**$1,250.00**
Ster.:	**£ 450.00**

HN 696
Lucy Lockett
Style Three
Designer: L. Harradine
Height: 6", 15.2 cm
Colour: Pale blue
Issued: 1925-1949
Varieties: HN 695
Series: Beggar's Opera

U.S.:	**None**
Can.:	**known**
Ster.:	**to exist**

HN 697
The Balloon Seller
Designer: L. Harradine
Height: 9", 22.9 cm
Colour: Red and blue
Issued: 1925-1938
Varieties: HN 479, 486, 548, 583; also called "The Balloon Woman"

U.S.:	**None**
Can.:	**known**
Ster.:	**to exist**

HN 698
Polly Peachum
Style Three
Designer: L. Harradine
Height: 2 1/4", 5.7 cm
Colour: Rose pink
Issued: 1925-1949
Varieties: HN 699, 757, 758, 759, 760, 761, 762, M21, M22, M23

U.S.:	**$1,200.00**
Can.:	**$1,350.00**
Ster.:	**£ 600.00**

HN 699
Polly Peachum
Style Three
Designer: L. Harradine
Height: 2 1/4", 5.7 cm
Colour: Pale blue
Issued: 1925-1949
Varieties: HN 698, 757, 758, 759, 760, 761, 762, M21, M22, M23

U.S.:	**$1,200.00**
Can.:	**$1,350.00**
Ster.:	**£ 600.00**

HN 700
Pretty Lady
Designer: H. Tittensor
Height: 9 1/2", 24.1 cm
Colour: Yellow and green
Issued: 1925-1938
Varieties: HN 69, 70, 302, 330, 361, 384, 565, 763, 783

U.S.:	**$2,500.00**
Can.:	**$2,500.00**
Ster.:	**£1,100.00**

HN 701
Myfanwy Jones
Designer: E.W. Light
Height: 12", 30.5 cm
Colour: Multi-coloured
Issued: 1925-1936
Varieties: HN 39, 92, 456, 514, 516, 519, 520, 660, 668, 669, 792; also called "The Welsh Girl"

U.S.:	**None**
Can.:	**known**
Ster.:	**to exist**

HN 702
A Lady of the Georgian Period
Designer: E. W. Light
Height: 10 1/4", 26.0 cm
Colour: Pink and green
Issued: 1925-1936
Varieties: HN 41, 331, 444, 690

U.S.:	**None**
Can.:	**known**
Ster.:	**to exist**

HN 703
Motherhood
Style Two
Designer: Unknown
Height: 9 1/4", 23.5 cm
Colour: Purple, black
        and red
Issued: 1925-1938
Varieties: HN 462, 570, 743

U.S.:	None
Can.:	known
Ster.:	to exist

HN 704
One of the Forty
Style Two
Designer: H. Tittensor
Height: 7 1/4", 18.4 cm
Colour: Red
Issued: 1925-1936
Varieties: HN 418, 494, 498,
        647, 666, 1353

U.S.:	None
Can.:	known
Ster.:	to exist

HN 705
The Gainsborough Hat
Designer: H. Tittensor
Height: 9", 22.9 cm
Colour: Blue
Issued: 1925-1936
Varieties: HN 46, 46A, 47, 329,
        352, 383, 453, 675

U.S.:	$3,750.00
Can.:	$3,750.00
Ster.:	£1,350.00

Earthenware

HN 706
Fruit Gathering
Designer: L. Harradine
Height: 7 1/4", 18.4 cm
Colour: Purple and yellow
Issued: 1925-1936
Varieties: HN 449, 476, 503,
        561, 562, 707

U.S.:	Extremely rare
Can.:	
Ster.:	

HN 707
Fruit Gathering
Designer: L. Harradine
Height: 7 1/4", 18.4 cm
Colour: Red
Issued: 1925-1936
Varieties: HN 449, 476, 503,
        561, 562, 706

U.S.:	$4,500.00
Can.:	$4,500.00
Ster.:	£1,500.00

Earthenware

HN 708
Shepherdess
Style One
Designer: L. Harradine
Height: 3 1/2", 8.8 cm
Colour: Red, yellow and pink
Issued: 1925-1948
Varieties: M18, M20

U.S.:	$3,200.00
Can.:	$2,500.00
Ster.:	£1,000.00

HN 709
Shepherd
Style Two
Designer: L. Harradine
Height: 3 1/2", 8.8 cm
Colour: Green, red
        and black
Issued: 1925-1938
Varieties: M17, M19

U.S.:	$3,200.00
Can.:	$2,500.00
Ster.:	£1,000.00

HN 710
Sleep
Designer: P. Stabler
Height: 6", 15.2 cm
Colour: Blue
Issued: 1925-1936
Varieties: HN 24, 24A, 25,
        25A, 424, 692

U.S.:	$2,700.00
Can.:	$2,700.00
Ster.:	£1,000.00

HN 711
Harlequinade
Designer: L. Harradine
Height: 7", 17.8 cm
Colour: White and black
Issued: 1925-1940
Varieties: HN 585, 635, 780

U.S.: $2,500.00
Can.: $2,500.00
Ster.: £ 800.00

HN 712
One of the Forty
Style Eleven
Designer: H. Tittensor
Height: Unknown
Colour: Red and black
Issued: 1925-1936
Varieties: HN 481, 483, 491, 646, 667, 1336, 1350; also known in flambé

U.S.: **Extremely rare**
Can.:
Ster.:

Photograph
Not
Available

HN 713
One of the Forty
Style Twelve
Designer: H. Tittensor
Height: 6", 15.2 cm
Colour: Red
Issued: 1925-1938
Varieties: HN 482, 484, 492, 645, 663

U.S.: **None**
Can.: **known**
Ster.: **to exist**

HN 714
One of the Forty
Style Ten
Designer: H. Tittensor
Height: 6 3/4", 17.2 cm
Colour: Red and blue
Issued: 1925-1938
Varieties: HN 480, 493, 497, 499, 664

U.S.: **Extremely rare**
Can.:
Ster.:

HN 715
Proposal (woman)
Designer: L. Harradine
Height: 5 3/4", 14.6 cm
Colour: Burgundy and black
Issued: 1925-1940
Varieties: HN 716, 788

U.S.: $2,500.00
Can.: $2,750.00
Ster.: £1,000.00

HN 716
Proposal (woman)
Designer: L. Harradine
Height: 5 3/4", 14.6 cm
Colour: White and black
Issued: 1925-1940
Varieties: HN 715, 788

U.S.: $2,500.00
Can.: $2,750.00
Ster.: £1,100.00

HN 717
Lady Clown
Designer: L. Harradine
Height: 7 1/2", 19.1 cm
Colour: White, red and black
Issued: 1925-1938
Varieties: HN 718, 738, 770; also called "Clownette" HN 1263

U.S.: $6,500.00
Can.: $6,500.00
Ster.: £3,000.00

HN 718
Lady Clown
Designer: L. Harradine
Height: 7 1/2", 19.1 cm
Colour: White, red and black
Issued: 1925-1938
Varieties: HN 717, 738, 770; also called "Clownette" HN1263

U.S.: **None**
Can.: **known**
Ster.: **to exist**

HN 719
Butterfly
Designer: L. Harradine
Height: 6 1/2", 16.5 cm
Colour: Pink, yellow
and black
Issued: 1925-1940
Varieties: HN 720, 730, 1203;
also called "Butterfly
Woman" HN 1456

U.S.: $3,500.00
Can.: $3,500.00
Ster.: £1,500.00

HN 720
Butterfly
Designer: L. Harradine
Height: 6 1/2", 16.5 cm
Colour: Orange, white
and black
Issued: 1925-1940
Varieties: HN 719, 730, 1203;
also called "Butterfly
Woman" HN 1456

U.S.: $3,500.00
Can.: $3,500.00
Ster.: £1,500.00

HN 721
Pierrette
Style One
Designer: L. Harradine
Height: 7 1/4", 18.4 cm
Colour: Black and white
Issued: 1925-1938
Varieties: HN 642, 643, 644,
691, 731, 732, 784

U.S.: $3,500.00
Can.: $3,500.00
Ster.: £1,500.00

HN 722
Mephisto
Designer: L. Harradine
Height: 6 1/2", 16.5 cm
Colour: Black and red
Issued: 1925-1938
Varieties: HN 723

U.S.: $5,000.00
Can.: $5,000.00
Ster.: £2,000.00

HN 723
Mephisto
Designer: L. Harradine
Height: 6 1/2", 16.5 cm
Colour: Red and black
Issued: 1925-1938
Varieties: HN 722

U.S.: $4,500.00
Can.: $4,500.00
Ster.: £2,000.00

HN 724
Mam'selle
Designer: L. Harradine
Height: 7", 17.8 cm
Colour: White, red
and yellow
Issued: 1925-1938
Varieties: HN 658, 659, 786

U.S.: $3,000.00
Can.: $3,000.00
Ster.: £1,500.00

HN 725
The Proposal (man)
Designer: Unknown
Height: 5 1/2", 14.0 cm
Colour: Red and black
Issued: 1925-1938
Varieties: HN 1209

U.S.: $2,500.00
Can.: $2,500.00
Ster.: £1,000.00

HN 726
A Victorian Lady
Style One
Designer: L. Harradine
Height: 7 1/2", 19.1 cm
Colour: Purple and yellow
Issued: 1925-1938
Varieties: HN 727, 728, 736, 739,
740, 742, 745, 1208,
1258, 1276, 1277,
1345, 1452, 1529

U.S.: $1,100.00
Can.: $1,000.00
Ster.: £ 350.00

HN 727
A Victorian Lady
Style One
Designer: L. Harradine
Height: 7 1/2", 19.1 cm
Colour: Pink and green
Issued: 1925-1938
Varieties: HN 726, 728, 736, 739,
740, 742, 745, 1208,
1258, 1276, 1277,
1345, 1452, 1529

U.S.: $650.00
Can.: $750.00
Ster.: £350.00

HN 728
A Victorian Lady
Style One
Designer: L. Harradine
Height: 7 3/4", 19.7 cm
Colour: Pink and purple
Issued: 1925-1952
Varieties: HN 726, 727, 736, 739,
740, 742, 745, 1208,
1258, 1276, 1277,
1345, 1452, 1529

U.S.: $650.00
Can.: $750.00
Ster.: £300.00

HN 729
The Mask
Designer: L. Harradine
Height: 6 3/4", 17.2 cm
Colour: Red and black
Issued: 1925-1938
Varieties: HN 656, 657, 733,
785, 1271

U.S.: $4,000.00
Can.: $4,000.00
Ster.: £1,750.00

HN 730
Butterfly
Designer: L. Harradine
Height: 6 1/2", 16.5 cm
Colour: Yellow , blue
and black
Issued: 1925-1940
Varieties: HN 719, 720, 1203;
also called "Butterfly
Woman" HN 1456

U.S.: $3,500.00
Can.: $3,500.00
Ster.: £1,500.00

HN 731
Pierrette
Style One
Designer: L. Harradine
Height: 7 1/4", 18.4 cm
Colour: Black and white
Issued: 1925-1938
Varieties: HN 642, 643, 644,
691, 721, 732, 784

U.S.: $3,500.00
Can.: $3,500.00
Ster.: £1,500.00

HN 732
Pierrette
Style One
Designer: L. Harradine
Height: 7 1/4", 18.4 cm
Colour: Black and white
Issued: 1925-1938
Varieties: HN 642, 643, 644,
691, 721, 731, 784

U.S.: **Extremely rare**
Can.:
Ster.:

HN 733
The Mask
Designer: L. Harradine
Height: 6 3/4", 17.2 cm
Colour: White and black
Issued: 1925-1938
Varieties: HN 656, 657, 729,
785, 1271

U.S.: $4,000.00
Can.: $4,000.00
Ster.: £1,500.00

HN 734
Polly Peachum
Style Two
Designer: L. Harradine
Height: 4 1/4", 10.8 cm
Colour: Black and white
Issued: 1925-1949
Varieties: HN 489, 549, 620,
694
Series: Beggar's Opera

U.S.: $1,800.00
Can.: $1,600.00
Ster.: £ 750.00

HN 735
Shepherdess
Style Two
Designer: L. Harradine
Height: 7", 17.8 cm
Colour: Blue and black
Issued: 1925-1938
Varieties: HN 750; also
called "Milkmaid"

U.S.:	$3,300.00
Can.:	$3,000.00
Ster.:	£1,100.00

HN 736
A Victorian Lady
Style One
Designer: L. Harradine
Height: 7 3/4", 19.7 cm
Colour: Pink and purple
Issued: 1925-1938
Varieties: HN 726, 727, 728, 739,
740, 742, 745, 1208,
1258, 1276, 1277,
1345, 1452, 1529

U.S.:	$850.00
Can.:	$850.00
Ster.:	£350.00 *

HN 738
Lady Clown
Designer: L. Harradine
Height: 7 1/2", 19.1 cm
Colour: Black, white and red
Issued: 1925-1938
Varieties: HN 717, 718, 770;
Also called
"Clownette," HN 1263

U.S.:	None
Can.:	known
Ster.:	to exist

HN 739
A Victorian Lady
Style One
Designer: L. Harradine
Height: 7 3/4", 19.7 cm
Colour: Red, blue, yellow
Issued: 1925-1938
Varieties: HN 726, 727, 728, 736,
740, 742, 745, 1208,
1258, 1276,1277,
1345, 1452, 1529

U.S.:	$1,300.00
Can.:	$1,200.00
Ster.:	£ 350.00

HN 740
A Victorian Lady
Style One
Designer: L. Harradine
Height: 7 3/4", 19.7 cm
Colour: Pink
Issued: 1925-1938
Varieties: HN 726, 727, 728, 736,
739, 742, 745, 1208,
1258, 1276, 1277,
1345, 1452, 1529

U.S.:	$1,300.00
Can.:	$1,200.00
Ster.:	£ 350.00

HN 741
A Geisha
Style One
Designer: H. Tittensor
Height: 10 3/4", 27.3 cm
Colour: Multi-coloured
Issued: 1925-1936
Varieties: HN 354, 376, 376A,
387, 634, 779, 1321,
1322; "Japanese Lady"

U.S.:	None
Can.:	known
Ster.:	to exist

HN 742
A Victorian Lady
Style One
Designer: L. Harradine
Height: 7 3/4", 19.7 cm
Colour: Black and white
Issued: 1925-1938
Varieties: HN 726, 727, 728, 736,
739, 740, 745, 1208,
1258, 1276, 1277,
1345, 1452, 1529

U.S.:	$1,500.00
Can.:	$1,500.00
Ster.:	£ 450.00

HN 743
Motherhood
Style Two
Designer: Unknown
Height: 9 1/4", 23.5 cm
Colour: Blue and yellow
Issued: 1925-1938
Varieties: HN 462, 570, 703

U.S.:	None
Can.:	known
Ster.:	to exist

HN 744
The Lavender Woman
Designer: P. Stabler
Height: 8 1/4", 21.0 cm
Colour: Blue
Issued: 1925-1936
Varieties: HN 22, 23, 23A, 342, 569

U.S.: $6,000.00
Can.: $6,000.00
Ster.: £2,000.00

HN 745
A Victorian Lady
Style One
Designer: L. Harradine
Height: 7 3/4", 19.7 cm
Colour: Pink and green
Issued: 1925-1938
Varieties: HN 726, 727, 728, 736, 739, 740, 742, 1208, 1258, 1276, 1277, 1345, 1452, 1529

U.S.: $1,300.00
Can.: $1,250.00
Ster.: £ 425.00

HN 746
A Mandarin
Style One
Designer: C.J. Noke
Height: 10 1/4", 26.0 cm
Colour: Yellow, black and lilac
Issued: 1925-1936
Varieties: HN 84, 316, 318, 382, 611, 787, 791; "Chinese Mandarin" and "The Mikado"

U.S.: $7,500.00
Can.: $7,500.00
Ster.: £2,500.00

HN 747
Tulips
Designer: Unknown
Height: 9 1/2", 24.1 cm
Colour: Blue and green
Issued: 1925-1936
Varieties: HN 466, 488, 672, 1334

U.S.: $4,000.00
Can.: $4,000.00
Ster.: £1,350.00

HN 748
Out For a Walk
Designer: E.W. Light
Height: 10", 25.4 cm
Colour: Green, red and white
Issued: 1925-1936
Varieties: HN 86, 443

U.S.: $6,000.00
Can.: $6,000.00
Ster.: £2,000.00

HN 749
London Cry, Strawberries
Designer: L. Harradine
Height: 6 3/4", 17.2 cm
Colour: Red and cream
Issued: 1925-1936
Varieties: HN 772

U.S.: $2,850.00
Can.: $2,750.00
Ster.: £1,250.00

HN 750
Shepherdess
Style Two
Designer: Leslie Harradine
Height: 7", 17.8 cm
Colour: Pink and yellow
Issued: 1925-1938
Varieties: HN 735; also called "Milkmaid"

U.S.: $3,300.00
Can.: $3,000.00
Ster.: £1,100.00

HN 751
Shepherd
Style Three
Designer: Leslie Harradine
Height: 7", 17.8 cm
Colour: Green, black, red and white
Issued: 1925-1938

U.S.: $3,600.00
Can.: $3,250.00
Ster.: £1,100.00

HN 752
London Cry,
Turnips and Carrots
Designer: L. Harradine
Height: 6 3/4". 17.2 cm
Colour: Purple, red,
black and green
Issued: 1925-1938
Varieties: HN 771

U.S.: **$2,850.00**
Can.: **$2,750.00**
Ster.: **£1,250.00**

HN 753
The Dandy
Designer: L. Harradine
Height: 6 3/4". 17.2 cm
Colour: Red, white,
black and green
Issued: 1925-1936

U.S.: **$2,250.00**
Can.: **$2,250.00**
Ster.: **£1,000.00**

HN 754
The Belle
Style One
Designer: L. Harradine
Height: 6 1/2", 16.5 cm
Colour: Multi-coloured
Issued: 1925-1938
Varieties: HN 776

U.S.: **$1,750.00**
Can.: **$1,750.00**
Ster.: **£ 750.00**

HN 755
Mephistopheles
and Marguerite
Designer: C.J. Noke
Height: 7 3/4", 19.7 cm
Colour: Orange and purple
Issued: 1925-1949
Varieties: HN 775

U.S.: **$2,800.00**
Can.: **$3,000.00**
Ster.: **£1,500.00**

HN 756
The Modern Piper
Designer: L. Harradine
Height: 8 1/2", 21.6 cm
Colour: Lavender
and green
Issued: 1925-1940

U.S.: **$3,600.00**
Can.: **$3,600.00**
Ster.: **£1,600.00**

HN 757
Polly Peachum
Style Three
Designer: L. Harradine
Height: 2 1/4", 5.7 cm
Colour: Red
Issued: 1925-1949
Varieties: HN 698, 699, 758,
759, 760, 761, 762;
M21, M22, M23
Series: Beggar's Opera

U.S.: **$1,200.00**
Can.: **$1,350.00**
Ster.: **£ 650.00**

HN 758
Polly Peachum
Style Three
Designer: L. Harradine
Height: 2 1/4", 5.7 cm
Colour: Pink and orange
Issued: 1925-1949
Varieties: HN 698, 699, 757,
759, 760, 761, 762;
M21, M22, M23
Series: Beggar's Opera

U.S.: **$1,200.00**
Can.: **$1,350.00**
Ster.: **£ 650.00**

HN 759
Polly Peachum
Style Three
Designer: L. Harradine
Height: 2 1/4", 5.7 cm
Colour: Yellow, white & black
Issued: 1925-1949
Varieties: HN 698, 699, 757,
758, 760, 761, 762;
M21, M22, M23
Series: Beggar's Opera

U.S.: **$1,200.00**
Can.: **$1,350.00**
Ster.: **£ 650.00**

HN 760
Polly Peachum
Style Three
Designer: L. Harradine
Height: 2 1/4", 5.7 cm
Colour: Multi-coloured
Issued: 1925-1949
Varieties: HN 698, 699, 757, 758, 759, 761, 762; M21, M22, M23
Series: Beggar's Opera
U.S.: $1,200.00
Can.: $1,350.00
Ster.: £ 650.00

HN 761
Polly Peachum
Style Three
Designer: L. Harradine
Height: 2 1/4", 5.7 cm
Colour: Blue and purple
Issued: 1925-1949
Varieties: HN 698, 699, 757, 758, 759, 760, 762 M21, M22, M23
Series: Beggar's Opera
U.S.: $1,200.00
Can.: $1,350.00
Ster.: £ 650.00

HN 762
Polly Peachum
Style Three
Designer: L. Harradine
Height: 2 1/4", 5.7 cm
Colour: Red and white
Issued: 1925-1949
Varieties: HN 698, 699, 757, 758, 759, 760, 761; M21, M22, M23
Series: Beggar's Opera
U.S.: $1,200.00
Can.: $1,350.00
Ster.: £ 650.00

HN 763
Pretty Lady
Designer: H. Tittensor
Height: 9 1/2", 24.1 cm
Colour: Orange, white and green
Issued: 1925-1938
Varieties: HN 69, 70, 302, 330, 361, 384, 565, 700, 783
U.S.: None
Can.: known
Ster.: to exist

HN 764
Madonna of the Square
Designer: P. Stabler
Height: 7", 17.8 cm
Colour: Blue, purple and yellow
Issued: 1925-1936
Varieties: HN 10, 10A, 11, 14, 27, 326, 573, 576, 594, 613, 1968, 1969, 2034
U.S.: Extremely rare
Can.:
Ster.:

HN 765
The Poke Bonnet
Designer: C.J. Noke
Height: 8 3/4", 22.2 cm
Colour: Green, blue, purple
Issued: 1925-1938
Varieties: HN 362, 612; "A Lilac Shawl" HN 44, 44A, "In Grandma's Days" HN339, 340, 388, 442
U.S.: None
Can.: known
Ster.: to exist

HN 766
Irish Colleen
Designer: L. Harradine
Height: 6 1/2", 16.5 cm
Colour: Red, black, white and grey
Issued: 1925-1936
Varieties: HN 767
U.S.: Extremely rare
Can.:
Ster.:

NOTES ON PRICING

The prices on the secondary market for Royal Doulton Figures, particularly the early HN Numbers, have risen considerably over the years. As values rise, the condition and quality of these figurines take on an increasingly important role.

The prices listed in *The Charlton Standard Catalogue of Royal Doulton Beswick Figurines* are for figures in mint condition.

Naturally, repaired or restored figures, no matter how professionally done, will sell at a substantial discount.

On Condition: For figures to command catalogue prices they must be in mint condition. This simply means that a figure will not have paint chips, scratches, hairline cracks, crazing or blemishes. Any of which will remove from the mint category figure.

On Quality: Some figures can be better moulded, assembled or painted than others. High quality figures will command catalogue prices. Low quality figures will not.

If the quality or condition of the figures is below the standard for mint, look for that figure to be priced at a percentage of the catalogue prices.

HN 767
Irish Collen
Designer: L. Harradine
Height: 6 1/2", 16.5 cm
Colour: Black, red and green
Issued: 1925-1936
Varieties: HN 766

U.S.: $4,500.00
Can.: $4,500.00
Ster.: £2,000.00

HN 768
Harlequinade Masked
Designer: L. Harradine
Height: 6 1/2", 16.5 cm
Colour: Black, red and green
Issued: 1925-1938
Varieties: HN 769, 1274, 1304

U.S.: **Extremely rare**
Can.:
Ster.:

HN 769
Harlequinade Masked
Designer: L. Harradine
Height: 6 1/2", 16.5 cm
Colour: Blue, red and yellow
Issued: 1925-1938
Varieties: HN 768, 1274, 1304

U.S.: $4,500.00
Can.: $4,500.00
Ster.: £2,000.00

HN 770
Lady Clown
Designer: L. Harradine
Height: 7 1/2", 19.1 cm
Colour: White and green
Issued: 1925-1938
Varieties: HN 717, 718, 738;
Also called
"Clownette," HN 1263

U.S.: **Extremely rare**
Can.:
Ster.:

HN 771
London Cry,
Turnips and Carrots
Designer: L. Harradine
Height: 6 3/4", 17.2 cm
Colour: Lavender, cream
and brown
Issued: 1925-1938
Varieties: HN 752

U.S.: $2,850.00
Can.: $2,750.00
Ster.: £1,250.00

HN 772
London Cry, Strawberries
Designer: L. Harradine
Height: 6 3/4", 17.2 cm
Colour: Lavender and cream
Issued: 1925-1936
Varieties: HN 749

U.S.: $2,850.00
Can.: $2,750.00
Ster.: £1,250.00

HN 773
The Bather
Style Two
Designer: L. Harradine
Height: 7 1/2", 19.1 cm
Colour: Red, purple and black
Issued: 1925-1938
Varieties: HN 774, 1227

U.S.: $4,000.00
Can.: $4,000.00
Ster.: £1,750.00

HN 774
The Bather
Style Two
Designer: L. Harradine
Height: 7 3/4", 19.7 cm
Colour: Blue and red
Issued: 1925-1938
Varieties: HN 773, 1227

U.S.: $4,000.00
Can.: $4,000.00
Ster.: £1,750.00

HN 775
Mephistopheles
and Marguerite
Designer: C.J. Noke
Height: 7 3/4", 19.7 cm
Colour: Orange and cream
Issued: 1925-1949
Varieties: HN 755

U.S.: $3,000.00
Can.: $3,000.00
Ster.: £1,500.00

HN 776
The Belle
Style One
Designer: L. Harradine
Height: 6 1/2", 16.5 cm
Colour: Unknown
Issued: 1925-1938
Varieties: HN 754

U.S.: **Extremely rare**
Can.:
Ster.:

HN 777
Bo-Peep
Style One
Designer: L. Harradine
Height: 6 3/4", 17.2 cm
Colour: Dark blue
Issued: 1926-1936
Varieties: HN 1202, 1327, 1328

U.S.: $3,250.00
Can.: $3,250.00
Ster.: £1,500.00

HN 778
Captain
Style One
Designer: L. Harradine
Height: 7", 17.8 cm
Colour: Red and white
Issued: 1926-1936

U.S.: $4,000.00
Can.: $4,000.00
Ster.: £1,500.00

HN 779
Geisha
Style One
Designer: H. Tittensor
Height: 10 3/4", 27.3 cm
Colour: Red and purple
Issued: 1926-1936
Varieties: HN 354, 376, 376A,
387, 634, 741, 1321,
1322; "The Japanese
Lady"

U.S.: $8,500.00
Can.: $8,500.00
Ster.: £2,750.00

HN 780
Harlequinade
Designer: L. Harradine
Height: 6 1/2", 16.5 cm
Colour: Pink, blue and brown
Issued: 1926-1940
Varieties: HN 585, 635, 711

U.S.: $2,500.00
Can.: $2,500.00
Ster.: £   600.00

HN 781
The Bather
Style One
Designer: L. Harradine
Height: 7 3/4", 19.7 cm
Colour: Blue and green
Issued: 1926-1938
Varieties: HN 597, 687, 782,
1238, 1708

U.S.: **Extremely rare**
Can.:
Ster.:

HN 782
The Bather
Style One
Designer: L. Harradine
Height: 7 3/4", 19.7 cm
Colour: Purple and black
Issued: 1926-1938
Varieties: HN 597, 687, 781,
1238, 1708

U.S.: **Extremely rare**
Can.:
Ster.:

HN 783
Pretty Lady
Designer: H. Tittensor
Height: 9 1/2", 24.1 cm
Colour: Blue
Issued: 1926-1938
Varieties: HN 69, 70, 302, 330,
361, 384, 565, 700,
763

U.S.: $2,500.00
Can.: $2,500.00
Ster.: £1,250.00

HN 784
Pierrette
Style One
Designer: L. Harradine
Height: 7 1/4", 18.4 cm
Colour: Pink and black
Issued: 1926-1938
Varieties: HN 642, 643, 644,
691, 721, 731, 732

U.S.: $3,500.00
Can.: $3,500.00
Ster.: £1,400.00

HN 785
The Mask
Designer: L. Harradine
Height: 6 3/4", 17.2 cm
Colour: Blue, black and pink
Issued: 1926-1938
Varieties: HN 656, 657, 729,
733, 1271

U.S.: $3,500.00
Can.: $3,500.00
Ster.: £1,500.00

HN 786
Mam'selle
Designer: L. Harradine
Height: 7", 17.8 cm
Colour: Pink and black
Issued: 1926-1938
Varieties: HN 658, 659, 724

U.S.: $4,000.00
Can.: $4,000.00
Ster.: £1,500.00

HN 787
A Mandarin
Style One
Designer: C.J. Noke
Height: 10 1/4", 26.0 cm
Colour: Pink and orange
Issued: 1926-1936
Varieties: HN 84, 316, 318, 382,
611, 746, 791;
"Chinese Mandarin"
and "The Mikado"

U.S.: **Extremely rare**
Can.:
Ster.:

HN 788
Proposal (woman)
Designer: Unknown
Height: 5 3/4", 14.6 cm
Colour: Pink
Issued: 1926-1940
Varieties: HN 715, 716

U.S.: **Extremely rare**
Can.:
Ster.:

HN 789
The Flower Seller
Designer: L. Harradine
Height: 8 3/4", 22.2 cm
Colour: Green, cream
and white
Issued: 1926-1938

U.S.: $1,350.00
Can.: $1,500.00
Ster.: £ 500.00

Earthenware

HN 790
The Parson's Daughter
Designer: H. Tittensor
Height: 10", 25.4 cm
Colour: Multicoloured
Issued: 1926-1938
Varieties: HN 337, 338, 441,
564, 1242, 1356,
2018

U.S.: $2,200.00
Can.: $2,200.00
Ster.: £ 900.00

HN 791
A Mandarin
Style One
Designer: C.J. Noke
Height: 10 1/4", 26.0 cm
Colour: Black and purple
Issued: 1926-1936
Varieties: HN 84, 316, 318,
            382, 611, 746, 787;
            "Chinese Mandarin"
            and "The Mikado"

U.S.: $7,500.00
Can.: $7,500.00
Ster.: £3,000.00

HN 792
Myfanwy Jones
Designer: E.W. Light
Height: 12", 30.5 cm
Colour: Pink and blue
Issued: 1926-1936
Varieties: HN 39, 92, 456, 514,
            516, 519, 520, 660,
            668, 669, 701; also
            called "The Welsh Girl"

U.S.:   **Extremely rare**
Can.:
Ster.:

HN 793
Katharine
Designer: C.J. Noke
Height: 5 3/4", 14.6 cm
Colour: Lavender
            and green
Issued: 1926-1938
Varieties: HN 61, 74, 341,
            471, 615

U.S.: $3,500.00
Can.: $3,500.00
Ster.: £1,500.00

HN 794
The Bouquet
Designer: G. Lambert
Height: 9", 22.9 cm
Colour: Blue, red and green
Issued: 1926-1936
Varieties: HN 406, 414, 422,
            428, 429, 567; also
            called "The Nosegay"

U.S.:   **Extremely rare**
Can.:
Ster.:

HN 795
Pierrette
Style Two
Designer: L. Harradine
Height: 3 1/2", 8.9 cm
Colour: Pink
Issued: 1926-1938
Varieties: HN 796

U.S.:   **Extremely rare**
Can.:
Ster.:

HN 796
Pierrette
Style Two
Designer: L. Harradine
Height: 3 1/2", 8.9 cm
Colour: White and silver
Issued: 1926-1938
Varieties: HN 795

U.S.:   **Extremely rare**
Can.:
Ster.:

HN 797
Moorish Minstrel
Designer: C.J. Noke
Height: 13 1/2", 34.3 cm
Colour: Purple
Issued: 1926-1949
Varieties: HN 34, 364, 415

U.S.: $4,250.00
Can.: $4,250.00
Ster.: £1,750.00

HN 798
Tete-a-Tete
Style One
Designer: L. Harradine
Height: 5 3/4", 14.6 cm
Colour: Pink and red
Issued: 1926-1938
Varieties: HN 799

U.S.: $3,500.00
Can.: $3,500.00
Ster.: £1,500.00

HN 799
Tete-a-Tete
Style One
Designer: L. Harradine
Height: 5 3/4", 14.6 cm
Colour: Blue and red
Issued: 1926-1940
Varieties: HN 798

U.S.: **$3,500.00**
Can.: **$3,500.00**
Ster.: **£1,500.00**

*

HN 1201
Hunts Lady
Designer: L. Harradine
Height: 8 1/4", 21.0 cm
Colour: Grey and cream
Issued: 1926-1938

U.S.: **$4,000.00**
Can.: **$4,000.00**
Ster.: **£1,750.00**

HN 1202
Bo-Peep
Style One
Designer: L. Harradine
Height: 6 3/4", 17.2 cm
Colour: Purple, green and pink
Issued: 1926-1936
Varieties: HN 777, 1327, 1328

U.S.: **Extremely rare**
Can.:
Ster.:

HN 1203
Butterfly
Designer: L. Harradine
Height: 6 1/2", 16.5 cm
Colour: Black and gold
Issued: 1926-1940
Varieties: HN 719, 720, 730; also called "Butterfly Woman" HN 1456

U.S.: **Extremely rare**
Can.:
Ster.:

HN 1204
Angela
Style One
Designer: L. Harradine
Height: 7 1/4", 18.4 cm
Colour: Purple and pink
Issued: 1926-1940
Varieties: HN 1303; also called "Fanny"

U.S.: **$3,000.00**
Can.: **$3,250.00**
Ster.: **£1,500.00**

HN 1205
Miss 1926
Designer: L. Harradine
Height: 7 1/4", 18.4 cm
Colour: Black and white
Issued: 1926-1938
Varieties: HN 1207

U.S.: **$4,500.00**
Can.: **$4,500.00**
Ster.: **£2,000.00**

HN 1206
The Flower Seller's Children
Designer: L. Harradine
Height: 8 1/4", 21.0 cm
Colour: Blue and purple
Issued: 1926-1949
Varieties: HN 525, 551, 1342, 1406

U.S.: **$1,850.00**
Can.: **$1,850.00**
Ster.: **£ 750.00**

HN 1207
Miss 1926
Designer: L. Harradine
Height: 7 1/4", 18.4 cm
Colour: Black
Issued: Unknown
Varieties: HN 1205

U.S.: **Extremely rare**
Can.:
Ster.:

HN 1208
A Victoria Lady
Style One
Designer: L. Harradine
Height: 7 3/4", 19.7 cm
Colour: Green and purple
Issued: 1926-1938
Varieties: HN 726, 727, 728,
736, 739, 740, 742,
745, 1258, 1276, 1277,
1345, 1452, 1529

U.S.: $1,000.00
Can.: $ 950.00
Ster.: £ 375.00

HN 1209
The Proposal (Man)
Designer: Unknown
Height: 5 1/2", 14.0 cm
Colour: Blue and pink
Issued: 1926-1938
Varieties: HN 725

U.S.: $3,000.00
Can.: $3,000.00
Ster.: £1,500.00

HN 1210
Boy with Turban
Designer: L. Harradine
Height: 3 3/4", 9.5 cm
Colour: Orange, black
and white
Issued: 1926-1936
Varieties: HN 586, 587, 661,
662, 1212, 1213,
1214, 1225

U.S.: $1,100.00
Can.: $1,250.00
Ster.: £ 550.00

HN 1211
Quality Street
Designer: Unknown
Height: 7 1/4", 18.4 cm
Colour: Red
Issued: 1926-1936
Varieties: HN 1211A

U.S.: $1,600.00
Can.: $1,800.00
Ster.: £ 750.00

HN 1211A
Quality Street
Designer: Unknown
Height: 7 1/4", 18.4 cm
Colour: Lavender
Issued: 1926-1936
Varieties: HN 1211

U.S.: $2,000.00
Can.: $2,200.00
Ster.: £ 750.00

HN 1212
Boy with Turban
Designer: L. Harradine
Height: 3 3/4", 9.5 cm
Colour: Purple and green
Issued: 1926-1936
Varieties: HN 586, 587, 661,
662, 1210, 1213,
214, 1225

U.S.: $1,100.00
Can.: $1,250.00
Ster.: £ 550.00

HN 1213
Boy with Turban
Designer: L. Harradine
Height: 3 3/4", 9.5 cm
Colour: White and black
Issued: 1926-1936
Varieties: HN 586, 587, 661,
662, 1210, 1212,
1214, 1225

U.S.: $1,100.00
Can.: $1,250.00
Ster.: £ 550.00

HN 1214
Boy with Turban
Designer: L. Harradine
Height: 3 1/2", 8.9 cm
Colour: Black, white
and green
Issued: 1926-1936
Varieties: HN 586, 587, 661,
662, 1210, 1212,
1213, 1225

U.S.: $1,100.00
Can.: $1,250.00
Ster.: £ 550.00

HN 1215
The Pied Piper
Style One
Designer: L. Harradine
Height: 8 1/4", 21.0 cm
Colour: Red, black and
yellow
Issued: 1926-1938
Varieties: HN 2102

U.S.: $2,500.00
Can.: $2,500.00
Ster.: £ 950.00

HN 1216
Falstaff
Style One
Designer: C.J. Noke
Height: 7", 17.8 cm
Colour: Multi-coloured
Issued: 1926-1949
Varieties: HN 571, 575, 608,
609, 619, 638, 1606

U.S.: $2,500.00
Can.: $2,500.00
Ster.: £ 900.00

HN 1217
The Prince of Wales
Designer: L. Harradine
Height: 7 1/2", 19.1 cm
Colour: Red and white
Issued: 1926-1938

U.S.: $2,850.00
Can.: $3,000.00
Ster.: £1,500.00

HN 1218
A Spook
Style Two
Designer: H. Tittensor
Height: 3", 7.6 cm
Colour: Multi-coloured
Issued: 1926-1936
Varieties: Colourway: Red
cloak, black cap

U.S.: $3,200.00
Can.: $3,200.00
Ster.: £1,250.00

HN 1219
Negligée
Designer: L. Harradine
Height: 5", 12.7 cm
Colour: Bluish-yellow,
blue hair band
Issued: 1927-1936
Varieties: HN 1228, 1272,
1273, 1454

U.S.: $2,500.00
Can.: $2,500.00
Ster.: £ 950.00

HN 1220
Lido Lady
Designer: L. Harradine
Height: 6 3/4", 17.2 cm
Colour: Pink
Issued: 1927-1936
Varieties: HN 1229

U.S.: $2,500.00
Can.: $2,500.00
Ster.: £ 950.00

HN 1221
Lady Jester
Style One
Designer: L. Harradine
Height: 7", 17.8 cm
Colour: Multi-coloured
Issued: 1927-1938
Varieties: HN 1222, 1332

U.S.: $3,500.00
Can.: $3,500.00
Ster.: £1,500.00

HN 1222
Lady Jester
Style One
Designer: L. Harradine
Height: 7", 17.8 cm
Colour: Black and white
Issued: 1927-1938
Varieties: HN 1221, 1332

U.S.: $3,500.00
Can.: $3,500.00
Ster.: £1,500.00

HN 1223
A Geisha
Style Two
Designer: C.J. Noke
Height: 6 3/4", 17.2 cm
Colour: Black and orange
Issued: 1927-1938
Varieties: HN 1234, 1292, 1310

U.S.: $2,000.00
Can.: $2,000.00
Ster.: £ 900.00

HN 1224
The Wandering Minstrel
Designer: L. Harradine
Height: 7", 17.8 cm
Colour: Purple and red
Issued: 1927-1936

U.S.: $4,000.00
Can.: $4,000.00
Ster.: £1,500.00

HN 1225
Boy with Turban
Designer: L. Harradine
Height: 3 3/4", 9.5 cm
Colour: Yellow and blue
Issued: 1927-1936
Varieties: HN 586, 587, 661,
     662, 1210, 1212,
     1213, 1214

U.S.: $1,100.00
Can.: $1,250.00
Ster.: £ 550.00

HN 1226
The Huntsman
Style One
Designer: L. Harradine
Height: 8 3/4", 22.2 cm
Colour: Red and white
Issued: 1927-1938

U.S.: $3,500.00
Can.: $3,500.00
Ster.: £1,500.00

HN 1227
The Bather
Style Two
Designer: L. Harradine
Height: 7 1/2", 19.1 cm
Colour: Pink and black
Issued: 1927-1938
Varieties: HN 773, 774

U.S.: $4,000.00
Can.: $4,000.00
Ster.: £1,750.00

HN 1228
Negligée
Designer: L. Harradine
Height: 5", 12.7 cm
Colour: Bluish-yellow,
     red hair band
Issued: 1927-1936
Varieties: HN 1219, 1272,
     1273, 1454

U.S.: $2,500.00
Can.: $2,500.00
Ster.: £ 950.00

HN 1229
Lido Lady
Designer: L. Harradine
Height: 6 3/4", 17.2 cm
Colour: Pink
Issued: 1927-1936
Varieties: HN 1220

U.S.: $3,500.00
Can.: $3,500.00
Ster.: £1,250.00

HN 1230
Baba
Designer: L. Harradine
Height: 3 1/4", 8.3 cm
Colour: Blue, yellow
     and purple
Issued: 1927-1938
Varieties: HN 1243, 1244, 1245,
     1246, 1247, 1248

U.S.: $1,100.00
Can.: $1,250.00
Ster.: £ 550.00

HN 1231
Cassim
Style One
Designer: L. Harradine
Height: 3", 7.6 cm
Colour: Blue, yellow and
turquoise
Issued: 1927-1938
Varieties: HN 1232
U.S.: **$1,100.00**
Can.: **$1,250.00**
Ster.: £ 550.00

HN 1232
Cassim
Style One
Designer: L. Harradine
Height: 3", 7.6 cm
Colour: Orange and black
Issued: 1927-1938
Varieties: HN 1231
U.S.: **$1,100.00**
Can.: **$1,250.00**
Ster.: £ 550.00

HN 1233
Susanna
Designer: L. Harradine
Height: 6", 15.2 cm
Colour: Pink
Issued: 1927-1936
Varieties: HN 1288, 1299
U.S.: **$2,750.00**
Can.: **$2,750.00**
Ster.: £1,250.00

HN 1234
A Geisha
Style Two
Designer: C.J. Noke
Height: 6 3/4", 17.2 cm
Colour: Green and red
Issued: 1927-1938
Varieties: HN 1223, 1292, 1310
U.S.: **$1,750.00**
Can.: **$1,750.00**
Ster.: £ 750.00

HN 1235
A Scribe
Designer: C.J. Noke
Height: 6", 15.2 cm
Colour: Brown, blue
and orange
Issued: 1927-1938
Varieties: HN 305, 324
U.S.: **$2,500.00**
Can.: **$2,250.00**
Ster.: £ 750.00

HN 1236
Tete-a-Tete
Style Two
Designer: C.J. Noke
Height: 3", 7.6 cm
Colour: Purple and red
Issued: 1927-1938
Varieties: HN 1237
U.S.: **$4,000.00**
Can.: **$3,500.00**
Ster.: £1,500.00

HN 1237
Tete-a-Tete
Style Two
Designer: C.J. Noke
Height: 3", 7.6 cm
Colour: Pink
Issued: 1927-1938
Varieties: HN 1236
U.S.: **$4,000.00**
Can.: **$3,500.00**
Ster.: £1,500.00

HN 1238
The Bather
Style One
Designer: L. Harradine
Height: 7 3/4", 19.7 cm
Colour: Red and black
Issued: 1927-1938
Varieties: HN 597, 687, 781,
782, 1708
U.S.: **$3,500.00**
Can.: **$3,500.00**
Ster.: £1,250.00

*

HN 1242
The Parson's Daughter
Designer: H. Tittesnor
Height: 10", 25.4 cm
Colour: Lavender and yellow
Issued: 1927-1938
Varieties: HN 337, 338, 441,
564, 790, 1356, 2018

U.S.: $2,200.00
Can.: $2,200.00
Ster.: £ 900.00

HN 1243
Baba
Designer: L. Harradine
Height: 3 1/4", 8.3 cm
Colour: Orange
Issued: 1927-1938
Varieties: HN 1230, 1244, 1245,
1246, 1247, 1248

U.S.: $1,100.00
Can.: $1,250.00
Ster.: £ 550.00

HN 1244
Baba
Designer: L. Harradine
Height: 3 1/4", 8.3 cm
Colour: Yellow and green
Issued: 1927-1938
Varieties: HN 1230, 1243, 1245,
1246, 1247, 1248

U.S.: $1,100.00
Can.: $1,250.00
Ster.: £ 550.00

HN 1245
Baba
Designer: L. Harradine
Height: 3 1/4", 8.3 cm
Colour: White and black
Issued: 1927-1938
Varieties: HN 1230, 1243, 1244,
1246, 1247, 1248

U.S.: $1,100.00
Can.: $1,250.00
Ster.: £ 550.00

HN 1246
Baba
Designer: L. Harradine
Height: 3 1/4", 8.3 cm
Colour: Green
Issued: 1927-1938
Varieties: HN 1230, 1243, 1244,
1245, 1247, 1248

U.S.: $1,100.00
Can.: $1,250.00
Ster.: £ 550.00

HN 1247
Baba
Designer: L. Harradine
Height: 3 1/4", 8.3 cm
Colour: Black, white
and orange
Issued: 1927-1938
Varieties: HN 1230, 1243, 1244,
1245, 1246, 1248

U.S.: $1,100.00
Can.: $1,250.00
Ster.: £ 550.00

HN 1248
Baba
Designer: L. Harradine
Height: 3 1/4", 8.3 cm
Colour: Green and orange
Issued: 1927-1938
Varieties: HN 1230, 1243, 1244,
1245, 1246, 1247

U.S.: $1,100.00
Can.: $1,250.00
Ster.: £ 550.00

HN 1249
Circe
Designer: L. Harradine
Height: 7 3/4", 19.7 cm
Colour: Green, orange
and pink
Issued: 1927-1936
Varieties: HN 1250, 1254, 1255

U.S.: $4,000.00
Can.: $4,000.00
Ster.: £1,750.00

HN 1250
Circe
Designer: L. Harradine
Height: 7 1/2", 19.1 cm
Colour: Orange and black
Issued: 1927-1936
Varieties: HN 1249, 1254, 1255

U.S.:	**$4,000.00**
Can.:	**$4,000.00**
Ster.:	**£1,750.00**

HN 1251
The Cobbler
Style Two
Designer: C.J. Noke
Height: 8 1/2", 21.6 cm
Colour: Black and red
Issued: 1927-1938
Varieties: HN 681, 1283

U.S.:	**$3,000.00**
Can.:	**$2,750.00**
Ster.:	**£ 950.00**

HN 1252
Kathleen
Style One
Designer: L. Harradine
Height: 7 3/4", 19.7 cm
Colour: Lavender, pink and purple
Issued: 1927-1938
Varieties: HN 1253,1275, 1279, 1291, 1357, 1512

U.S.:	**$1,400.00**
Can.:	**$1,400.00**
Ster.:	**£ 550.00**

HN 1253
Kathleen
Style One
Designer: L. Harradine
Height: 7 1/2", 19.1 cm
Colour: Red and purple
Issued: 1927-1938
Varieties: HN 1252, 1275, 1279, 1291, 1357, 1512

U.S.:	**$1,400.00**
Can.:	**$1,400.00**
Ster.:	**£ 550.00**

HN 1254
Circe
Designer: L. Harradine
Height: 7 1/2", 19.1 cm
Colour: Orange and red
Issued: 1927-1936
Varieties: HN 1249, 1250, 1255

U.S.:	**Extremely rare**
Can.:	
Ster.:	

HN 1255
Circe
Designer: L. Harradine
Height: 7 1/2", 19.1 cm
Colour: Blue
Issued: 1927-1938
Varieties: HN 1249, 1250, 1254

U.S.:	**Extremely rare**
Can.:	
Ster.:	

HN 1256
Captain MacHeath
Designer: L. Harradine
Height: 7", 17.8 cm
Colour: Red, yellow and black
Issued: 1927-1949
Varieties: HN 464, 590
Series: Beggar's Opera

U.S.:	**$1,300.00**
Can.:	**$1,250.00**
Ster.:	**£ 475.00**

Earthenware

HN 1257
Highwayman
Designer: L. Harradine
Height: 6 1/2", 16.5 cm
Colour: Green and red
Issued: 1927-1949
Varieties: HN 527, 592
Series: Beggar's Opera

U.S.:	**$1,200.00**
Can.:	**$1,200.00**
Ster.:	**£ 475.00**

Earthenware

HN 1258
A Victorian Lady
Style One
Designer: L. Harradine
Height: 7 3/4", 19.7 cm
Colour: Purple and blue
Issued: 1927-1938
Varieties: HN 726, 727, 728,
736, 739, 740, 742,
745, 1208, 1276,1277,
1345, 1452, 1529

U.S.:	$1,300.00
Can..:	$1,200.00
Ster.:	£ 425.00

HN 1259
The Alchemist
Designer: L. Harradine
Height: 11 1/2", 29.2 cm
Colour: Green and red
Issued: 1927-1938
Varieties: HN 1282

U.S.:	$3,000.00
Can.:	$2,750.00
Ster.:	£1,000.00

HN 1260
Carnival
Designer: L. Harradine
Height: 8 1/4", 21.0 cm
Colour: Red, black and purple
Issued: 1927-1936
Varieties: HN 1278

U.S.:	$5,500.00
Can.:	$5,500.00
Ster.:	£2,000.00

HN 1261
Sea Sprite
Style One
Designer: L. Harradine
Height: 5", 12.7 cm
Colour: Red, purple and black
Issued: 1927-1938

U.S.:	$1,400.00
Can.:	$1,200.00
Ster.:	£ 500.00

HN 1262
Spanish Lady
Designer: L. Harradine
Height: 8 1/2", 21.6 cm
Colour: Black with red flowers
Issued: 1927-1940
Varieties: HN 1290, 1293,
1294, 1309

U.S.:	$1,700.00
Can.:	$1,800.00
Ster.:	£ 750.00

HN 1263
Clownette
Designer: L. Harradine
Height: 7 1/4", 18.4 cm
Colour: Mottled purple
Issued: 1927-1938
Varieties: Also called "Lady
Clown" HN 717,
718, 738, 770

U.S.:	$6,500.00
Can.:	$6,500.00
Ster.:	£3,000.00

HN 1264
Judge and Jury
Designer: J.G. Hughes
Height: 6", 15.2 cm
Colour: Red and white
Issued: 1927-1938

U.S.:	**Extremely**
Can.:	**rare**
Ster.:	

HN 1265
Lady Fayre
Designer: L. Harradine
Height: 5 1/4", 13.3 cm
Colour: Lavender and red
Issued: 1928-1938
Varieties: HN 1557

U.S.:	$1,200.00
Can.:	$1,000.00
Ster.:	£ 450.00

HN 1266
Ko-Ko
Style One
Designer: L. Harradine
Height: 5", 12.7 cm
Colour: Black, white and yellow
Issued: 1928-1936
Varieties: HN 1286

U.S.: $1,500.00
Can.: $1,500.00
Ster.: £ 650.00

HN 1267
Carmen
Style One
Designer: L. Harradine
Height: 7", 17.8 cm
Colour: Red and black
Issued: 1928-1938
Varieties: HN 1300

U.S.: $1,500.00
Can.: $1,700.00
Ster.: £ 650.00

HN 1268
Yum-Yum
Style One
Designer: L. Harradine
Height: 5", 12.7 cm
Colour: Pink and cream
Issued: 1928-1936
Varieties: HN 1287

U.S.: $1,500.00
Can.: $1,500.00
Ster.: £ 650.00

HN 1269
Scotch Girl
Designer: L. Harradine
Height: 7 1/2", 19.1 cm
Colour: Red and green
Issued: 1928-1938

U.S.: $3,700.00
Can.: $3,700.00
Ster.: £1,500.00

HN 1270
The Swimmer
Designer: L. Harradine
Height: 7 1/4", 18.4 cm
Colour: Multi-coloured
Issued: 1928-1938
Varieties: HN 1326, 1329

U.S.: $3,500.00
Can.: $3,500.00
Ster.: £1,500.00

HN 1271
The Mask
Designer: L. Harradine
Height: 6 3/4", 17.2 cm
Colour: Black, blue and red
Issued: 1928-1938
Varieties: HN 656, 657, 729, 733, 785

U.S.: $4,000.00
Can.: $4,000.00
Ster.: £1,750.00

HN 1272
Negligée
Designer: L. Harradine
Height: 5", 12.7 cm
Colour: Red and black
Issued: 1928-1936
Varieties: HN 1219, 1228, 1273, 1454,

U.S.: $2,500.00
Can.: $2,500.00
Ster.: £ 950.00

HN 1273
Negligée
Designer: L. Harradine
Height: 5", 12.7 cm
Colour: White and pink
Issued: 1928-1936
Varieties: HN 1219, 1228, 1272, 1454

U.S.: $2,750.00
Can.: $2,750.00
Ster.: £ 950.00

HN 1274
Harlequinade Masked
Designer: L. Harradine
Height: 6 1/2", 16.5 cm
Colour: Orange and black
Issued: 1928-1938
Varieties: HN 768, 769, 1304

U.S.:	**$4,500.00**
Can.:	**$4,500.00**
Ster.:	**£2,000.00**

HN 1275
Kathleen
Style One
Designer: L. Harradine
Height: 7 1/2", 19.1 cm
Colour: Pink and black
Issued: 1928-1938
Varieties: HN 1252, 1253,
1279, 1291,
1357, 1512

U.S.:	**Extremely rare**
Can.:	
Ster.:	

HN 1276
A Victorian Lady
Style One
Designer: L. Harradine
Height: 7 1/2", 19.1 cm
Colour: Purple, red, yellow
Issued: 1928-1938
Varieties: HN 726, 727, 728, 736,
739, 740, 742, 745,
1208, 1258, 1277,
1345, 1452, 1529

U.S.:	**$1,350.00**
Can.:	**$1,150.00**
Ster.:	**£ 475.00**

HN 1277
A Victorian Lady
Style One
Designer: L. Harradine
Height: 7 3/4", 19.7 cm
Colour: Red, yellow, blue
Issued: 1928-1938
Varieties: HN 726, 727, 728,
736, 739, 740, 742,
745, 1208, 1258, 1276,
1345, 1452, 1529

U.S.:	**$1,350.00**
Can.:	**$1,150.00**
Ster.:	**£ 450.00**

HN 1278
Carnival
Designer: L. Harradine
Height: 8 1/2", 21.6 cm
Colour: Blue, orange
and purple
Issued: 1928-1936
Varieties: HN 1260

U.S.:	**$6,500.00**
Can.:	**$6,500.00**
Ster.:	**£2,250.00**

HN 1279
Kathleen
Style One
Designer: L. Harradine
Height: 7 3/4", 19.7 cm
Colour: Red
Issued: 1928-1938
Varieties: HN 1252, 1253,
1275, 1291,
1357, 1512

U.S.:	**$1,600.00**
Can.:	**$1,400.00**
Ster.:	**£ 600.00**

HN 1280
Blue Bird
Designer: L. Harradine
Height: 4 3/4", 12.0 cm
Colour: Pink base
Issued: 1928-1938

U.S.:	**$1,300.00**
Can.:	**$1,100.00**
Ster.:	**£ 450.00**

HN 1281
Scotties
Designer: L. Harradine
Height: 5 1/2", 14.0 cm
Colour: Red and black
Issued: 1928-1936
Varieties: HN 1349

U.S.:	**$3,000.00**
Can.:	**$3,000.00**
Ster.:	**£1,500.00**

HN 1282
The Alchemist
Designer: L. Harradine
Height: 11 1/4", 28.5 cm
Colour: Purple and red
Issued: 1928-1938
Varieties: HN 1259

U.S.: $2,000.00
Can.: $2,000.00
Ster.: £ 950.00

HN 1283
The Cobbler
Style Two
Designer: C.J. Noke
Height: 8 1/2", 21.6 cm
Colour: Light green
Issued: 1928-1949
Varieties: HN 681, 1251

U.S.: $1,600.00
Can.: $1,600.00
Ster.: £ 550.00

HN 1284
Lady Jester
Style Two
Designer: L. Harradine
Height: 4 1/4", 10.8 cm
Colour: Purple and red
Issued: 1928-1938
Varieties: HN 1285

U.S.: $3,800.00
Can.: $3,800.00
Ster.: £1,750.00

HN 1285
Lady Jester
Style Two
Designer: L. Harradine
Height: 4 1/4", 10.8 cm
Colour: Red, pink
           and blue
Issued: 1928-1938
Varieties: HN 1284

U.S.: $3,800.00
Can.: $3,800.00
Ster.: £1,750.00

Earthenware

HN 1286
Ko-Ko
Style One
Designer: L. Harradine
Height: 5", 12.7 cm
Colour: Red and purple
Issued: 1938-1949
Varieties: HN 1266

U.S.: $1,500.00
Can.: $1,500.00
Ster.: £ 650.00

HN 1287
Yum-Yum
Style One
Designer: L. Harradine
Height: 5", 12.7 cm
Colour: Purple and cream
Issued: 1928-1936
Varieties: HN 1268

U.S.: $1,500.00
Can.: $1,500.00
Ster.: £ 650.00

HN 1288
Susanna
Designer: L. Harradine
Height: 6", 15.2 cm
Colour: Red
Issued: 1928-1936
Varieties: HN 1233, 1299

U.S.: $3,000.00
Can.: $3,000.00
Ster.: £1,500.00

HN 1289
Midinette
Style One
Designer: L. Harradine
Height: 9", 22.9 cm
Colour: Purple and pink
Issued: 1928-1938
Varieties: HN 1306

U.S.: $5,000.00
Can.: $5,000.00
Ster.: £2,000.00

HN 1290
Spanish Lady
Designer: L. Harradine
Height: 8 1/4", 21.0 cm
Colour: Lavender, yellow and black
Issued: 1928-1940
Varieties: HN 1262, 1293, 1294, 1309
U.S.: **$1,700.00**
Can.: **$1,800.00**
Ster.: £ 850.00

HN 1291
Kathleen
Style One
Designer: L. Harradine
Height: 7 1/2", 19.1 cm
Colour: Red and yellow
Issued: 1928-1938
Varieties: HN 1252, 1253, 1275, 1279, 1357, 1512
U.S.: **$1,700.00**
Can.: **$1,750.00**
Ster.: £ 650.00

HN 1292
A Geisha
Style Two
Designer: C.J. Noke
Height: 6 3/4", 17.2 cm
Colour: Pink and lavender
Issued: 1928-1938
Varieties: HN 1223, 1234, 1310
U.S.: **$1,750.00**
Can.: **$1,750.00**
Ster.: £ 750.00

HN 1293
Spanish Lady
Designer: L. Harradine
Height: 8 1/4", 21.0 cm
Colour: Black with yellow flowers
Issued: 1928-1940
Varieties: HN 1262, 1290, 1294, 1309
U.S.: **$2,100.00**
Can.: **$2,000.00**
Ster.: £ 950.00

HN 1294
Spanish Lady
Designer: L. Harradine
Height: 8 1/4", 21.0 cm
Colour: Red and black
Issued: 1928-1940
Varieties: HN 1262, 1290, 1293, 1309
U.S.: **$1,750.00**
Can.: **$1,750.00**
Ster.: £ 850.00

HN 1295
A Jester
Style One
Designer: C.J. Noke
Height: 10", 25.4 cm
Colour: Brown and purple
Issued: 1928-1949
Varieties: HN 45, 71, 71A, 320, 367, 412, 426, 446, 552, 616, 627, 1702, 2016
U.S.: **$1,600.00**
Can.: **$1,750.00**
Ster.: £ 675.00

HN 1296
Columbine
Style One
Designer: L. Harradine
Height: 6", 15.2 cm
Colour: Orange and lavender
Issued: 1928-1940
Varieties: HN 1297, 1439
U.S.: **$1,750.00**
Can.: **$1,750.00**
Ster.: £ 650.00

HN 1297
Columbine
Style One
Designer: L. Harradine
Height: 6", 15.2 cm
Colour: Pink and purple
Issued: 1928-1940
Varieties: HN 1296, 1439
U.S.: **$1,750.00**
Can.: **$1,750.00**
Ster.: £ 650.00

HN 1298
Sweet and Twenty
Style One
Designer: L. Harradine
Height: 5 3/4", 14.6 cm
Colour: Red and blue-green
Issued: 1928-1969
Varieties: HN 1360, 1437, 1438,
1549, 1563, 1649

U.S.: **$500.00**
Can.: **$500.00**
Ster.: **£325.00**

HN 1299
Susanna
Designer: L. Harradine
Height: 6", 15.2 cm
Colour: Black, red and blue
Issued: 1928-1936
Varieties: HN 1233, 1288

U.S.: **$2,750.00**
Can.: **$2,750.00**
Ster.: **£1,200.00**

HN 1300
Carmen
Style One
Designer: L. Harradine
Height: 7", 17.8 cm
Colour: Pale blue-lavender
Issued: 1928-1938
Varieties: HN 1267

U.S.: **$3,500.00**
Can.: **$2,750.00**
Ster.: **£1,250.00**

HN 1301
Young Mother with Child
Designer: Unknown
Height: 14 1/2", 37.0 cm
Colour: Green and red
Issued: 1928-1938

U.S.: **Only**
Can.: **one**
Ster.: **known**

HN 1302
The Gleaner
Designer: Unknown
Height: 14 1/2", 36.2 cm
Colour: Red and cream
Issued: 1928-1936

U.S.: **Only**
Can.: **one**
Ster.: **known**

HN 1303
Angela
Style One
Designer: L. Harradine
Height: 7 1/4", 18.4 cm
Colour: Blue
Issued: 1928-1940
Varieties: HN 1204; also
called "Fanny"

U.S.: **$4,000.00**
Can.: **$4,000.00**
Ster.: **£1,500.00**

HN 1304
Harlequinade Masked
Designer: L. Harradine
Height: 6 1/2", 16.5 cm
Colour: Mottled blue
Issued: 1928-1938
Varieties: HN 768, 769, 1274

U.S.: **$4,500.00**
Can.: **$4,500.00**
Ster.: **£2,000.00**

HN 1305
Siesta
Designer: L. Harradine
Height: 4 3/4", 12.0 cm
Colour: Red
Issued: 1928-1940

U.S.: **$4,500.00**
Can.: **$4,500.00**
Ster.: **£2,000.00**

HN 1306
Midinette
Style One
Designer: L. Harradine
Height: 9", 22.9 cm
Colour: Red and green
Issued: 1928-1938
Varieties: HN 1289

U.S.: **$5,000.00**
Can.: **$5,000.00**
Ster.: **£2,000.00**

HN 1307
An Irishman
Designer: H. Fenton
Height: 6 3/4", 17.2 cm
Colour: Green coat with
brown striped trousers
Issued: 1928-1938

U.S.: **$5,500.00**
Can.: **$5,000.00**
Ster.: **£2,000.00**

HN 1308
The Moor
Designer: C.J. Noke
Height: 16 1/2", 41.9 cm
Colour: Blue and mottled red
Issued: 1929-1938
Varieties: HN 1366, 1425, 1657,
2082, 3642; Also
called "An Arab"
HN 33, 343, 378

U.S.: **$4,000.00**
Can.: **$3,500.00**
Ster.: **£1,500.00**

HN 1309
Spanish Lady
Designer: L. Harradine
Height: 8 1/4", 21.0 cm
Colour: Black and
multi-coloured
Issued: 1929-1940
Varieties: HN 1262, 1290,
1293, 1294

U.S.: **$1,800.00**
Can.: **$1,800.00**
Ster.: **£ 850.00**

HN 1310
A Geisha
Style Two
Designer: C.J. Noke
Height: 6 3/4", 17.2 cm
Colour: Green
Issued: 1929-1938
Varieties: HN 1223, 1234, 1292

U.S.: **$1,750.00**
Can.: **$1,750.00**
Ster.: **£ 650.00**

Photograph
Not
Available

HN 1311
Cassim
Style Two
Designer: L. Harradine
Height: 3 3/4", 9.5 cm
Colour: Unknown
Issued: 1929-1938
Varieties: HN 1312

U.S.: **$1,750.00**
Can.: **$1,750.00**
Ster.: **£ 750.00**

Photograph
Not
Available

HN 1312
Cassim
Style Two
Designer: L. Harradine
Height: 3 3/4", 9.5 cm
Colour: Unknown
Issued: 1929-1938
Varieties: HN 1311

U.S.: **$1,750.00**
Can.: **$1,750.00**
Ster.: **£ 750.00**

HN 1313
Sonny
Designer: L. Harradine
Height: 3 1/2", 8.9 cm
Colour: Pink
Issued: 1929-1938
Varieties: HN 1314

U.S.: **$2,200.00**
Can.: **$2,200.00**
Ster.: **£ 650.00**

HN 1314
Sonny
Designer: L. Harradine
Height: 3 1/2", 8.9 cm
Colour: Blue
Issued: 1929-1938
Varieties: HN 1313

U.S.: $1,600.00
Can.: $1,500.00
Ster.: £ 650.00

HN 1315
Old Balloon Seller
Style One
Designer: L. Harradine
Height: 7 1/2", 19.1 cm
Colour: Green, purple
and white
Issued: 1929 to the
present

U.S.: $306.25
Can.: $495.00
Ster.: £139.00

Earthenware and china

Photograph
Not
Available

HN 1316
Toys
Designer: L. Harradine
Height: Unknown
Colour: Green, red
and yellow
Issued: 1929-1938

U.S.: **Extremely rare**
Can.:
Ster.:

HN 1317
The Snake Charmer
Designer: Unknown
Height: 4", 10.1 cm
Colour: Green and black
Issued: 1929-1938

U.S.: $3,000.00
Can.: $3,000.00
Ster.: £1,250.00

HN 1318
Sweet Anne
Style One
Designer: L. Harradine
Height: 7 1/2", 19.1 cm
Colour: Blue and green
Issued: 1929-1949
Varieties: HN 1330, 1331, 1453,
1496, 1631, 1701

U.S.: $425.00
Can.: $475.00
Ster.: £200.00

HN 1319
Darling
Style One
Designer: C. Vyse
Height: 7 1/2", 19.1 cm
Colour: White, black base
Issued: 1929-1959
Varieties: HN 1, 1371, 1372

U.S.: $275.00
Can.: $375.00
Ster.: £150.00

HN 1320
Rosamund
Style One
Designer: L. Harradine
Height: 7 1/4", 18.4 cm
Colour: Lavender
Issued: 1929-1937

U.S.: $2,750.00
Can.: $2,750.00
Ster.: £1,200.00

HN 1321
A Geisha
Style One
Designer: H. Tittensor
Height: 10 3/4", 27.3 cm
Colour: Green
Issued: 1929-1936
Varieties: HN 354, 376, 376A,
387, 634, 741, 779,
1322; also called
"Japanese Lady"

U.S.: **Extremely rare**
Can.:
Ster.:

HN 1322
A Geisha
Designer: H. Tittensor
Height: 10 3/4", 27.3 cm
Colour: Pink and blue
Issued: 1929-1936
Varieties: HN 354, 376, 376A
387, 634, 741, 779,
1321; Also called
"Japanese Lady"

U.S.: **Extremely rare**
Can.:
Ster.:

HN 1323
Contentment
Designer: L. Harradine
Height: 7 1/4", 18.4 cm
Colour: Red and blue
Issued: 1929-1938
Varieties: HN 395, 396, 421,
468, 572, 685, 686

U.S.: **$2,100.00**
Can.: **$2,000.00**
Ster.: **£ 950.00**

HN 1324
Fairy
Style One
Designer: L. Harradine
Height: 6 1/2", 16.5 cm
Colour: Multi-coloured
Issued: 1929-1938

U.S.: **$2,250.00**
Can.: **$2,250.00**
Ster.: **£ 950.00**

HN 1325
The Orange Seller
Designer: L. Harradine
Height: 7", 17.8 cm
Colour: Green and
lavender
Issued: 1929-1940

U.S.: **$1,750.00**
Can.: **$1,750.00**
Ster.: **£ 750.00**

HN 1326
The Swimmer
Designer: L. Harradine
Height: 7 1/2", 19.1 cm
Colour: Pink and purple
Issued: 1929-1938
Varieties: HN 1270, 1329

U.S.: **$3,500.00**
Can.: **$3,500.00**
Ster.: **£1,750.00**

HN 1327
Bo-Peep
Style One
Designer: L. Harradine
Height: 6 3/4", 17.2 cm
Colour: Multi-coloured
Issued: 1929-1936
Varieties: HN 777, 1202, 1328

U.S.: **$3,500.00**
Can.: **$3,500.00**
Ster.: **£1,500.00**

HN 1328
Bo-Peep
Style One
Designer: L. Harradine
Height: 6 3/4", 17.2 cm
Colour: Purple and cream
Issued: 1929-1936
Varieties: HN 777, 1202, 1327

U.S.: **$3,500.00**
Can.: **$3,500.00**
Ster.: **£1,500.00**

HN 1329
The Swimmer
Designer: L. Harradine
Height: 7 1/2", 19.1 cm
Colour: Pink
Issued: 1929-1938
Varieties: HN 1270, 1326

U.S.: **$3,750.00**
Can.: **$3,750.00**
Ster.: **£1,750.00**

HN 1330
Sweet Anne
Style One
Designer: L. Harradine
Height: 7 1/4", 18.4 cm
Colour: Blue, pink-yellow
Issued: 1929-1949
Varieties: HN 1318, 1331,
1453, 1496,
1631, 1701

U.S.:	$550.00
Can.:	$675.00
Ster.:	£250.00

HN 1331
Sweet Anne
Style One
Designer: L. Harradine
Height: 7 1/4", 18.4 cm
Colour: Red, blue-yellow
Issued: 1929-1949
Varieties: HN 1318, 1330,
1453, 1496,
1631, 1701

U.S.:	$550.00
Can.:	$675.00
Ster.:	£250.00

HN 1332
Lady Jester
Style One
Designer: L. Harradine
Height: 7", 17.8 cm
Colour: Red, blue and black
Issued: 1929-1938
Varieties: HN 1221, 1222

U.S.:	$3,750.00
Can.:	$3,750.00
Ster.:	£1,750.00

HN 1333
A Jester
Style Two
Designer: C.J. Noke
Height: 10 1/4", 26.0 cm
Colour: Blue, yellow
and black
Issued: 1929-1949
Varieties: HN 45A, 45B,
55, 308, 630

U.S.:	$6,500.00
Can.:	$6,500.00
Ster.:	£1,750.00

HN 1334
Tulips
Designer: Unknown
Height: 9 1/2", 24.1 cm
Colour: Lavender and pink
Issued: 1929-1936
Varieties: HN 466, 488,
672, 747

U.S.:	$3,250.00
Can.:	$3,250.00
Ster.:	£1,350.00

HN 1335
Folly
Designer: L. Harradine
Height: 9", 22.9 cm
Colour: Lavender with orange
and yellow balloons
Issued: 1929-1938
Varieties: HN 1750

U.S.:	$3,500.00
Can.:	$4,000.00
Ster.:	£2,000.00

China

HN 1336
One of the Forty
Style Eleven
Designer: H. Tittensor
Height: Unknown
Colour: Red, orange and blue
Issued: 1929-1938
Varieties: HN 481, 483, 491,
646, 667, 712, 1350;
Also known in flambé

U.S.:	$3,000.00
Can.:	$3,000.00
Ster.:	£1,250.00

HN 1337
Priscilla
Style One
Designer: L. Harradine
Height: 8", 20.3 cm
Colour: Lavender and yellow
Issued: 1929-1938
Varieties: HN 1340, 1495,
1501, 1559

U.S.:	$1,100.00
Can.:	$1,250.00
Ster.:	£ 450.00

HN 1338
The Courtier
Designer: L. Harradine
Height: 4 1/2", 11.4 cm
Colour: Red and white
Issued: 1929-1938

U.S.:   **$4,500.00**
Can.:   **$4,500.00**
Ster.:   **£1,800.00**

HN 1339
Covent Garden
Style One
Designer: L. Harradine
Height: 9", 22.9 cm
Colour: Green and lavender
Issued: 1929-1938

U.S.:   **$2,750.00**
Can.:   **$2,750.00**
Ster.:   **£1,250.00**

HN 1340
Priscilla
Style One
Designer: L. Harradine
Height: 8", 20.3 cm
Colour: red and purple
Issued: 1929-1949
Varieties: HN 1337, 1495,
             1501, 1559

U.S.:   **$550.00**
Can.:   **$675.00**
Ster.:   **£300.00**

HN 1341
Marietta
Desgner: L. Harradine
Height: 8", 20.3 cm
Colour: Red and black
Issued: 1929-1940
Varieties: HN 1446, 1699

U.S.:   **$1,800.00**
Can.:   **$1,800.00**
Ster.:   **£ 750.00**

HN 1342
The Flower Seller's
Children
Designer: L. Harradine
Height: 8", 20.3 cm
Colour: Purple, red
             and yellow
Issued: 929-1993
Varieties: HN 525, 551,
             1206, 1406

U.S.:   **$800.00**
Can.:   **$950.00**
Ster.:   **£350.00**

HN 1343
Dulcinea
Designer: L. Harradine
Height: 5 1/2", 14.0 cm
Colour: Red, black, green
             and blue
Issued: 1929-1936
Varieties: HN 1419

U.S.:   **$3,500.00**
Can.:   **$3,500.00**
Ster.:   **£1,500.00**

HN 1344
Sunshine Girl
Designer: L. Harradine
Height: 5", 12.7 cm
Colour: Green, black and red
Issued: 1929-1938
Varieties: HN 1348

U.S.:   **$5,000.00**
Can.:   **$5,000.00**
Ster.:   **£2,500.00**

HN 1345
A Victorian Lady
Style One
Designer: L. Harradine
Height: 7 3/4", 19.7 cm
Colour: Green and purple
Issued: 1929-1949
Varieties: HN 726, 727, 728, 736,
             739, 740, 742, 745,
             1208, 1258, 1276,
             1277, 1452, 1529

U.S.:   **$1,000.00**
Can.:   **$1,100.00**
Ster.:   **£ 425.00**

HN 1346
Iona
Designer: L. Harradine
Height: 7 1/2", 19.1 cm
Colour: Green, black
and lavender
Issued: 1929-1938
U.S.: **$5,000.00**
Can.: **$5,000.00**
Ster.: **£2,250.00**

HN 1347
Moira
Designer: L. Harradine
Height: 6 1/2", 16.5 cm
Colour: Lavender, pink
and green
Issued: 1929-1938
U.S.: **$5,000.00**
Can.: **$5,000.00**
Ster.: **£2,250.00**

HN 1348
Sunshine Girl
Designer: L. Harradine
Height: 5", 12.7 cm
Colour: Black and orange
Issued: 1929-1937
Varieties: HN 1344
U.S.: **$5,000.00**
Can.: **$5,000.00**
Ster.: **£2,500.00**

HN 1349
Scotties
Designer: L. Harradine
Height: 5 1/4", 13.3 cm
Colour: Blue
Issued: 1929-1936
Varieties: HN 1281
U.S.: **$5,500.00**
Can.: **$5,500.00**
Ster.: **£1,750.00**

HN 1350
One of the Forty
Style Eleven
Designer: H. Tittensor
Height: Unknown
Colour: Multi-coloured
Issued: 1929-1949
Varieties: HN 481, 483, 491,
646, 667, 712, 1336,
Also known in flambé
U.S.: **none**
Can.: **known**
Ster.: **to exist**

HN 1351
One of the Forty
Style One
Designer: H. Tittensor
Height: 8 1/4", 21.0 cm
Colour: Mottled red
and purple
Issued: 1929-1949
Varieties: HN 417, 490, 495,
501, 528, 648, 677,
1352
U.S.: **$3,500.00**
Can.: **$3,500.00**
Ster.: **£1,250.00**

HN 1352
One of the Forty
Style One
Designer: H. Tittensor
Height: 8 1/4", 21.0 cm
Colour: Multi-coloured
Issued: 1929-1949
Varieties: HN 417, 490, 495,
501, 528, 648, 677,
1351
U.S.: **$3,500.00**
Can.: **$3,500.00**
Ster.: **£1,250.00**

HN 1353
One of the Forty
Style Two
Designer: H. Tittensor
Height: 7 1/4", 18.4 cm
Colour: Orange and purple
Issued: 1929-1936
Varieties: HN 418, 494, 498,
647, 666, 704
U.S.: **$3,500.00**
Can.: **$3,500.00**
Ster.: **£1,250.00**

HN 1354
One of the Forty
Style Thirteen
Designer: H. Tittensor
Height: 7 3/4", 19.7 cm
Colour: Multi-coloured
Issued: 1929-1949
Varieties: HN 496, 500,
649, 665

U.S.: **$3,000.00**
Can.: **$3,000.00**
Ster.: **£1,250.00**

HN 1355
The Mendicant
Designer: L. Harradine
Height: 8 1/4", 21.0 cm
Colour: Brown
Issued: 1929-1938
Varieties: HN 1365 (Minor
glaze difference)

U.S.:
Can.: **Rare**
Ster.:

Earthenware

HN 1356
The Parson's Daughter
Designer: H. Tittensor
Height: 9 1/4", 23.5 cm
Colour: Multi-coloured
Issued: 1929-1938
Varieties: HN 337, 338, 441,
564, 790, 1242, 2018

U.S.: **$1,350.00**
Can.: **$1,500.00**
Ster.: **£ 650.00**

HN 1357
Kathleen
Style One
Designer: L. Harradine
Height: 7 1/2", 19.1 cm
Colour: Pink and lavender
Issued: 1929-1938
Varieties: HN 1252, 1253, 1275,
1279, 1291, 1512

U.S.: **$1,500.00**
Can.: **$1,600.00**
Ster.: **£ 600.00**

HN 1358
Rosina
Designer: L. Harradine
Height: 5 3/4", 14.6 cm
Colour: Red
Issued: 1929-1937
Varieties: HN 1364, 1556

U.S.: **$1,400.00**
Can.: **$1,600.00**
Ster.: **£ 650.00**

HN 1359
Two-A-Penny
Designer: L. Harradine
Height: 8 1/4", 21.0 cm
Colour: Red and green
Issued: 1929-1938

U.S.: **$5,500.00**
Can.: **$5,500.00**
Ster.: **£2,500.00**

Earthenware

HN 1360
Sweet and Twenty
Style One
Designer: L. Harradine
Height: 6", 15.2 cm
Colour: Blue and green
Issued: 1929-1938
Varieties: HN 1298, 1437, 1438,
1549, 1563, 1649

U.S.: **$1,000.00**
Can.: **$1,000.00**
Ster.: **£ 425.00**

NOTE ON PRICING

Prices are given for three separate and distinct market areas.

Prices are given in the currency of each of these different trading areas.

Prices are not exchange rate calculations but are based on supply and demand in that market.

Prices listed are guidelines to the most current retail values but actual selling prices may vary slightly.

Prices for current figurines are those suggested by Royal Doulton.

Extremely rare or unique figurines have inconsistent retail values and their prices must therefore be determined between buyer and seller.

Prices given are for figurines in mint condition.

138

HN 1361
Mask Seller
Designer: L. Harradine
Height: 8 1/2", 21.6 cm
Colour: Black, white
                 and red
Issued: 1929-1938
Varieties: HN 2103

U.S.:	$2,500.00
Can.:	$2,250.00
Ster.:	£ 950.00

HN 1362
Pantalettes
Style Two
Designer: L. Harradine
Height: 7 3/4", 19.7 cm
Colour: Green and blue
Issued: 1929-1942
Varieties: HN 1412, 1507, 1709

U.S.:	$750.00
Can.:	$950.00
Ster.:	£400.00

HN 1363
Doreen
Designer: L. Harradine
Height: 5 1/4", 13.3 cm
Colour: Red
Issued: 1929-1940
Varieties: HN 1389, 1390

U.S.:	$1,750.00
Can.:	$1,750.00
Ster.:	£ 600.00

HN 1364
Rosina
Designer: L. Harradine
Height: 5 1/4", 13.3 cm
Colour: Purple and red
Issued: 1929-1937
Varieties: HN 1358, 1556

U.S.:	$1,750.00
Can.:	$1,750.00
Ster.:	£ 650.00

HN 1365
The Mendicant
Designer: L. Harradine
Height: 8 1/4", 21.0 cm
Colour: Brown
Issued: 1929-1969
Varieties: HN 1355 (Minor
                 glaze differences)

U.S.:	$350.00
Can.:	$475.00
Ster.:	£250.00

Earthenware

HN 1366
The Moor
Designer: C.J. Noke
Height: 16 1/2", 41.9 cm
Colour: Multi-coloured
Issued: 1930-1949
Varieties: HN 1308, 1425,
                 1657, 2082, 3642;
                 Also called "An Arab"
                 HN 33, 343, 378

U.S.:	$3,500.00
Can.:	$3,500.00
Ster.:	£1,500.00

Photograph
Not
Available

HN 1367
Kitty
Designer: Unknown
Height: 4", 10.1 cm
Colour: White, yellow
                 and purple
Issued: 1930-1938

U.S.:	**Extremely rare**
Can.:	
Ster.:	

HN 1368
Rose
Style One
Designer: L. Harradine
Height: 4 1/2", 11.4 cm
Colour: Pink
Issued: 1930-1995
Varieties: HN 1387, 1416,
                 1506, 1654, 2123

U.S.:	$100.00
Can.:	$150.00
Ster.:	£ 50.00

HN 1369
Boy on Pig
Designer: C.J. Noke
Height: 4", 10.1 cm
Colour: Green and brown
Issued: 1930-1938
Varieties: Also known in flambé

U.S.: **Extremely**
Can.: **Rare**
Ster.:

HN 1370
Marie
Style Two
Designer: L. Harradine
Height: 4 3/4", 12.0 cm
Colour: Purple
Issued: 1930-1988
Varieties: HN 1388, 1417, 1489,
1531, 1635, 1655

U.S.: **$150.00**
Can.: **$200.00**
Ster.: **£ 80.00**

HN 1371
Darling
Style One
Designer: C. Vyse
Height: 7 1/2", 19.1 cm
Colour: Green
Issued: 1930-1938
Varieties: HN 1, 1319, 1372

U.S.: **$1,700.00**
Can.: **$1,700.00**
Ster.: **£ 750.00**

HN 1372
Darling
Style One
Designer: C. Vyse
Height: 7 3/4", 19.7 cm
Colour: Pink, black base
Issued: 1930-1938
Varieties: HN 1, 1319, 1371

U.S.: **$1,700.00**
Can.: **$1,700.00**
Ster.: **£ 750.00**

HN 1373
Sweet Lavender
Designer: L. Harradine
Height: 9", 22.8 cm
Colour: Green, red and black
Issued: 1930-1949
Varieties: Also called "Any
Old Lavender"

U.S.: **$1,250.00**
Can.: **$1,250.00**
Ster.: **£ 575.00**

HN 1374
Fairy
Style Two
Designer: L. Harradine
Height: 4", 10.1 cm
Colour: Yellow flowers
Issued: 1930-1938
Varieties: HN 1380, 1532

U.S.: **$2,200.00**
Can.: **$2,500.00**
Ster.: **£1,250.00**

HN 1375
Fairy
Style Three
Designer: L. Harradine
Height: 3", 7.6 cm
Colour: Yellow flowers
Issued: 1930-1938
Varieties: HN 1395, 1533, 1536

U.S.: **$2,250.00**
Can.: **$2,250.00**
Ster.: **£ 900.00**

HN 1376
Fairy
Style Four
Designer: L. Harradine
Height: 2 1/2", 6.3 cm
Colour: Yellow flowers
Issued: 1930-1938
Varieties: HN 1536

U.S.: **$1,250.00**
Can.: **$1,250.00**
Ster.: **£ 650.00**

Earthenware

Photograph
Not
Available

HN 1377
Fairy
Style Five
Designer: L. Harradine
Height: 1 1/2", 3.8 cm
Colour: Lavender and yellow
Issued: 1930-1938
U.S.:   **$1,600.00**
Can.:   **$1,600.00**
Ster.:   £ 750.00

HN 1378
Fairy
Style Six
Designer: L. Harradine
Height: 2 1/2", 6.3 cm
Colour: Orange flowers
Issued: 1930-1938
Varieties: HN 1396, 1535
U.S.:   **$1,250.00**
Can.:   **$1,250.00**
Ster.:   £ 550.00

HN 1379
Fairy
Style Seven
Designer: L. Harradine
Height: 2 1/2", 6.3 cm
Colour: Blue flowers
Issued: 1930-1938
Varieties: HN 1394, 1534
U.S.:   **$1,250.00**
Can.:   **$1,250.00**
Ster.:   £ 600.00

HN 1380
Fairy
Style Two
Designer: L. Harradine
Height: 4", 10.1 cm
Colour: Multi-coloured
Issued: 1930-1938
Varieties: HN 1374, 1532
U.S.:   **$2,200.00**
Can.:   **$2,500.00**
Ster.:   £1.250.00

*

HN 1387
Rose
Style One
Designer: L. Harradine
Height: 4 1/2", 11.4 cm
Colour: Blue, pink and
             orange
Issued: 1930-1938
Varieties: HN 1368, 1416,
             1506, 1654, 2123
U.S.:   **$375.00**
Can.:   **$450.00**
Ster.:   £225.00

HN 1388
Marie
Style Two
Designer: L. Harradine
Height: 4 1/2", 11.4 cm
Colour: Pink
Issued: 1930-1938
Varieties: HN 1370, 1417,
             1489, 1531, 1635,
             1655
U.S.:   **$375.00**
Can.:   **$450.00**
Ster.:   £225.00

HN 1389
Doreen
Designer: L. Harradine
Height: 5 1/4", 13.3 cm
Colour: Green
Issued: 1930-1940
Varieties: HN 1363, 1390
U.S.:   **$1,750.00**
Can.:   **$1,750.00**
Ster.:   £ 600.00

HN 1390
Doreen
Designer: L. Harradine
Height: 5 3/4", 14.6 cm
Colour: Lavender
Issued: 1929-1940
Varieties: HN 1363, 1389
U.S.:   **$1,750.00**
Can.:   **$1,750.00**
Ster.:   £ 600.00

HN 1391
Pierrette
Style Three
Designer: L. Harradine
Height: 8 1/2", 21.6 cm
Colour: Red
Issued: 1930-1938
Varieties: HN 1749

U.S.: $3,000.00
Can.: $3,500.00
Ster.: £1,750.00

Earthenware

HN 1392
Paisley Shawl
Style One
Designer: L. Harradine
Height: 8 1/4", 21.0 cm
Colour: Red shawl, flowered
cream dress
Issued: 1930-1949
Varieties: HN 1460, 1707,
1739, 1987

U.S.: $600.00
Can.: $675.00
Ster.: £325.00

HN 1393
Fairy
Style Eight
Designer: L. Harradine
Height: 2 1/2", 6.3 cm
Colour: Yellow flowers
Issued: 1930-1938

U.S.: $1,250.00
Can.: $1,250.00
Ster.: £ 650.00

HN 1394
Fairy
Style Seven
Designer: L. Harradine
Height: 2 1/2", 6.3 cm
Colour: Yellow flowers
Issued: 1930-1938
Varieties: HN 1379, 1534

U.S.: $1,250.00
Can.: $1,250.00
Ster.: £ 750.00

HN 1395
Fairy
Style Three
Designer: L. Harradine
Height: 3", 7.6 cm
Colour: Blue flowers
Issued: 1930-1938
Varieties: HN 1375, 1533

U.S.: $2,250.00
Can.: $2,250.00
Ster.: £ 900.00

HN 1396
Fairy
Style Six
Designer: L. Harradine
Height: 2 1/2", 6.3 cm
Colour: Blue flowers
Issued: 1930-1938
Varieties: HN 1378, 1535

U.S.: $1,250.00
Can.: $1,250.00
Ster.: £ 550.00

HN 1397
Gretchen
Designer: L. Harradine
Height: 7 3/4", 19.7 cm
Colour: Blue and white
Issued: 1930-1940
Varieties: HN 1562

U.S.: $1,200.00
Can.: $1,350.00
Ster.: £ 550.00

HN 1398
Derrick
Designer: L. Harradine
Height: 8", 20.3 cm
Colour: Blue and white
Issued: 1930-1940

U.S.: $1,200.00
Can.: $1,350.00
Ster.: £ 550.00

HN 1399
The Young Widow
Designer: L. Harradine
Height: 8", 20.3 cm
Colour: Purple
Issued: 1930-1930
Varieties: Also called "Little
Mother" Style Two;
HN 1418, 1641

U.S.: $5,500.00
Can.: $5,500.00
Ster.: £1,700.00

HN 1400
The Windmill Lady
Designer: L. Harradine
Height: 8 1/2", 21.6 cm
Colour: Green, yellow
and orange
Issued: 1930-1937

U.S.: $7,000.00
Can.: $7,000.00
Ster.: £1,600.00

HN 1401
Chorus Girl
Designer: L. Harradine
Height: 8 1/2", 21.6 cm
Colour: Red and orange
Issued: 1930-1936

U.S.: $3,250.00
Can.: $3,250.00
Ster.: £1,500.00

HN 1402
Miss Demure
Designer: L. Harradine
Height: 7 1/2", 19.1 cm
Colour: Lavender and pink
Issued: 1930-1975
Varieties: HN 1440, 1463,
1499, 1560

U.S.: $325.00
Can.: $425.00
Ster.: £200.00

*

HN 1404
Betty
Style Two
Designer: L. Harradine
Height: 4 1/2", 11.4 cm
Colour: Lavender
Issued: 1930-1936
Varieties: HN 1405, 1435, 1436

U.S.: $4,000.00
Can.: $4,000.00
Ster.: £1,500.00

HN 1405
Betty
Style Two
Designer: L. Harradine
Height: 4 1/2", 11.4 cm
Colour: Green
Issued: 1930-1936
Varieties: HN 1404, 1435, 1436

U.S.: $4,000.00
Can.: $4,000.00
Ster.: £1,500.00

HN 1406
The Flower Seller's
Children
Designer: L. Harradine
Height: 8 1/4", 21.0 cm
Colour: Yellow and blue
Issued: 1930-1938
Varieties: HN 525, 551,
1206, 1342

U.S.: $2,500.00
Can.: $2,500.00
Ster.: £ 800.00

HN 1407
The Winner
Designer: Unknown
Height: 6 3/4", 17.2 cm
Colour: Red, blue and grey
Issued: 1930-1938

U.S.: Very
Can.: rare
Ster.:

HN 1408
John Peel
Designer: Unknown
Height: 9 1/2", 24.1 cm
Colour: Red and brown
Issued: 1930-1937
Varieties: Also called
"The Huntsman"
Style Two HN 1815

U.S.: $5,500.00
Can.: $5,500.00
Ster.: £2,500.00

HN 1409
Hunting Squire
Designer: Unknown
Height: 9 3/4", 24.7 cm
Colour: Red and grey
Issued: 1930-1938
Varieties: Also called "The
Squire" HN 1814

U.S.: $5,500.00
Can.: $5,500.00
Ster.: £2,500.00

HN 1410
Abdullah
Designer: L. Harradine
Height: 5 3/4", 14.6 cm
Colour: Blue, lavender
and green
Issued: 1930-1937
Varieties: HN 2104

U.S.: $2,000.00
Can.: $2,000.00
Ster.: £ 850.00

HN 1411
Charley's Aunt
Style Two
Designer: H. Fenton
Height: 8", 20.3 cm
Colour: Black
Issued: 1930-1938
Varieties: HN 1554

U.S.: $2,000.00
Can.: $2,000.00
Ster.: £ 950.00

HN 1412
Pantalettes
Style One
Designer: L. Harradine
Height: 7 3/4", 19.7 cm
Colour: Blue and pink
Issued: 1930-1949
Varieties: HN 1362, 1507, 1709

U.S.: $950.00
Can.: $950.00
Ster.: £400.00

HN 1413
Margery
Designer: L. Harradine
Height: 11", 27.9 cm
Colour: Maroon and purple
Issued: 1930-1949

U.S.: $1,000.00
Can.: $ 900.00
Ster.: £ 400.00

Earthenware

HN 1414
Patricia
Style One
Designer: L. Harradine
Height: 8 1/2", 21.6 cm
Colour: Yellow and green
Issued: 1930-1949
Varieties: HN 1431, 1462, 1567

U.S.: $1,200.00
Can.: $1,200.00
Ster.: £ 450.00

HN 1416
Rose
Style One
Designer: L. Harradine
Height: 4 1/2", 11.4 cm
Colour: Lavender
Issued: 1930-1949
Varieties: HN 1368, 1387,
1506, 1654, 2123

U.S.: $400.00
Can.: $500.00
Ster.: £225.00

HN 1417
Marie
Style Two
Designer: L. Harradine
Height: 4 3/4", 12.0 cm
Colour: Rose-pink
Issued: 1930-1949
Varieties: HN 1370, 1388, 1489,
1531, 1635, 1655

  U.S.: **$400.00**
 Can.: **$500.00**
 Ster.: **£225.00**

HN 1418
The Little Mother
Style Two
Designer: L. Harradine
Height: 8", 20.3 cm
Colour: Purple
Issued: 1930-1938
Varieties: HN 1641; also called
"Young Widow"
HN 1399

  U.S.: **$4,500.00**
 Can.: **$4,500.00**
 Ster.: **£1,500.00**

HN 1419
Dulcinea
Designer: L. Harradine
Height: 5 1/2", 14.0 cm
Colour: Red
Issued: 1930-1938
Varieties: HN 1343

  U.S.: **$3,750.00**
 Can.: **$3,750.00**
 Ster.: **£1,750.00**

HN 1420
Phyllis
Style One
Designer: L. Harradine
Height: 9", 22.9 cm
Colour: Purple and green
Issued: 1930-1949
Varieties: HN 1430, 1486, 1698

  U.S.: **$1,200.00**
 Can.: **$1,200.00**
 Ster.: **£ 450.00**

HN 1421
Barbara
Style One
Designer: L. Harradine
Height: 7 3/4", 19.7 cm
Colour: Cream and lavender
Issued: 1930-1937
Varieties: HN 1432, 1461

  U.S.: **$1,700.00**
 Can.: **$1,700.00**
 Ster.: **£ 750.00**

HN 1422
Joan
Style One
Designer: L. Harradine
Height: 5 1/2", 14.0 cm
Colour: Blue
Issued: 1930-1949
Varieties: HN 2023 (minor
glaze difference)

  U.S.: **$450.00**
 Can.: **$600.00**
 Ster.: **£300.00**

HN 1423
Babette
Designer: L. Harradine
Height: 5", 12.7 cm
Colour: Yellow, green and red
Issued: 1930-1938
Varieties: HN 1424

  U.S.: **$1,750.00**
 Can.: **$1,750.00**
 Ster.: **£ 650.00**

HN 1424
Babette
Designer: L. Harradine
Height: 5", 12.7 cm
Colour: Blue
Issued: 1930-1938
Varieties: HN 1423

  U.S.: **$1,500.00**
 Can.: **$1,500.00**
 Ster.: **£ 650.00**

HN 1425
The Moor
Designer: C.J. Noke
Height: 16 1/2", 41.9 cm
Colour: Multi-coloured
Issued: 1930-1949
Varieties: HN 1308, 1366,
1657, 2082, 3642;
Also called "An Arab"
HN 33, 343, 378
U.S.: **$4,000.00**
Can.: **$3,500.00**
Ster.: **£1,500.00**

HN 1426
The Gossips
Designer: L. Harradine
Height: 5 3/4", 14.6 cm
Colour: Turquoise and pink
Issued: 1930-1949
Varieties: HN 1429, 2025
U.S.: **$2,000.00**
Can.: **$2,000.00**
Ster.: **£ 800.00**

HN 1427
Darby
Designer: L. Harradine
Height: 5 1/2", 14.0 cm
Colour: Pink and blue
Issued: 1930-1949
Varieties: HN 2024 (minor
glaze difference)
U.S.: **$450.00**
Can.: **$600.00**
Ster.: **£295.00**

HN 1428
Calumet
Designer: C.J. Noke
Height: 6", 15.2 cm
Colour: Brown, blue
and yellow
Issued: 1930-1949
Varieties: HN 1689, 2068
U.S.: **$1,500.00**
Can.: **$1,500.00**
Ster.: **£ 650.00**

HN 1429
The Gossips
Designer: L. Harradine
Height: 5 3/4", 14.6 cm
Colour: Red and cream
Issued: 1930-1949
Varieties: HN 1426, 2025
U.S.: **$1,300.00**
Can.: **$1,300.00**
Ster.: **£ 600.00**

HN 1430
Phyllis
Style One
Designer: L. Harradine
Height: 9", 22.9 cm
Colour: Blue and pink
Issued: 1930-1938
Varieties: HN 1420, 1486, 1698
U.S.: **$2,000.00**
Can.: **$2,000.00**
Ster.: **£ 700.00**

HN 1431
Patricia
Style One
Designer: L. Harradine
Height: 8 1/2", 21.6 cm
Colour: Lavender
Issued: 1930-1949
Varieties: HN 1414, 1462, 1567
U.S.: **$1,250.00**
Can.: **$1,250.00**
Ster.: **£ 500.00**

HN 1432
Barbara
Style One
Designer: L. Harradine
Height: 7 3/4", 19.7 cm
Colour: Lavender
Issued: 1930-1937
Varieties: HN 1421, 1461
U.S.: **$1,650.00**
Can.: **$1,650.00**
Ster.: **£ 800.00**

HN 1433
The Little Bridesmaid
Style One
Designer: L. Harradine
Height: 5 1/4", 13.3 cm
Colour: Lavender and pink
Issued: 1930-1951
Varieties: HN 1434, 1530

U.S.:	$275.00
Can.:	$350.00
Ster.:	£150.00

HN 1434
The Little Bridesmaid
Style One
Designer: L. Harradine
Height: 5", 12.7 cm
Colour: Yellow-green
Issued: 1930-1949
Varieties: HN 1433, 1530

U.S.:	$475.00
Can.:	$500.00
Ster.:	£225.00

HN 1435
Betty
Style Two
Designer: L. Harradine
Height: 4 1/2", 11.4 cm
Colour: Multi-coloured
Issued: 1930-1936
Varieties: HN 1404, 1405, 1436

U.S.:	$3,800.00
Can.:	$3,800.00
Ster.:	£1,500.00

HN 1436
Betty
Style Two
Designer: L. Harradine
Height: 4 1/2", 11.4 cm
Colour: Green
Issued: 1930-1936
Varieties: HN 1404, 1405, 1435

U.S.:	$3,800.00
Can.:	$3,800.00
Ster.:	£1,500.00

HN 1437
Sweet and Twenty
Style One
Designer: L. Harradine
Height: 6", 15.2 cm
Colour: Red
Issued: 1930-1938
Varieties: HN 1298, 1360, 1438, 1549, 1563, 1649

U.S.:	$1,400.00
Can.:	$1,400.00
Ster.:	£ 500.00

HN 1438
Sweet and Twenty
Style One
Designer: L. Harradine
Height: 6", 15.2 cm
Colour: Multi-coloured
Issued: 1930-1938
Varieties: HN 1298, 1360, 1437, 1549, 1563, 1649

U.S.:	$1,400.00
Can.:	$1,400.00
Ster.:	£ 500.00

HN 1439
Columbine
Style One
Designer: L. Harradine
Height: 6", 15.2 cm
Colour: Mottled lavender and cream
Issued: 1930-1940
Varieties: HN 1296, 1297

U.S.:	$1,750.00
Can.:	$1,750.00
Ster.:	£ 775.00

HN 1440
Miss Demure
Designer: L. Harradine
Height: 7", 17.8 cm
Colour: Blue
Issued: 1930-1949
Varieties: HN 1402, 1463, 1499, 1560

U.S.:	$1,000.00
Can.:	$1,000.00
Ster.:	£ 425.00

HN 1441
Child Study
Style One
Designer: L. Harradine
Height: 5", 12.7 cm
Colour: Cream, green flowered base
Issued: 1931-1938
Varieties: HN 603A, 603B

U.S.: $1,000.00
Can.: $ 850.00
Ster.: £ 300.00

HN 1442
Child Study
Style Two
Designer: L. Harradine
Height: 6 1/4", 15.9 cm
Colour: Cream, green flowered base
Issued: 1931-1938
Varieties: HN 604A, 604B, 1443

U.S.: $1,000.00
Can.: $ 850.00
Ster.: £ 300.00

HN 1443
Child Study
Style Two
Designer: L. Harradine
Height: 5", 12.7 cm
Colour: Cream, green flowered base
Issued: 1931-1938
Varieties: HN 604A, 604B, 1442

U.S.: $1,000.00
Can.: $ 850.00
Ster.: £ 300.00

HN 1444
Pauline
Style One
Designer: L. Harradine
Height: 6", 15.2 cm
Colour: Blue
Issued: 1931-1940

U.S.: $650.00
Can.: $750.00
Ster.: £350.00

HN 1445
Biddy
Designer: L. Harradine
Height: 5 1/2", 14.0 cm
Colour: Yellow-green
Issued: 1931-1937
Varieties: HN 1500, 1513

U.S.: $450.00
Can.: $500.00
Ster.: £325.00

HN 1446
Marietta
Designer: L. Harradine
Height: 8", 20.3 cm
Colour: Green and lavender
Issued: 1931-1940
Varieties: HN 1341, 1699

U.S.: $2,200.00
Can.: $2,200.00
Ster.: £ 750.00

HN 1447
Marigold
Designer: L. Harradine
Height: 6", 15.2 cm
Colour: Lavender
Issued: 1931-1949
Varieties: HN 1451, 1555

U.S.: $675.00
Can.: $750.00
Ster.: £375.00

HN 1448
Rita
Designer: L. Harradine
Height: 7", 17.8 cm
Colour: Red dress with green shawl
Issued: 1931-1938
Varieties: HN 1450

U.S.: $1,650.00
Can.: $1,650.00
Ster.: £ 750.00

HN 1449
The Little Mistress
Designer: L. Harradine
Height: 5 3/4", 14.6 cm
Colour: Green and blue
Issued: 1931-1949
U.S.: $800.00
Can.: $900.00
Ster.: £350.00

HN 1450
Rita
Designer: L. Harradine
Height: 7", 17.8 cm
Colour: Blue dress
with red shawl
Issued: 1931-1938
Varieties: HN 1448
U.S.: $1,650.00
Can.: $1,650.00
Ster.: £ 750.00

HN 1451
Marigold
Designer: L. Harradine
Height: 6", 15.2 cm
Colour: Yellow
Issued: 1931-1938
Varieties: HN 1447, 1555
U.S.: $1,000.00
Can.: $1,000.00
Ster.: £ 475.00

HN 1452
A Victorian Lady
Style one
Designer: L. Harradine
Height: 7 3/4", 19.7 cm
Colour: Green
Issued: 1931-1949
Varieties: HN 726, 727, 728, 736,
739, 740, 742, 745,
1208, 1258, 1276,
1277, 1345, 1529
U.S.: $1,000.00
Can.: $1,000.00
Ster.: £ 325.00

HN 1453
Sweet Anne
Style One
Designer: L. Harradine
Height: 7", 17.8 cm
Colour: Green
Issued: 1931-1949
Varieties: HN 1318, 1330, 1331,
1496, 1631, 1701
U.S.: $1,100.00
Can.: $1,100.00
Ster.: £ 300.00

HN 1454
Negligée
Designer: L. Harradine
Height: 5", 12.7 cm
Colour: Pink
Issued: 1931-1936
Varieties: HN 1219, 1228,
1272, 1273
U.S.: $2,500.00
Can.: $2,500.00
Ster.: £ 950.00

HN 1455
Molly Malone
Designer: L. Harradine
Height: 7", 17.8 cm
Colour: Red and brown
Issued: 1931-1937
U.S.: $4,600.00
Can.: $4,600.00
Ster.: £1,750.00

HN 1456
The Butterfly Woman
Designer: L. Harradine
Height: 6 1/2", 16.5 cm
Colour: Lavender and green
Issued: 1931-1940
Varieties: Also called "Butterfly,"
HN 719, 720, 730,
1203
U.S.: $3,600.00
Can.: $3,500.00
Ster.: £1,500.00

HN 1457
All-A-Blooming
Designer: L. Harradine
Height: 6 1/2", 16.5 cm
Colour: Blue
Issued: 1931-1938
Varieties: HN 1466

U.S.: $2,750.00
Can.: $2,750.00
Ster.: £1,250.00

HN 1458
Monica
Style One
Designer: L. Harradine
Height: 4", 10.1 cm
Colour: Flowered cream dress
Issued: 1931-1949
Varieties: HN 1459, 1467, 3617

U.S.: $650.00
Can.: $650.00
Ster.: £300.00

HN 1459
Monica
Style One
Designer: L. Harradine
Height: 4", 10.1 cm
Colour: Lavender
Issued: 1931-1949
Varieties: HN 1458, 1467, 3617

U.S.: $750.00
Can.: $750.00
Ster.: £300.00

HN 1460
Paisley Shawl
Style One
Designer: L. Harradine
Height: 8 1/4", 21.0 cm
Colour: Green
Issued: 1931-1949
Varieties: HN 1392, 1707, 1739, 1987

U.S.: $ 950.00
Can.: $ 1,100.00
Ster.: £ 400.00

HN 1461
Barbara
Style One
Designer: L. Harradine
Height: 7 3/4", 19.7 cm
Colour: Green
Issued: 1931-1937
Varieties: HN 1421, 1432

U.S.: $2,000.00
Can.: $2,000.00
Ster.: £ 750.00

HN 1462
Patricia
Style One
Designer: L. Harradine
Height: 8", 20.3 cm
Colour: Green
Issued: 1931-1938
Varieties: HN 1414, 1431, 1567

U.S.: $1,400.00
Can.: $1,400.00
Ster.: £ 450.00

Earthenware

HN 1463
Miss Demure
Designer: L. Harradine
Height: 7", 17.8 cm
Colour: Green
Issued: 1931-1949
Varieties: HN 1402, 1440, 1499, 1560

U.S.: $1,000.00
Can.: $1,000.00
Ster.: £ 425.00

HN 1464
The Carpet Seller
(Hand Open)
Style One
Designer: L. Harradine
Height: 9 1/4", 23.5 cm
Colour: Green and orange
Issued: 1929-Unknown
Varieties: HN 1464A (Hand closed)

U.S.: $1,200.00
Can.: $1,000.00
Ster.: £ 450.00

Earthenware

HN 1464A
The Carpet Seller
(Hand Closed)
Style Two
Designer: L. Harradine
Height: 9", 22.9 cm
Colour: Green and orange
Issued: Unknown-1969
Varieties: HN 1464
               (Hand open)

U.S.:	**$350.00**
Can.:	**$450.00**
Ster.:	**£250.00**

Porcelain

HN 1465
Lady Clare
Designer: L. Harradine
Height: 7 3/4", 19.7 cm
Colour: Red
Issued: 1931-1937

U.S.:	**$1,400.00**
Can.:	**$1,400.00**
Ster.:	**£ 475.00**

HN 1466
All-A-Blooming
Designer: L. Harradine
Height: 6 1/2", 16.5 cm
Colour: Purple, green
               and red
Issued: 1931-1938
Varieties: HN 1457

U.S.:	**$2,750.00**
Can.:	**$2,750.00**
Ster.:	**£1,100.00**

HN 1467
Monica
Style One
Designer: L. Harradine
Height: 4", 10.1 cm
Colour: Flowered
               purple dress
Issued: 1931-1995
Varieties: HN 1458, 1459,
               3617

U.S.:	**$175.00**
Can.:	**$225.00**
Ster.:	**£ 75.00**

HN 1468
Pamela
Style One
Designer: L. Harradine
Height: 7 1/2", 19.1 cm
Colour: Blue
Issued: 1931-1937
Varieties: HN 1469, 1564

U.S.:	**$1,750.00**
Can.:	**$1,750.00**
Ster.:	**£ 850.00**

HN 1469
Pamela
Style One
Designer: L. Harradine
Height: 7 1/2", 19.1 cm
Colour: Yellow
Issued: 1931-1937
Varieties: HN 1468, 1564

U.S.:	**$1,750.00**
Can.:	**$1,750.00**
Ster.:	**£ 750.00**

HN 1470
Chloe
Style One
Designer: L. Harradine
Height: 5 1/2", 14.0 cm
Colour: Yellow and purple
Issued: 1931-1949
Varieties: HN 1476, 1479,
               1498, 1765, 1956

U.S.:	**$750.00**
Can.:	**$800.00**
Ster.:	**£375.00**

HN 1471
Annette
Style One
Designer: L. Harradine
Height: 6 1/4", 15.9 cm
Colour: Blue and white
Issued: 1931-1938
Varieties: HN 1472, 1550

U.S.:	**$750.00**
Can.:	**$800.00**
Ster.:	**£400.00**

HN 1472
Annette
Style One
Designer: L. Harradine
Height: 6", 15.2 cm
Colour: Green
Issued: 1931-1949
Varieties: HN 1471, 1550

U.S.: **$750.00**
Can.: **$800.00**
Ster.: **£400.00**

HN 1473
Dreamland
Designer: L. Harradine
Height: 4 3/4", 12.0 cm
Colour: Lavender
Issued: 1931-1937
Varieties: HN 1481

U.S.: **$5,500.00**
Can.: **$5,500.00**
Ster.: **£2,500.00**

HN 1474
In the Stocks
Style One
Designer: L. Harradine
Height: 5", 12.7 cm
Colour: Red and brown
Issued: 1931-1938
Varieties: HN 1475; also
called "Love in
the Stocks" and
"Love Locked In"

U.S.: **$3,250.00**
Can.: **$3,250.00**
Ster.: **£1,500.00**

HN 1475
In the Stocks
Style One
Designer: L. Harradine
Height: 5 1/4", 13.3 cm
Colour: Green
Issued: 1931-1937
Varieties: HN 1474; also
called "Love in
the Stocks" and
"Love Locked In"

U.S.: **$3,250.00**
Can.: **$3,250.00**
Ster.: **£1,500.00**

HN 1476
Chloe
Style One
Designer: L. Harradine
Height: 5 1/2", 14.0 cm
Colour: Blue
Issued: 1931-1938
Varieties: HN 1470, 1479,
1498, 1765, 1956

U.S.: **$575.00**
Can.: **$675.00**
Ster.: **£400.00**

*

HN 1478
Sylvia
Designer: L. Harradine
Height: 10 1/2", 26.7 cm
Colour: Orange and blue
Issued: 1931-1938

U.S.: **$1,200.00**
Can.: **$1,000.00**
Ster.: **£ 400.00**

Earthenware

HN 1479
Chloe
Style One
Designer: L. Harradine
Height: 5 1/2", 14.0 cm
Colour: Lavender
Issued: 1931-1949
Varieties: HN 1470, 1476,
1498, 1765, 1956

U.S.: **$1,000.00**
Can.: **$1,000.00**
Ster.: **£ 375.00**

HN 1480
Newhaven Fishwife
Designer: H. Fenton
Height: 7 3/4", 19.7 cm
Colour: Red, white and
black
Issued: 1931-1937

U.S.: **$5,500.00**
Can.: **$5,500.00**
Ster.: **£2,500.00**

HN 1481
Dreamland
Designer: L. Harradine
Height: 4 3/4", 12.0 cm
Colour: Orange and purple
Issued: 1931-1937
Varieties: HN 1473

U.S.:	**$5,500.00**
Can.:	**$5,500.00**
Ster.:	**£2,500.00**

HN 1482
Pearly Boy
Style One
Designer: L. Harradine
Height: 5 1/2", 14.0 cm
Colour: Brown suit, red vest
Issued: 1931-1949
Varieties: HN 1547

U.S.:	**$425.00**
Can.:	**$475.00**
Ster.:	**£225.00**

HN 1483
Pearly Girl
Style One
Designer: L. Harradine
Height: 5 1/2", 14.0 cm
Colour: Orange and brown
Issued: 1931-1949
Varieties: HN 1548

U.S.:	**$425.00**
Can.:	**$475.00**
Ster.:	**£225.00**

HN 1484
Jennifer
Style One
Designer: L. Harradine
Height: 6 1/2", 16.5 cm
Colour: Yellow flowers
           on cream dress
Issued: 1931-1949

U.S.:	**$900.00**
Can.:	**$950.00**
Ster.:	**£350.00**

HN 1485
Greta
Designer: L. Harradine
Height: 5 1/2", 14.0 cm
Colour: Lavender
Issued: 1931-1953

U.S.:	**$475.00**
Can.:	**$525.00**
Ster.:	**£325.00**

HN 1486
Phyllis
Style One
Designer: L. Harradine
Height: 9", 22.9 cm
Colour: Blue and pink
Issued: 1931-1949
Varieties: HN 1420, 1430, 1698

U.S.:	**$1,500.00**
Can.:	**$1,500.00**
Ster.:	**£ 500.00**

HN 1487
Suzette
Designer: L. Harradine
Height: 7 1/2", 19.1 cm
Colour: Flowered pink dress
Issued: 1931-1950
Varieties: HN 1577, 1585,
           1696, 2026

U.S.:	**$625.00**
Can.:	**$675.00**
Ster.:	**£300.00**

HN 1488
Gloria
Style One
Designer: L. Harradine
Height: 7 1/4", 18.4 cm
Colour: Green-blue
Issued: 1932-1938
Varieties: HN 1700

U.S.:	**$3,250.00**
Can.:	**$3,250.00**
Ster.:	**£1,500.00**

HN 1489
Marie
Style Two
Designer: L. Harradine
Height: 4 1/2", 11.4 cm
Colour: Pale green
Issued: 1932-1949
Varieties: HN 1370, 1388, 1417, 1531, 1635, 1655

U.S.: $600.00
Can.: $600.00
Ster.: £250.00

HN 1490
Dorcas
Designer: L. Harradine
Height: 7", 17.8 cm
Colour: Light blue
Issued: 1932-1938
Varieties: HN 1491, 1558

U.S.: $1,250.00
Can.: $1,250.00
Ster.: £ 400.00

HN 1491
Dorcas
Designer: L. Harradine
Height: 6 3/4", 17.2 cm
Colour: Pale green and lavender
Issued: 1932-1938
Varieties: HN 1490, 1558

U.S.: $950.00
Can.: $950.00
Ster.: £400.00

HN 1492
Old Lavender Seller
Designer: L. Harradine
Height: 6", 15.2 cm
Colour: Green and orange
Issued: 1932-1949
Varieties: HN 1571

U.S.: $1,100.00
Can.: $1,100.00
Ster.: £ 550.00

Earthenware

HN 1493
The Potter
Designer: C.J. Noke
Height: 7", 17.8 cm
Colour: Brown
Issued: 1932 -1992
Varieties: HN 1518, 1522

U.S.: $600.00
Can.: $600.00
Ster.: £275.00

HN 1494
Gwendolen
Designer: L. Harradine
Height: 6", 15.2 cm
Colour: Green and pink
Issued: 1932-1940
Varieties: HN 1503, 1570

U.S.: $2,000.00
Can.: $2,000.00
Ster.: £ 800.00

HN 1495
Priscilla
Style One
Designer: L. Harradine
Height: 8", 20.3 cm
Colour: Blue
Issued: 1932-1949
Varieties: HN 1337, 1340, 1501, 1559

U.S.: $1,100.00
Can.: $1,200.00
Ster.: £ 450.00

HN 1496
Sweet Anne
Style One
Designer: L. Harradine
Height: 7", 17.8 cm
Colour: Purple
Issued: 1932-1967
Varieties: HN 1318, 1330, 1331, 1453, 1631, 1701

U.S.: $375.00
Can.: $475.00
Ster.: £250.00

HN 1497
Rosamund
Style Two
Designer: L. Harradine
Height: 8 1/2", 21.6 cm
Colour: Red
Issued: 1932-1938
Varieties: HN 1551

U.S.: $2,500.00
Can.: $2,500.00
Ster.: £1,000.00

HN 1498
Chloe
Style One
Designer: L. Harradine
Height: 6", 15.2 cm
Colour: Peach-yellow
Issued: 1932-1938
Varieties: HN 1470, 1476,
1479, 1765, 1956

U.S.: $1,000.00
Can.: $1,000.00
Ster.: £ 450.00

HN 1499
Miss Demure
Designer: L. Harradine
Height: 7", 17.8 cm
Colour: Pink and yellow
Issued: 1932-1938
Varieties: HN 1402, 1440,
1463, 1560

U.S.: $1,000.00
Can.: $1,000.00
Ster.: £ 400.00

HN 1500
Biddy
Designer: L. Harradine
Height: 5 1/2", 14.0 cm
Colour: Yellow
Issued: 1932-1937
Varieties: HN 1445, 1513

U.S.: $950.00
Can.: $950.00
Ster.: £375.00

HN 1501
Priscilla
Style One
Designer: L. Harradine
Height: 8", 20.3 cm
Colour: Orange
Issued: 1932-1938
Varieties: HN 1337, 1340,
1495, 1559

U.S.: $1,200.00
Can.: $1,200.00
Ster.: £ 450.00

HN 1502
Lucy Ann
Designer: L. Harradine
Height: 5 1/4", 13.3 cm
Colour: Lavender
Issued: 1932-1951
Varieties: HN 1565

U.S.: $475.00
Can.: $550.00
Ster.: £325.00

HN 1503
Gwendolen
Designer: L. Harradine
Height: 6", 15.2 cm
Colour: Orange and yellow
Issued: 1932-1949
Varieties: HN 1494, 1570

U.S.: $2,000.00
Can.: $2,000.00
Ster.: £ 800.00

HN 1504
Sweet Maid
Style One
Designer: L. Harradine
Height: 8", 20.3 cm
Colour: Lavender and blue
Issued: 1932-1936
Varieties: HN 1505

U.S.: $2,000.00
Can.: $2,000.00
Ster.: £ 750.00

HN 1505
Sweet Maid
Style One
Designer: L. Harradine
Height: 8", 20.3 cm
Colour: Red and green
Issued: 1932-1936
Varieties: HN 1504

U.S.: **$2,000.00**
Can.: **$2,000.00**
Ster.: £ 750.00

HN 1506
Rose
Style One
Designer: L. Harradine
Height: 4 1/2", 11.4 cm
Colour: Yellow
Issued: 1932-1938
Varieties: HN 1368, 1387,
1416, 1654, 2123

U.S.: **$550.00**
Can.: **$650.00**
Ster.: £275.00

HN 1507
Pantalettes
Style One
Designer: L. Harradine
Height: 7 3/4", 19.7 cm
Colour: Yellow
Issued: 1932-1949
Varieties: HN 1362, 1412, 1709

U.S.: **$1,200.00**
Can.: **$1,200.00**
Ster.: £ 500.00

HN 1508
Helen
Style One
Designer: L. Harradine
Height: 8", 20.3 cm
Colour: Flowered
green dress
Issued: 1932-1938
Varieties: HN 1509, 1572

U.S.: **$1,750.00**
Can.: **$1,750.00**
Ster.: £ 750.00

Photograph
Not
Available

Photograph
Not
Available

HN 1509
Helen
Style One
Designer: L. Harradine
Height: 8", 20.3 cm
Colour: Flowered blue-
yellow dress
Issued: 1932-1938
Varieties: HN 1508, 1572

U.S.: **$1,750.00**
Can.: **$1,750.00**
Ster.: £ 750.00

HN 1510
Constance
Designer: L. Harradine
Height: 6 3/4", 17.1 cm
Colour: Yellow-purple
Issued: 1932-1936
Varieties: HN 1511

U.S.: **$1,800.00**
Can.: **$2,000.00**
Ster.: £ 950.00

HN 1511
Constance
Designer: L. Harradine
Height: 6 3/4", 17.1 cm
Colour: Lavender
Issued: 1932-1936
Varieties: HN 1510

U.S.: **$1,800.00**
Can.: **$2,000.00**
Ster.: £ 950.00

HN 1512
Kathleen
Style One
Designer: L. Harradine
Height: 7 1/2", 19.1 cm
Colour: Lavender and blue
Issued: 1932-1938
Varieties: HN 1252, 1253, 1275,
1279, 1291, 1357

U.S.: **$1,400.00**
Can.: **$1,500.00**
Ster.: £ 650.00

HN 1513
Biddy
Designer: L. Harradine
Height: 5 1/2", 14.0 cm
Colour: Pink dress with
mauve shawl
Issued: 1932-1937
Varieties: HN 1445, 1500

U.S.: **$325.00**
Can.: **$375.00**
Ster.: **£200.00**

HN 1514
Dolly Vardon
Designer: L. Harradine
Height: 8 1/2", 21.6 cm
Colour: Multi-coloured
Issued: 1932-1938
Varieties: HN 1515

U.S.: **$1,450.00**
Can.: **$1,450.00**
Ster.: **£ 750.00**

HN 1515
Dolly Vardon
Designer: L. Harradine
Height: 8 1/2", 21.6 cm
Colour: Red and lavender
Issued: 1932-1949
Varieties: HN 1514

U.S.: **$1,450.00**
Can.: **$1,450.00**
Ster.: **£ 750.00**

HN 1516
Cicely
Designer: L. Harradine
Height: 5 3/4", 14.6 cm
Colour: Purple and red
Issued: 1932-1949

U.S.: **$2,000.00**
Can.: **$2,000.00**
Ster.: **£ 800.00**

HN 1517
Veronica
Style One
Designer: L. Harradine
Height: 8", 20.3 cm
Colour: Red-cream
Issued: 1932-1951
Varieties: HN 1519, 1650, 1943

U.S.: **$475.00**
Can.: **$575.00**
Ster.: **£275.00**

HN 1518
The Potter
Designer: C.J. Noke
Height: 6 3/4", 17.2 cm
Colour: Green
Issued: 1932-1949
Varieties: HN 1493, 1522

U.S.: **$1,750.00**
Can.: **$1,750.00**
Ster.: **£ 600.00**

HN 1519
Veronica
Style One
Designer: L. Harradine
Height: 8", 20.3 cm
Colour: Blue-cream
Issued: 1932-1938
Varieties: HN 1517, 1650, 1943

U.S.: **$1,000.00**
Can.: **$1,000.00**
Ster.: **£ 450.00**

HN 1520
Eugene
Designer: L. Harradine
Height: 5 3/4", 14.6 cm
Colour: Green and pink
Issued: 1932-1936
Varieties: HN 1521

U.S.: **$2,000.00**
Can.: **$2,000.00**
Ster.: **£ 950.00**

HN 1521
Eugene
Designer: L. Harradine
Height: 5", 12.7 cm
Colour: Orange, yellow
and white
Issued: 1932-1936
Varieties: HN 1520
U.S.: $2,000.00
Can.: $2,000.00
Ster.: £ 950.00

HN 1522
The Potter
Designer: L. Harradine
Height: 6 3/4", 17.2 cm
Colour: Green and purple
Issued: 1932-1949
Varieties: HN 1493, 1518
U.S.: $2,250.00
Can.: $2,250.00
Ster.: £ 750.00

HN 1523
Lisette
Designer: L. Harradine
Height: 5 1/4", 13.3 cm
Colour: Yellow and red
Issued: 1932-1936
Varieties: HN 1524, 1684
U.S.: $2,250.00
Can.: $2,250.00
Ster.: £ 775.00

HN 1524
Lisette
Designer: L. Harradine
Height: 5 1/4", 13.3 cm
Colour: Blue, pink
and yellow
Issued: 1932-1936
Varieties: HN 1523, 1684
U.S.: $2,250.00
Can.: $2,250.00
Ster.: £ 775.00

HN 1525
Clarissa
Style One
Designer: L. Harradine
Height: 10", 25.4 cm
Colour: Green and red
Issued: 1932-1938
Varieties: HN 1687
U.S.: $1,250.00
Can.: $1,250.00
Ster.: £ 550.00

Earthenware

HN 1526
Anthea
Designer: L. Harradine
Height: 6 1/2", 16.5 cm
Colour: Green and blue
Issued: 1932-1940
Varieties: HN 1527, 1669
U.S.: $1,750.00
Can.: $1,750.00
Ster.: £ 775.00

HN 1527
Anthea
Designer: L. Harradine
Height: 6 1/2", 16.5 cm
Colour: Lavender
Issued: 1932-1940
Varieties: HN 1526, 1669
U.S.: $1,750.00
Can.: $1,750.00
Ster.: £ 775.00

HN 1528
Bluebeard
Style Two
Designer: L. Harradine
Height: 11 1/2", 29.2 cm
Colour: Red and purple
Issued: 1932-1949
Varieties: HN 2105
U.S.: $1,100.00
Can.: $1,200.00
Ster.: £ 650.00

Earthenware

HN 1529
A Victorian Lady
Style One
Designer: L. Harradine
Height: 7 3/4", 19.7 cm
Colour: Green and orange
Issued: 1932-1938
Varieties: HN 726, 727, 728,
736, 739, 740, 742,
745, 1208, 1258, 1276,
1277, 1345, 1452
U.S.: $1,000.00
Can.: $1,000.00
Ster.: £ 375.00

HN 1530
The Little Bridesmaid
Style One
Designer: L. Harradine
Height: 5", 12.7 cm
Colour: Yellow and green
Issued: 1932-1938
Varieties: HN 1433, 1434
U.S.: $750.00
Can.: $800.00
Ster.: £300.00

HN 1531
Marie
Style Two
Designer: L. Harradine
Height: 4 1/2", 11.4 cm
Colour: Yellow-green
Issued: 1932-1938
Varieties: HN 1370, 1388, 1417,
1489, 1635, 1655
U.S.: $675.00
Can.: $675.00
Ster.: £275.00

HN 1532
Fairy
Style Two
Designer: L. Harradine
Height: 4", 10.1 cm
Colour: Multi-coloured
Issued: 1932-1938
Varieties: HN 1374, 1380
U.S.: $2,100.00
Can.: $2,500.00
Ster.: £1,250.00

HN 1533
Fairy
Style Three
Designer: L. Harradine
Height: 3", 7.6 cm
Colour: Multi-coloured
Issued: 1932-1938
Varieties: HN 1375, 1395
U.S.: $2,100.00
Can.: $2,250.00
Ster.: £ 900.00

HN 1534
Fairy
Style Seven
Designer: L. Harradine
Height: 2 1/2", 6.3 cm
Colour: Yellow flowers
Issued: 1932-1938
Varieties: HN 1379, 1394
U.S.: $1,250.00
Can.: $1,250.00
Ster.: £ 600.00

HN 1535
Fairy
Style Six
Designer: L. Harradine
Height: 2 1/2", 6.3 cm
Colour: Yellow and blue
flowers
Issued: 1932-1938
Varieties: HN 1378, 1396
U.S.: $1,250.00
Can.: $1,250.00
Ster.: £ 550.00

HN 1536
Fairy
Style Four
Designer: L. Harradine
Height: 2 1/2", 6.3 cm
Colour: Yellow and blue
flowers
Issued: 1932-1938
Varieties: HN 1376
U.S.: $1,250.00
Can.: $1,250.00
Ster.: £ 650.00

HN 1537
Janet
Style One
Designer: L. Harradine
Height: 6 1/4", 15.9 cm
Colour: Red
Issued: 1932-1995
Varieties: HN 1538, 1652, 1737

U.S.: $200.00
Can.: $225.00
Ster.: £ 85.00

HN 1538
Janet
Style One
Designer: L. Harradine
Height: 6 1/4", 15.9 cm
Colour: Purple
Issued: 1932-1949
Varieties: HN 1537, 1652, 1737

U.S.: $850.00
Can.: $850.00
Ster.: £375.00

HN 1539
A Saucy Nymph
Designer: Unknown
Height: 4 1/2", 11.4 cm
Colour: Green base
Issued: 1933-1949
Varieties: Also with pearl glaze

U.S.: $650.00
Can.: $550.00
Ster.: £225.00

HN 1540
**"Little Child So
Rare and Sweet"**
Style One
Designer: Unknown
Height: 5", 12.7 cm
Colour: Green base
Issued: 1933-1949

U.S.: $1,000.00
Can.: $1,000.00
Ster.: £ 400.00

HN 1541
"Happy Joy, Baby Boy"
Designer: Unknown
Height: 6 1/4", 15.9 cm
Colour: Green base
Issued: 1933-1949

U.S.: $1,100.00
Can.: $1,100.00
Ster.: £ 450.00

HN 1542
**"Little Child So
Rare and Sweet"**
Style Two
Designer: Unknown
Height: 5", 12.7 cm
Colour: Blue base
Issued: 1933-1949

U.S.: $950.00
Can.: $950.00
Ster.: £400.00

HN 1543
**"Dancing Eyes
and Sunny Hair"**
Designer: Unknown
Height: 5", 12.7 cm
Colour: Blue base
Issued: 1933-1949

U.S.: $950.00
Can.: $950.00
Ster.: £400.00

HN 1544
**"Do You Wonder Where
Fairies Are That Folk
Declare Have Vanished"**
Designer: Unknown
Height: 5", 12.7 cm
Colour: Lavender with
 yellow base
Issued: 1933-1949

U.S.: $1,150.00
Can.: $1,150.00
Ster.: £ 475.00

HN 1545
"Called Love, A Little Boy,
Almost Naked, Wanton,
Blind, Cruel Now, and Then
as Kind"
Designer: Unknown
Height: 3 1/2", 8.9 cm
Colour: Tan base
Issued: 1933-1949
U.S.: **$1,150.00**
Can.: **$1,150.00**
Ster.: £ 475.00

HN 1546
"Here A Little Child I Stand"
Designer: Unknown
Height: 6 1/4", 15.9 cm
Colour: Lavender with
green base
Issued: 1933-1949
U.S.: **$1,150.00**
Can.: **$1,150.00**
Ster.: £ 475.00

HN 1547
Pearly Boy
Style One
Designer: L. Harradine
Height: 5 1/2", 14.0 cm
Colour: Green and purple
Issued: 1933-1949
Varieties: HN 1482
U.S.: **$775.00**
Can.: **$775.00**
Ster.: £325.00

HN 1548
Pearly Girl
Style One
Designer: L. Harradine
Height: 5 1/2", 14.0 cm
Colour: Green and purple
Issued: 1933-1949
Varieties: HN 1483
U.S.: **$775.00**
Can.: **$775.00**
Ster.: £325.00

HN 1549
Sweet and Twenty
Style One
Designer: L. Harradine
Height: 6", 15.2 cm
Colour: Multi-coloured
Issued: 1933-1949
Varieties: HN 1298, 1360, 1437,
1438, 1563, 1649
U.S.: **$875.00**
Can.: **$875.00**
Ster.: £325.00

HN 1550
Annette
Style One
Designer: L. Harradine
Height: 6 1/4", 15.9 cm
Colour: Red and green
Issued: 1933-1949
Varieties: HN 1471, 1472
U.S.: **$700.00**
Can.: **$775.00**
Ster.: £325.00

HN 1551
Rosamund
Style Two
Designer: L. Harradine
Height: 8 1/2", 21.6 cm
Colour: Blue
Issued: 1933-1938
Varieties: HN 1497
U.S.: **$4,000.00**
Can.: **$4,000.00**
Ster.: £1,500.00

HN 1552
Pinkie
Designer: L. Harradine
Height: 5", 12.7 cm
Colour: Pink
Issued: 1933-1938
Varieties: HN 1553
U.S.: **$1,650.00**
Can.: **$1,650.00**
Ster.: £ 750.00

HN 1553
Pinkie
Designer: L. Harradine
Height: 5", 12.7 cm
Colour: Yellow and blue
Issued: 1933-1938
Varieties: HN 1552

U.S.: **$1,750.00**
Can.: **$1,750.00**
Ster.: **£ 850.00**

HN 1554
Charley's Aunt
Style Two
Designer: H. Fenton
Height: 7 1/2", 19.1 cm
Colour: Purple
Issued: 1933-1938
Varieties: HN 1411

U.S.: **$2,000.00**
Can.: **$2,000.00**
Ster.: **£ 850.00**

HN 1555
Marigold
Designer: L. Harradine
Height: 6", 15.2 cm
Colour: Pink and blue
Issued: 1933-1949
Varieties: HN 1447, 1451

U.S.: **$875.00**
Can.: **$875.00**
Ster.: **£450.00**

HN 1556
Rosina
Designer: L. Harradine
Height: 5 3/4", 14.6 cm
Colour: Lavender
Issued: 1933-1937
Varieties: HN 1358, 1364

U.S.: **$1,500.00**
Can.: **$1,600.00**
Ster.: **£ 650.00**

HN 1557
Lady Fayre
Designer: L. Harradine
Height: 5 3/4", 14.6 cm
Colour: Red and purple
Issued: 1933-1938
Varieties: HN 1265

U.S.: **$1,750.00**
Can.: **$1,750.00**
Ster.: **£ 650.00**

HN 1558
Dorcas
Designer: L. Harradine
Height: 6 3/4", 17.2 cm
Colour: Purple
Issued: 1933-1952
Varieties: HN 1490, 1491

U.S.: **$400.00**
Can.: **$575.00**
Ster.: **£350.00**

HN 1559
Priscilla
Style One
Designer: L. Harradine
Height: 8", 20.3 cm
Colour: Purple
Issued: 1933-1949
Varieties: HN 1337, 1340,
1495, 1501

U.S.: **$1,200.00**
Can.: **$1,200.00**
Ster.: **£ 400.00**

HN 1560
Miss Demure
Designer: L. Harradine
Height: 7", 17.8 cm
Colour: Blue dress with
red shawl
Issued: 1933-1949
Varieties: HN 1402, 1440,
1463, 1499

U.S.: **$850.00**
Can.: **$850.00**
Ster.: **£300.00**

HN 1561
Willy-Won't He
Designer: L. Harradine
Height: 6", 15.2 cm
Colour: Blue, pink and white
Issued: 1933-1949
Varieties: HN 1584, 2150

U.S.: $1,750.00
Can.: $1,750.00
Ster.: £ 600.00

HN 1562
Gretchen
Designer: L. Harradine
Height: 7 3/4", 19.7 cm
Colour: Purple and white
Issued: 1933-1940
Varieties: HN 1397

U.S.: $1,600.00
Can.: $1,750.00
Ster.: £ 750.00

HN 1563
Sweet and Twenty
Style One
Designer: L. Harradine
Height: 6", 15.2 cm
Colour: Black and light pink
Issued: 1933-1938
Varieties: HN 1298, 1360, 1437, 1438, 1549, 1649

U.S.: $1,200.00
Can.: $1,500.00
Ster.: £ 450.00

HN 1564
Pamela
Style One
Designer: L. Harradine
Height: 8", 20.3 cm
Colour: Pink
Issued: 1933-1937
Varieties: HN 1468, 1469

U.S.: $1,750.00
Can.: $1,750.00
Ster.: £ 650.00

HN 1565
Lucy Ann
Designer: L. Harradine
Height: 5 1/4", 13.3 cm
Colour: Light green
Issued: 1933-1938
Varieties: HN 1502

U.S.: $800.00
Can.: $800.00
Ster.: £350.00

HN 1566
Estelle
Designer: L. Harradine
Height: 8", 20.3 cm
Colour: Lavender
Issued: 1933-1940
Varieties: HN 1802

U.S.: $1,650.00
Can.: $1,650.00
Ster.: £ 750.00

HN 1567
Patricia
Style One
Designer: L. Harradine
Height: 8 1/2", 21.6 cm
Colour: Red
Issued: 1933-1949
Varieties: HN 1414, 1431, 1462

U.S.: $2,000.00
Can.: $2,000.00
Ster.: £ 500.00

HN 1568
Charmian
Designer: L. Harradine
Height: 6 1/2", 16.5 cm
Colour: Red and cream
Issued: 1933-1940
Varieties: HN 1569, 1651

U.S.: $1,200.00
Can.: $1,200.00
Ster.: £ 525.00

HN 1569
Charmian
Designer: L. Harradine
Height: 6 1/2", 16.5 cm
Colour: Cream and lavender
Issued: 1933-1940
Varieties: HN 1568, 1651

U.S.: $1,200.00
Can.: $1,200.00
Ster.: £ 525.00

HN 1570
Gwendolen
Designer: L. Harradine
Height: 6", 15.2 cm
Colour: Pink
Issued: 1933-1949
Varieties: HN 1494, 1503

U.S.: $2,000.00
Can.: $2,000.00
Ster.: £ 850.00

HN 1571
Old Lavender Seller
Designer: L. Harradine
Height: 6 1/2", 16.5 cm
Colour: Orange and black
Issued: 1933-1949
Varieties: HN 1492

U.S.: $1,350.00
Can.: $1,350.00
Ster.: £ 575.00

HN 1572
Helen
Style One
Designer: L. Harradine
Height: 8", 20.3 cm
Colour: Red
Issued: 1933-1938
Varieties: HN 1508, 1509

U.S.: $1,900.00
Can.: $1,900.00
Ster.: £ 850.00

HN 1573
Rhoda
Designer: L. Harradine
Height: 10 1/4", 26.7 cm
Colour: Green and orange
Issued: 1933-1940
Varieties: HN 1574, 1688

U.S.: $1,200.00
Can.: $1,000.00
Ster.: £ 450.00

HN 1574
Rhoda
Designer: L. Harradine
Height: 10 1/4", 26.7 cm
Colour: Burgundy and orange
Issued: 1933-1940
Varieties: HN 1573, 1688

U.S.: $1,250.00
Can.: $1,100.00
Ster.: £ 475.00

HN 1575
Daisy
Style One
Designer: L. Harradine
Height: 3 3/4", 9.5 cm
Colour: Blue dress
with flowers
Issued: 1933-1949
Varieties: HN 1961

U.S.: $500.00
Can.: $600.00
Ster.: £325.00

HN 1576
Tildy
Designer: L. Harradine
Height: 5", 12.7 cm
Colour: Red and pink-cream
Issued: 1933-1939
Varieties: HN 1859

U.S.: $1,600.00
Can.: $1,600.00
Ster.: £ 750.00

Earthenware

HN 1577
Suzette
Designer: L. Harradine
Height: 7 1/2", 19.1 cm
Colour: Flowered
lavender dress
Issued: 1933-1949
Varieties: HN 1487, 1585,
1696, 2026
U.S.: **$1,000.00**
Can.: **$1,000.00**
Ster.: **£ 450.00**

HN 1578
The Hinged Parasol
Designer: L. Harradine
Height: 6 1/2", 16.5 cm
Colour: Red and yellow
dress with spots
Issued: 1933-1949
Varieties: HN 1579
U.S.: **$1,500.00**
Can.: **$1,500.00**
Ster.: **£ 600.00**

HN 1579
The Hinged Parasol
Designer: L. Harradine
Height: 6 1/2", 16.5 cm
Colour: Red and purple
Issued: 1933-1949
Varieties: HN 1578
U.S.: **$1,500.00**
Can.: **$1,500.00**
Ster.: **£ 600.00**

HN 1580
Rosebud
Style One
Designer: L. Harradine
Height: 3", 7.6 cm
Colour: Pink
Issued: 1933-1938
Varieties: HN 1581
U.S.: **$1,200.00**
Can.: **$1,250.00**
Ster.: **£ 500.00**

HN 1581
Rosebud
Style One
Designer: L. Harradine
Height: 3", 7.6 cm
Colour: Blue dress
with flowers
Issued: 1933-1938
Varieties: HN 1580
U.S.: **$1,200.00**
Can.: **$1,250.00**
Ster.: **£ 500.00**

HN 1582
Marion
Designer: L. Harradine
Height: 6 1/2", 16.5 cm
Colour: Purple
Issued: 1933-1940
Varieties: HN 1583
U.S.: **$2,500.00**
Can.: **$2,500.00**
Ster.: **£ 850.00**

HN 1583
Marion
Designer: L. Harradine
Height: 6 1/2", 16.5 cm
Colour: Blue dress,
patterned shawl
Issued: 1933-1940
Varieties: HN 1582
U.S.: **$2,200.00**
Can.: **$2,200.00**
Ster.: **£ 850.00**

HN 1584
Willy-Won't He
Designer: L. Harradine
Height: 6", 15.2 cm
Colour: Red, green,
blue and white
Issued: 1933-1949
Varieties: HN 1561, 2150
(minor glaze
difference)
U.S.: **$600.00**
Can.: **$700.00**
Ster.: **£375.00**

HN 1585
Suzette
Designer: L. Harradine
Height: 7 1/2", 19.1 cm
Colour: Green and yellow
Issued: 1933-1938
Varieties: HN 1487, 1577, 1696, 2026

U.S.: **$1,000.00**
Can.: **$1,000.00**
Ster.: £ 350.00

HN 1586
Camille
Style One
Designer: L. Harradine
Height: 6 1/2", 16.5 cm
Colour: Red and pink
Issued: 1933-1949
Varieties: HN 1648, 1736

U.S.: **$1,650.00**
Can.: **$1,650.00**
Ster.: £ 425.00

HN 1587
Fleurette
Designr: L. Harradine
Height: 6 1/2", 16.5 cm
Colour: Red and pink
Issued: 1933-1949

U.S.: **$900.00**
Can.: **$850.00**
Ster.: £350.00

HN 1588
The Bride
Style One
Designer: L. Harradine
Height: 8 3/4", 22.2 cm
Colour: Cream
Issued: 1933-1938
Varieties: HN 1600, 1762, 1841

U.S.: **$1,650.00**
Can.: **$1,750.00**
Ster.: £ 650.00

HN 1589
Sweet and Twenty
Style Two
Designer: L. Harradine
Height: 3 1/2", 8.9 cm
Colour: Red dress, pale green sofa
Issued: 1933-1949
Varieties: HN 1610

U.S.: **$500.00**
Can.: **$525.00**
Ster.: £325.00

HN 1598
Clothilde
Designer: L. Harradine
Height: 7 1/4", 18.4 cm
Colour: Yellow and red
Issued: 1933-1949
Varieties: HN 1599

U.S.: **$1,250.00**
Can.: **$1,250.00**
Ster.: £ 650.00

HN 1599
Clothilde
Designer: L. Harradine
Height: 7 1/4", 18.4 cm
Colour: Purple and red
Issued: 1933-1949
Varieties: HN 1598

U.S.: **$1,250.00**
Can.: **$1,250.00**
Ster.: £ 650.00

HN 1600
The Bride
Style One
Designer: L. Harradine
Height: 8 3/4", 22.2 cm
Colour: Pale pink
Issued: 1933-1949
Varieties: HN 1588, 1762, 1841

U.S.: **$1,750.00**
Can.: **$1,750.00**
Ster.: £ 750.00

HN 1604
The Emir
Designer: C.J. Noke
Height: 7 1/2", 19.1 cm
Colour: Yellow and red
Issued: 1933-1949
Varieties: HN 1605; also called
 "Ibrahim" HN 2095

U.S.: **$1,200.00**
Can.: **$1,200.00**
Ster.: £ 550.00

HN 1605
The Emir
Designer: C.J. Noke
Height: 7 1/4", 18.4 cm
Colour: Yellow and purple
Issued: 1933-1949
Varieties: HN 1604; also called
 "Ibrahim" HN 2095

U.S.: **$1,200.00**
Can.: **$1,200.00**
Ster.: £ 550.00

HN 1606
Falstaff
Style One
Designer: C.J. Noke
Height: 7", 17.8 cm
Colour: Red and brown
Issued: 1933-1949
Varieties: HN 571, 575, 608,
 609, 619, 638, 1216

U.S.: **$2,500.00**
Can.: **$2,500.00**
Ster.: £ 900.00

HN 1607
Cerise
Designer: L. Harradine
Height: 5 1/4", 13.3 cm
Colour: Lavender dress
 with flowers
Issued: 1933-1949

U.S.: **$650.00**
Can.: **$650.00**
Ster.: £325.00

*

HN 1610
Sweet and Twenty
Style Two
Designer: L. Harradine
Height: 3 1/2", 8.9 cm
Colour: Red dress, green sofa
Issued: 1933-1938
Varieties: HN 1589

U.S.: **$475.00**
Can.: **$575.00**
Ster.: £325.00

*

HN 1617
Primroses
Designer: L. Harradine
Height: 6 1/2", 16.5 cm
Colour: Purple, red, white
 and yellow
Issued: 1934-1949

U.S.: **$1,350.00**
Can.: **$1,350.00**
Ster.: £ 650.00

Earthenware

HN 1618
Maisie
Designer: L. Harradine
Height: 6 1/4", 15.9 cm
Colour: Yellow and blue
Issued: 1934-1949
Varieties: HN 1619

U.S.: **$850.00**
Can.: **$950.00**
Ster.: £450.00

HN 1619
Maisie
Designer: L. Harradine
Height: 6 1/4", 15.9 cm
Colour: Red and pink
Issued: 1934-1949
Varieties: HN 1618

U.S.: **$500.00**
Can.: **$650.00**
Ster.: £350.00

HN 1620
Rosabell
Designer: L. Harradine
Height: 6 3/4", 17.1 cm
Colour: Red and green
Issued: 1934-1940
U.S.: **$1,900.00**
Can.: **$1,900.00**
Ster.: **£ 650.00**

HN 1621
Irene
Designer: L. Harradine
Height: 6 1/2", 16.5 cm
Colour: Yellow
Issued: 1934-1951
Varieties: HN 1697, 1952
U.S.: **$600.00**
Can.: **$700.00**
Ster.: **£350.00**

HN 1622
Evelyn
Designer: L. Harradine
Height: 6 1/4", 15.9 cm
Colour: Red and cream
Issued: 1934-1940
Varieties: HN 1637
U.S.: **$2,000.00**
Can.: **$2,000.00**
Ster.: **£ 750.00**

HN 1626
Bonnie Lassie
Designer: L. Harradine
Height: 5 1/4", 13.3 cm
Colour: Red
Issued: 1934-1953
U.S.: **$650.00**
Can.: **$700.00**
Ster.: **£450.00**

HN 1627
Curly Knob
Designer: L. Harradine
Height: 6", 15.2 cm
Colour: Blue and red
Issued: 1934-1949
U.S.: **$1,250.00**
Can.: **$1,250.00**
Ster.: **£ 650.00**

HN 1628
Margot
Designer: L. Harradine
Height: 5 1/2", 14.0 cm
Colour: Blue and yellow
Issued: 1934-1940
Varieties: HN 1636, 1653
U.S.: **$1,500.00**
Can.: **$1,500.00**
Ster.: **£ 700.00**

HN 1629
Grizel
Designer: L. Harradine
Height: 6 3/4", 17.2 cm
Colour: Red and cream
Issued: 1934-1938
U.S.: **$2,100.00**
Can.: **$2,100.00**
Ster.: **£ 850.00**

HN 1631
Sweet Anne
Style One
Designer: L. Harradine
Height: 7", 17.8 cm
Colour: Green, red, pink
and yellow
Issued: 1934-1938
Varieties: HN 1318, 1330, 1331,
1453, 1496, 1701
U.S.: **$1,400.00**
Can.: **$1,400.00**
Ster.: **£ 575.00**

HN 1632
A Gentlewoman
Designer: L. Harradine
Height: 7 1/2", 19.1 cm
Colour: Lavender dress,
green hat
Issued: 1934-1949
U.S.: $1,100.00
Can.: $1,100.00
Ster.: £ 500.00

HN 1633
Clemency
Designer: L. Harradine
Height: 7", 17.8 cm
Colour: Lavender jacket,
cream flowered dress
Issued: 1934-1938
Varieties: HN 1634, 1643
U.S.: $1,600.00
Can.: $1,600.00
Ster.: £ 675.00

HN 1634
Clemency
Designer: L. Harradine
Height: 7", 17.8 cm
Colour: Green and orange
patterned jacket,
green dress
Issued: 1934-1949
Varieties: HN 1633, 1643
U.S.: $1,850.00
Can.: $1,850.00
Ster.: £ 750.00

HN 1635
Marie
Style Two
Designer: L. Harradine
Height: 4 3/4", 12.0 cm
Colour: Blue, pink and
white, pink flowers
Issued: 1934-1949
Varieties: HN 1370, 1388, 1417,
1489, 1531, 1655
U.S.: $725.00
Can.: $750.00
Ster.: £250.00

HN 1636
Margot
Designer: L. Harradine
Height: 5 3/4", 14.6 cm
Colour: Red, pink and yellow
Issued: 1934-1940
Varieties: HN 1628, 1653
U.S.: $1,600.00
Can.: $1,700.00
Ster.: £ 750.00

HN 1637
Evelyn
Designer: L. Harradine
Height: 6", 15.2 cm
Colour: Blue and cream
Issued: 1934-1940
Varieties: HN 1622
U.S.: $2,000.00
Can.: $2,000.00
Ster.: £ 750.00

HN 1638
Ladybird
Designer: L. Harradine
Height: 7 3/4", 19.7 cm
Colour: Pink
Issued: 1934-1949
Varieties: HN 1640
U.S.: $2,800.00
Can.: $2,800.00
Ster.: £1,500.00

HN 1639
Dainty May
Style One
Designer: L. Harradine
Height: 6", 15.2 cm
Colour: Red and green
Issued: 1934-1949
Varieties: HN 1656
U.S.: $575.00
Can.: $675.00
Ster.: £395.00

HN 1640
Ladybird
Designer: L. Harradine
Height: 7 3/4", 19.7 cm
Colour: Blue
Issued: 1934-1938
Varieties: HN 1638

U.S.: **$3,250.00**
Can.: **$3,250.00**
Ster.: **£1,800.00**

HN 1641
The Little Mother
Style Two
Designer: L. Harradine
Height: 8", 20.3 cm
Colour: Red, green, white
and purple
Issued: 1934-1949
Varieties: HN 1418; also
called "Young
Widow" HN 1399

U.S.: **$5,000.00**
Can.: **$5,000.00**
Ster.: **£1,750.00**

HN 1642
Granny's Shawl
Designer: L. Harradine
Height: 5 3/4", 14.6 cm
Colour: Cream dress,
red shawl
Issued: 1934-1949
Varieties: HN 1647

U.S.: **$700.00**
Can.: **$750.00**
Ster.: **£325.00**

HN 1643
Clemency
Designer: L. Harradine
Height: 7", 17.8 cm
Colour: Red jacket, white
and green dress
Issued: 1934-1938
Varieties: HN 1633, 1634

U.S.: **$1,850.00**
Can.: **$1,850.00**
Ster.: **£ 850.00**

HN 1644
Herminia
Designer: L. Harradine
Height: 6 1/2", 16.5 cm
Colour: Flowered cream dress
Issued: 1934-1938
Varieties: HN 1646, 1704

U.S.: **$2,000.00**
Can.: **$2,000.00**
Ster.: **£ 850.00**

HN 1645
Aileen
Designer: L. Harradine
Height: 6", 15.2 cm
Colour: Green dress,
flowered shawl
Issued: 1934-1938
Varieties: HN 1664, 1803

U.S.: **$2,200.00**
Can.: **$2,200.00**
Ster.: **£ 850.00**

HN 1646
Herminia
Designer: L. Harradine
Height: 6 1/2", 16.5 cm
Colour: Red dress with
cream stripe
Issued: 1934-1938
Varieties: HN 1644, 1704

U.S.: **$2,000.00**
Can.: **$2,000.00**
Ster.: **£ 950.00**

HN 1647
Granny's Shawl
Designer: L. Harradine
Height: 5 3/4", 14.6 cm
Colour: Cream dress
with blue shawl
Issued: 1934-1949
Varieties: HN 1642

U.S.: **$625.00**
Can.: **$750.00**
Ster.: **£325.00**

HN 1648
Camille
Style One
Designer: L. Harradine
Height: 6 1/2", 16.5 cm
Colour: Pale green
flowered dress
Issued: 1934-1949
Varieties: HN 1586, 1736

U.S.: $2,100.00
Can.: $2,100.00
Ster.: £ 750.00

HN 1649
Sweet and Twenty
Style One
Designer: L. Harradine
Height: 6", 15.2 cm
Colour: Green and cream
dress, brown sofa
Issued: 1934-1936
Varieties: HN 1298, 1360, 1437,
1438, 1549, 1563

U.S.: $1,200.00
Can.: $1,200.00
Ster.: £ 450.00

HN 1650
Veronica
Style One
Designer: L. Harradine
Height: 8", 20.3 cm
Colour: Green
Issued: 1934-1949
Varieties: HN 1517, 1519, 1943

U.S.: $1,200.00
Can.: $1,200.00
Ster.: £ 450.00

HN 1651
Charmian
Designer: L. Harradine
Height: 6 1/2", 16.5 cm
Colour: Red and green
Issued: 1934-1940
Varieties: HN 1568, 1569

U.S.: $1,750.00
Can.: $1,750.00
Ster.: £ 650.00

HN 1652
Janet
Style One
Designer: L. Harradine
Height: 6 1/2", 16.5 cm
Colour: Red with pink
flowered skirt
Issued: 1934-1949
Varieties: HN 1537, 1538, 1737

U.S.: $1,000.00
Can.: $1,000.00
Ster.: £ 450.00

HN 1653
Margot
Designer: L. Harradine
Height: 5 3/4", 14.6 cm
Colour: White and red
Issued: 1934-1940
Varieties: HN 1628, 1636

U.S.: $1,600.00
Can.: $1,600.00
Ster.: £ 750.00

HN 1654
Rose
Style One
Designer: L. Harradine
Height: 4 1/2", 11.4 cm
Colour: Green and cream
Issued: 1934-1938
Varieties: HN 1368, 1387,
1416, 1506, 2123

U.S.: $550.00
Can.: $625.00
Ster.: £250.00

HN 1655
Marie
Style Two
Designer: L. Harradine
Height: 4 1/2", 11.4 cm
Colour: Pink and white
Issued: 1934-1938
Varieties: HN 1370, 1388,
1417, 1489, 1531,
1635

U.S.: $650.00
Can.: $700.00
Ster.: £300.00

HN 1656
Dainty May
Style One
Designer: L. Harradine
Height: 6", 15.2 cm
Colour: Lavender
Issued: 1934-1949
Varieties: HN 1639

U.S.: $800.00
Can.: $800.00
Ster.: £350.00

HN 1657
The Moor
Designer: C.J. Noke
Height: 16 1/2", 41.9 cm
Colour: Red and black
Issued: 1934-1949
Varieties: HN 1308, 1366, 1425, 2082, 3642; "An Arab" HN 33, 343, 378

U.S.: $4,000.00
Can.: $3,500.00
Ster.: £1,500.00

*

HN 1662
Delicia
Designer: L. Harradine
Height: 5 3/4", 14.6 cm
Colour: Pink and lavender
Issued: 1934-1938
Varieties: HN 1663, 1681

U.S.: $1,900.00
Can.: $1,900.00
Ster.: £ 750.00

HN 1663
Delicia
Designer: L. Harradine
Height: 5 3/4", 14.6 cm
Colour: Lavender, pink and green
Issued: 1934-1938
Varieties: HN 1662, 1681

U.S.: $1,900.00
Can.: $1,900.00
Ster.: £ 750.00

HN 1664
Aileen
Designer: L. Harradine
Height: 6", 15.2 cm
Colour: Pink dress, patterned shawl
Issued: 1934-1938
Varieties: HN 1645, 1803

U.S.: $2,200.00
Can.: $2,200.00
Ster.: £ 900.00

HN 1665
Miss Winsome
Designer: L. Harradine
Height: 6 3/4", 17.2 cm
Colour: Lavender dress, patterned shawl
Issued: 1934-1949
Varieties: HN 1666

U.S.: $1,350.00
Can.: $1,350.00
Ster.: £ 550.00

HN 1666
Miss Winsome
Designer: L. Harradine
Height: 6 3/4", 17.2 cm
Colour: Green dress, patterned shawl
Issued: 1934-1938
Varieties: HN 1665

U.S.: $1,550.00
Can.: $1,550.00
Ster.: £ 650.00

NOTE ON PRICING

Prices are given for three separate and distinct market areas.

Prices are given in the currency of each of these different trading areas.

Prices are not exchange rate calculations but are based on supply and demand in that market.

Prices listed are guidelines to the most current retail values but actual selling prices may vary slightly.

Prices for current figurines are taken from the Royal Doulton suggested retail lists.

Extremely rare figurines have widely fluctuating retail values and their prices must therefore be determined between buyer and seller.

Figurines where there are only one or two known are possibly best priced in an auction environment.

Prices given are for figurines in mint condition.

HN 1667
Blossom
Designer: L. Harradine
Height: 6 3/4", 17.2 cm
Colour: Orange and blue
Issued: 1934-1949

U.S.: $2,800.00
Can.: $2,800.00
Ster.: £1,250.00

HN 1668
Sibell
Designer: L. Harradine
Height: 6 1/2", 16.5 cm
Colour: Red and green
Issued: 1934-1949
Varieties: HN 1695, 1735

U.S.: $1,300.00
Can.: $1,300.00
Ster.: £ 500.00

HN 1669
Anthea
Designer: L. Harradine
Height: 6 1/2", 16.5 cm
Colour: Pink dress,
green shawl
Issued: 1934-1940
Varieties: HN 1526, 1527

U.S.: $1,750.00
Can.: $1,750.00
Ster.: £ 750.00

HN 1670
Gillian
Style One
Designer: L. Harradine
Height: 7 3/4", 19.7 cm
Colour: Pink
Issued: 1934-1949
Varieties: HN 1670A

U.S.: $1,500.00
Can.: $1,500.00
Ster.: £ 675.00

HN 1670A
Gillian
Style One
Designer: L. Harradine
Height: 7 3/4", 19.7 cm
Colour: Green jacket, white
flowered skirt
Issued: Unknown
Varieties: HN 1670

U.S.: $1,700.00
Can.: $1,700.00
Ster.: £ 675.00

HN 1677
Tinkle Bell
Designer: L. Harradine
Height: 4 3/4", 12.0 cm
Colour: Pink
Issued: 1935-1988

U.S.: $135.00
Can.: $150.00
Ster: £ 75.00

HN 1678
Dinky Doo
Designer: L. Harradine
Height: 4 3/4", 12.0 cm
Colour: Lavender
Issued: 1934-1996
Varieties: HN 2120, 3618

U.S.: $143.75
Can.: $205.00
Ster.: £ 49.95

HN 1679
Babie
Designer: L. Harradine
Height: 4 3/4", 12.0 cm
Colour: Green
Issued: 1935-1992
Varieties: HN 1842, 2121

U.S.: $125.00
Can.: $150.00
Ster.: £ 65.00

HN 1680
Tootles
Designer: L. Harradine
Height: 4 3/4", 12.0 cm
Colour: Pink
Issued: 1935-1975

U.S.: $135.00
Can.: $150.00
Ster.: £ 95.00

HN 1681
Delicia
Designer: L. Harradine
Height: 5 3/4", 14.6 cm
Colour: Green and purple
Issued: 1935-1938
Varieties: HN 1662, 1663

U.S.: $1,850.00
Can.: $1,850.00
Ster.: £ 750.00

HN 1682
Teresa
Style One
Designer: L. Harradine
Height: 5 3/4", 14.6 cm
Colour: Red and brown
Issued: 1935-1949
Varieties: HN 1683

U.S.: $2,750.00
Can.: $2,750.00
Ster.: £1,250.00

HN 1683
Teresa
Style One
Designer: L. Harradine
Height: 5 3/4", 14.6 cm
Colour: Light blue and brown
Issued: 1935-1938
Varieties: HN 1682

U.S.: $4,000.00
Can.: $4,000.00
Ster.: £2,000.00

HN 1684
Lisette
Designer: L. Harradine
Height: 5 1/4", 13.3 cm
Colour: Pink and green
Issued: 1935-1936
Varieties: HN 1523, 1524

U.S.: $2,250.00
Can.: $2,250.00
Ster.: £ 750.00

HN 1685
Cynthia
Style One
Designer: L. Harradine
Height: 5 3/4", 14.6 cm
Colour: Pink and turquoise
Issued: 1935-1949
Varieties: HN 1686, 1686A

U.S.: $1,750.00
Can.: $1,750.00
Ster.: £ 750.00

HN 1686
Cynthia
Style One
Designer: L. Harradine
Height: 5 3/4", 14.6 cm
Colour: Blue and red
Issued: 1935-1949
Varieties: HN 1685, 1686A

U.S.: $1,750.00
Can.: $1,750.00
Ster.: £ 750.00

HN 1686A
Cynthia
Style One
Designer: L. Harradine
Height: 5 3/4", 14.6 cm
Colour: Red and purple
Issued: 1935-1949
Varieties: HN 1685, 1686

U.S.: $1,750.00
Can.: $1,750.00
Ster.: £ 750.00

HN 1687
Clarissa
Style One
Designer: L. Harradine
Height: 9 3/4", 24.8 cm
Colour: Blue, green and orange
Issued: 1935-1949
Varieties: HN 1525

  U.S.:   **$1,400.00**
  Can.:   **$1,400.00**
  Ster.:   £ **400.00**

Earthenware

HN 1688
Rhoda
Designer: L. Harradine
Height: 10 1/4", 26.7 cm
Colour: Orange and red
Issued: 1935-1940
Varieties: HN 1573, 1574

  U.S.:   **$1,200.00**
  Can.:   **$1,200.00**
  Ster.:   £ **450.00**

Earthenware

HN 1689
Calumet
Designer: C.J. Noke
Height: 6 1/2", 16.5 cm
Colour: Green and brown
Issued: 1935-1949
Varieties: HN 1428, 2068

  U.S.:   **$1,200.00**
  Can.:   **$1,200.00**
  Ster.:   £ **550.00**

Earthenware

HN 1690
June
Style One
Designer: L. Harradine
Height: 7 1/4", 18.4 cm
Colour: Pale green and pink
Issued: 1935-1949
Varieties: HN 1691, 1947, 2027

  U.S.:   **$1,100.00**
  Can.:   **$1,100.00**
  Ster.:   £ **475.00**

HN 1691
June
Style One
Designer: L. Harradine
Height: 7 1/4", 18.4 cm
Colour: Yellow and pink
Issued: 1935-1949
Varieties: HN 1690, 1947, 2027

  U.S.:   **$1,100.00**
  Can.:   **$1,100.00**
  Ster.:   £ **475.00**

HN 1692
Sonia
Designer: L. Harradine
Height: 6 1/4", 15.9 cm
Colour: Pink, white and green
Issued: 1935-1949
Varieties: HN 1738

  U.S.:   **$1,900.00**
  Can.:   **$1,900.00**
  Ster.:   £ **850.00**

HN 1693
Virginia
Designer: L. Harradine
Height: 7 1/2", 19.1 cm
Colour: Yellow and red
Issued: 1935-1949
Varieties: HN 1694

  U.S.:   **$1,900.00**
  Can.:   **$1,900.00**
  Ster.:   £ **725.00**

HN 1694
Virginia
Designer: L. Harradine
Height: 7 1/2", 19.1 cm
Colour: Green
Issued: 1935-1949
Varieties: HN 1693

  U.S.:   **$2,000.00**
  Can.:   **$2,000.00**
  Ster.:   £ **750.00**

HN 1695
Sibell
Designer: L. Harradine
Height: 6 1/2", 16.5 cm
Colour: Green and orange
Issued: 1935-1949
Varieties: HN 1668, 1735

U.S.: $1,250.00
Can.: $1,250.00
Ster.: £ 550.00

HN 1696
Suzette
Designer: L. Harradine
Height: 7 1/2", 19.1 cm
Colour: Flowered green dress
Issued: 1935-1949
Varieties: HN 1487, 1577,
1585, 2026

U.S.: $ 950.00
Can.: $1,100.00
Ster.: £ 375.00

HN 1697
Irene
Designer: L. Harradine
Height: 7", 17.8 cm
Colour: Pink
Issued: 1935-1949
Varieties: HN 1621, 1952

U.S.: $1,250.00
Can.: $1,250.00
Ster.: £ 450.00

HN 1698
Phyllis
Style One
Designer: L. Harradine
Height: 9", 22.9 cm
Colour: Green
Issued: 1935-1949
Varieties: HN 1420, 1430, 1486

U.S.: $1,500.00
Can.: $1,500.00
Ster.: £ 600.00

HN 1699
Marietta
Designer: L. Harradine
Height: 8", 20.3 cm
Colour: Green and red
Issued: 1935-1940
Varieties: HN 1341, 1446

U.S.: $2,800.00
Can.: $2,800.00
Ster.: £ 900.00

HN 1700
Gloria
Style One
Designer: L. Harradine
Height: 7", 17.8 cm
Colour: Green and black
Issued: 1935-1938
Varieties: HN 1488

U.S.: $3,250.00
Can.: $3,250.00
Ster.: £1,500.00

HN 1701
Sweet Anne
Style One
Designer: L. Harradine
Height: 7", 17.8 cm
Colour: Pink and blue
Issued: 1935-1938
Varieties: HN 1318, 1330, 1331,
1453, 1496, 1631

U.S.: $1,200.00
Can.: $1,200.00
Ster.: £ 550.00

HN 1702
A Jester
Style One
Designer: C.J. Noke
Height: 10", 25.4 cm
Colour: Brown and mauve
Issued: 1935-1949
Varieties: HN 45, 71, 71A,
320, 367, 412, 426,
446, 552, 616, 627,
1295, 2016

U.S.: $1,100.00
Can.: $1,000.00
Ster.: £ 475.00

176

HN 1703
Charley's Aunt
Style Three
Designer: A. Toft
Height: 6", 15.2 cm
Colour: Lilac and white,
no base
Issued: 1935-1938
U.S.: **$2,000.00**
Can.: **$2,000.00**
Ster.: £ 750.00

HN 1704
Herminia
Designer: L. Harradine
Height: 6 3/4", 17.2 cm
Colour: Red
Issued: 1935-1938
Varieties: HN 1644, 1646
U.S.: **$1,900.00**
Can.: **$1,900.00**
Ster.: £ 875.00

HN 1705
The Cobbler
Style Three
Designer: C.J. Noke
Height: 8", 20.3 cm
Colour: Purple and blue
Issued: 1935-1949
Varieties: HN 1706
U.S.: **$1,300.00**
Can.: **$1,300.00**
Ster.: £ 400.00

Earthenware

HN 1706
The Cobbler
Style Three
Designer: C.J. Noke
Height: 8 1/4", 21.0 cm
Colour: Green and brown
Issued: 1935-1969
Varieties: HN 1705
U.S.: **$400.00**
Can.: **$500.00**
Ster.: £275.00

Earthenware

HN 1707
Paisley Shawl
Style One
Designer: L. Harradine
Height: 8 1/4", 21.0 cm
Colour: Purple
Issued: 1935-1949
Varieties: HN 1392, 1460,
1739, 1987
U.S.: **$1,200.00**
Can.: **$1,200.00**
Ster.: £ 450.00

HN 1708
The Bather
Style One
Designer: L. Harradine
Height: 7 3/4", 19.7 cm
Colour: Black, red and
turquoise
Issued: 1935-1938
Varieties: HN 597, 687,
781, 782, 1238
U.S.: **$4,000.00**
Can.: **$4,000.00**
Ster.: £1,500.00

HN 1709
Pantalettes
Style One
Designer: L. Harradine
Height: 8", 20.3 cm
Colour: Red
Issued: 1935-1938
Varieties: HN 1362, 1412, 1507
U.S.: **$1,500.00**
Can.: **$1,500.00**
Ster.: £ 675.00

HN 1710
Camilla
Designer: L. Harradine
Height: 7", 17.8 cm
Colour: Red and yellow
Issued: 1935-1949
Varieties: HN 1711
U.S.: **$1,950.00**
Can.: **$1,950.00**
Ster.: £ 750.00

HN 1711
Camilla
Designer: L. Harradine
Height: 7", 17.8 cm
Colour: Green and yellow
Issued: 1935-1949
Varieties: HN 1710

U.S.: $1,950.00
Can.: $1,950.00
Ster.: £ 750.00

HN 1712
Daffy Down Dilly
Designer: L. Harradine
Height: 7 3/4", 19.7 cm
Colour: Green
Issued: 1935-1975
Varieties: HN 1713

U.S.: $500.00
Can.: $625.00
Ster.: £375.00

HN 1713
Daffy Down Dilly
Designer: L. Harradine
Height: 8 1/4", 21.0 cm
Colour: Turquoise
Issued: 1935-1949
Varieties: HN 1712

U.S.: $1,500.00
Can.: $1,500.00
Ster.: £ 525.00

HN 1714
Millicent
Designer: L. Harradine
Height: 8", 20.3 cm
Colour: Red
Issued: 1935-1949
Varieties: HN 1715, 1860

U.S.: $2,400.00
Can.: $2,400.00
Ster.: £ 850.00

HN 1715
Millicent
Designer: L. Harradine
Height: 8", 20.3 cm
Colour: Lavender
Issued: 1935-1949
Varieties: HN 1714, 1860

U.S.: $2,600.00
Can.: $2,600.00
Ster.: £1,000.00

HN 1716
Diana
Style One
Designer: L. Harradine
Height: 5 3/4", 14.6 cm
Colour: Pink and blue
Issued: 1935-1949
Varieties: HN 1717, 1986

U.S.: $725.00
Can.: $850.00
Ster.: £325.00

HN 1717
Diana
Style One
Designer: L. Harradine
Height: 5 3/4", 14.6 cm
Colour: Turquoise
Issued: 1935-1949
Varieties: HN 1716, 1986

U.S.: $725.00
Can.: $850.00
Ster.: £325.00

HN 1718
Kate Hardcastle
Designer: L. Harradine
Height: 8", 20.3 cm
Colour: Pink and green
Issued: 1935-1949
Varieties: HN 1719, 1734,
1861, 1919, 2028

U.S.: $1,600.00
Can.: $1,600.00
Ster.: £ 600.00

HN 1719
Kate Hardcastle
Designer: L. Harradine
Height: 8", 20.3 cm
Colour: Red and green
Issued: 1935-1949
Varieties: HN 1718, 1734,
1861, 1919, 2028

U.S.: $1,150.00
Can.: $1,150.00
Ster.: £ 495.00

HN 1720
Frangçon
Designer: L. Harradine
Height: 7 1/2", 19.1 cm
Colour: Lavender dress
with orange and
red flowers
Issued: 1935-1949
Varieties: HN 1721

U.S.: $2,750.00
Can.: $2,750.00
Ster.: £1,000.00

HN 1721
Frangçon
Designer: L. Harradine
Height: 7 1/4", 18.4 cm
Colour: Green
Issued: 1935-1949
Varieties: HN 1720

U.S.: $2,100.00
Can.: $2,100.00
Ster.: £ 750.00

HN 1722
The Coming of Spring
Designer: L. Harradine
Height: 12 1/2", 31.7 cm
Colour: Yellow-pink
Issued: 1935-1949
Varieties: HN 1723

U.S.: $3,500.00
Can.: $3,500.00
Ster.: £1,750.00

HN 1723
The Coming of Spring
Designer: L. Harradine
Height: 12 1/2", 31.7 cm
Colour: Pale green
Issued: 1935-1949
Varieties: HN 1722

U.S.: $3,500.00
Can.: $3,500.00
Ster.: £1,750.00

HN 1724
Ruby
Designer: L. Harradine
Height: 5 1/4", 13.3 cm
Colour: Red
Issued: 1935-1949
Varieties: HN 1725

U.S.: $700.00
Can.: $775.00
Ster.: £375.00

HN 1725
Ruby
Designer: L. Harradine
Height: 5 1/4", 13.3 cm
Colour: Blue
Issued: 1935-1949
Varieties: HN 1724

U.S.: $850.00
Can.: $895.00
Ster.: £400.00

HN 1726
Celia
Designer: L. Harradine
Height: 11 1/2", 29.2 cm
Colour: Pale lavender
Issued: 1935-1949
Varieties: HN 1727

U.S.: $2,500.00
Can.: $2,500.00
Ster.: £1,250.00

HN 1727
Celia
Designer: L. Harradine
Height: 11 1/2", 29.2 cm
Colour: Pale green
Issued: 1935-1949
Varieties: HN 1726

U.S.: $1,750.00
Can.: $1,750.00
Ster.: £1,250.00

HN 1728
The New Bonnet
Designer: L. Harradine
Height: 7", 17.8 cm
Colour: Pink
Issued: 1935-1949
Varieties: HN 1957

U.S.: $1,350.00
Can.: $1,350.00
Ster.: £ 625.00

HN 1729
Vera
Designer: L. Harradine
Height: 4 1/4", 10.8 cm
Colour: Pink
Issued: 1935-1940
Varieties: HN 1730

U.S.: $1,350.00
Can.: $1,350.00
Ster.: £ 650.00

HN 1730
Vera
Designer: L. Harradine
Height: 4 1/4", 10.8 cm
Colour: Green
Issued: 1935-1938
Varieties: HN 1729

U.S.: $1,250.00
Can.: $1,250.00
Ster.: £ 650.00

HN 1731
Daydreams
Designer: L. Harradine
Height: 5 3/4", 14.6 cm
Colour: Pink
Issued: 1935 to the present
Varieties: HN 1732, 1944

U.S.: $350.00
Can.: $445.00
Ster.: £139.00

HN 1732
Daydreams
Designer: L. Harradine
Height: 5 1/2", 14.0 cm
Colour: Light blue and pink
Issued: 1935-1949
Varieties: HN 1731, 1944

U.S.: $1,150.00
Can.: $1,250.00
Ster.: £ 400.00

HN 1734
Kate Hardcastle
Designer: L. Harradine
Height: 8 1/4", 21.0 cm
Colour: Green and white
Issued: 1935-1949
Varieties: HN 1718, 1719,
1861, 1919, 2028

U.S.: $1,850.00
Can.: $1,850.00
Ster.: £ 700.00

HN 1735
Sibell
Designer: L. Harradine
Height: 6 1/2", 16.5 cm
Colour: White and blue
Issued: 1935-1949
Varieties: HN 1668, 1695

U.S.: $1,500.00
Can.: $1,500.00
Ster.: £ 650.00

HN 1736
Camille
Style One
Designer: L. Harradine
Height: 6 1/2", 16.5 cm
Colour: Pink and cream
Issued: 1935-1949
Varieties: HN 1586, 1648

U.S.: **$2,250.00**
Can.: **$2,250.00**
Ster.: £ 900.00

HN 1737
Janet
Style One
Designer: L. Harradine
Height: 6 1/4", 15.9 cm
Colour: Green
Issued: 1935-1949
Varieties: HN 1537, 1538, 1652

U.S.: **$900.00**
Can.: **$900.00**
Ster.: £350.00

HN 1738
Sonia
Designer: L. Harradine
Height: 6 1/2", 16.5 cm
Colour: Green
Issued: 1935-1949
Varieties: HN 1692

U.S.: **$1,900.00**
Can.: **$1,900.00**
Ster.: £ 950.00

HN 1739
Paisley Shawl
Style One
Designer: L. Harradine
Height: 8 1/4", 21.0 cm
Colour: Green and red
Issued: 1935-1949
Varieties: HN 1392, 1460,
1707, 1987

U.S.: **$950.00**
Can.: **$950.00**
Ster.: £400.00

HN 1740
Gladys
Designer: L. Harradine
Height: 5 1/4", 13.3 cm
Colour: Green
Issued: 1935-1949
Varieties: HN 1741

U.S.: **$1,350.00**
Can.: **$1,350.00**
Ster.: £ 625.00

HN 1741
Gladys
Designer: L. Harradine
Height: 5", 12.7 cm
Colour: Pink
Issued: 1935-1938
Varieties: HN 1740

U.S.: **$1,350.00**
Can.: **$1,350.00**
Ster.: £ 625.00

HN 1742
Sir Walter Raleigh
Designer: L. Harradine
Height: 10 1/2", 26.7 cm
Colour: Green, purple
and orange
Issued: 1935-1949
Varieties: HN 1751, 2015

U.S.: **$5,000.00**
Can.: **$5,000.00**
Ster.: £1,500.00

HN 1743
Mirabel
Style One
Designer: L. Harradine
Height: 7 3/4", 19.7 cm
Colour: Pale blue
Issued: 1935-1949
Varieties: HN 1744

U.S.: **$1,950.00**
Can.: **$1,950.00**
Ster.: £ 850.00

HN 1744
Mirabel
Style One
Designer: L. Harradine
Height: 7 3/4", 19.7 cm
Colour: Pink
Issued: 1935-1949
Varieties: HN 1743

U.S.: $1,750.00
Can.: $1,750.00
Ster.: £ 800.00

HN 1745
The Rustic Swain
Designer: L. Harradine
Height: 5 1/4", 13.3 cm
Colour: Green, white and brown
Issued: 1935-1949
Varieties: HN 1746

U.S.: $2,750.00
Can.: $2,750.00
Ster.: £1,250.00

HN 1746
The Rustic Swain
Designer: L. Harradine
Height: 5 1/4", 13.3 cm
Colour: Green, blue and pink
Issued: 1935-1949
Varieties: HN 1745

U.S.: $3,500.00
Can.: $3,500.00
Ster.: £1,450.00

HN 1747
Afternoon Tea
Designer: P. Railston
Height: 5 3/4", 14.6 cm
Colour: Pink and blue
Issued: 1935-1982
Varieties: HN 1748

U.S.: $600.00
Can.: $575.00
Ster.: £375.00

HN 1748
Afternoon Tea
Designer: P. Railston
Height: 5 1/4", 13.3 cm
Colour: Green
Issued: 1935-1949
Varieties: HN 1747

U.S.: $2,200.00
Can.: $2,200.00
Ster.: £ 950.00

HN 1749
Pierrette
Style Three
Designer: L. Harradine
Height: 8 1/2", 21.6 cm
Colour: Purple
Issued: 1936-1949
Varieties: HN 1391

U.S.: $2,900.00
Can.: $3,250.00
Ster.: £1,500.00

Earthenware

HN 1750
Folly
Designer: L. Harradine
Height: 9 1/2", 24.1 cm
Colour: Black-purple
Issued: 1936-1949
Varieties: HN 1335

U.S.: $2,700.00
Can.: $4,000.00
Ster.: £2,000.00

Earthenware

HN 1751
Sir Walter Raleigh
Designer: L. Harradine
Height: 11 1/2", 29.2 cm
Colour: Orange and purple
Issued: 1936-1949
Varieties: HN 1742, 2015

U.S.: $1,600.00
Can.: $1,600.00
Ster.: £ 750.00

Earthenware

HN 1752
Regency
Designer: L. Harradine
Height: 8", 20.3 cm
Colour: Lavender and green
Issued: 1936-1949
U.S.: $1,900.00
Can.: $1,900.00
Ster.: £ 750.00

HN 1753
Eleanore
Designer: L. Harradine
Height: 7", 17.8 cm
Colour: Blue, green and pink
Issued: 1936-1949
Varieties: HN 1754
U.S.: $2,200.00
Can.: $2,200.00
Ster.: £ 800.00

HN 1754
Eleanore
Designer: L. Harradine
Height: 7", 17.8 cm
Colour: Orange and cream
Issued: 1936-1949
Varieties: HN 1753
U.S.: $2,000.00
Can.: $2,000.00
Ster.: £ 800.00

HN 1755
The Court Shoemaker
Designer: L. Harradine
Height: 6 3/4", 17.2 cm
Colour: Purple, brown
        and green
Issued: 1936-1949
U.S.: $3,400.00
Can.: $3,400.00
Ster.: £1,250.00

HN 1756
Lizana
Designer: L. Harradine
Height: 8 1/2", 21.6 cm
Colour: Green, pink and
        purple
Issued: 1936-1949
Varieties: HN 1761
U.S.: $1,600.00
Can.: $1,600.00
Ster.: £ 750.00

HN 1757
Romany Sue
Designer: L. Harradine
Height: 9 1/4", 23.5 cm
Colour: Green and red
Issued: 1936-1949
Varieties: HN 1758
U.S.: $1,600.00
Can.: $1,600.00
Ster.: £ 750.00

HN 1758
Romany Sue
Designer: L. Harradine
Height: 9 1/2", 24.1 cm
Colour: Lavender
Issued: 1936-1949
Varieties: HN 1757
U.S.: $2,100.00
Can.: $2,100.00
Ster.: £ 750.00

HN 1759
The Orange Lady
Designer: L. Harradine
Height: 8 3/4", 22.2 cm
Colour: Pink
Issued: 1936-1975
Varieties: HN 1953
U.S.: $400.00
Can.: $475.00
Ster.: £175.00

1. Earlier pieces have holes in
   the oranges
2. Earthenware

HN 1760
4 O'Clock
Designer: L. Harradine
Height: 6", 15.2 cm
Colour: Lavender
Issued: 1936-1949
U.S.: **$2,100.00**
Can.: **$2,100.00**
Ster.: £ 750.00

HN 1761
Lizana
Designer: L. Harradine
Height: 8 1/2", 21.6 cm
Colour: Green
Issued: 1936-1938
Varieties: HN 1756
U.S.: **$1,400.00**
Can.: **$1,400.00**
Ster.: £ 750.00

HN 1762
The Bride
Style One
Designer: L. Harradine
Height: 8 3/4", 22.2 cm
Colour: Cream
Issued: 1936-1949
Varieties: HN 1588, 1600, 1841
U.S.: **$1,750.00**
Can.: **$1,750.00**
Ster.: £ 700.00

HN 1763
Windflower
Style One
Designer: L. Harradine
Height: 7 1/4", 18.4 cm
Colour: Pink
Issued: 1936-1949
Varieties: HN 1764, 2029
U.S.: **$650.00**
Can.: **$750.00**
Ster.: £425.00

HN 1764
Windflower
Style One
Designer: L. Harradine
Height: 7 1/4", 18.4 cm
Colour: Blue
Issued: 1936-1949
Varieties: HN 1763, 2029
U.S.: **$1,200.00**
Can.: **$1,200.00**
Ster.: £ 650.00

HN 1765
Chloe
Style One
Designer: L. Harradine
Height: 6", 15.2 cm
Colour: Blue
Issued: 1936-1950
Varieties: HN 1470, 1476,
1479, 1498, 1956
U.S.: **$425.00**
Can.: **$550.00**
Ster.: £325.00

HN 1766
Nana
Designer: L. Harradine
Height: 4 3/4", 12.0 cm
Colour: Pink
Issued: 1936-1949
Varieties: HN 1767
U.S.: **$475.00**
Can.: **$650.00**
Ster.: £300.00

HN 1767
Nana
Designer: L. Harradine
Height: 4 3/4", 12.0 cm
Colour: Lavender
Issued: 1936-1949
Varieties: HN 1766
U.S.: **$550.00**
Can.: **$650.00**
Ster.: £300.00

HN 1768
Ivy
Designer: L. Harradine
Height: 4 3/4", 12.0 cm
Colour: Purple
Issued: 1936-1979
Varieties: HN 1769

U.S.: $150.00
Can.: $175.00
Ster.: £110.00

HN 1769
Ivy
Designer: L. Harradine
Height: 4 3/4", 12.0 cm
Colour: Unknown
Issued: 1936-1938
Varieties: HN 1768

U.S.: $600.00
Can.: $675.00
Ster.: £250.00

HN 1770
Maureen
Style One
Designer: L. Harradine
Height: 7 1/2", 19.1 cm
Colour: Pink
Issued: 1936-1959
Varieties: HN 1771

U.S.: $500.00
Can.: $600.00
Ster.: £350.00

HN 1771
Maureen
Style One
Designer: L. Harradine
Height: 7 1/2", 19.1 cm
Colour: Lavender
Issued: 1936-1949
Varieties: HN 1770

U.S.: $1,600.00
Can.: $1,600.00
Ster.: £ 650.00

HN 1772
Delight
Designer: L. Harradine
Height: 7", 17.8 cm
Colour: Red
Issued: 1936-1967
Varieties: HN 1773

U.S.: $300.00
Can.: $400.00
Ster.: £275.00

HN 1773
Delight
Designer: L. Harradine
Height: 6 3/4", 17.2 cm
Colour: Turquoise
Issued: 1936-1949
Varieties: HN 1772

U.S.: $1,100.00
Can.: $1,100.00
Ster.: £ 450.00

HN 1774
Spring (Matte)
Style Three
Designer: R. Garbe
Height: 21", 53.3 cm
Colour: Ivory
Issued: 1933 in a limited
edition of 100
Varieties: HN 1827

U.S.: Only
Can.: five
Ster.: known

HN 1775
Salome (Matte)
Style One
Designer: R. Garbe
Height: 8", 20.3 cm
Colour: Ivory
Issued: 1933 in a limited
edition of 100
Varieties: HN 1828

U.S.: Only
Can.: two
Ster.: known

HN 1776
West Wind (Matte)
Designer: R. Garbe
Height: 14 1/2", 36.8 cm
Colour: Ivory
Issued: 1933 in a limited
edition of 25
Varieties: HN 1826

U.S.:	**Only**
Can.:	**three**
Ster.:	**known**

Photograph
Not
Available

HN 1777
Spirit of the Wind (Matte)
Designer: R. Garbe
Height: Unknown
Colour: Ivory
Issued: 1933 in a limited
edition of 50
Varieties: HN 1825

U.S.:	**None**
Can.:	**known**
Ster.:	**to exist**

HN 1778
Beethoven (Matte)
Designer: R. Garbe
Height: 22", 55.8 cm
Colour: Ivory
Issued: 1933 in a limited
edition of 25

U.S.:	**Only**
Can.:	**two**
Ster.:	**known**

Photograph
Not
Available

HN 1779
Macaw (Matte)
Designer: R. Garbe
Height: 14 1/2", 35.6 cm
Colour: Ivory
Issued: 1933-1949
Varieties: HN 1829

U.S.:	**Only**
Can.:	**one**
Ster.:	**known**

HN 1780
Lady of the Snows
Designer: R. Garbe
Height: Unknown
Colour: Unknown
Issued: 1933 in a limited
edition of 50
Varieties: HN 1830

U.S.:	**Only**
Can.:	**one**
Ster.:	**known**

HN 1791
Old Balloon Seller and
Bulldog
Designer: L. Harradine
Height: 7", 17.8 cm
Colour: Green, red and white
Issued: 1932-1938
Varieties: HN 1912

U.S.:	**Only**
Can.:	**one**
Ster.:	**known**

HN 1792
Henry VIII
Style Two
Designer: C. J. Noke
Height: 11 1/2", 29.2 cm
Colour: Multi-coloured
Issued: 1933 in a limited
edition of 200

U.S.:	**$7,500.00**
Can.:	**$7,500.00**
Ster.:	**£2,750.00**

HN 1793
This Little Pig
Designer: L. Harradine
Height: 4", 10.1 cm
Colour: Red
Issued: 1936-1995
Varieties: HN 1794, 2125

U.S.:	**$175.00**
Can.:	**$200.00**
Ster.:	**£ 65.00**

HN 1794
This Little Pig
Designer: L. Harradine
Height: 4", 10.1 cm
Colour: Blue
Issued: 1936-1949
Varieties: HN 1793, 2125

U.S.:	**$800.00**
Can.:	**$700.00**
Ster.:	**£350.00**

HN 1795
M'Lady's Maid
Designer: L. Harradine
Height: 9", 22.9 cm
Colour: Red
Issued: 1936-1949
Varieties: HN 1822

U.S.:	**$3,000.00**
Can.:	**$3,000.00**
Ster.:	**£1,250.00**

HN 1796
Hazel
Style One
Designer: L. Harradine
Height: 5 1/4", 13.3 cm
Colour: Green and red
Issued: 1936-1949
Varieties: HN 1797

U.S.:	**$750.00**
Can.:	**$850.00**
Ster.:	**£350.00**

HN 1797
Hazel
Style One
Designer: L. Harradine
Height: 5 1/4", 13.3 cm
Colour: Pink and blue
Issued: 1936-1949
Varieties: HN 1796

U.S.:	**$700.00**
Can.:	**$800.00**
Ster.:	**£350.00**

HN 1798
Lily
Style One
Designer: L. Harradine
Height: 5", 12.7 cm
Colour: Pink
Issued: 1936-1971
Varieties: HN 1799

U.S.:	**$200.00**
Can.:	**$275.00**
Ster.:	**£130.00**

HN 1799
Lily
Style One
Designer: L. Harradine
Height: 5", 12.7 cm
Colour: Green and blue
Issued: 1936-1949
Varieties: HN 1798

U.S.:	**$650.00**
Can.:	**$700.00**
Ster.:	**£275.00**

HN 1800
St. George
Style One
Designer: S. Thorogood
Height: 16", 40.6 cm
Colour: Purple, green and grey
Issued: 1934-1950
Varieties: HN 385, 386, 2067

U.S.:	**$5,000.00**
Can.:	**$5,000.00**
Ster.:	**£2,000.00**

Earthenware

HN 1801
An Old King
Designer: C.J. Noke
Height: 9 3/4", 24.7 cm
Colour: Unknown
Issued: 1937-1954
Varieties: HN 358, 623, 2134

U.S.:	**Extremely rare**
Can.:	
Ster.:	

HN 1802
Estelle
Designer: L. Harradine
Height: 8", 20.3 cm
Colour: Pink
Issued: 1937-1940
Varieties: HN 1566

U.S.: $1,900.00
Can.: $1,900.00
Ster.: £ 950.00

HN 1803
Aileen
Designer: L. Harradine
Height: 6", 15.2 cm
Colour: Cream dress
with blue shawl
Issued: 1937-1949
Varieties: HN 1645, 1664

U.S.: $2,600.00
Can.: $2,600.00
Ster.: £ 975.00

HN 1804
Granny
Designer: L. Harradine
Height: 7", 17.8 cm
Colour: Grey, purple
and brown
Issued: 1937-1949
Varieties: HN 1832

U.S.: Only
Can.: three
Ster.: known

HN 1805
To Bed
Designer: L. Harradine
Height: 6", 15.2 cm
Colour: Green
Issued: 1937-1959
Varieties: HN 1806

U.S.: $250.00
Can.: $300.00
Ster.: £175.00

HN 1806
To Bed
Designer: L. Harradine
Height: 6", 15.2 cm
Colour: Lavender
Issued: 1937-1949
Varieties: HN 1805

U.S.: $700.00
Can.: $700.00
Ster.: £325.00

HN 1807
Spring Flowers
Designer: L. Harradine
Height: 7 1/4", 18.4 cm
Colour: Green and blue
Issued: 1937-1959
Varieties: HN 1945

U.S.: $525.00
Can.: $650.00
Ster.: £350.00

HN 1808
Cissie
Designer: L. Harradine
Height: 5", 12.7 cm
Colour: Green
Issued: 1937-1951
Varieties: HN 1809

U.S.: $675.00
Can.: $750.00
Ster.: £275.00

HN 1809
Cissie
Designer: L. Harradine
Height: 5", 12.7 cm
Colour: Pink
Issued: 1937-1993
Varieties: HN 1808

U.S.: $185.00
Can.: $225.00
Ster.: £ 90.00

HN 1810
Bo-Peep
Style Two
Designer: L. Harradine
Height: 5", 12.7 cm
Colour: Blue
Issued: 1937-1949
Varieties: HN 1811

U.S.: $800.00
Can.: $900.00
Ster.: £300.00

HN 1811
Bo-Peep
Style Two
Designer: L. Harradine
Height: 5", 12.7 cm
Colour: Pink
Issued: 1937-1995
Varieties: HN 1810

U.S.: $175.00
Can.: $200.00
Ster.: £ 75.00

HN 1812
Forget-Me-Not
Style One
Designer: L. Harradine
Height: 6", 15.2 cm
Colour: Pink and green
Issued: 1937-1949
Varieties: HN 1813

U.S.: $1,000.00
Can.: $1,150.00
Ster.: £ 525.00

HN 1813
Forget-Me-Not
Style One
Designer: L. Harradine
Height: 6", 15.2 cm
Colour: Red and blue
Issued: 1937-1949
Varieties: HN 1812

U.S.: $850.00
Can.: $950.00
Ster.: £500.00

HN 1814
The Squire
Designer: Unknown
Height: 9 3/4", 24.7 cm
Colour: Red and grey
Issued: 1937-1949
Varieties: Also called "Hunting
Squire" HN 1409

U.S.: $5,500.00
Can.: $5,500.00
Ster.: £2,250.00

Earthenware

HN 1815
The Huntsman
Style Two
Designer: Unknown
Height: 9 1/2", 24.1 cm
Colour: Red and brown
Issued: 1937-1949
Varieties: Also called "John
Peel" HN 1408

U.S.: $5,500.00
Can.: $5,500.00
Ster.: £2,250.00

Earthenware

HN 1818
Miranda
Style One
Designer: L. Harradine
Height: 8 1/2", 21.6 cm
Colour: Red and blue
Issued: 1937-1949
Varieties: HN 1819

U.S.: $2,800.00
Can.: $2,800.00
Ster.: £1,100.00

HN 1819
Miranda
Style One
Designer: L. Harradine
Height: 8 1/2", 21.6 cm
Colour: Green
Issued: 1937-1949
Varieties: HN 1818

U.S.: $3,000.00
Can.: $3,000.00
Ster.: £1,250.00

HN 1820
Reflections
Style One
Designer: L. Harradine
Height: 5", 12.7 cm
Colour: Red and green
Issued: 1937-1938
Varieties: HN 1821, 1847, 1848

U.S.:	**$3,500.00**
Can.:	**$3,500.00**
Ster.:	**£2,000.00**

HN 1821
Reflections
Style One
Designer: L. Harradine
Height: 5", 12.7 cm
Colour: Green and red
Issued: 1937-1938
Varieties: HN 1820, 1847, 1848

U.S.:	**$3,500.00**
Can.:	**$3,500.00**
Ster.:	**£2,000.00**

HN 1822
M'Lady's Maid
Designer: L. Harradine
Height: 9", 22.9 cm
Colour: Multi-coloured
Issued: 1937-1949
Varieties: HN 1795

U.S.:	**$4,750.00**
Can.:	**$4,750.00**
Ster.:	**£1,500.00**

*

Photograph
Not
Available

HN 1825
Spirit of the Wind
Designer: R. Garbe
Height: Unknown
Colour: Green and ivory
Issued: 1937-1949
Varieties: HN 1777

U.S.:	**Only**
Can.:	**four**
Ster.:	**Known**

HN 1826
West Wind
Designer: R. Garbe
Height: 14 1/2", 36.8 cm
Colour: Antique ivory
Issued: 1937-1949
Varieties: HN 1776

U.S.:	**Only**
Can.:	**two**
Ster.:	**known**

HN 1827
Spring
Style Three
Designer: R. Garbe
Height: 21", 53.3 cm
Colour: Green and ivory
Issued: 1937-1949
Varieties: HN 1774

U.S.:	**Only**
Can.:	**four**
Ster.:	**known**

HN 1828
Salome
Style One
Designer: R. Garbe
Height: 8", 20.3 cm
Colour: Pale blue
Issued: 1937-1949
Varieties: HN 1775

U.S.:	**Only**
Can.:	**two**
Ster.:	**known**

Photograph
Not
Available

HN 1829
Macaw
Designer: R. Garbe
Height: 14 1/2", 35.6 cm
Colour: Antique ivory
Issued: 1933-1949
Varieties: HN 1779

U.S.:	**Only**
Can.:	**two**
Ster.:	**known**

HN 1830
Lady of the Snows
Designer: R. Garbe
Height: Unknown
Colour: Antique ivory
Issued: 1937-1949
Varieties: HN 1780

U.S.:   **Only**
Can.:   **two**
Ster.: **known**

Photograph
Not
Available

HN 1831
The Cloud
Designer: R. Garbe
Height: 23", 58.4 cm
Colour: Ivory and gold
Issued: 1937-1949

U.S.:   **Only**
Can.:   **two**
Ster.: **known**

HN 1832
Granny
Designer: L. Harradine
Height: 6 3/4", 17.1 cm
Colour: Red and yellow
Issued: 1937-1949
Varieties: HN 1804

U.S.:   **$3,750.00**
Can.:   **$3,750.00**
Ster.: **£1,400.00**

HN 1833
Top o' the Hill
Style One
Designer: L. Harradine
Height: 7", 17.8 cm
Colour: Green and blue
Issued: 1937-1971
Varieties: HN 1834, 1849, 2127

U.S.:   **$350.00**
Can.:   **$450.00**
Ster.: **£175.00**

HN 1834
Top o' the Hill
Style One
Designer: L. Harradine
Height: 7", 17.8 cm
Colour: Red
Issued: 1937 to the present
Varieties: HN 1833, 1849, 2127

U.S.:   **$350.00**
Can.:   **$490.00**
Ster.: **£139.00**

HN 1835
Verena
Designer: L. Harradine
Height: 8 1/4", 21.0 cm
Colour: Green and peach
Issued: 1938-1949
Varieties: HN 1854

U.S.:   **$2,100.00**
Can.:   **$2,100.00**
Ster.: **£ 650.00**

HN 1836
Vanessa
Style One
Designer: L. Harradine
Height: 7 1/2", 19.1 cm
Colour: Green and blue
Issued: 1938-1949
Varieties: HN 1838

U.S.:   **$1,650.00**
Can.:   **$1,650.00**
Ster.: **£ 695.00**

HN 1837
Mariquita
Designer: L. Harradine
Height: 8", 20.3 cm
Colour: Red and purple
Issued: 1938-1949

U.S.:   **$3,500.00**
Can.:   **$3,500.00**
Ster.: **£1,250.00**

HN 1838
Vanessa
Style One
Designer: L. Harradine
Height: 7 1/2", 19.1 cm
Colour: Pink and green
Issued: 1938-1949
Varieties: HN 1836

U.S.:	**$1,850.00**
Can.:	**$1,850.00**
Ster.:	**£ 675.00**

HN 1839
Christine
Style One
Designer: L. Harradine
Height: 7 3/4", 19.6 cm
Colour: Lavender and blue
Issued: 1938-1949
Varieties: HN 1840

U.S.:	**$1,850.00**
Can.:	**$1,850.00**
Ster.:	**£ 750.00**

HN 1840
Christine
Style One
Designer: L. Harradine
Height: 7 3/4", 19.6 cm
Colour: Pink and blue
Issued: 1938-1949
Varieties: HN 1839

U.S.:	**$1,500.00**
Can.:	**$1,500.00**
Ster.:	**£ 750.00**

HN 1841
The Bride
Style One
Designer: L. Harradine
Height: 9 1/2", 24.1 cm
Colour: Blue
Issued: 1938-1949
Varieties: HN 1588, 1600, 1762

U.S.:	**$2,000.00**
Can.:	**$2,000.00**
Ster.:	**£ 850.00**

HN 1842
Babie
Designer: L. Harradine
Height: 4 3/4", 12.0 cm
Colour: Rose and green
Issued: 1938-1949
Varieties: HN 1679, 2121

U.S.:	**$450.00**
Can.:	**$475.00**
Ster.:	**£200.00**

HN 1843
Biddy Penny Farthing
Designer: L. Harradine
Height: 9", 22.9 cm
Colour: Green and lavender
Issued: 1938 to the present

U.S.:	**$306.25**
Can.:	**$495.00**
Ster.:	**£139.00**

Earthenware and China

HN 1844
Odds and Ends
Designer: L. Harradine
Height: 7 3/4", 19.6 cm
Colour: Orange and green
Issued: 1938-1949

U.S.:	**$3,250.00**
Can.:	**$3,250.00**
Ster.:	**£1,500.00**

Earthenware

NOTES ON PRICING

The prices on the secondary market for Royal Doulton Figures, particularly the early HN Numbers, have risen considerably over the years. As values rise, the condition and quality of these figurines take on an increasingly important role.

The prices listed in *The Charlton Standard Catalogue of Royal Doulton Beswick Figurines* are for figures in mint condition.

Naturally, repaired or restored figures, no matter how professionally done, will sell at a substantial discount.

On Condition: For figures to command catalogue prices they must be in mint condition. This simply means that a figure will not have paint chips, scratches, hairline cracks, crazing or blemishes. Any of which will remove from the mint category figure.

On Quality: Some figures can be better moulded, assembled or painted than others. High quality figures will command catalogue prices. Low quality figures will not.

If the quality or condition of the figures is below the standard for mint, look for that figure to be priced at a percentage of the catalogue prices.

192

HN 1845
Modena
Designer: L. Harradine
Height: 7 1/4", 18.4 cm
Colour: Blue and pink
Issued: 1938-1949
Varieties: HN 1846

U.S.: $2,750.00
Can.: $2,750.00
Ster.: £1,250.00

HN 1846
Modena
Designer: L. Harradine
Height: 7 1/4", 18.4 cm
Colour: Red and green
Issued: 1938-1949
Varieties: HN 1845

U.S.: $2,500.00
Can.: $2,500.00
Ster.: £1,250.00

HN 1847
Reflections
Style One
Designer: L. Harradine
Height: 4 1/2", 11.4 cm
Colour: Red and green
Issued: 1938-1949
Varieties: HN 1820, 1821, 1848

U.S.: $2,500.00
Can.: $2,500.00
Ster.: £1,250.00

HN 1848
Reflections
Style One
Designer: L. Harradine
Height: 5", 12.7 cm
Colour: Green, blue and pink
Issued: 1938-1949
Varieties: HN 1820, 1821, 1847

U.S.: $2,750.00
Can.: $2,750.00
Ster.: £1,250.00

HN 1849
Top o' the Hill
Style One
Designer: L. Harradine
Height: 7 1/4", 18.4 cm
Colour: Pink
Issued: 1938-1975
Varieties: HN 1833, 1834, 2127

U.S.: $275.00
Can.: $400.00
Ster.: £175.00

HN 1850
Antoinette
Style One
Designer: L. Harradine
Height: 8 1/4", 21.0 cm
Colour: Red and pink
Issued: 1938-1949
Varieties: HN 1851

U.S.: $2,000.00
Can.: $2,000.00
Ster.: £ 950.00

HN 1851
Antoinette
Style One
Designer: L. Harradine
Height: 8 1/4", 21.0 cm
Colour: Blue and lavender
Issued: 1938-1949
Varieties: HN 1850

U.S.: $2,200.00
Can.: $2,200.00
Ster.: £ 950.00

HN 1852
The Mirror
Designer: L. Harradine
Height: 7 1/2", 18.4 cm
Colour: Pink
Issued: 1938-1949
Varieties: HN 1853

U.S.: $4,000.00
Can.: $4,000.00
Ster.: £1,750.00

HN 1853
The Mirror
Designer: L. Harradine
Height: 7 1/2", 18.4 cm
Colour: Blue
Issued: 1938-1949
Varieties: HN 1852

U.S.: $5,250.00
Can.: $5,250.00
Ster.: £2,250.00

HN 1854
Verena
Designer: L. Harradine
Height: 8 1/4", 21.0 cm
Colour: Blue and pink
Issued: 1938-1949
Varieties: HN 1835

U.S.: $2,700.00
Can.: $2,700.00
Ster.: £ 950.00

HN 1855
Memories
Designer: L. Harradine
Height: 6", 15.2 cm
Colour: Green and red
Issued: 1938-1949
Varieties: HN 1856, 1857, 2030

U.S.: $1,100.00
Can.: $1,100.00
Ster.: £ 550.00

HN 1856
Memories
Designer: L. Harradine
Height: 6", 15.2 cm
Colour: Blue and white
Issued: 1938-1949
Varieties: HN 1855, 1857, 2030

U.S.: $1,250.00
Can.: $1,250.00
Ster.: £ 550.00

HN 1857
Memories
Designer: L. Harradine
Height: 6", 15.2 cm
Colour: Red and lavender
Issued: 1938-1949
Varieties: HN 1855, 1856, 2030

U.S.: $1,400.00
Can.: $1,400.00
Ster.: £ 550.00

HN 1858
Dawn
(With head-dress)
Style One
Designer: L. Harradine
Height: 10", 25.4 cm
Colour: Green
Issued: 1938-Unknown
Varieties: HN 1858A

U.S.: $4,000.00
Can.: $4,000.00
Ster.: £1,500.00

HN 1858A
Dawn
(Without head-dress)
Style One
Designer: L. Harradine
Height: 9 3/4", 24.7 cm
Colour: Green
Issued: Unknown-1949
Varieties: HN 1858

U.S.: $2,750.00
Can.: $2,500.00
Ster.: £1,250.00

HN 1859
Tildy
Designer: L. Harradine
Height: 5 1/2", 14.0 cm
Colour: Red and green
Issued: 1934-1939
Varieties: HN 1576

U.S.: $1,750.00
Can.: $1,750.00
Ster.: £ 800.00

HN 1860
Millicent
Designer: L. Harradine
Height: 8", 20.3 cm
Colour: Red and blue
Issued: 1938-1949
Varieties: HN 1714, 1715

U.S.:	**$2,500.00**
Can.:	**$2,500.00**
Ster.:	**£ 900.00**

HN 1861
Kate Hardcastle
Designer: L. Harradine
Height: 8", 20.3 cm
Colour: Red and blue
Issued: 1938-1949
Varieties: HN 1718, 1719,
1734, 1919, 2028

U.S.:	**$2,200.00**
Can.:	**$2,200.00**
Ster.:	**£ 775.00**

HN 1862
Jasmine
Designer: L. Harradine
Height: 7 1/4", 18.4 cm
Colour: Green, blue
and orange
Issued: 1938-1949
Varieties: HN 1863, 1876

U.S.:	**$1,750.00**
Can.:	**$1,750.00**
Ster.:	**£ 750.00**

HN 1863
Jasmine
Designer: L. Harradine
Height: 7 1/2", 19.1 cm
Colour: Blue and green
Issued: 1938-1949
Varieties: HN 1862, 1876

U.S.:	**$2,000.00**
Can.:	**$1,750.00**
Ster.:	**£ 850.00**

HN 1864
Sweet and Fair
Designer: L. Harradine
Height: 7 1/2", 19.1 cm
Colour: Pink
Issued: 1938-1949
Varieties: HN 1865

U.S.:	**$3,250.00**
Can.:	**$3,250.00**
Ster.:	**£1,250.00**

HN 1865
Sweet and Fair
Designer: L. Harradine
Height: 7 1/4", 18.4 cm
Colour: Green
Issued: 1938-1949
Varieties: HN 1864

U.S.:	**$3,250.00**
Can.:	**$3,250.00**
Ster.:	**£1,250.00**

HN 1866
Wedding Morn
Style One
Designer: L. Harradine
Height: 10 1/2", 26.7 cm
Colour: Cream
Issued: 1938-1949
Varieties: HN 1867

U.S.:	**$3,750.00**
Can.:	**$3,750.00**
Ster.:	**£1,500.00**

HN 1867
Wedding Morn
Style One
Designer: L. Harradine
Height: 10 1/2", 26.7 cm
Colour: Red and cream
Issued: 1938-1949
Varieties: HN 1866

U.S.:	**$3,750.00**
Can.:	**$3,750.00**
Ster.:	**£1,500.00**

HN 1868
Serena
Designer: L. Harradine
Height: 11", 27.9 cm
Colour: Red, pink and blue
Issued: 1938-1949

U.S.: $1,850.00
Can.: $1,850.00
Ster.:   £   750.00

Earthenware

Photograph
Not
Available

HN 1869
Dryad of the Pines
Designer: R. Garbe
Height: 23", 58.4 cm
Colour: Ivory and gold
Issued: 1938-1949

U.S.:   **Extremely rare**
Can.:
Ster.:

HN 1870
Little Lady Make Believe
Designer: L. Harradine
Height: 6 1/4", 15.9 cm
Colour: Red and blue
Issued: 1938-1949

U.S.: $700.00
Can.: $850.00
Ster.:   £475.00

HN 1871
Annabella
Designer: L. Harradine
Height: 5 1/4", 13.3 cm
Colour: Pink and green
Issued: 1938-1949
Varieties: HN 1872, 1875

U.S.: $1,300.00
Can.: $1,300.00
Ster.:   £   550.00

HN 1872
Annabella
Designer: L. Harradine
Height: 5 1/4", 13.3 cm
Colour: Green and blue
Issued: 1938-1949
Varieties: HN 1871, 1875

U.S.: $1,300.00
Can.: $1,300.00
Ster.:   £   550.00

HN 1873
Granny's Heritage
Designer: L. Harradine
Height: 6 3/4", 17.2 cm
Colour: Pink, blue and grey
Issued: 1938-1949
Varieties: HN 1874, 2031

U.S.: $1,350.00
Can.: $1,350.00
Ster.:   £   650.00

HN 1874
Granny's Heritage
Designer: L. Harradine
Height: 6 1/4", 15.9 cm
Colour: Blue and green
Issued: 1938-1949
Varieties: HN 1873, 2031

U.S.: $ 950.00
Can.: $1,100.00
Ster.:   £   650.00

HN 1875
Annabella
Designer: L. Harradine
Height: 4 3/4", 12.0 cm
Colour: Red
Issued: 1938-1949
Varieties: HN 1871, 1872

U.S.: $1,300.00
Can.: $1,300.00
Ster.:   £   525.00

HN 1876
Jasmine
Designer: L. Harradine
Height: 7 1/2", 19.1 cm
Colour: Green and blue
Issued: 1938-1949
Varieties: HN 1862, 1863

U.S.: $2,000.00
Can.: $2,000.00
Ster.: £ 750.00

HN 1877
Jean
Style One
Designer: L. Harradine
Height: 7 1/2", 19.0 cm
Colour: Pink and purple
Issued: 1938-1949
Varieties: HN 1878, 2032

U.S.: $1,100.00
Can.: $1,100.00
Ster.: £ 450.00

HN 1878
Jean
Style One
Designer: L. Harradine
Height: 7 1/2", 19.0 cm
Colour: Green and red
Issued: 1938-1949
Varieties: HN 1877, 2032

U.S.: $725.00
Can.: $775.00
Ster.: £395.00

HN 1879
Bon Jour
Designer: L. Harradine
Height: 6 3/4", 17.2 cm
Colour: Green
Issued: 1938-1949
Varieties: HN 1888

U.S.: $1,750.00
Can.: $1,750.00
Ster.: £ 850.00

HN 1880
The Lambeth Walk
Designer: L. Harradine
Height: 10", 25.4 cm
Colour: Blue
Issued: 1938-1949
Varieties: HN 1881

U.S.: $3,750.00
Can.: $3,750.00
Ster.: £1,650.00

HN 1881
The Lambeth Walk
Designer: L. Harradine
Height: 10", 25.4 cm
Colour: Pink
Issued: 1938-1949
Varieties: HN 1880

U.S.: $3,200.00
Can.: $3,200.00
Ster.: £1,450.00

HN 1882
Nell Gwynn
Designer: L. Harradine
Height: 6 3/4", 17.2 cm
Colour: Blue and pink
Issued: 1938-1949
Varieties: HN 1887

U.S.: $1,500.00
Can.: $1,500.00
Ster.: £ 650.00

HN 1883
Prudence
Designer: L. Harradine
Height: 6 3/4", 17.2 cm
Colour: Blue
Issued: 1938-1949
Varieties: HN 1884

U.S.: $1,150.00
Can.: $1,150.00
Ster.: £ 475.00

HN 1884
Prudence
Designer: L. Harradine
Height: 6 3/4", 17.2 cm
Colour: Pink
Issued: 1938-1949
Varieties: HN 1883

U.S.: $1,250.00
Can.: $1,250.00
Ster.: £ 475.00

HN 1885
Nadine
Designer: L. Harradine
Height: 7 3/4", 19.7 cm
Colour: Turquoise
Issued: 1938-1949
Varieties: HN 1886

U.S.: $1,950.00
Can.: $1,950.00
Ster.: £ 775.00

HN 1886
Nadine
Designer: L. Harradine
Height: 7 3/4", 19.7 cm
Colour: Pink
Issued: 1938-1949
Varieties: HN 1885

U.S.: $1,950.00
Can.: $1,950.00
Ster.: £ 775.00

HN 1887
Nell Gwynn
Designer: L. Harradine
Height: 6 3/4", 17.2 cm
Colour: Green and pink
Issued: 1938-1949
Varieties: HN 1882

U.S.: $1,700.00
Can.: $1,700.00
Ster.: £ 750.00

HN 1888
Bon Jour
Designer: L. Harradine
Height: 6 3/4", 17.2 cm
Colour: Red
Issued: 1938-1949
Varieties: HN 1879

U.S.: $1,750.00
Can.: $1,750.00
Ster.: £ 850.00

HN 1889
Goody Two Shoes
Style One
Designer: L. Harradine
Height: 4 3/4", 12.0 cm
Colour: Green and purple
Issued: 1938-1949
Varieties: HN 1905, 2037

U.S.: $750.00
Can.: $750.00
Ster.: £275.00

HN 1890
Lambing Time
Style One
Designer: W.M. Chance
Height: 9 1/4", 23.5 cm
Colour: Light brown
Issued: 1938-1981

U.S.: $325.00
Can.: $400.00
Ster.: £175.00

Earthenware

HN 1891
Pecksniff
Style Two
Designer: L. Harradine
Height: 7", 17.8 cm
Colour: Black and brown
Issued: 1938-1952
Varieties: HN 553
Series: Dickens (Series Two)

U.S.: $525.00
Can.: $625.00
Ster.: £300.00

HN 1892
Uriah Heep
Style Two
Designer: L. Harradine
Height: 7", 17.8 cm
Colour: Black
Issued: 1938-1952
Varieties: HN 554
Series: Dickens (Series Two)

U.S.: $525.00
Can.: $625.00
Ster.: £300.00

HN 1893
Fat Boy
Style Two
Designer: L. Harradine
Height: 7", 17.8 cm
Colour: Blue and cream
Issued: 1938-1952
Varieties: HN 555
Series: Dickens (Series Two)

U.S.: $525.00
Can.: $625.00
Ster.: £300.00

HN 1894
Mr Pickwick
Style Two
Designer: L. Harradine
Height: 7", 17.8 cm
Colour: Blue, tan and cream
Issued: 1938-1952
Varieties: HN 556
Series: Dickens (Series Two)

U.S.: $525.00
Can.: $625.00
Ster.: £300.00

Earthenware and porcelain

HN 1895
Mr Micawber
Style Two
Designer: L. Harradine
Height: 7", 17.8 cm
Colour: Brown, black
           and tan
Issued: 1938-1952
Varieties: HN 557
Series: Dickens (Series Two)

U.S.: $525.00
Can.: $625.00
Ster.: £300.00

HN 1896
Sairey Gamp
Style Two
Designer: L. Harradine
Height: 7", 17.8 cm
Colour: Green
Issued: 1938-1952
Varieties: HN 558
Series: Dickens (Series Two)

U.S.: $675.00
Can.: $750.00
Ster.: £375.00

HN 1897
Miss Fortune
Designer: L. Harradine
Height: 6", 15.2 cm
Colour: Pink and blue
Issued: 1938-1949
Varieties: HN 1898

U.S.: $1,150.00
Can.: $1,150.00
Ster.: £ 650.00

HN 1898
Miss Fortune
Designer: L. Harradine
Height: 5 3/4", 14.6 cm
Colour: Blue
Issued: 1938-1949
Varieties: HN 1897

U.S.: $1,750.00
Can.: $1,750.00
Ster.: £ 725.00

HN 1899
Midsummer Noon
Designer: L. Harradine
Height: 4 3/4", 12.0 cm
Colour: Pink
Issued: 1939-1949
Varieties: HN 1900, 2033

U.S.: $900.00
Can.: $900.00
Ster.: £550.00

HN 1900
Midsummer Noon
Designer: L. Harradine
Height: 4 3/4", 12.0 cm
Colour: Blue
Issued: 1939-1949
Varieties: HN 1899, 2033

U.S.:	$2,500.00
Can.:	$2,500.00
Ster.:	£ 850.00

HN 1901
Penelope
Designer: L. Harradine
Height: 7", 17.8 cm
Colour: Red
Issued: 1939-1975
Varieties: HN 1902

U.S.:	$500.00
Can.:	$600.00
Ster.:	£325.00

HN 1902
Penelope
Designer: L. Harradine
Height: 7", 17.8 cm
Colour: Lavender and green
Issued: 1939-1949
Varieties: HN 1901

U.S.:	$2,100.00
Can.:	$2,100.00
Ster.:	£ 750.00

HN 1903
Rhythm
Designer: L. Harradine
Height: 6 3/4", 17.2 cm
Colour: Pink
Issued: 1939-1949
Varieties: HN 1904

U.S.:	$3,500.00
Can.:	$3,500.00
Ster.:	£1,500.00

HN 1904
Rhythm
Designer: L. Harradine
Height: 6 3/4", 17.2 cm
Colour: Blue
Issued: 1939-1949
Varieties: HN 1903

U.S.:	$4,500.00
Can.:	$4,500.00
Ster.:	£1,750.00

HN 1905
Goody Two Shoes
Style One
Designer: L. Harradine
Height: 4 3/4", 12.0 cm
Colour: Pink and red
Issued: 1939-1949
Varieties: HN 1889, 2037

U.S.:	$250.00
Can.:	$350.00
Ster.:	£175.00

HN 1906
Lydia
Designer: L. Harradine
Height: 4 1/4", 10.8 cm
Colour: Orange and pink
Issued: 1939-1949
Varieties: HN 1907, 1908

U.S.:	$ 950.00
Can.:	$1,000.00
Ster.:	£ 375.00

HN 1907
Lydia
Designer: L. Harradine
Height: 4 3/4", 12.0 cm
Colour: Green
Issued: 1939-1949
Varieties: HN 1906, 1908

U.S.:	$950.00
Can.:	$950.00
Ster.:	£300.00

HN 1908
Lydia
Designer: L. Harradine
Height: 4 3/4", 12.0 cm
Colour: Red
Issued: 1939-1995
Varieties: HN 1906, 1907

U.S.:	$175.00
Can.:	$225.00
Ster.:	£ 85.00

HN 1909
Honey
Designer: L. Harradine
Height: 7", 17.8 cm
Colour: Pink
Issued: 1939-1949
Varieties: HN 1910, 1963

U.S.:	$650.00
Can.:	$725.00
Ster.:	£350.00

HN 1910
Honey
Designer: L. Harradine
Height: 6 3/4", 17.2 cm
Colour: Blue
Issued: 1939-1949
Varieties: HN 1909, 1963

U.S.:	$1,500.00
Can.:	$1,500.00
Ster.:	£ 575.00

HN 1911
Autumn Breezes
Style One
Designer: L. Harradine
Height: 7 1/2", 19.1 cm
Colour: Green and pink
Issued: 1939-1976
Varieties: HN 1913, 1934, 2131, 2147

U.S.:	$285.00
Can.:	$375.00
Ster.:	£175.00

HN 1912
Old Balloon Seller and Bulldog
Designer: L. Harradine
Height: 7", 17.8 cm
Colour: Unknown
Issued: 1939-1949
Varieties: HN 1791

U.S.:	Only
Can.:	one
Ster.:	Known

HN 1913
Autumn Breezes
Style One
Designer: L. Harradine
Height: 7 1/2", 19.1 cm
Colour: Green and blue
Issued: 1939-1971
Varieties: HN 1911, 1934, 2131, 2147

U.S.:	$325.00
Can.:	$425.00
Ster.:	£175.00

HN 1914
Paisley Shawl
Style Three
Designer: L. Harradine
Height: 6 1/2", 16.5 cm
Colour: Green and red
Issued: 1939-1949
Varieties: HN 1988

U.S.:	$350.00
Can.:	$450.00
Ster.:	£225.00

HN 1915
Veronica
Style Three
Designer: L. Harradine
Height: 5 3/4", 14.6 cm
Colour: Red and cream
Issued: 1939-1949

U.S.:	$450.00
Can.:	$550.00
Ster.:	£275.00

HN 1916
Janet
Style Three
Designer: L. Harradine
Height: 5 1/4", 13.3 cm
Colour: Pink and blue
Issued: 1939-1949
Varieties: HN 1964

U.S.:	**$350.00**
Can.:	**$475.00**
Ster.:	**£225.00**

HN 1917
Meryll
Designer: L. Harradine
Height: 6 3/4", 17.2 cm
Colour: Red and green
Issued: 1939-1940
Varieties: Also called "Toinette"
HN 1940

U.S.:	**$4,000.00**
Can.:	**$4,000.00**
Ster.:	**£1,750.00**

HN 1918
Sweet Suzy
Designer: L. Harradine
Height: 6 1/2", 16.5 cm
Colour: Pink and green
Issued: 1939-1949

U.S.:	**$1,200.00**
Can.:	**$1,200.00**
Ster.:	**£ 550.00**

HN 1919
Kate Hardcastle
Designer: L. Harradine
Height: 8 1/4", 21.0 cm
Colour: Red and green
Issued: 1939-1949
Varieties: HN 1718, 1719, 1734,
1861, 2028

U.S.:	**$2,200.00**
Can.:	**$2,200.00**
Ster.:	**£ 700.00**

HN 1920
Windflower
Style Two
Designer: L. Harradine
Height: 11", 27.9 cm
Colour: Multi-coloured
Issued: 1939-1949
Varieties: HN 1939

U.S.:	**$3,750.00**
Can.:	**$3,750.00**
Ster.:	**£1,500.00**

HN 1921
Roseanna
Designer: L. Harradine
Height: 8", 20.3 cm
Colour: Green
Issued: 1940-1949
Varieties: HN 1926

U.S.:	**$2,500.00**
Can.:	**$2,500.00**
Ster.:	**£ 775.00**

HN 1922
Spring Morning
Style One
Designer: L. Harradine
Height: 7 1/2", 19.1 cm
Colour: Pink and blue
Issued: 1940-1973
Varieties: HN 1923

U.S.:	**$375.00**
Can.:	**$475.00**
Ster.:	**£225.00**

HN 1923
Spring Morning
Style One
Designer: L. Harradine
Height: 7 1/2", 19.1 cm
Colour: Green and cream
Issued: 1940-1949
Varieties: HN 1922

U.S.:	**$1,400.00**
Can.:	**$1,400.00**
Ster.:	**£ 600.00**

HN 1924
Fiona
Style One
Designer: L. Harradine
Height: 5 3/4", 14.6 cm
Colour: Pink and lavender
Issued: 1940-1949
Varieties: HN 1925, 1933

U.S.: $1,600.00
Can.: $1,600.00
Ster.: £ 750.00

HN 1925
Fiona
Style One
Designer: L. Harradine
Height: 5 3/4", 14.6 cm
Colour: Blue
Issued: 1940-1949
Varieties: HN 1924, 1933

U.S.: $1,600.00
Can.: $1,600.00
Ster.: £ 750.00

HN 1926
Roseanna
Designer: L. Harradine
Height: 8", 20.3 cm
Colour: Pink
Issued: 1940-1959
Varieties: HN 1921

U.S.: $625.00
Can.: $675.00
Ster.: £325.00

HN 1927
The Awakening
Style One
Designer: L. Harradine
Height: 10 1/4", 26.0 cm
Colour: Pale pink
Issued: 1940-1949

U.S.: $4,000.00
Can.: $4,000.00
Ster.: £1,500.00

HN 1928
Marguerite
Designer: L. Harradine
Height: 8", 20.3 cm
Colour: Pink
Issued: 1940-1959
Varieties: HN 1929, 1930, 1946

U.S.: $550.00
Can.: $625.00
Ster.: £325.00

HN 1929
Marguerite
Designer: L. Harradine
Height: 8", 20.3 cm
Colour: Pale pink and yellow
Issued: 1940-1949
Varieties: HN 1928, 1930, 1946

U.S.: $1,000.00
Can.: $1,000.00
Ster.: £ 325.00

HN 1930
Marguerite
Designer: L. Harradine
Height: 8", 20.3 cm
Colour: Blue and purple
Issued: 1940-1949
Varieties: HN 1928, 1929, 1946

U.S.: $2,000.00
Can.: $2,000.00
Ster.: £ 600.00

HN 1931
Meriel
Designer: L. Harradine
Height: 7 1/4", 18.4 cm
Colour: Pink
Issued: 1940-1949
Varieties: HN 1932

U.S.: $2,500.00
Can.: $2,500.00
Ster.: £1,000.00

HN 1932
Meriel
Designer: L. Harradine
Height: 7 1/4", 18.4 cm
Colour: Green
Issued: 1940-1949
Varieties: HN 1931

U.S.: $2,500.00
Can.: $2,500.00
Ster.: £ 950.00

HN 1933
Fiona
Style One
Designer: L. Harradine
Height: 5 3/4", 14.6 cm
Colour: Multi-coloured
Issued: 1940-1949
Varieties: HN 1924, 1925

U.S.: $1,600.00
Can.: $1,600.00
Ster.: £ 750.00

HN 1934
Autumn Breezes
Style One
Designer: L. Harradine
Height: 7 1/2", 19.1 cm
Colour: Red
Issued: 1940 to the present
Varieties: HN 1911, 1913, 2131, 2147

U.S.: $375.00
Can.: $490.00
Ster.: £139.00

HN 1935
Sweeting
Designer: L. Harradine
Height: 6", 15.2 cm
Colour: Pink
Issued: 1940-1973
Varieties: HN 1938

U.S.: $200.00
Can.: $275.00
Ster.: £100.00

HN 1936
Miss Muffet
Designer: L. Harradine
Height: 5 1/2", 14.0 cm
Colour: Red
Issued: 1940-1967
Varieties: HN 1937

U.S.: $250.00
Can.: $300.00
Ster.: £150.00

HN 1937
Miss Muffet
Designer: L. Harradine
Height: 5 1/2", 14.0 cm
Colour: Green
Issued: 1940-1952
Varieties: HN 1936

U.S.: $500.00
Can.: $575.00
Ster.: £225.00

HN 1938
Sweeting
Designer: L. Harradine
Height: 6", 15.2 cm
Colour: Purple and red
Issued: 1940-1949
Varieties: HN 1935

U.S.: $650.00
Can.: $750.00
Ster.: £250.00

HN 1939
Windflower
Style Two
Designer: L. Harradine
Height: 11", 27.9 cm
Colour: Pink
Issued: 1940-1949
Varieties: HN 1920

U.S.: $3,750.00
Can.: $3,750.00
Ster.: £1,500.00

HN 1940
Toinette
Designer: L. Harradine
Height: 6 3/4", 17.1 cm
Colour: Red
Issued: 1940-1949
Varieties: Also called "Meryll"
HN 1917

U.S.:	**$2,400.00**
Can.:	**$2,400.00**
Ster.:	**£ 975.00**

HN 1941
Peggy
Designer: L. Harradine
Height: 5", 12.7 cm
Colour: Red and white
Issued: 1940-1949
Varieties: HN 2038 (Minor
glaze difference)

U.S.:	**$250.00**
Can.:	**$400.00**
Ster.:	**£200.00**

HN 1942
Pyjams
Designer: L. Harradine
Height: 5 1/4", 13.3 cm
Colour: Pink
Issued: 1940-1949

U.S.:	**$1,250.00**
Can.:	**$1,250.00**
Ster.:	**£ 450.00**

HN 1943
Veronica
Style One
Designer: L. Harradine
Height: 8", 20.3 cm
Colour: Red and blue
Issued: 1940-1949
Varieties: HN 1517, 1519, 1650

U.S.:	**$1,350.00**
Can.:	**$1,350.00**
Ster.:	**£ 600.00**

HN 1944
Daydreams
Designer: L. Harradine
Height: 5 1/2", 14.0 cm
Colour: Red
Issued: 1940-1949
Varieties: HN 1731, 1732

U.S.:	**$1,350.00**
Can.:	**$1,350.00**
Ster.:	**£ 350.00**

HN 1945
Spring Flowers
Designer: L. Harradine
Height: 7 1/4", 18.4 cm
Colour: Red and green
Issued: 1940-1949
Varieties: HN 1807

U.S.:	**$1,900.00**
Can.:	**$1,900.00**
Ster.:	**£ 650.00**

HN 1946
Marguerite
Designer: L. Harradine
Height: 8", 20.3 cm
Colour: Pink
Issued: 1940-1949
Varieties: HN 1928, 1929, 1930

U.S.:	**$1,200.00**
Can.:	**$1,200.00**
Ster.:	**£ 500.00**

HN 1947
June
Style One
Designer: L. Harradine
Height: 7 1/4", 18.4 cm
Colour: Red
Issued: 1940-1949
Varieties: HN 1690, 1691, 2027

U.S.:	**$1,500.00**
Can.:	**$1,500.00**
Ster.:	**£ 450.00**

HN 1948
Lady Charmian
Designer: L. Harradine
Height: 8", 20.3 cm
Colour: Green dress with red shawl
Issued: 1940-1973
Varieties: HN 1949

U.S.: $350.00
Can.: $425.00
Ster.: £250.00

HN 1949
Lady Charmian
Designer: L. Harradine
Height: 8", 20.3 cm
Colour: Red dress with green shawl
Issued: 1940-1975
Varieties: HN 1948

U.S.: $325.00
Can.: $425.00
Ster.: £220.00

HN 1950
Claribel
Designer: L. Harradine
Height: 4 3/4", 12.0 cm
Colour: Purple and pink
Issued: 1940-1949
Varieties: HN 1951

U.S.: $650.00
Can.: $775.00
Ster.: £275.00

HN 1951
Claribel
Designer: L. Harradine
Height: 4 3/4", 12.0 cm
Colour: Red
Issued: 1940-1949
Varieties: HN 1950

U.S.: $600.00
Can.: $675.00
Ster.: £275.00

HN 1952
Irene
Designer: L. Harradine
Height: 6 3/4", 17.2 cm
Colour: Blue and purple
Issued: 1940-1950
Varieties: HN 1621, 1697

U.S.: $1,500.00
Can.: $1,500.00
Ster.: £ 650.00

HN 1953
Orange Lady
Designer: L. Harradine
Height: 8 1/2", 21.6 cm
Colour: Light green dress, dark green shawl
Issued: 1940-1975
Varieties: HN 1759

U.S.: $300.00
Can.: $450.00
Ster.: £175.00

HN 1954
The Balloon Man
Designer: L. Harradine
Height: 7 1/4", 18.4 cm
Colour: Black and gray
Issued: 1940 to the present

U.S.: $306.25
Can.: $495.00
Ster.: £139.00

Earthenware and China

HN 1955
Lavinia
Designer: L. Harradine
Height: 5", 12.7 cm
Colour: Red
Issued: 1940-1979

U.S.: $175.00
Can.: $225.00
Ster.: £110.00

HN 1956
Chloe
Style One
Designer: L. Harradine
Height: 6", 15.2 cm
Colour: Red and green
Issued: 1940-1949
Varieties: HN 1470, 1476, 1479, 1498, 1765

U.S.:	**$1,200.00**
Can.:	**$1,200.00**
Ster.:	**£ 395.00**

HN 1957
The New Bonnet
Designer: L. Harradine
Height: 7", 17.8 cm
Colour: Red
Issued: 1940-1949
Varieties: HN 1728

U.S.:	**$1,950.00**
Can.:	**$1,950.00**
Ster.:	**£ 650.00**

HN 1958
Lady April
Designer: L. Harradine
Height: 7", 17.8 cm
Colour: Red and purple
Issued: 1940-1959
Varieties: HN 1965

U.S.:	**$475.00**
Can.:	**$550.00**
Ster.:	**£300.00**

HN 1959
The Choice
Designer: L. Harradine
Height: 7 1/4", 18.4 cm
Colour: Red
Issued: 1941-1949
Varieties: HN 1960

U.S.:	**$2,250.00**
Can.:	**$2,250.00**
Ster.:	**£ 950.00**

HN 1960
The Choice
Designer: L. Harradine
Height: 7 1/4", 18.4 cm
Colour: Purple
Issued: 1941-1949
Varieties: HN 1959

U.S.:	**$2,700.00**
Can.:	**$2,700.00**
Ster.:	**£1,000.00**

HN 1961
Daisy
Style One
Designer: L. Harradine
Height: 3 1/2", 8.9 cm
Colour: Pink
Issued: 1941-1949
Varieties: HN 1575

U.S.:	**$650.00**
Can.:	**$750.00**
Ster.:	**£350.00**

HN 1962
Genevieve
Designer: L. Harradine
Height: 7", 17.8 cm
Colour: Red
Issued: 1941-1975

U.S.:	**$425.00**
Can.:	**$550.00**
Ster.:	**£250.00**

HN 1963
Honey
Designer: L. Harradine
Height: 6 3/4", 17.2 cm
Colour: Red and blue
Issued: 1941-1949
Varieties: HN 1909, 1910

U.S.:	**$1,250.00**
Can.:	**$1,250.00**
Ster.:	**£ 400.00**

HN 1964
Janet
Style Three
Designer: L. Harradine
Height: 5", 12.7 cm
Colour: Pink
Issued: 1941-1949
Varieties: HN 1916

U.S.: $975.00
Can.: $975.00
Ster.: £325.00

HN 1965
Lady April
Designer: L. Harradine
Height: 7", 17.8 cm
Colour: Green and pink
Issued: 1941-1949
Varieties: HN 1958

U.S.: $1,400.00
Can.: $1,400.00
Ster.: £ 650.00

HN 1966
An Orange Vendor
Designer: C.J. Noke
Height: 6 1/4", 15.9 cm
Colour: Purple
Issued: 1941-1949
Varieties: HN 72, 508, 521

U.S.: $1,350.00
Can.: $1,250.00
Ster.: £ 500.00

Earthenware

HN 1967
Lady Betty
Designer: L. Harradine
Height: 6 1/2", 16.5 cm
Colour: Red
Issued: 1941-1951

U.S.: $650.00
Can.: $700.00
Ster.: £325.00

HN 1968
Madonna of the Square
Designer: P. Stabler
Height: 7", 17.8 cm
Colour: Light green
Issued: 1941-1949
Varieties: HN 10, 10A, 11, 14,
27, 326, 573, 576,
594, 613, 764, 1969,
2034

U.S.: $2,500.00
Can.: $2,000.00
Ster.: £ 750.00

HN 1969
Madonna of the Square
Designer: P. Stabler
Height: 7", 17.8 cm
Colour: Lavender
Issued: 1941-1949
Varieties: HN 10, 10A, 11, 14,
27, 326, 573, 576,
594, 613, 764, 1968,
2034

U.S.: $2,500.00
Can.: $2,000.00
Ster.: £ 750.00

HN 1970
Milady
Designer: L. Harradine
Height: 6 1/2", 16.5 cm
Colour: Pink
Issued: 1941-1949

U.S.: $1,700.00
Can.: $1,700.00
Ster.: £ 750.00

HN 1971
Springtime
Style One
Designer: L. Harradine
Height: 6", 15.2 cm
Colour: Pink and blue
Issued: 1941-1949

U.S.: $1,500.00
Can.: $1,500.00
Ster.: £ 750.00

HN 1972
Regency Beau
Designer: H. Fenton
Height: 8", 20.3 cm
Colour: Green and pink
Issued: 1941-1949

U.S.: $1,500.00
Can.: $1,500.00
Ster.: £ 750.00

HN 1973
The Corinthian
Designer: H. Fenton
Height: 7 3/4", 19.7 cm
Colour: Green, red and cream
Issued: 1941-1949

U.S.: $1,750.00
Can.: $1,750.00
Ster.: £ 800.00

HN 1974
Forty Winks
Designer: H. Fenton
Height: 6 3/4", 17.2 cm
Colour: Green and tan
Issued: 1945-1973

U.S.: $375.00
Can.: $450.00
Ster.: £175.00

HN 1975
The Shepherd
Style Four
Designer: H. Fenton
Height: 8 1/2", 21.6 cm
Colour: Light brown
Issued: 1945-1975

U.S.: $375.00
Can.: $450.00
Ster.: £175.00

HN 1976
Easter Day
Designer: L. Harradine
Height: 7 1/4", 18.4 cm
Colour: White, lilac and green
Issued: 1945-1951
Varieties: HN 2039

U.S.: $700.00
Can.: $900.00
Ster.: £375.00

HN 1977
Her Ladyship
Designer: L. Harradine
Height: 7 1/4", 18.4 cm
Colour: Red and cream
Issued: 1945-1959

U.S.: $475.00
Can.: $575.00
Ster.: £275.00

HN 1978
Bedtime
Style One
Designer: L. Harradine
Height: 5 3/4", 14.6 cm
Colour: White, black base
Issued: 1945 to the present
Varieties: HN 2219

U.S.: $106.25
Can.: $160.00
Ster.: £ 39.95

HN 1979
Gollywog
Designer: L. Harradine
Height: 5 1/4", 13.3 cm
Colour: Patterned white
         dungarees
Issued: 1945-1959
Varieties: HN 2040

U.S.: $975.00
Can.: $975.00
Ster.: £450.00

HN 1980
Gwynneth
Designer: L. Harradine
Height: 7", 17.8 cm
Colour: Red
Issued: 1945-1952

U.S.:	$525.00
Can.:	$575.00
Ster.:	£275.00

HN 1981
The Ermine Coat
Designer: L. Harradine
Height: 6 3/4", 17.2 cm
Colour: White and red
Issued: 1945-1967

U.S.:	$425.00
Can.:	$525.00
Ster.:	£275.00

HN 1982
Sabbath Morn
Designer: L. Harradine
Height: 7 1/4", 18.4 cm
Colour: Red
Issued: 1945-1959

U.S.:	$375.00
Can.:	$495.00
Ster.:	£250.00

HN 1983
Rosebud
Style Two
Designer: L. Harradine
Height: 7 1/2", 19.1 cm
Colour: Pink and red
Issued: 1945-1952

U.S.:	$650.00
Can.:	$750.00
Ster.:	£400.00

HN 1984
The Patchwork Quilt
Designer: L. Harradine
Height: 6", 15.2 cm
Colour: Multi-coloured
Issued: 1945-1959

U.S.:	$475.00
Can.:	$600.00
Ster.:	£375.00

HN 1985
Darling
Style Two
Designer: C. Vyse
 Height: 5 1/4", 13.3 cm
Colour: White, black base
Issued: 1946 to the present
Varieties: HN 3613

U.S.:	$106.25
Can.:	$160.00
Ster.:	£ 39.95

HN 1986
Diana
Style One
Designer: L. Harradine
Height: 5 3/4", 14.6 cm
Colour: Red
Issued: 1946-1975
Varieties: HN 1716, 1717

U.S.:	$250.00
Can.:	$300.00
Ster.:	£150.00

HN 1987
Paisley Shawl
Style One
Designer: L. Harradine
Height: 8 1/4", 21.0 cm
Colour: Red and cream
Issued: 1946-1959
Varieties: HN 1392, 1460,
           1707, 1739

U.S.:	$450.00
Can.:	$550.00
Ster.:	£300.00

HN 1988
Paisley Shawl
Style Three
Designer: L. Harradine
Height: 6 1/4", 15.9 cm
Colour: Red and pink
Issued: 1946-1975
Varieties: HN 1914

U.S.: $250.00
Can.: $375.00
Ster.: £250.00

HN 1989
Margaret
Style One
Designer: L. Harradine
Height: 7 1/4", 18.4 cm
Colour: Red and green
Issued: 1947-1959

U.S.: $550.00
Can.: $650.00
Ster.: £300.00

HN 1990
Mary Jane
Designer: L. Harradine
Height: 7 1/2", 19.1 cm
Colour: Flowered pink dress
Issued: 1947-1952

U.S.: $650.00
Can.: $750.00
Ster.: £395.00

HN 1991
Market Day
Designer: L. Harradine
Height: 7 1/4", 18.4 cm
Colour: Blue, pink and white
Issued: 1947-1955
Varieties: Also called "Country
Lass" HN 1991A

U.S.: $375.00
Can.: $450.00
Ster.: £225.00

HN 1991A
A Country Lass
Designer: L. Harradine
Height: 7 1/4", 18.4 cm
Colour: Blue, brown and white
Issued: 1975-1981
Varieties: Also called "Market
Day" HN 1991

U.S.: $250.00
Can.: $325.00
Ster.: £175.00

HN 1992
Christmas Morn
Style One
Designer: M. Davies
Height: 7", 17.8 cm
Colour: Red and white
Issued: 1947-1996

U.S.: $268.75
Can.: $425.00
Ster.: £129.00

HN 1993
Griselda
Designer: L. Harradine
Height: 5 3/4", 14.6 cm
Colour: Lavender and cream
Issued: 1947-1953

U.S.: $575.00
Can.: $700.00
Ster.: £395.00

HN 1994
Karen
Style One
Designer: L. Harradine
Height: 8", 20.3 cm
Colour: Red
Issued: 1947-1955

U.S.: $750.00
Can.: $850.00
Ster.: £395.00

HN 1995
Olivia
Style One
Designer: L. Harradine
Height: 7 1/2", 19.1 cm
Colour: Red and green
Issued: 1947-1951

U.S.:	$900.00
Can.:	$975.00
Ster.:	£495.00

HN 1996
Prue
Designer: L. Harradine
Height: 6 3/4", 17.2 cm
Colour: Red, white and black
Issued: 1947-1955

U.S.:	$600.00
Can.:	$675.00
Ster.:	£375.00

HN 1997
Belle o' the Ball
Designer: R. Asplin
Height: 6", 15.2 cm
Colour: Red and white
Issued: 1947-1979

U.S.:	$450.00
Can.:	$550.00
Ster.:	£300.00

HN 1998
Collinette
Designer: L. Harradine
Height: 7 1/4", 18.4 cm
Colour: Turquoise and cream
Issued: 1947-1949
Varieties: HN 1999

U.S.:	$1,000.00
Can.:	$1,100.00
Ster.:	£ 500.00

HN 1999
Collinette
Designer: L. Harradine
Height: 7 1/4", 18.4 cm
Colour: Red and cream
Issued: 1947-1949
Varieties: HN 1998

U.S.:	$ 900.00
Can.:	$1,000.00
Ster.:	£ 400.00

HN 2000
Jacqueline
Style One
Designer: L. Harradine
Height: 7 1/4", 18.4 cm
Colour: Lavender
Issued: 1947-1951
Varieties: HN 2001

U.S.:	$800.00
Can.:	$925.00
Ster.:	£450.00

HN 2001
Jacqueline
Style One
Designer: L. Harradine
Height: 7 1/4", 18.4 cm
Colour: Pink
Issued: 1947-1951
Varieties: HN 2000

U.S.:	$700.00
Can.:	$800.00
Ster.:	£325.00

HN 2002
Bess
Designer: L. Harradine
Height: 7 1/4", 18.4 cm
Colour: Red cloak, flowered cream dress
Issued: 1947-1969
Varieties: HN 2003

U.S.:	$450.00
Can.:	$550.00
Ster.:	£275.00

HN 2003
Bess
Designer: L. Harradine
Height: 7 1/4", 18.4 cm
Colour: Pink dress, purple
cloak
Issued: 1947-1950
Varieties: HN 2002

U.S.: $ 900.00
Can.: $1,000.00
Ster.: £ 400.00

HN 2004
A'Courting
Designer: L. Harradine
Height: 7 1/4", 18.4 cm
Colour: Red, black and grey
Issued: 1947-1953

U.S.: $700.00
Can.: $800.00
Ster.: £375.00

HN 2005
Henrietta Maria
Designer: M. Davies
Height: 9 1/2", 24.1 cm
Colour: Yellow and red
Issued: 1948-1953
Series: Period Figures in
English History

U.S.: $800.00
Can.: $800.00
Ster.: £450.00

HN 2006
The Lady Anne Nevill
Designer: M. Davies
Height: 9 3/4", 24.7 cm
Colour: Purple and white
Issued: 1948-1953
Series: Period Figures in
English History

U.S.: $1,100.00
Can.: $1,100.00
Ster.: £ 550.00

HN 2007
Mrs. Fitzherbert
Designer: M. Davies
Height: 9 1/4", 23.5 cm
Colour: Yellow and cream
Issued: 1948-1953
Series: Period Figures in
English History

U.S.: $975.00
Can.: $975.00
Ster.: £400.00

HN 2008
Philippa of Hainault
Designer: M. Davies
Height: 9 3/4", 24.7 cm
Colour: Blue, brown and red
Issued: 1948-1953
Series: Period Figures in
English History

U.S.: $900.00
Can.: $900.00
Ster.: £400.00

HN 2009
Eleanor of Provence
Designer: M. Davies
Height: 9 1/2", 24.1 cm
Colour: Purple and red
Issued: 1948-1953
Series: Period Figures in
English History

U.S.: $900.00
Can.: $900.00
Ster.: £400.00

HN 2010
The Young
Miss Nightingale
Designer: M. Davies
Height: 9 1/4", 23.5 cm
Colour: Red and green
Issued: 1948-1953
Series: Period Figures in
English History

U.S.: $1,100.00
Can.: $1,100.00
Ster.: £ 450.00

FOR A LIMITED TIME . . .

Now you can complete your Doulton library with the addition of *Royal Doulton Figures*.
This is the third edition of this invaluable reference book and it functions as the perfect
companion piece to *The Charlton Standard Catalogue of Royal Doulton Beswick
Figurines*. With 1450 colour plates and 150 black and white illustrations this fascinating
work lists and illustrates all the figures made at the Burslem factory between 1913 and 1994.
In addition to the authoritative introduction this new edition contains a chapter on
experimental glazes and extended information on both early and unusual figures.

ABOUT THE AUTHORS

The book was written by Louise Irvine, Valerie Baynton and the late Desmond Eyles, three
renowned Doulton experts. Desmond Eyles, the former Head of publicity for Royal Doulton,
tells the history of figure production at Burslem. Louise Irvine worked as Director of
Historical Promotions for Doulton and initiated the International Collectors Club. Valerie
Baynton joined Royal Doulton as Curator of the Sir Henry Doulton Gallery and is now the
Press Officer.

Order your copy today
at the special price of $85.00 Cdn.
or $65.00 US.
- plus $9.50 for shipping
and handling
Call:1-800-442-6042

Fax: 1-800-442-1542

Write:

The Charlton Press
**2010 Yonge Street Toronto, ON
M4S 1Z9**

Royal Doulton Figures
**Produced at Burslem,
Staffordshire
1892-1994**

310 x 215 mm, cloth

408pp, 1450 colour plates

ISBN 0 903685 35 3

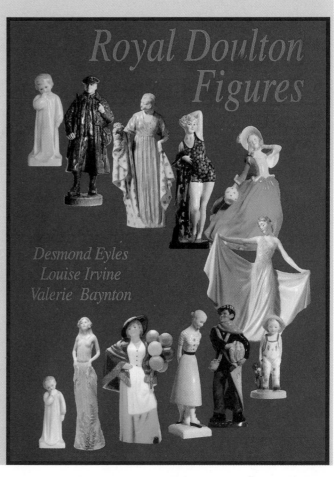

ROYAL DOULTON FIGURES

Christie's South Kensington hosts more auctions devoted to decorative arts than any other auction house. Royal Doulton Beswick Figurines will be featured at sales during the upcoming year. For advice on all aspects of buying and selling decorative arts at auction or for a free verbal valuation and sales calendar please contact:

Mark Wilkinson or Michael Jeffrey   0171-321 3236/3237

CHRISTIE'S

85 OLD BROMPTON RD.
LONDON SW7 3LD
TEL: (0171) 581 7611
FAX: (0171) 321 3321

HN 2011
Matilda
Designer: M. Davies
Height: 9 1/4", 23.5 cm
Colour: Red and purple
Issued: 1948-1953
Series: Period Figures in
English History

U.S.: $900.00
Can.: $900.00
Ster.: £450.00

HN 2012
Margaret of Anjou
Designer: M. Davies
Height: 9 1/4", 23.5 cm
Colour: Green and yellow
Issued: 1948-1953
Series: Period Figures in
English History

U.S.: $1,000.00
Can.: $1,000.00
Ster.: £ 600.00

HN 2013
Angelina
Designer: L. Harradine
Height: 6 3/4", 17.1 cm
Colour: Red
Issued: 1948-1951

U.S.: $1,400.00
Can.: $1,400.00
Ster.: £ 650.00

HN 2014
Jane
Style One
Designer: L. Harradine
Height: 6 1/4", 15.9 cm
Colour: Red and pink
Issued: 1948-1951

U.S.: $2,000.00
Can.: $2,000.00
Ster.: £ 950.00

HN 2015
Sir Walter Raleigh
Designer: L. Harradine
Height: 11 1/2", 29.2 cm
Colour: Orange and purple
Issued: 1948-1955
Varieties: HN 1742, 1751

U.S.: $900.00
Can.: $900.00
Ster.: £500.00

Earthenware

HN 2016
A Jester
Style One
Designer: C.J. Noke
Height: 10", 25.4 cm
Colour: Brown and mauve
Issued: 1949 to the present
Varieties: HN 45, 71, 71A, 320,
367, 412, 426, 446,
552, 616, 627, 1295,
1702

U.S.: $493.75
Can.: $530.00
Ster.: £169.00

HN 2017
Silks and Ribbons
Designer: L. Harradine
Height: 6", 15.2 cm
Colour: Green, red and white
Issued: 1949 to the present

U.S.: $306.25
Can.: $495.00
Ster.: £115.00

NOTES ON PRICING

The prices on the secondary market for Royal Doulton Figures, particularly the early HN Numbers, have risen considerably over the years. As values rise, the condition and quality of these figurines take on an increasingly important role.

The prices listed in The Charlton Standard Catalogue of Royal Doulton Beswick Figurines are for figures in mint condition.

Naturally, repaired or restored figures, no matter how professionally done, will sell at a substantial discount.

On Condition: For figures to command catalogue prices they must be in mint condition. This simply means that a figure will not have paint chips, scratches, hairline cracks, crazing or blemishes. Any of which will remove from the mint category figure.

On Quality: Some figures can be better moulded, assembled or painted than others. High quality figures will command catalogue prices. Low quality figures will not.

If the quality or condition of the figures is below the standard for mint, look for that figure to be priced at a percentage of the catalogue prices.

HN 2018
The Parson's Daughter
Designer: H. Tittensor
Height: 9 3/4", 24.7 cm
Colour: Multi-coloured
Issued: 1949-1953
Varieties: HN 337, 338, 441,
564, 790, 1242, 1356

U.S.: $1,100.00
Can.: $1,000.00
Ster.: £ 450.00

HN 2019
Minuet
Designer: M. Davies
Height: 7 1/4", 18.4 cm
Colour: Patterned white dress
Issued: 1949-1971
Varieties: HN 2066

U.S.: $425.00
Can.: $530.00
Ster.: £275.00

HN 2020
Deidre
Designer: L. Harradine
Height: 7", 17.8 cm
Colour: Blue and pink
Issued: 1949-1955

U.S.: $650.00
Can.: $750.00
Ster.: £400.00

HN 2021
Blithe Morning
Designer: L. Harradine
Height: 7 1/4", 18.4 cm
Colour: Mauve and pink
Issued: 1949-1971
Varieties: HN 2065

U.S.: $325.00
Can.: $450.00
Ster.: £195.00

HN 2022
Janice
Style One
Designer: M. Davies
Height: 7 1/4", 18.4 cm
Colour: Green and cream
Issued: 1949-1955
Varieties: HN 2165

U.S.: $700.00
Can.: $825.00
Ster.: £375.00

HN 2023
Joan
Style One
Designer: L. Harradine
Height: 5 3/4", 14.6 cm
Colour: Blue
Issued: 1949-1959
Varieties: HN 1422 (Minor
glaze difference)

U.S.: $300.00
Can.: $475.00
Ster.: £225.00

HN 2024
Darby
Designer: L. Harradine
Height: 5 3/4", 14.6 cm
Colour: Pink and blue
Issued: 1949-1959
Varieties: HN 1427 (Minor
glaze difference)

U.S.: $300.00
Can.: $475.00
Ster.: £225.00

HN 2025
Gossips
Designer: L. Harradine
Height: 5 1/2", 14.0 cm
Colour: Red and cream
Issued: 1949-1967
Varieties: HN 1426, 1429

U.S.: $600.00
Can.: $700.00
Ster.: £350.00

HN 2026
Suzette
Designer: L. Harradine
Height: 7 1/4", 18.4 cm
Colour: Flowered pink dress
Issued: 1949-1959
Varieties: HN 1487, 1577, 1585, 1696

U.S.: $550.00
Can.: $675.00
Ster.: £325.00

HN 2027
June
Style One
Designer: L. Harradine
Height: 7 1/4", 18.4 cm
Colour: Yellow and pink
Issued: 1949-1952
Varieties: HN 1690, 1691, 1947

U.S.: $775.00
Can.: $850.00
Ster.: £450.00

HN 2028
Kate Hardcastle
Designer: L. Harradine
Height: 7 3/4", 19.7 cm
Colour: Green and red
Issued: 1949-1952
Varieties: HN 1718, 1719, 1734, 1861, 1919

U.S.: $875.00
Can.: $950.00
Ster.: £450.00

HN 2029
Windflower
Style One
Designer: L. Harradine
Height: 7 1/4", 18.4 cm
Colour: Pink
Issued: 1949-1952
Varieties: HN 1763, 1764

U.S.: $775.00
Can.: $875.00
Ster.: £650.00

HN 2030
Memories
Designer: L. Harradine
Height: 6", 15.2 cm
Colour: Pink and green
Issued: 1949-1959
Varieties: HN 1855, 1856, 1857

U.S.: $650.00
Can.: $775.00
Ster.: £350.00

HN 2031
Granny's Heritage
Designer: L. Harradine
Height: 6 3/4", 17.2 cm
Colour: Lavender and green
Issued: 1949-1969
Varieties: HN 1873, 1874

U.S.: $725.00
Can.: $800.00
Ster.: £500.00

HN 2032
Jean
Style One
Designer: L. Harradine
Height: 7 1/2", 19.1 cm
Colour: Green and red
Issued: 1949-1959
Varieties: HN 1877, 1878

U.S.: $550.00
Can.: $675.00
Ster.: £300.00

HN 2033
Midsummer Noon
Designer: L. Harradine
Height: 4 3/4", 12.0 cm
Colour: Pink
Issued: 1949-1955
Varieties: HN 1899, 1900

U.S.: $725.00
Can.: $825.00
Ster.: £450.00

HN 2034
Madonna of the Square
Designer:	P. Stabler
Height:	7", 17.8 cm
Colour:	Pale green
Issued:	1949-1951
Varieties:	HN 10, 10A, 11, 14, 27, 326, 573, 576, 594, 613, 764,1968, 1969

U.S.:	**$1,000.00**
Can.:	**$1,100.00**
Ster.:	**£ 550.00**

HN 2035
Pearly Boy
Style Two
Designer:	L. Harradine
Height:	5 1/4", 13.3 cm
Colour:	Reddish-brown
Issued:	1949-1959

U.S.:	**$250.00**
Can.:	**$325.00**
Ster.:	**£175.00**

HN 2036
Pearly Girl
Style Two
Designer:	L. Harradine
Height:	5 1/4", 13.3 cm
Colour:	Reddish-brown
Issued:	1949-1959

U.S.:	**$250.00**
Can.:	**$325.00**
Ster.:	**£175.00**

HN 2037
Goody Two Shoes
Style One
Designer:	L. Harradine
Height:	5", 12.7 cm
Colour:	Red and pink
Issued:	1949-1989
Varieties:	HN 1889, 1905

U.S.:	**$170.00**
Can.:	**$225.00**
Ster.:	**£120.00**

HN 2038
Peggy
Designer:	L. Harradine
Height:	5", 12.7 cm
Colour:	Red and white
Issued:	1949-1979
Varieties:	HN 1941 (Minor glaze difference)

U.S.:	**$170.00**
Can.:	**$250.00**
Ster.:	**£120.00**

HN 2039
Easter Day
Designer:	L. Harradine
Height:	7 1/4", 18.4 cm
Colour:	Multi-coloured
Issued:	1949-1969
Varieties:	HN 1976

U.S.:	**$525.00**
Can.:	**$600.00**
Ster.:	**£350.00**

HN 2040
Gollywog
Designer:	L. Harradine
Height:	5 1/4", 13.3 cm
Colour:	Blue dungarees
Issued:	1949-1959
Varieties:	HN 1979

U.S.:	**$400.00**
Can.:	**$500.00**
Ster.:	**£275.00**

HN 2041
The Broken Lance
Designer:	M. Davies
Height:	8 3/4", 22.2 cm
Colour:	Blue, red and yellow
Issued:	1949-1975

U.S.:	**$700.00**
Can.:	**$850.00**
Ster.:	**£450.00**

HN 2042
Owd Willum
Designer: L. Harradine
Height: 6 3/4", 17.2 cm
Colour: Green and brown
Issued: 1949-1973

U.S.: **$375.00**
Can.: **$495.00**
Ster.: **£225.00**

"Harradine" incised on figurine

HN 2043
The Poacher
Designer: L. Harradine
Height: 6", 15.2 cm
Colour: Black and brown
Issued: 1949-1959

U.S.: **$425.00**
Can.: **$525.00**
Ster.: **£225.00**

HN 2044
Mary, Mary
Designer: L. Harradine
Height: 5", 12.7 cm
Colour: Pink
Issued: 1949-1973
Series: Nursery Rhymes
(Series One)

U.S.: **$300.00**
Can.: **$350.00**
Ster.: **£175.00**

HN 2045
She Loves Me Not
Designer: L. Harradine
Height: 5 1/2", 14.0 cm
Colour: Blue
Issued: 1949-1962
Series: Nursery Rhymes
(Series One)

U.S.: **$300.00**
Can.: **$375.00**
Ster.: **£175.00**

HN 2046
He Loves Me
Designer: L. Harradine
Height: 5 1/2", 14.0 cm
Colour: Flowered pink dress
Issued: 1949-1962
Series: Nursery Rhymes
(Series One)

U.S.: **$300.00**
Can.: **$375.00**
Ster.: **£175.00**

HN 2047
Once Upon a Time
Designer: L. Harradine
Height: 4 1/4", 10.8 cm
Colour: Pink dress with
white spots
Issued: 1949-1955
Series: Nursery Rhymes
(Series One)

U.S.: **$600.00**
Can.: **$700.00**
Ster.: **£375.00**

HN 2048
Mary Had a Little Lamb
Designer: M. Davies
Height: 3 1/2", 8.9 cm
Colour: Lavender
Issued: 1949-1988
Series: Nursery Rhymes
(Series One)

U.S.: **$200.00**
Can.: **$235.00**
Ster.: **£165.00**

HN 2049
Curly Locks
Designer: M. Davies
Height: 4 1/2", 11.4 cm
Colour: Pink flowered dress
Issued: 1949-1953
Series: Nursery Rhymes
(Series One)

U.S.: **$625.00**
Can.: **$700.00**
Ster.: **£425.00**

HN 2050
Wee Willie Winkie
Style One
Designer: M. Davies
Height: 5 1/4", 13.3 cm
Colour: Blue
Issued: 1949-1953
Series: Nursery Rhymes
(Series One)
U.S.: **$425.00**
Can.: **$500.00**
Ster.: **£295.00**

HN 2051
St. George
Style Two
Designer: M. Davies
Height: 7 1/2", 19.1 cm
Colour: Green and white
Issued: 1950-1985
U.S.: **$675.00**
Can.: **$775.00**
Ster.: **£375.00**

HN 2052
Grandma
Designer: L. Harradine
Height: 6 3/4", 17.2 cm
Colour: Blue shawl with
red and cream dress
Issued: 1950-1959
Varieties: HN 2052A
U.S.: **$525.00**
Can.: **$625.00**
Ster.: **£325.00**

Earthenware

HN 2052A
Grandma
Designer: L. Harradine
Height: 6 3/4", 17.2 cm
Colour: Brown shawl with
red and cream dress
Issued: Unknown
Varieties: HN 2052
U.S.: **$600.00**
Can.: **$675.00**
Ster.: **£325.00**

Earthenware

HN 2053
The Gaffer
Designer: L. Harradine
Height: 7 3/4", 19.7 cm
Colour: Green and brown
Issued: 1950-1959
U.S.: **$550.00**
Can.: **$725.00**
Ster.: **£295.00**

Earthenware

HN 2054
Falstaff
Style Two
Designer: C.J. Noke
Height: 7", 17.8 cm
Colour: Brown
Issued: 1950-1992
Varieties: HN 618
U.S.: **$250.00**
Can.: **$300.00**
Ster.: **£165.00**

Earthenware and China

HN 2055
The Leisure Hour
Designer: M. Davies
Height: 7", 17.8 cm
Colour: Green, yellow
and brown
Issued: 1950-1965
U.S.: **$650.00**
Can.: **$750.00**
Ster.: **£400.00**

HN 2056
Susan
Style One
Designer: L. Harradine
Height: 7", 17.8 cm
Colour: Lavender dress
with flowered apron
Issued: 1950-1959
U.S.: **$600.00**
Can.: **$675.00**
Ster.: **£350.00**

HN 2057
The Jersey Milkmaid
Designer: L. Harradine
Height: 6 1/2", 16.5 cm
Colour: Blue, white and red
Issued: 1950-1959
Varieties: Also called
"The Milkmaid"
HN 2057A

U.S.: $350.00
Can.: $425.00
Ster.: £250.00

HN 2057A
The Milkmaid
Designer: L. Harradine
Height: 6 1/2", 16.5 cm
Colour: Green, white
and brown
Issued: 1975-1981
Varieties: Also called
"Jersey Milkmaid"
HN 2057

U.S.: $225.00
Can.: $300.00
Ster.: £175.00

HN 2058
Hermione
Designer: M. Davies
Height: 7 3/4", 19.7 cm
Colour: Cream and lavender
Issued: 1950-1952

U.S.: $2,400.00
Can.: $2,400.00
Ster.: £1,000.00

HN 2059
The Bedtime Story
Designer: L. Harradine
Height: 4 3/4", 12.0 cm
Colour: Pink, white, yellow
and blue
Issued: 1950-1996

U.S.: $493.75
Can.: $585.00
Ster.: £169.00

HN 2060
Jack
Designer: L. Harradine
Height: 5 1/2", 14.0 cm
Colour: Green, white
and black
Issued: 1950-1971
Series: Nursery Rhymes
(Series One)

U.S.: $250.00
Can.: $300.00
Ster.: £165.00

HN 2061
Jill
Designer: L. Harradine
Height: 5 1/2", 14.0 cm
Colour: Pink and white
Issued: 1950-1971
Series: Nursery Rhymes
(Series One)

U.S.: $250.00
Can.: $300.00
Ster.: £165.00

HN 2062
Little Boy Blue
Style One
Designer: L. Harradine
Height: 5 1/2", 14.0 cm
Colour: Blue
Issued: 1950-1973
Series: Nursery Rhymes
(Series One)

U.S.: $225.00
Can.: $325.00
Ster.: £165.00

HN 2063
Little Jack Horner
Style One
Designer: L. Harradine
Height: 4 1/2", 11.4 cm
Colour: Red and white
Issued: 1950-1953
Series: Nursery Rhymes
(Series One)

U.S.: $625.00
Can.: $700.00
Ster.: £425.00

HN 2064
My Pretty Maid
Designer: L. Harradine
Height: 5 1/2", 14.0 cm
Colour: Turquoise
Issued: 1950-1954
Series: Nursery Rhymes
(Series One)
U.S.: $625.00
Can.: $650.00
Ster.: £425.00

HN 2065
Blithe Morning
Designer: L. Harradine
Height: 7 1/4", 18.4 cm
Colour: Red
Issued: 1950-1973
Varieties: HN 2021
U.S.: $350.00
Can.: $400.00
Ster.: £165.00

HN 2066
Minuet
Designer: M. Davies
Height: 7 1/4", 18.4 cm
Colour: Red
Issued: 1950-1955
Varieties: HN 2019
U.S.: $1,500.00
Can.: $1,500.00
Ster.: £ 600.00

HN 2067
St. George
Style One
Designer: S. Thorogood
Height: 15 3/4", 40.0 cm
Colour: Multi-coloured
Issued: 1950-1979
Varieties: HN 385, 386, 1800;
Fair and dark hair
U.S.: $3,500.00
Can.: $3,500.00
Ster.: £1,500.00

HN 2068
Calumet
Designer: C.J. Noke
Height: 6 1/4", 15.9 cm
Colour: Green and brown
Issued: 1950-1953
Varieties: HN 1428, 1689
U.S.: $1,000.00
Can.: $1,000.00
Ster.: £ 550.00

Earthenware

HN 2069
Farmer's Wife
Style One
Designer: L. Harradine
Height: 9", 22.9 cm
Colour: Red, green
and brown
Issued: 1951-1955
U.S.: $800.00
Can.: $875.00
Ster.: £495.00

Earthenware

HN 2070
Bridget
Designer: L. Harradine
Height: 7 3/4", 19.7 cm
Colour: Green, brown
and lavender
Issued: 1951-1973
U.S.: $475.00
Can.: $550.00
Ster.: £225.00

Earthenware

HN 2071
Bernice
Designer: M. Davies
Height: 7 3/4", 19.7 cm
Colour: Pink and red
Issued: 1951-1953
U.S.: $1,750.00
Can.: $1,750.00
Ster.: £ 850.00

HN 2072
The Rocking Horse
Designer: L. Harradine
Height: 7", 17.8 cm
Colour: Red, white, blue
             and yellow
Issued: 1951-1953
U.S.:   **$3,500.00**
Can.:   **$3,500.00**
Ster.:   **£1,500.00**

HN 2073
Vivienne   X
Designer: L. Harradine
Height: 7 3/4", 19.7 cm
Colour: Red
Issued: 1951-1967
U.S.:   **$400.00**
Can.:   **$500.00**
Ster.:   **£245.00**

HN 2074
Marianne
Designer: L. Harradine
Height: 7 1/4", 18.4 cm
Colour: Red
Issued: 1951-1953
U.S.:   **$1,600.00**
Can.:   **$1,600.00**
Ster.:   **£ 675.00**

HN 2075
French Peasant
Designer: L. Harradine
Height: 9 1/4", 23.5 cm
Colour: Brown and green
Issued: 1951-1955
U.S.:   **$700.00**
Can.:   **$875.00**
Ster.:   **£475.00**

Earthenware

HN 2076
Promenade
Style One
Designer: M. Davies
Height: 8", 20.3 cm
Colour: Blue and orange
Issued: 1951-1953
U.S.:   **$2,750.00**
Can.:   **$2,750.00**
Ster.:   **£1,500.00**

HN 2077
Rowena
Designer: L. Harradine
Height: 7 1/4", 18.4 cm
Colour: Red and green
Issued: 1951-1955
U.S.:   **$850.00**
Can.:   **$950.00**
Ster.:   **£425.00**

HN 2078
Elfreda
Designer: L. Harradine
Height: 7 1/4", 18.4 cm
Colour: Red and purple
Issued: 1951-1955
U.S.:   **$1,100.00**
Can.:   **$1,100.00**
Ster.:   **£ 475.00**

HN 2079
Damaris
Designer: M. Davies
Height: 7 1/4", 18.4 cm
Colour: Green, white
             and purple
Issued: 1951-1952
U.S.:   **$2,500.00**
Can.:   **$2,500.00**
Ster.:   **£1,250.00**

HN 2080
Jack Point
Designer: C.J. Noke
Height: 16", 40.6 cm
Colour: Purple, green
            and lavender
Issued: 1952 to the present
Varieties: HN 85, 91, 99, 3920
U.S.:   **$3,400.00**
Can.:   **$3,850.00**
Ster.: **£1,450.00**

HN 2081
Princess Badoura
Designer: H. Tittensor, Harry
            E. Stanton and F.
            Van Allen Phillips
Height: 20", 50.8 cm
Colour: Multi-coloured
Issued: 1952 to the present
Varieties: HN 3921
U.S.:   **$33,000.00**
Can.:   **$43,750.00**
Ster.: **£12,500.00**

HN 2082
The Moor
Designer: C.J. Noke
Height: 16 1/4", 41.2 cm
Colour: Red and black
Issued: 1952 to the present
Varieties: HN 1308, 1366,
            1425, 1657, 3642;
            also called "An Arab"
            HN 33, 343, 378
U.S.:   **$3,000.00**
Can.:   **$3,350.00**
Ster.: **£1,450.00**

*

HN 2084
King Charles
Designer: C.J. Noke,
            H. Tittensor
Height: 16", 40.6 cm
Colour: Black with
            yellow base
Issued: 1952-1992
Varieties: HN 404, 3459
U.S.:   **$2,500.00**
Can.:   **$2,500.00**
Ster.: **£1,250.00**

HN 2085
Spring
Style Four
Designer: M. Davies
Height: 7 3/4", 19.6 cm
Colour: Lavender and cream
Issued: 1952-1959
Series: The Seasons
            (Series Two)
U.S.:   **$600.00**
Can.:   **$750.00**
Ster.: **£365.00**

HN 2086
Summer
Style Two
Designer: M. Davies
Height: 7 1/4", 18.4 cm
Colour: Red flowered dress
Issued: 1952-1959
Series: The Seasons
            (Series Two)
U.S.:   **$600.00**
Can.:   **$750.00**
Ster.: **£365.00**

HN 2087
Autumn
Style Two
Designer: M. Davies
Height: 7 1/4", 18.4 cm
Colour: Red and lavender
Issued: 1952-1959
Series: The Seasons
            (Series Two)
U.S.:   **$700.00**
Can.:   **$850.00**
Ster.: **£400.00**

HN 2088
Winter
Style Two
Designer: M. Davies
Height: 6 1/4", 15.9 cm
Colour: Lavender, green
            and red
Issued: 1952-1959
Series: The Seasons
            (Series Two)
U.S.:   **$600.00**
Can.:   **$750.00**
Ster.: **£365.00**

HN 2089
Judith
Style One
Designer: L. Harradine
Height: 7", 17.8 cm
Colour: Red and blue
Issued: 1952-1959

U.S.:	**$425.00**
Can.:	**$575.00**
Ster.:	**£250.00**

HN 2090
Midinette
Style Two
Designer: L. Harradine
Height: 7 1/4", 18.4 cm
Colour: Blue
Issued: 1952-1965

U.S.:	**$425.00**
Can.:	**$525.00**
Ster.:	**£295.00**

HN 2091
Rosemary
Style One
Designer: L. Harradine
Height: 7", 17.8 cm
Colour: Red and blue
Issued: 1952-1959

U.S.:	**$650.00**
Can.:	**$775.00**
Ster.:	**£350.00**

HN 2092
Sweet Maid
Style Two
Designer: L. Harradine
Height: 7", 17.8 cm
Colour: Lavender
Issued: 1952-1955

U.S.:	**$625.00**
Can.:	**$775.00**
Ster.:	**£375.00**

HN 2093
Georgiana
Designer: M. Davies
Height: 8 1/4", 21.0 cm
Colour: Orange and blue
Issued: 1952-1955

U.S.:	**$2,250.00**
Can.:	**$2,250.00**
Ster.:	**£1,000.00**

HN 2094
Uncle Ned
Designer: H. Fenton
Height: 6 3/4", 17.2 cm
Colour: Brown
Issued: 1952-1965

U.S.:	**$600.00**
Can.:	**$750.00**
Ster.:	**£225.00**

Earthenware

HN 2095
Ibrahim
Designer: C.J. Noke
Height: 7 3/4", 19.7 cm
Colour: Brown and yellow
Issued: 1952-1955
Varieties: Also called "The
 Emir" HN 1604, 1605

U.S.:	**$700.00**
Can.:	**$850.00**
Ster.:	**£450.00**

Earthenware

HN 2096
Fat Boy
Style Three
Designer: L. Harradine
Height: 7 1/4", 18.4 cm
Colour: Blue and cream
Issued: 1952-1967
Series: Dickens
 (Series Three)

U.S.:	**$500.00**
Can.:	**$600.00**
Ster.:	**£250.00**

Earthenware

HN 2097
Mr. Micawber
Style Three
Designer: L. Harradine
Height: 7 1/2", 19.1 cm
Colour: Black and brown
Issued: 1952-1967
Series: Dickens
(Series Three)
U.S.: $450.00
Can.: $550.00
Ster.: £250.00

Earthenware

HN 2098
Pecksniff
Style Three
Designer: L. Harradine
Height: 7 1/4", 18.4 cm
Colour: Black and brown
Issued: 1952-1967
Series: Dickens
(Series Three)
U.S.: $450.00
Can.: $550.00
Ster.: £250.00

Earthenware

HN 2099
Mr. Pickwick
Style Three
Designer: L. Harradine
Height: 7 1/2", 19.1 cm
Colour: Blue and brown
Issued: 1952-1967
Series: Dickens
(Series Three)
U.S.: $500.00
Can.: $600.00
Ster.: £250.00

Earthenware

HN 2100
Sairey Gamp
Style Three
Designer: L. Harradine
Height: 7 1/4", 18.4 cm
Colour: Green
Issued: 1952-1967
Series: Dickens
(Series Three)
U.S.: $550.00
Can.: $650.00
Ster.: £325.00

Earthenware

HN 2101
Uriah Heep
Style Three
Designer: L. Harradine
Height: 7 1/2", 19.1 cm
Colour: Black
Issued: 1952-1967
Series: Dickens
(Series Three)
U.S.: $450.00
Can.: $550.00
Ster.: £250.00

Earthenware

HN 2102
Pied Piper
Style One
Designer: L. Harradine
Height: 8 3/4", 22.2 cm
Colour: Black, red and yellow
Issued: 1953-1976
Varieties: HN 1215
U.S.: $400.00
Can.: $500.00
Ster.: £225.00

HN 2103
Mask Seller
Designer: L. Harradine
Height: 8 1/2", 21.6 cm
Colour: Green and yellow
Issued: 1953-1995
Varieties: HN 1361
U.S.: $275.00
Can.: $350.00
Ster.: £125.00

Earthenware

HN 2104
Abdullah
Designer: L. Harradine
Height: 6", 15.2 cm
Colour: Multi-coloured
Issued: 1953-1962
Varieties: HN 1410
U.S.: $675.00
Can.: $750.00
Ster.: £350.00

HN 2105
Bluebeard
Style Two
Designer: L. Harradine
Height: 11", 27.9 cm
Colour: Purple, green
  and brown
Issued: 1953-1992
Varieties: HN 1528

U.S.: **$725.00**
Can.: **$775.00**
Ster.: **£300.00**

HN 2106
Linda
Style One
Designer: L. Harradine
Height: 4 3/4", 12.0 cm
Colour: Red
Issued: 1953-1976

U.S.: **$250.00**
Can.: **$300.00**
Ster.: **£145.00**

HN 2107
Valerie
Designer: M. Davies
Height: 4 3/4", 12.0 cm
Colour: Red, pink and white
Issued: 1953-1995
Varieties: HN 3620

U.S.: **$175.00**
Can.: **$200.00**
Ster.: **£ 65.00**

HN 2108
Baby Bunting
Designer: M. Davies
Height: 5 1/4", 13.3 cm
Colour: Brown and cream
Issued: 1953-1959

U.S.: **$475.00**
Can.: **$525.00**
Ster.: **£250.00**

HN 2109
Wendy
Designer: L. Harradine
Height: 5", 12.7 cm
Colour: Blue
Issued: 1953-1995

U.S.: **$100.00**
Can.: **$150.00**
Ster.: **£ 50.00**

HN 2110
Christmas Time
Designer: M. Davies
Height: 6 1/2", 16.5 cm
Colour: Red with white frills
Issued: 1953-1967

U.S.: **$600.00**
Can.: **$750.00**
Ster.: **£350.00**

HN 2111
Betsy
Designer: L. Harradine
Height: 7", 17.8 cm
Colour: Lavender with
  flowered apron
Issued: 1953-1959

U.S.: **$550.00**
Can.: **$650.00**
Ster.: **£325.00**

HN 2112
Carolyn
Style One
Designer: L. Harradine
Height: 7", 17.8 cm
Colour: White and green
  flowered dress
Issued: 1953-1965

U.S.: **$525.00**
Can.: **$600.00**
Ster.: **£275.00**

HN 2113
Maytime
Designer: L. Harradine
Height: 7", 17.8 cm
Colour: Pink dress
with blue scarf
Issued: 1953-1967
U.S.: $450.00
Can.: $575.00
Ster.: £275.00

HN 2114
Sleepyhead
Style One
Designer: M. Davies
Height: 5", 12.7 cm
Colour: Orange, blue
and white
Issued: 1953-1955
U.S.: $2,500.00
Can.: $2,500.00
Ster.: £1,250.00

HN 2115
Coppelia
Designer: M. Davies
Height: 7 1/4", 18.4 cm
Colour: Blue, red and white
Issued: 1953-1959
U.S.: $800.00
Can.: $925.00
Ster.: £575.00

HN 2116
Ballerina
Style One
Designer: M. Davies
Height: 7 1/4", 18.4 cm
Colour: Lavender
Issued: 1953-1973
U.S.: $450.00
Can.: $550.00
Ster.: £275.00

HN 2117
The Skater
Style One
Designer: M. Davies
Height: 7 1/4", 18.4 cm
Colour: Red, white and brown
Issued: 1953-1971
U.S.: $625.00
Can.: $675.00
Ster.: £295.00

HN 2118
Good King Wenceslas
Style One
Designer: M. Davies
Height: 8 1/2", 21.6 cm
Colour: Brown and purple
Issued: 1953-1976
U.S.: $550.00
Can.: $600.00
Ster.: £250.00

Earthenware

HN 2119
Town Crier
Style One
Designer: M. Davies
Height: 8 1/2", 21.6 cm
Colour: Purple, green
and yellow
Issued: 1953-1976
U.S.: $400.00
Can.: $500.00
Ster.: £250.00

Earthenware

HN 2120
Dinky Doo
Designer: L. Harradine
Height: 4 3/4" 12.0 cm
Colour: Red
Issued: 1983-1996
Varieties: HN 1678, 3618
U.S.: $143.75
Can.: $205.00
Ster.: £ 49.95

HN 2121
Babie

Designer:	L. Harradine
Height:	4 3/4", 12.0 cm
Colour:	Pink
Issued:	1983-1992
Varieties:	HN 1679, 1842
U.S.:	**$160.00**
Can.:	**$185.00**
Ster.:	**£ 90.00**

HN 2122
Yeoman of the Guard

Designer:	L. Harradine
Height:	5 3/4", 14.6 cm
Colour:	Red, gold and brown
Issued:	1954-1959
Varieties:	HN 688
U.S.:	**$1,300.00**
Can.:	**$1,300.00**
Ster.:	**£ 650.00**

HN 2123
Rose
Style One

Designer:	L. Harradine
Height:	4 1/2", 11.4 cm
Colour:	Lavender
Issued:	1983-1995
Varieties:	HN 1368, 1387, 1416, 1506, 1654
U.S.:	**$115.00**
Can.:	**$125.00**
Ster.:	**£ 50.00**

*

HN 2125
This Little Pig

Designer:	L. Harradine
Height:	4", 10.1 cm
Colour:	White
Issued:	1984-1995
Varieties:	HN 1793, 1794
U.S.:	**$ 80.00**
Can.:	**$100.00**
Ster.:	**£ 30.00**

HN 2126
Top o' The Hill
Style Two

Designer:	L. Harradine
Remodeller:	P. Gee
Height:	4", 10.1 cm
Colour:	Green and mauve
Issued:	1988-1988
Series:	R.D.I.C.C. and Miniatures
Varieties:	HN 2180, 3499
U.S.:	**$175.00**
Can.:	**$200.00**
Ster.:	**£125.00**

HN 2127
Top o' The Hill
Style One

Designer:	L. Harradine
Height:	7", 17.8 cm
Colour:	Gold
Issued:	1988-1988
Varieties:	HN 1833, 1834, 1849
U.S.:	**$425.00**
Can.:	**$475.00**
Ster.:	**£225.00**

Commissioned for
Australian Bicentenary

HN 2128
River Boy

Designer:	M. Davies
Height:	4", 10.1 cm
Colour:	Blue and green
Issued:	1962-1975
U.S.:	**$325.00**
Can.:	**$350.00**
Ster.:	**£195.00**

HN 2129
The Old Balloon Seller
Style Two

Designer:	L. Harradine
Remodeller:	W.K. Harper
Height:	3 1/2", 8.9 cm
Colour:	Green and white
Issued:	1989-1991
Series:	Miniatures
U.S.:	**$200.00**
Can.:	**$250.00**
Ster.:	**£125.00**

HN 2130
The Balloon Seller
Style Two
Designer: L. Harradine
Remodeller: R. Tabbenor
Height: 3 3/4", 8.9 cm
Colour: Green and cream
Issued: 1989-1991
Series: Miniatures
U.S.:   **$200.00**
Can.:   **$225.00**
Ster.:   **£110.00**

HN 2131
Autumn Breezes
Style One
Designer: L. Harradine
Height: 7 1/2", 19.1 cm
Colour: Orange, yellow
                   and black
Issued: 1990-1994
Varieties: HN1911, 1913,
                   1934, 2147
U.S.:   **$325.00**
Can.:   **$400.00**
Ster.:   **£175.00**

HN 2132
The Suitor
Designer: M. Davies
Height: 7 1/4", 18.4 cm
Colour: Green, yellow
                   and blue
Issued: 1962-1971
U.S.:   **$550.00**
Can.:   **$650.00**
Ster.:   **£350.00**

HN 2133
Faraway
Designer: M. Davies
Height: 2 1/2", 6.3 cm
Colour: Blue and white
Issued: 1958-1962
Series: Teenagers
U.S.:   **$525.00**
Can.:   **$600.00**
Ster.:   **£300.00**

HN 2134
An Old King
Designer: C.J. Noke
Height: 10 3/4", 27.3 cm
Colour: Purple, red, green
                   and brown
Issued: 1954-1992
Varieties: HN 358, 623, 1801
U.S.:   **$725.00**
Can.:   **$950.00**
Ster.:   **£350.00**

HN 2135
Gay Morning
Designer: M. Davies
Height: 7", 17.8 cm
Colour: Pink
Issued: 1954-1967
U.S.:   **$475.00**
Can.:   **$550.00**
Ster.:   **£225.00**

HN 2136
Delphine
Designer: M. Davies
Height: 7 1/4", 18.4 cm
Colour: Blue and lavender
Issued: 1954-1967
U.S.:   **$475.00**
Can.:   **$600.00**
Ster.:   **£250.00**

HN 2137
Lilac Time
Designer: M. Davies
Height: 7 1/4", 18.4 cm
Colour: Red
Issued: 1954-1969
U.S.:   **$500.00**
Can.:   **$550.00**
Ster.:   **£250.00**

HN 2138
La Sylphide
Designer: M. Davies
Height: 7", 17.8 cm
Colour: White and blue
Issued: 1954-1965
U.S.: **$600.00**
Can.: **$700.00**
Ster.: **£350.00**

HN 2139
Giselle
Designer: M. Davies
Height: 6", 15.2 cm
Colour: Blue and white
Issued: 1954-1969
U.S.: **$600.00**
Can.: **$675.00**
Ster.: **£350.00**

HN 2140
Giselle, The Forest Glade
Designer: M. Davies
Height: 7", 17.8 cm
Colour: White and blue
Issued: 1954-1965
U.S.: **$600.00**
Can.: **$675.00**
Ster.: **£350.00**

HN 2141
Choir Boy
Designer: M. Davies
Height: 4 3/4", 12.0 cm
Colour: White and red
Issued: 1954-1975
U.S.: **$200.00**
Can.: **$250.00**
Ster.: **£110.00**

HN 2142
Rag Doll
Designer: M. Davies
Height: 4 3/4", 12.0 cm
Colour: White, blue and red
Issued: 1954-1986
U.S.: **$165.00**
Can.: **$200.00**
Ster.: **£120.00**

HN 2143
Friar Tuck
Designer: M. Davies
Height: 7 1/2", 19.1 cm
Colour: Brown
Issued: 1954-1965
U.S.: **$700.00**
Can.: **$800.00**
Ster.: **£450.00**

Earthenware

HN 2144
The Jovial Monk
Designer: M. Davies
Height: 7 3/4", 19.7 cm
Colour: Brown
Issued: 1954-1976
U.S.: **$375.00**
Can.: **$450.00**
Ster.: **£245.00**

Earthenware

HN 2145
Wardrobe Mistress
Designer: M. Davies
Height: 5 3/4", 14.6 cm
Colour: Green, red, white
and blue
Issued: 1954-1967
U.S.: **$700.00**
Can.: **$825.00**
Ster.: **£395.00**

Earthenware

HN 2146
The Tinsmith
Designer: M. Nicoll
Height: 6 1/2", 16.5 cm
Colour: Green and brown
Issued: 1962-1967

U.S.: $625.00
Can.: $800.00
Ster.: £375.00

HN 2147
Autumn Breezes
Style One
Designer: L. Harradine
Height: 7 1/2", 19.1 cm
Colour: Black and white
Issued: 1955-1971
Varieties: HN 1911, 1913, 1934, 2131

U.S.: $475.00
Can.: $550.00
Ster.: £225.00

HN 2148
The Bridesmaid
Style Three
Designer: M. Davies
Height: 5 1/2", 14.0 cm
Colour: Yellow
Issued: 1955-1959

U.S.: $300.00
Can.: $375.00
Ster.: £225.00

HN 2149
Love Letter
Style One
Designer: M. Davies
Height: 5 1/2", 14.0 cm
Colour: Pink and blue
Issued: 1958-1976

U.S.: $650.00
Can.: $750.00
Ster.: £350.00

HN 2150
Willy-Won't He
Designer: L. Harradine
Height: 5 1/2", 14.0 cm
Colour: Red, green, blue and white
Issued: 1955-1959
Varieties: HN 1561, 1584 (Minor glaze differences)

U.S.: $550.00
Can.: $650.00
Ster.: £275.00

HN 2151
Mother's Help
Designer: M. Davies
Height: 5", 12.7 cm
Colour: Black and white
Issued: 1962-1969

U.S.: $300.00
Can.: $350.00
Ster.: £140.00

HN 2152
Adrienne
Designer: M. Davies
Height: 7 1/2", 19.1 cm
Colour: Purple
Issued: 1964-1976
Varieties: HN 2304, also called "Fiona" HN 3748; "Joan" HN 3217

U.S.: $250.00
Can.: $295.00
Ster.: £165.00

HN 2153
The One That Got Away
Designer: M. Davies
Height: 6 1/4", 15.9 cm
Colour: Brown
Issued: 1955-1959

U.S.: $550.00
Can.: $625.00
Ster.: £300.00

HN 2154
A Child From Williamsburg
Designer: M. Davies
Height: 5 1/2", 14.0 cm
Colour: Blue
Issued: 1964-1983
Series: Figures of
Williamsburg

U.S.: **$275.00**
Can.: **$275.00**
Ster.: **£145.00**

HN 2156
The Polka
Designer: M. Davies
Height: 7 1/2", 19.1 cm
Colour: Pink
Issued: 1955-1969

U.S.: **$500.00**
Can.: **$575.00**
Ster.: **£225.00**

HN 2157
A Gypsy Dance
Style One
Designer: M. Davies
Height: 7", 17.8 cm
Colour: Lavender
Issued: 1955-1957

U.S.: **$1,300.00**
Can.: **$1,300.00**
Ster.: **£ 475.00**

HN 2158
Alice
Style One
Designer: M. Davies
Height: 5", 12.7 cm
Colour: Blue
Issued: 1960-1981

U.S.: **$225.00**
Can.: **$275.00**
Ster.: **£145.00**

HN 2159
Fortune Teller
Designer: L. Harradine
Height: 6 1/2", 16.5 cm
Colour: Green and brown
Issued: 1955-1967

U.S.: **$625.00**
Can.: **$750.00**
Ster.: **£350.00**

HN 2160
The Apple Maid
Designer: L. Harradine
Height: 6 1/2", 16.5 cm
Colour: Blue, black
and white
Issued: 1957-1962

U.S.: **$650.00**
Can.: **$750.00**
Ster.: **£350.00**

HN 2161
The Hornpipe
Designer: M. Nicoll
Height: 9 1/4", 23.5 cm
Colour: Blue and white
Issued: 1955-1962

U.S.: **$ 950.00**
Can.: **$1,100.00**
Ster.: **£ 500.00**

HN 2162
The Foaming Quart
Designer: M. Davies
Height: 6", 15.2 cm
Colour: Brown
Issued: 1955-1992

U.S.: **$250.00**
Can.: **$325.00**
Ster.: **£165.00**

Earthenware

Earthenware

HN 2163
In The Stocks
Style Two
Designer: M. Nicoll
Height: 5 3/4", 14.6 cm
Colour: Red, brown
  and black
Issued: 1955-1959

U.S.: $1,000.00
Can.: $1,100.00
Ster.: £ 550.00

HN 2165
Janice
Style One
Designer: M. Davies
Height: 7 1/4", 18.4 cm
Colour: Black and pale blue
Issued: 1955-1965
Varieties: HN 2022

U.S.: $650.00
Can.: $800.00
Ster.: £395.00

HN 2166
The Bride
Style Two
Designer: M. Davies
Height: 8", 20.3 cm
Colour: Pink
Issued: 1956-1976

U.S.: $275.00
Can.: $375.00
Ster.: £175.00

HN 2167
Home Again
Designer: M. Davies
Height: 3 1/4", 8.3 cm
Colour: Red and white
Issued: 1956-1995

U.S.: $175.00
Can.: $250.00
Ster.: £ 75.00

HN 2168
Esmeralda
Designer: M. Davies
Height: 5 1/2", 14.0 cm
Colour: Yellow and red
Issued: 1956-1959

U.S.: $600.00
Can.: $675.00
Ster.: £300.00

HN 2169
Dimity
Designer: L. Harradine
Height: 5 3/4", 14.6 cm
Colour: Green, lavender
  and cream
Issued: 1956-1959

U.S.: $500.00
Can.: $625.00
Ster.: £250.00

HN 2170
Invitation
Designer: M. Davies
Height: 5 1/2", 14.0 cm
Colour: Pink
Issued: 1956-1975

U.S.: $250.00
Can.: $325.00
Ster.: £145.00

HN 2171
The Fiddler
Designer: M. Nicoll
Height: 8 3/4", 22.2 cm
Colour: Green, cream
  and red
Issued: 1956-1962

U.S.: $1,200.00
Can.: $1,200.00
Ster.: £ 550.00

Earthenware

HN 2172
Jolly Sailor
Designer:	M. Nicoll
Height:	6 1/2", 16.5 cm
Colour:	Black, brown, blue and white
Issued:	1956-1965
U.S.:	**$925.00**
Can.:	**$975.00**
Ster.:	**£500.00**

Earthenware

HN 2173
The Organ Grinder
Designer:	M. Nicoll
Height:	8 3/4", 22.2 cm
Colour:	Green, cream and brown
Issued:	1956-1965
U.S.:	**$1,100.00**
Can.:	**$1,100.00**
Ster.:	**£ 500.00**

Earthenware

HN 2174
The Tailor
Designer:	M. Nicoll
Height:	5", 12.7 cm
Colour:	Blue, cream and orange
Issued:	1956-1959
U.S.:	**$1,100.00**
Can.:	**$1,100.00**
Ster.:	**£ 550.00**

Earthenware

HN 2175
The Beggar
Style Two
Designer:	L. Harradine
Height:	6 3/4", 17.2 cm
Colour:	Green
Issued:	1956-1962
Series:	Beggar's Opera
U.S.:	**$625.00**
Can.:	**$725.00**
Ster.:	**£425.00**

Earthenware
*

HN 2176
Autumn Breezes
Style Two
Designer:	L. Harradine
Remodeller:	D. Frith
Height:	3 1/2", 8.9 cm
Colour:	Red
Issued:	1991-1995
Varieties:	HN 2180
Series:	Miniatures
U.S.:	**$125.00**
Can.:	**$175.00**
Ster.:	**£ 60.00**

HN 2177
My Teddy
Designer:	M. Davies
Height:	3 1/4", 8.3 cm
Colour:	Turquoise and brown
Issued:	1962-1967
U.S.:	**$675.00**
Can.:	**$750.00**
Ster.:	**£350.00**

HN 2178
Enchantment
Designer:	M. Davies
Height:	7 1/2", 19.1 cm
Colour:	Blue
Issued:	1957-1982
U.S.:	**$275.00**
Can.:	**$325.00**
Ster.:	**£145.00**

HN 2179
Noelle
Designer:	M. Davies
Height:	6 3/4", 17.2 cm
Colour:	Orange, white and black
Issued:	1957-1967
U.S.:	**$650.00**
Can.:	**$750.00**
Ster.:	**£275.00**

HN 2180
Autumn Breezes, Style Two
Designer: L. Harradine
Remodeller: D. Frith
Height: 3 1/2", 8.9 cm
Colour: Red, lavender, 22kt gold trim
Issued: 1991-1995
Varieties: HN 2176, 3499
Series: Signature Collection

U.S.: $150.00
Can.: $200.00
Ster.: £ 90.00

HN 2181
Summer's Day
Style One
Designer: M. Davies
Height: 5 3/4", 14.6 cm
Colour: White
Issued: 1957-1962

U.S.: $475.00
Can.: $525.00
Ster.: £225.00

*

HN 2183
Boy from Williamsburg
Designer: M. Davies
Height: 5 1/2", 14.0 cm
Colour: Blue and pink
Issued: 1969-1983
Series: Figures of Williamsburg

U.S.: $250.00
Can.: $275.00
Ster.: £145.00

HN 2184
Sunday Morning
Designer: M. Davies
Height: 7 1/2", 19.1 cm
Colour: Red and brown
Issued: 1963-1969

U.S.: $500.00
Can.: $550.00
Ster.: £225.00

HN 2185
Columbine
Style Two
Designer: M. Davies
Height: 7", 17.8 cm
Colour: Pink
Issued: 1957-1969
Series: Teenagers

U.S.: $350.00
Can.: $450.00
Ster.: £225.00

HN 2186
Harlequin
Style One
Designer: M. Davies
Height: 7 1/4", 18.4 cm
Colour: Blue
Issued: 1957-1969
Series: Teenagers

U.S.: $350.00
Can.: $450.00
Ster.: £225.00

*

HN 2191
Sea Sprite
Style Two
Designer: M. Davies
Height: 7", 17.8 cm
Colour: Pink and blue
Issued: 1958-1962
Series: Teenagers

U.S.: $450.00
Can.: $500.00
Ster.: £275.00

HN 2192
Wood Nymph
Designer: M. Davies
Height: 7 1/4", 18.4 cm
Colour: Blue and white
Issued: 1958-1962
Series: Teenagers

U.S.: $450.00
Can.: $500.00
Ster.: £275.00

HN 2193
Fair Lady
Style One
Designer: M. Davies
Height: 7 1/4", 18.4 cm
Colour: Green
Issued: 1963-1996
Varieties: HN 2832, 2835,
Also called
"Kay" HN 3340

U.S.:	$268.75
Can.:	$415.00
Ster.:	£105.00

*

HN 2196
The Bridesmaid
Style Four
Designer: M. Davies
Height: 5 1/4", 13.3 cm
Colour: Pale blue
Issued: 1960-1976

U.S.:	$175.00
Can.:	$250.00
Ster.:	£110.00

*

HN 2202
Melody
Designer: M. Davies
Height: 6 1/4", 15.9 cm
Colour: Blue and peach
Issued: 1957-1962
Series: Teenagers

U.S.:	$450.00
Can.:	$500.00
Ster.:	£225.00

HN 2203
Teenager
Designer: M. Davies
Height: 7 1/4", 18.4 cm
Colour: Orange and white
Issued: 1957-1962
Series: Teenagers

U.S.:	$400.00
Can.:	$475.00
Ster.:	£250.00

HN 2204
Long John Silver
Style One
Designer: M. Nicoll
Height: 9", 22.9 cm
Colour: Green, black
and white
Issued: 1957-1965

U.S.:	$700.00
Can.:	$850.00
Ster.:	£450.00

Earthenware

HN 2205
Master Sweep
Designer: M. Nicoll
Height: 8 1/2", 21.6 cm
Colour: Green, black
and brown
Issued: 1957-1962

U.S.:	$900.00
Can.:	$975.00
Ster.:	£495.00

Earthenware

HN 2206
Sunday Best
Style One
Designer: M. Davies
Height: 7 1/2", 19.1 cm
Colour: Yellow
Issued: 1979-1984
Varieties: HN 2698

U.S.:	$275.00
Can.:	$375.00
Ster.:	£145.00

HN 2207
Stayed at Home
Designer: M. Davies
Height: 5", 12.7 cm
Colour: Green and white
Issued: 1958-1969

U.S.:	$300.00
Can.:	$350.00
Ster.:	£145.00

HN 2208
Silversmith of Williamsburg
Designer: M. Davies
Height: 6 1/4", 15.9 cm
Colour: Blue, white and
brown
Issued: 1960-1983
Series: Figures of
Williamsburg

U.S.: $250.00
Can.: $295.00
Ster.: £145.00

HN 2209
Hostess of Williamsburg
Designer: M. Davies
Height: 7 1/4", 18.4 cm
Colour: Pink
Issued: 1960-1983
Series: Figures of
Williamsburg

U.S.: $300.00
Can.: $350.00
Ster.: £145.00

HN 2210
Debutante
Style One
Designer: M. Davies
Height: 5", 12.7 cm
Colour: Blue
Issued: 1963-1967

U.S.: $450.00
Can.: $550.00
Ster.: £250.00

HN 2211
Fair Maiden
Designer: M. Davies
Height: 5 1/4", 13.3 cm
Colour: Green
Issued: 1967-1994
Varieties: HN 2434

U.S.: $185.00
Can.: $200.00
Ster.: £ 70.00

HN 2212
Rendezvous
Designer: M. Davies
Height: 7 1/4", 18.4 cm
Colour: Red and white
Issued: 1962-1971

U.S.: $575.00
Can.: $650.00
Ster.: £325.00

HN 2213
Contemplation
Designer: M. Davies
Height: 12", 30.5 cm
Colour: White
Issued: 1982-1986
Varieties: HN 2241
Series: Images

U.S.: $225.00
Can.: $200.00
Ster.: £145.00

HN 2214
Bunny
Designer: M. Davies
Height: 5", 12.7 cm
Colour: Turquoise
Issued: 1960-1975

U.S.: $250.00
Can.: $325.00
Ster.: £150.00

HN 2215
Sweet April
Designer: M. Davies
Height: 7 1/4", 18.4 cm
Colour: Pink
Issued: 1965-1967

U.S.: $575.00
Can.: $675.00
Ster.: £295.00

HN 2216
Pirouette
Designer: M. Davies
Height: 5 3/4", 14.6 cm
Colour: Pale blue
Issued: 1959-1967

U.S.: $250.00
Can.: $400.00
Ster.: £175.00

HN 2217
Old King Cole
Designer: M. Davies
Height: 6 1/2", 16.5 cm
Colour: Brown, yellow
and white
Issued: 1963-1967

U.S.: $775.00
Can.: $950.00
Ster.: £450.00

HN 2218
Cookie
Designer: M. Davies
Height: 4 3/4", 12.0 cm
Colour: Pink and white
Issued: 1958-1975

U.S.: $265.00
Can.: $325.00
Ster.: £140.00

HN 2219
Bedtime
Style One
Designer: L. Harradine
Height: 5 1/2", 14.0 cm
Colour: Pink
Issued: 1992
Varieties: HN 1978

U.S.: $100.00
Can.: $130.00
Ster.: £ 50.00

Commissioned by Peter Jones
China, Wakefield, England

HN 2220
Winsome
Designer: M. Davies
Height: 8", 20.3 cm
Colour: Red
Issued: 1960-1985

U.S.: $265.00
Can.: $350.00
Ster.: £145.00

HN 2221
Nanny
Designer: M. Nicoll
Height: 6", 15.2 cm
Colour: Blue and white
Issued: 1958-1991

U.S.: $325.00
Can.: $375.00
Ster.: £165.00

Earthenware

HN 2222
Camellia
Designer: M. Davies
Height: 7 3/4", 19.7 cm
Colour: Pink
Issued: 1960-1971

U.S.: $350.00
Can.: $450.00
Ster.: £165.00

HN 2223
Schoolmarm
Designer: M. Davies
Height: 6 3/4", 17.2 cm
Colour: Purple, grey
and brown
Issued: 1958-1981

U.S.: $375.00
Can.: $450.00
Ster.: £225.00

HN 2224
Make Believe
Designer: M. Nicoll
Height: 5 3/4", 14.6 cm
Colour: White
Issued: 1984-1988
Varieties: HN 2225

U.S.: **$175.00**
Can.: **$225.00**
Ster.: **£145.00**

HN 2225
Make Believe
Designer: M. Nicoll
Height: 5 3/4", 14.6 cm
Colour: Blue
Issued: 1962-1988
Varieties: HN 2224

U.S.: **$200.00**
Can.: **$250.00**
Ster.: **£145.00**

HN 2226
The Cellist
Designer: M. Nicoll
Height: 8", 20.3 cm
Colour: Black and brown
Issued: 1960-1967

U.S.: **$650.00**
Can.: **$775.00**
Ster.: **£395.00**

HN 2227
Gentleman from
Williamsburg
Designer: M. Davies
Height: 6 1/4", 15.9 cm
Colour: Green and white
Issued: 1960-1983
Series: Figures of
Williamsburg

U.S.: **$275.00**
Can.: **$350.00**
Ster.: **£145.00**

HN 2228
Lady from Williamsburg
Designer: M. Davies
Height: 6", 15.2 cm
Colour: Green
Issued: 1960-1983
Series: Figures of
Williamsburg

U.S.: **$275.00**
Can.: **$350.00**
Ster.: **£145.00**

HN 2229
Southern Belle
Style One
Designer: M. Davies
Height: 7 1/2", 19.1 cm
Colour: Red and cream
Issued: 1958 to the present
Varieties: HN 2425

U.S.: **$493.75**
Can.: **$490.00**
Ster.: **£139.00**

HN 2230
A Gypsy Dance
Style Two
Designer: M. Davies
Height: 7", 17.8 cm
Colour: Lavender
Issued: 1959-1971

U.S.: **$475.00**
Can.: **$575.00**
Ster.: **£275.00**

HN 2231
Sweet Sixteen
Style One
Designer: M. Davies
Height: 7 1/4", 18.4 cm
Colour: Blue and white
Issued: 1958-1965
Series: Teenagers

U.S.: **$400.00**
Can.: **$475.00**
Ster.: **£275.00**

*

HN 2233
Royal Governor's Cook
Designer: M. Davies
Height: 6", 15.2 cm
Colour: Dark blue, white
and brown
Issued: 1960-1983
Series: Figures of
Williamsburg
U.S.: **$675.00**
Can.: **$750.00**
Ster.: **£325.00**

HN 2234
Michele
Designer: M. Davies
Height: 7", 17.8 cm
Colour: Green
Issued: 1967-1993
Varieties: Also called "Autumn
Attraction" HN 3612
U.S.: **$275.00**
Can.: **$325.00**
Ster.: **£145.00**

HN 2235
Dancing Years
Designer: M. Davies
Height: 6 3/4", 17.2 cm
Colour: Lavender
Issued: 1965-1971
U.S.: **$500.00**
Can.: **$575.00**
Ster.: **£275.00**

HN 2236
Affection
Designer: M. Davies
Height: 4 1/2", 11.4 cm
Colour: Purple
Issued: 1962-1994
U.S.: **$200.00**
Can.: **$250.00**
Ster.: **£ 90.00**

HN 2237
Celeste
Style One
Designer: M. Davies
Colour: Pale blue
Height: 6 3/4", 17.2 cm
Issued: 1959-1971
U.S.: **$325.00**
Can.: **$425.00**
Ster.: **£165.00**

HN 2238
My Pet
Designer: M. Davies
Height: 2 3/4", 7.0 cm
Colour: Blue and white
Issued: 1962-1975
U.S.: **$265.00**
Can.: **$350.00**
Ster.: **£165.00**

HN 2239
Wigmaker of Williamsburg
Designer: M. Davies
Height: 7 1/2", 19.1 cm
Colour: White and brown
Issued: 1960-1983
Series: Figures of
Williamsburg
U.S.: **$250.00**
Can.: **$325.00**
Ster.: **£145.00**

HN 2240
Blacksmith of Willliamsburg
Designer: M. Davies
Height: 6 3/4", 17.2 cm
Colour: Grey and white
Issued: 1960-1983
Series: Figures of
Williamsburg
U.S.: **$250.00**
Can.: **$325.00**
Ster.: **£145.00**

HN 2241
Contemplation
Designer: M. Davies
Height: 12", 30.5 cm
Colour: Black
Issued: 1982-1986
Varieties: HN 2213
Series: Images

U.S.: $225.00
Can.: $250.00
Ster.: £165.00

HN 2242
First Steps
Style One
Designer: M. Davies
Height: 6 1/2", 16.5 cm
Colour: Blue and yellow
Issued: 1959-1965

U.S.: $675.00
Can.: $800.00
Ster.: £375.00

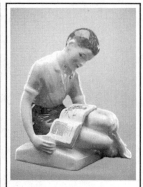

HN 2243
Treasure Island
Designer: M. Davies
Height: 4 3/4", 12.0 cm
Colour: Blue and yellow
Issued: 1962-1975

U.S.: $300.00
Can.: $350.00
Ster.: £150.00

HN 2244
Newsboy
Designer: M. Nicoll
Height: 8 1/2, 21.6 cm
Colour: Green, brown and blue
Issued: 1959-1965
Varieties: Limited edition of 250 for Evening Sentinel

U.S.: $775.00
Can.: $875.00
Ster.: £395.00

HN 2245
The Basket Weaver
Designer: M. Nicoll
Height: 5 3/4", 14.6 cm
Colour: Pale blue and yellow
Issued: 1959-1962

U.S.: $625.00
Can.: $700.00
Ster.: £325.00

HN 2246
Cradle Song
Designer: M. Davies
Height: 5 1/2", 14.0 cm
Colour: Green and brown
Issued: 1959-1962

U.S.: $650.00
Can.: $750.00
Ster.: £350.00

HN 2247
Omar Khayyam
Style Two
Designer: M. Nicoll
Height: 6 1/4", 15.9 cm
Colour: Brown
Issued: 1965-1983

U.S.: $250.00
Can.: $300.00
Ster.: £165.00

Earthenware

HN 2248
Tall Story
Designer: M. Nicoll
Height: 6 1/2", 16.5 cm
Colour: Blue and grey
Issued: 1968-1975
Series: Sea Characters

U.S.: $350.00
Can.: $450.00
Ster.: £225.00

HN 2249
The Favourite
Designer: M. Nicoll
Height: 7 3/4", 19.7 cm
Colour: Blue and white
Issued: 1960-1990

U.S.:	**$275.00**
Can.:	**$350.00**
Ster.:	**£150.00**

HN 2250
The Toymaker
Designer: M. Nicoll
Height: 6", 15.2 cm
Colour: Brown and red
Issued: 1959-1973

U.S.:	**$600.00**
Can.:	**$700.00**
Ster.:	**£325.00**

HN 2251
Masquerade
Style Two
Designer: M. Davies
Height: 8 1/2", 21.6 cm
Colour: Blue and white
Issued: 1960-1965
Varieties: HN 2259

U.S.:	**$425.00**
Can.:	**$550.00**
Ster.:	**£275.00**

HN 2252
The Joker
Style Two
Designer: M. Nicoll
Height: 8 1/2", 21.6 cm
Colour: White
Issued: 1990-1992
Series: Clowns

U.S.:	**$300.00**
Can.:	**$350.00**
Ster.:	**£145.00**

HN 2253
The Puppetmaker
Designer: M. Nicoll
Height: 8", 20.3 cm
Colour: Green, brown and red
Issued: 1962-1973

U.S.:	**$650.00**
Can.:	**$750.00**
Ster.:	**£395.00**

HN 2254
Shore Leave
Designer: M. Nicoll
Height: 7 1/2", 19.1 cm
Colour: Black
Issued: 1965-1979
Series: Sea Characters

U.S.:	**$300.00**
Can.:	**$375.00**
Ster.:	**£225.00**

HN 2255
Teatime
Designer: M. Nicoll
Height: 7 1/4", 18.4 cm
Colour: Brown
Issued: 1972-1995

U.S.:	**$300.00**
Can.:	**$325.00**
Ster.:	**£100.00**

HN 2256
Twilight
Designer: M. Nicoll
Height: 5", 12.7 cm
Colour: Green and black
Issued: 1971-1976

U.S.:	**$325.00**
Can.:	**$400.00**
Ster.:	**£175.00**

HN 2257
Sea Harvest
Designer: M. Nicoll
Height: 7 1/2", 19.1 cm
Colour: Blue and brown
Issued: 1969-1976
Series: Sea Characters
U.S.: $350.00
Can.: $425.00
Ster.: £225.00

HN 2258
A Good Catch
Designer: M. Nicoll
Height: 7 1/4", 18.4 cm
Colour: Green and grey
Issued: 1966-1986
Series: Sea Characters
U.S.: $285.00
Can.: $375.00
Ster.: £175.00

HN 2259
Masquerade
Style Two
Designer: M. Davies
Height: 8 1/2", 21.6 cm
Colour: Red and cream
Issued: 1960-1965
Varieties: HN 2251
U.S.: $400.00
Can.: $525.00
Ster.: £275.00

HN 2260
The Captain
Style Two
Designer: M. Nicoll
Height: 9 1/2", 24.1 cm
Colour: Black and white
Issued: 1965-1982
Series: Sea Characters
U.S.: $300.00
Can.: $375.00
Ster.: £225.00

HN 2261
Marriage of Art and Industry
Designer: M. Davies
Height: 19", 48.3 cm
Colour: Green
Issued: 1958 in a limited edition of 12
U.S.: $10,000.00
Can.: $10,000.00
Ster.: £ 4,000.00

HN 2262
Lights Out
Designer: M. Davies
Height: 5", 12.7 cm
Colour: Blue trousers with yellow spotted shirt
Issued: 1965-1969
U.S.: $350.00
Can.: $425.00
Ster.: £185.00

HN 2263
Seashore
Designer: M. Davies
Height: 3 1/2", 8.9 cm
Colour: Yellow, red and cream
Issued: 1961-1965
U.S.: $375.00
Can.: $450.00
Ster.: £225.00

HN 2264
Elegance
Designer: M. Davies
Height: 7 1/4", 18.4 cm
Colour: Green
Issued: 1961-1985
U.S.: $250.00
Can.: $325.00
Ster.: £165.00

HN 2265
Sara
Style One
Designer: M. Davies
Height: 7 1/2", 19.1 cm
Colour: Red and white
Issued: 1981-1996
Varieties HN 3308

U.S.:	$493.75
Can.:	$490.00
Ster.:	£169.00

HN 2266
Ballad Seller
Designer: M. Davies
Height: 7 1/2", 19.1 cm
Colour: Pink
Issued: 1968-1973

U.S.:	$425.00
Can.:	$500.00
Ster.:	£225.00

HN 2267
Rhapsody
Designer: M. Davies
Height: 6 3/4", 17.2 cm
Colour: Green
Issued: 1961-1973

U.S.:	$350.00
Can.:	$400.00
Ster.:	£175.00

HN 2268
Daphne
Designer: M. Davies
Height: 8 1/4", 21.0 cm
Colour: Pink
Issued: 1963-1975

U.S.:	$300.00
Can.:	$375.00
Ster.:	£175.00

HN 2269
Leading Lady
Designer: M. Davies
Height: 7 3/4", 19.7 cm
Colour: Blue and yellow
Issued: 1965-1976

U.S.:	$300.00
Can.:	$375.00
Ster.:	£175.00

HN 2270
Pillow Fight
Designer: M. Davies
Height: 5", 12.7 cm
Colour: Patterned pink
nightdress
Issued: 1965-1969

U.S.:	$350.00
Can.:	$430.00
Ster.:	£180.00

HN 2271
Melanie
Designer: M. Davies
Height: 7 3/4", 19.7 cm
Colour: Blue
Issued: 1965-1981

U.S.:	$275.00
Can.:	$350.00
Ster.:	£165.00

HN 2272
Repose
Designer: M. Davies
Height: 5 1/4", 13.3 cm
Colour: Pink and green
Issued: 1972-1979

U.S.:	$375.00
Can.:	$450.00
Ster.:	£245.00

HN 2273
Denise
Style Two
Designer: M. Davies
Height: 7", 17.8 cm
Colour: Red
Issued: 1964-1971
U.S.: $425.00
Can.: $550.00
Ster.: £225.00

HN 2274
Golden Days
Designer: M. Davies
Height: 3 3/4", 9.5 cm
Colour: Yellow , white
and blue
Issued: 1964-1973
U.S.: $275.00
Can.: $325.00
Ster.: £175.00

HN 2275
Sandra
Designer: M. Davies
Height: 7 3/4", 19.7 cm
Colour: Gold
Issued: 1969 to the present
Varieties: HN 2401; Also
called "Annette"
(Style Two) HN 3495
U.S.: $250.00
Can.: $445.00
Ster.: £119.00

HN 2276
Heart to Heart
Designer: M. Davies
Height: 5 1/2", 14.0 cm
Colour: Lavender, green
and yellow
Issued: 1961-1971
U.S.: $725.00
Can.: $850.00
Ster.: £350.00

HN 2277
Slapdash
Designer: M.Nicoll
Height: 10", 25.4 cm
Colour: Green, white
and blue
Issued: 1990 -1994
Series: Clowns
U.S.: $325.00
Can.: $450.00
Ster.: £135.00

HN 2278
Judith
Style Two
Designer: M. Nicoll
Height: 6 3/4", 17.2 cm
Colour: Yellow
Issued: 1986 N.America
1987 Worldwide
- 1989
Varieties: HN 2313
U.S.: $325.00
Can.: $375.00
Ster.: £200.00

HN 2279
The Clockmaker
Designer: M. Nicoll
Height: 7", 17.8 cm
Colour: Green and brown
Issued: 1961-1975
U.S.: $450.00
Can.: $550.00
Ster.: £325.00

HN 2280
The Mayor
Designer: M. Nicoll
Height: 8 1/4", 21.0 cm
Colour: Red and white
Issued: 1963-1971
Varieties: Two sizes 7 1/2"
and 8 1/4"
U.S.: $575.00
Can.: $675.00
Ster.: £325.00

HN 2281
The Professor
Designer: M. Nicoll
Height: 7 1/4", 18.4 cm
Colour: Brown and black
Issued: 1965-1981

U.S.:	$275.00
Can.:	$325.00
Ster.:	£165.00

HN 2282
The Coachman
Designer: M. Nicoll
Height: 7 1/4", 18.4 cm
Colour: Purple, grey and blue
Issued: 1963-1971

U.S.:	$675.00
Can.:	$775.00
Ster.:	£350.00

HN 2283
Dreamweaver (matte)
Designer: M. Nicoll
Height: 8 1/4", 21.0 cm
Colour: Blue, grey and brown
Issued: 1972-1976

U.S.:	$325.00
Can.:	$400.00
Ster.:	£180.00

HN 2284
The Craftsman
Designer: M. Nicoll
Height: 6", 15.2 cm
Colour: Blue, tan and brown
Issued: 1961-1965

U.S.:	$750.00
Can.:	$900.00
Ster.:	£475.00

*

HN 2287
Symphony
Designer: D.B. Lovegrove
Height: 5 1/4", 13.3 cm
Colour: Brown
Issued: 1961-1965

U.S.:	$325.00
Can.:	$500.00
Ster.:	£200.00

*

HN 2304
Adrienne
Designer: M. Davies
Height: 7 1/2", 19.1 cm
Colour: Blue
Issued: 1964-1991
Varieties: HN 2152, also called
"Fiona" HN 3748;
"Joan" HN 3217

U.S.:	$250.00
Can.:	$295.00
Ster.:	£145.00

HN 2305
Dulcie
Designer: M. Davies
Height: 7 1/4", 18.4 cm
Colour: Blue
Issued: 1981-1984

U.S.:	$325.00
Can.:	$375.00
Ster.:	£175.00

HN 2306
Reverie
Designer: M. Davies
Height: 6 1/2", 16.5 cm
Colour: Peach
Issued: 1964-1981

U.S.:	$375.00
Can.:	$450.00
Ster.:	£170.00

HN 2307
Coralie
Designer: M. Davies
Height: 7 1/4", 18.4 cm
Colour: Yellow
Issued: 1964-1988
U.S.: $250.00
Can.: $300.00
Ster.: £165.00

HN 2308
Picnic
Designer: M. Davies
Height: 3 3/4", 9.5 cm
Colour: Yellow
Issued: 1965-1988
U.S.: $240.00
Can.: $275.00
Ster.: £125.00

HN 2309
Buttercup
Designer: M. Davies
Height: 7", 17.8 cm
Colour: Green dress with
yellow sleeves
Issued: 1964 to the present
Varieties: HN 2399
U.S.: $268.75
Can.: $425.00
Ster.: £139.00

HN 2310
Lisa (matte)
Designer: M. Davies
Height: 7 1/4", 18.4 cm
Colour: Blue and white
Issued: 1969-1982
U.S.: $225.00
Can.: $325.00
Ster.: £145.00

HN 2311
Lorna
Designer: M. Davies
Height: 8 1/4", 21.0 cm
Colour: Green dress
yellow shawl
Issued: 1965-1985
U.S.: $265.00
Can.: $325.00
Ster.: £165.00

HN 2312
Soiree
Designer: M. Davies
Height: 7 1/2", 19.1 cm
Colour: Green and cream
Issued: 1967-1984
U.S.: $225.00
Can.: $300.00
Ster.: £145.00

HN 2313
Judith
Designer: M. Nicholl
Height: 6 1/4". 15.9 cm
Colour: Red and cream
Issued: 1988 in a limited
edition of 1,000
U.S.: $325.00
Can.: $450.00
Ster.: £225.00

HN 2314
Old Mother Hubbard
Designer: M. Nicholl
Height: 8", 20.3 cm
Colour: Green and white
Issued: 1964-1975
U.S.: $500.00
Can.: $600.00
Ster.: £275.00

HN 2315
Last Waltz
Designer: M. Nicoll
Height: 7 3/4", 19.7 cm
Colour: Yellow and white
Issued: 1967-1993
Varieties: HN 2316

U.S.: **$250.00**
Can.: **$300.00**
Ster.: **£145.00**

HN 2316
Last Waltz
Designer: M. Nicoll
Height: 7 3/4", 19.7 cm
Colour: Pink and cream
Issued: 1987 in a limited
 edition of 2000
Varieties: HN 2315

U.S.: **$300.00**
Can.: **$375.00**
Ster.: **£175.00**

Issued for Royal Doulton
special events during 1987

HN 2317
The Lobster Man
Designer: M. Nicoll
Height: 7 1/4", 18.4 cm
Colour: Blue, grey and brown
Issued: 1964-1994
Varieties: HN 2323
Series: Sea Characters

U.S.: **$225.00**
Can.: **$325.00**
Ster.: **£110.00**

HN 2318
Grace
Style One
Designer: M. Nicoll
Height: 7 3/4", 19.7 cm
Colour: Green
Issued: 1966-1981

U.S.: **$300.00**
Can.: **$395.00**
Ster.: **£175.00**

HN 2319
The Bachelor
Designer: M. Nicoll
Height: 7", 17.8 cm
Colour: Green and brown
Issued: 1964-1975

U.S.: **$450.00**
Can.: **$525.00**
Ster.: **£275.00**

HN 2320
Tuppence a Bag
Designer: M. Nicoll
Height: 5 1/2", 14.0 cm
Colour: Blue and green
Issued: 1968-1995

U.S.: **$250.00**
Can.: **$300.00**
Ster.: **£100.00**

HN 2321
Family Album
Designer: M. Nicholl
Height: 6 1/4", 15.9 cm
Colour: Lavender and green
Issued: 1966-1973

U.S.: **$550.00**
Can.: **$650.00**
Ster.: **£295.00**

NOTE ON PRICING

Prices are given for three separate and distinct market areas.

Prices are given in the currency of each of these different trading areas.

Prices are not exchange rate calculations but are based on supply and demand in that market.

Prices listed are guidelines to the most current retail values but actual selling prices may vary slightly.

Prices for current figurines are taken from the Royal Doulton suggested retail lists.

Extremely rare figurines have widely fluctuating retail values and their prices must therefore be determined between buyer and seller.

Figurines where there are only one or two known are possibly best priced in an auction environment.

Prices given are for figurines in mint condition

HN 2322
The Cup of Tea
Designer: M. Nicoll
Height: 7", 17.8 cm
Colour: Dark blue and grey
Issued: 1964-1983
U.S.: $265.00
Can. : $325.00
Ster.: £165.00

HN 2323
The Lobster Man
Designer: M. Nicoll
Height: 7 1/4", 18.4 cm
Colour: Cream, blue,
gold and grey
Issued: 1987-1995
Varieties: HN 2317
Series: Sea Characters
U.S.: $250.00
Can.: $350.00
Ster.: £125.00

HN 2324
Matador and the Bull
Designer: M. Davies
Height: 16", 40.6 cm
Colour: Black and yellow
Issued: 1964 to the present
U.S.: $25,200.00
Can.: $28,800.00
Ster.: £ 9,950.00

HN 2325
The Master
Designer: M. Davies
Height: 6 1/4", 15.9 cm
Colour: Green and brown
Issued: 1967-1992
U.S.: $325.00
Can.: $400.00
Ster.: £165.00

HN 2326
Antoinette
Style Two
Designer: M. Davies
Height: 6 1/4", 15.9 cm
Colour: White, white rose
Issued: 1967-1979
Varieties: Also called
"My Love," HN 2339
U.S.: $225.00
Can.: $325.00
Ster.: £145.00

HN 2327
Katrina
Designer: M. Davies
Height: 7 1/2", 19.1 cm
Colour: Red
Issued: 1965-1969
U.S.: $450.00
Can.: $525.00
Ster.: £225.00

HN 2328
Queen of Sheba
Designer: M. Davies
Height: 9", 22.9 cm
Colour: Purple and brown
with green base
Issued: 1982 in a limited
edition of 750
Series: Les Femmes
Fatales
U.S.: $1,900.00
Can.: $1,750.00
Ster.: £ 850.00

HN 2329
Lynne
Designer: M. Davies
Height: 7", 17.8 cm
Colour: Green
Issued: 1971-1996
Varieties: HN 3740; Also called
"Kathy" (Style Two)
HN 3305
U.S.: $375.00
Can.: $445.00
Ster.: £105.00

HN 2330
Meditation
Designer: M. Davies
Height: 5 3/4", 14.6 cm
Colour: Peach and cream
Issued: 1971-1983
U.S.: $375.00
Can.: $495.00
Ster.: £225.00

HN 2331
Cello
Style One
Designer: M. Davies
Height: 6", 15.2 cm
Colour: Yellow and brown
Issued: 1970 in a limited
edition of 750
Series: Lady Musicians
U.S.: $2,000.00
Can.: $2,000.00
Ster.: £ 750.00

HN 2332
Monte Carlo
Designer: M. Davies
Height: 8 1/4", 21.0 cm
Colour: Green
Issued: 1982 in a limited
edition of 1500
Series: Sweet and Twenties
U.S.: $375.00
Can.: $450.00
Ster.: £175.00

HN 2333
Jacqueline
Style Two
Designer: M. Davies
Height: 7 1/2", 19.1 cm
Colour: Purple
Issued: 1982 Canada,
1983 Worldwide
- 1991
U.S.: $250.00
Can.: $325.00
Ster.: £145.00

HN 2334
Fragrance
Style One
Designer: M. Davies
Height: 7 1/4", 18.4 cm
Colour: Blue
Issued: 1966-1995
Varieties: HN3311
U.S.: $250.00
Can.: $300.00
Ster.: £100.00

HN 2335
Hilary
Designer: M. Davies
Height: 7 1/4", 18.4 cm
Colour: Blue
Issued: 1967-1981
U.S.: $250.00
Can.: $350.00
Ster.: £165.00

HN 2336
Alison
Designer: M. Davies
Height: 7 1/2", 19.1 cm
Colour: Blue and white
Issued: 1966-1992
Varieties: HN 3264
U.S.: $250.00
Can.: $335.00
Ster.: £145.00

HN 2337
Loretta
Designer: M. Davies
Height: 7 3/4", 19.7 cm
Colour: Purple dress,
yellow shawl
Issued: 1966-1981
U.S.: $250.00
Can.: $325.00
Ster.: £165.00

HN 2338
Penny
Designer: M. Davies
Height: 4 3/4", 12.0 cm
Colour: Green and white
Issued: 1968-1995
Varieties: HN 2424

U.S.:	**$110.00**
Can.:	**$150.00**
Ster.:	**£ 65.00**

HN 2339
My Love
Designer: M. Davies
Height: 6 1/4", 15.9 cm
Colour: White, red rose
Issued: 1969 to the present
Varieties: Also called
         "Antoinette" (Style
         Two), HN 2326

U.S.:	**$406.25**
Can.:	**$490.00**
Ster.:	**£139.00**

HN 2340
Belle
Style Two
Designer: M. Davies
Height: 4 1/2", 11.4 cm
Colour: Green
Issued: 1968-1988

U.S.:	**$100.00**
Can.:	**$125.00**
Ster.:	**£ 90.00**

HN 2341
Cherie
Designer: M. Davies
Height: 5 1/2", 14.0 cm
Colour: Blue
Issued: 1966-1992

U.S.:	**$200.00**
Can.:	**$225.00**
Ster.:	**£100.00**

HN 2342
Lucrezia Borgia
Designer: M. Davies
Height: 8", 20.3 cm
Colour: Yellow
Issued: 1985 in a limited
        edition of 750
Series: Les Femmes
        Fatales

U.S.:	**$1,600.00**
Can.:	**$1,800.00**
Ster.:	**£ 750.00**

HN 2343
Premiere
(Hand holds cloak)
Designer: M. Davies
Height: 7 1/2", 19.1 cm
Colour: Green
Issued: 1969-Unknown
Varieties: HN 2343A

U.S.:	**$240.00**
Can.:	**$350.00**
Ster.:	**£165.00**

HN 2343A
Premiere
(Hand rests on cloak)
Designer: M. Davies
Height: 7 1/2", 19.1 cm
Colour: Green
Issued: Unknown-1979
Varieties: HN 2343

U.S.:	**$240.00**
Can.:	**$300.00**
Ster.:	**£165.00**

HN 2344
Deauville
Designer: M. Davies
Height: 8 1/4", 21.0 cm
Colour: Yellow and white
Issued: 1982 in a limited
        edition of 1,500
Series: Sweet and Twenties

U.S.:	**$350.00**
Can.:	**$425.00**
Ster.:	**£175.00**

HN 2345
Clarissa
Style Two
Designer: M. Davies
Height: 7 1/2", 19.1 cm
Colour: Green
Issued: 1968-1981

U.S.: **$240.00**
Can.: **$350.00**
Ster.: **£165.00**

HN 2346
Kathy
Style One
Designer: M. Davies
Height: 4 3/4", 12.0 cm
Colour: Cream flowered
dress
Issued: 1981-1987
Series: Kate Greenaway

U.S.: **$225.00**
Can.: **$275.00**
Ster.: **£145.00**

HN 2347
Nina (matte)
Designer: M. Davies
Height: 7 1/2", 19.1 cm
Colour: Blue
Issued: 1969-1976

U.S.: **$200.00**
Can.: **$275.00**
Ster.: **£145.00**

HN 2348
Geraldine (matte)
Designer: M. Davies
Height: 7 1/4", 18.4 cm
Colour: Green
Issued: 1972-1976

U.S.: **$200.00**
Can.: **$275.00**
Ster.: **£145.00**

HN 2349
Flora
Designer: M. Nicoll
Height: 7 3/4", 19.7 cm
Colour: Brown and white
Issued: 1966-1973

U.S.: **$475.00**
Can.: **$550.00**
Ster.: **£225.00**

HN 2352
A Stitch in Time
Designer: M. Nicoll
Height: 6 1/4", 15.9 cm
Colour: Purple, brown
and turquoise
Issued: 1966-1981

U.S.: **$275.00**
Can.: **$350.00**
Ster.: **£175.00**

HN 2356
Ascot
Style One
Designer: M. Nicoll
Height: 5 3/4", 14.6 cm
Colour: Green dress with
yellow shawl
Issued: 1968-1995

U.S.: **$250.00**
Can.: **$350.00**
Ster.: **£110.00**

HN 2359
The Detective
Designer: M. Nicoll
Height: 9 1/4", 23.5 cm
Colour: Brown
Issued: 1977-1983

U.S.: **$375.00**
Can.: **$450.00**
Ster.: **£175.00**

HN 2361
The Laird
(Small Base)
Designer: M. Nicoll
Height: 8", 20.3 cm
Colour: Green and brown
Issued: 1969-Unknown
Varieties: HN 2361A (Large base)

U.S.: $400.00
Can.: $445.00
Ster.: £125.00

HN 2361A
The Laird
(Large Base)
Designer: M. Nicoll
Height: 8", 20.3 cm
Colour: Green and brown
Issued: Unknown- to the present
Varieties: HN 2361 (Small base)

U.S.: $406.25
Can.: $445.00
Ster.: £125.00

HN 2362
The Wayfarer
Designer: M. Nicoll
Height: 5 1/2", 14.0 cm
Colour: Green, grey and brown
Issued: 1970-1976

U.S.: $275.00
Can.: $350.00
Ster.: £195.00

*

HN 2368
Fleur
Designer: J. Bromley
Height: 7 1/4", 18.4 cm
Colour: Green
Issued: 1968-1995
Varieties: HN 2369; also called "Flower of Love" HN 2460, 3970

U.S.: $275.00
Can.: $325.00
Ster.: £130.00

HN 2369
Fleur
Designer: J. Bromley
Height: 7 1/4", 18.4 cm
Colour: Orange and blue
Issued: 1983-1986
Varieties: HN 2368; also called "Flower of Love" HN 2460, 3970

U.S.: $300.00
Can.: $375.00
Ster.: £175.00

HN 2370
Sir Edward
Designer: J. Bromley
Height: 11", 27.9 cm
Colour: Red and grey
Issued: 1979 in a limited edition of 500
Series: Age of Chivalry

U.S.: $600.00
Can.: $600.00
Ster.: £250.00

HN 2371
Sir Ralph
Designer: J. Bromley
Height: 10 3/4", 27. 3cm
Colour: Turquoise and grey
Issued: 1979 in a limited edition of 500
Series: Age of Chivalry

U.S.: $600.00
Can.: $600.00
Ster.: £250.00

HN 2372
Sir Thomas
Designer: J. Bromley
Height: 11", 27.9 cm
Colour: Black
Issued: 1979 in a limited edition of 500
Series: Age of Chivalry

U.S.: $600.00
Can.: $600.00
Ster.: £250.00

HN 2373
Joanne
Style One
Designer: J. Bromley
Height: 5 1/4", 13.3 cm
Colour: White
Issued: 1982-1988
Series: Vanity Fair Ladies

U.S.: **$250.00**
Can.: **$375.00**
Ster.: **£165.00**

HN 2374
Mary
Style One
Designer: J. Bromley
Height: 7 3/4", 19.7 cm
Colour: White
Issued: 1984-1986
Series: Vanity Fair Ladies

U.S.: **$400.00**
Can.: **$475.00**
Ster.: **£175.00**

HN 2375
The Viking (matte)
Designer: J. Bromley
Height: 8 3/4", 22.2 cm
Colour: Blue and brown
Issued: 1973-1976

U.S.: **$350.00**
Can.: **$475.00**
Ster.: **£225.00**

HN 2376
Indian Brave
Designer: M. Davies
Height: 16", 40.6 cm
Colour: Multi-coloured
Issued: 1967 in a limited
edition of 500

U.S.: **$7,500.00**
Can.: **$7,500.00**
Ster.: **£3,000.00**

HN 2377
Georgina
Designer: M. Davies
Height: 5 3/4", 14.6 cm
Colour: Red and yellow
Issued: 1981-1986
Series: Kate Greenaway

U.S.: **$225.00**
Can.: **$300.00**
Ster.: **£165.00**

HN 2378
Simone
Designer: M. Davies
Height: 7 1/4", 18.4 cm
Colour: Green
Issued: 1971-1981

U.S.: **$225.00**
Can.: **$350.00**
Ster.: **£165.00**

HN 2379
Ninette
Style One
Designer: M. Davies
Height: 7 1/2", 19.1 cm
Colour: Yellow and cream
Issued: 1971 to the present
Varieties: HN 3417; Also called
Olivia HN 3339

U.S.: **$406.25**
Can.: **$445.00**
Ster.: **£139.00**

HN 2380
Sweet Dreams
Style One
Designer: M. Davies
Height: 5", 12.7 cm
Colour: Multi-coloured
Issued: 1971-1990

U.S.: **$250.00**
Can.: **$325.00**
Ster.: **£165.00**

HN 2381
Kirsty
Style One
Designer: M. Davies
Height: 7 1/2", 19.1 cm
Colour: Orange
Issued: 1971 to the present
Varieties: Also called
"Janette" HN 3415

U.S.: $306.25
Can.: $445.00
Ster.: £139.00

HN 2382
Secret Thoughts
Designer: M. Davies
Height: 6 1/4", 15.9 cm
Colour: Green
Issued: 1971-1988

U.S.: $325.00
Can.: $450.00
Ster.: £195.00

HN 2383
Breton Dancer
Designer: M. Davies
Height: 8 1/2", 21.6 cm
Colour: Blue and white
Issued: 1981 in a limited
edition of 750
Series: Dancers of the
World

U.S.: $1,000.00
Can.: $1,150.00
Ster.: £ 500.00

HN 2384
West Indian Dancer
Designer: M. Davies
Height: 8 3/4", 22.2 cm
Colour: Yellow and white
Issued: 1981 in a limited
edition of 750
Series: Dancers of the
World

U.S.: $1,000.00
Can.: $1,150.00
Ster.: £ 500.00

HN 2385
Debbie
Designer: M. Davies
Height: 5 1/2", 14.0 cm
Colour: Blue and white
Issued: 1969-1982
Varieties: HN 2400; "Lavender
Rose," HN 3481;
"Moonlight Rose,"
HN3483; "Old Country
Roses," HN 3482

U.S.: $175.00
Can.: $250.00
Ster.: £110.00

HN 2386
HRH Prince Philip
Duke of Edinburgh
Designer: M. Davies
Height: 8 1/4", 21.0 cm
Colour: Black and gold
Issued: 1981 in a limited
edition of 1500

U.S.: $575.00
Can.: $600.00
Ster.: £250.00

HN 2387
Helen of Troy
Designer: M. Davies
Height: 9 1/4", 23.5 cm
Colour: Green and pink
Issued: 1981 in a limited
edition of 750
Series: Les Femmes
Fatales

U.S.: $2,000.00
Can.: $2,000.00
Ster.: £ 900.00

HN 2388
Karen
Style Two
Designer: M. Davies
Height: 8", 20.3 cm
Colour: Red and white
Issued: 1982 to the present

U.S.: $493.75
Can.: $490.00
Ster.: £175.00

HN 2389
Angela
Style Two
Designer: M. Davies
Height: 7 1/2", 19.1 cm
Colour: White
Issued: 1983-1986
Series Vanity Fair Ladies
U.S.: **$225.00**
Can.: **$275.00**
Ster.: **£150.00**

HN 2390
Spinning
Designer: M. Davies
Height: 7 1/4", 18.4 cm
Colour: Yellow, pink, blue
and white
Issued: 1984 in a limited
edition of 750
Series: Gentle Arts
U.S.: **$2,000.00**
Can.: **$2,000.00**
Ster.: **£ 900.00**

HN 2391
T'zu-hsi, Empress Dowager
Designer: M. Davis
Height: 8", 20.3 cm
Colour: Red, white and blue
Issued: 1983 in a limited
edition of 750
Series: Les Femmes
Fatales
US.:. **$1,500.00**
Can.: **$1,500.00**
Ster.: **£ 750.00**

HN 2392
Jennifer
Style Two
Designer: M. Davies
Height: 7", 17.8 cm
Colour: Blue
Issued: 1982-1992
U.S.: **$300.00**
Can.: **$375.00**
Ster.: **£150.00**

HN 2393
Rosalind
Designer: M. Davies
Height: 5 1/2", 14.0 cm
Colour: Blue
Issued: 1970-1975
U.S.: **$300.00**
Can.: **$350.00**
Ster.: **£175.00**

HN 2394
Lisa
Designer: M. Davies
Height: 7 1/4", 18.4 cm
Colour: Purple-yellow
Issued: 1983 -1990
Varieties: HN 2310, 3265
U.S.: **$250.00**
Can.: **$300.00**
Ster.: **£145.00**

HN 2395
Catherine
Style One
Designer: M. Davies
Height: 7 1/2", 19.1 cm
Colour: Red and yellow
Issued: 1983-1984
Series: Ladies of Covent
Garden
U.S.: **$500.00**
Can.: **$600.00**
Ster.: **£225.00**

Commissioned by Amex

HN 2396
Wistful
Style One
Designer: M. Davies
Height: 6 1/2", 16.5 cm
Colour: Peach and cream
Issued: 1979-1990
Varieties: HN 2472
U.S.: **$375.00**
Can.: **$475.00**
Ster.: **£165.00**

HN 2397
Margaret
Style Two
Designer: M. Davies
Height: 7 1/2", 19.1 cm
Colour: White dress, blue sash
Issued: 1982 to present
Varieties: HN 3496;
"Adele" HN 2480;
"Camille" HN 3171
Series: Vanity Fair Ladies
U.S.: $187.50
Can.: $280.00
Ster.: £ 79.95

HN 2398
Alexandra
Style One
Designer: M. Davies
Height: 7 3/4", 19.7 cm
Colour: Patterned green
dress, yellow cape
Issued: 1970-1976
U.S.: $250.00
Can.: $350.00
Ster.: £165.00

HN 2399
Buttercup
Style One
Designer: M. Davies
Height: 7", 17.8 cm
Colour: Red dress with
yellow sleeves
Issued: 1983 to the present
Varieties: HN 2309
U.S.: $268.75
Can.: $490.00
Ster.: £139.00

HN 2400
Debbie
Designer: M. Davies
Height: 5 1/2", 14.0 cm
Colour: Peach
Issued: 1983-1995
Varieties: HN 2385; "Lavender
Rose" HN 3481;
"Moonlight Rose"
HN 3483; "Old Country
Roses" HN 3482
U.S.: $165.00
Can.: $225.00
Ster.: £ 85.00

HN 2401
Sandra
Designer: M. Davies
Height: 7 3/4", 19.7 cm
Colour: Green
Issued: 1983-1992
Varieties: HN 2275; Also
called "Annette"
(Style Two) HN 3495
U.S.: $275.00
Can.: $375.00
Ster.: £165.00

HN 2408
A Penny's Worth
Designer: M. Nicoll
Height: 7", 17.8 cm
Colour: Pale blue, yellow
and white
Issued: 1986-1990
U.S.: $225.00
Can.: $325.00
Ster.: £165.00

HN 2410
Lesley
Designer: M. Nicoll
Height: 8", 20.3 cm
Colour: Orange and yellow
Issued: 1986-1990
U.S.: $250.00
Can.: $375.00
Ster.: £165.00

HN 2417
The Boatman
Designer: M. Nicoll
Height: 6 1/2", 16.5 cm
Colour: Yellow
Issued: 1971-1987
Series: Sea Characters
Varieties: HN 2417A
U.S.: $275.00
Can.: $350.00
Ster.: £175.00

HN2417A
The Boatman
Designer: M. Nicoll
Height: 6 1/2", 16.5 cm
Colour: Yellow
Issued: 1971-1987
Series: Sea Characters
Varieties: HN 2417

U.S.:	**$275.00**
Can.:	**$350.00**
Ster.:	**£175.00**

Commissioned by Pilot
Insurance

HN 2418
Country Love
Designer: J. Bromley
Height: 8", 20.3 cm
Colour: Pink flowered dress
Issued: 1990 in a limited
edition of 12,500

U.S.:	**$300.00**
Can.:	**$400.00**
Ster.:	**£175.00**

Commissioned by Lawleys

HN 2419
The Goose Girl
Style Two
Designer: J. Bromley
Height: 8", 20.3 cm
Colour: Blue and white
Issued: 1990 in a limited
edition of 12,500

U.S.:	**$300.00**
Can.:	**$400.00**
Ster.:	**£175.00**

Commissioned by Lawleys

HN 2420
The Shepherdess
Style Four
Designer: J. Bromley
Height: 9", 22.9 cm
Colour: Peach, blue
and white
Issued: 1991 in a limited
edition of 12,500

U.S.:	**$300.00**
Can.:	**$400.00**
Ster.:	**£175.00**

Commissioned by Lawleys

HN 2421
Charlotte
Style One
Designer: J. Bromley
Height: 6 1/2", 16.5 cm
Colour: Purple
Issued: 1972-1986
Varieties: HN 2423

U.S.:	**$300.00**
Can.:	**$350.00**
Ster.:	**£165.00**

HN 2422
Francine
(Bird's tail up)
Designer: J. Bromley
Height: 5", 12.7 cm
Colour: Green and white
Issued: 1972-1981
Varieties: HN 2422A (Bird's tail
moulded to hand)

U.S.:	**$175.00**
Can.:	**$225.00**
Ster.:	**£120.00**

HN 2422A
Francine
(Bird's tail moulded to hand)
Designer: J. Bromley
Height: 5", 12.7 cm
Colour: Green and white
Issued: 1972-1981
Varieties: HN 2422 (Bird's
tail up)

U.S.:	**$175.00**
Can.:	**$225.00**
Ster.:	**£120.00**

HN 2423
Charlotte
Style One
Designer: J. Bromley
Height: 6 1/2", 16.5 cm
Colour: Pale blue
and pink
Issued: 1986-1992
Varieties: HN 2421

U.S.:	**$275.00**
Can.:	**$375.00**
Ster.:	**£175.00**

HN 2424
Penny
Designer: M. Davies
Height: 4 3/4", 12.0 cm
Colour: Yellow and white
Issued: 1983-1992
Varieties: HN 2338

U.S.:	$125.00
Can.:	$150.00
Ster.:	£ 90.00

Note: Also known with yellow underskirt

HN 2425
Southern Belle
Designer: M. Davies
Height: 7 1/2", 19.1 cm
Colour: Pale blue and pink
Issued: 1983-1994
Varieties: HN 2229

U.S.:	$275.00
Can.:	$350.00
Ster.:	£120.00

HN 2426
Tranquility
Designer: M. Davies
Height: 12", 30.5 cm
Colour: Black
Issued: 1981-1986
Varieties: HN 2469
Series: Images

U.S.:	$200.00
Can.:	$250.00
Ster.:	£125.00

HN 2427
Virginals
Designer: M. Davies
Height: 6 1/4", 15.9 cm
Colour: Green, gold and brown
Issued: 1971 in a limited edition of 750
Series: Lady Musicians

U.S.:	$2,300.00
Can.:	$2,300.00
Ster.:	£ 750.00

HN 2428
The Palio
Designer: M. Davies
Height: 17 1/2", 44.5 cm
Colour: Blue, yellow and brown
Issued: 1971 in a limited edition of 500

U.S.:	$12,000.00
Can.:	$12,000.00
Ster.:	£ 5,000.00

HN 2429
Elyse
Designer: M. Davies
Height: 5 3/4", 14.6 cm
Colour: Blue
Issued: 1972-1995
Varieties: HN 2474

U.S.:	$275.00
Can.:	$350.00
Ster.:	£120.00

HN 2430
Romance
Designer: M. Davies
Height: 5 1/4", 13.3 cm
Colour: Gold and green
Issued: 1972-1981

U.S.:	$240.00
Can.:	$350.00
Ster.:	£175.00

HN 2431
Lute
Designer: M. Davies
Height: 6 1/4", 15.9 cm
Colour: Blue, white and brown
Issued: 1972 in a limited edition of 750
Series: Lady Musicians

U.S.:	$1,250.00
Can.:	$1,250.00
Ster.:	£ 700.00

HN 2432
Violin
Designer: M. Davies
Height: 6 1/4", 15.9 cm
Colour: Brown and gold
Issued: 1972 in a limited
 edition of 750
Series: Lady Musicians
U.S.: **$1,250.00**
Can.: **$1,250.00**
Ster.: **£ 700.00**

HN 2433
Peace
Designer: M. Davies
Height: 8", 20.3 cm
Colour: Black
Issued: 1981 to the present
Varieties: HN 2470
Series: Images
U.S.: **$141.25**
Can.: **$135.00**
Ster.: **£ 49.95**

HN 2434
Fair Maiden
Designer: M. Davies
Height: 5 1/4", 13.3 cm
Colour: Red and white
Issued: 1983-1994
Varieties: HN 2211
U.S.: **$185.00**
Can.: **$225.00**
Ster.: **£ 70.00**

HN 2435
Queen of the Ice
Designer: M. Davies
Height: 8", 20.3 cm
Colour: Cream
Issued: 1983-1986
Series: Enchantment
U.S.: **$300.00**
Can.: **$375.00**
Ster.: **£165.00**

HN 2436
Scottish Highland Dancer
Designer: M. Davies
Height: 9 1/2", 24.1 cm
Colour: Red, black
 and white
Issued: 1978 in a limited
 edition of 750
Series: Dancers of the
 World
U.S.: **$1,750.00**
Can.: **$1,750.00**
Ster.: **£ 600.00**

HN 2437
Queen of the Dawn
Designer: M. Davies
Height: 8 1/2", 21.6 cm
Colour: Cream
Issued: 1983-1986
Series: Enchantment
U.S.: **$300.00**
Can.: **$375.00**
Ster.: **£165.00**

HN 2438
Sonata
Designer: M. Davies
Height: 6 1/2", 16.5 cm
Colour: Cream
Issued: 1983-1985
Series: Enchantment
U.S.: **$250.00**
Can.: **$300.00**
Ster.: **£145.00**

HN 2439
Philippine Dancer
Designer: M. Davies
Height: 9 1/2", 24.1 cm
Colour: Green and cream
Issued: 1978 in a limited
 edition of 750
Series: Dancers of the
 World
U.S.: **$1,100.00**
Can.: **$1,100.00**
Ster.: **£ 500.00**

HN 2440
Cynthia
Style Two
Designer: M. Davies
Height: 7 1/4", 18.4 cm
Colour: Green and yellow
Issued: 1984-1992
U.S.: $275.00
Can.: $350.00
Ster.:   £165.00

HN 2441
Pauline
Style Two
Designer: M. Davies
Height: 5", 12.7 cm
Colour: Peach
Issued: 1983 Canada,
          1984 Worldwide
          - 1989
U.S.: $300.00
Can.: $375.00
Ster.:   £175.00

HN 2442
Sailor's Holiday
Designer: M. Nicoll
Height: 6 1/4", 15.9 cm
Colour: Gold, brown
          and white
Issued: 1972-1979
Series: Sea Characters
U.S.: $325.00
Can.: $450.00
Ster.:   £225.00

HN 2443
The Judge (matte)
Designer: M. Nicoll
Height: 6 1/2", 16.5 cm
Colour: Red and white
Issued: 1972-1976
Varieties: HN 2443A (gloss)
U.S.: $250.00
Can.: $375.00
Ster.:   £165.00

HN 2443A
The Judge (gloss)
Designer: M. Nicoll
Height: 6 1/2", 16.5 cm
Colour: Red and white
Issued: 1976-1992
Varieties: HN 2443 (matte)
U.S.: $250.00
Can.: $300.00
Ster.:   £165.00

HN 2444
Bon Appetit (matte)
Designer: M. Nicoll
Height: 6", 15.2 cm
Colour: Grey and brown
Issued: 1972-1976
U.S.: $275.00
Can.: $350.00
Ster.:   £145.00

HN 2445
Parisian (matte)
Designer: M. Nicoll
Height: 8", 20.3 cm
Colour: Blue and grey
Issued: 1972-1975
U.S.: $250.00
Can.: $350.00
Ster.:   £150.00

HN 2446
Thanksgiving (matte)
Designer: M. Nicoll
Height: 8", 20.3 cm
Colour: Blue, pink and grey
Issued: 1972-1976
U.S.: $300.00
Can.: $400.00
Ster.:   £145.00

HN 2455
The Seafarer (matte)
Designer: M. Nicoll
Height: 8 1/2", 21.6 cm
Colour: Gold, blue and grey
Issued: 1972-1976
Series: Sea Characters

U.S.: **$300.00**
Can.: **$450.00**
Ster.: **£225.00**

*

HN 2460
Flower of Lover
Designer: John Bromley
Height: 7 1/2" 19.1 cm
Colour: White and yellow
Issued: 1991 Canada
1992 Worldwide
to the present
Varieties: HN 3970; "Fleur"
HN 2368, 2369
Series: Vanity Fair Ladies

U.S.: **$187.50**
Can.: **$300.00**
Ster.: **£ 79.95**

HN 2461
Janine
Designer: J. Bromley
Height: 7 1/2", 19.1 cm
Colour: Turquoise and white
Issued: 1971-1995

U.S.: **$275.00**
Can.: **$325.00**
Ster.: **£115.00**

*

HN 2463
Olga
Designer: J. Bromley
Height: 8 1/4", 21.0 cm
Colour: Turquoise and gold
Issued: 1972-1975

U.S.: **$325.00**
Can.: **$350.00**
Ster.: **£145.00**

*

HN 2465
Elizabeth
Style Two
Designer: J. Bromley
Height: 8 1/2", 21.6 cm
Colour: Blue
Issued: 1990 to the present

U.S.: **$306.25**
Can.: **$425.00**
Ster.: **£129.00**

HN 2466
Eve
Designer: M. Davies
Height: 9 1/4", 23.5 cm
Colour: Green and brown
Issued: 1984 in a limited
edition of 750
Series: Les Femmes
Fatales

U.S.: **$1,500.00**
Can.: **$1,500.00**
Ster.: **£ 700.00**

HN 2467
Melissa
Designer: M. Davies
Height: 6 3/4", 17.2 cm
Colour: Purple and cream
Issued: 1981-1994

U.S.: **$275.00**
Can.: **$350.00**
Ster.: **£125.00**

HN 2468
Diana
Style Two
Designer: M. Davies
Height: 8", 20.3 cm
Colour: Flowered white dress
Issued: 1986 N. America,
1987 Worldwide
to the present
Varieties: HN 3266

U.S.: **$243.75**
Can.: **$370.00**
Ster.: **£109.00**

HN 2469
Tranquility
Designer: M. Davies
Height: 12", 30.5 cm
Colour: White
Issued: 1981-1986
Varieties: HN 2426
Series: Images

U.S.:	$200.00
Can.:	$225.00
Ster.:	£125.00

HN 2470
Peace
Designer: M. Davies
Height: 8", 20.3 cm
Colour: White
Issued: 1981 to the present
Varieties: HN 2433
Series: Images

U.S.:	$131.25
Can.:	$140.00
Ster.:	£ 49.95

HN 2471
Victoria
Style One
Designer: M. Davies
Height: 6 1/2", 16.5 cm
Colour: Patterned pink dress
Issued: 1973 to the present
Varieties: HN 3416

U.S.:	$375.00
Can.:	$560.00
Ster.:	£139.00

HN 2472
Wistful
Style One
Designer: M. Davies
Height: 6 1/2", 16.5 cm
Colour: Blue and white
Issued: 1985-1985
Varieties: HN 2396
Series: Michael Doulton
Events

U.S.:	$350.00
Can.:	$425.00
Ster.:	£195.00

HN 2473
At Ease
Designer: M. Davies
Height: 6", 15.2 cm
Colour: Yellow
Issued: 1973-1979

U.S.:	$325.00
Can.:	$400.00
Ster.:	£225.00

HN 2474
Elyse
Designer: M. Davies
Height: 5 3/4", 14.6 cm
Colour: Patterned green
dress
Issued: 1986 N. America,
1987 Worldwide
to the present
Varieties: HN 2429

U.S.:	$306.25
Can.:	$560.00
Ster.:	£139.00

HN 2475
Vanity
Designer: M. Davies
Height: 5 1/4", 13.3 cm
Colour: Red
Issued: 1973-1992

U.S.:	$175.00
Can.:	$250.00
Ster.:	£110.00

HN 2476
Mandy
Designer: M. Davies
Height: 4 1/2", 11.4 cm
Colour: White
Issued: 1982-1992

U.S.:	$125.00
Can.:	$155.00
Ster.:	£ 90.00

HN 2477
Denise
Style Three
Designer: M. Davies
Height: 7 1/2", 19.1 cm
Colour: White
Issued: 1987-1996
Varieties: Also called
"Summer Rose"
(Style Two) HN 3309
Series: Vanity Fair Ladies
U.S.: $187.50
Can.: $280.00
Ster.: £ 79.95

HN 2478
Kelly
Designer: M. Davies
Height: 7 1/2", 19.1 cm
Colour: White with blue
flowers
Issued: 1985-1992
Varieties: HN 3222
U.S.: $250.00
Can.: $300.00
Ster.: £145.00

HN 2479
Pamela
Style Two
Designer: M. Davies
Height: 7", 17.8 cm
Colour: White
Issued: 1986-1994
Varieties: HN 3223
Series: Vanity Fair Ladies
U.S.: $225.00
Can.: $250.00
Ster.: £ 75.00

HN 2480
Adele
Designer: M. Davies
Height: 8", 20.3 cm
Colour: Flowered white dress
Issued: 1987-1992
Varieties: "Camille" (Style
Two) HN 3171;
"Margaret" (Style
Two) HN 2397, 3496
U.S.: $250.00
Can.: $300.00
Ster.: £165.00

HN 2481
Maureen
Style Three
Designer: M. Davies
Height: 7 1/2", 19.1 cm
Colour: White dress,
purple flowers
Issued: 1987-1992
Varieties: Also called "Tina"
HN 3494
Series: Vanity Fair Ladies
U.S.: $250.00
Can.: $300.00
Ster.: £145.00

HN 2482
Harp
Designer: M. Davies
Height: 8 3/4", 22.2 cm
Colour: Purple, green
and gold
Issued: 1973 in a limited
edition of 750
Series: Lady Musicians
U.S.: $2,500.00
Can.: $2,500.00
Ster.: £ 950.00

HN 2483
Flute
Designer: M. Davies
Height: 6", 15.2 cm
Colour: Red and white
Issued: 1973 in a limited
edition of 750
Series: Lady Musicians
U.S.: $1,350.00
Can.: $1,350.00
Ster.: £ 700.00

HN 2484
Past Glory
Designer: M. Nicoll
Height: 7 1/2", 19.1 cm
Colour: Red and black
Issued: 1973-1979
U.S.: $325.00
Can.: $500.00
Ster.: £275.00

HN 2485
Lunchtime
Designer: M. Nicoll
Height: 8", 20.3 cm
Colour: Brown
Issued: 1973-1981
U.S.: **$300.00**
Can.: **$400.00**
Ster.: **£195.00**

HN 2487
Beachcomber (matte)
Designer: M. Nicoll
Height: 6 1/2", 15.9 cm
Colour: Purple and grey
Issued: 1973-1976
U.S.: **$275.00**
Can.: **$375.00**
Ster.: **£150.00**

HN 2492
Huntsman
Style Three
Designer: M. Nicoll
Height: 7 1/2", 19.1 cm
Colour: Grey and cream
Issued: 1974-1979
U.S.: **$325.00**
Can.: **$400.00**
Ster.: **£225.00**

HN 2494
Old Meg (matte)
Designer: M. Nicoll
Height: 8 1/4", 21.0 cm
Colour: Blue and grey
Issued: 1974-1976
U.S.: **$275.00**
Can.: **$425.00**
Ster.: **£195.00**

HN 2499
Helmsman
Designer: M. Nicoll
Height: 9", 22.9 cm
Colour: Brown
Issued: 1974-1986
Series: Sea Characters
U.S.: **$300.00**
Can.: **$400.00**
Ster.: **£225.00**

HN 2502
Queen Elizabeth II
Style One
Designer: M. Davies
Height: 7 3/4", 19.7 cm
Colour: Pale blue
Issued: 1973 in a limited
edition of 750
U.S.: **$2,200.00**
Can.: **$2,200.00**
Ster.: **£ 900.00**

HN 2520
The Farmer's Boy
Designer: W.M. Chance
Height: 8 1/2", 21.6 cm
Colour: White, brown
and green
Issued: 1938-1960
U.S.: **$2,500.00**
Can.: **$3,000.00**
Ster.: **£1,500.00**

HN 2521
Dapple Grey
Designer: W.M. Chance
Height: 7 1/4", 18.4 cm
Colour: White, red and
brown
Issued: 1938-1960
U.S.: **$3,500.00**
Can.: **$4,000.00**
Ster.: **£1,500.00**

HN 2542
Boudoir
Designer: E.J. Griffiths
Height: 12 1/4", 31.1 cm
Colour: Pale blue
Issued: 1974-1979
Series: Haute Ensemble
U.S.: $450.00
Can.: $600.00
Ster.: £245.00

HN 2543
Eliza
(Handmade flowers)
Style One
Designer: E. J. Griffiths
Height: 11 3/4", 29.8 cm
Colour: Gold
Issued: 1974-1979
Varieties: HN 2543A
Series: Haute Ensemble
U.S.: $325.00
Can.: $475.00
Ster.: £245.00

HN 2543A
Eliza
(Painted flowers)
Style One
Designer: E. J. Griffiths
Height: 11 3/4", 29.8 cm
Colour: Gold
Issued: 1974-1979
Varieties: HN 2543
Series: Haute Ensemble
U.S.: $300.00
Can.: $425.00
Ster.: £225.00

HN 2544
A la Mode
Designer: E.J. Griffiths
Height: 12 1/4", 31.1 cm
Colour: Green
Issued: 1974-1979
Series: Haute Ensemble
U.S.: $225.00
Can.: $425.00
Ster.: £245.00

HN 2545
Carmen
Style Two
Designer: E.J. Griffiths
Height: 11 1/2", 29.2 cm
Colour: Blue
Issued: 1974-1979
Series: Haute Ensemble
U.S.: $325.00
Can.: $425.00
Ster.: £245.00

HN 2546
Buddies (matte)
Style One
Designer: E.J. Griffiths
Height: 6", 15.2 cm
Colour: Blue and brown
Issued: 1973-1976
U.S.: $275.00
Can.: $475.00
Ster.: £195.00

HN 2547
R.C.M.P. 1973
Designer: D.V. Tootle
Height: 8", 20.3 cm
Colour: Red
Issued: 1973 in a limited edition of 1,500
U.S.: $1,000.00
Can.: $1,000.00
Ster.: £ 475.00

HN 2554
Masque
(Hand holds wand of mask)
Designer: D.V. Tootle
Height: 8 1/2", 21.6 cm
Colour: Blue
Issued: 1973-1975
Varieties: HN 2554A
U.S.: $500.00
Can.: $500.00
Ster.: £275.00

HN 2554A
Masque
(Hand holds mask to face)
Designer: D.V. Tootle
Height: 8 1/2", 21.6 cm
Colour: Blue
Issued: 1975-1982
Varieties: HN 2554

U.S.:	**$350.00**
Can.:	**$400.00**
Ster.:	**£245.00**

HN 2555
R.C.M.P. 1873
Designer: D.V. Tootle
Height: 8 1/4", 21.0 cm
Colour: Red
Issued: 1973 in a limited
edition of 1,500

U.S.:	**$1,000.00**
Can.:	**$1,000.00**
Ster.:	**£ 400.00**

*

HN 2671
Good Morning (matte)
Designer: M. Nicoll
Height: 8", 20.3 cm
Colour: Blue, pink
and brown
Issued: 1974-1976

U.S.:	**$225.00**
Can.:	**$375.00**
Ster.:	**£150.00**

*

HN 2677
Taking Things Easy
Designer: M. Nicoll
Height: 6 3/4", 17.2 cm
Colour: Blue, white
and brown
Issued: 1975-1987
Varieties: HN 2680

U.S.:	**$240.00**
Can.:	**$400.00**
Ster.:	**£175.00**

HN 2678
The Carpenter
Designer: M. Nicoll
Height: 8", 20.3 cm
Colour: Blue, white
and brown
Issued: 1986-1992

U.S.:	**$325.00**
Can.:	**$375.00**
Ster.:	**£195.00**

HN 2679
Drummer Boy
Designer: M. Nicoll
Height: 8 1/2", 21.6 cm
Colour: Multi-coloured
Issued: 1976-1981

U.S.:	**$500.00**
Can.:	**$650.00**
Ster.:	**£375.00**

HN 2680
Taking Things Easy
Designer: M. Nicoll
Height: 6 3/4", 17.2 cm
Colour: Cream and blue
Issued: 1987 to the present
Varieties: HN 2677

U.S.:	**$375.00**
Can.:	**$425.00**
Ster.:	**£135.00**

*

HN 2683
Stop Press
Designer: M. Nicoll
Height: 7 1/2", 19.1 cm
Colour: Brown, blue
and white
Issued: 1977-1981

U.S.:	**$240.00**
Can.:	**$325.00**
Ster.:	**£165.00**

*

HN 2693
October
Style One
Designer: M. Davies
Height: 7 3/4", 19.5 cm
Colour: White with blue dress, cosmos flowers
Issued: 1987-1987
Series: Flower of the Month
U.S.: $200.00
Can.: $275.00
Ster.: £120.00

HN 2694
Fiona
Style Two
Designer: M. Davies
Height: 7 1/2", 19.1 cm
Colour: Red and white
Issued: 1974-1981
U.S.: $275.00
Can.: $350.00
Ster.: £165.00

HN 2695
November
Style One
Designer: M. Davies
Height: 7 3/4", 19.7 cm
Colour: White with pink dress, chrysanthemum flowers
Issued: 1987-1987
Series: Flower of the Month
U.S.: $200.00
Can.: $275.00
Ster.: £120.00

HN 2696
December
Style One
Designer: M. Davies
Height: 7 3/4", 19.7 cm
Colour: White with green dress, Christmas rose flowers
Issued: 1987-1987
Series: Flower of the Month
U.S.: $200.00
Can.: $275.00
Ster.: £120.00

HN 2697
January
Style One
Designer: M. Davies
Height: 7 3/4", 19.7 cm
Colour: White with green dress, snowdrop flowers
Issued: 1987-1987
Series: Flower of the Month
U.S.: $200.00
Can.: $275.00
Ster.: £120.00

HN 2698
Sunday Best
Style One
Designer: M. Davies
Height: 7 1/2", 19.1 cm
Colour: Pink and white
Issued: 1985-1995
Varieties: HN 2206
U.S.: $225.00
Can.: $325.00
Ster.: £125.00

HN 2699
Cymbals
Designer: M. Davies
Height: 7 1/2", 19.1 cm
Colour: Green and gold
Issued: 1974 in a limited edition of 750
Series: Lady Musicians
U.S.: $1,000.00
Can.: $1,100.00
Ster.: £ 500.00

HN 2700
Chitarrone
Designer: M. Davies
Height: 7 1/2", 19.1 cm
Colour: Blue
Issued: 1974 in a limited edition of 750
Series: Lady Musicians
U.S.: $1,100.00
Can.: $1,250.00
Ster.: £ 550.00

HN 2701
Deborah
Designer:	M. Davies
Height:	7 3/4", 19.7 cm
Colour:	Green and white
Issued:	1983-1984
Series:	Ladies of Covent Garden
U.S.:	**$500.00**
Can.:	**$600.00**
Ster.:	**£250.00**

Commissioned by Amex

HN 2702
Shirley
Designer:	M. Davies
Height:	7 1/4", 18.4 cm
Colour:	White dress with pink flowers
Issued:	1985 to the present
U.S.:	**$243.75**
Can.:	**$370.00**
Ster.:	**£109.00**

HN 2703
February
Style One
Designer:	M. Davies
Height:	7 3/4", 19.7 cm
Colour:	White with purple dress, violet flowers
Issued:	1987-1987
Series:	Flower of the Month
U.S.:	**$200.00**
Can.:	**$275.00**
Ster.:	**£120.00**

HN 2704
Pensive Moments
Designer:	M. Davies
Height:	5", 12.7 cm
Colour:	Blue
Issued:	1975-1981
U.S.:	**$275.00**
Can.:	**$350.00**
Ster.:	**£175.00**

HN 2705
Julia
Designer:	M. Davies
Height:	7 1/2", 19.1 cm
Colour:	Gold
Issued:	1975-1990
Varieties:	HN 2706
U.S.:	**$240.00**
Can.:	**$300.00**
Ster.:	**£165.00**

HN 2706
Julia
Designer:	M. Davies
Height:	7 1/2", 19.1 cm
Colour:	Pink and green
Issued:	1985-1993
Varieties:	HN 2705
U.S.:	**$200.00**
Can.:	**$275.00**
Ster.:	**£125.00**

HN 2707
March
Style One
Designer:	M. Davies
Height:	7 3/4", 19.7 cm
Colour:	White with green dress, anemone flowers
Issued:	1987-1987
Series:	Flower of the Month
U.S.:	**$200.00**
Can.:	**$295.00**
Ster.:	**£120.00**

HN 2708
April
Style One
Designer:	M. Davies
Height:	7 3/4", 19.7 cm
Colour:	White with tan dress, sweet pea flowers
Issued:	1987-1987
Series:	Flower of the Month
U.S.:	**$200.00**
Can.:	**$295.00**
Ster.:	**£120.00**

HN 2709
Regal Lady
Designer: M. Davies
Height: 7 1/2", 19.1 cm
Colour: Turquoise
and cream
Issued: 1975-1983
U.S.: **$275.00**
Can.: **$375.00**
Ster.: **£165.00**

HN 2710
Jean
Style Two
Designer: M. Davies
Height: 5 3/4", 14.6 cm
Colour: White
Issued: 1983-1986
Series: Vanity Fair Ladies
U.S.: **$200.00**
Can.: **$275.00**
Ster.: **£145.00**

HN 2711
May
Style Two
Designer: M. Davies
Height: 7 3/4", 19.7 cm
Colour: White with green
dress, lily of the
valley flowers
Issued: 1987-1987
Series: Flower of the Month
U.S.: **$200.00**
Can.: **$275.00**
Ster.: **£120.00**

HN 2712
Mantilla
Designer: E.J. Griffiths
Height: 11 1/2", 29.2 cm
Colour: Red, black and white
Issued: 1974-1979
Varieties: HN 3192
Series: Haute Ensemble
U.S.: **$450.00**
Can.: **$575.00**
Ster.: **£325.00**

HN 2713
Tenderness
Designer: E.J. Griffiths
Height: 12", 30.5 cm
Colour: White
Issued: 1982 to the present
Varieties: HN 2714
Series: Images
U.S.: **$200.00**
Can.: **$210.00**
Ster.: **£ 69.95**

HN 2714
Tenderness
Designer: E.J. Griffiths
Height: 12", 30.5 cm
Colour: Black
Issued: 1982-1992
Varieties: HN 2713
Series: Images
U.S.: **$150.00**
Can.: **$175.00**
Ster.: **£110.00**

HN 2715
Patricia
Style Three
Designer: M. Davies
Height: 7 1/2", 19.1 cm
Colour: White
Issued: 1982-1985
Series: Vanity Fair Ladies
U.S.: **$250.00**
Can.: **$450.00**
Ster.: **£175.00**

HN 2716
Cavalier
Style Two
Designer: E.J. Griffiths
Height: 9 3/4", 24.7 cm
Colour: Brown and green
Issued: 1976-1982
U.S.: **$275.00**
Can.: **$375.00**
Ster.: **£195.00**

Flambé pilot piece known

HN 2717
Private, 2nd South Carolina
Regiment, 1781
Designer: E.J. Griffiths
Height: 11 1/2", 29.2 cm
Colour: Blue and cream
Issued: 1975 in a limited
edition of 350
Series: Soldiers of the
Revolution
U.S.: $1,750.00
Can.: $1,750.00
Ster.: £ 700.00

HN 2718
Lady Pamela
Designer: D.V. Tootle
Height: 8", 20.3 cm
Colour: Purple
Issued: 1974-1981
U.S.: $275.00
Can.: $375.00
Ster.: £165.00

HN 2719
Laurianne
Designer: D.V. Tootle
Height: 6 1/4", 15.9 cm
Colour: Dark blue and white
Issued: 1974-1979
U.S.: $225.00
Can.: $350.00
Ster.: £175.00

HN 2720
Family
Designer: E.J. Griffiths
Height: 12", 30.5 cm
Colour: White
Issued: 1981 to the present
Varieties: HN 2721
Series: Images
U.S.: $200.00
Can.: $325.00
Ster.: £ 99.95

HN 2721
Family
Designer: E.J. Griffiths
Height: 12", 30.5 cm
Colour: Black
Issued: 1981-1992
Varieties: HN 2720
Series: Images
U.S.: $200.00
Can.: $250.00
Ster.: £145.00

HN 2722
Veneta
Designer: W.K. Harper
Height: 8", 20.3 cm
Colour: Green and white
Issued: 1974-1981
U.S.: $225.00
Can.: $350.00
Ster.: £165.00

HN 2723
Grand Manner
Designer: W.K. Harper
Height: 7 3/4", 19.7 cm
Colour: Lavender-yellow
Issued: 1975-1981
U.S.: $275.00
Can.: $350.00
Ster.: £165.00

HN 2724
Clarinda
Designer: W.K. Harper
Height: 8 1/2", 21.6 cm
Colour: Blue and white
Issued: 1975-1981
U.S.: $240.00
Can.: $350.00
Ster.: £175.00

HN 2725
Santa Claus
Designer: W.K. Harper
Height: 9 3/4", 24.7 cm
Colour: Red and white
Issued: 1982-1993

U.S.: $450.00
Can.: $500.00
Ster.: £225.00

HN 2726
Centurian
Designer: W.K. Harper
Height: 9 1/4", 23.5 cm
Colour: Grey and purple
Issued: 1982-1984

U.S.: $250.00
Can.: $350.00
Ster.: £225.00

HN 2727
Little Miss Muffet
Designer: W.K. Harper
Height: 6 1/4", 15.9 cm
Colour: White and pink
Issued: 1984-1987
Series: Nursery Rhymes
(Series Two)

U.S.: $175.00
Can.: $225.00
Ster.: £110.00

HN 2728
Rest Awhile
Designer: W.K. Harper
Height: 8", 20.3 cm
Colour: Blue, white
and purple
Issued: 1981-1984

U.S.: $265.00
Can.: $325.00
Ster.: £165.00

HN 2729
Song of the Sea
Designer: W.K. Harper
Height: 7 1/4", 18.4 cm
Colour: Blue and grey
Issued: 1982 Canada,
1983 Worldwide
-1991
Series: Sea Characters

U.S.: $325.00
Can.: $375.00
Ster.: £195.00

HN 2731
Thanks Doc
Designer: W.K. Harper
Height: 8 3/4", 22.2 cm
Colour: White and brown
Issued: 1975-1990

U.S.: $325.00
Can.: $425.00
Ster.: £175.00

HN 2732
Thank You
Style One
Designer: W.K. Harper
Height: 8 1/4", 21.0 cm
Colour: White, brown
and blue
Issued: 1982 Canada,
1983 Worldwide
-1986

U.S.: $250.00
Can.: $325.00
Ster.: £165.00

HN 2733
Officer of the Line
Designer: W.K. Harper
Height: 9", 22.9 cm
Colour: Red and yellow
Issued: 1982 Canada,
1983 Worldwide
-1986
Series: Sea Characters

U.S.: $325.00
Can.: $375.00
Ster.: £225.00

*

HN 2734
Sweet Seventeen
Designer: D.V. Tootle
Height: 7 1/2", 19.1 cm
Colour: White with
gold trim
Issued: 1975-1993

U.S.: $300.00
Can.: $375.00
Ster.: £145.00

HN 2735
Young Love
Designer: D.V. Tootle
Height: 10", 25.4 cm
Colour: Cream, green,
blue and brown
Issued: 1975-1990

U.S.: $675.00
Can.: $800.00
Ster.: £400.00

HN 2736
Tracy
Designer: D.V. Tootle
Height: 7 1/2", 19.1 cm
Colour: White
Issued: 1983-1994
Varieties: HN 3291
Series: Vanity Fair Ladies

U.S.: $175.00
Can.: $225.00
Ster.: £ 85.00

HN 2737
Harlequin
Style Two
Designer: D.V. Tootle
Height: 12 1/2", 31.7 cm
Colour: Multi-coloured
Issued: 1982 to the present
Varieties: HN 3287

U.S.: $1,350.00
Can.: $2,588.00
Ster.: £ 995.00

HN 2738
Columbine
Style Three
Designer: D.V. Tootle
Height: 12 1/2", 31.7 cm
Colour: Flowered pink
and blue dress
Issued: 1982 to the present
Varieties: HN 3288

U.S.: $1,350.00
Can.: $2,588.00
Ster.: £ 995.00

HN 2739
Ann
Style One
Designer: D.V. Tootle
Height: 7 3/4", 19.7 cm
Colour: White
Issued: 1983-1985
Series: Vanity Fair Ladies

U.S.: $225.00
Can.: $300.00
Ster.: £145.00

HN 2740
Becky
Designer: D.V. Tootle
Height: 8", 20.3 cm
Colour: Green, yellow
and cream
Issued: 1987-1992

U.S.: $250.00
Can.: $325.00
Ster.: £145.00

HN 2741
Sally
Style One
Designer: D.V. Tootle
Height: 5 1/2", 14.0 cm
Colour: Red and lavender
Issued: 1987-1991

U.S.: $200.00
Can.: $300.00
Ster.: £145.00

HN 2742
Sheila
Designer: D.V. Tootle
Height: 8 1/4", 21.0 cm
Colour: Pale blue
flowered dress
Issued: 1983 Canada,
1984 Worldwide
-1991
U.S.: $225.00
Can.: $275.00
Ster.: £145.00

HN 2743
Meg
Designer: D.V. Tootle
Height: 8", 20.3 cm
Colour: Lavender and
yellow
Issued: 1987-1991
U.S.: $225.00
Can.: $325.00
Ster.: £145.00

HN 2744
Modesty
Designer: D.V. Tootle
Height: 8 1/2", 21.6 cm
Colour: White
Issued: 1987-1991
U.S.: $300.00
Can.: $325.00
Ster.: £145.00

HN 2745
Florence
Designer: D.V. Tootle
Height: 8", 20.3 cm
Colour: Purple
Issued: 1987-1992
U.S.: $275.00
Can.: $400.00
Ster.: £145.00

HN 2746
May
Style One
Designer: D.V. Tootle
Height: 8", 20.3 cm
Colour: Blue, red
and green
Issued: 1987-1992
Varieties: HN 3251
U.S.: $325.00
Can.: $375.00
Ster.: £165.00

HN 2747
First Love
Designer: D.V. Tootle
Height: 13", 33.0 cm
Colour: White
Issued: 1987 to the present
Series: Images
U.S.: $200.00
Can.: $265.00
Ster.: £ 79.95

HN 2748
Wedding Day
Designer: D.V. Tootle
Height: 12 1/2", 31.7 cm
Colour: White
Issued: 1987 to the present
Series: Images
U.S.: $200.00
Can.: $325.00
Ster.: £149.00

HN 2749
Lizzie
Designer: D.V. Tootle
Height: 8 1/4", 21.0 cm
Colour: Green, white
and red
Issued: 1988-1991
U.S.: $225.00
Can.: $325.00
Ster.: £145.00

HN 2750
Wedding Vows
Designer: D.V. Tootle
Height: 8", 20.3 cm
Colour: White
Issued: 1988-1992

U.S.: $275.00
Can.: $350.00
Ster.: £165.00

HN 2751
Encore
Designer: D.V. Tootle
Height: 10". 25.4 cm
Colour: Lavender, white and blue
Issued: 1988 to 1989
Series: Reflections

U.S.: $225.00
Can.: $275.00
Ster.: £145.00

HN 2752
Major, 3rd New Jersey Regiment, 1776
Designer: E.J. Griffiths
Height: 10", 25.4 cm
Colour: Blue and brown
Issued: 1975 in a limited edition of 350
Series: Soldiers of the Revolution

U.S.: $2,500.00
Can.: $2,500.00
Ster.: £ 950.00

HN 2753
Serenade
Designer: E.J. Griffiths
Height: 9", 22.9 cm
Colour: Cream
Issued: 1983-1985
Series: Enchantment

U.S.: $250.00
Can.: $300.00
Ster.: £145.00

HN 2754
Private, 3rd North Carolina Regiment, 1778
Designer: E.J. Griffiths
Height: 11", 27.9 cm
Colour: Tan
Issued: 1976 in a limited edition of 350
Series: Soldiers of the Revolution

U.S.: $1,250.00
Can.: $1,250.00
Ster.: £ 650.00

HN 2755
Captain, 2nd New York Regiment, 1775
Designer: E.J. Griffiths
Height: 10", 25.4 cm
Colour: Brown
Issued: 1976 in a limited edition of 350
Series: Soldiers of the Revolution

U.S.: $1,250.00
Can.: $1,250.00
Ster.: £ 650.00

HN 2756
Musicale
Designer: E.J. Griffiths
Height: 9", 22.9 cm
Colour: Cream
Issued: 1983-1985
Series: Enchantment

U.S.: $250.00
Can.: $300.00
Ster.: £145.00

HN 2757
Lyric
Designer: E.J. Griffiths
Height: 6 1/4", 15.9 cm
Colour: Cream
Issued: 1983-1985
Series: Enchantment

U.S.: $250.00
Can.: $275.00
Ster.: £145.00

HN 2758
Linda
Style Two
Designer: E.J. Griffiths
Height: 7 3/4", 19.7 cm
Colour: White with pink trim
Issued: 1984 to 1988
Series: Vanity Fair Ladies
U.S.: **$200.00**
Can.: **$300.00**
Ster.: **£165.00**

HN 2759
Private, Rhode Island
Regiment, 1781
Designer: E.J. Griffiths
Height: 11 3/4", 29.8 cm
Colour: Grey
Issued: 1977 in a limited
 edition of 350
Series: Soldiers of the
 Revolution
U.S.: **$1,250.00**
Can.: **$1,250.00**
Ster.: **£ 650.00**

HN 2760
Private, Massachusetts
Regiment, 1778
Designer: E.J. Griffiths
Height: 12 1/2", 31.7 cm
Colour: Blue and tan
Issued: 1977 in a limited
 edition of 350
Series: Soldiers of the
 Revolution
U.S.: **$1,250.00**
Can.: **$1,250.00**
Ster.: **£ 650.00**

HN 2761
Private, Delaware
Regiment, 1776
Designer: E.J. Griffiths
Height: 12", 30.5 cm
Colour: Blue and tan
Issued: 1977 in a limited
 edition of 350
Series: Soldiers of the
 Revolution
U.S.: **$1,250.00**
Can.: **$1,250.00**
Ster.: **£ 650.00**

HN 2762
Lovers
Designer: D.V. Tootle
Height: 12", 30.5 cm
Colour: White
Issued: 1981 to the present
Varieties: HN 2763
Series: Images
U.S.: **$200.00**
Can.: **$325.00**
Ster.: **£ 99.95**

HN 2763
Lovers
Designer: D.V. Tootle
Height: 12", 30.5 cm
Colour: Black
Issued: 1981-1992
Varieties: HN 2762
Series: Images
U.S.: **$200.00**
Can.: **$250.00**
Ster.: **£125.00**

HN 2764
The Lifeboat Man
Designer: W.K. Harper
Height: 9 1/4", 23.5 cm
Colour: Yellow
Issued: 1987-1991
Series: Sea Characters
U.S.: **$275.00**
Can.: **$375.00**
Ster.: **£165.00**

HN 2765
Punch and Judy Man
Designer: W.K. Harper
Height: 9", 22.9 cm
Colour: Green and yellow
Issued: 1981-1990
U.S.: **$475.00**
Can.: **$600.00**
Ster.: **£175.00**

HN 2766
Autumn Glory
Designer: W.K. Harper
Height: 11 3/4", 29.9 cm
Colour: Blue-grey and tan
Issued: 1988 in a limited
edition of 1,000
Series: Reflections

U.S.: $300.00
Can.: $400.00
Ster.: £200.00

Commissioned by Home
Shopping Network, Florida

HN 2767
Pearly Boy
Style Three
Designer: W.K. Harper
Height: 7 1/2", 19.1 cm
Colour: Black, white and blue
Issued: 1988
Varieties: HN 2767A

U.S.: $250.00
Can.: $300.00
Ster.: £165.00

Guild of Specialist China and Glass
Retailers

HN 2767A
Pearly Boy
Style Three
Designer: W.K. Harper
Height: 7 1/2", 19.1 cm
Colour: Black, white and blue
Issued: 1989-1992
Varieties: HN 2767

U.S.: $250.00
Can.: $300.00
Ster.: £150.00

HN 2768
Pretty Polly
Designer: W.K. Harper
Height: 6", 15.2 cm
Colour: Pink and white
Issued: 1984-1986

U.S.: $250.00
Can.: $300.00
Ster.: £165.00

HN 2769
Pearly Girl
Style Three
Designer: W.K. Harper
Height: 7 1/2", 19.1 cm
Colour: Black, white and blue
Issued: 1988
Varieties: HN 2769A

U.S.: $250.00
Can.: $300.00
Ster.: £165.00

Guild of Specialist and Glass Retailers

HN 2769A
Pearly Girl
Style Three
Designer: W.K. Harper
Height: 7 1/2", 19.1 cm
Colour: Black, white and blue
Issued: 1989-1992
Varieties: HN 2769

U.S.: $250.00
Can.: $300.00
Ster.: £150.00

HN 2770
New Companions
Designer: W.K. Harper
Height: 7 3/4", 19.7 cm
Colour: Purple, white
and black
Issued: 1982-1985

U.S.: $285.00
Can.: $325.00
Ster.: £175.00

HN 2771
Charlie Chaplin
Designer: W.K. Harper
Height: 9", 22.9 cm
Colour: Grey
Issued: 1989 in a limited
edition of 9,500
Series: Entertainers

U.S.: $450.00
Can.: $350.00
Ster.: £225.00

HN 2772
Ritz Bell Boy
Designer: W.K. Harper
Height: 8", 20.3 cm
Colour: Black
Issued: 1989-1993

U.S.: $250.00
Can.: $275.00
Ster.: £125.00

HN 2773
Robin Hood
Style One
Designer: W.K. Harper
Height: 7 3/4", 19.7 cm
Colour: Green
Issued: 1985-1990

U.S.: $275.00
Can.: $330.00
Ster.: £165.00

HN 2774
Stan Laurel
Designer: W.K. Harper
Height: 9 1/4", 23.5 cm
Colour: Grey-black
Issued: 1990 in a limited
edition of 9,500
Series: Entertainers

U.S.: $300.00
Can.: $400.00
Ster.: £145.00

Commissioned by Lawleys

HN 2775
Oliver Hardy
Designer: W.K. Harper
Height: 10", 25.4 cm
Colour: Black and grey
Issued: 1990 in a limited
edition of 9,500
Series: Entertainers

U.S.: $300.00
Can.: $400.00
Ster.: £145.00

Commissioned by Lawleys

HN 2776
Carpet Seller
(Standing)
Style Three
Designer: W.K. Harper
Height: 9", 22.9 cm
Colour: Flambé
Issued: 1990-1995
Series: Flambé

U.S.: $250.00
Can.: $350.00
Ster.: £125.00

HN 2777
Groucho Marx
Designer: W.K. Harper
Height: 9 1/2", 24.1 cm
Colour: Black and grey
Issued: 1991 in a limited
edition of 9,500
Series: Entertainers

U.S.: $400.00
Can.: $450.00
Ster.: £145.00

Commissioned by Lawleys

HN 2778
The Bobby
Designer: W.K. Harper
Height: 9", 22.9 cm
Colour: Black
Issued: 1992-1995

U.S.: $200.00
Can.: $275.00
Ster.: £ 95.00

HN 2779
Private, 1st Georgia
Regiment, 1777
Designer: E.J. Griffiths
Height: 11", 27.9 cm
Colour: Light brown
Issued: 1975 in a limited
edition of 350
Series: Soldiers of the
Revolution

U.S.: $1,250.00
Can.: $1,250.00
Ster.: £ 650.00

HN 2780
Corporal, 1st New
Hampshire Regiment, 1778
Designer: E.J. Griffiths
Height: 13", 33.0 cm
Colour: Green
Issued: 1975 in a limited
           edition of 350
Series: Soldiers of the
           Revolution
U.S.:   **$1,250.00**
Can.:   **$1,250.00**
Ster.: **£ 650.00**

HN 2781
The Lifeguard
Designer: W.K. Harper
Height: 9 1/2", 24.1 cm
Colour: Red, black and
           white
Issued: 1992-1995
U.S.:   **$250.00**
Can.:   **$325.00**
Ster.: **£130.00**

HN 2782
The Blacksmith
Designer: W.K. Harper
Height: 9", 22.9 cm
Colour: Brown, white
           and grey
Issued: 1987-1991
U.S..:   **$275.00**
Can.:   **$325.00**
Ster.: **£175.00**

HN 2783
Good Friends
Designer: W.K. Harper
Height: 9", 22.9 cm
Colour: Blue and brown
Issued: 1985-1990
U.S.:   **$250.00**
Can.:   **$300.00**
Ster.: **£165.00**

HN 2784
The Guardsman
Designer: W.K. Harper
Height: 9 3/4", 24.8 cm
Colour: Red, black and
           white
Issued: 1992-1995
U.S.:   **$250.00**
Can.:   **$325.00**
Ster.: **£130.00**

HN 2788
Marjorie
Designer: M. Davies
Height: 5 1/4", 13.3 cm
Colour: Pale blue
Issued: 1980-1984
U.S.:   **$325.00**
Can.:   **$425.00**
Ster.: **£175.00**

HN 2789
Kate
Style One
Designer: M. Davies
Height: 7 1/2", 19.1 cm
Colour: Flowered
           white dress
Issued: 1978-1987
U.S.:   **$250.00**
Can.:   **$350.00**
Ster.: **£145.00**

HN 2790
June
Style Three
Designer: M. Davies
Height: 7 3/4", 19.7 cm
Colour: White with pink
           dress, roses
Issued: 1987-1987
Series: Flower of the Month
U.S.:   **$200.00**
Can.:   **$275.00**
Ster.: **£120.00**

*

HN 2791
Elaine
Style One
Designer: M. Davies
Height: 7 1/2", 19.1 cm
Colour: Blue
Issued: 1980 to the present
Varieties: HN 3307, 3741
U.S.: $406.25
Can.: $490.00
Ster.: £129.00

HN 2792
Christine
Style Two
Designer: M. Davies
Height: 7 1/2", 19.1 cm
Colour: Flowered blue
and white dress
Issued: 1978-1994
Varieties: HN 3172
U.S.: $450.00
Can.: $500.00
Ster.: £175.00

HN 2793
Clare
Designer: M. Davies
Height: 7 1/2", 19.1 cm
Colour: Flowered
lavender dress
Issued: 1980-1984
U.S.: $300.00
Can.: $400.00
Ster.: £175.00

HN 2794
July
Style One
Designer: M. Davies
Height: 7 3/4", 19.7 cm
Colour: White dress,
forget-me-not
flowers
Issued: 1987-1987
Series: Flower of the Month
U.S.: $200.00
Can.: $275.00
Ster.: £120.00

HN 2795
French Horn
Designer: M. Davies
Height: 6", 15.2 cm
Colour: Purple and
turquoise
Issued: 1976 in a limited
edition of 750
Series: Lady Musicians
U.S.: $1,250.00
Can.: $1,250.00
Ster.: £ 650.00

HN 2796
Hurdy Gurdy
Designer: M. Davies
Height: 6", 15.2 cm
Colour: Turquoise
and white
Issued: 1975 in a limited
edition of 750
Series: Lady Musicians
U.S.: $1,250.00
Can.: $1,250.00
Ster.: £ 650.00

HN 2797
Viola d'Amore
Designer: M. Davies
Height: 6", 15.2 cm
Colour: Pale blue
and yellow
Issued: 1976 in a limited
edition of 750
Series: Lady Musicians
U.S.: $1,250.00
Can.: $1,250.00
Ster.: £ 650.00

HN 2798
Dulcimer
Designer: M. Davies
Height: 6 1/2", 16.5 cm
Colour: Lavender
and cream
Issued: 1975 in a limited
edition of 750
Series: Lady Musicians
U.S.: $1,250.00
Can.: $1,250.00
Ster.: £ 650.00

HN 2799
Ruth
Designer: M. Davies
Height: 6", 15.2 cm
Colour: Green
Issued: 1976-1981
Series: Kate Greenaway

U.S.:	**$375.00**
Can.:	**$400.00**
Ster.:	**£165.00**

HN 2800
Carrie
Designer: M. Davies
Height: 6", 15.2 cm
Colour: Turquoise
Issued: 1976-1981
Series: Kate Greenaway

U.S.:	**$275.00**
Can.:	**$325.00**
Ster.:	**£145.00**

HN 2801
Lori
Designer: M. Davies
Height: 5 3/4", 14.6 cm
Colour: Yellow-cream
Issued: 1976-1987
Series: Kate Greenaway

U.S.:	**$275.00**
Can.:	**$325.00**
Ster.:	**£150.00**

HN 2802
Anna
Designer: M. Davies
Height: 5 3/4", 14.6 cm
Colour: Purple and white
Issued: 1976-1982
Series: Kate Greenaway

U.S.:	**$275.00**
Can.:	**$325.00**
Ster.:	**£140.00**

HN 2803
First Dance
Designer: M. Davies
Height: 7 1/4", 18.4 cm
Colour: Pale blue
Issued: 1977-1992
Varieties: Also called
"Samantha" (Style
Two) HN 3304

U.S.:	**$300.00**
Can.:	**$375.00**
Ster.:	**£165.00**

HN 2804
Nicola
Designer: M. Davies
Height: 7", 17.8 cm
Colour: Red and lilac
Issued: 1987-1987
Varieties: HN 2839; also
called "Tender
Moment" HN 3303
Series: M. Doulton Events

U.S.:	**$300.00**
Can.:	**$325.00**
Ster.:	**£175.00**

HN 2805
Rebecca
Style One
Designer: M. Davies
Height: 7 1/4", 18.4 cm
Colour: Pale blue and
lavender
Issued: 1980 to the present

U.S.:	**$656.25**
Can.:	**$750.00**
Ster.:	**£199.00**

HN 2806
Jane
Style Two
Designer: M. Davies
Height: 8", 20.3 cm
Colour: Yellow
Issued: 1982-1986

U.S.:	**$250.00**
Can.:	**$400.00**
Ster.:	**£165.00**

HN 2807
Stephanie
Designer: M. Davies
Height: 7 1/4", 18.4 cm
Colour: Gold
Issued: 1977-1982
Varieties: HN 2811

U.S.: $275.00
Can.: $375.00
Ster.: £165.00

HN 2808
Balinese Dancer
Designer: M. Davies
Height: 8 3/4", 22.2 cm
Colour: Green and yellow
Issued: 1982 in a limited
edition of 750
Series: Dancers of the
World

U.S.: $925.00
Can.: $975.00
Ster.: £450.00

HN 2809
North American Indian
Dancer
Designer: M. Davies
Height: 8 1/2", 21.6 cm
Colour: Yellow
Issued: 1982 in a limited
edition of 750
Series: Dancers of the
World

U.S.: $925.00
Can.: $975.00
Ster.: £450.00

HN 2810
Solitude
Designer: M. Davies
Height: 5 1/2", 14.0 cm
Colour: Cream, blue
and orange
Issued: 1977-1983

U.S.: $375.00
Can.: $450.00
Ster.: £245.00

HN 2811
Stephanie
Designer: M. Davies
Height: 7 1/4", 18.4 cm
Colour: Red and white
Issued: 1983-1994
Varieties: HN 2807

U.S.: $300.00
Can.: $400.00
Ster.: £125.00

HN 2814
Eventide
Designer: W.K. Harper
Height: 7 3/4", 19.7 cm
Colour: Blue, white, red,
yellow and green
Issued: 1977-1991

U.S.: $325.00
Can.: $400.00
Ster.: £175.00

HN 2815
Sergeant, 6th Maryland
Regiment, 1777
Designer: E.J. Griffiths
Height: 13 3/4", 34.9 cm
Colour: Light grey
Issued: 1976 in a limited
edition of 350
Series: Soldiers of the
Revolution

U.S.: $1,250.00
Can.: $1,250.00
Ster.: £ 650.00

HN 2816
Votes for Women
Designer: W.K. Harper
Height: 9 3/4", 24.7 cm
Colour: Gold and grey
Issued: 1978-1981

U.S.: $325.00
Can.: $450.00
Ster.: £200.00

HN 2818
Balloon Girl
Designer: W.K. Harper
Height: 6 1/2", 16.5 cm
Colour: Green, white,
grey and red
Issued: 1982 to the present
U.S.: $212.50
Can.: $375.00
Ster.: £ 95.00

HN 2824
Harmony
Designer: R. Jefferson
Height: 8", 20.3 cm
Colour: Grey
Issued: 1978-1984
U.S.: $275.00
Can.: $325.00
Ster.: £165.00

HN 2825
Lady and the Unicorn
Designer: R. Jefferson
Height: 8 3/4", 22.2 cm
Colour: Blue, white and red
Issued: 1982 in a limited
edition of 300
Series: Myths and Maidens
U.S.: $3,000.00
Can.: $3,000.00
Ster.: £1,250.00

HN 2826
Leda and the Swan
Designer: R. Jefferson
Height: 9 3/4", 24.7 cm
Colour: Yellow, green,
red and blue
Issued: 1983 in a limited
edition of 300
Series: Myths and Maidens
U.S.: $2,600.00
Can.: $2,600.00
Ster.: £1,250.00

HN 2827
Juno and the Peacock
Designer: R. Jefferson
Height: 11", 27.9 cm
Colour: Turquoise,
lavender and gold
Issued: 1984 in a limited
edition of 300
Series: Myths and Maidens
U.S.: $2,600.00
Can.: $2,600.00
Ster.: £1,250.00

HN 2828
Europa and the Bull
Style Two
Designer: R. Jefferson
Height: 10 1/2", 26.5 cm
Colour: Yellow, orange,
white and lavender
Issued: 1985 in a limited
edition of 300
Series: Myths and
Maidens
U.S.: $2,600.00
Can.: $2,600.00
Ster.: £1,250.00

HN 2829
Diana the Huntress
Designer: R. Jefferson
Height: 11 1/4", 28.6 cm
Colour: Green and gold
Issued: 1986 in a limited
edition of 300
Series: Myths and
Maidens
U.S.: $2,600.00
Can.: $2,600.00
Ster.: £1,250.00

HN 2830
Indian Temple Dancer
Designer: M. Davies
Height: 9 1/4", 23.5 cm
Colour: Gold
Issued: 1977 in a limited
edition of 750
Series: Dancers of the
World
U.S.: $1,850.00
Can.: $1,850.00
Ster.: £ 575.00

HN 2831
Spanish Flamenco Dancer
Designer: M. Davies
Height: 9 1/2", 24.1 cm
Colour: Red and white
Issued: 1977 in a limited
edition of 750
Series: Dancers of the
World
U.S.: **$2,200.00**
Can.: **$2,200.00**
Ster.: **£ 625.00**

HN 2832
Fair Lady
Style One
Designer: M. Davies
Height: 7 1/4", 18.4 cm
Colour: Red and white
Issued: 1977-1996
Varieties: HN 2193, 2835;
Also called "Kay,"
HN 3340
U.S.: **$268.75**
Can.: **$425.00**
Ster.: **£105.00**

HN 2833
Sophie
Style One
Designer: M. Davies
Height: 6", 15.2 cm
Colour: Red and grey
Issued: 1977-1987
Series: Kate Greenaway
U.S.: **$275.00**
Can.: **$325.00**
Ster.: **£145.00**

HN 2834
Emma
Style One
Designer: M. Davies
Height: 5 3/4", 14.6 cm
Colour: Pink and white
Issued: 1977-1981
Series: Kate Greenaway
U.S.: **$325.00**
Can.: **$350.00**
Ster.: **£195.00**

HN 2835
Fair Lady
Style One
Designer: M. Davies
Height: 7 1/4", 18.4 cm
Colour: Peach
Issued: 1977-1996
Varieties: HN 2193, 2832;
Also called "Kay,"
HN 3340
U.S.: **$268.75**
Can.: **$425.00**
Ster.: **£105.00**

HN 2836
Polish Dancer
Designer: M. Davies
Height: 9 1/2", 24.1 cm
Colour: Multi-coloured
Issued: 1980 in a limited
edition of 750
Series: Dancers of the
World
U.S.: **$1,000.00**
Can.: **$1,000.00**
Ster.: **£ 500.00**

HN 2837
Awakening
Style Two
Designer: M. Davies
Height: 8 1/2", 21.6 cm
Colour: Black
Issued: 1981 to the present
Varieties: HN 2875
Series: Images
U.S.: **$131.25**
Can.: **$180.00**
Ster.: **£ 49.95**

HN 2838
Sympathy
Designer: M. Davies
Height: 11 3/4", 29.8 cm
Colour: Black
Issued: 1981-1986
Varieties: HN 2876
Series: Images
U.S.: **$200.00**
Can.: **$230.00**
Ster.: **£125.00**

HN 2839
Nicola
Designer: M. Davies
Height: 7", 17.8 cm
Colour: Flowered lavender dress
Issued: 1978-1995
Varieties: HN 2804; also called "Tender Moment" HN 3303
U.S.: $375.00
Can.: $450.00
Ster.: £200.00

HN 2840
Chinese Dancer
Designer: M. Davies
Height: 9", 22.9 cm
Colour: Red, green, purple and lavender
Issued: 1980 in a limited edition of 750
Series: Dancers of the World
U.S.: $1,000.00
Can.: $1,000.00
Ster.: £ 500.00

HN 2841
Mother and Daughter
Designer: E.J. Griffiths
Height: 8 1/2", 21.6 cm
Colour: White
Issued: 1981 to the present
Varieties: HN 2843
Series: Images
U.S.: $200.00
Can.: $325.00
Ster.: £ 99.95

HN 2842
Innocence
Style One
Designer: E.J. Griffiths
Height: 7 1/2", 19.1 cm
Colour: Red
Issued: 1979-1983
U.S.: $225.00
Can.: $350.00
Ster.: £145.00

NH 2843
Mother and Daughter
Designer: E.J. Griffiths
Height: 8 1/2", 21.6 cm
Colour: Black
Issued: 1981-1992
Varieties: HN 2841
Series: Images
U.S.: $185.00
Can.: $225.00
Ster.: £125.00

HN 2844
Sergeant, Virginia 1st Regiment Continental Light Dragoons, 1777
Designer: E.J. Griffiths
Height: 14 1/4", 36.1 cm
Colour: Brown and green
Issued: 1978 in a limited edition of 350
Series: Soldiers of the Revolution
U.S.: $6,000.00
Can.: $6,000.00
Ster.: £1,750.00

HN 2845
Private, Connecticut Regiment, 1777
Designer: E.J. Griffiths
Height: 11 1/4", 28.5 cm
Colour: Brown and cream
Issued: 1978 in a limited edition of 350
Series: Soldiers of the Revolution
U.S.: $1,250.00
Can.: $1,250.00
Ster.: £ 650.00

HN 2846
Private, Pennsylvania Rifle Battalion, 1776
Designer: E.J. Griffiths
Height: 8", 20.3 cm
Colour: Grey
Issued: 1978 in a limited edition of 350
Series: Soldiers of the Revolution
U.S.: $1,250.00
Can.: $1,250.00
Ster.: £ 650.00

*

HN 2851
Christmas Parcels
Style One
Designer: W.K. Harper
Height: 8 3/4", 22.2 cm
Colour: Black
Issued: 1978-1982

U.S.:	**$350.00**
Can.:	**$400.00**
Ster.:	**£175.00**

*

HN 2855
Embroidering
Designer: W.K. Harper
Height: 7 1/4", 18.4 cm
Colour: Grey
Issued: 1980-1990

U.S.:	**$325.00**
Can.:	**$400.00**
Ster.:	**£175.00**

HN 2856
St. George
Style Three
Designer: W.K. Harper
Height: 6", 40.6 cm
Colour: Cream and grey
Issued: 1978 to the present

U.S.:	**$14,500.00**
Can.:	**$17,300.00**
Ster.:	**£ 5,650.00**

HN 2857
Covent Garden
Style Two
Designer: W.K. Harper
Height: 10", 25.4 cm
Colour: Pale blue and white
Issued: 1988-1990
Series: Reflections

U.S.:	**$275.00**
Can.:	**$325.00**
Ster.:	**£165.00**

HN 2858
The Doctor
Designer: W.K. Harper
Height: 7 1/2", 19.1 cm
Colour: Black and grey
Issued: 1979-1992

U.S.:	**$375.00**
Can.:	**$475.00**
Ster.:	**£165.00**

HN 2859
The Statesman
Designer: W.K. Harper
Height: 9", 22.9 cm
Colour: Black and grey
Issued: 1988-1990
Varieties: also called "Sir John A. MacDonald," HN 2860

U.S.:	**$225.00**
Can.:	**$300.00**
Ster.:	**£160.00**

HN 2860
Sir John A. MacDonald
Designer: W.K. Harper
Height: 9", 22.9 cm
Colour: Black and grey
Issued: 1987-1987
Varieties: Also called "The Statesman," HN 2859

U.S.:	**$275.00**
Can.:	**$350.00**
Ster.:	**£175.00**

NOTES ON PRICING

The prices on the secondary market for Royal Doulton Figures, particularly the early HN Numbers, have risen considerably over the years. As values rise, the condition and quality of these figurines take on an increasingly important role.

The prices listed in The Charlton Standard Catalogue of Royal Doulton Beswick Figurines are for figures in mint condition.

Naturally, repaired or restored figures, no matter how professionally done, will sell at a substantial discount.

On Condition: For figures to command catalogue prices they must be in mint condition. This simply means that a figure will not have paint chips, scratches, hairline cracks, crazing or blemishes. Any of which will remove from the mint category figure.

On Quality: Some figures can be better moulded, assembled or painted than others. High quality figures will command catalogue prices. Low quality figures will not.

If the quality or condition of the figures is below the standard for mint, look for that figure to be priced at a percentage of the catalogue prices.

HN 2861
George Washington at Prayer
Designer: L. Ispanky
Height: 12 1/2", 31.7 cm
Colour: Blue and tan
Issued: 1977 in a limited edition of 750

U.S.: $3,750.00
Can.: $3,750.00
Ster.: £1,250.00

HN 2862
First Waltz
Designer: M. Davies
Height: 7 1/4", 18.4 cm
Colour: Red
Issued: 1979-1983

U.S.: $350.00
Can.: $450.00
Ster.: £175.00

HN 2863
Lucy
Style One
Designer: M. Davies
Height: 6", 15.2 cm
Colour: Blue and white
Issued: 1980-1984
Series: Kate Greenaway

U.S.: $225.00
Can.: $325.00
Ster.: £175.00

HN 2864
Tom
Designer: M. Davies
Height: 5 3/4", 14.6 cm
Colour: Blue and yellow
Issued: 1978-1981
Series: Kate Greenaway

U.S.: $425.00
Can.: $450.00
Ster.: £270.00

HN 2865
Tess
Designer: M. Davies
Height: 5 3/4", 14.6 cm
Colour: Green
Issued: 1978-1983
Series: Kate Greenaway

U.S.: $325.00
Can.: $400.00
Ster.: £200.00

HN 2866
Mexican Dancer
Designer: M. Davies
Height: 8 1/4", 21.0 cm
Colour: Gold and white
Issued: 1979 in a limited edition of 750
Series: Dancers of the World

U.S.: $1,100.00
Can.: $1,100.00
Ster.: £ 500.00

HN 2867
Kurdish Dancer
Designer: M. Davies
Height: 8 1/4", 21.0 cm
Colour: Blue
Issued: 1979 in a limited edition of 750
Series: Dancers of the World

U.S.: $1,200.00
Can.: $1,200.00
Ster.: £ 500.00

HN 2868
Cleopatra
Designer: M. Davies
Height: 7 1/4", 18.4 cm
Colour: White, blue and black
Issued: 1979 in a limited edition of 750
Series: Les Femmes Fatales

U.S.: $2,400.00
Can.: $2,400.00
Ster.: £ 925.00

HN 2869
Louise
Stlye One
Designer: M. Davies
Height: 6", 15.2 cm
Colour: Brown
Issued: 1979-1986
Series: Kate Greenaway

U.S.: **$275.00**
Can.: **$325.00**
Ster.: **£145.00**

HN 2870
Beth
Designer: M. Davies
Height: 5 3/4", 14.6 cm
Colour: Pink and white
Issued: 1979-1983
Series: Kate Greenaway

U.S.: **$350.00**
Can.: **$400.00**
Ster.: **£195.00**

HN 2871
Beat You To It
Designer: M. Davies
Height: 6 1/2", 16.5 cm
Colour: Pink, gold and blue
Issued: 1980-1987

U.S.: **$425.00**
Can.: **$525.00**
Ster.: **£225.00**

HN 2872
Young Master
Designer: M. Davies
Height: 7", 17.8 cm
Colour: Purple, grey
and brown
Issued: 1980-1989

U.S.: **$375.00**
Can.: **$500.00**
Ster.: **£225.00**

HN 2873
The Bride
Style Three
Designer: M. Davies
Height: 8", 20.3 cm
Colour: White with
gold trim
Issued: 1980-1989

U.S.: **$175.00**
Can.: **$300.00**
Ster.: **£145.00**

HN 2874
The Bridesmaid
Style Five
Designer: M. Davies
Height: 5 1/4", 13.3 cm
Colour: White with
gold trim
Issued: 1980-1989

U.S.: **$100.00**
Can.: **$200.00**
Ster.: **£110.00**

HN 2875
Awakening
Style Two
Designer: M. Davies
Height: 8 1/2", 21.6 cm
Colour: White
Issued: 1981 to the present
Varieties: HN 2837
Series: Images

U.S.: **$131.25**
Can.: **$180.00**
Ster.: **£ 49.95**

HN 2876
Sympathy
Designer: M. Davies
Height: 11 3/4", 29.8 cm
Colour: White
Issued: 1981-1986
Varieties: HN 2838
Series: Images

U.S.: **$200.00**
Can.: **$230.00**
Ster.: **£125.00**

HN 2877
The Wizard
Style One
Designer: A. Maslankowski
Height: 9 3/4", 24.8 cm
Colour: Blue
Issued: 1979 to the present
Varieties: HN 3121

U.S.: $493.75
Can.: $530.00
Ster.: £149.00

HN 2878
Her Majesty
Queen Elizabeth II
Style Two
Designer: E.J. Griffiths
Height: 10 1/2", 26.7 cm
Colour: Blue, red and cream
Issued: 1983 in a limited
edition of 2500

U.S.: $600.00
Can.: $650.00
Ster.: £325.00

HN 2879
The Gamekeeper
Designer: E.J. Griffiths
Height: 7 1/4", 18.4 cm
Colour: Green, black and tan
Issued: 1984-1992

U.S.: $325.00
Can.: $375.00
Ster.: £165.00

HN 2880
Monique
Designer: E.J. Griffiths
Height: 12 1/2", 31.7 cm
Colour: Pale green
Issued: 1984-1984
Varieties: Also called "Allure,"
HN 3080
Series: Elegance

U.S.: $500.00
Can.: $625.00
Ster.: £275.00

HN 2881
Lord Olivier as Richard III
Designer: E.J. Griffiths
Height: 11 1/2", 29.2 cm
Colour: Red, blue
and black
Issued: 1985 in a limited
edition of 750

U.S.: $ 975.00
Can.: $1,000.00
Ster.: £ 425.00

HN 2882
HM Queen Elizabeth
The Queen Mother
Style One
Designer: E.J. Griffiths
Height: 8", 20.3 cm
Colour: Pink
Issued: 1980 in a limited
edition of 1500

U.S.: $1,500.00
Can.: $1,500.00
Ster.: £ 700.00

HN 2883
HRH The Prince of Wales
Style One
Designer: E.J. Griffiths
Height: 8", 20.3 cm
Colour: Purple, white
and black
Issued: 1981 in a limited
edition of 1500

U.S.: $750.00
Can.: $750.00
Ster.: £325.00

HN 2884
HRH The Prince of Wales
Style Two
Designer: E.J. Griffiths
Height: 8", 20.3 cm
Colour: Red and black
Issued: 1981 in a limited
edition of 1500

U.S.: $950.00
Can.: $950.00
Ster.: £550.00

HN 2885
Lady Diana Spencer
Designer: E.J. Griffiths
Height: 7 3/4", 19.7 cm
Colour: Blue and white
Issued: 1982 in a limited edition of 1500

U.S.:	$750.00
Can.:	$750.00
Ster.:	£275.00

*

HN 2886
Margaret Thatcher (Bust)
Designer: E.J. Griffiths
Height: 4 1/2", 11.5 cm
Colour: Blue
Issued: 1983-1983

U.S.:	$350.00
Can.:	$450.00
Ster.:	£275.00

HN 2887
HRH The Princess of Wales
Designer: E.J. Griffiths
Height: 7 3/4", 19.7 cm
Colour: Cream
Issued: 1982 in a limited edition of 1500

U.S.:	$1,750.00
Can.:	$1,750.00
Ster.:	£ 950.00

HN 2888
His Holiness Pope John-Paul II
Designer: E.J. Griffiths
Height: 10", 25.4 cm
Colour: White
Issued: 1982-1992

U.S.:	$250.00
Can.:	$325.00
Ster.:	£165.00

HN 2889
Captain Cook
Designer: W.K. Harper
Height: 8", 20.3 cm
Colour: Black and cream
Issued: 1980-1984
Series: Sea Characters

U.S.:	$475.00
Can.:	$500.00
Ster.:	£250.00

HN 2890
The Clown
Designer: W.K. Harper
Height: 9", 22.9 cm
Colour: Gold and grey
Issued: 1979 to 1988

U.S.:	$350.00
Can.:	$500.00
Ster.:	£175.00

HN 2891
The Newsvendor
Designer: W.K. Harper
Height: 8", 20.3 cm
Colour: Gold and grey
Issued: 1986 in a limited edition of 2,500

U.S.:	$275.00
Can.:	$350.00
Ster.:	£150.00

HN 2892
The Chief
Designer: W.K. Harper
Height: 7", 17.8 cm
Colour: Gold
Issued: 1979-1988

U.S.:	$275.00
Can.:	$375.00
Ster.:	£165.00

*

HN 2894
Balloon Clown
Designer: W.K. Harper
Height: 9 1/4", 23.5 cm
Colour: White and blue
Issued: 1986-1992

U.S.: $300.00
Can.: $325.00
Ster.: £150.00

HN 2895
Morning Ma'am
Designer: W.K. Harper
Height: 9", 23.5 cm
Colour: Pale blue
Issued: 1986-1989

U.S.: $225.00
Can.: $300.00
Ster.: £165.00

HN 2896
Good Day Sir
Designer: W.K. Harper
Height: 8 1/2", 21.6 cm
Colour: Purple
Issued: 1986-1989

U.S. $225.00
Can.: $300.00
Ster.: £165.00

Photograph
Not
Available

HN 2897
Francoise
Designer: W.K. Harper
Height: 12 1/2", 31.7 cm
Colour: Cream
Issued: 1984-1984
Series: Elegance

U.S.: $500.00
Can.: $600.00
Ster.: £175.00

HN 2898
Ko-Ko
Style Two
Designer: W.K. Harper
Height: 11 1/2", 29.2 cm
Colour: Yellow and blue
Issued: 1980-1985
Series: Gilbert and Sullivan

U.S.: $900.00
Can.: $900.00
Ster.: £450.00

HN 2899
Yum-Yum
Style Two
Designer: W.K. Harper
Height: 10 3/4", 27.3 cm
Colour: Green and yellow
Issued: 1980-1985
Series: Gilbert and Sullivan

U.S.: $1,000.00
Can.: $1,000.00
Ster.: £ 500.00

HN 2900
Ruth, The Pirate Maid
Designer: W.K. Harper
Height: 11 3/4", 29.8 cm
Colour: Brown and blue
Issued: 1981-1985
Series: Gilbert and Sullivan

U.S.: $900.00
Can.: $900.00
Ster.: £400.00

HN 2901
The Pirate King
Designer: W.K. Harper
Height: 10", 25.4 cm
Colour: Blue and gold
Issued: 1981-1985
Series: Gilbert and Sullivan

U.S.: $900.00
Can.: $900.00
Ster.: £425.00

HN 2902
Elsie Maynard
Style Two
Designer: W.K. Harper
Height: 12", 30.5 cm
Colour: Green and white
Issued: 1982-1985
Series: Gilbert and Sullivan
U.S.: $950.00
Can.: $950.00
Ster.: £425.00

HN 2903
Colonel Fairfax
Designer: W.K. Harper
Height: 11 1/2", 29.2 cm
Colour: Red and gold
Issued: 1982-1985
Series: Gilbert and Sullivan
U.S.: $1,000.00
Can.: $1,000.00
Ster.: £ 450.00

*

HN 2906
Paula
Designer: P. Parsons
Height: 7", 17.8 cm
Colour: Yellow with
green trim
Issued: 1980-1986
Varieties: HN 3234
U.S.: $300.00
Can.: $400.00
Ster.: £165.00

HN 2907
The Piper
Style One
Designer: M. Abberley
Height: 8", 20.3 cm
Colour: Green
Issued: 1980-1992
U.S.: $475.00
Can.: $450.00
Ster.: £195.00

HN 2908
HMS Ajax
Designer: S. Keenan
Height: 9 3/4", 24.8 cm
Colour: Red, green
and gold
Issued: 1980 in a limited
edition of 950
Series: Ships Figureheads
U.S.: $600.00
Can.: $600.00
Ster.: £300.00

HN 2909
Benmore
Designer: S. Keenan
Height: 9 1/4", 23.5 cm
Colour: Blue, red,
white and gold
Issued: 1980 in a limited
edition of 950
Series: Ships Figureheads
U.S.: $600.00
Can.: $600.00
Ster.: £300.00

HN 2910
Lalla Rookh
Designer: S. Keenan
Height: 9", 22.9 cm
Colour: Brown, green
with gold trim
Issued: 1981 in a limited
edition of 950
Series: Ships Figureheads
U.S.: $700.00
Can.: $750.00
Ster.: £325.00

HN 2911
Gandalf
Designer: D. Lyttleton
Height: 7", 17.8 cm
Colour: Green and white
Issued: 1980-1984
Series: Middle Earth
U.S.: $300.00
Can.: $350.00
Ster.: £185.00

HN 2912
Frodo
Designer: D. Lyttleton
Height: 4 1/2", 11.4 cm
Colour: Black and white
Issued: 1980-1984
Series: Middle Earth

U.S.:	$150.00
Can.:	$200.00
Ster.:	£130.00

HN 2913
Gollum
Designer: D. Lyttleton
Height: 3 1/4", 8.3 cm
Colour: Brown
Issued: 1980-1984
Series: Middle Earth

U.S.:	$190.00
Can.:	$225.00
Ster.:	£145.00

HN 2914 ✗
Bilbo
Designer: D. Lyttleton
Height: 4 1/2", 11.4 cm
Colour: Brown
Issued: 1980-1984
Series: Middle Earth

U.S.:	$150.00
Can.:	$200.00
Ster.:	£130.00

HN 2915
Galadriel
Designer: D. Lyttleton
Height: 5 1/2", 14.0 cm
Colour: White
Issued: 1981-1984
Series: Middle Earth

U.S.:	$175.00
Can.:	$225.00
Ster.:	£130.00

HN 2916
Aragorn
Designer: D. Lyttleton
Height: 6 1/4", 15.9 cm
Colour: Brown and green
Issued: 1981-1984
Series: Middle Earth

U.S.:	$165.00
Can.:	$200.00
Ster.:	£130.00

HN 2917
Legolas
Designer: D. Lyttleton
Height: 6 1/4", 15.9 cm
Colour: Cream and tan
Issued: 1981-1984
Series: Middle Earth

U.S.:	$150.00
Can.:	$200.00
Ster.:	£130.00

HN 2918
Boromir
Designer: D Lyttleton
Height: 6 3/4", 17.2 cm
Colour: Brown and green
Issued: 1981-1984
Series: Middle Earth

U.S.:	$375.00
Can.:	$450.00
Ster.:	£195.00

HN 2919
Rachel
Designer: P. Gee
Height: 7 1/2", 19.1 cm
Colour: Gold and green
Issued: 1981-1984
Varieties: HN 2936

U.S.:	$325.00
Can.:	$400.00
Ster.:	£195.00

HN 2920
Yearning
Designer: P. Gee
Height: 11 3/4", 29.8 cm
Colour: White
Issued: 1982-1986
Varieties: HN 2921
Series: Images

U.S.: $200.00
Can.: $230.00
Ster.: £125.00

HN 2921
Yearning
Designer: P. Gee
Height: 11 3/4", 29.8 cm
Colour: Black
Issued: 1982-1986
Varieties: HN 2920
Series: Images

U.S.: $200.00
Can.: $230.00
Ster.: £125.00

HN 2922
Gimli
Designer: D. Lyttleton
Height: 5 1/2", 14.0 cm
Colour: Brown and blue
Issued: 1981-1984
Series: Middle Earth

U.S.: $200.00
Can.: $275.00
Ster.: £150.00

HN 2923
Barliman Butterbur
Designer: D. Lyttleton
Height: 5 1/4", 13.3 cm
Colour: Brown, tan and white
Issued: 1982-1984
Series: Middle Earth

U.S.: $475.00
Can.: $550.00
Ster.: £295.00

HN 2924
Tom Bombadil
Designer: D. Lyttleton
Height: 5 3/4", 14.6 cm
Colour: Black and yellow
Issued: 1982-1984
Series: Middle Earth

U.S.: $525.00
Can.: $625.00
Ster.: £295.00

HN 2925
Samwise
Designer: D. Lyttleton
Height: 4 1/2", 11.4 cm
Colour: Black and brown
Issued: 1982-1984
Series: Middle Earth

U.S.: $500.00
Can.: $600.00
Ster.: £295.00

HN 2926
Tom Sawyer
Designer: D. Lyttleton
Height: 5 1/4", 13.3 cm
Colour: Blue
Issued: 1982-1985
Series: Characters from
Children's Literature

U.S.: $175.00
Can.: $225.00
Ster.: £125.00

HN 2927
Huckleberry Finn
Designer: D. Lyttleton
Height: 7", 17.8 cm
Colour: Tan and brown
Issued: 1982-1985
Series: Characters from
Children's Literature

U.S.: $175.00
Can.: $225.00
Ster.: £125.00

HN 2928
Nelson

Designer:	S. Keenan
Height:	8 3/4", 22.2 cm
Colour:	Blue, gold and green
Issued:	1981 in a limited edition of 950
Series:	Ships Figureheads
U.S.:	**$1,000.00**
Can.:	**$1,000.00**
Ster.:	**£ 425.00**

HN 2929
Chieftain

Designer:	S. Keenan
Height:	8 3/4", 22.2 cm
Colour:	Green and brown
Issued:	1982 in a limited edition of 950
Series:	Ships Figureheads
U.S.:	**$1,200.00**
Can.:	**$1,200.00**
Ster.:	**£ 395.00**

HN 2930
Pocahontas

Designer:	S. Keenan
Height:	8", 20.3 cm
Colour:	White, red and gold
Issued:	1982 in a limited edition of 950
Series:	Ships Figureheads
U.S.:	**$1,200.00**
Can.:	**$1,200.00**
Ster.:	**£ 395.00**

HN 2931
Mary Queen of Scots
Style One

Designer:	S. Keenan
Height:	9 1/2", 24.1 cm
Colour:	Purple, red and white
Issued:	1983 in a limited edition of 950
Series:	Ships Figureheads
U.S.:	**$1,500.00**
Can.:	**$1,500.00**
Ster.:	**£ 425.00**

HN 2932
Hibernia

Designer:	S. Keenan
Height:	9 1/2", 24.1 cm
Colour:	Black, white and gold
Issued:	1983 in a limited edition of 950
Series:	Ships Figureheads
U.S.:	**$1,500.00**
Can.:	**$1,500.00**
Ster.:	**£ 395.00**

HN 2933
Kathleen
Style Two

Designer:	S. Keenan
Height:	6 1/2", 16.5 cm
Colour:	Orange, yellow and green
Issued:	1983 Canada, 1984 Worldwide -1987
Varieties:	HN 3100
U.S.:	**$275.00**
Can.:	**$350.00**
Ster.:	**£175.00**

HN 2934
Balloon Boy

Designer:	P. Gee
Height:	7 1/2", 19.1 cm
Colour:	Green and black
Issued:	1984 to the present
U.S.:	**$212.50**
Can.:	**$375.00**
Ster.:	**£ 95.00**

HN 2935
Balloon Lady

Designer:	P. Gee
Height:	8 1/4", 21.0 cm
Colour:	Purple, gold and white
Issued:	1984 to the present
U.S.:	**$212.50**
Can.:	**$495.00**
Ster.:	**£ 99.95**

HN 2936
Rachel
Designer: P. Gee
Height: 7 1/2", 19.1 cm
Colour: Red and cream
Issued: 1985 to the present
Varieties: HN 2919

U.S.:   **$375.00**
Can.:   **$490.00**
Ster.:   **£149.00**

HN 2937
Gail
Style One
Designer: P. Gee
Height: 7 1/2", 19.1 cm
Colour: Red and cream
Issued: 1986 to the present

U.S.:   **$375.00**
Can.:   **$490.00**
Ster.:   **£139.00**

HN 2938
Isadora
Designer: P. Gee
Height: 8", 20.3 cm
Colour: Lavender
Issued: 1986-1992
Varieties: Also called
            "Celeste," HN 3322

U.S.:   **$350.00**
Can.:   **$425.00**
Ster.:   **£195.00**

HN 2939
Donna
Designer: P. Gee
Height: 7 3/4", 19.7 cm
Colour: White
Issued: 1982-1994
Series: Vanity Fair Ladies

U.S.:   **$225.00**
Can.:   **$250.00**
Ster.:   **£ 75.00**

HN 2940
All Aboard
Designer: R. Tabbenor
Height: 9 1/4", 23.5 cm
Colour: Blue, cream
            and brown
Issued: 1982-1986
Series: Sea characters

U.S.:   **$285.00**
Can.:   **$350.00**
Ster.:   **£165.00**

HN 2941
Tom Brown
Designer: R. Tabbenor
Height: 6 3/4", 17.2 cm
Colour: Blue and cream
Issued: 1983-1985
Series: Characters from
            Children's Literature

U.S.:   **$150.00**
Can.:   **$200.00**
Ster.:   **£125.00**

HN 2942
Prized Possessions
Designer: R. Tabbenor
Height: 6 1/2", 16.5 cm
Colour: Cream, purple
            and green
Issued: 1982-1982
Series: R.D.I.C.C.

U.S.:   **$750.00**
Can.:   **$800.00**
Ster.:   **£395.00**

HN 2943
The China Repairer
Designer: R. Tabbenor
Height: 6 3/4", 17.2 cm
Colour: Blue, white and tan
Issued: 1982 Canada,
            1983 Worldwide
            -1988

U.S.:   **$275.00**
Can.:   **$400.00**
Ster.:   **£165.00**

HN 2944
The Rag Doll Seller
Designer: R. Tabbenor
Height: 7", 17.8 cm
Colour: Green, lavender
and white
Issued: 1983-1995
U.S.: **$300.00**
Can.: **$375.00**
Ster.: **£150.00**

HN 2945
Pride and Joy
Designer: R. Tabbenor
Height: 7", 17.8 cm
Colour: Brown, gold
and green
Issued: 1984-1984
Series: R.D.I.C.C.
U.S.: **$350.00**
Can.: **$500.00**
Ster.: **£300.00**

HN 2946
Elizabeth
Style One
Designer: B. Franks
Height: 8", 20.3 cm
Colour: Green and yellow
Issued: 1982-1986
U.S.: **$375.00**
Can.: **$475.00**
Ster.: **£195.00**

*

HN 2952
Susan
Style Two
Designer: P. Parsons
Height: 8 1/2", 21.6 cm
Colour: Blue, black and pink
Issued: 1982-1993
Varieties: HN 3050
U.S.: **$325.00**
Can.: **$450.00**
Ster.: **£165.00**

HN 2953
Sleepy Darling
Designer: P. Parsons
Height: 7 1/4", 18.4 cm
Colour: Pale blue and pink
Issued: 1981-1981
Series: R.D.I.C.C.
U.S.: **$275.00**
Can.: **$425.00**
Ster.: **£200.00**

HN 2954
Samantha
Style One
Designer: P. Parsons
Height: 7", 17.8 cm
Colour: White
Issued: 1982-1984
Series: Vanity Fair Ladies
U.S.: **$225.00**
Can.: **$300.00**
Ster.: **£145.00**

HN 2955
Nancy
Designer: P. Parsons
Height: 7 1/2", 19.1 cm
Colour: White
Issued: 1982-1994
Series: Vanity Fair Ladies
U.S.: **$175.00**
Can.: **$225.00**
Ster.: **£ 75.00**

HN 2956
Heather
Designer: P. Parsons
Height: 6", 15.2 cm
Colour: White
Issued: 1982 to the present
Varieties: Also called "Marie"
(Style Three) HN 3357
Series: Vanity Fair Ladies
U.S.: **$187.50**
Can.: **$280.00**
Ster.: **£ 79.95**

HN 2957
Edith
Designer:	P. Parsons
Height:	5 3/4", 14.6 cm
Colour:	Green and white
Issued:	1982-1985
Series:	Kate Greenaway
U.S.:	**$285.00**
Can.:	**$350.00**
Ster.:	**£200.00**

HN 2958
Amy
Style One	
Designer:	P. Parsons
Height:	6", 15.2 cm
Colour:	White and blue
Issued:	1982-1987
Series:	Kate Greenaway
U.S.:	**$190.00**
Can.:	**$275.00**
Ster.:	**£165.00**

HN 2959
Save Some For Me
Designer:	P. Parsons
Height:	7 1/4", 18.4 cm
Colour:	Blue and white
Issued:	1982-1985
Series:	Childhood Days
U.S.:	**$275.00**
Can.:	**$325.00**
Ster.:	**£165.00**

HN 2960
Laura - Style One
Designer:	P. Parsons
Height:	7 1/4", 18.4 cm
Colour:	Pale blue and white, yellow flowers
Issued:	1982 Canada, 1984 Worldwide - 1994
Varieties:	HN 3136
U.S.:	**$250.00**
Can.:	**$350.00**
Ster.:	**£150.00**

HN 2961
Carol
Designer:	P. Parsons
Height:	7 1/2", 19.1 cm
Colour:	White
Issued:	1982-1995
Series:	Vanity Fair Ladies
U.S.:	**$200.00**
Can.:	**$225.00**
Ster.:	**£100.00**

HN 2962
Barbara
Style Two	
Designer:	P. Parsons
Height:	8", 20.3 cm
Colour:	White
Issued:	1982-1984
Series:	Vanity Fair Ladies
U.S.:	**$275.00**
Can.:	**$400.00**
Ster.:	**£165.00**

HN 2963
It Won't Hurt
Designer:	P. Parsons
Height:	7 1/2", 19.1 cm
Colour:	White, brown and blue
Issued:	1982-1985
Series:	Childhood Days
U.S.:	**$175.00**
Can.:	**$250.00**
Ster.:	**£145.00**

HN 2964
Dressing Up
Style One	
Designer:	P. Parsons
Height:	7 1/2", 19.1 cm
Colour:	White and blue
Issued:	1982-1985
Series:	Childhood Days
U.S.:	**$200.00**
Can.:	**$250.00**
Ster.:	**£195.00**

HN 2965
Pollyanna
Designer: P. Parsons
Height: 6 1/2", 16.5 cm
Colour: White, grey and tan
Issued: 1982-1985
Series: Characters
         from Children's
         Literature
U.S.: **$200.00**
Can.: **$250.00**
Ster.: **£145.00**

HN 2966
And So To Bed
Designer: P. Parsons
Height: 7 1/2", 19.1 cm
Colour: Cream and gold
Issued: 1982-1985
Series: Childhood Days
U.S.: **$200.00**
Can.: **$250.00**
Ster.: **£145.00**

HN 2967
Please Keep Still
Designer: P. Parsons
Height: 4 1/2", 11.4 cm
Colour: Yellow and blue
Issued: 1982-1985
Series: Childhood Days
U.S.: **$240.00**
Can.: **$275.00**
Ster.: **£150.00**

HN 2968
Juliet
Style One
Designer: P. Parsons
Height: 7", 17.8 cm
Colour: Blue and white
Issued: 1983-1984
Series: Ladies of
         Covent Garden
U.S.: **$500.00**
Can.: **$600.00**
Ster.: **£250.00**

Commissioned by Amex

HN 2969
Kimberley Style One
Designer: P. Parsons
Height: 8", 20.3 cm
Colour: Yellow and white
Issued: 1983-1984
Varieties: Also called "Yours
           Forever," HN 3354
Series: Ladies of Covent Garden
U.S.: **$500.00**
Can.: **$600.00**
Ster.: **£250.00**

Commissioned by Amex   *

HN 2970
And One For You
Designer: A. Hughes
Height: 6 1/2", 16.5 cm
Colour: White and brown
Issued: 1982-1985
Series: Childhood Days
U.S.: **$240.00**
Can.: **$275.00**
Ster.: **£145.00**

HN 2971
As Good As New
Designer: A. Hughes
Height: 6 1/2", 16.5 cm
Colour: Blue, green and tan
Issued: 1982-1985
Series: Childhood Days
U.S.: **$200.00**
Can.: **$250.00**
Ster.: **£145.00**

HN 2972
Little Lord Fauntleroy
Designer: A. Hughes
Height: 6 1/4", 15.9 cm
Colour: Blue and white
Issued: 1982-1985
Series: Characters from
         Children's Literature
U.S.: **$165.00**
Can.: **$225.00**
Ster.: **£125.00**

*

HN 2974
Carolyn
Style Two
Designer: A. Hughes
Height: 5 1/2", 14.0 cm
Colour: Green
Issued: 1982 Canada,
1984 Worldwide
-1986

U.S.: $250.00
Can.: $300.00
Ster.: £165.00

HN 2975
Heidi
Designer: A. Hughes
Height: 4 1/2", 11.4 cm
Colour: Green and white
Issued: 1983-1985
Series: Characters from
Children's Literature
U.S.: $200.00
Can.: $250.00
Ster.: £165.00

HN 2976
I'm Nearly Ready
Designer: A. Hughes
Height: 7 1/2", 19.1 cm
Colour: Black, white and
brown
Issued: 1983 Canada,
1984 Worldwide
-1985
Series: Childhood Days
U.S.: $225.00
Can.: $275.00
Ster.: £145.00

HN 2977
Magic Dragon
Designer: A. Hughes
Height: 4 3/4", 12.0 cm
Colour: Cream
Issued: 1983-1986
Series: Enchantment
U.S.: $225.00
Can.: $300.00
Ster.: £145.00

HN 2978
The Magpie Ring
Designer: A. Hughes
Height: 8", 20.3 cm
Colour: Cream
Issued: 1983-1986
Series: Enchantment
U.S.: $225.00
Can.: $300.00
Ster.: £145.00

HN 2979
Fairyspell
Designer: A. Hughes
Height: 5 1/4", 13.3 cm
Colour: Cream
Issued: 1983-1986
Series: Enchantment
U.S. $225.00
Can.: $300.00
Ster.: £165.00

HN 2980
Just One More
Designer: A. Hughes
Height: 7", 17.8 cm
Colour: Gold and blue
Issued: 1983 Canada,
1984 Worldwide
-1985
Series: Childhood Days
U.S.: $200.00
Can.: $250.00
Ster.: £145.00

HN 2981
Stick 'em Up
Designer: A. Hughes
Height: 7", 17.8 cm
Colour: Blue and tan
Issued: 1983 Canada,
1984 Worldwide
-1985
Series: Childhood Days
U.S.: $200.00
Can.: $250.00
Ster.: £165.00

*

HN 2988
The Auctioneer
Designer:	R. Tabbenor
Height:	8 1/2", 21.6 cm
Colour:	Black, grey and brown
Issued:	1986-1986
Series:	R.D.I.C.C.
U.S.:	**$325.00**
Can.:	**$425.00**
Ster.:	**£245.00**

HN 2989
The Genie
Designer:	R. Tabbenor
Height:	9 3/4", 24.7 cm
Colour:	Blue
Issued:	1983-1990
Varieties:	HN 2999
U.S.:	**$275.00**
Can.:	**$300.00**
Ster.:	**£165.00**

HN 2990
Shepherdess
Style Three
Designer:	R. Tabbenor
Height:	8", 20.3 cm
Colour:	Pale blue, white and tan
Issued:	1987-1988
Series:	Reflections
U.S.:	**$275.00**
Can.:	**$325.00**
Ster.:	**£150.00**

HN 2991
June
Style Four
Designer:	R. Tabbenor
Height:	9", 22.9 cm
Colour:	Lavender and red
Issued:	1988-1994
U.S.:	**$275.00**
Can.:	**$350.00**
Ster.:	**£120.00**

HN 2992
Golfer
Designer:	R. Tabbenor
Height:	9 1/2", 24.1 cm
Colour:	Blue, white and pale brown
Issued:	1988-1991
Series:	Reflections
U.S.:	**$275.00**
Can.:	**$325.00**
Ster.:	**£165.00**

HN 2993
Old Father Thames
Designer:	R. Tabbenor
Height:	5 3/4", 14.6 cm
Colour:	Cream with gold trim
Issued:	1988 in a limited edition of 500
U.S.:	**$275.00**
Can.:	**$325.00**
Ster.:	**£150.00**

Commissioned by Thames Water
*

HN 2994
Helen
Style Two
Designer:	R. Tabbenor
Height:	5", 12.7 cm
Colour:	White
Issued:	1985-1987
Series:	Vanity Fair Children
U.S.:	**$100.00**
Can.:	**$175.00**
Ster.:	**£110.00**

HN 2995
Julie
Designer:	R. Tabbenor
Height:	5", 12.7 cm
Colour:	White
Issued:	1985-1995
Varieties:	HN 3407
Series:	Vanity Fair Children
U.S.:	**$ 90.00**
Can.:	**$125.00**
Ster.:	**£ 50.00**

HN 2996
Amanda
Designer: R. Tabbenor
Height: 5 1/4", 13.3 cm
Colour: White and pink
Issued: 1986 to the present
Varieties: HN 3406, 3632
Series: Vanity Fair Children
Also called "Figure
of the Month, Child"

U.S.: $106.25
Can.: $190.00
Ster.: £ 39.95

HN 2997
Chic
Designer: R. Tabbenor
Height: 13", 33.0 cm
Colour: Pale blue
Issued: 1987 N. America,
1988 Worldwide
-1990
Series: Reflections

U.S.: $225.00
Can.: $275.00
Ster.: £120.00

HN 2998
Aperitif
Designer: P. Gee
Height: 12", 30.5 cm
Colour: Pale green
Issued: 1988-1988
Series: Reflections

U.S.: $375.00
Can.: $450.00
Ster.: £175.00

Commissioned by Home
Shopping Network, Florida

HN 2999
The Genie
Designer: R. Tabbenor
Height: 9 3/4", 24.7 cm
Colour: Red
Issued: 1990-1995t
Varieties: HN 2989
Series: Flambé

U.S.: $300.00
Can.: $325.00
Ster.: £120.00

Photograph
Not
Available

HN 3000
Sweet Bouquet
Designer: R. Tabbenor
Height: 13", 33.0 cm
Colour: Blue and white
Issued: 1988-1988
Series: Reflections

U.S.: $300.00
Can.: $400.00
Ster.: £175.00

Commissioned by Home
Shopping Network, Florida

HN 3001
Danielle
Style Two
Designer: P. Gee
Height: 7", 17.8 cm
Colour: Pink and white
Issued: 1990-1995
Varieties: Also called "Spring
Song," HN 3446
Series: Vanity Fair Ladies

U.S.: $200.00
Can.: $250.00
Ster.: £100.00

HN 3002
Marilyn
Designer: P. Gee
Height: 7 1/4", 18.4 cm
Colour: White dress
with flowers
Issued: 1985 Canada,
1986-1995
Worldwide

U.S.: $225.00
Can.: $275.00
Ster.: £120.00

HN 3003
Lilian In Summer
Designer: P. Gee
Height: 8 1/2", 21.6 cm
Colour: White, blue and pink
Issued: 1985
Series: Four Seasons
(Series Three)

U.S.: $450.00
Can.: $550.00
Ster.: £225.00

Commissioned by Danbury Mint

HN 3004
Emily In Autumn
Style One
Designer: P. Gee
Height: 8", 20.3 cm
Colour: Yellow and white
Issued: 1986
Series: Four Seasons
(SeriesThree)
U.S.: $450.00
Can.: $550.00
Ster.: £225.00

Commissioned by Danbury Mint

HN 3005
Sarah In Winter
Style One
Designer: P. Gee
Height: 8", 20.3 cm
Colour: Pale green, white
Issued: 1986
Series: Four Seasons
(SeriesThree)
U.S.: $450.00
Can.: $550.00
Ster.: £225.00

Commissioned by Danbury Mint

HN 3006
Catherine In Spring
Style Two
Designer: P. Gee
Height: 8 1/2", 21.6 cm
Colour: Pink and white
Issued: 1985
Series: Four Seasons
(Series Three)
U.S.: $450.00
Can.: $550.00
Ster.: £225.00

Commissioned by Danbury Mint

HN 3007
Mary, Countess Howe
Designer: P. Gee
Height: 9 1/4", 23.5 cm
Colour: Pink and blue
Issued: 1990 in a limited
edition of 5,000
Series: Gainsborough
Ladies
U.S.: $700.00
Can.: $750.00
Ster.: £350.00

HN 3008
Sophia Charlotte,
Lady Sheffield
Designer: P. Gee
Height: 10", 25.4 cm
Colour: Yellow, turquoise
Issued: 1990 in a limited
edition of 5,000
Series: Gainsborough
Ladies
U.S.: $700.00
Can.: $750.00
Ster.: £350.00

HN 3009
Honourable
Frances Duncombe
Designer: P. Gee
Height: 9 3/4", 24.7 cm
Colour: Blue and yellow
Issued: 1991 in a limited
edition of 5,000
Series: Gainsborough
Ladies
U.S.: $700.00
Can.: $750.00
Ster.: £350.00

HN 3010
Isabella,
Countess of Sefton
Designer: P. Gee
Height: 9 3/4", 24.7 cm
Colour: Yellow and black
Issued: 1991 in a limited
edition of 5,000
Series: Gainsborough
Ladies
U.S.: $700.00
Can.: $750.00
Ster.: £350.00

HN 3011
My Best Friend
Designer: P. Gee
Height: 8", 20.3 cm
Colour: Pink
Issued: 1990 to the present
U.S.: $350.00
Can.: $445.00
Ster.: £149.00

HN 3012
Painting
Designer: P. Parsons
Height: 7 142", 18.4 cm
Colour: Purple
Issued: 1987 in a limited
edition of 750
Series: Gentle Arts
U.S.: **$1,750.00**
Can.: **$1,750.00**
Ster.: **£ 750.00**

HN 3013
James
Designer: P. Parsons
Height: 6", 15.2 cm
Colour: White
Issued: 1983-1987
Series: Kate Greenaway
U.S.: **$550.00**
Can.: **$600.00**
Ster.: **£325.00**

HN 3014
Nell
Designer: P. Parsons
Height: 4", 10.1 cm
Colour: White and pink
Issued: 1982-1987
Series: Kate Greenaway
U.S.: **$200.00**
Can.: **$275.00**
Ster.: **£165.00**

HN 3015
Adornment
Designer: P. Parsons
Height: 7 1/4", 18.4 cm
Colour: Pink and lavender
stripes
Issued: 1989 in a limited
edition of 750
Series: Gentle Arts
U.S.: **$1,250.00**
Can.: **$1,250.00**
Ster.: **£ 550.00**

HN 3016
The Graduate (female)
Designer: P. Parsons
Height: 8 3/4", 22.2 cm
Colour: Black, pink
and yellow
Issued: 1984-1992
U.S.: **$275.00**
Can.: **$325.00**
Ster.: **£195.00**

HN 3017
The Graduate (male)
Designer: P. Parsons
Height: 9 1/4", 23.5 cm
Colour: Black and grey
Issued: 1984-1992
U.S.: **$275.00**
Can.: **$325.00**
Ster.: **£195.00**

HN 3018
Sisters
Designer: P. Parsons
Height: 8 1/2", 21.6 cm
Colour: White
Issued: 1983 to the present
Varieties: HN 3019
Series: Images
U.S.: **$106.25**
Can.: **$210.00**
Ster.: **£ 49.95**

HN 3019
Sisters
Designer: P. Parsons
Height: 8 1/2", 21.6 cm
Colour: Black
Issued: 1983 to the present
Varieties: HN 3018
Series: Images
U.S.: **$ 90.00**
Can.: **N/I**
Ster.: **£ 49.95**

HN 3020
Ellen
Designer:	P. Parsons
Height:	3 1/2", 8.9 cm
Colour:	Blue and yellow
Issued:	1984-1987
Series:	Kate Greenaway
U.S.:	**$500.00**
Can.:	**$500.00**
Ster.:	**£225.00**

HN 3021
Polly Put The Kettle On
Designer:	P. Parsons
Height:	8", 20.3 cm
Colour:	White and pink
Issued:	1984-1987
Series:	Nursery Rhymes (Series Two)
U.S.:	**$225.00**
Can.:	**$275.00**
Ster.:	**£145.00**

*

HN 3024
April Shower
Designer:	R. Jefferson
Height:	4 3/4", 12.0 cm
Colour:	Cream
Issued:	1983-1986
Series:	Enchantment
U.S.:	**$225.00**
Can.:	**$275.00**
Ster.:	**£175.00**

HN 3025
Rumpelstiltskin
Designer:	R. Jefferson
Height:	8", 20.3 cm
Colour:	Cream
Issued:	1983-1986
Series:	Enchantment
U.S.:	**$250.00**
Can.:	**$275.00**
Ster.:	**£225.00**

HN 3026
Carefree
Designer:	R. Jefferson
Height:	12 1/4", 31.1 cm
Colour:	White
Issued:	1986 to the present
Varieties:	HN 3029
Series:	Images
U.S.:	**$200.00**
Can.:	**$210.00**
Ster.:	**£ 69.95**

HN 3027
Windswept
Style One	
Designer:	R. Jefferson
Height:	12 3/4", 32.0 cm
Colour:	Pale blue
Issued:	1985 N. America 1987 Worldwide -1994
Series:	Reflections
U.S.:	**$225.00**
Can.:	**$275.00**
Ster.:	**£115.00**

HN 3028
Panorama
Designer:	R. Jefferson
Height:	12 3/4", 32.5 cm
Colour:	Pale blue
Issued:	1985 N. America, 1987 Worldwide -1988
Series:	Reflections
U.S.:	**$225.00**
Can.:	**$275.00**
Ster.:	**£145.00**

HN 3029
Carefree
Designer:	R. Jefferson
Height:	12 1/4", 31.1 cm
Colour:	Black
Issued:	1986 to the present
Varieties:	HN 3026
Series:	Images
U.S.:	**$160.00**
Can.:	**N/I**
Ster.:	**£ 69.95**

HN 3030
Little Bo Peep
Designer: A. Hughes
Height: 8", 20.3 cm
Colour: White with blue trim
Issued: 1984-1987
Series: Nursery Rhymes (Series Two)

U.S.: $150.00
Can.: $200.00
Ster.: £145.00

HN 3031
Wee Willie Winkie
Style Two
Designer: A. Hughes
Height: 7 3/4", 19.7 cm
Colour: White and blue
Issued: 1984-1987
Series: Nursery Rhymes (Series Two)

U.S.: $185.00
Can.: $300.00
Ster.: £165.00

HN 3032
Tom, Tom, the Piper's Son
Designer: A. Hughes
Height: 7", 17.8 cm
Colour: White, yellow and pink
Issued: 1984-1987
Series: Nursery Rhymes (Series Two)

U.S.: $135.00
Can.: $200.00
Ster.: £125.00

HN 3033
Springtime
Style Two
Designer: A. Hughes
Height: 8", 20.3 cm
Colour: Yellow, cream and green
Issued: 1983-1983
Series: R.D.I.C.C and Four Seasons (Series Four)

U.S.: $350.00
Can.: $450.00
Ster.: £300.00

HN 3034
Little Jack Horner
Style Two
Designer: A. Hughes
Height: 7", 17.8 cm
Colour: White, yellow and green
Issued: 1984-1987
Series: Nursery Rhymes (Series Two)

U.S.: $140.00
Can.: $200.00
Ster.: £165.00

HN 3035
Little Boy Blue
Style Two
Designer: A. Hughes
Height: 7 3/4", 19.7 cm
Colour: Blue and white
Issued: 1984-1987
Series: Nursery Rhymes (Series Two)

U.S.: $160.00
Can.: $200.00
Ster.: £125.00

HN 3036
Kerry
Designer: A. Hughes
Height: 5 1/4", 13.3 cm
Colour: White
Issued: 1986-1992
Varieties: HN 3461
Series: Vanity Fair Children

U.S.: $100.00
Can.: $125.00
Ster.: £ 75.00

HN 3037
Miranda
Style Two
Designer: A. Hughes
Height: 8 1/2", 21.5 cm
Colour: Cream, yellow and purple
Issued: 1987-1990

U.S.: $300.00
Can.: $375.00
Ster.: £165.00

HN 3038
Yvonne
Designer: A. Hughes
Height: 8 1/2", 21.6 cm
Colour: Turquoise
Issued: 1987-1992

U.S.: **$250.00**
Can.: **$330.00**
Ster.: **£165.00**

HN 3039
Reflection
Designer: A. Hughes
Height: 8", 20.3 cm
Colour: Pale blue, pale
brown and white
Issued: 1987-1991
Series: Reflections

U.S.: **$250.00**
Can.: **$300.00**
Ster.: **£145.00**

HN 3040
Flower Arranging
Designer: D. Brindley
Height: 7 1/4", 18.4 cm
Colour: Green, purple
and pink
Issued: 1988 in a limited
edition of 750
Series: Gentle Arts

U.S.: **$1,250.00**
Can.: **$1,250.00**
Ster.: **£ 550.00**

HN 3041
The Lawyer
Designer: P. Parsons
Height: 8 3/4", 22.2 cm
Colour: Grey and black
Issued: 1985-1995

U.S.: **$250.00**
Can.: **$275.00**
Ster.: **£135.00**

HN 3042
Gillian
(With shoulder straps)
Style Two
Designer: P. Parsons
Height: 8 1/4", 21.0 cm
Colour: Green
Issued: 1984 - Unknown
Varieties: HN 3042A (without
shoulder straps)
Series: M. Doulton Events

U.S.: **$225.00**
Can.: **$300.00**
Ster.: **£145.00**

HN 3042A
Gillian
(Without shoulder straps)
Style Two
Designer: P. Parsons
Height: 8 1/4", 21.0 cm
Colour: Green
Issued: Unknown-1990
Varieties: HN 3042 (with
shoulder straps)

U.S.: **$225.00**
Can.: **$250.00**
Ster.: **£145.00**

HN 3043
Lynsey
Designer: P. Parsons
Height: 4 3/4", 12.0 cm
Colour: White
Issued: 1985-1995
Series: Vanity Fair
Children

U.S.: **$ 95.00**
Can.: **$130.00**
Ster.: **£ 45.00**

HN 3044
Catherine
Style Three
Designer: P. Parsons
Height: 5", 12.7 cm
Colour: White with blue
flowers
Issued: 1985-1996
Varieties: HN 3451
Series: Vanity Fair Children

U.S.: **$106.25**
Can.: **$190.00**
Ster.: **£ 39.95**

HN 3045
Demure
Designer: P. Parsons
Height: 12 3/4", 32.5 cm
Colour: Grey-blue
and white
Issued: 1985 N. America,
1987 Worldwide
-1988
Series: Reflections
U.S.: $250.00
Can.: $295.00
Ster.: £145.00

HN 3046
Debut
Designer: P. Parsons
Height: 12 1/2", 32.0 cm
Colour: Pale blue ,
white and green
Issued: 1985 N. America,
1986 Worldwide
-1989
Series: Reflections
U.S. $250.00
Can.: $295.00
Ster.: £145.00

HN 3047
Sharon
Style One
Designer: P. Parsons
Height: 5 1/2", 14.0 cm
Colour: White and blue
Issued: 1984-1993
Varieties: HN 3455
U.S.: $175.00
Can.: $225.00
Ster.: £ 90.00

HN 3048
Tapestry Weaving
Designer: P. Parsons
Height: 7 1/2", 19.1 cm
Colour: Flowered pink dress
Issued: 1985 in a limited
edition of 750
Series: Gentle Arts
U.S.: $1,650.00
Can.: $1,650.00
Ster.: £ 750.00

HN 3049
Writing
Designer: P. Parsons
Height: 7 1/4", 18.4 cm
Colour: Flowered yellow
dress
Issued: 1986 in a limited
edition of 750
Series: Gentle Arts
U.S.: $1,500.00
Can.: $1,500.00
Ster.: £ 800.00

HN 3050
Susan
Style Two
Designer: P. Parsons
Height: 8 1/2", 21.6 cm
Colour: Pink and red
Issued: 1986-1995
Varieties: HN 2952
U.S.: $300.00
Can.: $375.00
Ster.: £120.00

HN 3051
Country Girl
Style One
Designer: A. Hughes
Height: 7 3/4", 19.7 cm
Colour: Blue and white
Issued: 1987-1992
Series: Reflections
U.S.: $150.00
Can.: $200.00
Ster.: £125.00

HN 3052
A Winter's Walk
Designer: A. Hughes
Height: 12 1/4", 31.1 cm
Colour: Pale blue and white
Issued: 1987 N. America,
1988-1995
Worldwide
Series: Reflections
U.S.: $300.00
Can.: $300.00
Ster.: £130.00

HN 3053
Martine
Designer: A. Hughes
Height: 13 1/2", 34.3 cm
Colour: Cream
Issued: 1984-1984
Varieties: Also called
             "Promenade" (Style
             Two) HN 3072
Series: Elegance
U.S.: $425.00
Can.: $500.00
Ster.:   £225.00

HN 3054
Dominique
Designer: A. Hughes
Height: 14", 35.6 cm
Colour: Cream
Issued: 1984-1984
Varieties: Also called
             "Paradise" HN 3074
Series: Elegance
U.S.: $ 425.00
Can.: $ 550.00
Ster.:   £ 175.00

Photograph
Not
Available

HN 3055
Claudine
Designer: A. Hughes
Height: 12", 30.5 cm
Colour: Cream
Issued: 1984-1984
Series: Elegance
U.S.: $ 425.00
Can.: $ 550.00
Ster.:   £ 175.00

HN 3056
Danielle
Style One
Designer: A. Hughes
Height: 12", 30.5 cm
Colour: Cream
Issued: 1984-1984
Series: Elegance
U.S.: $ 425.00
Can.: $ 550.00
Ster.:   £ 175.00

HN 3057
Sir Winston Churchill
Style One
Designer: A. Hughes
Height: 10 1/2", 26.7 cm
Colour: White
Issued: 1985 to the present
U.S.: $306.25
Can.: $425.00
Ster.:   £ 95.00

HN 3058
Andrea
Designer: A. Hughes
Height: 5 1/4", 13.3 cm
Colour: Blue and white
Issued: 1985-1995
Series: Vanity Fair Children
U.S.: $ 95.00
Can.: $130.00
Ster.:   £ 50.00

HN 3059
Sophistication
Designer: A. Hughes
Height: 11 1/2", 29.2 cm
Colour: Pale blue and white
Issued: 1987 N. America,
             1988 Worldwide
             -1990
Series: Reflections
U.S.: $250.00
Can.: $275.00
Ster.:   £165.00

NOTES ON PRICING

The prices on the secondary market for Royal Doulton Figures, particularly the early HN Numbers, have risen considerably over the years. As values rise, the condition and quality of figurines take on an increasingly important role.

The prices listed in the The Charlton Standard Catalogue of Royal Doulton Beswick Figurines are for figures in **mint condition.**

Naturally, repaired or restored figures, no matter how professionally done, will sell at a substantial discount.

On Condition: For figures to command catalogue prices they must be in mint condition. This simply means that a figure will not have paint chips, scratches, hairline cracks, crazing or blemishes. Any of which will remove the figure from the mint category.

On Quality: Some figures can be better moulded, assembled or painted than others. High quality figures will command catalogue prices. Low quality figures will not.

If the quality or condition of the figures is below the standard for mint, look for that figure to be priced at a percentage of the catalogue prices.

HN 3060
Wintertime
Style One
Designer: A. Hughes
Height: 8 1/2", 21.6 cm
Colour: Red and white
Issued: 1985-1985
Series: R.D.I.C.C. and
Four Seasons
(Series Four)
U.S.: $275.00
Can.: $400.00
Ster.: £225.00

HN 3061
Hope
Designer: S. Mitchell
Height: 8 1/4", 21.0 cm
Colour: Pale blue
Issued: 1984 in a limited
edition of 9500
Series: N.S.P.C.C. Charity
U.S.: $600.00
Can.: $750.00
Ster.: £295.00

Commissioned by Lawleys
*

HN 3066
Printemps (Spring)
Designer: R. Jefferson
Height: 11 1/4", 28.6 cm
Colour: White, brown and
green
Issued: 1987 in a limited
edition of 300
Series: Les Saisons
U.S.: $1,000.00
Can.: $1,250.00
Ster.: £ 675.00

HN 3067
Ete (Summer)
Designer: R. Jefferson
Height: 11 3/4", 29.8 cm
Colour: Yellow and green
Issued: 1989 in a limited
edition of 300
Series: Les Saisons
U.S.: $1,100.00
Can.: $1,250.00
Ster.: £ 675.00

HN 3068
Automne (Autumn)
Designer: R. Jefferson
Height: 11 1/2", 29.2 cm
Colour: Lavender and
cream
Issued: 1986 in a limited
edition of 300
Series: Les Saisons
U.S.: $1,100.00
Can.: $1,250.00
Ster.: £ 675.00

HN 3069
Hiver (Winter)
Designer: R. Jefferson
Height: 11 3/4", 29.8 cm
Colour: White
Issued: 1988 in a limited
edition of 300
Series: Les Saisons
U.S.: $1,000.00
Can.: $1,250.00
Ster.: £ 675.00

HN 3070
Cocktails
Designer: A. Hughes
Height: 11", 28.0 cm
Colour: Pale brown
Issued: 1985 N. America,
1987-1995
Worldwide
Series: Reflections
U.S.: $275.00
Can.: $300.00
Ster.: £120.00

HN 3071
Flirtation
Designer: A. Hughes
Height: 10", 25.4 cm
Colour: Pale blue
Issued: 1985 N. America,
1987-1995
Worldwide
Series: Reflections
U.S.: $275.00
Can.: $300.00
Ster.: £120.00

HN 3072
Promenade
Style Two
Designer: A. Hughes
Height: 13 1/4", 33.5 cm
Colour: Pale brown
Issued: 1985 N. America,
1987 Worldwide
-1995
Varieties: "Martine," HN 3053
Series: Reflections

U.S.: **$275.00**
Can.: **$325.00**
Ster.: **£135.00**

HN 3073
Strolling
Style One
Designer: A. Hughes
Height: 13 1/2", 34.3 cm
Colour: Pale green and
white
Issued: 1985 N. America,
1987 Worldwide
-1995
Series: Reflections

U.S.: **$325.00**
Can.: **$375.00**
Ster.: **£150.00**

HN 3074
Paradise
Designer: A. Hughes
Height: 14", 35.5 cm
Colour: Pale brown
Issued: 1985 N. America,
1987 Worldwide
-1992
Varieties: "Dominique,"
HN 3054
Series: Reflections

U.S.: **$250.00**
Can.: **$300.00**
Ster.: **£145.00**

HN 3075
Tango
Designer: A. Hughes
Height: 13", 33.0 cm
Colour: Pale blue and
cream
Issued: 1985 N. America,
1987 Worldwide
-1992
Series: Reflections

U.S.: **$250.00**
Can.: **$300.00**
Ster.: **£165.00**

HN 3076
Bolero
Designer: A. Hughes
Height: 13 1/2", 34.3 cm
Colour: Pale blue and pink
Issued: 1985 N. America,
1987 Worldwide
-1992
Series: Reflections

U.S.: **$250.00**
Can.: **$300.00**
Ster.: **£165.00**

HN 3077
Windflower
Style Four
Designer: A. Hughes
Height: 12 1/4", 31.1 cm
Colour: Pale blue
Issued: 1986 N. America,
1987 Worldwide
-1992
Series: Reflections

U.S.: **$225.00**
Can.: **$275.00**
Ster.: **£145.00**

HN 3078
Dancing Delight
Designer: A. Hughes
Height: 12 3/4", 32.0 cm
Colour: Pale brown
Issued: 1986 N. America,
1987 Worldwide
-1988
Series: Reflections

U.S.: **$250.00**
Can.: **$300.00**
Ster.: **£145.00**

HN 3079
Sleeping Beauty
Designer: A. Hughes
Height: 4 1/2", 11.4 cm
Colour: Green and white
Issued: 1987-1989

U.S.: **$300.00**
Can.: **$325.00**
Ster.: **£195.00**

HN 3080
Allure
Designer: E. J. Griffiths
Height: 12 1/2", 32.0 cm
Colour: Pale green
Issued: 1985 N. America,
1987 Worldwide
-1988
Varieties: "Monique," HN 2880
Series: Reflections
U.S.: **$250.00**
Can.: **$300.00**
Ster.: **£145.00**
*

HN 3082
Faith
Designer: E. J. Griffiths
Height: 8 1/2", 21.6 cm
Colour: Pink
Issued: 1986 in a limited
edition of 9,500
Series: N.S.P.C.C. Charity
U.S.: **$275.00**
Can.: **$375.00**
Ster.: **£195.00**

Commissioned by Lawleys

HN 3083
Sheikh
Designer: E.J. Griffiths
Height: 9 3/4", 24.7 cm
Colour: White
Issued: 1987-1989
Series: Reflections
U.S.: **$250.00**
Can.: **$275.00**
Ster.: **£165.00**

HN 3084
Harvestime
Designer: E.J. Griffiths
Height: 8", 20.3 cm
Colour: Blue and blue-grey
Issued: 1988-1990
Series: Reflections
U.S.: **$250.00**
Can.: **$275.00**
Ster.: **£150.00**

HN 3085
Summer Rose
Style One
Designer: E.J. Griffiths
Height: 8 1/2", 21.6 cm
Colour: Blue
Issued: 1987 N. America,
1988 Worldwide
-1992
Series: Reflections
U.S.: **$225.00**
Can.: **$275.00**
Ster.: **£145.00**

HN 3086
The Duchess of York
Designer: E.J. Griffiths
Height: 8 1/4", 21.0 cm
Colour: Cream
Issued: 1986 in a limited
edition of 1,500
U.S.: **$800.00**
Can.: **$800.00**
Ster.: **£450.00**

Commissioned by Lawleys

Photograph
Not
Available

HN 3087
Charity
Designer: E.J. Griffiths
Height: 8 1/2", 21.6 cm
Colour: Yellow and purple
Issued: 1987 in a limited
edition of 9,500
Series: N.S.P.C.C. Charity
U.S.: **$500.00**
Can.: **$650.00**
Ster.: **£225.00**

Commissioned by Lawleys

HN 3088
Kate Hannigan
Designer: E.J. Griffiths
Height: 9", 22.9 cm
Colour: Light brown
Issued: 1989 in a limited
edition of 9,500
U.S.: **$450.00**
Can.: **$550.00**
Ster.: **£300.00**

Commissioned by Lawleys

HN 3089
Grace Darling
Designer: E.J. Griffiths
Height: 9", 22.9 cm
Colour: Blue, yellow
             and rose
Issued: 1987 in a limited
             edition of 9500
U.S.:   **$375.00**
Can.:   **$450.00**
Ster.:   **£275.00**

Commissioned by Lawleys

HN 3090
Charisma
Designer: P. Parsons
Height: 12 1/2", 31.7 cm
Colour: Pale blue, white
             and brown
Issued: 1986 N. America,
             1987 Worldwide
             -1990
Series: Reflections
U.S.:   **$250.00**
Can.:   **$275.00**
Ster.:   **£145.00**

HN 3091
Summer's Darling
Designer: P. Parsons
Height: 11 1/2", 29.0 cm
Colour: Pale blue
Issued: 1986 N. America,
             1987 Worldwide
             -1995
Series: Reflections
U.S.:   **$300.00**
Can.:   **$325.00**
Ster.:   **£145.00**

HN 3092
Cherry Blossom
Designer: P. Parsons
Height: 12 3/4", 32.0 cm
Colour: Pale green and
             pale brown
Issued: 1986 N. America,
             1987 Worldwide
             -1989
Series: Reflections
U.S.:   **$250.00**
Can.:   **$275.00**
Ster.:   **£145.00**

HN 3093
Morning Glory
Designer: P. Parsons
Height: 13", 33.0 cm
Colour: Green and blue
Issued: 1986 N. America,
             1987 Worldwide
             -1989
Series: Reflections
U.S.:   **$250.00**
Can.:   **$275.00**
Ster.:   **£145.00**

HN 3094
Sweet Perfume
Designer: P. Parsons
Colour: Pale blue and white
Height: 13", 33.0 cm
Issued: 1986 N. America,
             1987 Worldwide
             -1995
Series: Reflections
U.S.:   **$250.00**
Can.:   **$275.00**
Ster.:   **£125.00**

HN 3095
Happy Birthday
Style One
Designer: P. Parsons
Height: 8 1/2", 21.6 cm
Colour: Yellow and white
Issued: 1987-1994
Series: Special Occasions
U.S.:   **$275.00**
Can.:   **$350.00**
Ster.:   **£135.00**

HN 3096
Merry Christmas
Designer: P. Parsons
Height: 8 1/2", 21.6 cm
Colour: Green and white
Issued: 1987-1992
Series: Special Occasions
U.S.:   **$325.00**
Can.:   **$375.00**
Ster.:   **£165.00**

HN 3097
Happy Anniversary
Style One
Designer: P. Parsons
Height: 6 1/2", 16.5 cm
Colour: Purple and white
Issued: 1987-1993
Series: Special Occasions
U.S.: $250.00
Can.: $350.00
Ster.: £165.00

HN 3098
Dorothy
Designer: P. Parsons
Height: 7", 17.8 cm
Colour: Grey
Issued: 1987-1990
U.S.: $400.00
Can.: $475.00
Ster.: £225.00

HN 3099
Queen Elizabeth I
Designer: P. Parsons
Height: 9", 22.9 cm
Colour: Red and gold
Issued: 1986 U.K., 1987
Worldwide in a
limited edition
of 5000
Series: Queens of the
Realm
U.S.: $650.00
Can.: $725.00
Ster.: £295.00

HN 3100
Kathleen
Style Two
Designer: S. Keenan
Height: 6 1/2", 16.5 cm
Colour: Purple, cream
and pink
Issued: 1986-1986
Varieties: HN 2933
Series: M. Doulton Events
U.S.: $275.00
Can.: $375.00
Ster.: £195.00
*

HN 3105
The Love Letter
Style Two
Designer: R. Jefferson
Height: 12", 30.5 cm
Colour: Pale blue and
pale brown
Issued: 1986 N. America,
1987 Worldwide
-1988
Series: Reflections
U.S.: $250.00
Can.: $300.00
Ster.: £145.00

HN 3106
Secret Moment
Designer: R. Jefferson
Height: 12 1/4", 31.1 cm
Colour: Pale blue, green
flowers
Issued: 1986 N. America
1987 Worldwide
-1988
Series: Reflections
U.S.: $250.00
Can.: $300.00
Ster.: £145.00

HN 3107
Daybreak
Designer: R. Jefferson
Height: 11 3/4", 29.8 cm
Colour: White, pale green
borders with
yellow flowers
Issued: 1986 N. America,
1987 Worldwide
-1988
Series: Reflections
U.S.: $250.00
Can.: $300.00
Ster.: £145.00

HN 3108
Enchanting Evening
Designer: R. Jefferson
Height: 11 3/4", 29.8 cm
Colour: Pale pink
Issued: 1986 N. America,
1987 Worldwide
- 1992
Series: Reflections
U.S.: $250.00
Can.: $300.00
Ster.: £145.00

HN 3109
Pensive
Designer: R. Jefferson
Height: 13", 33.0 cm
Colour: White with yellow
flowers on skirt
Issued: 1986 N. America,
1987 Worldwide
-1988
Series: Reflections
U.S.: **$250.00**
Can.: **$300.00**
Ster.: **£145.00**

HN 3110
Enigma
Designer: R. Jefferson
Height: 12 3/4", 32.0 cm
Colour: Cream
Issued: 1986 N. America,
1987 Worldwide
-1995
Series: Reflections
U.S.: **$235.00**
Can.: **$300.00**
Ster.: **£145.00**

HN 3111
**Robin Hood and Maid
Marion**
Designer: R. Jefferson
Height: 12 3/4", 33.0 cm
Colour: Blue, green
and cream
Issued: 1994 in a limited
edition of 150
Series: Great Lovers
U.S.: **$5,250.00**
Can.: **$7,000.00**
Ster.: **£1,995.00**

HN 3112
Lancelot and Guinivere
Designer: R. Jefferson
Height: 12 3/4", 33.0 cm
Colour: Lilac, purple, cream,
green and yellow
Issued: 1996 in a limited
edition of 150
Series: Great Lovers
U.S.: **$5.250.00**
Can.: **$7,000.00**
Ster.: **£1,995.00** .

HN 3113
Romeo and Juliet
Designer: R. Jefferson
Height: 12", 30.5 cm
Colour: Lilac, purple, cream,
yellow and green
Issued: 1993 in a limited
edition of 150
Series: Great Lovers
U.S.: **$5,250.00**
Can.: **$7,000.00**
Ster.: **£1,995.00**

HN 3114
Antony and Cleopatra
Designer: R. Jefferson
Height: 11 3/4", 29.8 cm
Colour: Pale blue and cream
Issued: 1995 in a limited
edition of 150
Series: Great Lovers
U.S.: **$5,250.00**
Can.: **$7,000.00**
Ster.: **£1,995.00**

HN 3115
Idle Hours
Designer: A. Maslankowski
Length: 12 1/4", 31.1 cm
Colour: Blue-white and
pale green
Issued: 1986 N. America,
1987 Worldwide
-1988
Series: Reflections
U.S.: **$275.00**
Can.: **$325.00**
Ster.: **£165.00**

HN 3116
Park Parade
Designer: A. Maslankowski
Height: 11 3/4", 29.8 cm
Colour: Pale green
and pale blue
Issued: 1987 N. America,
1988 Worldwide
-1994
Series: Reflections
U.S.: **$300.00**
Can.: **$350.00**
Ster.: **£150.00**

HN 3117
Indian Maiden
Designer: A. Maslankowski
Height: 12", 30.5 cm
Colour: Pale tan and
pale blue
Issued: 1987-1990
Series: Reflections
U.S.: **$300.00**
Can.: **$300.00**
Ster.: **£145.00**

HN 3118
Lorraine
Designer: A. Maslankowski
Height: 7 3/4", 19.7 cm
Colour: Blue
Issued: 1988-1995
U.S.: **$300.00**
Can.: **$350.00**
Ster.: **£145.00**

HN 3119
Partners
Designer: A. Maslankowski
Height: 6 3/4", 17.2 cm
Colour: Black, blue
and grey
Issued: 1990-1992
Series: Clowns
U.S.: **$325.00**
Can.: **$375.00**
Ster.: **£150.00**

HN 3120
Spring Walk
Designer: A. Maslankowski
Height: 13", 32.9 cm
Colour: Blue with
white poodle
Issued: 1990-1992
Series: Reflections
U.S.: **$300.00**
Can.: **$325.00**
Ster.: **£165.00**

HN 3121
Wizard
Style One
Designer: A. Maslankowski
Height: 10", 25.4 cm
Colour: Flambé
Issued: 1990-1995
Varieties: HN 2877
Series: Flambé
U.S.: **$275.00**
Can.: **$325.00**
Ster.: **£125.00**

HN 3122
My First Pet
Designer: A. Maslankowski
Height: 4 1/2", 11.4 cm
Colour: Blue and white
Issued: 1991 to the present
Series: Vanity Fair
Children
U.S.: **$106.25**
Can.: **$190.00**
Ster.: **£ 49.95**

HN 3123
Sit
Designer: A. Maslankowski
Height: 4 1/2", 11.4 cm
Colour: White and yellow
Issued: 1991 to the present
Varieties: HN 3430
Series: Vanity Fair
Children
U.S.: **$106.25**
Can.: **$190.00**
Ster.: **£ 49.95**

HN 3124
Thinking of You
Designer: A. Maslankowski
Height: 6 3/4", 17.1 cm
Colour: White
Issued: 1991 to the present
Varieties: HN 3490
Series: Sentiments
U.S.: **$ 81.25**
Can.: **$135.00**
Ster.: **£ 39.95**

HN 3125
Queen Victoria
Designer: P. Parsons
Height: 8", 20.3 cm
Colour: Pink and white
Issued: 1987 U.K., 1988
Worldwide in a
limited edition
of 5,000
Series: Queens of the
Realm
U.S.: **$1,500.00**
Can.: **$1,500.00**
Ster.: **£ 650.00**

HN 3126
Storytime
Style One
Designer: P. Parsons
Height: 6", 15.2 cm
Colour: Pale blue
Issued: 1987-1992
Series: Reflections
U.S.: **$225.00**
Can.: **$275.00**
Ster.: **£125.00**

HN 3127
Playmates
Designer: P. Parsons
Height: 8 1/2", 21.6 cm
Colour: Pale blue,
green and white
Issued: 1987-1992
Series: Reflections
U.S.: **$225.00**
Can.: **$275.00**
Ster.: **£125.00**

HN 3128
Tomorrow's Dreams
Style One
Designer: P. Parsons
Height: 6 1/2", 16.5 cm
Colour: White and green
Issued: 1987-1992
Series: Reflections
U.S.: **$250.00**
Can.: **$275.00**
Ster.: **£125.00**

HN 3129
Thankful
Designer: P. Parsons
Height: 8 1/2", 21.6 cm
Colour: White
Issued: 1987 to the present
Varieties: HN 3135
Series: Images
U.S.: **$131.25**
Can.: **$140.00**
Ster.: **£ 49.95**

HN 3130
Sisterly Love
Designer: P. Parsons
Height: 8 1/2", 21.6 cm
Colour: Pale blue and white
Issued: 1987-1995
Series: Reflections
U.S.: **$200.00**
Can.: **$250.00**
Ster.: **£125.00**

HN 3132
Good Pals
Designer: P. Parsons
Height: 6 1/4", 15.9 cm
Colour: Pale blue and white
Issued: 1987-1992
Series: Reflections
U.S.: **$200.00**
Can.: **$250.00**
Ster.: **£125.00**

HN 3133
Dreaming
Designer: P. Parsons
Height: 9", 22.9 cm
Colour: Pale pink
Issued: 1987-1995
Series: Reflections
U.S.: **$200.00**
Can.: **$225.00**
Ster.: **£ 95.00**

HN 3134
Ballet Class
Style One
Designer: P. Parsons
Height: 6", 15.2 cm
Colour: White and tan
Issued: 1987 N. America,
1988 Worldwide
-1992
Series: Reflections
U.S.: $250.00
Can.: $275.00
Ster.: £125.00

HN 3135
Thankful
Designer: P. Parsons
Height: 8 1/2", 21.6 cm
Colour: Black
Issued: 1987-1994
Varieties: HN 3129
Series: Images
U.S.: $100.00
Can.: $125.00
Ster.: £ 50.00

HN 3136
Laura
Style One
Designer: P. Parsons
Height: 7 1/4", 18.4 cm
Colour: Dark blue and white
Issued: 1988-1988
Varieties: HN 2960
Series: Michael Doulton
Events
U.S.: $250.00
Can.: $350.00
Ster.: £195.00

HN 3137
Summertime
Style One
Designer: P. Parsons
Height: 8", 20.3 cm
Colour: White and blue
Issued: 1987-1987
Series: R.D.I.C.C and
Four Seasons
(Series Four)
U.S.: $225.00
Can.: $350.00
Ster.: £175.00

HN 3138
Eastern Grace
Designer: P. Parsons
Height: 12", 30.5 cm
Colour: Cream
Issued: 1988-1989
Series: Reflections
Varieties: HN 3683
U.S.: $250.00
Can.: $275.00
Ster.: £165.00

HN 3139
Free As The Wind
Designer: P. Parsons
Height: 9 1/2". 24.1 cm
Colour: Pale blue
Issued: 1988 N. America,
1989 Worldwide
-1995
Series: Reflections
U.S.: $250.00
Can.: $325.00
Ster.: £150.00

HN 3140
Gaiety
Designer: P. Parsons
Height: 10 1/4". 26.0 cm
Colour: Pale green and
pale blue
Issued: 1988-1990
Series: Reflections
U.S.: $250.00
Can.: $300.00
Ster.: £165.00

HN 3141
Queen Anne
Designer: P. Parsons
Height: 9". 22.9 cm
Colour: Green, red and white
Issued: 1988 in a limited
edition of 5,000
Series: Queens of the
Realm
U.S.: $650.00
Can.: $600.00
Ster.: £275.00

Commissioned by Lawleys

HN 3142
Mary, Queen of Scots
Style Two
Designer: P. Parsons
Height: 9". 22.9 cm
Colour: Blue and purple
Issued: 1989 in a limited
edition of 5000
Series: Queens of the Realm
U.S.: $900.00
Can.: $975.00
Ster.: £450.00

Commissioned by Lawleys

HN 3143
Rosemary
Style Two
Designer: P. Parsons
Height: 7 1/2", 19.1 cm
Colour: White dress with
pink flowers
Issued: 1988-1991
U.S.: $250.00
Can.: $300.00
Ster.: £135.00

HN 3144
Florence Nightingale
Designer: P. Parsons
Height: 8 1/4", 21.0 cm
Colour: Red
Issued: 1988 in a limited
edition of 5,000
U.S.: $1,400.00
Can.: $1,250.00
Ster.: £ 550.00

Commissioned by Lawleys

HN 3145
Rose Arbour
Designer: D. Brindley
Height: 12", 30.5 cm
Colour: Pale blue and white
Issued: 1987 N. America,
1988 Worldwide
-1990
Series: Reflections
U.S.: $250.00
Can.: $275.00
Ster.: £145.00

*

HN 3155
Water Maiden
Designer: A. Hughes
Height: 12", 30.5 cm
Colour: Blue
Issued: 1987-1991
Series: Reflections
U.S.: $225.00
Can.: $275.00
Ster.: £145.00

HN 3156
Bathing Beauty
Designer: A. Hughes
Height: 9 3/4", 24.7 cm
Colour: Pale grey
Issued: 1987-1989
Series: Reflections
U.S.: $450.00
Can.: $500.00
Ster.: £225.00

HN 3157
Free Spirit
Style One
Designer: A. Hughes
Height: 10 1/2", 26.5 cm
Colour: White
Issued: 1987-1992
Varieties: HN 3159
Series: Images
U.S.: $150.00
Can.: $175.00
Ster.: £100.00

*

HN 3159
Free Spirit
Style One
Designer: A. Hughes
Height: 10 1/2", 26.5 cm
Colour: Black
Issued: 1987-1992
Varieties: HN 3157
Series: Images
U.S.: $150.00
Can.: $175.00
Ster.: £100.00

HN 3160
Shepherd
Style Five
Designer: A. Hughes
Height: 8 1/2", 21.6 cm
Colour: Grey-blue and black
Issued: 1988-1989
Series: Reflections
U.S.: **$275.00**
Can.: **$325.00**
Ster.: **£175.00**

HN 3161
The Gardener
Designer: A. Hughes
Height: 8 1/4", 21.0 cm
Colour: Blue and pale brown
Issued: 1988-1991
Series: Reflection
U.S.: **$275.00**
Can.: **$325.00**
Ster.: **£175.00**

HN 3162
Breezy Day
Designer: A. Hughes
Height: 8 1/2", 21.6 cm
Colour: Pale blue, pale brown and white
Issued: 1988-1990
Series: Reflections
U.S.: **$225.00**
Can.: **$300.00**
Ster.: **£145.00**

HN 3163
Country Maid
Designer: A. Hughes
Height: 8 1/4", 21.0 cm
Colour: Blue, pink, white and black
Issued: 1988-1991
U.S.: **$275.00**
Can.: **$300.00**
Ster.: **£165.00**

HN 3164
Farmer's Wife
Style Two
Designer: A. Hughes
Height: 8 3/4", 22.2 cm
Colour: Brown and blue
Issued: 1988-1991
U.S.: **$250.00**
Can.: **$300.00**
Ster.: **£165.00**

HN 3165
August
Style One
Designer: M. Davies
Height: 7 3/4", 19.7 cm
Colour: White and blue dress, poppies
Issued: 1987-1987
Series: Flower of the Month
U.S.: **$200.00**
Can.: **$275.00**
Ster.: **£120.00**

HN 3166
September
Style One
Designer: M. Davies
Height: 7 3/4", 19.7 cm
Colour: White and yellow dress, michaelmas daisies
Issued: 1987-1987
Series: Flower of the Month
U.S.: **$200.00**
Can.: **$275.00**
Ster.: **£120.00**

HN 3167
Hazel
Style Two
Designer: M. Davies
Height: 8", 20.3 cm
Colour: Flowered white dress
Issued: 1988-1991
U.S.: **$225.00**
Can.: **$300.00**
Ster.: **£120.00**

HN 3168
Jemma
Designer: M. Davies
Height: 7 1/4", 18.4 cm
Colour: Red and blue
Issued: 1988-1991
Series: Vanity Fair Ladies
U.S.: $250.00
Can.: $325.00
Ster.: £145.00

HN 3169
Jessica
Designer: M. Davies
Height: 7", 17.8 cm
Colour: White
Issued: 1988-1995
Varieties: HN 3497
Series: Vanity Fair Ladies
U.S.: $225.00
Can.: $250.00
Ster.: £115.00

HN 3170
Caroline
Style One
Designer: M. Davies
Height: 7 1/2", 19.1 cm
Colour: White dress with blue flowers
Issued: 1988-1992
Varieties: Also called "Winter Welcome," HN 3611
U.S.: $275.00
Can.: $325.00
Ster.: £125.00

HN 3171
Camille
Style Two
Designer: M. Davies
Height: 7 1/2", 19.1 cm
Colour: Orange-yellow, white and green
Issued: 1987
Varieties: "Adéle," HN 2480; "Margaret" (Style Two) HN 2397, 3496
U.S.: $275.00
Can.: $350.00
Ster.: £100.00

HN 3172
Christina
Style Two
Designer: M. Davies
Height: 7 1/2", 19.1 cm
Colour: Pink and white
Issued: 1987 in a limited edition of 1,000
Varieties: HN 2792
U.S.: $325.00
Can.: $375.00
Ster.: £175.00
Commissioned for Guild of China & Glass Retailers

HN 3173
Natalie
Designer: M. Davies
Height: 8", 20.3 cm
Colour: Yellow and white
Issued: 1988-1996
Varieties: HN 3498
Series: Vanity Fair Ladies
U.S.: $187.50
Can.: $300.00
Ster.: £ 95.00

HN 3174
Southern Belle
Style Two
Designer: M. Davies
Remodeller: R. Tabbenor
Height: 4", 10.1 cm
Colour: Red and yellow
Issued: 1988 to the present
Varieties: HN 3244
Series: Miniatures
U.S.: $125.00
Can.: $230.00
Ster.: £ 59.95

HN 3175
Sweet Violets
Designer: D.V. Tootle
Height: 10 1/4", 26.0 cm
Colour: Pale blue and white
Issued: 1988-1989
Series: Reflections
U.S.: $225.00
Can.: $275.00
Ster.: £125.00

HN 3176
Young Dreams
Designer: D.V. Tootle
Height: 6 1/4", 15.9 cm
Colour: Pink
Issued: 1988-1992
U.S.: $275.00
Can.: $350.00
Ster.: £175.00

HN 3177
Harriet
Style One
Designer: D.V. Tootle
Height: 7 1/4", 18.4 cm
Colour: Pink
Issued: 1988-1991
U.S.: $400.00
Can.: $475.00
Ster.: £175.00

HN 3178
Polly
Designer: D.V. Tootle
Height: 8", 20.3 cm
Colour: Green and lavender
Issued: 1988-1991
U.S.: $250.00
Can.: $325.00
Ster.: £175.00

HN 3179
Eliza
Style Two
Designer: D. V. Tootle
Height: 7 1/2", 19.1 cm
Colour: Red and lilac
Issued: 1988-1992
U.S.: $250.00
Can.: $350.00
Ster.: £165.00

HN 3180
Phyllis
Style Two
Designer: D.V. Tootle
Height: 7 1/4", 18.4 cm
Colour: Red, white and purple
Issued: 1988-1991
U.S.: $300.00
Can.: $330.00
Ster.: £145.00

HN 3181
Moondancer
Designer: D.V. Tootle
Height: 11 3/4", 29.8 cm
Colour: Blue, white and pale green
Issued: 1988-1990
Series: Reflections
U.S.: $325.00
Can.: $375.00
Ster.: £165.00

HN 3182
Stargazer
Designer: D.V. Tootle
Height: 10 1/2", 26.7 cm
Colour: Blue and pale blue
Issued: 1988-1990
Series: Reflections
U.S.: $300.00
Can.: $375.00
Ster.: £165.00

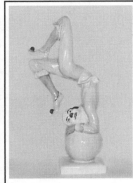

HN 3183
Tumbler
Designer: D.V. Tootle
Height: 9", 22.9 cm
Colour: Pink and yellow
Issued: 1989-1991
Varieties: Also called Tumbling; HN 3283, 3289
Series: Reflections, Clowns
U.S.: $275.00
Can.: $350.00
Ster.: £145.00

HN 3184
Joy
Designer:	D.V. Tootle
Height:	6 3/4", 17.2 cm
Colour:	Blue and pink
Issued:	1988-1990
Series:	Reflections
U.S.:	**$275.00**
Can.:	**$350.00**
Ster.:	**£145.00**

HN 3185
Traveller's Tale
Designer:	E.J. Griffiths
Height:	9 1/4", 23.5 cm
Colour:	Pale blue and pale green
Issued:	1988-1989
Series:	Reflections
U.S.:	**$275.00**
Can.:	**$325.00**
Ster.:	**£145.00**

HN 3186
Entranced
Designer:	E.J. Griffiths
Height:	7 1/4", 18.4 cm
Colour:	Green, white and tan
Issued:	1988-1989
Series:	Reflections
U.S.:	**$200.00**
Can.:	**$225.00**
Ster.:	**£145.00**

HN 3187
Balloons
Designer:	E.J. Griffiths
Height:	9 1/4", 23.5 cm
Colour:	Pale blue
Issued:	1988-in a limited edition of 1,000
Series:	Reflections
U.S.:	**$500.00**
Can.:	**$625.00**
Ster.:	**£275.00**

Commissioned by Home Shopping Network

HN 3188
Debutante
Style Two
Designer:	E.J. Griffiths
Height:	12", 30.5 cm
Colour:	Grey-pink
Issued:	1988 in a limited edition of 1,000
Series:	Reflections
U.S.:	**$325.00**
Can.:	**$400.00**
Ster.:	**£225.00**

Commissioned by Home Shopping

HN 3189
HM Queen Elizabeth, The Queen Mother
Style Two
Designer:	E.J. Griffiths
Height:	8", 20.3 cm
Colour:	Lavender, blue and pink
Issued:	1990 in a limited edition of 2,500
U.S.:	**$750.00**
Can:	**$750.00**
Ster.:	**£325.00**

HN 3190
Old Ben
Designer:	M. Nicholl
Height:	8 1/2", 21.6 cm
Colour:	Green, brown and blue
Issued:	1990 in a limited editon of 1,500
U.S.:	**$200.00**
Can.:	**$250.00**
Ster.:	**£120.00**

Commissioned by the News-vendors Benevelent Society

HN 3191
Brothers
Designer:	E.J. Griffiths
Height:	8 1/4", 21.0 cm
Colour:	White
Issued:	1991 to the present
Series:	Images
U.S.:	**$106.25**
Can.:	**$210.00**
Ster.:	**£ 49.95**

HN 3192
Mantilla
Designer: E.J. Griffiths
Height: 11 1/2", 29.2 cm
Colour: Red, black and white
Issued: 1992 in a limited
edition of 1992
Varieties: HN 2712

U.S.:	**$550.00**
Can.:	**$650.00**
Ster.:	**£350.00**

To commemorate Expo '92,
Seville, Spain
*

HN 3195
The Farmer
Designer: A. Hughes
Height: 9", 22.9 cm
Colour: Brown and white
Issued: 1988-1991

U.S.:	**$250.00**
Can.:	**$300.00**
Ster.:	**£165.00**

HN 3196
The Joker
Style One
Designer: A. Hughes
Height: 9 1/4", 23.5 cm
Colour: White and blue
Issued: 1988-1990
Series: Reflections, Clowns
Varieties: Also called "Tip-Toe"
HN 3293

U.S.:	**$275.00**
Can.:	**$300.00**
Ster.:	**£145.00**

Photograph
Not
Available

HN 3197
Ballerina
Style Two
Designer: A. Hughes
Height: 14", 35.5 cm
Colour: White and beige
Issued: 1988 in a limited
edition of 1,000
Series: Reflections

U.S.:	**$325.00**
Can.:	**$400.00**
Ster.:	**£225.00**

Commissioned by Home
Shopping Network

HN 3198
Vanessa
Style Two
Designer: A. Hughes
Height: 8 1/2", 21.6 cm
Colour: Green and black
Issued: 1989-1990

U.S.:	**$275.00**
Can.:	**$300.00**
Ster.:	**£175.00**

HN 3199
Maxine
Style One
Designer: A. Hughes
Height: 8 1/2", 21.6 cm
Colour: Pink and purple
Issued: 1989-1990

U.S.:	**$275.00**
Can.:	**$300.00**
Ster.:	**£175.00**

HN 3200
Gloria
Style Two
Designer: A. Hughes
Height: 8 3/4", 22.2 cm
Colour: Pink
Issued: 1989-1990

U.S.:	**$275.00**
Can.:	**$300.00**
Ster.:	**£165.00**

HN 3201
Liberty
Designer: A. Hughes
Height: 8 1/4", 21.0 cm
Colour: White, blue
and red
Issued: 1989-1990

U.S.:	**$275.00**
Can.:	**$300.00**
Ster.:	**£165.00**

324

HN 3202
The Boy Evacuee
Designer: A. Hughes
Height: 8 1/2", 21.6 cm
Colour: Green and blue
Issued: 1989 in a limited
edition of 9,500
Series: Children of the Blitz

U.S.:	$375.00
Can.:	$500.00
Ster.:	£325.00

Commissioned by Lawleys

HN 3203
The Girl Evacuee
Designer: A. Hughes
Height: 8", 20.3 cm
Colour: Red, blue and brown
Issued: 1989 in a limited
edition of 9,500
Series: Children of the Blitz

U.S.:	$375.00
Can.:	$500.00
Ster.:	£375.00

Commissioned by Lawleys

HN 3204
Emily
Style Two
Designer: A. Hughes
Height: 8 1/4", 21.0 cm
Colour: White and blue
Issued: 1989-1994
Series: Vanity Fair Ladies

U.S.:	$225.00
Can.:	$275.00
Ster.:	£135.00

HN 3205
Veronica
Style Four
Designer: A. Hughes
Height: 8", 20.3 cm
Colour: White and pink
Issued: 1989-1992
Series: Vanity Fair Ladies

U.S.:	$250.00
Can.:	$275.00
Ster.:	£140.00

HN 3206
Teresa
Style Two
Designer: A. Hughes
Height: 7 3/4", 19.7 cm
Colour: White with flowers
Issued: 1989-1992

U.S.:	$250.00
Can.:	$300.00
Ster.:	£125.00

HN 3207
Louise
Style Two
Designer: A. Hughes
Height: 7 1/2", 19.1 cm
Colour: Red
Issued: 1990-1996

U.S.:	$306.25
Can.:	$490.00
Ster.:	£135.00

HN 3208
Emma
Style Two
Designer: A. Hughes
Height: 4 1/4", 10.8 cm
Colour: Red
Issued: 1990 to the present
Series: Miniatures

U.S.:	$131.25
Can.:	$230.00
Ster.:	£ 59.95

NOTES ON PRICING

The prices on the secondary market for Royal Doulton Figures, particularly the early HN Numbers, have risen considerably over the years. As values rise, the condition and quality of these figurines take on an increasingly important role.

The prices listed in The Charlton Standard Catalogue of Royal Doulton Beswick Figurines are for figures in mint condition.

Naturally, repaired or restored figures, no matter how professionally done, will sell at a substantial discount.

On Condition: For figures to command catalogue prices they must be in mint condition. This simply means that a figure will not have paint chips, scratches, hairline cracks, crazing or blemishes. Any of which will remove from the mint category figure.

On Quality: Some figures can be better moulded, assembled or painted than others. High quality figures will command catalogue prices. Low quality figures will not.

If the quality or condition of the figures is below the standard for mint, look for that figure to be priced at a percentage of the catalogue prices.

HN 3209
Claire
Style One
Designer: A. Hughes
Height: 8 1/2", 21.6 cm
Colour: Pink and with dress
with flowers
Issued: 1990-1992

U.S.:	**$250.00**
Can.:	**$300.00**
Ster.:	**£125.00**

HN 3210
Christening Day
Designer: P.A. Northcroft
Height: 8 1/2", 21.6 cm
Colour: White, baby's
shawl blue
Issued: 1988-1990
Varieties: HN 3211
Series: Special Occasions

U.S.:	**$225.00**
Can.:	**$300.00**
Ster.:	**£145.00**

HN 3211
Christening Day
Designer: P.A. Northcroft
Height: 8 1/2", 21.6 cm
Colour: White, baby's
shawl pink
Issued: 1988-1990
Varieties: HN 3210
Series: Special Occasions

U.S.:	**$225.00**
Can.:	**$300.00**
Ster.:	**£145.00**

HN 3212
Christmas Morn
Style Two
Designer: M. Davies
Remodeller: R. Tabbenor
Height: 4", 10.1 cm
Colour: Red and white
Issued: 1988 to the present
Varieties: HN 3245
Series: Miniatures

U.S.:	**$131.25**
Can.:	**$230.00**
Ster.:	**£ 49.95**

HN 3213
Kirsty
Style Two
Designer: M. Davies
Remodeller: P. Gee
Height: 3 3/4", 9.5 cm
Colour: Red
Issued: 1988 to the present
Varieties: HN 3246, 3480,
3743
Series: Miniatures

U.S.:	**$131.25**
Can.:	**$230.00**
Ster.:	**£ 49.95**

HN 3214
Elaine
Style Two
Designer: M. Davies
Remodeller: P. Gee
Height: 4", 10.1 cm
Colour: Blue
Issued: 1988 to the present
Varieties: HN 3247
Series: Miniatures

U.S.:	**$131.25**
Can.:	**$230.00**
Ster.:	**£ 59.95**

HN 3215
Ninette
Style Two
Designer: M. Davies
Remodeller: P. Gee
Height: 3 1/2", 8.9 cm
Colour: Cream and
lavender
Issued: 1988 to the present
Varieties: HN 3248
Series: Miniatures

U.S.:	**$131.25**
Can.:	**$185.00**
Ster.:	**£ 49.95**

HN 3216
Fair Lady
Style Two
Designer: M. Davies
Remodeller: P. Gee
Height: 3 3/4", 9.5 cm
Colour: Lemon and blue
Issued: 1988-1995
Varieties: HN 3336
Series: Miniatures

U.S.:	**$100.00**
Can.:	**$150.00**
Ster.:	**£ 65.00**

HN 3217
Joan
Style Two
Designer: M. Davies
Height: 8", 20.3 cm
Colour: Yellow and green
Issued: 1988 in a limited
edition of 2,000
Varieties: "Adrienne," HN 2152,
2304; "Fiona"
HN 3748

U.S.:	**$400.00**
Can.:	**$500.00**
Ster.:	**£195.00**

HN 3218
Sunday Best
Style Two
Designer: M. Davies
Remodeller: P. Gee
Height: 3 3/4", 9.5 cm
Colour: Green and blue
Issued: 1988-1993
Varieties: HN 3312
Series: Miniatures

U.S.:	**$145.00**
Can.:	**$175.00**
Ster.:	**£ 75.00**

HN 3219
Sara
Style Two
Designer: M. Davies
Remodeller: P. Gee
Height: 3 3/4", 9.5 cm
Colour: Pink and green
Issued: 1988 to the present
Varieties: HN 3249
Series: Miniatures

U.S.:	**$131.25**
Can.:	**$185.00**
Ster.:	**£ 49.95**

HN 3220
Fragrance
Style Two
Designer: M. Davies
Remodeller: P. Gee
Height: 3 3/4", 9.5 cm
Colour: Gold
Issued: 1988-1992
Varieties: HN 3250
Series: Miniatures

U.S.:	**$150.00**
Can.:	**$175.00**
Ster.:	**£ 75.00**

HN 3221
Country Rose
Designer: M. Davies
Height: 8 1/2", 21.6 cm
Colour: White dress,
red flowers
Issued: 1989 to the present

U.S.:	**$243.75**
Can.:	**$370.00**
Ster.:	**£109.00**

HN 3222
Kelly
Designer: M. Davies
Height: 7 1/2", 19.1 cm
Colour: White and blue
Issued: 1989
Varieties: HN 2478

U.S.:	**$175.00**
Can.:	**$225.00**
Ster.:	**$ 95.00**

Commissioned for Kay's Mail
Order Catalogue

HN 3223
Pamela
Style Two
Designer: M. Davies
Height: 7", 17.8 cm
Colour: Blue and white
Issued: 1989-1989
Varieties: HN 2479
Series: Michael Doulton
Events

U.S.:	**$225.00**
Can.:	**$295.00**
Ster.:	**£165.00**
*	

HN 3228
Devotion
Designer: P. Parsons
Height: 9 1/2", 24.1 cm
Colour: Pale green
Issued: 1989-1995
Series: Reflections

U.S.:	**$300.00**
Can.:	**$350.00**
Ster.:	**£150.00**

HN 3229
The Geisha
Style Three
Designer: P. Parsons
Height: 9 1/2", 24.1 cm
Colour: Flambé
Issued: 1989-1989
Series: R.D.I.C.C. and
Flambé

U.S.:	$375.00
Can.:	$450.00
Ster.:	£225.00

HN 3230
HM Queen Elizabeth the
Queen Mother as the
Duchess of York
Designer: P. Parsons
Height: 9", 22.9 cm
Colour: Pale blue and pink
Issued: 1989 in a limited
edition of 9,500

U.S.:	$700.00
Can.:	$750.00
Ster.:	£375.00

Commissioned by Lawleys

HN 3231
Autumntime
Style One
Designer: P. Parsons
Height: 8", 20.3 cm
Colour: Golden brown
Issued: 1989-1989
Series: R.D.I.C.C. Four
Seasons (Series
Four)

U.S.:	$275.00
Can.:	$375.00
Ster.:	£175.00

HN 3232
Anne Bolelyn
Designer: P. Parsons
Height: 8", 20.3 cm
Colour: Red and grey
Issued: 1990 in a limited
edition of 9,500
Series: Six Wives of
Henry VIII

U.S.:	N/I
Can.:	N/I
Ster.:	£195.00

Commissioned by Lawleys

HN 3233
Catherine of Aragon
Designer: P. Parsons
Height: 6 1/2", 16.5 cm
Colour: Green, blue and white
Issued: 1990 in a limited
edition of 9,500
Series: Six Wives of
Henry VIII

U.S.:	N/I
Can.:	N/I
Ster.:	£195.00

Commissioned by Lawleys

HN 3234
Paula
Designer: P. Parsons
Height: 7", 17.8 cm
Colour: White and blue
Issued: 1990-1996
Varieties: HN 2906
Series: Vanity Fair Ladies

U.S.:	$187.50
Can.:	$300.00
Ster.:	£ 95.00

HN 3235
Mother and Child
Designer: P. Parsons
Height: 7 1/2", 19.1 cm
Colour: White and blue
Issued: 1991-1993
Varieties: HN 3348, 3353

U.S.:	$275.00
Can.:	$325.00
Ster.:	£165.00

HN 3236
Falstaff
Style Three
Designer: C.J. Noke
Remodeller: R. Tabbenor
Height: 3 3/4", 9.5 cm
Colour: Brown, yellow
and lavender
Issued: 1989-1990
Series: Miniatures

U.S.:	$175.00
Can.:	$200.00
Ster.:	£ 95.00
*

HN 3244
Southern Belle
Designer:	M. Davies
Remodeller:	R. Tabbenor
Height:	4", 10.1 cm
Colour:	Turquoise with 22 kt gold trim
Issued:	1989 to the present
Varieties:	HN 3174
Series:	M. Doulton Signature Collection

U.S.:	**$150.00**
Can.:	**$200.00**
Ster.:	**£ 90.00**

HN 3245
Christmas Morn - Style Two
Designer:	M. Davies
Remodeller:	R. Tabbenor
Height:	3 1/2", 8.9 cm
Colour:	Green, blue, white, with 22 kt gold trim
Issued:	1991 to the present
Varieties:	HN 3212
Series:	M. Doulton Signature Collection

U.S.:	**$150.00**
Can.:	**$200.00**
Ster.:	**£ 90.00**

HN 3246
Kirsty
Style Two
Designer:	M. Davies
Remodeller:	Peter Gee
Height:	3 3/4", 9.5 cm
Colour:	Purple, 22 kt gold trim
Issued:	1989 to the present
Varieties:	HN 3213, 3480, 3743
Series:	M. Doulton Signature Collection

U.S.:	**$150.00**
Can.:	**$200.00**
Ster.:	**£ 90.00**

HN 3247
Elaine
Style Two
Designer:	M. Davies
Remodeller:	P. Gee
Height:	4", 10.1 cm
Colour:	Blue, 22kt gold trim
Issued:	1989 to the present
Varieties:	HN 3214
Series:	M. Doulton Signature Collection

U.S.:	**$150.00**
Can.:	**$200.00**
Ster.:	**£ 90.00**

HN 3248
Ninette - Style Two
Designer:	M. Davies
Remodeller:	P. Gee
Height:	3 1/2", 8.9 cm
Colour:	Red and green, 22 kt gold trim
Issued:	1989 to the present
Varieties:	HN 3215
Series:	M. Doulton Signature Collection

U.S.:	**$150.00**
Can.:	**$200.00**
Ster.:	**£ 90.00**

HN 3249
Sara - Style Two
Designer:	M. Davies
Remodeller:	P. Gee
Height:	3 3/4", 9.5 cm
Colour:	Blue and pink, 22 kt gold trim
Issued:	1989 to the present
Varieties:	HN 3219
Series:	M. Doulton Signature Collection

U.S.:	**$150.00**
Can.:	**$200.00**
Ster.:	**£ 90.00**

HN 3250
Fragrance - Style Two
Designer:	M. Davies
Remodeller:	P. Gee
Height:	3 3/4", 9.5 cm
Colour:	Red, 22 kt gold trim
Issued:	1989-1992
Varieties:	HN 3220
Series:	M. Doulton Signature Collection

U.S.:	**$150.00**
Can.:	**$200.00**
Ster.:	**£ 90.00**

Commissioned by Lawleys

HN 3251
May
Style One
Designer:	D.V. Tootle
Height:	8", 20.3 cm
Colour:	Blue, red and pink
Issued:	1989 in a limited edition of 2,000
Varieties:	HN 2746

U.S.:	**$275.00**
Can.:	**$350.00**
Ster.:	**£175.00**

Exclusively for U.S.A.
Direct Mail Service

HN 3252
Fiona
Style Three
Designer: D.V. Tootle
Height: 7", 17.8 cm
Colour: Red
Issued: 1989-1992

U.S.: $350.00
Can.: $450.00
Ster.: £175.00

HN 3253
Cheryl
Designer: D.V. Tootle
Height: 7 1/2", 19.1 cm
Colour: Red and white
Issued: 1989-1994

U.S.: $350.00
Can.: $400.00
Ster.: £175.00

HN 3254
Happy Anniversary
Style Two
Designer: D.V. Tootle
Height: 12", 30.5 cm
Colour: White
Issued: 1989 to the present
Series: Images

U.S.: $200.00
Can.: $325.00
Ster.: £ 99.95

HN 3255
Madaleine
Designer: D.V. Tootle
Height: 7 1/2", 19.1 cm
Colour: Blue, pink
           and cream
Issued: 1989-1992

U.S.: $275.00
Can.: $325.00
Ster.: £150.00

HN 3256
Queen Victoria and
Prince Albert
Designer: D.V. Tootle
Height: 9 1/4", 20.3 cm
Colour: Yellow-pink,
           cream and red
Issued: 1990 in a limited
           edition of 2,500

U.S.: $1,000.00
Can.: $1,000.00
Ster.: £ 395.00

Commissioned by Lawleys

HN 3257
Sophie
Style Two
Designer: D.V. Tootle
Height: 8", 20.3 cm
Colour: Blue and red
Issued: 1990-1992

U.S.: $350.00
Can.: $450.00
Ster.: £175.00

HN 3258
Dawn
Style Two
Designer: D.V. Tootle
Height: 8", 20.3 cm
Colour: Purple, red
           and white
Issued: 1990-1992

U.S.: $250.00
Can.: $325.00
Ster.: £140.00

HN 3259
Ann
Style Two
Designer: D.V. Tootle
Height: 8", 20.3 cm
Colour: Pink, green
           and blue
Issued: 1990 to the present
Varieties: Also called "Lauren"
           HN 3290

U.S.: $406.25
Can.: $460.00
Ster.: £149.00

HN 3260
Jane
Style Three
Designer: D.V. Tootles
Height: 7 3/4", 19.7 cm
Colour: Green, blue
 and yellow
Issued: 1990-1993
U.S.: $275.00
Can.: $350.00
Ster.: £150.00

HN 3261
The Town Crier
Style Two
Designer: M. Davies
Remodeller: R. Tabbenor
Height: 4", 10.1 cm
Colour: Purple, green
 and black
Issued: 1989-1991
Series: Miniatures
U.S.: $185.00
Can.: $225.00
Ster.: £ 95.00

HN 3262
Good King Wenceslas
Style Two
Designer: M. Davies
Remodeller: R. Tabbenor
Height: 4", 10.1 cm
Colour: Black and purple
Issued: 1989-1992
Series: Miniatures
U.S.: $185.00
Can.: $225.00
Ster.: £ 95.00

HN 3263
Beatrice
Designer: M. Davies
Height: 7", 17.8 cm
Colour: Blue flowered dress
Issued: 1989 to the present
Varieties: HN 3631, Summer
 Serenade HN 3610,
 Kathryn HN 3413, and
 Wildflower of the Month
U.S.: $243.75
Can.: $370.00
Ster.: £109.00

HN 3264
Alison
Designer: M. Davies
Height: 7 1/2", 19.1 cm
Colour: White and pastel pink
Issued: 1989-1993
Varieties: HN 2336
U.S.: $200.00
Can.: $325.00
Ster.: £125.00

HN 3265
Lisa
Designer: M. Davies
Height: 7 1/2", 19.1 cm
Colour: White and rose
Issued: 1989-1995
Varieties: HN 2310, 2394
U.S.: $175.00
Can.: $225.00
Ster.: £100.00

HN 3266
Diana
Style Two
Designer: M. Davies
Height: 8", 20.3 cm
Colour: Pink, blue and white
Issued: 1990-1990
Varieties: HN 2468
Series: Michael Doulton
 Events
U.S.: $225.00
Can.: $300.00
Ster.: £165.00

HN 3267
Salome
Style Two
Designer: M. Davies
Height: 9 1/2", 24.1cm
Colour: Red, blue, lavender
 and green
Issued: 1990 in a limited
 edition of 1,000
U.S.: $1,350.00
Can.: $1,350.00
Ster.: £ 600.00

HN 3268
Buttercup
Style Two
Designer: M. Davies
Remodeller: R. Tabbenor
Height: 4", 10.1 cm
Colour: Green
Issued: 1990 to the present
Series: Miniatures

U.S.: $131.25
Can.: $230.00
Ster.: £ 49.95

HN 3269
Christine
Style Three
Designer: M. Davies
Remodeller: P. Gee
Height: 3 3/4", 9.5 cm
Colour: Orange and pink
Issued: 1990-1994
Varieties: HN 3337
Series: Miniatures

U.S.: $150.00
Can.: $175.00
Ster.: £ 65.00

HN 3270
Karen
Style Three
Designer: M. Davies
Remodeller: R. Tabbenor
Height: 4", 10.1 cm
Colour: Red
Issued: 1990-1995
Varieties: HN 3338
Series: Miniatures

U.S.: $150.00
Can.: $175.00
Ster.: £ 65.00

HN 3271
Guy Fawkes
Style Two
Designer: C.J. Nokes
Remodeller: P. Gee
Height: 4", 10.1 cm
Colour: Red and black
Issued: 1989-1991
Series: Miniatures

U.S.: $185.00
Can.: $200.00
Ster.: £ 95.00

HN 3272
Dick Turpin
Style One
Designer: G. Tongue
Height: 12", 30.5 cm
Colour: Brown and black
Issued: 1989 in a limited
edition of 5,000

U.S.: $750.00
Can.: $850.00
Ster.: £395.00

Commissioned by Lawleys

HN 3273
Annabel
Designer: R. Tabbenor
Height: 6", 15.2 cm
Colour: White and blue
Issued: 1989-1992

U.S.: $325.00
Can.: $425.00
Ster.: £175.00

HN 3274
Over The Threshold
Designer: R. Tabbenor
Height: 12", 30.5 cm
Colour: White
Issued: 1989 to the present
Series: Images

U.S.: $200.00
Can.: $355.00
Ster.: £149.00

HN 3275
Will He, Won't He
Designer: R. Tabbenor
Height: 9", 22.9 cm
Colour: Green
Issued: 1990-1994
Series: Clowns

U.S.: $300.00
Can.: $350.00
Ster.: £150.00

HN 3276
Teeing Off
Designer: R. Tabbenor
Height: 9", 22.9 cm
Colour: Yellow and green
Issued: 1990 to the present
U.S.: $212.50
Can.: $375.00
Ster.: £135.00

HN 3277
The Carpet Seller
(Seated)
Style Four
Designer: R. Tabbenor
Height: 7 1/2", 19.0 cm
Colour: Red
Issued: 1990-1995
Series: Flambé
U.S.: $275.00
Can.: $325.00
Ster.: £135.00

HN 3278
Lamp Seller
Designer: R. Tabbenor
Height: 9", 22.9 cm
Colour: Red
Issued: 1990-1995
Series: Flambé
U.S.: $450.00
Can.: $450.00
Ster.: £195.00

HN 3279
Winning Put
Designer: R. Tabbenor
Height: 8", 20.3 cm
Colour: Blue and yellow
Issued: 1991-1995
U.S.: $225.00
Can.: $275.00
Ster.: £125.00

HN 3280
Bridesmaid
Style Five
Designer: R. Tabbenor
Height: 8 1/2", 21.6 cm
Colour: White
Issued: 1991 to the present
Series: Images
U.S.: $ 93.75
Can.: $160.00
Ster.: £ 39.95

HN 3281
Bride and Groom
Designer: R. Tabbenor
Height: 6 1/4", 15.9 cm
Colour: White
Issued: 1991 to the present
Series: Images
U.S.: $ 93.75
Can.: $135.00
Ster.: £ 39.95

HN 3282
First Steps
Style Two
Designer: R. Tabbenor
Height: 9 1/2", 24.0 cm
Colour: White
Issued: 1991 to the present
Series: Images
U.S.: $200.00
Can.: $210.00
Ster.: £ 59.95

HN 3283
Tumbling
Designer: D. V. Tootle
Height: 8 3/4", 22.2 cm
Colour: White, yellow,
blue and green
Issued: 1990-1994
Varieties: 3289; Also called
"Tumbler," HN 3183
Series: Clowns
U.S.: $300.00
Can.: $375.00
Ster.: £160.00

PASCOE & COMPANY

FINE COLLECTABLES

Cavalier
Prototype

Robin Hood
Prototype

Shepard HN751
Prototype
Designer L. Harradine

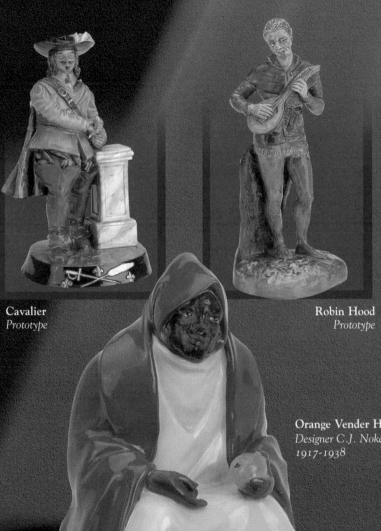

Orange Vender HN72
Designer C.J. Noke
1917-1938

1971-1996
25TH
ANNIVERSARY
PASCOE & COMPANY
FINE COLLECTABLES

101 Almeria Avenue
Coral Gables, FL 33134, USA
(800) 872-0195
(305) 445-3229

IN U.S.A. AND CANADA
Call Toll Free (800) 872-0195 Fax: (305) 445-3305

PASCOE & COMPANY
FINE COLLECTABLES

Butterfly HN720
Designer L. Harradine
1925-1940

Fairy HN1532
Designer L. Harradine
1932-1938

Dolly Varden HN1515
Designer L. Harradine
1932-1949

Siesta HN72
Designer L. Harradine
1928-1940

THE

ROYAL DOULTON
SPECIALIST

*The #1 Expert
in Rare and
Discontinued Pieces*

WE BUY
AND SELL

IN U.S.A. AND CANADA
Call Toll Free (800) 872-0195 Fax: (305) 445-3305

HN 3284
The Bride
Style Four
Designer: D. V. Tootle
Height: 8 1/4", 21.0 cm
Colour: White
Issued: 1990 to the present
Varieties: HN 3285

U.S.:	**$268.75**
Can.:	**$375.00**
Ster.:	**£135.00**

HN 3285
The Bride
Style Four
Designer: D. V. Tootle
Height: 8 1/4", 21.0 cm
Colour: Ivory
Issued: 1990 to the present
Varieties: HN 3284

U.S.:	**$268.75**
Can.:	**$375.00**
Ster.:	**£135.00**

HN 3286
Alexandra
Style Two
Designer: D. V. Tootle
Height: 7 3/4", 19.7 cm
Colour: Yellow
Issued: 1990 to the present
Varieties: HN 3292

U.S.:	**$268.75**
Can.:	**$445.00**
Ster.:	**£139.00**

HN 3287
Harlequin
Style Two
Designer: D. V. Tootle
Height: 12 1/2", 31.7 cm
Colour: Black, gold and yellow
Issued: 1993-1993
Varieties: HN 2737

U.S.:	**$1,350.00**
Can.:	**$1,750.00**
Ster.:	**£ 950.00**

Commissioned by Harrod's

HN 3288
Columbine
Style Three
Designer: D. V. Tootle
Height: 12 1/2", 31.7 cm
Colour: Red, yellow, black
and gold
Issued: 1993-1993
Varieties: HN 2738

U.S.:	**$1,350.00**
Can.:	**$1,750.00**
Ster.:	**£ 950.00**

Commissioned by Harrod's

HN 3289
Tumbling
Designer: D.V. Tootle
Height: 8 3/4", 22.2 cm
Colour: Pink and blue
Issued: 1991 in a limited
edition of 2,500
Varieties: HN 3283; "Tumbler,"
HN 3183
Series: Clowns

U.S.:	**$275.00**
Can.:	**$375.00**
Ster.:	**£200.00**

National Playing Fields Ass.

HN 3290
Lauren
Designer: D.V. Tootle
Height: 8", 20.3 cm
Colour: Mauve and yellow
Issued: 1992-1992
Varieties: Also called "Ann"
(Style One), HN 3259

U.S.:	**$275.00**
Can.:	**$350.00**
Ster.:	**£165.00**

Commissioned by Great
Universal Stores

HN 3291
Tracy
Designer: D.V. Toole
Height: 7 1/2", 19.1 cm
Colour: White and pink
Issued: 1993 to the present
Varieties: HN 2736

U.S.:	**$160.00**
Can.:	**N/I**
Ster.:	**N/I**

Exclusive to U.S.A.

HN 3292
Alexandra
Style Two
Designer: D.V. Tootle
Height: 7 3/4", 19.7 cm
Colour: Pink and white
Issued: 1994 to the present
Varieties: HN 3286

U.S.$ **$268.75**
Can.:   **$445.00**
Ster.: **$119.00**

HN 3293
Tip-toe
Designer: A. Hughes
Height: 9", 22.9 cm
Colour: Black, white
           and yellow
Issued: 1990-1994
Varieties: Also called "Joker"
           HN 3196
Series: Clowns

U.S.:   **$225.00**
Can.:   **$325.00**
Ster.: **£150.00**

HN 3294
Daddy's Joy
Designer: A. Hughes
Height: 8", 20.3 cm
Colour: Pink, yellow
           and white
Issued: 1990 in a limited
           edition of 12,500

U.S.:   **$350.00**
Can.:   **$475.00**
Ster.: **£200.00**

Commissioned by Lawleys

HN 3295
The Homecoming
Designer: A. Hughes
Height: 7", 17.8 cm
Colour: Blue, pink and green
Issued: 1990 in a limited
           edition of 9,500
Series: Children of the Blitz

U.S.:   **$275.00**
Can.:   **$300.00**
Ster.: **£150.00**

Commissioned by Lawleys

HN 3296
Fantasy
Designer: A. Hughes
Height: 12 1/2", 31.7 cm
Colour: White
Issued: 1990-1992
Series: Reflections

U.S.:   **$325.00**
Can.:   **$350.00**
Ster.: **£175.00**

HN 3297
Milestone
Designer: A. Hughes
Height: 7 1/4", 18.4 cm
Colour: Red and blue
Issued: 1990-1994

U.S.:   **$350.00**
Can.:   **$450.00**
Ster.: **£175.00**

HN 3298
Hold Tight
Designer: A. Hughes
Height: 8 1/2", 21.6 cm
Colour: Red, blue and green
Issued: 1990-1993

U.S.:   **$450.00**
Can.:   **$550.00**
Ster.: **£250.00**

HN 3299
Welcome Home
Designer: A. Hughes
Height: 8 1/2", 21.6 cm
Colour: Grey and turquoise
Issued: 1991 in a limited
           edition of 9,500
Series: Children of the Blitz

U.S.:   **$275.00**
Can.:   **$300.00**
Ster.: **£125.00**

Commissioned by Lawleys

HN 3300
Dressing Up
Style Two
Designer: A. Hughes
Height: 6 3/4", 17.5 cm
Colour: Yellow and blue
Issued: 1991 in a limited
edition of 9,500

U.S.: $250.00
Can.: $325.00
Ster.: £150.00

Commissioned by Lawleys

HN 3301
Santa's Helper
Designer: A. Hughes
Height: 6 1/2", 16.5 cm
Colour: Green, red and white
Issued: 1991-1995

U.S.: $275.00
Can.: $325.00
Ster.: $150.00

Commissioned by Lawleys

HN 3302
Please Sir
Designer: A. Hughes
Height: 8", 20.3 cm
Colour: Blue, grey and beige
Issued: 1992 in a limited
edition of 7,500

U.S.: $275.00
Can.: $325.00
Ster.: $175.00

"National Children's Home"
Commissioned by Lawleys

HN 3303
Tender Moment
Designer: M. Davies
Height: 7", 17.8 cm
Colour: Pink
Issued: 1990 to the present
Varieties: Also called "Nicola"
HN 2804, 2839
Series: Vanity Fair Ladies

U.S.: $187.50
Can.: $300.00
Ster.: £ 95.00

HN 3304
Samantha
Style Two
Designer: M. Davies
Height: 7 1/2", 19.1 cm
Colour: White/green dress,
flowered border
Issued: 1990-1996
Varieties: Also called "First
Dance" HN 2803

U.S.: $243.75
Can.: $370.00
Ster.: £105.00

HN 3305
Kathy
Style Two
Designer: M. Davies
Height: 7 1/4", 18.4 cm
Colour: Blue/white dress,
flowered border
Issued: 1990-1996
Varieties: Also called "Lynne"
HN 2329; 3740

U.S.: $243.75
Can.: $370.00
Ster.: £109.00

HN 3306
Megan
Designer: M. Davies
Height: 7 1/2", 19.0 cm
Colour: White and yellow
Issued: 1991-1994
Series: Vanity Fair Ladies

U.S.: $150.00
Can.: $225.00
Ster.: £ 90.00

HN 3307
Elaine
Style One
Designer: M. Davies
Height: 7 1/4", 18.4 cm
Colour: Pink
Issued: 1990 to the present
Varieties: HN 2791

U.S.: $350.00
Can.: $445.00
Ster.: £129.00

HN 3308
Sara
Style One
Designer: M. Davies
Height: 7 3/4", 19.7 cm
Colour: Blue, pink and white
Issued: 1990-1996
Varieties: HN 2265

U.S.:	**$350.00**
Can.:	**$490.00**
Ster.:	**£169.00**

HN 3309
Summer Rose
Style Two
Designer: M. Davies
Height: 7 1/2", 19.1 cm
Colour: White with
pink flowers
Issued: 1991 to the present
Variations: "Denise," (Style
Three) HN 2477

U.S.:	**$243.75**
Can.:	**$370.00**
U.S.:	**£109.00**

HN 3310
Diana
Style Three
Designer: M. Davies
Remodeller: D. Frith
Height: 4 1/4", 10.8 cm
Colour: Pale pink and blue
Issued: 1991-1995
Series: Miniatures

U.S.:	**$ 95.00**
Can.:	**$150.00**
Ster.:	**£ 65.00**

HN 3311
Fragrance
Style One
Designer: M. Davies
Height: 7 1/4", 18.4 cm
Colour: Red
Issued: 1991-1991
Varieties: HN 2334
Series: Michael Doulton
Events

U.S.:	**$275.00**
Can.:	**$350.00**
Ster.:	**£145.00**

HN 3312
Sunday Best - Style Two
Designer: M. Davies
Remodeller: P. Gee
Height: 3", 7.6 cm,
Colour: Green, blue and
white, gold trim
Issued: 1991-1993
Varieties: HN 3218
Series: Signature

U.S.:	**$150.00**
Can.:	**$200.00**
Ster.:	**£ 90.00**

Commissioned by Lawleys

HN 3313
Morning Breeze
Designer: P. Gee
Height: 8", 20.3 cm
Colour: Mottled blue
and orange
Issued: 1990-1994

U.S.:	**$250.00**
Can.:	**$350.00**
Ster.:	**£150.00**

HN 3314
Confucius
Designer: P. Gee
Height: 9", 22.9 cm
Colour: Flambé
Issued: 1990-1995
Series: Flambé

U.S.:	**$250.00**
Can.:	**$325.00**
Ster.:	**£130.00**

HN 3315
Waiting For A Train
Designer: P. Gee
Height: 8 1/2", 21.6 cm
Colour: Cashmere coat,
black hat,
"biscuit" finish
Issued: 1991 in a limited
edition of 9,500

U.S.:	**$375.00**
Can.:	**$425.00**
Ster.:	**£150.00**

Commissioned by Lawleys

HN 3316
Amy
Style Two
Designer: P. Gee
Height: 8" 20.3 cm
Colour: Blue and rose
Issued: 1991-1991
Series: Figure of the Year

U.S.:	$950.00
Can.:	$950.00
Ster.:	£400.00

HN 3317
Countess of Harrington
Designer: P. Gee
Height: 9 1/2", 24.3 cm
Colour: Pale green
Issued: 1992 in a limited
edition of 5,000
Series: Reynolds Ladies

U.S.:	$675.00
Can.:	$750.00
Ster.:	£275.00

HN 3318
Lady Worsley
Designer: P. Gee
Height: 9 1/2", 24.3 cm
Colour: Red, black and gold
Issued: 1991 in a limited
edition of 5,000
Series: Reynolds Ladies

U.S.:	$700.00
Can.:	$750.00
Ster.:	£275.00

HN 3319
Mrs. Hugh Bonfoy
Designer: P. Gee
Height: 9 1/2", 24.3 cm
Colour: Blue-pink
Issued: 1992 in a limited
edition of 5,000
Series: Reynolds Ladies

U.S.:	$625.00
Can.:	$750.00
Ster.:	£275.00

HN 3320
Countess Spencer
Designer: P. Gee
Height: 9 1/2", cm
Colour: Red, blue and white
Issued: 1993 in a limited
edition of 5,000
Series: Reynolds Ladies

U.S.:	$600.00
Can.:	$750.00
Ster.:	£275.00

HN 3321
Gail
Style Two
Designer: P. Gee
Height: 3 3/4", cm
Colour: Red and white
Issued: 1992 to the present
Series: Miniatures

U.S.:	$131.25
Can.:	$230.00
Ster.:	£ 59.95

HN 3322
Celeste
Style Two
Designer: P. Gee
Height: 8", 20.3 cm
Colour: Yellow
Issued: 1992-1992
Varieties: Also called
"Isadora" HN 2938

U.S.:	$250.00
Can.:	$350.00
Ster.:	£175.00

Commissioned by G.U.S.

HN 3323
June - Style Five
Designer: R. Tabbenor
Height: 5 1/4", 13.3 cm
Colour: White, pink flowers
Issued: 1990-1990
Varieties: "Amanda" HN 2996,
3406, 3632, 3634,
3635
Series: Figure of the Month,
Child

U.S.$	$100.00
Can.:	$135.00
Ster.:	$ 75.00

HN 3324
July - Style Two
Designer: R. Tabbenor
Height: 5 1/4", 13.3 cm
Colour: White, blue flowers
Issued: 1990-1990
Varieties: "Amanda" HN 2996,
             3406, 3632, 3634,
             3635
Series: Figure of the Month,
             Child
U.S.$ **$100.00**
Can.:   **$135.00**
Ster.:   **$ 75.00**

HN 3325
August - Style Two
Designer: R. Tabbenor
Height: 5 1/4", 13.3 cm
Colour: White,purple flowers
Issued: 1990-1990
Varieties: "Amanda" HN 2996,
             3406, 3632, 3634, 3635
Series: Figure of the Month,
             Child
U.S.$ **$100.00**
Can.:   **$135.00**
Ster.:   **$ 75.00**

HN 3326
September - Style Two
Designer: R. Tabbenor
Height: 5 1/4", 13.3 cm
Colour: White, lilac flowers
Issued: 1990-1990
Varieties: "Amanda" HN 2996,
             3406, 3632, 3634
             3635
Series: Figure of the Month,
             Child
U.S.$ **$100.00**
Can.:   **$135.00**
Ster.:   **$ 75.00**

HN 3327
October - Style Two
Designer: R. Tabbenor
Height: 5 1/4", 13.3 cm
Colour: White, lilac and
             white flowers
Issued: 1990-1990
Varieties: "Amanda" HN 2996,
             3406, 3632, 3634, 3635
Series: Figure of the Month,
             Child
U.S.$ **$100.00**
Can.:   **$135.00**
Ster.:   **$ 75.00**

HN 3328
November - Style Two
Designer: R. Tabbenor
Height: 5 1/4", 13.3 cm
Colour: White, lilac flowers
Issued: 1990-1990
Varieties: "Amanda" HN 2996,
             3406, 3632, 3634,
             3635
Series: Figure of the Month,
             Child
U.S.$ **$100.00**
Can.:   **$135.00**
Ster.:   **$ 75.00**

HN 3329
December - Style Two
Designer: R. Tabbenor
Height: 5 1/4", 13.3 cm
Colour: White, holly berries
Issued: 1990-1990
Varieties: "Amanda" HN 2996,
             3406, 3632
Series: Figure of the Month
             Child
U.S.$ **$100.00**
Can.:   **$135.00**
Ster.:   **$ 75.00**

HN 3330
January - Style Two
Designer: R. Tabbenor
Height: 5 1/4", 13.3 cm
Colour: White, yellow flowers
Issued: 1990-1990
Varieties: "Amanda" HN 2996,
             3406, 3632, 3634
Series: Figure of the Month,
             Child
U.S.$ **$100.00**
Can.:   **$135.00**
Ster.:   **$ 75.00**

HN 3331
February - Style Two
Designer: R. Tabbenor
Height: 5 1/4", 13.3 cm
Colour: White, blue flowers
Issued: 1990-1990
Varieties: "Amanda" HN 2996,
             3406, 3632, 3634,
             3635
Series: Figure of the Month,
             Child
U.S.$ **$100.00**
Can.:   **$135.00**
Ster.:   **$ 75.00**

HN 3332
March - Style Two
Designer: R. Tabbenor
Height: 5 1/4", 13.3 cm
Colour: White, purple flowers
Issued: 1990-1990
Varieties: "Amanda" HN 2996, 3406, 3632, 3634, 3635
Series: Figure of the Month, Child

U.S.$	**$100.00**
Can.:	**$135.00**
Ster.:	**$ 75.00**

HN 3333
April - Style Two
Designer: R. Tabbenor
Height: 5 1/4", 13.3 cm
Colour: White, purple flowers
Issued: 1990-1990
Varieties: "Amanda" HN 2996, 3406, 3632, 3634, 3635
Series: Figure of the Month, Child

U.S.$	**$100.00**
Can.:	**$135.00**
Ster.:	**$ 75.00**

HN 3334
May - Style Three
Designer: R. Tabbenor
Height: 5 1/4", 13.3 cm
Colour: White with lily-of-the-valley flowers
Issued: 1990-1990
Varieties: "Amanda" HN 2996, 3406, 3632, 3634, 3635
Series: Figure of the Month, Child

U.S.$	**$100.00**
Can.:	**$135.00**
Ster.:	**$ 75.00**

HN 3335
A Jester
Style Three
Designer: C.J. Noke
Remodeller: R. Tabbenor
Height: 4", 10.1 cm
Colour: Brown and purple
Issued: 1990-1990
Series: Miniatures, R.D.I.C.C.

U.S.:	**$175.00**
Can.:	**$200.00**
Ster.:	**£110.00**

HN 3336
Fair Lady - Style Two
Designer: M. Davies
Remodeller: P. Gee
Height: 3 1/2", 8.9 cm
Colour: ed, white, purple, 2 kt gold trim
Issued: 1991-1994
Varieties: HN 3216
Series: M. Doulton Signature Collection

U.S.:	**$150.00**
Can.:	**$200.00**
Ster.:	**£ 90.00**

HN 3337
Christine - Style Three
Designer: M. Davies
Remodeller: P. Gee
Height: 3 1/2", 8.9 cm
Colour: Yellow, black, white with 22 kt gold trim
Issued: 1991-1994
Varieties: HN 3269
Series: M. Doulton Signature Collection

U.S.:	**$150.00**
Can.:	**$200.00**
Ster.:	**£ 90.00**

HN 3338
Karen - Style Three
Designer: M. Davies
Remodeller: R. Tabbenor
Height: 3 /12", 8.9 cm
Colour: Purple with 22 kt gold trim
Issued: 1991-1994
Varieties: HN 3270
Series: M. Doulton Signature Collection

U.S.:	**$150.00**
Can.:	**$200.00**
Ster.:	**£ 90.00**

NOTE ON PRICING

Prices are given for three separate and distinct market areas.

Prices are given in the currency of each of these different trading areas.

Prices are not exchange rate calculations but are based on supply and demand in that market.

Prices listed are guidelines to the most current retail values but actual selling prices may vary slightly.

Prices for current figurines are taken from the Royal Doulton suggested retail lists.

Extremely rare figurines have widely fluctuating retail values and their prices must therefore be determined between buyer and seller.

Figurines where there are only one or two known are possibly best priced in an auction environment.

HN 3339
Olivia
Style Two
Designer: M. Davies
Height: 8", 20.3 cm
Colour: Red
Issued: 1992
Varieties: Also called "Ninette"
(Style One), HN 2379,
3417

U.S.:	$350.00
Can.:	$450.00
Ster.:	£190.00

Commissioned by G.U.S.

HN 3340
Kay
Designer: M. Davies
Height: 7 1/4", 18.4 cm
Colour: Dark blue and white
Issued: 1991 to the present
Varieties: Also called "Fair
Lady" (Style One),
HN 2193, 2832, 2835

U.S.:	$275.00
Can.:	$350.00
Ster.:	£125.00

Commissioned by Sears

HN 3341
January
Style Three
Designer: M. Davies
Height: 7 1/2", 19.0 cm
Colour: White and pale
blue, snowdrops
Issued: 1991-1991
Varieties: "Beatrice," HN 3263
3631
Series: Wildflower of the Month

U.S.:	$200.00
Can.:	$250.00
Ster.:	£125.00

HN 3342
February
Style Three
Designer: M. Davies
Height: 7 1/2", 19.0 cm
Colour: White and pink, wood
anemone flowers
Issued: 1991-1991
Varieties: "Beatrice," HN 3263,
3631
Series: Wildflower of the Month

U.S.:	$200.00
Can.:	$250.00
Ster.:	£125.00

HN 3343
March
Style Three
Designer: M. Davies
Height: 7 1/2", 19.0 cm
Colour: White; violet flowers
Issued: 1991-1991
Varieties: "Beatrice," HN 3263
3631
Series: Wildflower of the Month

U.S.:	$200.00
Can.:	$250.00
Ster.:	£125.00

HN 3344
April
Style Three
Designer: M. Davies
Height: 7 1/2", 19.0 cm
Colour: White and blue,
primrose flowers
Issued: 1991-1991
Varieties: "Beatrice," HN 3263
3631
Series: Wildflower of the Month

U.S.:	$200.00
Can.:	$250.00
Ster.:	£125.00

HN 3345
May
Style Four
Designer: M. Davies
Height: 7 1/2", 19.0 cm
Colour: White with lady's
smock flowers
Issued: 1991-1991
Varieties: "Beatrice," HN 3263
3631
Series: Wildflower of the Month

U.S.:	$200.00
Can.:	$250.00
Ster.:	£125.00

HN 3346
June
Style Six
Designer: M. Davies
Height: 7 1/2", 19.0 cm
Colour: White with briar
rose flowers
Issued: 1991-1991
Varieties: "Beatrice," HN 3263
3631
Series: Wildflower of the Month

U.S.:	$200.00
Can.:	$250.00
Ster.:	£125.00

HN 3347
July
Style Three
Designer: M. Davies
Height: 7 1/2", 19.0 cm
Colour: White with hare
bell flowers
Issued: 1991-1991
Varieties: "Beatrice," HN 3263
3631
Series: Wildflower of the Month
U.S.: $200.00
Can.: $250.00
Ster.: $125.00

HN 3348
Mother and Child
Designer: P. Parsons
Height: 7 1/2", 19.0 cm
Colour: White and pink
Issued: 1991-1993
Varieties: HN 3235, 3353
U.S.: $275.00
Can.: $325.00
Ster.: £165.00

HN 3349
Jane Seymour
Designer: P. Parsons
Height: 9", 22.9 cm
Colour: Orange and blue
Issued: 1991 in a limited
edition of 9,500
Series: Six Wives of
Henry VIII
U.S.: N/I
Can.: N/I
Ster.: £215.00

Commissioned by Lawleys

HN 3350
Henry VIII
Style Three
Designer: P. Parsons
Height: 9 1/2", 24.0 cm
Colour: Gold-brown and red
Issued: 1991 in a limited
edition of 1991
U.S.: N/I
Can.: N/I
Ster.: £750.00

Commissioned by Lawleys

HN 3351
Congratulations
Designer: P. Parsons
Height: 11", 27.9 cm
Colour: White
Issued: 1991 to the present
Series: Images
U.S.: $200.00
Can.: $325.00
Ster.: £ 99.95

HN 3353
Mother and Child
Designer: P. Parsons
Height: 7 1/2", 19.0 cm
Colour: White
Issued: 1992 to the present
Varieties: HN 3235, 3348
Series: Vanity Fair Series
U.S.: N/I
Can.: $300.00
Ster.: £ 79.95

HN 3354
Yours Forever
Designer: P. Parsons
Height: 8", 20.3 cm
Colour: Yellow and pink
Issued: 1992 - Canada
1993 - Worldwide
to the present
Varieties: "Kimberley," HN 2969
Series: Vanity Fair Ladies
U.S.: N/I
Can.: $425.00
Ster.: £109.00

HN 3355
Just For You
Designer: P. Parsons
Height: 8 1/4", 21 cm
Colour: White
Issued: 1992 to the present
Series: Vanity Fair Ladies
U.S.: $268.75
Can.: $375.00
Ster.: £109.00

HN 3356
Anne of Cleves
Designer: P. Parsons
Height: 6 1/4", 15.9 cm
Colour: Green and gold
Issued: 1991 in a limited
edition of 9,500
Series: Six Wives of
Henry VIII

U.S.: N/I
Can.: N/I
Ster.: £215.00

Commissioned by Lawleys

HN 3357
Marie
Style Three
Designer: P. Parson
Height: 6", 15.2 cm
Colour: Pink and yellow
Issued: 1992
Varieties: "Heather" HN 2956

U.S.: $175.00
Can.: $225.00
Ster.: £ 75.00

Commissioned by G.U.S.

HN 3358
Loyal Friend
Designer: V. Annand
Height: 8 1/4", 20.9 cm
Colour: Pale green and
white
Issued: 1991-1995

U.S.: $350.00
Can.: $450.00
Ster.: £200.00

HN 3359
L'Ambitieuse
Designer: V. Annand
Height: 8 1/4 ", 20.9 cm
Colour: Rose and pale blue
Issued: 1991 in a limited
edition of 5,000
Series: R.D.I.C.C.

U.S.: $375.00
Can.: $400.00
Ster.: £175.00

HN 3360
Katie
Designer: V. Annand
Height: 8 1/4", 21.0 cm
Colour: Yellow and pink
Issued: 1992 to the present

U.S.: $375.00
Can.: $445.00
Ster.: £139.00

HN 3361
First Steps
Style Three
Designer: V. Annand
Height: 5", 12.7 cm
Colour: Pink
Issued: 1992
Series: Little Cherubs

U.S.: $125.00
Can.: $150.00
Ster.: £ 75.00

Commissioned by Lawleys

HN 3362
Well Done
Designer: V. Annand
Height: 4", 10.1 cm
Colour: Pink
Issued: 1992
Series: Little Cherubs

U.S.: $125.00
Can.: $150.00
Ster.: £ 75.00

Commissioned by Lawleys

HN 3363
Peek a Boo
Designer: V. Annand
Height: 2 1/2", 6.4 cm
Colour: Pink
Issued: 1992
Series: Little Cherubs

U.S.: $125.00
Can.: $150.00
Ster.: £ 75.00

Commissioned by Lawleys

HN 3364
What Fun
Designer: V. Annand
Height: 3 3/4", 9.5 cm
Colour: Pink
Issued: 1992
Series: Little Cherubs

U.S.: $125.00
Can.: $150.00
Ster.: £ 75.00

Commissioned by Lawleys

HN 3365
Patricia
Style Four
Designer: V. Annand
Height: 8 1/2", 21.6 cm
Colour: Red and black
Issued: 1993-1993
Series: Figure of the Year

U.S.: $425.00
Can.: $475.00
Ster.: £200.00

HN 3366
Wimbledon
Designer: V. Annand
Height: 7 3/4", 19.8 cm
Colour: Cream, pink
and green
Issued: 1995 in a limited
edition of 5,000
Series: British Sporting
Heritage

U.S.: $475.00
Can.: $685.00
Ster.; £195.00

HN 3367
Henley
Designer: V. Annand
Height: 8", 20.3 cm
Colour: Green and pink
Issued: 1993 in a limited
edition of 5,000
Series: British Sporting
Heritage

U.S.: $475.00
Can.: $685.00
Ster.: £195.00

HN 3368
Alice
Style Two
Designer: N. Pedley
Height: 8 1/4", 21.0 cm
Colour: Light blue and pink
Issued: 1991 to the present

U.S.: $350.00
Can.: $445.00
Ster.: £139.00

HN 3369
Hannah
Style One
Designer: N. Pedley
Height: 8 1/4", 19.0 cm
Colour: Pale pink, yellow
and blue
Issued: 1991 to the present
Variations: HN 3655

U.S.: $268.75
Can.: $445.00
Ster.: £139.00

HN 3370
Bunny's Bedtime
Designer: N. Pedley
Height: 6", 15.2 cm
Colour: Pale blue,
pink ribbon
Issued: 1991 in a limited
edition of 9,500
Series: R.D.I.C.C.

U.S.: $250.00
Can.: $350.00
Ster.: £200.00

HN 3371
Puppy Love
Designer: N. Pedley
Height: 7 1/2", 19.0 cm
Colour: Yellow-orange
and brown
Issued: 1991 in a limited
edition of 9,500
Series: Age of Innocence

U.S.: $300.00
Can.: $450.00
Ster.: £150.00

HN 3372
Making Friends
Designer: N. Pedley
Height: 5 1/2", 14.0 cm
Colour: Pinkish yellow and white
Issued: 1991 in a limited edition of 9,500
Series: Age of Innocence
U.S.: **$300.00**
Can.: **$475.00**
Ster.: **£150.00**

HN 3373
Feeding Time
Designer: N. Pedley
Height: 7", 17.8 cm
Colour: Yellow and white
Issued: 1991 in a limited edition of 9,500
Series: Age of Innocence
U.S.: **$300.00**
Can.: **$450.00**
Ster.: **£150.00**

HN 3374
Linda
Style Three
Designer: N. Pedley
Height: 8 1/4", 21.0 cm
Colour: Turquoise and white
Issued: 1990 Canada
1991 Worldwide
-1995
U.S.: **$250.00**
Can.: **$325.00**
Ster.: **£125.00**

HN 3375
Mary
Style Two
Designer: N. Pedley
Height: 8 1/2", 21.6 cm
Colour: Blue and white
Issued: 1992-1992
Series: Figure of the Year
U.S.: **$750.00**
Can.: **$850.00**
Ster.: **£275.00**

HN 3376
Single Red Rose
Designer: N. Pedley
Height: 8", 20.3 cm
Colour: Red
Issued: 1992-1995
U.S.: **$300.00**
Can.: **$400.00**
Ster.: **£150.00**

HN 3377
First Outing
Designer: N. Pedley
Height: 7 1/2", 19.0 cm
Colour: Peach and white
Issued: 1992 in a limited edition of 9,500
Series: Age of Innocence
U.S.: **$300.00**
Can.: **$450.00**
Ster.: **£150.00**

HN 3378
Summer's Day
Style Two
Designer: T. Potts
Height: 8 1/2", 21.6 cm
Colour: Rose and white
Issued: 1991 to the present
U.S.: **$268.75**
Can.: **$445.00**
Ster.: **£129.00**

HN 3379
Kimberley
Style Two
Designer: T. Potts
Height: 8 1/2", 21.6 cm
Colour: White and blue
Issued: 1992 to the present
Varieties: HN 3382
Series: Vanity Fair Ladies
U.S.: **$187.50**
Can.: **$300.00**
Ster.: **£ 79.95**

HN 3380
Sarah
Style Two
Designer: T. Potts
Height: 8", 20.3 cm
Colour: Yellow and pink
Issued: 1993-1993
Series: M. Doulton Events

U.S.:	**$300.00**
Can.:	**$400.00**
Ster.:	**£225.00**

HN 3381
Maria
Designer: T. Potts
Height: 8 ", 20.3 cm
Colour: White and yellow
Issued: 1993 to the present
Series: Collectors Roadshow
Events / Vanity
Fair Ladies

U.S.:	**$143.75**
Can.:	**$300.00**
Ster.:	**£ 79.95**

HN 3382
Kimberley
Style Two
Designer: T. Potts
Height: 8 1/2", 21.6 cm
Colour: Yellow, pink and white
Issued: 1993 to the present
Varieties: HN 3379

U.S.:	**$200.00**
Can.:	**N/I**
Ster.:	**N/I**

Exclusive to U.S.A.
*

HN 3383
Sally
Style Two
Designer: T. Potts
Height: 8 1/4", 21.0 cm
Colour: Red
Issued: 1995
Varieties: HN 3851

U.S.:	**N/I**
Can.:	**N/I**
Ster.:	**£99.99**

Commissioned by Freemans

HN 3384
Sarah
Style Three
Designer: Tim Potts
Height: 8", 20.3 cm
Colour: Red and pink
Issued: 1995 to the present
Varieties: HN 3852, 3857

U.S.:	**$243.75**
Can.:	**$425.00**
Ster.:	**£ 99.95**

*

HN 3388
Forget-Me-Not
Style Two
Designer: A. Maslankowski
Height: 6", 15.2 cm
Colour: White
Issued: 1991 to the present
Series: Sentiments

U.S.:	**$ 81.25**
Can.:	**$135.00**
Ster.:	**£ 39.95**

HN 3389
Loving You
Designer: A. Maslankowski
Height: 6 1/4", 15.8 cm
Colour: White
Issued: 1991 to the present
Series: Sentiments

U.S.:	**$ 81.25**
Can.:	**$135.00**
Ster.:	**£ 39.95**

HN 3390
Thank You
Style Two
Designer: A. Maslankowski
Height: 6 1/4", 15.8 cm
Colour: White
Issued: 1991 to the present
Series: Sentiments

U.S.:	**$ 81.25**
Can.:	**$135.00**
Ster.:	**£ 39.95**

HN 3391
Reward
Designer: A. Maslankowski
Height: 4 1/2", 11.4 cm
Colour: White and pink
Issued: 1992 to the present
Series: Vanity Fair
Children
U.S.: $106.25
Can.: $190.00
Ster.: £ 49.95

HN 3392
Christopher Columbus
Designer: A. Maslankowski
Height: 12", 30.5 cm
Colour: Green, brown
and red
Issued: 1992 in a limited
edition of 1,492
U.S.: $1,950.00
Can.: $2,500.00
Ster.: £ 750.00

HN 3393
With Love
Designer: A. Maslankowski
Height: 6", 15.2 cm
Colour: White
Issued: 1992 to the present
Varieties: HN 3492
Series: Sentiments
U.S.: $ 81.25
Can.: $135.00
Ster.: £ 39.95

HN 3394
Sweet Dreams
Style Two
Designer: A. Maslankowski
Height: 6", 15.2 cm
Colour: White
Issued: 1992 to the present
Series: Sentiments
U.S.: $ 81.25
Can.: $135.00
Ster.: £ 39.95

HN 3395
Little Ballerina
Designer: A. Maslankowski
Height: 6", 15.2 cm
Colour: White
Issued: 1992 to the present
Varieties: HN 3431
U.S.: $ 81.25
Can.: $190.00
Ster.: £ 39.95

HN 3396
Buddies
Style Two
Designer: A. Maslankowski
Height: 4 1/4", 10.8 cm
Colour: Pink and beige
Issued: 1992 to the present
Series: Vanity Fair Children
U.S.: $106.25
Can.: $190.00
Ster.: £ 49.95

HN 3397
Let's Play
Designer: A. Maslankowski
Height: 4", 10.0 cm
Colour: Pale green and white
Issued: 1992 to the present
Series: Vanity Fair Children
U.S.: $106.25
Can.: $190.00
Ster.: £ 49.95

HN 3398
The Ace
Designer: R. Tabbenor
Height: 10", 25.4 cm
Colour: White
Issued: 1991-1995
U.S.: $225.00
Can.: $300.00
Ster.: £125.00

HN 3399
Father Christmas
Designer: R. Tabbenor
Height: 9", 22.9 cm
Colour: Red and white
Issued: 1992 to the present

U.S.:	**$212.50**
Can.:	**$375.00**
Ster.:	**£149.00**

HN 3400
God Bless You
Designer: R. Tabbenor
Height: 8", 20.3 cm
Colour: White
Issued: 1992 to the present
Series: Images

U.S.:	**$150.00**
Can.:	**$140.00**
Ster.:	**£ 29.95**

HN 3401
Gardening Time
Designer: R. Tabbenor
Height: 5", 12.7 cm
Colour: Yellow, blue
            and green
Issued: 1992-1994

U.S.:	**$225.00**
Can.:	**$300.00**
Ster.:	**£125.00**

HN 3402
Samurai Warrior
Designer: R. Tabbenor
Height: 9", 22.7 cm
Colour: Red
Issued: 1992 in a limited
            edition of 950
Series: Flambé

U.S.:	**$500.00**
Can.:	**$650.00**
Ster.:	**£250.00**

HN 3403
Lt. General Ulysses S.
Grant
Designer: R. Tabbenor
Height: 11 3/4", 29.8 cm
Colour: Blue and brown
Issued: 1993 in a limited
            edition of 5,000

U.S.:	**$1,200.00**
Can.:	**$1,000.00**
Ster.:	**£ 500.00**

HN 3404
General Robert E. Lee
Designer: R. Tabbenor
Height: 11 1/2", 29.2 cm
Colour: Grey and brown
Issued: 1993 in a limited
            edition of 5,000

U.S.:	**$1,300.00**
Can.:	**$1,000.00**
Ster.:	**£ 500.00**

HN 3405
Field Marshall Montgomery
Designer: R. Tabbenor
Height: 11 3/4", 29.2 cm
Colour: Browns
Issued: 1994 in a limited
            edition of 1,944

U.S.:	**$1,100.00**
Can.:	**$1,000.00**
Ster.:	**£ 500.00**

HN 3406
Amanda
Style One
Designer: R. Tabbenor
Height: 5 1/4", 13.3 cm
Colour: White and pink
Issued: 1993 to the present
Varieties: HN 2996, 3632,
            3634, 3635
Series: Vanity Fair Children

U.S.:	**$105.00**
Can.:	**N/I**
Ster.:	**N/I**

Exclusive to U.S.A.

HN 3407
Julie
Designer: R. Tabbenor
Height: 5", 12.7 cm
Colour: White and blue
Issued: 1993 to the present
Varieties: HN 2995

U.S.:	**$106.25**
Can.:	**N/I**
Ster.:	**N/I**

Exclusive to U.S.A.

HN 3408
August
Style Three
Designer: M. Davies
Height: 7 1/2", 19.1 cm
Colour: White and green, poppy flowers
Issued: 1991-1991
Varieties: "Beatrice" HN 3263 3631
Series: Wildflower of the Month

U.S.:	**$200.00**
Can.:	**$250.00**
Ster.:	**£125.00**

HN 3409
September
Style Three
Designer: M. Davies
Height: 7 1/2", 19.1 cm
Colour: White and pink, blue flowers
Issued: 1991-1991
Varieties: "Beatrice" HN 3263 3631
Series: Wildflower of the Month

U.S.:	**$200.00**
Can.:	**$250.00**
Ster.:	**£125.00**

HN 3410
October
Style Three
Designer: M. Davies
Height: 7 1/2", 19.1 cm
Colour: White and blue, buttercup flowers
Issued: 1991-1991
Varieties: "Beatrice" HN 3263 3631
Series: Wildflower of the Month

U.S.:	**$200.00**
Can.:	**$250.00**
Ster.:	**£125.00**

HN 3411
November
Style Three
Designer: M. Davies
Height: 7 1/2", 19.1 cm
Colour: White and blue, pink campion flowers
Issued: 1991-1991
Varieties: "Beatrice" HN 3263 3631
Series: Wildflower of the Month

U.S.:	**$200.00**
Can.:	**$250.00**
Ster.:	**£125.00**

HN 3412
December
Style Three
Designer: M. Davies
Height: 7 1/2", 19.1 cm
Colour: White and pink trim; Christmas roses
Issued: 1991-1991
Varieties: "Beatrice" HN 3263 3631
Series: Wildflower of the Month

U.S.:	**$200.00**
Can.:	**$250.00**
Ster.:	**£125.00**

HN 3413
Kathryn
Designer: M. Davies
Height: 7", 17.8 cm
Colour: Blue and white
Issued: 1992-1992
Varieties: "Beatrice," HN 3263, 3631; Lucy (Style Two), HN 3653; "Summer Serenade," HN 3610

U.S.:	**$300.00**
Can.:	**$375.00**
Ster.:	**£125.00**

HN 3414
Rebecca
Style Two
Designer: M. Davies
Remodeller: D. Frith
Height: 3 1/2", 8.9 cm
Colour: Pale blue and pink
Issued: 1992 to the present
Series: Miniatures

U.S.:	**$131.25**
Can.:	**$230.00**
Ster.:	**£ 59.95**

HN 3415
Janette
Designer: M. Davies
Height: 7 1/2" 19.1 cm
Colour: Blue and green
Issued: 1992-1992
Varieties: Also called "Kirsty"
(Style One) HN 2381

U.S.: **$250.00**
Can.: **$350.00**
Ster.: **£145.00**

Commissioned by G.U.S.

HN 3416
Victoria
Style One
Designer: M. Davies
Height: 6 1/2", 16.5 cm
Colour: Blue and rose
22kt gold trim
Issued: 1992-1992
Varieties: HN 2471
Series: Collector's Roadshow
Events

U.S.: **$400.00**
Can.: **$475.00**
Ster.: **£200.00**

HN 3417
Ninette
Style One
Designer: M. Davies
Height: 7 1/2", 19.1 cm
Colour: Orange and green
dress, 22kt gold trim
Issued: 1992-1992
Varieties: HN 2379; Olivia
HN 339
Series: Roadshow Events

U.S.: **$400.00**
Can.: **$475.00**
Ster.: **£200.00**

HN 3418
Bedtime
Style Two
Designer: N. Pedley
Height: 7 1/4", 18.4 cm
Colour: Pink-yellow
Issued: 1992 in a limited
edition of 9,000

U.S.: **$250.00**
Can.: **$375.00**
Ster.: **£175.00**

Commissioned by Lawleys

HN 3419
Angela
Style Three
Designer: N. Pedley
Height: 8 1/2", 21.6 cm
Colour: Blue, pink and white
Issued: 1992-1992
Series: Michael Doulton
Events

U.S.: **$300.00**
Can.: **$375.00**
Ster.: **£200.00**

HN 3420
Ashley
Designer: N. Pedley
Height: 8", 20.3 cm
Colour: Lavender
Issued: 1992 to the present
Series: Vanity Fair Ladies

U.S.: **$187.50**
Can.: **$300.00**
Ster.: **£ 79.95**

HN 3421
Nicole
Designer: N. Pedley
Height: 7 1/2", 19.1 cm
Colour: Pink and cream
Issued: 1993 to the present
Varieties: HN 3686

U.S.: **$168.75**
Can.: **$280.00**
Ster.: **£ 89.95**

HN 3422
Joanne
Style Two
Designer: N. Pedley
Height: 7 1/2", 19.1 cm
Colour: White and pink dress
flowered border
Issued: 1993 to the present

U.S.: **$243.75**
Can.: **$370.00**
Ster.: **£109.00**

HN 3423
Birthday Girl
Designer: N. Pedley
Height: 6", 15.2 cm
Colour: White
Issued: 1993 to the present
Series: Vanity Fair Children

U.S.: $143.75
Can.: $205.00
Ster.: £ 59.95

HN 3424
My First Figurine
Designer: N. Pedley
Height: 4 1/4", 10.8 cm
Colour: Red and pink
Issued: 1993 to the present

U.S.: $106.25
Can.: $205.00
Ster.: £ 49.95

HN 3425
Almost Grown
Designer: N. Pedley
Height: 4 1/2", 11.4 cm
Colour: White and pale green
Issued: 1993 to the present

U.S.: $ 81.25
Can.: $160.00
Ster.: £ 39.95

HN 3426
Best Wishes
Designer: N. Pedley
Height: 6", 15.2 cm
Colour: Red and white
Issued: 1993-1995

U.S.: $160.00
Can.: $225.00
Ster.: £ 80.00

HN 3427
Gift of Love
Designer: N. Pedley
Height: 7 1/2", 19.1 cm
Colour: White, yellow and
pink
Issued: 1993 to the present
Series: Vanity Fair Ladies

U.S.: $143.75
Can.: $300.00
Ster.: £ 79.95

HN 3428
Discovery
Designer: A. Munslow
Height: 12", 30.5 cm
Colour: Matte white
Issued: 1992-1992
Series: R.D.I.C.C.

U.S.: $160.00
Can.: $225.00
Ster.: £150.00

HN 3429
Napoleon at Waterloo
Designer: A. Maslankowski
Height: 11 1/2", 29.2 cm
Colour: Black, cream and
green
Issued: 1992 in a limited
edition of 1,500

U.S.: $1,900.00
Can.: $2,000.00
Ster.: £ 850.00

HN 3430
Sit
Designer: A. Maslankowski
Height: 4 1/2", 11.4 cm
Colour: Pink and white
Issued: 1992 to the present
Varieties: HN 3123
Series: Vanity Fair Children

U.S.: $99.00
Can.: $280.00
Ster.: N/I

Exclusive to N. America

HN 3431
Little Ballerina
Designer: A. Maslankowski
Height: 6", 15.2 cm
Colour: Pink
Issued: 1993 in a limited
edition of 2,000
Varieties: HN 3395

U.S.:	**$100.00**
Can.:	**$200.00**
Ster.:	**£ 90.00**

Exclusive to N. America

HN 3432
Duke of Wellington
Designer: A. Maslankowski
Height: 12", 30.5 cm
Colour: Dark blue and
cream
Issued: 1993 in a limited
edition of 1,500

U.S.:	**$1,750.00**
Can.:	**$2,000.00**
Ster.:	**£ 850.00**

HN 3433
Winston S. Churchill
Style Two
Designer: A. Maslankowski
Height: 12", 30.5 cm
Colour: Black and grey
Issued: 1993 in a limited
edition of 5,000

U.S.:	**$595.00**
Can.:	**$795.00**
Ster.:	**£295.00**

HN 3434
Ballet Shoes
Designer: A. Maslankowski
Height: 3 3/4", 9.5 cm
Colour: White
Issued: 1993 to the present

U.S.:	**$ 81.25**
Can.:	**$190.00**
Ster.:	**£ 39.95**

HN 3435
Daddy's Girl
Designer: A. Maslankowski
Height: 4 1/2" , 11.4 cm
Colour: Pink and white
Issued: 1993 to the present
Series: Vanity Fair Children

U.S.:	**$ 81.25**
Can.:	**$190.00**
Ster.:	**£ 35.00**

HN 3436
HM Queen Elizabeth II
Style Four
Designer: A. Maslankowski
Height: 8 1/4", 21.0 cm
Colour: Lilac and yellow
Issued: 1992 in a limited
edition of 2,500

U.S.:	**$1300.00**
Can.:	**$1300.00**
Ster.:	**£ 495.00**

Commissioned by Lawleys

HN 3437
Mary
Style Three
Designer: A. Maslankowski
Height: 3 1/4", 8.3 cm
Colour: White
Issued: 1993 to the present
Varieties: HN 3485
Series: Holy Family

U.S.:	**$50.00**
Can.:	**$60.00**
Ster.:	**£75.00**

Exclusive to N. America

NOTES ON PRICING

The prices on the secondary market for Royal Doulton Figures, particularly the early HN Numbers, have risen considerably over the years. As values rise, the condition and quality of these figurines take on an increasingly important role.

The prices listed in The Charlton Standard Catalogue of Royal Doulton Beswick Figurines are for figures in mint condition.

Naturally, repaired or restored figures, no matter how professionally done, will sell at a substantial discount.

On Condition: For figures to command catalogue prices they must be in mint condition. This simply means that a figure will not have paint chips, scratches, hairline cracks, crazing or blemishes. Any of which will remove from the mint category figure.

On Quality: Some figures can be better moulded, assembled or painted than others. High quality figures will command catalogue prices. Low quality figures will not.

HN 3438
Joseph
Designer:	A. Maslankowski
Height:	5 3/4", 14.6 cm
Colour:	White
Issued:	1993 to the present
Varieties:	HN 3486
Series:	Holy Family
U.S.:	**$50.00**
Can.:	**$70.00**
Ster.:	**N/I**

HN 3439
The Skater
Style Two
Designer:	P. Gee
Height:	8", 20.3 cm
Colour:	Red
Issued:	1992 to the present
U.S.:	**$406.25**
Can.:	**$490.00**
Ster.:	**£149.00**

HN 3440
HM Queen Elizabeth II
Style Three
Designer:	P. Gee
Height:	7 1/2", 19.0 cm
Colour:	Yellow and pink
Issued:	1992 in a limited edition of 3,500
U.S.:	**$500.00**
Can.:	**$550.00**
Ster.:	**£250.00**

HN 3441
Barbara
Style Three
Designer:	P. Gee
Height:	8", 20.3 cm
Colour:	Pink and lavender
Issued:	1993 in a limited edition of 9,500
Series:	R.D.I.C.C.
U.S.:	**$300.00**
Can.:	**$425.00**
Ster.:	**£150.00**

HN 3442
Eliza Farren,
Countess of Derby
Designer:	P. Gee
Height:	8 3/4", 22.2 cm
Colour:	Pale blue, white and beige
Issued:	1993 in a limited edition of 5,000
Series:	R.D.I.C.C.
U.S.:	**$335.00**
Can.:	**$395.00**
Ster.:	**£195.00**

HN 3443
Gift of Freedom
Designer:	P. Gee
Height:	9 3/4", 24.8 cm
Colour:	White
Issued:	1993 to the present
Series:	Images
U.S.:	**$106.25**
Can.:	**$210.00**
Ster.:	**£ 59.95**

HN 3444
Piper
Style Two
Designer:	P. Gee
Height:	9 1/4", 23.4 cm
Colour:	Black, red and green
Issued:	1993 in a limited edition of 750
U.S.:	**$300.00**
Can.:	**$325.00**
Ster.:	**£125.00**

Site of the Green

HN 3445
Amy's Sister
Designer:	P. Gee
Height:	8", 20.3 cm
Colour:	Red, cream and blue
Issued:	1993 to the present
U.S.:	**$268.75**
Can.:	**$425.00**
Ster.:	**£109.00**

HN 3446
Spring Song
Designer: P. Gee
Height: 7 1/4", 18.4 cm
Colour: Yellow and white
Issued: 1993
Varieties: Also called Danielle
             (Style Two), HN 3001
Series: Seasons, (Series Five)

U.S.:   **$200.00**
Can.:   **$250.00**
Ster.:   **£ 80.00**

HN 3447
Jennifer
Style Three
Designer: P. Gee
Height: 7 1/4", 18.4 cm
Colour: Pink
Issued: 1994-1994
Series: Figure of the Year

U.S.:   **$325.00**
Can.:   **$375.00**
Ster.:   **£125.00**

HN 3448
Charles Dickens
Designer: P. Gee
Height: 4", 10.1 cm
Colour: Black and grey
Issued: 1994 in a limited
             editon of 5,000

U.S.:   **$115.00**
Can.:   **$125.00**
Ster.:   **£ 75.00**

Commissioned by Pascoe
and Company

HN 3449
Catherine Howard
Designer: P. Parsons
Height: 8 1/4", 21.0 cm
Colour: Purple
Issued: 1992 in a limited
             edition of 9,500
Series: Six Wives of
             Henry VIII

U.S.:   **N/I**
Can.:   **N/I**
Ster.:   **£225.00**

Commissioned by Lawleys

HN 3450
Catherine Parr
Designer: P. Parsons
Height: 6 1/4", 15.9 cm
Colour: Red
Issued: 1992 in a limited
             edition of 9,500
Series: Six Wives of
             Henry VIII

U.S.:   **N/I**
Can.:   **N/I**
Ster.:   **£235.00**

Commissioned by Lawleys

HN 3451
Catherine
Style Three
Designer: P. Parsons
Height: 5", 12,7 cm
Colour: White and lemon
Issued: 1993 to the present
Varieties: HN 3044

U.S.:   **$106.25**
Can.:   **N/I**
Ster.:   **N/I**

Exclusive to U.S.A.

HN 3452
Our First Christmas
Designer: P. Parsons
Height: 11 1/2", 29.2 cm
Colour: White
Issued: 1993 to the present
Series: Images

U.S.:   **$200.00**
Can.:   **$325.00**
Ster.:   **£ 85.00**

HN 3453
Juliet
Style Two
Designer: P. Parsons
Height: 6", 15.2 cm
Colour: Red, pink and green
Issued: 1994 in a limited
             edition of 5,000
Series: Shakespearian Ladies

U.S.:   **N/I**
Can.:   **N/I**
Ster.:   **£195.00**

Commissioned by Lawleys

HN 3454
Flowers For Mother
Designer:	P. Parsons
Height:	5 3/4", 14.6 cm
Colour:	White and pink
Issued:	1994 to the present
U.S.:	**$106.25**
Can.:	**$190.00**
Ster.:	**£ 49.95**

HN 3455
Sharon
Style One	
Designer:	P. Parsons
Height:	5 1/2", 14.0 cm
Colour:	White dress with pink flowers
Issued:	1994 to the present
Varieties:	HN 3047
U.S.:	**$106.25**
Can.:	**N/I**
Ster.:	**N/I**

HN 3456
Grandpa's Story
Designer:	P. Parsons
Height:	6", 15.2 cm
Colour:	Black, pink and blue
Issued:	1994 to the present
U.S.:	**$306.25**
Can.:	**$495.00**
Ster.:	**£135.00**

HN 3457
When I Was Young
Designer:	P. Parsons
Height:	5 1/2", 14.0 cm
Colour:	Pink, green and purple
Issued:	1994 to the present
U.S.:	**$306.25**
Can.:	**$495.00**
Ster.:	**£135.00**

HN 3458
Henry VIII
Style Four	
Designer:	P. Parsons
Height:	9 1/4", 23.5 cm
Colour:	Browns, black and white
Issued:	1994 in a limited edition of 9,500
U.S.:	**N/I**
Can.:	**N/I**
Ster.:	**£295.00**

Commissioned by Lawleys

HN 3459
King Charles
Designer:	C.J. Noke and H. Tittensor
Height:	16 3/4", 42.5 cm
Colour:	Red, dark blue, purple and white
Issued:	1992 in a limited edition of 350
Varieties:	HN 404, 2084
U.S.:	**$4,000.00**
Can.:	**$4,000.00**
Ster.:	**£1,600.00**

HN 3460
Brother and Sister
Designer:	A. Hughes
Height:	8", 20.3 cm
Colour:	White
Issued:	1993 to the present
Series:	Images
U.S.:	**$106.25**
Can.:	**$210.00**
Ster.:	**£ 49.95**

HN 3461
Kerry
Designer:	A. Hughes
Height:	5 1/4", 13.3 cm
Colour:	White and green
Issued:	1993 to the present
Varieties:	HN 3036
U.S.:	**$106.25**
Can.:	**N/I**
Ster.:	**N/I**

Exclusive to U.S.A.

HN 3462
Boy Scout
Designer: A. Hughes
Height: 7 3/4", 19.7 cm
Colour: Brown and black
Issued: 1994 in a limited
edition of 9,500
U.S.: **$300.00**
Can.: **$400.00I**
Ster.: **£175.00**

Commissioned by Lawleys
*

HN 3470
Croquet
Designer: V. Annand
Height: 8 1/2", 21.6 cm
Colour: Red and blue
Issued: 1994 in a limited
edition of 5,000
Series: British Sporting
Heritage
U.S.: **$475.00**
Can.: **$685.00**
Ster.: **£195.00**

HN 3471
Ascot
Style Two
Designer: V. Annand
Height: 8 1/2", 21.6 cm
Colour: Pink and purple
Issued: 1994 in a limited
edition of 5,000
Series: British Sporting
Heritage
U.S.: **$475.00**
Can.: **$685.00**
Ster.: **£195.00**

HN 3472
La Loge
Designer: V. Annand
Height: 8 1/2", 21.6 cm
Colour: White and black
Issued: 1992 in a limited
edition of 7,500
U.S.: **$475.00**
Can.: **$685.00**
Ster.: **£195.00**

Commissioned by Lawleys

HN 3473
Les Parapluies
Designer: V. Annand
Height: 8 1/4", 21.0 cm
Colour: Blue
Issued: 1993 in a limited
edition of 7,500
U.S.: **$475.00**
Can.: **$685.00**
Ster.: **£195.00**

Commissioned by Lawleys

HN 3474
Lise
Designer: V. Annand
Height: 8 1/2", 21.6 cm
Colour: Lavender and
purple
Issued: 1994 in a limited
edition of 7,500
U.S.: **$475.00**
Can.: **$685.00**
Ster.: **£175.00**

Commissioned by Lawleys

HN 3475
Marie Sisley
Designer: V. Annand
Height: 8 1/2", 21.6 cm
Colour: Red, yellow and
grey
Issued: 1994 in a limited
edition of 7,500
U.S.: **$475.00**
Can.: **$685.00**
Ster.: **£175.00**

Commissioned by Lawleys

HN 3476
Bridesmaid
Style Seven
Designer: V. Annand
Height: 5 1/2", 13.3 cm
Colour: Pink
Issued: 1994 to the present
Varieties: Also called
"Flowergirl," (Style
One), HN 3479
U.S.: **$106.25**
Can.: **$280.00**
Ster.: **£ 69.95**

HN 3477
Springtime
Style Three
Designer: V. Annand
Height: 8", 20.3 cm
Colour: Pink and cream
Issued: 1993 to the present
Series: Four Seasons
(Series Six)

U.S.:	**$350.00**
Can.:	**$490.00**
Ster.:	**£175.00**

HN 3478
Summertime
Style Two
Designer: V. Annand
Height: 8 1/2", 21.6 cm
Colour: Lilac and green
Issued: 1994 to the present
Series: Four Seasons
(Series Six)

U.S.:	**$350.00**
Can.:	**$490.00**
Ster.:	**£175.00**

HN 3479
Flowergirl
Style One
Designer: V. Annand
Height: 5 ", 12.7 cm
Colour: White and pink
Issued: 1994 to the present
Varieties: Also called
"Bridesmaid," (Style
Seven), HN 3476

U.S.:	**$131.25**
Can.:	**$280.00**
Ster.:	**N/I**

Exclusive to N. America

HN 3480
Kirsty
Style Two
Designer: M. Davies
Remodeller: P. Gee
Height: 3 3/4", 9.5 cm
Colour: Blue
Issued: 1993 to the present
Varieties: HN 3213, 3246, 3743
Series: Miniatures

U.S.:	**N/I**
Can.:	**$205.00**
Ster.:	**N/I**

Exclusive to Canada

HN 3481
Lavender Rose
Designer: M. Davies
Height: 6", 15.2 cm
Colour: White with pink flowers
Issued: 1993-1995
Varieties: "Debbie", HN 2385, 2400;
"Lavender Rose",
HN 3481; "Old Country
Roses", HN 3483

U.S.:	**$150.00**
Can.:	**$200.00**
Ster.:	**£ 75.00**

HN 3482
Old Country Roses
Style One
Designer: M. Davies
Height: 6", 15.2 cm
Colour: White flowered dress
Issued: 1993-1995
Varieties: "Debbie", HN 2385, 2400;
"Lavender Rose",
HN 3481; "Old Country
Roses", HN 3483

U.S.:	**$150.00**
Can.:	**$200.00**
Ster.:	**£ 75.00**

HN 3483
Moonlight Rose
Designer: M. Davies
Height: 6", 15.2 cm
Colour: White with blue flowers
Issued: 1993-1995
Varieties: "Debbie", HN 2385, 2400;
"Lavender Rose",
HN 3481; "Old Country
Roses", HN 3482

U.S.:	**$150.00**
Can.:	**$200.00**
Ster.:	**£ 75.00**

HN 3484
Jesus
Designer: A. Maslankowski
Width: 2 1/2", 6.4 cm
Colour: White
Issued: 1993 to the present
Varieties: HN 3487
Series: Holy Family

U.S.:	**$30.00**
Can.:	**$5500**
Ster.:	**N/I**

Exclusive to N. America

HN 3485
Mary
Style Three
Designer: A. Maslankowski
Height: 3 1/4", 8.3 cm
Colour: Blue and white
Issued: 1993 to the present
Varieties: HN 3437
Series: Holy Family

U.S.: $ 60.00
Can.: $105.00
Ster.: N/I

Exclusive to N. America

HN 3486
Joseph
Designer: A. Maslankowski
Height: 5 3/4", 14.6 cm
Colour: Brown and white
Issued: 1993 to the present
Varieties: HN 3438
Series: Holy Family

U.S.: $ 65.00
Can.: $105.00
Ster.: N/I

Exclusive to N. America

HN 3487
Jesus
Designer: A. Maslankowski
Width: 2 1/2", 6.4 cm
Colour: White and brown
Issued: 1993 to the present
Varieties: HN 3484
Series: Holy Family

U.S.: $60.00
Can.: $85.00
Ster.: N/I

Exclusive to N. America

HN 3488
Christmas Day
Designer: A. Maslankowski
Height: 6", 15.2 cm
Colour: White
Issued: 1993 to the present
Series: Sentiments

U.S.: $ 68.75
Can.: $125.00
Ster.: £ 39.95

HN 3489
Vice Admiral Lord Nelson
Designer: A. Maslankowski
Height: 12 1/2", 31.7 cm
Colour: Dark blue, gold
        and cream
Issued: 1993 in a limited
        edition of 950

U.S.: $1,750.00
Can.: $2,850.00
Ster.: £ 850.00

HN 3490
Thinking of You
Designer: A. Maslankowski
Height: 6 3/4", 17.2 cm
Colour: White with pink sash
Issued: 1993
Varieties: HN 3124
Series: Sentiments

U.S.: $187.50
Can.: N/I
Ster.: £ 39.95

Commisssioned for Collectors
events in the U.K.

HN 3491
Friendship
Designer: A. Maslankowski
Height: 6", 15.2 cm
Colour: White
Issued: 1994 to the present
Series: Sentiments

U.S.: $187.50
Can.: $135.00
Ster.: £ 39.95

HN 3492
With Love
Designer: A. Maslankowski
Height: 5 3/4", 14.6 cm
Colour: White dress and
        sash
Issued: 1994 to the present
Varieties: HN 3393
Series: Sentiments

U.S.: $ 68.75
Can.: $102.00
Ster.: £ 39.95

Canadian exclusive

HN 3493
Christmas Parcels
Style Two
Designer:	A. Maslankowski
Height:	6", 15.2 cm
Colour:	White
Issued:	1994 to the present
Series:	Sentiments
U.S.:	**$ 68.75**
Can.:	**$125.00**
Ster.:	**£ 39.95**

HN 3494
Tina
Designer:	M. Davies
Height:	7 1/2", 19.1 cm
Colour:	Blue and white
Issued:	1993
Varieties:	Also called "Maureen," (Style Three), HN 2481
U.S.:	**$200.00**
Can.:	**$250.00**
Ster.:	**£ 95.00**

Commissioned by G.U.S.

HN 3495
Annette
Style Two
Designer:	M. Davies
Height:	8", 20.3 cm
Colour:	Pale green
Issued:	1993-1993
Varieties:	Also called "Sandra," HN 2275, 2401
U.S.:	**$200.00**
Can.:	**$250.00**
Ster.:	**£ 95.00**

HN 3496
Margaret
Style Two
Designer:	M. Davies
Height:	7 1/2", 19.1 cm
Colour:	White and green
Issued:	1993 to the present
Varieties:	HN 2397; "Adele" HN 2480; "Camille" HN 3171 (Style Two)
U.S.:	**$175.00**
Can.:	**N/I**
Ster.:	**N/I**

Exclusive to U.S.A.

HN 3497
Jessica
Designer:	M. Davies
Height:	7", 17.8 cm
Colour:	White and blue
Issued:	1993
Varieties:	HN 3169
U.S.:	**$175.00**
Can.:	**$200.00**
Ster.:	**£ 85.00**

HN 3498
Natalie
Designer:	M. Davies
Height:	8", 20.3 cm
Colour:	White and lemon
Issued:	1993 to the present
Varieties:	HN 3173
U.S.:	**$175.00**
Can.:	**N/I**
Ster.:	**N/I**

Exclusive to U.S.A.

HN 3499
Top o' the Hill
Style Two
Designer:	L. Harradine
Remodeller:	P. Gee
Height:	3 3/4", 9.5 cm
Colour:	Red
Issued:	1993 to present
Varieties:	HN 2126, 2180
Series:	Miniatures
U.S.:	**$131.25**
Can.:	**$230.00**
Ster.:	**£ 49.95**
*	

HN 3600
Dawn
Style Three
Designer:	N. Pedley
Height:	7 1/2", 19.1 cm
Colour:	White and pink
Issued:	1993 to the present
Series:	Vanity Fair
U.S.:	**$143.75**
Can.:	**$300.00**
Ster.:	**£ 79.95**

HN 3601
Helen
Style Three
Designer: N. Pedley
Height: 8 1/4", 21.0 cm
Colour: Blue and white
Issued: 1993 to the present
Varieties: HN 3687, 3763;
Also called "Miss
Kay," HN 3659

U.S.: $268.75
Can.: $425.00
Ster.: £ 99.95

HN 3602
Flowergirl
Style Two
Designer: N. Pedley
Height: 5 1/4", 13.3. cm
Colour: Pink and cream
Issued: 1993 to the present

U.S.: $106.25
Can.: N/I
Ster.: £ 39.95

HN 3603
Sharon
Style Two
Designer: N. Pedley
Height: 8 3/4", 22.2 cm
Colour: Peach, cream
and blue
Issued: 1994-1994
Series: Michael Doulton
Events

U.S.: $250.00
Can.: $350.00
Ster.: £105.00

HN 3604
Diane
Designer: N. Pedley
Height: 8 1/2", 21.6 cm
Colour: Pink and blue
Issued: 1994-1994
Series: R.D.I.C.C.

U.S.: $275.00
Can.: $375.00
Ster.: £160.00

HN 3605
First Performance
Designer: N. Pedley
Height: 6", 15.2 cm
Colour: White and pink
Issued: 1994 to the present

U.S.: $106.25
Can.: $205.00
Ster.: £ 59.95

HN 3606
A Posy For You
Designer: N. Pedley
Height: 4 1/4", 10.8 cm
Colour: Blue and white
Issued: 1994 to the present

U.S.: $106.25
Can.: $205.00
Ster.: £ 49.95

HN 3607
Special Friend
Designer: N. Pedley
Height: 4 1/4", 10.8 cm
Colour: Blue and white
Issued: 1994 to the present

U.S.: $106.25
Can.: $205.00
Ster.: £ 49.95

HN 3608
Good Companion
Designer: N. Pedley
Height: 8 1/2", 21.6 cm
Colour: Pink and white
Issued: 1994 to the present
Series: Vanity Fair

U.S.: $187.50
Can.: $300.00
Ster.: £ 89.95

HN 3609
Kathleen
Style Three
Designer: N. Pedley
Height: 8 1/2", 21.6 cm
Colour: White and yellow
Issued: 1994 to the present
Series: Vanity Fair Ladies
U.S.: **$187.50**
Can.: **$300.00**
Ster.: **£ 79.95**

HN 3610
Summer Serenade
Designer: M. Davies
Height: 7", 17.8 cm
Colour: Blue and white
Issued: 1993
Varieties: "Beatrice" HN 3263,
3631; "Lucy" HN 3653;
"Kathryn" HN 3413;
Wildflower of the Month
Series: Seasons (Series Five)
U.S.: **$200.00**
Can.: **$250.00**
Ster.: **£ 80.00**

HN 3611
Winter Welcome
Designer: M. Davies
Height: 7 1/2", 19.1 cm
Colour: Rust and white
Issued: 1993
Varieties: Also called
"Caroline" HN 3170
Series: Seasons (Series Five)
U.S.: **$200.00**
Can.: **$250.00**
Ster.: **£ 80.00**

HN 3612
Autumn Attraction
Designer: M. Davies
Height: 6 3/4", 17.2 cm
Colour: Gold and white
Issued: 1993
Varieties: Also called
"Michele" HN 2234
Series: Seasons
(Series Five)
U.S.: **$200.00**
Can.: **$250.00**
Ster.: **£ 80.00**

HN 3613
Darling
Style Two
Designer: C. Vyse
Height: 5 1/4", 13.3 cm
Colour: Pale blue
Issued: 1993
Varieties: HN 1985
U.S.: **$ 85.00**
Can.: **$125.00**
Ster.: **£ 50.00**

*

HN 3617
Monica
Style One
Designer: L. Harradine
Height: 4 1/4", 10.8 cm
Colour: Rose, lemon and
white
Issued: 1993 to the present
Varieties: HN 1458, 1459,
1467
U.S.: **N/I**
Can.: **N/I**
Ster.: **£69.95**

HN 3618
Dinky Doo
Designer: L. Harradine
Height: 4 1/2", 11.9 cm
Colour: White and blue
Issued: 1994 to the present
Varieties: HN 1678, 2120
U.S.: **N/I**
Can.: **N/I**
Ster.: **£43.00**

*

HN 3620
Valerie
Designer: M. Davies
Height: 5 1/4", 13.3 cm
Colour: Blue, pink and
white
Issued: 1994 to the present
Varieties: HN 2107
U.S.: **N/I**
Can.: **N/I**
Ster.: **£69.95**

HN 3621
Autumntime
Style Two
Designer: V. Annand
Height: 8 3/4", 22.2 cm
Colour: Turquoise and brown
Issued: 1994 to the present
Series: Four Seasons (Series Six)

U.S.: $350.00
Can.: $490.00
Ster.: £175.00

HN 3622
Wintertime
Style Two
Designer: Valerie Annand
Height: 8 1/2", 21.6 cm
Colour: Red, white and green
Issued: 1995 to the present
Series: Four Seasons (Series Six)

U.S.: $350.00
Can.: $490.00
Ster.: £175.00

HN 3623
Lady Eaton
Designer: V. Annand
Height: 7 1/2", 19.1 cm
Colour: Blue, white and yellow
Issued: 1994 in a limited edition of 2,500
Varieties: Also called "Janice" (Style Two), HN 3624

U.S.: $450.00
Can.: $500.00
Ster.: £250.00

HN 3624
Janice
Style Two
Designer: V. Annand
Height: 7 1/2", 19.1 cm
Colour: Blue, pink, white and yellow
Issued: 1994 to the present
Varieties: Also called "Lady Eaton" HN 3623

U.S.: N/I
Can.: $369.99
Ster.: £125.00

Commissioned by G.U.S.

HN 3625
Anniversary
Designer: V. Annand
Height: 8 3/4", 22.2 cm
Colour: Blue, black and pink
Issued: 1994 to the present

U.S.: $656.25
Can.: $880.00
Ster.: £275.00

HN 3626
Lily
Style Two
Designer: Valerie Annand
Height: 9 1/2", 24.0 cm
Colour: Mauve and yellow
Issued: 1995-1995
Series: 1. M. Doulton Events
2. Lady Doulton 1995

U.S.: $275.00
Can.: $375.00
Ster.: £150.00

HN 3627
England
Designer: Valerie Annand
Height: 8", 20.3 cm
Colour: Blue and pink
Issued: 1996 to the present
Series: Ladies of the British Isles

U.S.: $370.00
Can.: $490.00
Ster.: £159.00

HN 3628
Ireland
Designer: Valerie Annand
Height: 7 3/4", 19.7 cm
Colour: Green and white
Issued: 1996 to the present
Series: Ladies of the British Isles

U.S.: $370.00
Can. : $490.00
Ster.: £159.00

HN 3629
Scotland
Designer: V. Annand
Height: 7 3/4", 19.7 cm
Colour: Green, white and pink
Issued: 1995 to the present
Series:: Ladies of the British Isles
U.S.: $370.00
Can.: $490.00
Ster.: £159.00

HN 3630
Wales
Designer: V. Annand
Height: 8 1/2", 21.6 cm
Colour: Red, white and green
Issued: 1995 to the present
Series: Ladies of the British Isles
U.S.: $370.00
Can.: $490.00
Ster.: £159.00

HN 3631
Beatrice
Designer: M. Davies
Height: 7", 17.8 cm
Colour: White
Issued: 1994 to the present
Varieties: HN 3263; "Summer Serenade" HN3610; "Kathryn" HN 3413, "Lucy" HN 3653
U.S.: N/I
Can.: N/I
Ster.: £79.95

HN 3632
Amanda
Designer: R. Tabbenor
Height: 5 1/4", 13.3 cm
Colour: White and pink
Issued: 1994 to the present
Varieties: HN 2996, 3406, 3634, 3635; Also called "Figureof the Month, Child"
Series: Vanity Fair Children
U.S.: N/I
Can.: N/I
Ster.: £41.95

HN 3633
Shakespeare
Designer: R. Tabbenor
Height: 11 3/4", 29.8 cm
Colour: Browns and cream
Issued: 1994 in a limited edition of 1564
U.S.: N/I
Can.: N/I
Ster.: £695.00

Commissioned by Lawleys

HN 3634
Amanda
Designer: R. Tabbenor
Height: 5 1/4", 13.3 cm
Colour: White and blue
Issued: 1995
Varieties: HN 2996, 3406, 3632; Also Called Figure Of The Month, Child
U.S.: $100.00
Can.: $100.00
Ster.: £ 50.00

Commissioned by Youngs, London, Canada

HN 3635
Amanda
Designer: R. Tabbenor
Height: 5 1/4", 13.3 cm
Colour: White and pink
Issued: 1995-1995
Varieties: HN 2996, 3406, 3632; Also Called Figure Of The Month, Child
U.S.: $100.00
Can.: $100.00
Ster.: £ 50.00

HN 3636
Captain Hook
Designer: R. Tabbenor
Height: 9 1/4", 23.5 cm
Colour: Red, blue and brown
Issued: 1993 to the present
Series: Character Sculptures
U.S.: $268.75
Can.: $425.00
Ster.: £109.00

HN 3637
Dick Turpin
Designer: R. Tabbenor
Height: 9", 22.9 cm
Colour: Brown, black, red
and white
Issued: 1993 to the present
Series: Character
Sculptures
U.S.: **$268.75**
Can.: **$425.00**
Ster.: **£ 99.95**

HN 3638
D'Artagnan
Designer: R. Tabbenor
Height: 9", 22.9 cm
Colour: Maroon, black, blue
and brown
Issued: 1993 to the present
Series: Character
Sculptures
U.S.: **$268.75**
Can.: **$425.00**
Ster.: **£109.00**

HN 3639
Sherlock Holmes
Designer: R. Tabbenor
Height: 7 1/2", 19.1 cm
Colour: Brown and grey
Issued: 1995 to the present
Series: Character
Sculptures
U.S.: **$268.75**
Can.: **$425.00**
Ster.: **£ 99.95**

HN 3640
W. G. Grace
Designer: R. Tabbenor
Height: 8", 20.3 cm
Colour: White, beige and
red
Issued: 1995 in a limited
edition of 9,500
U.S.: **N/I**
Can.: **N/I**
Ster.: **£125.00**

Commissioned by Lawleys

HN 3641
Robert Burns
Style Two
Designer: R. Tabbenor
Height: 7 1/2", 19.1 cm
Colour: Green and brown
Issued: 1996 to the present
U.S.: **$356.25**
Can.: **$495.00**
Ster.: **£125.00**

HN 3642
The Moor
Designer: C.J. Noke
Height: 13 1/2", 34.3 cm
Colour: Flambé
Issued: 1994-1995
Varieties: HN 1308, 1366,
1425, 1657, 2082;
Also called The Arab
HN 33, 343, 378
Series: Flambe
U.S.: **$3,000.00**
Can.: **$3,000.00**
Ster.: **£ 950.00**

HN 3643
Pauline
Style Three
Designer: N. Pedley
Height: 7 1/4", 18.4 cm
Colour: Red and white
Issued: 1994-1994
Varieties: HN 3656
Series: Collector's
Roadshow Events
U.S.: **$250.00**
Can.: **$325.00**
Ster.: **£145.00**

HN 3644
Deborah
Designer: N. Pedley
Height: 7 1/2", 19.1 cm
Colour: Yellow and white
Issued: 1995-1995
Series: Figure of the Year
U.S.: **$225.00**
Can.: **$385.00**
Ster.: **£105.00**

HN 3645
Lindsay
Designer: N. Pedley
Height: 8", 20.3 cm
Colour: White, blue
and cream
Issued: 1994 to the present
U.S.: **$143.75**
Can.: **$300.00**
Ster.: **£ 89.95**

HN 3646
Claire
Style Three
Designer: N. Pedley
Height: 8", 20.3 cm
Colour: White and blue
Issued: 1994 to the present
Varieties: Also called "Rosemary"
(Style Three)
HN 3691, 3698
U.S.: **$187.50**
Can.: **$300.00**
Ster.: **£ 79.95**

HN 3647
Holly
Designer: N. Pedley
Height: 8", 20.3 cm
Colour: Green and red
Issued: 1994 to the present
U.S.: **$212.50**
Can.: **$395.00**
Ster.: **£ 99.95**

HN 3648
Sweet Sixteen
Style Two
Designer: N. Pedley
Height: 8", 20.3 cm
Colour: Dark pink and white
Issued: 1994 to the present
Varieties: Also called "Angela"
HN 3690
U.S.: **$175.00**
Can.: **$395.00**
Ster.: **£ 95.00**

HN 3649
Hannah
Style Two
Designer: N. Pedley
Height: 4", 10.1 cm
Colour: Pink, yellow and blue
Issued: 1994 to the present
Varieties: HN 3870
Series: Miniatures
U.S.: **$131.25**
Can.: **$230.00**
Ster.: **£ 49.95**

HN 3650
Mother's Helper
Designer: N. Pedley
Height: 4 1/2", 11.4 cm
Colour: White, pink
and yellow
Issued: 1994 to the present
U.S.: **$106.25**
Can.: **$190.00**
Ster.: **£ 49.95**

HN 3651
Hello Daddy
Designer: N. Pedley
Height: 5 3/4", 14.6 cm
Colour: White and green
Issued: 1994 to the present
U.S.: **$143.75**
Can.: **$205.00**
Ster.: **£ 59.95**

HN 3652
First Recital
Designer: N. Pedley
Height: 4 1/2", 11.4 cm
Colour: Blue, pink and white
Issued: 1994 to the present
U.S.: **$106.25**
Can.: **$190.00**
Ster.: **£ 49.95**

HN 3653
Lucy
Style Two
Designer: M. Davies
Height: 7", 17.8 cm
Colour: White
Issued: 1994
Varieties: "Beatrice" HN3263, 3631; "Kathryn" HN 3413; HN 3610

U.S.: N/I
Can.: N/I
Ster.: £70.00

Commissioned by G.U.S.

HN 3654
Young Melody
Designer: N. Pedley
Height: 4 1/4", 10.8 cm
Colour: Yellow and white
Issued: 1994 to the present

U.S.: $106.25
Can.: $190.00
Ster.: £ 49.95

HN 3655
Hannah
Style Two
Designer: N. Pedley
Height: 8 1/4", 19.0 cm
Colour: Blue
Issued: 1995 to the present
Varieties: HN 3369

U.S.: $250.00
Can.: $425.00
Ster.: £ 99.95

HN 3656
Pauline
Style Three
Designer: N. Pedley
Height: 7 1/4", 18.4 cm
Colour: Red and white
Issued: 1994-1994
Series: Collector's Roadshow Events
Varieties: HN 3643

U.S.: $250.00
Can.: $325.00
Ster.: £145.00

HN 3657
Quiet, They're Sleeping
Designer: N. Pedley
Height: 5 1/2", 14.0 cm
Colour: Blue, pink and white
Issued: 1994 to the present

U.S.: N/I
Can.: $179.00
Ster.: £75.00

Commissioned by Lawleys

HN 3658
Charlotte
Style Two
Designer: N. Pedley
Height: Unknown
Colour: Blue
Issued: 1995

U.S.: N/I
Can.: N/I
Ster.: £99.99

Commissioned by Littlewoods

HN 3659
Miss Kay
Designer: N. Pedley
Height: 8 1/4", 21.0 cm
Colour: Pink
Issued: 1994
Varieties: Also called "Helen" HN 3601, 3763

U.S.: N/I
Can.: N/I
Ster.: £79.99

Issued to celebrate Bicentenary Kay's Catalogue Company

HN 3660
Happy Birthday
Style Two
Designer: N. Pedley
Height: 8", 20.3 cm
Colour: Green
Issued: 1995 to the present

U.S.: $268.75
Can.: $445.00
Ster.: £109.00

HN 3661
Gemma
Designer: N. Pedley
Height: 8", 20.3 cm
Colour: Green and pink
Issued: 1995 to the present
U.S.: $212.50
Can.: $425.00
Ster.: £ 89.95

HN 3662
Take Me Home
Designer: N. Pedley
Height: 8", 20.3 cm
Colour: White dress,
pink roses
Issued: 1995 to the present
U.S.: $212.50
Can.: $300.00
Ster.: £ 89.95

HN 3663
Special Treat
Designer: N. Pedley
Height: 6", 15.0 cm
Colour: Pink and white
Issued: 1995 to the present
U.S.: $135.00
Can.: $220.00
Ster.: £ 69.95

HN 3664
Wistful
Style Two
Designer: P. Gee
Height: 12 1/4", 31.1 cm
Colour: White
Issued: 1994 to the present
Series: Images
U.S.: $187.50
Can.: $210.00
Ster.: £ 49.95

HN 3665
Tomorrow's Dreams
Style Two
Designer: P. Gee
Height: 8 1/2", 21.6 cm
Colour: White
Issued: 1995 to the present
Series: Images
U.S.: $187.50
Can.: $150.00
Ster.: £ 69.95

*

HN 3674
Ophelia
Designer: P. Parsons
Height: 7", 17.8 cm
Colour: Rose, yellow and
white
Issued: 1995 in a limited
edition of 5,000
Series: Shakespeare's
Ladies
U.S.: N/I
Can.: N/I
Ster.: £195.00

Commissioned by Lawleys

HN 3675
Richard the Lionheart
Designer: P. Parsons
Height: 10", 25.4 cm
Colour: Grey and white
Issued: 1995 to the present
U.S.: $550.00
Can.: $740.00
Ster.: £225.00

HN 3676
Desdemona
Designer: P. Parsons
Height: 9", 22.9 cm
Colour: Blue, orange and
white
Issued: 1995 in a limited
edition of 5,000
Series: Shakespeare's
Ladies
U.S.: N/I
Can.: N/I
Ster.: £195.00

HN 3677
Cinderella
Designer: P. Parsons
Height: 8", 20.3 cm
Colour: Blue and white
Issued: 1995 in a limited
           edition of 2,000
Series: The Disney Princess
           Collection
U.S.: $300.00
Can.: $375.00
Ster.:   £175.00

HN 3678
Snow White
Designer: P. Parsons
Height: 8", 20.3 cm
Colour: Yellow, blue and red
Issued: 1995 in a limited
           edition of 2,000
Series: The Disney Princess
           Collection
U.S.: $300.00
Can.: $375.00
Ster.:   £175.00

HN 3679
Titania
Designer: P. Parsons
Height: 8 3/4", 22.2 cm
Colour: Rose-yellow and
           blue
Issued: 1995 in a limited
           edition of 5,000
Series: Shakespeare's
           Ladies
U.S.:   N/I
Can.:   N/I
Ster.:   £195.00

HN 3680
Lady Jane Grey
Designer: P. Parsons
Height: 8 1/4", 19.0 cm
Colour: Green and gold
Issued: 1995 in a limited
           edition of 5,000
Series: Tudor Roses
U.S.:   N/I
Can.:   N/I
Ster.:   £225.00

Commissioned by Lawleys

HN 3681
Joan Of Arc
Designer: P. Parsons
Height: 10", 25.4 cm
Colour: Cream and blue
Issued: 1996 to the present
U.S.: $600.00
Can.: $845.00
Ster.:   £225.00

HN 3682
Princess Elizabeth
Designer: P. Parsons
Height: 8 1/2", 21.6 cm
Colour: Red and pink
Issued: 1996 in a limited
           edition of 5,000
Series: Tudor Roses
U.S.:   N/I
Can.:   N/I
Ster.:   £235.00

Commissioned by Lawleys

HN 3683
Eastern Grace
Designer: P. Parsons
Height: 12 1/2", 31.7 cm
Colour: Flambé
Issued: 1995 in a limited
           edition of 2,500
Variaties: HN 3138
Series: Flambé
U.S.: $493.75
Can.:   N/I
Ster.:   £195.00

HN 3684
What's The Matter?
Designer: N. Pedley
Height: 5 1/2", 14.0 cm
Colour: Yellow and white
Issued: 1995 to the present
U.S.: $143.75
Can.: $220.00
Ster.:   £ 69.95

HN 3685
Hometime
Designer: N. Pedley
Height: 6", 15.0 cm
Colour: White and blue
Issued: 1995 to the present

U.S.:	**$143.75**
Can.:	**$220.00**
Ster.:	**£ 69.95**

HN 3686
Nicole
Designer: N. Pedley
Height: 7 1/2", 19.1 cm
Colour: Pink and cream
Issued: 1995
Varieties: HN 3421

U.S.:	**$170.00**
Can.:	**$280.00**
Ster.:	**£ 90.00**

Commissioned by Birks, Canada

HN 3687
Helen
Style Three
Designer: N. Pedley
Height: 7 1/2", 19.1 cm
Colour: Green
Issued: 1995
Varieties: HN 3601, 3763; Also
called "Miss Kay"
HN 3659

U.S.:	**N/I**
Can.:	**N/I**
Ster.:	**£79.99**

Commissioned by Express Gifts

HN 3688
Emily
Style Three
Designer: N. Pedley
Height: 8 1/4", 21.0 cmm
Colour: Blue and yellow
Issued: 1995-1995
Series: R.D.I.C.C.

U.S.:	**$225.00**
Can.:	**$300.00**
Ster.:	**£125.00**

HN 3689
Jacqueline
Style Three
Designer: N. Pedley
Height: 8", 20.3 cm
Colour: White and green
Issued: 1995-1995
Series: Collector's Roadshow
Events

U.S.:	**N/I**
Can.:	**$229.00**
Ster.:	**£ 69.95**

HN 3690
Angela
Style Four
Designer: N. Pedley
Height: 8", 20.3 cm
Colour: Unknown
Issued: 1995
Varieties: Also called "Sweet
Sixteen" HN 3648

U.S.:	**N/I**
Can.:	**N/I**
Ster.:	**£69.99**

Commissioned by G.U.S.

HN 3691
Rosemary
Style Three
Designer: N. Pedley
Height: 8", 20.3 cm
Colour: Mauve and yellow
Issued: 1995 U.K.
1996 Canada
Varieties: HN 3698; Also called
"Claire" (Style Two)
HN 3646

U.S.:	**$300.00**
Can.:	**$375.00**
Ster.:	**£150.00**

HN 3692
Old Country Roses
Style Two
Designer: N. Pedley
Height: 8", 20.3 cm
Colour: Red, white and
yellow
Issued: 1995 to the present

U.S.:	**$350.00**
Can.:	**$495.00**
Ster.:	**£149.00**

HN 3693
April
Style Four
Designer: N. Pedley
Height: 8", 20.3 cm
Colour: Green, yellow and white
Issued: 1995 to the present
U.S.: $306.25
Can.: $445.00
Ster.: £129.00

HN 3694
Caroline
Style Two
Designer: N. Pedley
Height: 8", 20.3 cm
Colour: Pink and yellow
Issued: 1995 to the present
U.S.: $306.25
Can.: $445.00
Ster.: £129.00

HN 3695
Storytime
Style Two
Designer: N. Pedley
Height: 4", 10.1 cm
Colour: White dress with red flowers
Issued: 1995 to the present
U.S.: $143.75
Can.: $220.00
Ster.: £ 69.96

HN 3696
Faithful Friend
Designer: N. Pedley
Height: 6", 15.0 cm
Colour: Reddish-pink, yellow and white
Issued: 1995 to the present
U.S.: $143.75
Can.: $220.00
Ster.: £ 69.95

HN 3697
Home at Last
Designer: N. Pedley
Height: 5 3/4", 14.6 cm
Colour: Green and cream
Issued: 1995 to the present
U.S.: $143.75
Can.: $220.00
Ster.: £ 69.95

HN 3698
Rosemary
Style Three
Designer: N. Pedley
Height: 8", 20.3 cm
Colour: Mauve and yellow
Issued: 1995
Varieties: HN 3691; Also called "Claire" (Style Two) HN 3646
U.S.: $350.00
Can.: $375.00
Ster.: £150.00

HN 3699
Grace
Style Two
Designer: N. Pedley
Height: 8", 20.3 cm
Colour: Green
Issued: 1996 to the present
U.S.: $187.50
Can.: $300.00
Ster.: £ 79.95

HN 3700
Forget-Me-Nots
Designer: V. Annand
Height: 9", 22.9 cm
Colour: Lavender
Issued: 1995 to the present
Series: Flowers of Love
U.S.: $350.00
Can.: $445.00
Ster.: £129.00

HN 3701
Camellias
Designer: V. Annand
Height: 8 1/2", 21.6 cm
Colour: Pink
Issued: 1995 to the present
Series: Flowers of Love

U.S.:	**$350.00**
Can.:	**$445.00**
Ster.:	**£129.00**

HN 3702
Le Bal
Designer: V. Annand
Height: 8 1/2", 21.6 cm
Colour: Yellow and pink
Issued: 1995 in a limited
edition of 5,000
Series: R.D.I.C.C.

U.S.:	**$350.00**
Can.:	**$385.00**
Ster.:	**£175.00**

HN 3703
Belle
Style Three
Designer: V. Annand
Height: 8", 20.3 cm
Colour: Red and gold
Issued: 1996-1996
Series: Figure of the year

U.S.:	**$231.25**
Can.:	**$425.00**
Ster.:	**£109.00**

HN 3704
First Violin
Designer: V. Annand
Height: 9", 22.9 cm
Colour: Grey, yellow ribbon
Issued: 1995 in a limited
edition of 1,500
Series: Edwardian String
Quartet

U.S.:	**N/I**
Can.:	**N/I**
Ster.:	**£295.00**

Commissioned by Lawleys

HN 3705
Second Violin
Designer: V. Annand
Height: 9", 22.9 cm
Colour: Grey, pink ribbon
Issued: 1995 in a limited
edition of 1,500
Series: Edwardian String
Quartet

U.S.:	**N/I**
Can.:	**N/I**
Ster.:	**£295.00**

Commissioned by Lawleys

HN 3706
Viola
Designer: V. Annand
Height: 8 3/4", 22.2 cm
Colour: Grey, green ribbon
Issued: 1995 in a limited
edition of 1,500
Series: Edwardian String
Quartet

U.S.:	**N/I**
Can.:	**N/I**
Ster.:	**£295.00**

Commissioned by Lawleys

HN 3707
Cello
Style Two
Designer: V. Annand
Height: 7", 17.8 cm
Colour: Grey, blue ribbon
Issued: 1995 in a limited
edition of 1,500
Series: Edwardian String
Quartet

U.S.:	**N/I**
Can.:	**N/I**
Ster.:	**£295.00**

Commissioned by Lawleys

HN 3708
Katherine
Style
Designer: V. Annand
Height: 9", 22.9 cm
Colour: Peach
Issued: 1996-1996
Series: 1. M. Doulton Exclusive
2. Lady Doulton 1996

U.S.:	**$275.00**
Can.:	**$385.00**
Ster.:	**£149.00**

HN 3709
Rose
Style Two
Designer: V. Annand
Height: 8 1/2", 21.6 cm
Colour: Peach and white
Issued: 1996 to the present
Series: Flowers of Love
U.S.: $356.25
Can.: $445.00
Ster.: £129.00

HN 3710
Primrose
Designer: V. Annand
Height: 9", 22.9 cm
Colour: Yellow and pink
Issued: 1996 to the present
Series: Flowers of Love
U.S.: $356.25
Can.: $445.00
Ster.: £129.00

*

HN 3718
The Charge of the Light Brigade
Designer: A. Maslankowski
Height: 17", 43.2 cm
Colour: Dark blue, brown and black
Issued: 1995 to the present
Series: Prestige Figures
U.S.: $17,500.00
Can.: $17,000.00
Ster.: £ 7,500.00

HN 3719
Long John Silver
Style Two
Designer: A. Maslankowski
Height: 8 3/4", 22.2 cm
Colour: Browns and yellow
Issued: 1993 to the present
Series: Character Sculptures
U.S.: $268.75
Can.: $425.00
Ster.: £ 99.95

HN 3720
Robin Hood
Style Two
Designer: A. Maslankowski
Height: 10 1/2", 26.7 cm
Colour: Greens and browns
Issued: 1993 to the present
Series: Character Sculptures
U.S.: $268.75
Can.: $425.00
Ster.: £109.00

HN 3721
Pied Piper
Style Two
Designer: A. Maslankowski
Height: 8 3/4", 22.2 cm
Colour: Red, yellow and black
Issued: 1993 to the present
Series: Character Sculptures
U.S.: $268.75
Can.: $425.00
Ster.: £109.00

HN 3722
The Wizard
Style Two
Designer: A. Maslankowski
Height: 10", 25.4 cm
Colour: Unknown
Issued: 1994
Series: Character Sculptures
Varieties: HN 3732
U.S.: $300.00
Can.: $500.00
Ster.: £140.00

HN 3723
Au Revoir
Style One
Designer: A. Maslankowski
Height: 7 3/4", 19.7 cm
Colour: Cream with gold trim
Issued: 1995 to the present
Series: Elegance Collection
U.S.: $168.75
Can.: $300.00
Ster.: £ 69.95

HN 3724
Summer Breeze
Designer: A. Maslankowski
Height: 7 3/4", 19.7 cm
Colour: Cream with gold trim
Issued: 1995 to the present
Series: Elegance Collection

U.S.: $168.75
Can.: $300.00
Ster.: £ 69.95

HN 3725
Spring Morning
Style Two
Designer: A. Maslankowski
Height: 7 3/4", 19.7 cm
Colour: Cream with gold trim
Issued: 1995 to the present
Series: Elegance Collection

U.S.: $168.75
Can.: $300.00
Ster.: £ 69.95

HN 3726
Dinnertime
Designer: A. Maslankowski
Height: 4 1/2", 11.9 cm
Colour: White and green
Issued: 1995 to the present
Series: Vanity Fair Children

U.S.: $106.25
Can.: $190.00
Ster.: £ 49.95

HN 3727
Christmas Carols
Designer: A. Maslankowski
Height: 6", 15.0 cm
Colour: White
Issued: 1995 to the present
Series: Sentiments

U.S.: $ 68.75
Can.: $125.00
Ster.: £ 39.95

HN 3728
Free Spirit
Style Two
Designer: A. Maslankowski
Height: 7 1/2", 19.1 cm
Colour: Cream with gold trim
Issued: 1995 to the present
Series: Elegance Collection

U.S.: $168.75
Can.: $300.00
Ster.: £ 69.95

HN 3729
Au Revoir
Style Two
Designer: A. Maslankowski
Height: 6 1/2", 16.5 cm
Colour: White
Issued: 1996 to the present
Series: Sentiments

U.S.: $ 81.25
Can.: $135.00
Ster.: £ 39.95

HN 3730
Innocence
Style Two
Designer: A. Maslankowski
Height: 3 1/2", 8.9 cm
Colour: Pink and white
Issued: 1996 to the present

U.S.: $ 81.25
Can.: $140.00
Ster.: £ 29.95

HN 3731
Ballet Class
Style Two
Designer: A. Maslankowski
Height: 6", 15.0 cm
Colour: White and yellow
Issued: 1996 to the present

U.S.: $ 81.25
Can.: $190.00
Ster.: £ 39.95

HN3732
The Wizard
Style Two
Designer: A. Maslankowski
Height: 10", 25.4 cm
Colour: Blue and orange
Issued: 1995 to the present
Varieties: HN 3722
Series: Character Sculptures

U.S.:	**$306.25**
Can.:	**$515.00**
Ster.:	**£139.00**

Commissioned by Lawleys

HN 3733
Christmas Angel
Designer: A. Maslankowski
Height: 5 3/4", 14.6 cm
Colour: White
Issued: 1996 to the present
Series: Sentiments

U.S.:	**$ 68.75**
Can.:	**$135.00**
Ster.:	**£ 39.95**

*

HN 3735
Victoria
Style Two
Designer: M. Davies
Remodeller: P. Gee
Height: 3 1/2", 8.9 cm
Colour: Purple
Issued: 1995
Series: M. Doulton Signature
Varieties: HN 3744

U.S.:	**N/I**
Can.:	**N/I**
Ster.:	**£69.00**

Commissioned by Lawleys *

HN 3740
Lynne
Designer: M. Davies
Height: 7", 17.8 cm
Colour: Multi-coloured with gold trim
Issued: 1995-1995
Varieties: HN 2329; Also called "Kathy" (Style Two) HN3305
Series: Roadshow Events

U.S.:	**N/I**
Can.:	**N/I**
Ster.:	**£149.00**

HN 3741
Elaine
Style One
Designer: M. Davies
Height: 7 1/2", 19.1 cm
Colour: Red with gold trim
Issued: 1995-1995
Varieties: HN 2791, 3307
Series: Collector's Roadshow Events

U.S.:	**N/I**
Can.:	**N/I**
Ster.:	**£125.00**

HN 3742
Gillian
Style Three
Designer: M. Davies
Height: 7 3/4", 19.7 cm
Colour: White and pink
Issued: 1995 to the present
Varieties: "June" (Style Three) HN 2790 and Flower of the month

U.S.:	**N/I**
Can.:	**N/I**
Ster.:	**£69.99**

Commissioned by G.U.S.

HN 3743
Kirsty
Style Two
Designer: M. Davies
Remodeller: P. Gee
Height: 3 3/4", 9.5 cm
Colour: Yellow
Issued: 1995
Varieties: HN 3213, 3246, 3480
Series: Miniatures

U.S.:	**N/I**
Can.:	**N/I**
Ster.:	**£39.95**

HN 3744
Victoria
Style Two
Designer: M. Davies
Remodeller: P. Gee
Height: 3 1/2", 8.9 cm
Colour: Patterned pink dress
Issued: 1995 to the present
Varieties: HN 3735
Series: Miniatures

U.S.:	**$131.25**
Can.:	**$230.00**
Ster.:	**£ 49.95**

*

HN 3748
Fiona
Style Four
Designer: M. Davies
Height: 7 1/2", 19.1 cm
Colour: Lemon-yellow, tartan shawl
Issued: 1996 to the present
Varieties: "Adrienne" HN 2152, 2304; Joan HN 3217

U.S.:	**N/I**
Can.:	**N/I**
Ster.:	**£ 99.98**

Available in Scotland only.　*

HN 3750
Gulliver
Designer: D. Biggs
Height: 8 1/2", 21.6 cm
Colour: Blue, yellow, green and red
Issued: 1995 to the present
Series: Character Sculptures

U.S.:	**$306.25**
Can.:	**$515.00**
Ster.:	**£129.00**

HN 3751
Cyrano de Bergerac
Designer: D. Biggs
Height: 8 1/2", 21.6 cm
Colour: Red, blue, black and brown
Issued: 1995 to the present
Series: Character Sculptures

U.S.:	**$268.75**
Can.:	**$425.00**
Ster.:	**£109.00**

HN 3752
Fagin
Style Two
Designer: A. Dobson
Height: 8 1/2", 21.6 cm
Colour: Browns, black and green
Issued: 1995 to the present
Series: Character Sculptuures

U.S.:	**$268.75**
Can.:	**$425.00**
Ster.:	**£ 99.95**

*

HN 3754
For You
Designer: T. Potts
Height: 8 1/2", 21.6 cm
Colour: White, blue and pink
Issued: 1996 to the present

U.S.:	**$187.50**
Can.:	**$289.00**
Ster.:	**£ 79.95**

Metal plaque on base for engraved name

HN 3755
Strolling
Style Two
Designer: T. Potts
Height: 8", 20.3 cm
Colour: Red and yellow
Issued: 1996 to the present

U.S.:	**$206.25**
Can.:	**$395.00**
Ster.:	**£ 89.95**

HN 3756
Pamela
Style Three
Designer: T. Potts
Height: 8", 20.3 cm
Colour: Blue and pink
Issued: 1996-1996
Series: R.D.I.C.C.

U.S.:	**$275.00**
Can.:	**$305.00**
Ster.:	**£129.00**

HN 3757
Jean
Style Three
Designer: T. Potts
Height: 6 3/4", 17.2 cm
Colour: White and blue
Issued: 1996

U.S.:	**N/I**
Can.:	**N/I**
Ster.:	**£89.99**

Commissioned for Kay's mail order catalogue

HN 3758
Bride of the Year
Designer: T. Potts
Height: 8", 20.3 cm
Colour: White and peach
Issued: 1996
Varieties: Also called "Wedding
Morn" HN 3853
U.S.: N/I
Can.: N/I
Ster.: £149.99

Commissioned for Kay's Mail
Order Catalogue

HN 3759
Stephanie
Style Two
Designer: T. Potts
Height: 8 1/4", 21.0 cm
Colour: Pink and lavender
Issued: 1996-1996
Series: Collector's Roadshow
Events
U.S.: N/I
Can.: $229.00
Ster.: N/I

HN 3760
Laura
Style Two
Designer: N. Pedley
Height: 8", 20.3 cm
Colour: White and blue
Issued: 1996 to the present
U.S.: $150.00
Can.: $300.00
Ster.: £ 79.95

HN 3761
Sleepyhead
Style Two
Designer: N. Pedley
Height: 4", 10.1 cm
Colour: White, green and
brown
Issued: 1996 to the present
U.S.: $ 93.75
Can.: $190.00
Ster.: £ 39.95

HN 3762
Time For Bed
Designer: N. Pedley
Height: 5 1/4", 13.3 cm
Colour: Pink
Issued: 1996 to the present
U.S.: $143.75
Can.: $220.00
Ster.: £ 69.95

HN 3763
Helen
Style Three
Designer: N. Pedley
Height: 8 1/4", 21.0 cm
Colour: Pink
Issued: 1996
Varieties: HN 3601, 3687;
"Miss Kay" HN 3659
U.S.: N/I
Can.: $
Ster.: N/I

Commissioned by Sears, Canada

HN 3764
Welcome
Designer: N. Pedley
Height: 5 3/4", 14.6 cm
Colour: White
Issued: 1996-1996
Series: R.D.I.C.C.
Complimentary
figure 1996
U.S.: $ 80.00
Can.: $140.00
Ster.: £ 60.00

Photograph
Not
Available

HN 3765
Kate
Style Two
Designer: N. Pedley
Height: 8", 20.3 cm
Colour: Red and orange
with flowers
Issued: 1996
U.S.: N/I
Can.: N/I
Ster.: £129.99

Commissioned for Kay's Mail
Order Catalogue

HN 3766
Anita
Designer: N. Pedley
Height: 8", 20.3 cm
Colour: White, green and yellow
Issued: 1996

U.S.:	N/I
Can.:	N/I
Ster.:	£79.99

Commissioned for Kay's Mail Order Catalogue

HN 3767
Christine
Style Four
Designer: N. Pedley
Height: 8", 20.3 cm
Colour: Blue
Issued: 1996

U.S.:	$306.25
Can.:	$445.00
Ster.:	£125.00

HN 3768
Off To School
Designer: N. Pedley
Height: 5 1/4", 13.3 cm
Colour: Navy and grey
Issued: 1996 to the present

U.S.:	$187.50
Can.:	$300.00
Ster.:	£ 69.95

HN 3769
Winter's Day
Designer: N. Pedley
Height: 7 3/4", 19.7 cm
Colour: Red and white
Issued: 1996-1997
Series: R.D.I.C.C.

U.S.:	$325.00
Can.:	$380.00
Ster.:	£129.00

HN 3770
Sir Francis Drake
Designer: D. Biggs
Height: 8 1/2", 21.6 cm
Colour: Red, yellow, brown and green
Issued: 1996 to the present
Series: Character Sculptures

U.S.:	$275.00
Can.:	$400.00
Ster.:	£ 99.95

*

HN 3780
The Bowls Player
Designer: J. Jones
Height: 6", 15.0 cm
Colour: Yellow, white and green
Issued: 1996 to the present
Series: Character Sculptures

U.S.:	$137.50
Can.:	$250.00
Ster.:	£ 69.95

*

HN 3785
Bill Sikes
Designer: A. Dobson
Height: 9", 22.9 cm
Colour: Brown
Issued: 1996 to the present
Series: Character Sculptures

U.S.:	$306.25
Can.:	$400.00
Ster.:	£ 99.95

HN 3786
Oliver Twist and
The Artful Dodger
Designer: A. Dobson
Height: 8", 20.3 cm
Colour: Browns, blue and black
Issued: 1996 to the present
Series: Character Sculptures

U.S.:	$275.00
Can.:	$515.00
Ster.:	£129.00

*

HN 3790
Sophie
Style Three
Designer: A. Maslankowski
Height: 9 1/2", 24.1 cm
Colour: Cream and green
Issued: 1996 to the present
Varieties: HN 3791, 3792, 3793
Series: Charleston

U.S.: **$212.50**
Can.: **$370.00**
Ster.: **£ 79.95**

HN 3791
Sophie
Style Three
Designer: A. Maslankowski
Height: 9 1/2", 24.1 cm
Colour: Cream and blue
Issued: 1996 to the present
Varieties: HN 3790, 3792, 3793
Series: Charleston

U.S.: **$212.50**
Can.: **$370.00**
Ster.: **£ 79.95**

HN 3792
Sophie
Style Three
Designer: A. Maslankowski
Height: 9 1/2", 24.1 cm
Colour: Cream and pink
Issued: 1996 to the present
Varieties: HN 3790, 3791, 3793
Series: Charleston

U.S.: **$212.50**
Can.: **$370.00**
Ster.: **£ 79.95**

HN 3793
Sophie
Style Three
Designer: A. Maslankowski
Height: 9 1/2", 24.1 cm
Colour: Ivory and gold
Issued: 1996 to the present
Varieties: HN 3790, 3791, 3792
Series: Charleston

U.S.: **$212.50**
Can.: **$370.00**
Stir.: **£ 79.95**

HN 3794
Harriet
Style Two
Designer: A. Maslankowski
Height: 9 1/4", 23.5 cm
Colour: Cream and green
Issued: 1996 to the present
Varieties: HN 3795, 3796, 3797
Series: Charleston

U.S.: **$268.75**
Can.: **$395.00**
Ster.: **£ 99.95**

HN 3795
Harriet
Style Two
Designer: A. Maslankowski
Height: 9 1/4", 23.5 cm
Colour: Cream and blue
Issued: 1996 to the present
Varieties: HN 3794, 3796, 3797
Series: Charleston

U.S.: **$268.75**
Can.: **$395.00**
Ster.: **£ 99.95**

HN 3796
Harriet
Style Two
Designer: A. Maslankowski
Height: 9 1/4", 23.5 cm
Colour: Cream and pink
Issued: 1996 to the present
Varieties: HN 3794, 3795, 3797
Series: Charleston

U.S.: **$268.75**
Can.: **$395.00**
Ster.: **£ 99.95**

HN 3797
Harriet
Style Two
Designer: A. Maslankowski
Height: 9 1/4", 23.5 cm
Colour: Cream, ivory and
gold
Issued: 1996 to the present
Varieties: HN 3794, 3795, 3796
Series: Charleston

U.S.: **$268.75**
Can.: **$395.00**
Ster.: **£ 99.95**

HN 3798
Eliza
Style Three
Designer: A. Maslankowski
Height: 9 1/2", 24.1 cm
Colour: Cream and green
Issued: 1996 to the present
Varieties: HN 3799, 3800, 3801
Series: Charleston

U.S.:	**$212.50**
Can.:	**$370.00**
Ster.:	**£ 79.95**

HN 3799
Eliza
Style Three
Designer: A. Maslankowski
Height: 9 1/2", 24.1 cm
Colour: Cream and blue
Issued: 1996 to the present
Varieties: HN 3798, 3800, 3801
Series: Charleston

U.S.:	**$212.50**
Can.:	**$370.00**
Ster.:	**£ 79.95**

HN 3800
Eliza
Style Three
Designer: A. Maslankowski
Height: 9 1/2", 24.1 cm
Colour: Cream and pink
Issued: 1996 to the present
Varieties: HN 3798, 3799, 3801
Series: Charleston

U.S.:	**$212.50**
Can.:	**$370.00**
Ster.:	**£ 79.95**

HN 3801
Eliza
Style Three
Designer: A. Maslankowski
Height: 9 1/2", 24.1 cm
Colour: Ivory and gold
Issued: 1996 to the present
Varieties: HN 3798, 3799, 3800
Series: Charleston

U.S.:	**$212.50**
Can.:	**$370.00**
Ster.:	**£ 79.95**

HN 3802
Daisy
Style Two
Designer: A. Maslankowski
Height: 9 1/4", 23.5 cm
Colour: Cream and green
Issued: 1996 to the present
Varieties: HN 3803, 3804, 3805
Series: Charleston

U.S.:	**$268.75**
Can.:	**$395.00**
Ster.:	**£ 99.95**

HN 3803
Daisy
Style Two
Designer: A. Maslankowski
Height: 9 1/4", 23.5 cm
Colour: Cream and blue
Issued: 1996 to the present
Varieties: HN 3802, 3804, 3805
Series: Charleston

U.S.:	**$268.75**
Can.:	**$395.00**
Ster.:	**£ 99.95**

HN 3804
Daisy
Style Two
Designer: A. Maslankowski
Height: 9 1/4", 23.5 cm
Colour: Cream and pink
Issued: 1996 to the present
Varieties: 3802, 3803, 3805
Series: Charleston

U.S.:	**$268.75**
Can.:	**$395.00**
Ster.:	**£ 99.95**

HN 3805
Daisy
Style Two
Designer: A. Maslankowski
Height: 9 1/4", 23.5 cm
Colour: Ivory and gold
Issued: 1996 to the present
Varieties: HN 3802, 3803, 3804
Series: Charleston

U.S.:	**$268.75**
Can.:	**$395.00**
Ster.:	**£ 99.95**

HN 3806
Emily
Style Three
Designer: A. Maslankowski
Height: 9", 22.9 cm
Colour: Cream and green
Issued: 1996 to the present
Series: Charleston
Varieties: HN 3807, 3808, 3809

U.S.: $212.50
Can.: $395.00
Ster.: £ 99.95

HN 3807
Emily
Style Three
Designer: A. Maslankowski
Height: 9", 22.9 cm
Colour: Cream and blue
Issued: 1996 to the present
Series: Charleston
Varieties: HN 3806, 3808, 3809

U.S.: $212.50
Can.: $395.00
Ster.: £ 99.95

HN 3808
Emily
Style Three
Designer: A. Maslankowski
Height: 9", 22.9 cm
Colour: Cream and pink
Issued: 1996 to the present
Series: Charleston
Varieties: HN 3806, 3807, 3809

U.S.: $212.50
Can.: $395.00
Ster.: £ 99.95

HN 3809
Emily
Style Three
Designer: A. Maslankowski
Height: 9", 22.9 cm
Colour: Ivory and gold
Issued: 1996 to the present
Series: Charleston
Varieties: HN 3806. 3807, 3808

U.S.: $212.50
Can.: $395.00
Ster.: £ 99.95

HN 3810
Charlotte
Style Two
Designer: A. Maslankowski
Height: 9 1/4", 23.5 cm
Colour: Cream and green
Issued: 1996 to the present
Series: Charleston
Varieties: HN 3811, 3812, 3813

U.S.: $268.75
Can.: $395.00
Ster.: £ 99.95

HN 3811
Charlotte
Style Two
Designer: A. Maslankowski
Height: 9 1/4", 23.5 cm
Colour: Cream and blue
Issued: 1996 to the present
Series: Charleston
Varieties: HN 3810, 3812, 3813

U.S.: $268.75
Can.: $395.00
Ster.: £ 99.95

HN 3812
Charlotte
Style Two
Designer: A. Maslankowski
Height: 9 1/4", 23.5 cm
Colour: Cream and pink
Issued: 1996 to the present
Series: Charleston
Varieties: HN 3810, 3811, 3813

U.S.: $268.75
Can.: $395.00
Ster.: £ 99.95

HN 3813
Charlotte
Style Two
Designer: A. Maslankowski
Height: 9 1/4", 23.5 cm
Colour: Ivory and gold
Issued: 1996 to the present
Series: Charleston
Varieties: HN 3810, 3811, 3812

U.S.: $268.75
Can.: $395.00
Ster.: £ 99.95

HN 3814
The Cricketer
Designer: A. Maslankowski
Height: 8 1/4", 21.0 cm
Colour: White
Issued: 1996 to the present

U.S.:	$171.25
Can.:	$250.00
Ster.:	£ 69.95

*

HN 3820
Lillie Langtry
Designer: D. V. Tootle
Height: 8 3/4", 22.2 cm
Colour: Pink
Issued: 1996 in a limited
edition of 5,000
Series: Victorian and
Edwardian actresses

U.S.:	N/I
Can.:	N/I
Ster.:	£175.00

Commissioned by Lawleys

HN 3821
Alfred The Great
Designer: D. V. Tootle
Height: 9 1/4", 23.5 cm
Colour: Gold, red and green
Issued: 1996 to the present

U.S.:	$550.00
Can.:	$845.00
Ster.:	£225.00

HN 3822
King James I
Designer: D. V. Tootle
Height: 9", 22.9 cm
Colour: Red, grey , gold trim
Issued: 1996 in a limited
edition of 1,500
Series: Stuart Kings

U.S.:	N/I
Can.:	N/I
Ster.:	£495.00

Commissioned by Lawleys
*

Photograph
Not
Available

HN 3825
King Charles II
Designer: D.V. Tootle
Height: 9", 22.9 cm
Colour: Black and white
Issued: 1996 in a limited
edition of 5,000
Series: Stuart Kings

U.S.:	N/I
Can.:	N/I
Ster.:	£495.00

Commissioned by Lawleys

Photograph
Not
Available

HN 3826
Ellen Terry
Designer: D.V. Tootle
Height: 9", 22.9 cm
Colour: Blue and yellow
Issued: 1996 in a limited
edition of 5,000
Series: Victorian Actresses

U.S.:	N/I
Can.:	N/I
Ster.:	£175.00

Commissioned by Lawleys
*

HN 3830
Belle
Style Three
Designer: P. Parsons
Height: 8", 20.3 cm
Colour: Yellow
Issued: 1996 in a limited
ediiton of 2,000
Series: The Disney Princess
Collection

U.S.:	N/I
Can.:	N/I
Ster.:	£150.00

HN 3831
Ariel
Designer: P. Parsons
Height: 8 1/4", 21.0 cm
Colour: White
Issued: 1996 in a limited
edition of 2,000
Series: The Disney Princess
Collection

U.S.:	N/I
Can.:	N/I
Ster.:	£150.00

HN 3832
Jasmine
Designer: P. Parsons
Height: 7 1/2", 19.1 cm
Colour: Lilac dress
Issued: 1996 in a limited edition of 2,000
Series: The Disney Princess Collection

U.S.: N/I
Can.: N/I
Ster.: £150.00

HN 3833
Aurora
Designer: P. Parsons
Height: 7 1/2", 19.1 cm
Colour: Blue dress
Issued: 1996 in a limited edition of 2,000
Series: The Disney Princess Collection

U.S.: N/I
Can.: N/I
Ster.: £150.00

HN 3834
Mary Tudor
Designer: P. Parsons
Height: 6 1/4", 15.9 cm
Colour: Purple and yellow
Issued: 1996 in a limited edition of 5,000
Series: Tudor Roses

U.S.: N/I
Can.: N/I
Ster.: £235.00

Commissioned by Lawleys

HN 3835
Scheherazade
Designer: P. Parsons
Height: 10 1/2", 26.7 cm
Colour: Red and green
Issued: 1996 in a limited edition of 1,500
Series: Fabled Beauties

U.S.: N/I
Can.: N/I
Ster.: £395.00

Commissioned by Lawleys
*

HNHN 3851
Sally
Style Two
Designer: T. Potts
Height: 8 1/4", 21.0 cm
Colour: Blue
Issued: 1996 to the present
Varieties: HN 3383

U.S.: N/I
Can.: $395.00
Ster.: £ 99.95

HN 3852
Sarah
Designer: T. Potts
Height: 8", 20.3 cm
Colour: Green
Issued: 1996 to the present
Varieties: HN 3384, 3857

U.S.: N/I
Can.: $445.00
Ster.: £125.00

HN 3853
Wedding Morn
Style Two
Designer: T. Potts
Height: 8", 20.3 cm
Colour: Ivory and gold
Issued: 1996 to the present
Varieties: Also called "Bride of the Year" HN 3758

U.S.: N/I
Can.: $490.00
Ster.: £149.00

HN 3854
Amy
Style Three
Designer: T. Potts
Height: 8", 20.3 cm
Colour: Pink
Issued: 1996 to the present

U.S.: N/I
Can.: $269.99
Ster.: £ 99.95

HN 3855
Lambing Time
Style Two
Designer: T. Potts
Height: 8", 20.3 cm
Colour: White, gold trim
Issued: 1996 to the present
Series: Elegance Collection

U.S.: N/I
Can.: $300.00
Ster.: £ 69.95

HN 3856
Country Girl
Style Two
Designer: T. Potts
Height: 8", 20.3 cm
Colour: White, gold trim
Issued: 1996 to the present
Series: Elegance Collection

U.S.: N/I
Can.: $300.00
Ster.: £ 69.95

HN 3857
Sarah
Designer: T. Potts
Height: 8", 20.3 cm
Colour: Pink and yellow
Issued: In a limited edition
of 1,996
Varieties: HN 3384, 3852

U.S.: N/I
Can.: N/I
Ster.: £ 99.95

To commemorate the opening of
the R.D. Visitor's Centre
*

HN3890
Geoffrey Boycott
Designer: R. Tabbenor
Height: 9 1/2", 24.0 cm
Colour: White
Issued: 1996 in a limited
edition of 8,114

U.S.: N/I
Can.: N/I
Ster.: £125.00

Commissioned by Lawleys
*

HN 3920
Jack Point
Designer: C. J. Noke
Height: 17", 43.2 cm
Colour: Blue, gold and red
Issued: 1996 in a limited
edition of 250
Varieties: HN 85, 91, 99, 2080

U.S.: $6300.00
Can.: $8,755.00
Ster.: £2,500.00

HN 3921
Princess Badoura
Designer: H. Tittensor, Harry
E. Stanton and
F. Van Allen Phillips
Height: 20", 50.8 cm
Colour: Blue, gold and red
Issued: 1996 to the present
Varieties: HN 2081

U.S.: N/I
Can.: $43,750.00
Ster.: £12,500.00

M SERIES

M 1
Victorian Lady
Style Two
Designer: L. Harradine
Height: 3 3/4", 9.5 cm
Colour: Pink and green
Issued: 1932-1945
Varieties: M 2, 25

US: $550.00
Can.: $625.00
Ster.: £295.00

M 2
Victorian Lady
Style Two
Designer: L. Harradine
Height: 3 3/4", 9.5 cm
Colour: Lavender and green
Issued: 1932-1945
Varieties: M 1, 25

US: $550.00
Can.: $650.00
Ster.: £295.00

M 3
Paisley Shawl
Style Two
Designer: L. Harradine
Height: 4", 10.1 cm
Colour: Lavender
Issued: 1932-1938
Varieties: M 4, 26

US: $600.00
Can.: $675.00
Ster.: £295.00

M 4
Paisley Shawl
Style Two
Designer: L. Harradine
Height: 4", 10.1 cm
Colour: Purple and green
Issued: 1932-1945
Varieties: M 3, 26

US: $525.00
Can.: $600.00
Ster.: £295.00

M 5
Sweet Anne
Style Two
Designer: L. Harradine
Height: 4", 10.1 cm
Colour: Lavender and green
Issued: 1932-1945
Varieties: HN 6, 27

US: $550.00
Can.: $625.00
Ster.: £295.00

M 6
Sweet Anne
Style Two
Designer: L. Harradine
Height: 4", 10.1 cm
Colour: Blue
Issued: 1932-1945
Varieties: HN 5, 27

US: $600.00
Can.: $675.00
Ster.: £295.00

M 7
Patricia
Style Two
Designer: L. Harradine
Height: 4", 10.1 cm
Colour: Pink and green
Issued: 1932-1945
Varieties: HN 8, 28

US: $700.00
Can.: $775.00
Ster.: £375.00

M 8
Patricia
Style Two
Designer: L. Harradine
Height: 4", 10.1 cm
Colour: Orange and yellow
Issued: 1932-1938
Varieties: HN 7, 28

US: $650.00
Can.: $775.00
Ster.: £375.00

M 9
Chloe
Style Two
Designer: L. Harradine
Height: 2 3/4", 7.0 cm
Colour: Pink
Issued: 1932-1945
Varieties: HN 10, 29

US:	$600.00
Can.:	$750.00
Ster.:	£350.00

M 10
Chloe
Style Two
Designer: L. Harradine
Height: 2 3/4", 7.0 cm
Colour: Lavender
Issued: 1932-1945
Varieties: HN 9, 29

US:	$600.00
Can.:	$750.00
Ster.:	£350.00

M 11
Bridesmaid
Style Two
Designer: L. Harradine
Height: 3 3/4", 9.5 cm
Colour: Pink and lavender
Issued: 1932-1938
Varieties: M 12, 30

US:	$700.00
Can.:	$875.00
Ster.:	£295.00

M 12
Bridesmaid
Style Two
Designer: L. Harradine
Height: 3 3/4", 9.5 cm
Colour: Yellow and lavender
Issued: 1932-1945
Varieties: M 11, 30

US:	$500.00
Can.:	$600.00
Ster.:	£295.00

M 13
Priscilla
Style Two
Designer: L. Harradine
Height: 4", 10.1 cm
Colour: Green and yellow
Issued: 1932-1938
Varieties: M 14, 24

US:	$700.00
Can.:	$875.00
Ster.:	£350.00

M 14
Priscilla
Style Two
Designer: L. Harradine
Height: 4", 10.1 cm
Colour: Lavender and pink
Issued: 1932-1945
Varieties: M 13, 24

US:	$575.00
Can.:	$650.00
Ster.:	£350.00

M 15
Pantalettes
Style Two
Designer: L. Harradine
Height: 3 3/4", 9.5 cm
Colour: Lavender
Issued: 1932-1945
Varieties: M 16, 31

US:	$700.00
Can.:	$800.00
Ster.:	£375.00

M 16
Pantalettes
Style Two
Designer: L. Harradine
Height: 3 3/4", 9.5 cm
Colour: Pink
Issued: 1932-1945
Varieties: M 15, 31

US:	$675.00
Can.:	$700.00
Ster.:	£375.00

M 17
Shepherd
Style Two
Designer: Unknown
Height: 3 3/4", 9.5 cm
Colour: Purple, pink
and green
Issued: 1932-1938
Varieties: HN 709, M 19

US: $4,000.00
Can.: $4,000.00
Ster.: £1,500.00

M 18
Shepherdess
Style One
Designer: Unknown
Height: 3 1/2", 8.9 cm
Colour: Green and lavender
Issued: 1932-1938
Varieties: HN 708, M 20

US: $4,000.00
Can.: $4,000.00
Ster.: £1,500.00

M 19
Shepherd
Style Two
Designer: Unknown
Height: 3 3/4", 9.5 cm
Colour: Purple, green
and brown
Issued: 1932-1938
Varieties: HN 709, M 17

US: $4,000.00
Can.: $4,000.00
Ster.: £1,500.00

M 20
Shepherdess
Style One
Designer: Unknown
Height: 3 3/4", 9.5 cm
Colour: Yellow
Issued: 1932-1938
Varieties: HN 708, M 18

US: $4,000.00
Can.: $4,000.00
Ster.: £1,500.00

M 21
Polly Peachum
Style Three
Designer: L. Harradine
Height: 2 1/4", 5.7 cm
Colour: Pink
Issued: 1932-1945
Varieties: HN 698, 699, 757,
758, 759, 760, 761,
762, M 22, 23

US: $950.00
Can.: $950.00
Ster.: £295.00

M 22
Polly Peachum
Style Three
Designer: L. Harradine
Height: 2 1/4", 5.7 cm
Colour: Red and blue
Issued: 1932-1938
Varieties: HN 698, 699, 757,
758, 759, 760, 761,
762, M 21, 23

US: $1,250.00
Can.: $1,250.00
Ster.: £ 450.00

M 23
Polly Peachum
Style Three
Designer: L. Harradine
Height: 2 1/4", 5.7 cm
Colour: Purple, pink
and white
Issued: 1932-1938
Varieties: HN 698, 699, 757,
758, 759, 760, 761,
762, M 21, 22

US: $1,750.00
Can.: $1,750.00
Ster.: £ 650.00

M 24
Priscilla
Style Two
Designer: L. Harradine
Height: 3 3/4", 9.5 cm
Colour: Red
Issued: 1932-1945
Varieties: M 13, 14

US: $650.00
Can.: $800.00
Ster.: £395.00

M 25
Victorian Lady
Style Two
Designer: L. Harradine
Height: 3 3/4", 9.5 cm
Colour: Lavender and pink
Issued: 1932-1945
Varieties: M 1, 2

US:	**$600.00**
Can.:	**$750.00**
Ster.:	**£295.00**

M 26
Paisley Shawl
Style Two
Designer: L. Harradine
Height: 3 3/4", 9.5 cm
Colour: Green
Issued: 1932-1945
Varieties: M 3, 4

US:	**$675.00**
Can.:	**$775.00**
Ster.:	**£295.00**

M 27
Sweet Anne
Style Two
Designer: L. Harradine
Height: 4", 10.1 cm
Colour: Red, blue and yellow
Issued: 1932-1945
Varieties: M 5, 6

US:	**$600.00**
Can.:	**$675.00**
Ster.:	**£295.00**

M 28
Patricia
Style Two
Designer: L. Harradine
Height: 4", 10.1 cm
Colour: Lavender
Issued: 1932-1945
Varieties: M 7, 8

US:	**$700.00**
Can.:	**$800.00**
Ster.:	**£395.00**

M 29
Chloe
Style Two
Designer: L. Harradine
Height: 2 3/4", 7.0 cm
Colour: Pink and yellow
Issued: 1932-1945
Varieties: M 9, 10

US:	**$775.00**
Can.:	**$875.00**
Ster.:	**£295.00**

M 30
Bridesmaid
Style Two
Designer: L. Harradine
Height: 3 3/4", 9.5 cm
Colour: Pink and lavender
Issued: 1932-1945
Varieties: M 11, 12

US:	**$525.00**
Can.:	**$600.00**
Ster.:	**£295.00**

M 31
Pantalettes
Style Two
Designer: L. Harradine
Height: 4", 10.1 cm
Colour: Green and blue
Issued: 1932-1945
Varieties: M 15, 16

US:	**$825.00**
Can.:	**$900.00**
Ster.:	**£350.00**

M 32
Rosamund
Style Three
Designer: L. Harradine
Height: 4 1/4", 10.8 cm
Colour: Yellow
Issued: 1932-1945
Varieties: M 33

US:	**$1,250.00**
Can.:	**$1,250.00**
Ster.:	**£ 475.00**

M 33
Rosamund
Style Three
Designer: L. Harradine
Height: 4", 10.1 cm
Colour: Red
Issued: 1932-1945
Varieties: M 32

US:	**$1,100.00**
Can.:	**$1,100.00**
Ster.:	**£ 475.00**

M 34
Denise
Style One
Designer: L. Harradine
Height: 4 1/2", 11.4 cm
Colour: Green, red and blue
Issued: 1933-1945
Varieties: M 35

US:	**$1,350.00**
Can.:	**$1,350.00**
Ster.:	**£ 650.00**

M 35
Denise
Style One
Designer: L. Harradine
Height: 4 1/2", 11.4 cm
Colour: Blue and pink
Issued: 1933-1945
Varieties: M 34

US:	**$1,600.00**
Can.:	**$1,600.00**
Ster.:	**£ 650.00**

M 36
Norma
Designer: L. Harradine
Height: 4 1/2", 11.4 cm
Colour: Red and green
Issued: 1933-1945
Varieties: M 37

US:	**$1,500.00**
Can.:	**$1,500.00**
Ster.:	**£ 650.00**

M 37
Norma
Designer: L. Harradine
Height: 4 1/2", 11.4 cm
Colour: Blue, red
and white
Issued: 1933-1945
Varieties: M 36

US:	**$1,750.00**
Can.:	**$1,750.00**
Ster.:	**£ 650.00**

M 38
Robin
Designer: L. Harradine
Height: 2 1/2", 6.4 cm
Colour: Pink and lavender
Issued: 1933-1945
Varieties: M 39

US:	**$1,100.00**
Can.:	**$1,100.00**
Ster.:	**£ 475.00**

M 39
Robin
Designer: L. Harradine
Height: 2 1/2", 6.4 cm
Colour: Blue and green
Issued: 1933-1945
Varieties: M 38

US:	**$1,100.00**
Can.:	**$1,100.00**
Ster.:	**£ 475.00**

M 40
Erminie
Designer: L. Harradine
Height: 4", 10.1 cm
Colour: White and pink
Issued: 1933-1945

US:	**$1,350.00**
Can.:	**$1,350.00**
Ster.:	**£ 600.00**

M 41
Mr. Pickwick
Style One
Designer: L. Harradine
Height: 4", 10.1 cm
Colour: Yellow and black
Issued: 1932-1983
Varieties: HN 529
Series: Dickens (Series One)

  US: **$125.00**
  Can.: **$125.00**
  Ster.: **£ 45.00**

M 42
Mr. Micawber
Style One
Designer: L. Harradine
Height: 4", 10.1 cm
Colour: Yellow and black
Issued: 1932-1983
Varieties: HN 532
Series: Dickens (Series One)

  US: **$125.00**
  Can.: **$125.00**
  Ster.: **£ 45.00**

M 43
Pecksniff
Style One
Designer: L. Harradine
Height: 4 1/4", 10.8 cm
Colour: Black
Issued: 1932-1982
Varieties: HN 535
Series: Dickens (Series One)

  US: **$125.00**
  Can.: **$125.00**
  Ster.: **£ 45.00**

M 44
Fat Boy
Style One
Designer: L. Harradine
Height: 4 1/4", 10.8 cm
Colour: Blue and white
Issued: 1932-1983
Varieties: HN 530
Series: Dickens (Series One)

  US: **$125.00**
  Can.: **$125.00**
  Ster.: **£ 45.00**

M 45
Uriah Heep
Style One
Designer: L. Harradine
Height: 4", 10.1 cm
Colour: Black
Issued: 1932-1983
Varieties: HN 545
Series: Dickens (Series One)

  US: **$125.00**
  Can.: **$125.00**
  Ster.: **£ 45.00**

M 46
Sairey Gamp
Style One
Designer: L. Harradine
Height: 4", 10.1 cm
Colour: Green
Issued: 1932-1983
Varieties: HN 533
Series: Dickens (Series One)

  US: **$135.00**
  Can.: **$125.00**
  Ster.: **£ 45.00**

M 47
Tony Weller
Style One
Designer: L. Harradine
Height: 4", 10.1 cm
Colour: Green, black,
             red and yellow
Issued: 1932-1981
Varieties: HN 544
Series: Dickens (Series One)

  US: **$125.00**
  Can.: **$125.00**
  Ster.: **£ 45.00**

M 48
Sam Weller
Designer: L. Harradine
Height: 4", 10.1 cm
Colour: Yellow and
             brown
Issued: 1932-1981
Varieties: HN 531
Series: Dickens (Series One)

  US: **$125.00**
  Can.: **$125.00**
  Ster.: **£ 45.00**

M 49
Fagin
Style One
Designer: L. Harradine
Height: 4", 10.1 cm
Colour: Brown
Issued: 1932-1983
Varieties: HN 534
Series: Dickens (Series One)
US: **$125.00**
Can.: **$125.00**
Ster.: £ 45.00

M 50
Stiggins
Designer: L. Harradine
Height: 4", 10.1 cm
Colour: Black
Issued: 1932-1981
Varieties: HN 536
Series: Dickens (Series One)
US: **$125.00**
Can.: **$125.00**
Ster.: £ 45.00

M 51
Little Nell
Designer: L. Harradine
Height: 4 1/4", 10.8 cm
Colour: Pink
Issued: 1932-1983
Varieties: HN 540
Series: Dickens (Series One)
US: **$135.00**
Can.: **$125.00**
Ster.: £ 45.00

M 52
Alfred Jingle
Designer: L. Harradine
Height: 3 3/4", 9.5 cm
Colour: Black and white
Issued: 1932-1981
Varieties: HN 541
Series: Dickens (Series One)
US: **$125.00**
Can.: **$125.00**
Ster.: £ 45.00

M 53
Buz Fuz
Designer: L. Harradine
Height: 4", 10.1 cm
Colour: Black and red
Issued: 1932-1983
Varieties: HN 538
Series: Dickens (Series One)
US: **$130.00**
Can.: **$125.00**
Ster.: £ 45.00

M 54
Bill Sykes
Designer: L. Harradine
Height: 4 1/4", 10.8 cm
Colour: Black and brown
Issued: 1932-1981
Varieties: HN 537
Series: Dickens (Series One)
US: **$125.00**
Can.: **$125.00**
Ster.: £ 45.00

M 55
Artful Dodger
Designer: L. Harradine
Height: 4 1/4", 10.8 cm
Colour: Black and brown
Issued: 1932-1983
Varieties: HN 546
Series: Dickens (Series One)
US: **$125.00**
Can.: **$125.00**
Ster.: £ 45.00

M 56
Tiny Tim
Designer: L. Harradine
Height: 3 3/4", 9.5 cm
Colour: Black and brown
Issued: 1932-1983
Varieties: HN 539
Series: Dickens (Series One)
US: **$125.00**
Can.: **$125.00**
Ster.: £ 45.00

M 64
Veronica
Style Two
Designer: L. Harradine
Height: 4 1/2", 10.8 cm
Colour: Pink
Issued: 1934-1949
Varieties: M 70

US:	**$1,200.00**
Can.:	**$1,200.00**
Ster.:	**£ 550.00**

M 65
June
Style Two
Designer: L. Harradine
Height: 4 1/4", 10.8 cm
Colour: Pink and lavender
Issued: 1935-1949
Varieties: M 71

US:	**$1,100.00**
Can.:	**$1,100.00**
Ster.:	**£ 650.00**

M 66
Monica
Style Two
Designer: L. Harradine
Height: 3", 7.6 cm
Colour: Blue and pink
Issued: 1935-1949
Varieties: M 72

US:	**$1,350.00**
Can.:	**$1,350.00**
Ster.:	**£ 550.00**

M 67
Dainty May
Style Two
Designer: L. Harradine
Height: 4", 10.1 cm
Colour: Turquoise and pink
Issued: 1935-1949
Varieties: M 73

US:	**$1,300.00**
Can.:	**$1,300.00**
Ster.:	**£ 550.00**

M 68
Mirabel
Style Two
Designer: L. Harradine
Height: 4", 10.1 cm
Colour: Pink and green
Issued: 1936-1949
Varieties: M 74

US:	**$1,250.00**
Can.:	**$1,250.00**
Ster.:	**£ 650.00**

M 69
Janet
Style Two
Designer: L. Harradine
Height: 4", 10.1 cm
Colour: Blue and white
Issued: 1936-1949
Varieties: M 75

US:	**$1,100.00**
Can.:	**$1,100.00**
Ster.:	**£ 495.00**

M 70
Veronica
Style Two
Designer: L. Harradine
Height: 4 1/4", 10.8 cm
Colour: Green
Issued: 1936-1949
Varieties: M 64

US:	**$1,500.00**
Can.:	**$1,500.00**
Ster.:	**£ 495.00**

M 71
June
Style Two
Designer: L. Harradine
Height: 4 1/4", 10.8 cm
Colour: Lavender and green
Issued: 1936-1949
Varieties: M 65

US:	**$1,250.00**
Can.:	**$1,250.00**
Ster.:	**£ 650.00**

M 72
Monica
Style Two
Designer: L. Harradine
Height: 3", 7.6 cm
Colour: Blue and white
Issued: 1936-1949
Varieties: M 66

  US: $1,450.00
  Can.: $1,450.00
  Ster.:   £ 650.00

M 73
Dainty May
Style Two
Designer: L. Harradine
Height: 4", 10.1 cm
Colour: Pink and turquoise
Issued: 1936-1949
Varieties: M 67

  US: $1,600.00
  Can.: $1,600.00
  Ster.:   £ 650.00

M 74
Mirabel
Style Two
Designer: L. Harradine
Height: 4", 10.1 cm
Colour: Turquoise and red
Issued: 1936-1949
Varieties: M 68

  US: $1,375.00
  Can.: $1,375.00
  Ster.:   £ 650.00

M 75
Janet
Style Two
Designer: L. Harradine
Height: 4", 10.1 cm
Colour: Purple
Issued: 1936-1949
Varieties: M 69

  US: $1,250.00
  Can.: $1,250.00
  Ster.:   £ 650.00

M 76
Bumble
Designer: L. Harradine
Height: 4", 10.1 cm
Colour: Green and red
Issued: 1939-1982
Series: Dickens (Series One)

  US: $125.00
  Can.: $125.00
  Ster.:   £ 45.00

M 77
Captain Cuttle
Designer: L. Harradine
Height: 4", 10.1 cm
Colour: Yellow and black
Issued: 1939-1982
Series: Dickens (Series One)

  US: $125.00
  Can.: $125.00
  Ster.:   £ 45.00

M 78
Windflower
Style Three
Designer: L. Harradine
Height: 4", 10.1 cm
Colour: Red and pink
Issued: 1939-1949
Varieties: M 79

  US: $1,600.00
  Can.: $1,600.00
  Ster.:   £ 850.00

M 79
Windflower
Style Three
Designer: L. Harradine
Height: 4", 10.1 cm
Colour: Blue and green
Issued: 1939-1949
Varieties: M 78

  US: $1,600.00
  Can.: $1,600.00
  Ster.:   £ 850.00

M 80
Goody Two Shoes
Style Two
Designer: L. Harradine
Height: 4", 10.1 cm
Colour: Pink and blue
Issued: 1939-1949
Varieties: M 81

US: $1,750.00
Can.: $1,750.00
Ster.: £ 650.00

M 81
Goody Two Shoes
Style Two
Designer: L. Harradine
Height: 4", 10.1 cm
Colour: Lavender and pink
Issued: 1939-1949
Varieties: M 80

US: $1,500.00
Can.: $1,500.00
Ster.: £ 650.00

M 82
Bo-Peep
Style Three
Designer: L. Harradine
Height: 4", 10.1 cm
Colour: Pink
Issued: 1939-1949
Varieties: M 83

US: $1,500.00
Can.: $1,500.00
Ster.: £ 750.00

M 83
Bo-Peep
Style Three
Designer: L. Harradine
Height: 4", 10.1 cm
Colour: Purple
Issued: 1939-1949
Varieties: M 82

US: $1,650.00
Can.: $1,650.00
Ster.: £ 750.00

M 84
Maureen
Style Two
Designer: L. Harradine
Height: 4", 10.1 cm
Colour: Pink
Issued: 1939-1949
Varieties: M 85

US: $1,500.00
Can.: $1,500.00
Ster.: £ 750.00

M 85
Maureen
Style Two
Designer: L. Harradine
Height: 4", 10.1 cm
Colour: Purple
Issued: 1939-1949
Varieties: M 84

US: $1,750.00
Can.: $1,750.00
Ster.: £ 750.00

M 86
Mrs. Bardell
Designer: L. Harradine
Height: 4 1/4", 10.8 cm
Colour: Green
Issued: 1949-1982
Series: Dickens (Series One)

US: $100.00
Can.: $125.00
Ster.: £ 45.00

M 87
Scrooge
Designer: L. Harradine
Height: 4", 10.1 cm
Colour: Brown
Issued: 1949-1982
Series: Dickens (Series One)

US: $ 95.00
Can.: $125.00
Ster.: £ 45.00

M 88
David Copperfield
Designer: L. Harradine
Height: 4 1/4", 10.8 cm
Colour: Black and tan
Issued: 1949-1983
Series: Dickens (Series One)

US: $100.00
Can.: $125.00
Ster.:   £ 45.00

M 89
Oliver Twist
Designer: L. Harradine
Height: 4 1/4", 10.8 cm
Colour: Black and tan
Issued: 1949-1983
Series: Dickens (Series One)

US: $100.00
Can.: $125.00
Ster.:   £ 45.00

M 90
Dick Swiveller
Designer: L. Harradine
Height: 4 1/4", 10.8 cm
Colour: Black and tan
Issued: 1949-1981
Series: Dickens (Series One)

US: $ 95.00
Can.: $125.00
Ster.:   £ 45.00

M 91
Trotty Veck
Designer: L. Harradine
Height: 4 1/4", 10.8 cm
Colour: Black and brown
Issued: 1949-1982
Series: Dickens (Series One)

US: $ 95.00
Can.: $125.00
Ster.:   £ 45.00

BESWICK

303
Policeman
Designer: Mr. Symcox
Height: Unknown
Colour: Unknown
Issued: 1935-1954
U.S.:
Can.: Very rare
Ster.:

374
Girl With Pot Of Honey
Designer: Miss Greaves
Height: 5", 12.7 cm
Colour: 1: Green coat;
pink dress
2: Pink coat; green
dress
3: All blue
Issued: 1936-1954
U.S.: $325.00
Can.: $450.00
Ster.: £200.00

375
Boy (on base)
Designer: Miss Greaves
Height: Unknown
Colour: Unknown
Issued: 1936-1954
U.S.:
Can.: Very rare
Ster.:

388
Girl With Finger In Mouth
Designer: Miss Greaves
Height: 5 3/4", 14.6 cm
Colour: Unknown
Issued: 1936-1954
U.S.:
Can.: Very rare
Ster.:

389
Man On Rock
Designer: Miss Greaves
Height: Unknown
Colour: Unknown
Issued: 1936-1954
U.S.:
Can.: Very rare
Ster.:

390
Girl In Breeze
Designer: Miss Greaves
Height: 5 1/2", 14.0 cm
Colour: Pink
Issued: 1936-1954
U.S.: $400.00
Can.: $550.00
Ster.: £250.00

391
Girl With Hands In Muff
Designer: Miss Greaves
Height: 7 1/4", 18.4 cm
Colour: Blue and pink
Issued: 1936-1954
U.S.: $400.00
Can.: $550.00
Ster.: £250.00

437
Girl With Flared Dress
Designer: Miss Greaves
Height: 4 3/4", 12.1 cm
Colour: Yellow and pink
Issued: 1936-1954
U.S.: $575.00
Can.: $700.00
Ster.: £300.00

438
Girl With Frilled Dress
Designer: Miss Greaves
Height: Unknown
Colour: Unknown
Issued: 1936-1954

U.S.:
Can.: **Very rare**
Ster.:

441
Lady Standing On Base
Designer: Miss Greaves
Height: Unknown
Colour: Unknown
Issued: 1936-1954

U.S.:
Can.: **Very rare**
Ster.:

442
Boy Standing On Base
Designer: Miss Greaves
Height: 8", 20.3 cm
Colour: Blue
Issued: 1936-1954

U.S.: **$375.00**
Can.: **$500.00**
Ster.: **£225.00**

443
Child Sitting
Designer: Miss Greaves
Height: Unknown
Colour: Unknown
Issued: 1936-1954

U.S.:
Can.: **Very rare**
Ster.:

501
Clown
Designer: Mr. Watkin
Height: Unknown
Colour: Unknowm
Issued: 1937-1954

U.S.:
Can.: **Very rare**
Ster.:

622
Mr. Chamberlain
Designer: Mr. Owen
Height: Unknown
Colour: Unknown
Issued: 1938-1940

U.S.:
Can.: **Very rare**
Ster.:

751
Boy Soldier
(Left bookend)
Designer: Mr. Watkin
Height: 6", 15.0 cm
Colour: Red, black, green
and brown
Issued: 1939-1954

U.S.: **$150.00**
Can.: **$225.00**
Ster.: **£100.00**

751A
Boy Soldier
(Right bookend)
Designer: Mr. Watkin
Height: 6", 15.0 cm
Colour: Red, black, green
and brown
Issued: 1939-1954

U.S.: **$150.00**
Can.: **$225.00**
Ster.: **£100.00**

903
Trumpet Boy
Designer: Arthur Gredington
Height: 4 1/2", 11.9 cm
Colour: Green and black
Issued: 1940-1948
U.S.: $300.00
Can.: $400.00
Ster.: £175.00

904
Book Worm
Designer: Arthur Gredington
Height: 5 1/2", 14.0 cm
Colour: Green and browns
Issued: 1940-1948
U.S.: $575.00
Can.: $775.00
Ster.: £350.00

905
Goose Girl
Designer: Arthur Gredington
Height: 6", 15.0 cm
Colour: Yellow, black and white
Issued: 1940-1948
U.S.: $500.00
Can.: $675.00
Ster.: £300.00

906
Strolling Along
Designer: Arthur Gredington
Height: 4 3/4", 12.1 cm
Colour: Browns and green
Issued: 1941-1948
U.S.: $500.00
Can.: $675.00
Ster.: £300.00

908
Stormy Weather
Designer: Arthur Gredington
Height: 6", 15.0 cm
Colour: Green, brown and yellow
Issued: 1941-1948
U.S.: $425.00
Can.: $550.00
Ster.: £250.00

909
Puppy Love
Designer: Arthur Gredington
Height: 5 1/2", 14.0 cm
Colour: Browns and green
Issued: 1941-1948
U.S.: $500.00
Can.: $675.00
Ster.: £300.00

910
Meditation
Designer: Arthur Gredington
Height: 5", 12.7 cm
Colour: Browns and white
Issued: 1941-1948
U.S.: $475.00
Can.: $625.00
Ster.: £275.00

911
Max & Moritz
Designer: Arthur Gredington
Height: 5 1/2",14.0 cm
Colour: Green, black and brown
Issued: 1941-1948
U.S.: $500.00
Can.: $675.00
Ster.: £300.00

912
Farm Boy
Designer: Arthur Gredington
Height: 5 3/4", 14.6 cm
Colour: Green, brown and black
Issued: 1941-1948

U.S.: **$500.00**
Can.: **$675.00**
Ster.: **£300.00**

913
Globe Trotter
Designer: Arthur Gredington
Height: 5 1/4", 13.3 cm
Colour: Browns, green and yellow
Issued: 1941-1948

U.S.: **$500.00**
Can.: **$675.00**
Ster.: **£300.00**

914
Shepherd's Boy
Designer: Arthur Gredington
Height: 5 1/2", 14.0 cm
Colour: Browns, green and white
Issued: 1941-1948

U.S.: **$500.00**
Can.: **$675.00**
Ster.: **£300.00**

924
Winston Churchill
Designer: Unknown
Height: 6", 15.0 cm
Colour: Black
Issued: 1941-1954

U.S.: **$425.00**
Can.: **$550.00**
Ster.: **£250.00**

940 Family In Bunker
(Left Bookend)
Designer: Unknown
Height: 6", 15.0 cm
Colour: White
Issued: 1941-1946

U.S.: **$150.00**
Can.: **$225.00**
Ster.: **£100.00**

940A A.R.P. Warden
(Right Bookend)
Designer: Unknown
Height: 6 1/2", 16.5 cm
Colour: White
Issued: 1941-1946

U.S.: **$150.00**
Can.: **$225.00**
Ster.: **£100.00**

Photograph
Not
Available

952
Army Co-operation;
Embracing Couple,
Soldier With Hand Grenade
Designer: Arthur Gredington
Height: Unknown
Colour: Unknown
Issued: 1941-1946

U.S.: **$300.00**
Can.: **$450.00**
Ster.: **£200.00**

990 Happiness
Designer: Arthur Gredington
Height: 5", 12.7 cm
Colour: Brown
Issued: 1942

U.S.: **$ 850.00**
Can.: **$1,000.00**
Ster.: **£ 500.00**

1010
Fairy, Crying
Designer: Arthur Gredington
Height: 6", 15.0 cm
Colour: Pale mauve dress, yellow hair, green base
Issued: 1944
Set: 1011, 1012, 1013
U.S.:
Can.: **Very rare**
Ster.:

1011
Fairy, Drinking
Designer: Arthur Gredington
Height: 4", 10.1 cm
Colour: Pale mauve dress, yellow hair, green base
Issued: 1944
Set: 1010, 1012, 1013
U.S.:
Can.: **Very rare**
Ster.:

1012
Fairy, Sewing
Designer: Arthur Gredington
Height: 4 1/4", 10.8 cm
Colour: Pale mauve dress, yellow hair green base
Issued: 1944-1954
Set: 1010, 1011, 1013
U.S.:
Can.: **Very rare**
Ster.:

Only known example in Beswick Museum

1013
Fairy, Baking
Designer: Arthur Gredington
Height: 6 1/4", 15.9 cm
Colour: Pale mauve dress, yellow hair, green base
Issued: 1944-1954
Set: 1010, 1011, 1012
U.S.:
Can.: **Very rare**
Ster.:

Only known example in Beswick Museum

1020
Madonna
Designer: Arthur Gredington
Height: 14", 35.5 cm
Colour: 1: Maroon/yellow cloak, blue dress
2: All cream
Issued: 1945-1954
U.S.:
Can.: **Rare**
Ster.:

1086
Clown and Dog
Designer: Arthur Gredington
Height: 7 1/4", 18.4 cm
Colour: Pink jacket, blue trousers
Issued: 1947-1958
U.S.: **$425.00**
Can.: **$550.00**
Ster.: **£250.00**

Note: Dog available separately as No. 1239

1087
Jester Sitting
Designer: Arthur Gredington
Height: 5 ", 12.7 cm
Colour: Burgundy, pale green and blue
Issued: 1947-1958
U.S.: **$425.00**
Can.: **$550.00**
Ster.: **£250.00**

1091
Gypsy Girl
Designer: Arthur Gredington
Height: 7 1/4", 18.4 cm
Colour: Blue bodice, with blue and yellow striped skirt
Issued: 1947-1958
U.S.: **$425.00**
Can.: **$550.00**
Ster.: **£250.00**

1093
Boy Hiker
Designer: Arthur Gredington
Height: 6", 15.0 cm
Colour: Pale green shirt, dark green trousers
Issued: 1947-1954

U.S.: $425.00
Can.: $550.00
Ster.: £250.00

Photograph
Not
Available

1094
Girl Hiker
Designer: Arthur Gredington
Height: 6", 15.0 cm
Colour: Unknown
Issued: 1947-1954

U.S.: $425.00
Can.: $550.00
Ster.: £250.00

1096
Sportsman and Dog
Designer: Arthur Gredington
Height: 6 3/4", 17.2 cm
Colour: Green, tan and blue
Issued: 1947-1958

U.S.: $425.00
Can.: $550.00
Ster.: £250.00

Photograph
Not
Available

1097
Fruit Seller (Pedlar)
Designer: Arthur Gredington
Height: Unknown
Colour: Unknown
Issued: 1947-1958

U.S.:
Can.: Rare
Ster.:

1122
Butcher Boy
Designer: Arthur Gredington
Height: 5 1/4", 13.3 cm
Colour: Blue, white, yellow and green
Issued: 1948-1958

U.S.: $ 850.00
Can.: $1, 000.00
Ster.: £   500.00

1123
Gardener
Designer: Arthur Gredington
Height: 6 1/4", 15.9 cm
Colour: Yellow, green and olive green
Issued: 1948-1954

U.S.: $325.00
Can.: $450.00
Ster.: £200.00

1124
Shepherd Boy
Designer: Arthur Gredington
Height: 6 1/4", 15.9 cm
Colour: Pale blue jacket, light brown trousers
Issued: 1948-1956

U.S.: $325.00
Can.: $450.00
Ster.: £200.00

1125
Scotsman
Designer: Arthur Gredington
Height: 6 1/4", 15.9 cm
Colour: Blue jacket, green kilt
Issued: 1948-1954

U.S.: $500.00
Can.: $650.00
Ster.: £300.00

1221
Hungarian Girl With Turkey
Designer: Miss Granoska
Height: 7 1/4", 18.4 cm
Colour: Maroon bodice
           green skirt
Issued: 1951-1962

U.S.:   **$375.00**
Can.:   **$500.00**
Ster.: **£225.00**

1222
Polish Girl With Hen
Designer: Miss Granoska
Height: 7", 17.8 cm
Colour: Green and yellow
           bodice, light and
           dark green skirts
Issued: 1951-1962

U.S.:   **$425.00**
Can.:   **$550.00**
Ster.: **£250.00**

1223
Spaniard Pulling Donkey
Designer: Miss Granoska
Height: 4 1/2", 11.9 cm
Colour: Cream shirt and
           dark blue trousers
Issued: 1951-1962

U.S.:   **$325.00**
Can.:   **$450.00**
Ster.: **£200.00**

Pair with 1224

1224
Spaniard Pushing Donkey
Designer: Miss Granoska
Height: 4 1/2", 11.9 cm
Colour: Cream shirt and
           pale brown trousers
Issued: 1951-1962

U.S.:   **$325.00**
Can.:   **$450.00**
Ster.: **£200.00**

Pair with 1223

1227
Swedish Girl With Cockerel
Designer: Miss Granoska
Height: 7", 17.8 cm
Colour: Dark purple bodice,
           green shirt, red and
           white striped apron
Issued: 1952-1962

U.S.:   **$375.00**
Can.:   **$500.00**
Ster.: **£225.00**

1230
Danish Girl With Pig
Designer: Miss Granoska
Height: 5 3/4", 14.6 cm
Colour: Dark purple bodice,
           green skirt and white
           apron
Issued: 1952-1962

U.S.:   **$425.00**
Can.:   **$550.00**
Ster.: **£250.00**

1234
Italian Girl Leading Goat
Designer: Miss Granoska
Height: 5 1/2", 14.0 cm
Colour: White and dark
           purple, yellow and
           green apron
Issued: 1952-1962

U.S.:   **$325.00**
Can.:   **$450.00**
Ster.: **£200.00**

1238
Italian Girl With Goat
Eating Hat
Designer: Miss Gransoka
Height: 6", 15.0 cm
Colour: Dark purple bodice,
           decorated skirt and
           blouse
Issued: 1952-1962

U.S.:   **$325.00**
Can.:   **$450.00**
Ster.: **£200.00**

1244
Spanish Girl on Donkey
Designer: Miss Granoska
Height: 5 1/2", 14.0 cm
Colour: Green dress with pink and dark purple
Issued: 1952-1962

U.S.: **$425.00**
Can.: **$550.00**
Ster.: **£250.00**

1245
Spanish Children on Donkey
Designer: Miss Granoska
Height: 4 1/2", 11.9 cm
Colour: Yellow dress with dark purple and green
Issued: 1952-1962

U.S.: **$425.00**
Can.: **$550.00**
Ster.: **£250.00**

1247
Finnish Girl With Duck
Designer: Miss Granoska
Height: 7", 17.8 cm
Colour: Two shades of green, white and dark purple
Issued: 1952-1962

U.S.: **$325.00**
Can.: **$450.00**
Ster.: **£200.00**

Photograph
Not
Available

1262
Balinese Dancer
Designer: Miss Granoska
Height: 3 1/2", 8.9 cm
Colour: Unknown
Issued: 1952-1962

U.S.: **$250.00**
Can.: **$325.00**
Ster.: **£150.00**

1263
Indian Dancer
Designer: Miss Granoska
Height: 3 1/2", 8.9 cm
Colour: Pink and green dress, beige trousers
Issued: 1952-1962

U.S.: **$250.00**
Can.: **$325.00**
Ster.: **£150.00**

1320
Siamese Dancer
Designer: Miss Granoska
Height: 3 1/2", 8.9 cm
Colour: Green and pink dress, blue cape
Issued: 1953-1962

U.S.: **$250.00**
Can.: **$325.00**
Ster.: **£150.00**

1321
Javanese Dancer
Designer: Miss Granoska
Height: 3 1/2", 8.9 cm
Colour: Pink skirt, green bodice, dark blue trim
Issued: 1953-1962

U.S.: **$250.00**
Can.: **$325.00**
Ster.: **£150.00**

1333
Chinese Dancer
Designer: Miss Granoska and Mr. Haywood
Height: 3 1/2", 8.9 cm
Colour: Dark blue jacket beige trousers and headress
Issued: 1953-1962

U.S.: **$175.00**
Can.: **$225.00**
Ster.: **£100.00**

1334
Hawaiian Dancer
Designer: Miss Granoska
Height: Unknown
Colour: Unknown
Issued: 1954
U.S.: **Possibly**
Can.: **not put into**
Ster.: **production**

1347
Susie Jamaica
Designer: Mr. Orwell
Height: 7", 17.8 cm
Colour: Yellow blouse and
 skirt with red trim
Issued: 1954-1975
U.S.: **$375.00**
Can.: **$500.00**
Ster.: **£225.00**

1626
Toy Drummer
Designer: J. Lawson
Height: 2 1/2", 6.4 cm
Colour: 1. Red and white
 2. Blue and white
Issued: 1959-1966
Set: 1627, 1628
U.S.: **$ 75.00**
Can.: **$100.00**
Ster.: **£ 40.00**

1627
Toy Buglers
Designer: J. Lawson
Height: 1 1/2", 5.0 cm
Colour: 1. Red and white
 2. Blue and white
Issued: 1959-1966
Set: 1626, 1628
U.S.: **$ 75.00**
Can.: **$100.00**
Ster.: **£ 40.00**

1628
Toy Guards
Designer: J. Lawson
Height: 1 1/2", 5.0 cm
Colour: 1. Red and white
 2. Blue and white
Issued: 1959-1966
Set: 1626, 1627
U.S.: **$ 75.00**
Can.: **$100.00**
Ster.: **£ 40.00**

1737
Couple Sitting
Designer: Mr. Brumbie
Height: 8 1/2", 21.6 cm
Colour: White and brown
Issued: 1961-1963
U.S.: **$575.00**
Can.: **$775.00**
Ster.: **£350.00**

1766
Road Gang - Foreman
Designer: Mr. Sales
Height: Unknown
Colour: Unknown
Issued: 1961
Set: 1767, 1768, 1769
U.S.: **Possibly**
Can.: **not put into**
Ster.: **production**

1767
Road Gang - Digger
Designer: Mr. Sales
Height: Unknown
Colour: Red jacket, blue cap
Issued: 1961
Set: 1766, 1768, 1769
U.S.:
Can.: **Very rare**
Ster.:

1768
Road Gang - Driller
Designer: Mr. Sales
Height: Unknown
Colour: Red jacket, blue cap
Issued: 1961
Set: 1766, 1767, 1769

U.S.:
Can.: **Very rare**
Ster.:

Photograph
Not
Available

1769
Road Gang - At Ease
Designer: Mr. Sales
Height: Unknown
Colour: Unknown
Issued: 1961
Set: 1766, 1767, 1768

U.S.: **Possibly**
Can.: **not put into**
Ster.: **production**

1878
Welsh Lady
Designer: Albert Hallam
Height: 5", 12.7 cm
Colour: 1: Shawl - Black
and red
2: Shawl - Black
and white
Issued: 1963-1969

U.S.: $ 95.00
Can.: $125.00
Ster.: £ 50.00

Photograph
Not
Available

1937
Bust of Lady
(C.M.C. on base)
Designer: Albert Hallam
Height: 6", 15.0 cm
Colour: Unknown
Issued: 1964-1965

U.S.:
Can.: **Rare**
Ster.:

Photograph
Not
Available

1993
Lady With Fan
Designer: Unknown
Height: 7 1/2", 19.1 cm
Colour: Unknown
Issued: 1964-1965

U.S.: $425.00
Can.: $575.00
Ster.: £250.00

Photograph
Not
Available

1994
Lady With Hat
Designer: Unknown
Height: 7 1/2", 19.1 cm
Colour: Unknown
Issued: 1964-1965

U.S.: $425.00
Can.: $575.00
Ster.: £250.00

1995
Lady In Ball Gown
Designer: Unknown
Height: 7", 17.8 cm
Colour: Blue and white
Issued: 1964-1965

U.S.: $425.00
Can.: $575.00
Ster.: £250.00

2181
Knight of St. John
Designer: Albert Hallam
Height: 6 3/4", 17.2 cm
Colour: Black and grey
Issued: 1968 in a limited
edition of 500

U.S.: $325.00
Can.: $450.00
Ster.: £200.00

To commemorate Golden
Jubilee year of the Priory for Wales

C OLLECTING BY
TYPE OR SERIES

AGE OF CHIVALRY

Sir Edward	HN 2370
Sir Ralph	HN 2371
Sir Thomas	HN 2372

AGE OF INNOCENCE

Feeding Time	HN 3373
First Outing	HN 3377
Making Friends	HN 3372
Puppy Love	HN 3371

BEGGAR'S OPERA

Beggar (The) (Style One)	HN 526, 591
Beggar (The) (Style Two)	HN 2175
Captain MacHeath	HN 464, 590, 1256
Highwayman (The)	HN 527, 592, 1257
Lucy Lockett, (Style One)	HN 485
Lucy Lockett, (Style Two)	HN 524
Polly Peachum (Style One)	HN 463, 465, 550, 589, 614, 680, 693
Polly Peachum (Style Two)	HN 549, 620, 694, 734
Polly Peachum (Style Three)	HN 698, 699, 757, 758, 759, 760, 761, 762, M21, 22, 23

BRITISH SPORTING HERITAGE

Ascot (Style Two)	HN 3471
Croquet	HN 3470
Henley	HN 3367
Wimbledon	HN 3366

CHARACTER SCULPTURES (RESIN)

Bill Sikes	HN 3785
Bowls Player, The	HN 3780
Captain Hook	HN 3636
Cyrano de Bergerac	HN 3751
D'Artagnan	HN 3838
Dick Turpin (Style Two)	HN 3637
Fagin (Style Two)	HN 3752
Guliver	HN 3750
Long John Silver (Style Two)	HN 3719
Oliver Twist and The Artful Dodger	HN 3786
Pied Piper (Style Two)	HN 3721
Robin Hood (Style Two)	HN 3720
Sherlock Holmes	HN 3639
Sir Francis Drake	HN 3770
Wizard, The (Style Two)	HN 3722, 3732

CHARACTERS FROM CHILDREN'S LITERATURE

Heidi	HN 2975
Huckleberry Finn	HN 2927
Little Lord Fauntleroy	HN 2972
Pollyanna	HN 2965
Tom Brown	HN 2941
Tom Sawyer	HN 2926

CHARLESTON

Charlotte (Style Two)	HN 3810, 3811, 3812, 3813
Daisy (Style Two)	HN 3802, 3803, 3804, 2805
Eliza (Style Three)	HN 3798, 3799, 3800, 3801
Emily (Style Three)	HN 3806, 3807, 3808, 3809
Harriet (Style Two)	HN 3794, 3795, 3796, 3997
Sophie (Style Three)	HN 3790, 3791. 3792, 3793

CHILDHOOD DAYS

And One For You	HN 2970
And So To Bed	HN 2966
As Good As New	HN 2971
Dressing Up	HN 2964
I'm Nearly Ready	HN 2976
It Won't Hurt	HN 2963
Just One More	HN 2980
Please Keep Still	HN 2967
Save Some For Me	HN 2959
Stick 'em Up	HN 2981

CHILDREN OF THE BLITZ

Boy Evacuee (The)	HN 3202
Girl Evacuee (The)	HN 3203
Homecoming (The)	HN 3295
Welcome Home	HN 3299

CLOWNS

Joker (The) (Style One)	HN 3196
Joker (The) (Style Two)	HN 2252
Partners	HN 3119
Slapdash	HN 2277
Tip-Toe	HN 3293
Tumbler	HN 3183
Tumbling	HN 3283, 3289
Will He, Won't He	HN 3275

DANCERS OF THE WORLD

Balinese Dancer	HN 2808
Breton Dancer	HN 2383
Chinese Dancer	HN 2840
Indian Temple Dancer	HN 2830
Kurdish Dancer	HN 2867
Mexican Dancer	HN 2866
North American Indian Dancer	HN 2809
Philippine Dancer	HN 2439
Polish Dancer	HN 2836
Scottish Highland Dancer	HN 2436
Spanish Flamenco Dancer	HN 2831
West Indian Dancer	HN 2384

DICKENS
Series One

Alfred Jingle	HN 541, M52
Artful Dodger	HN 546, M55
Bill Sykes	HN 537, M54
Buz Fuz	HN 538, M53
Fagin	HN 534, M49
Fat Boy (Style One)	HN 530, M44
Little Nell	HN 540, M51
Mr. Micawber (Style One)	HN 532, M42
Mr. Pickwick (Style One)	HN 529, M41
Pecksniff (Style One)	HN 535, M43
Sairey Gamp (Style One)	HN 533, M46
Sam Weller	HN 531, M48
Stiggins	HN 536, M50
Tiny Tim	HN 539, M56
Tony Weller (Style Two)	HN 544, M47
Uriah Heep (Style One)	HN 545, M45

Series Two

Fat Boy (Style Two)	HN 555, 1893
Mr. Micawber (Style Two)	HN 557, 1895
Mr. Pickwick (Style Two)	HN 556, 1894
Pecksniff (Style Two)	HN 553, 1891
Sairey Gamp (Style Two)	HN 558, 1896
Uriah Heep (Style Two)	HN 554, 1892

Series Three

Fat Boy (Style Three)	HN 2096
Mr. Micawber (Style Three)	HN 2097
Mr. Pickwick (Style Three)	HN 2099
Pecksniff (Style Three)	HN 2098
Sairey Gamp (Style Three)	HN 2100
Uriah Heep (Style Three)	HN 2101

DISNEY PRINCESS COLLECTION

Ariel	HN 3831
Aurora	HN 3833
Belle (Style Three)	HN 3830
Cinderella	HN 3677
Jasmine	HN 3832
Snow White	HN 3678

DOULTON COLLECTORS ROADSHOW EVENTS

Elaine 1995	HN 3741
Jacqueline (Style Two) 1995	HN 3689
Lynne 1995	HN 3740
Maria 1993	HN 3381
Ninette (Style One) 1992	HN 3417
Pauline 1994	HN 3643, 3656
Stephanie (Style Two) 1996	HN 3759
Victoria 1992	HN 3416

EDWARDIAN STRING QUARTET

Cello (Style Two)	HN 3707
First Violin	HN 3704
Second Violin	HN 3705
Viola	HN 3706

ELEGANCE

Claudine	HN 3055
Danielle (Style One)	HN 3056
Dominique	HN 3054
Francoise	HN 2897
Martine	HN 3053
Monique	HN 2880

ELEGANCE COLLECTION

Au Revoir (Style One)	HN 3723
Country Girl (Style Two)	HN 3856
Free Spirit (Style Two)	HN 3728
Lambing Time (Style Two)	HN 3855
Spring Morning (Style Two)	HN 3725
Summer Breeze	HN 3724

ENCHANTMENT

April Shower	HN 3024
Fairyspell	HN 2979
Lyric	HN 2757
Magic Dragon	HN 2977
Magpie Ring (The)	HN 2978
Musicale	HN 2756
Queen of the Dawn	HN 2437
Queen of the Ice	HN 2435

Rumpelstiltskin	HN 3025
Serenade	HN 2753
Sonata	HN 2438

ENTERTAINERS

Charlie Chaplin	HN 2771
Groucho Marx	HN 2777
Oliver Hardy	HN 2775
Stan Laurel	HN 2774

FABLED BEAUTIES

Scheherazade	HN 3835

FIGURE OF THE MONTH, CHILD

January (Style Two)	HN 3330
February (Style Two)	HN 3331
March (Style Two)	HN 3332
April (Style Two)	HN 3333
May (Style Three)	HN 3334
June (Style Five)	HN 3323
July (Style Two)	HN 3324
August (Style Two)	HN 3325
September (Style Two)	HN 3326
October (Style Two)	HN 3327
November (Style Two)	HN 3328
December (Style Two)	HN 3329

FIGURE OF THE YEAR

Amy (Style Two) 1991	HN 3316
Belle (Style Three) 1996	HN 3703
Deborah 1995	HN 3644
Jennifer (Style Three) 1994	HN 3447
Mary (Style Two) 1992	HN 3375
Patricia (Style Four) 1993	HN 3365

FIGURES OF WILLIAMSBURG

A Child From Williamsburg	HN 2154
Blacksmith Of Williamsburg	HN 2240
Boy From Williamsburg	HN 2183
Gentlemen From Williamsburg	HN 2227
Hostess of Williamsburg	HN 2209
Lady From Williamsburg	HN 2228
Royal Governor's Cook	HN 2233
Silversmith of Williamsburg	HN 2208
Wigmaker Of Williamsburg	HN 2239

FLAMBÉ

Carpet Seller (Seated)	HN 3277
Carpet Seller (Standing) (Style Three)	HN 2776
Confucius	HN 3314
Eastern Grace	HN 3683
Geisha (The)	HN 3229
Genie (The)	HN 2999
Lamp Seller	HN 3278
Moor (The)	HN 3642
Samurai Warrior	HN 3402
Wizard	HN 3121

FLOWER OF THE MONTH

January (Style One)	HN 2697
February (Style One)	HN 2703
March (Style One)	HN 2707
April (Style One)	HN 2708
May (Style Two)	HN 2711
June (Style Three)	HN 2790
July (Style One)	HN 2794

August (Style One)	HN 3165
September (Style One)	HN 3166
October (Style One)	HN 2693
November (Style One)	HN 2695
December (Style One)	HN 2696

FLOWERS OF LOVE

Camelias	HN 3701
Forget-Me—Nots	HN 3700
Primrose	HN 3710
Rose	HN 3709

GAINSBOROUGH LADIES

Honourable Frances Duncombe	HN 3009
Isabella, Countess of Shefton	HN 3010
Mary, Countess Howe	HN 3007
Sophia Charlotte, Lady Sheffield	HN 3008

GENTLE ARTS

Adornment	HN 3015
Flower Arranging	HN 3040
Painting	HN 3012
Spinning	HN 2390
Tapestry Weaving	HN 3048
Writing	HN 3049

GILBERT AND SULLIVAN

Colonel Fairfax	HN 2903
Elsie Maynard (Style Two)	HN 2902
Ko-ko (Style Two)	HN 2898
Pirate King (The)	HN 2901
Ruth, The Pirate Maid	HN 2900
Yum-Yum (Style Two)	HN 2899

GREAT LOVERS

Antony and Cleopatra	HN 3114
Lancelot and Guinivere	HN 3112
Robin Hood and Maid Marion	HN 3111
Romeo and Juliet	HN 3113

HAUTE ENSEMBLE

A la Mode	HN 2544
Boudoir	HN 2542
Carmen (Style Two)	HN 2545
Eliza	HN 2543, 2543A
Mantilla (Style One)	HN 2712

HOLY FAMILY

Jesus	HN 3484, 3487
Joseph	HN 3438, 3486
Mary (Style Three)	HN 3437, 3485

IMAGES

Awakening	HN 2837, 2875
Bride and Groom	HN 3281
Bridesmaid (Style Five)	HN 3280
Brother and Sister	HN 3460
Brothers	HN 3191
Carefree	HN 3026, 3029
Congratulations	HN 3351
Contemplation	HN 2213, 2241
Family	HN 2720, 2721
First Love	HN 2747
First Steps (Style Two)	HN 3282
Free Spirit	HN 3157, 3159
Gift of Freedom	HN 3443

God Bless You	HN 3400
Happy Anniversary (Style Two)	HN 3254
Lovers	HN 2762, 2763
Mother and Daughter	HN 2841, 2843
Our First Christmas	HN 3452
Over the Threshold	HN 3274
Peace	HN 2433, 2470
Sisters	HN 3018, 3019
Sympathy	HN 2838, 2876
Tenderness	HN 2713, 2714
Thankful	HN 3129, 3135
Tomorrow's Dreams	HN 3665
Tranquility	HN 2426, 2469
Wedding Day	HN 2748
Wistful (Style Two)	HN 3664
Yearning	HN 2920, 2921

KATE GREENAWAY

Amy	HN 2958
Anna	HN 2802
Beth	HN 2870
Carrie	HN 2800
Edith	HN 2957
Ellen	HN 3020
Emma (Style One)	HN 2834
Georgina	HN 2377
James	HN 3013
Kathy (Style One)	HN 2346
Lori	HN 2801
Louise (Style One)	HN 2869
Lucy	HN 2863
Nell	HN 3014
Ruth	HN 2799
Sophie (Style One)	HN 2833
Tess	HN 2865
Tom	HN 2864

LADIES OF THE BRITISH ISLES

England	HN 3627
Ireland	HN 3628
Scotland	HN 3629
Wales	HN 3630

LADIES OF COVENT GARDENS

Catherine (Style One)	HN 2395
Deborah	HN 2701
Juliet (Style One)	HN 2968
Kimberley (Style One)	HN 2969

LADY DOULTON

| Lily 1995 | HN 3626 |
| Katherine 1996 | HN 3708 |

LITTLE CHERUBS

First Steps (Style Three)	HN 3361
Peek a Boo	HN 3363
Well Done	HN 3362
What Fun	HN 3364

LADY MUSICIANS

Cello	HN 2331
Chitarrone	HN 2700
Cymbals	HN 2699
Dulcimer	HN 2798
Flute	HN 2483
French Horn	HN 2795
Harp	HN 2482

Hurdy Gurdy	HN 2796
Lute	HN 2431
Viola d'Amore	HN 2797
Violin	HN 2432
Virginals	HN 2427

LES FEMMES FATALES

Cleopatra	HN 2868
Eve	HN 2466
Helen of Troy	HN 2387
Lucrezia Borgia	HN 2342
Queen of Sheba	HN 2328
T'zu-hsi, Empress Dowager	HN 2391

LES SAISONS

Printemps (Spring)	HN 3066
Ete (Summer)	HN 3067
Automne (Autumn)	HN 3068
Hiver (Winter)	HN 3069

MICHAEL DOULTON EVENTS

1984 Gillian (Style Two)	HN 3042
1985 Wistful (Style One)	HN 2472
1986 Kathleen (Style Two)	HN 3100
1987 Nicola	HN 2804
1988 Laura	HN 3136
1989 Pamela (Style Two)	HN 3223
1990 Diana (Style Two)	HN 3266
1991 Fragrance (Style One)	HN 3311
1992 Angela (Style Three)	HN 3419
1993 Sarah (Style Two)	HN 3380
1994 Sharon (Style Two)	HN 3603
1995 Lily (Style Two)	HN 3626
1996 Katherine	HN 3708

MICHAEL DOULTON SIGNATURE COLLECTION

Autumn Breezes (Style Two)	HN 2180
Christine (Style Three)	HN 3337
Christmas Morn (Style Two)	HN 3245
Elaine (Style Two)	HN 3247
Fair Lady (Style Two)	HN 3336
Fragrance (Style Two)	HN 3250
Karen (Style Three)	HN 3338
Kirsty (Style Two)	HN 3246
Ninette (Style Two)	HN 3248
Sara (Style Two)	HN 3249
Southern Belle (Style Two)	HN 3244
Sunday Best (Style Two)	HN 3312
Victoria (Style Two)	HN 3735

MIDDLE EARTH

Aragorn	HN 2916
Barliman Butterbur	HN 2923
Bilbo	HN 2914
Boromir	HN 2918
Frodo	HN 2912
Galadriel	HN 2915
Gandalf	HN 2911
Gimli	HN 2922
Gollum	HN 2913
Legolas	HN 2917
Samwise	HN 2925
Tom Bombadil	HN 2924

MINIATURES
Ladies

Autumn Breezes (Style Two)	HN 2176, 2180
Buttercup (Style Two)	HN 3268
Christine (Style Three)	HN 3269, 3337
Christmas Morn (Style Two)	HN 3212, 3245
Diana (Style Three)	HN 3310
Elaine (Style Two)	HN 3214, 3247
Emma (Style Two)	HN 3208
Fair Lady (Style Two)	HN 3216, 3336
Fragrance (Style Two)	HN 3220, 3250
Gail (Style Two)	HN 3321
Hannah (Style Two)	HN 3649
Karen (Style Three)	HN 3270, 3338
Kirsty (Style Two)	HN 3213, 3246, 3480, 3743
Ninette (Style Two)	HN 3215, 3248
Rebecca (Style Two)	HN 3414
Sara (Style Two)	HN 3219, 3249
Southern Belle (Style Two)	HN 3174, 3244
Sunday Best (Style Two)	HN 3218, 3312
Top o' the Hill (Style Two)	HN 2126, 3499
Victoria (Style Two)	HN 3735, 3744

Character Studies

Balloon Seller (The)	HN 2130
Falstaff (Style Three)	HN 3236
Good King Wenceslas (Style Two)	HN 3262
Guy Fawkes (Style Two)	HN 3271
Jester (Style Three)	HN 3335
Old Balloon Seller (The)	HN 2129
Town Crier (Style Two)	HN 3261

MYTHS AND MAIDENS

Diana the Huntress	HN 2829
Europa and the Bull (Style Two)	HN 2828
Juno and the Peacock	HN 2827
Lady and the Unicorn	HN 2825
Leda and the Swan	HN 2826

NATIONAL SOCIETY FOR THE PREVENTION OF CRUELTY TO CHILDREN CHARITY

Charity	HN 3087
Faith	HN 3082
Hope	HN 3061

NURSERY RHYMES
Series One

Curly Locks	HN 2049
He Loves Me	HN 2046
Jack	HN 2060
Jill	HN 2061
Little Boy Blue (Style One)	HN 2062
Little Jack Horner (Style One)	HN 2063
Mary Had a Little Lamb	HN 2048
Mary, Mary	HN 2044
My Pretty Maid	HN 2064
Once Upon a Time	HN 2047
She Loves Me Not	HN 2045
Wee Willie Winkie (Style One)	HN 2050

Series Two

Little Bo Peep	HN 3030
Little Boy Blue (Style Two)	HN 3035
Little Jack Horner (Style Two)	HN 3034
Little Miss Muffet	HN 2727
Polly Put the Kettle On	HN 3021
Tom, Tom, the Piper's Son	HN 3032
Wee Willie Winkie (Style Two)	HN 3031

PERIOD FIGURES IN ENGLISH HISTORY

Eleanor of Provence	HN 2009
Henrietta Maria	HN 2005
Lady Anne Nevill (The)	HN 2006
Margaret of Anjou	HN 2012
Matilda	HN 2011
Mrs. Fitzherbert	HN 2007
Philippa of Hainault	HN 2008
Young Miss Nightingale (The)	HN 2010

QUEENS OF THE REALM

Mary, Queen of Scots (Style Two)	HN 3142
Queen Anne	HN 3141
Queen Elizabeth I	HN 3099
Queen Victoria	HN 3125

REFLECTIONS

A Winter's Walk	HN 3052
Allure	HN 3080
Aperitif	HN 2998
Autumn Glory	HN 2766
Ballerina (Style Two)	HN 3197
Ballet Class	HN 3135
Balloons	HN 3187
Bathing Beauty	HN 3156
Bolero	HN 3076
Breezy Day	HN 3162
Charisma	HN 3090
Cherry Blossom	HN 3092
Chic	HN 2997
Cocktails	HN 3070
Country Girl	HN 3051
Covent Garden (Style Two)	HN 2857
Dancing Delight	HN 3078
Daybreak	HN 3107
Debut	HN 3046
Debutante (Style Two)	HN 3189
Demure	HN 3045
Devotion	HN 3228
Dreaming	HN 3133
Eastern Grace	HN 3138
Enchanting Evening	HN 3108
Encore	HN 2751
Enigma	HN 3110
Entranced	HN 3186
Fantasy	HN 3296
Flirtation	HN 3071
Free As The Wind	HN 3139
Gaiety	HN 3140
Gardener (The)	HN 3161
Golfer	HN 2992
Good Pals	HN 3132
Harvestime	HN 3084
Idle Hours	HN 3115
Indian Maiden	HN 3117
Joker (The) (Style One)	HN 3196
Joy	HN 3184
Love Letter (The) (Style Two)	HN 3105
Moondancer	HN 3181

Morning Glory	HN 3093
Panorama	HN 3028
Paradise	HN 3074
Park Parade	HN 3116
Pensive	HN 3109
Playmates	HN 3127
Promenade	HN 3072
Reflection	HN 3039
Rose Arbour	HN 3145
Secret Moment	HN 3106
Sheikh	HN 3083
Shepherd (Style Five)	HN 3160
Shepherdess (Style Three)	HN 2990
Sisterly Love	HN 3130
Sophistication	HN 3059
Spring Walk	HN 3120
Stargazer	HN 3182
Storytime	HN 3126
Strolling	HN 3073
Summer Rose	HN 3085
Summer's Darling	HN 3091
Sweet Bouquet	HN 3000
Sweet Perfume	HN 3094
Sweet Violets	HN 3175
Tango	HN 3075
Tomorrow's Dreams	HN 3128
Traveller's Tale	HN 3185
Tumbler	HN 3183
Water Maiden	HN 3155
Windflower (Style Three)	HN 3077
Windswept	HN 3027

REYNOLDS LADIES

Countess Harrington	HN 3317
Countess Spencer	HN 3320
Lady Worsley	HN 3318
Mrs Hugh Bonfoy	HN 3319

ROYAL DOULTON INTERNATIONAL COLLECTORS CLUB

Auctioneer (The)	HN 2988
Autumntime (Style One)	HN 3231
Barbara	HN 3441
Bunny's Bedtime	HN 3370
Diane	HN 3604
Discovery	HN 3428
Eliza Farren, Countess of Derby	HN 3442
Emily (Style Three)	HN 3688
Geisha (Style Three)	HN 3229
Jester (Style Three)	HN 3335
L'Ambitieuse	HN 3359
Le Bal	HN 3702
Pamela (Style Three)	HN 3756
Pride and Joy	HN 2945
Prized Possessions	HN 2942
Sleepy Darling	HN 2953
Springtime (Style Two)	HN 3033
Summertime (Style One)	HN 3137
Top o' the Hill (Style Two)	HN 2126
Wintertime (Style One)	HN 3060
Winter's Day	HN 3769

SEA CHARACTERS

A Good Catch	HN 2258
All Aboard	HN 2940
Boatman (The)	HN 2417
Captain (The)	HN 2260
Captain Cook	HN 2889
Helmsman	HN 2499

Lifeboat Man (The)	HN 2764
Lobster Man (The)	HN 2317, 2323
Officer of the Line	HN 2733
Sailor's Holiday	HN 2442
Sea Harvest	HN 2257
Seafarer (The)	HN 2455
Shore Leave	HN 2254
Song of the Sea	HN 2729
Tall Story	HN 2248

SEASONS
Series One

Spring (Style One)	HN 312, 472
Summer (Style One)	HN 313, 473
Autumn (Style One)	HN 314, 474
Winter (Style One)	HN 315, 475

Series Two

Spring (Style Four)	HN 2085
Summer (Style Two)	HN 2086
Autumn (Style Two)	HN 2087
Winter (Style Two)	HN 2088

Series Three

Catherine (in Spring)(Style Two)	HN 3006
Lilian (in Summer)	HN 3003
Emily (in Autumn)	HN 3004
Sarah (in Winter)	HN 3005

Series Four

Springtime (Style One)	HN 3033
Summertime (Style One)	HN 3137
Autumntime (Style One)	HN 3231
Wintertime (Style One)	HN 3060

Series Five

Spring Song	HN 3446
Summer Serenade	HN 3610
Autumn Attraction	HN 3612
Winter Welcome	HN 3611

Series Six

Springtime (Style Three)	HN 3477
Summertime (Style Two)	HN 3478
Autumntime (Style Two)	HN 3621
Wintertime (Style Two)	HN 3622

SENTIMENTS

Christmas Angel	HN 3733
Christmas Carols	HN 3727
Christmas Day	HN 3488
Christmas Parcels (Style Two)	HN 3493
Forget-Me-Not (Style Two)	HN 3388
Friendship	HN 3491
Loving You	HN 3389
Sweet Dreams (Style Two)	HN 3394
Thank You (Style Two)	HN 3390
Thinking of You	HN 3124, 3490
With Love	HN 3393, 3492

SHAKESPEARE'S LADIES

Desdemona	HN 3676
Juliet (Style Two)	HN 3453
Ophelia	HN 3674
Titania	HN 3679

SHIPS FIGUREHEADS

Benmore	HN 2909
Chieftain	HN 2929
Hibernia	HN 2932
HMS Ajax	HN 2908
Lalla Rookh	HN 2910
Mary Queen of Scots	HN 2931
Nelson	HN 2928
Pocahontas	HN 2930

SIX WIVES OF HENRY VIII

Anne Bolelyn	HN 3232
Anne of Cleves	HN 3356
Catherine Howard	HN 3449
Catherine of Aragon	HN 3233
Catherine Parr	HN 3450
Jane Seymour	HN 3349

SOLDIERS OF THE REVOLUTION

Captain, 2nd New York Regiment, 1775	HN 2755
Corporal, 1st New Hamshire Regiment, 1778	HN 2780
Major, 3rd New Jersey Regiment, 1776	HN 2752
Private, 1st Georgia Regiment, 1777	HN 2779
Private, 2nd South Carolina Regiment, 1781	HN 2717
Private, 3rd North Carolina Regiment, 1778	HN 2754
Private, Connecticut Regiment, 1777	HN 2845
Private, Delaware Regiment, 1776	HN 2761
Private, Massachusetts Regiment, 1778	HN 2760
Private, Pennsylvania Rifle Battalion, 1776	HN 2846
Private, Rhode Island Regiment, 1781	HN 2759
Sergeant, 6th Maryland Regiment, 1777	HN 2815
Sergeant, Virginia 1st Regiment Continental Light Dragoons, 1777	HN 2844

SPECIAL OCCASIONS

Christening Day	HN 3210, 3211
Happy Anniversary (Style One)	HN 3097
Happy Birthday	HN 3095
Merry Christmas	HN 3096

STUART KINGS

King Charles II	HN 3825
King James I	HN 3822

SWEET AND TWENTIES

Deauville	HN 2344
Monte Carlo	HN 2332

TEENAGERS

Columbine (Style Two)	HN 2185
Faraway	HN 2133
Harlequin (Style One)	HN 2186
Melody	HN 2202
Sea Sprite (Style Two)	HN 2191
Sweet Sixteen	HN 2231
Teenager	HN 2203
Wood Nymph	HN 2192

TUDOR ROSES

Lady Jane Grey	HN 3680
Mary Tudor	HN 3834
Princess Elizabeth	HN 3682

VANITY FAIR LADIES

Angela (Style Two)	HN 2389
Ann (Style One)	HN 2739
Ashley	HN 3420
Barbara (Style Two)	HN 2962
Carol	HN 2961
Danielle (Style Two)	HN 3001
Dawn (Style Three)	HN 3600
Denise (Style Three)	HN 2477
Donna	HN 2939
Emily (Style Two)	HN 3204
Flower of Love	HN 2460
Gift of Love	HN 3427
Good Companion	HN 3608
Heather	HN 2956
Jean (Style Two)	HN 2710
Jemma	HN 3168
Jessica	HN 3169
Joanne (Style One)	HN 2373
Just For You	HN 3355
Kathleen (Style Three)	HN 3609
Kimberley (Style Two)	HN 3379
Linda (Style Two)	HN 2758
Margaret (Style Two)	HN 2397
Maria	HN 3381
Mary (Style One)	HN 2374
Maureen (Style Three)	HN 2481
Megan	HN 3306
Mother and Child	HN 3353
Nancy	HN 2955
Natalie	HN 3173
Pamela (Style Two)	HN 2479
Patricia (Style Three)	HN 2715
Paula	HN 3234
Samantha (Style One)	HN 2954
Tender Moment	HN 3303
Tracy	HN 2736
Veronica (Style Four)	HN 3205
Yours Forever	HN 3354

VANITY FAIR CHILDREN

Amanda	HN 2996, 3406, 3632
Andrea	HN 3058
Birthday Girl	HN 3423
Buddies (Style Two)	HN 3396
Catherine (Style Three)	HN 3044
Daddy's Girl	HN 3435
Dinnertime	HN 3726
Helen	HN 2994
Julie	HN 2995
Kerry	HN 3036
Let's Play	HN 3397
Lindsey	HN 3043
My First Pet	HN 3122
Reward	HN 3391
Sit	HN 3123, 3430

VICTORIAN AND EDWARDIAN ACTRESSES

Ellen Terry	HN 3826
Lillie Langtry	HN 3820

WILDFLOWER OF THE MONTH

January (Style Three)	HN 3341
February (Style Three)	HN 3342
March (Style Three)	HN 3343
April (Style Three)	HN 3344
May (Style Four)	HN 3345
June (Style Six)	HN 3346
July (Style Three)	HN 3347
August (Style Three)	HN 3408
September (Style Three)	HN 3409
October (Style Three)	HN 3410
November (Style Three)	HN 3411
December (Style Three)	HN 3412

ALPHABETICAL
INDEX

A

A la Mode, HN 2544
A Penny's Worth, HN 2408
A Posy for You, HN 3606
A Winter's Walk, HN 3052
Abdullah, HN 1410, 2104
Ace (The), HN 3398
A'Courting, HN 2004
Adele, HN 2480; Also called Camille (Style Two), HN 3171;
    Margaret (Style Two), HN 2397, 3496
Adornment, HN 3015
Adrienne, HN 2152, 2304; Also called Joan (Style Two),
    HN 3217
Affection, HN 2236
Afternoon Call see Lady With an Ermine Muff
Afternoon Tea, HN 1747, 1748
Aileen, HN 1645, 1664, 1803
Ajax, HMS, HN 2908
Alchemist, HN 1259, 1282
Alexandra (Style One), HN 2398
Alexandra (Style Two), HN 3286, 3292
Alfred Jingle, HN 541; M 52
Alfred The Great, HN 3821
Alice (Style One), HN 2158
Alice (Style Two), HN 3368
Alison, HN 2336, 3264
All Aboard, HN 2940
All-A-Blooming, HN 1457, 1466
Allure, HN 3080; Also called Monique, HN 2880
Almost Grown, HN 3425
Amanda (Style One), HN 2996, 3406, 3632, 3634, 3635; Also
    called Figure of the Month, Child
Amy Style One), HN 2958
Amy (Style Two), HN 3316
Amy (Style Three), HN 3854
Amy's Sister, HN 3445
And One For You, HN 2970
And So To Bed, HN 2966
Andrea, HN 3058
Anita, HN 3766
Angela (Style One), HN 1204, 1303
Angela (Style Two), HN 2389
Angela (Style Three), HN 3419
Angela (Style Four), HN 3690
Angelina, HN 2013
Ann (Style One), HN 2739
Ann (Style Two), HN 3259; Also called Lauren, HN 3290
Anna, HN 2802
Annabel, HN 3273
Annabella, HN 1871, 1872, 1875
Anne Bolelyn, HN 3232
Anne of Cleves, HN 3356
Annette (Style One), HN 1471, 1472, 1550
Annette (Style Two), HN 3495; Also called Sandra, HN 2275,
    2401
Anniversary, HN 3625
Anthea, HN 1526, 1527, 1669
Antoinette (Style One), HN 1850, 1851
Antoinette (Style Two), HN 2326; Also called My Love, HN
    2339
Antony and Cleopatra, HN 3114
Any Old Lavender, see Sweet Lavender
Aperitif, HN 2998
Apple Maid, HN 2160
April (Style One), HN 2708

April (Style Two), HN 3333
April (Style Three), HN 3344
April (Style Four), HN 3693
April Shower, HN 3024
Arab, HN 33, 343, 378; Also called The Moor, HN 1308, 1366,
    1425, 1657, 2082, 3642
Aragorn, HN 2916
Ariel, HN 3831
Artful Dodger, HN 546; M 55
As Good As New, HN 2971
Ascot (Style One), HN 2356
Ascot (Style Two), HN 3471
Ashley, HN 3420
At Ease, HN 2473
Attentive Scholar see Diligent Scholar
Auctioneer, HN 2988
August (Style One), HN 3165
August (Style Two), HN 3325
August (Style Three), HN 3408
Au Revoir (Style One), HN 3723
Au Revoir (Style Two), HN 3729
Aurora, HN 3833
Automne, HN 3068
Autumn (Style One), HN 314, 474
Autumn (Style Two), HN 2087
Autumn Attraction, HN 3612; Also called "Michele,"HN 2234
Autumn Breezes (Style One), HN 1911, 1913, 1934, 2131, 2147
Autumn Breezes (Style Two) HN 2176, 2180
Autumn Glory, HN 2766
Autumntime (Style One), HN 3231
Autumntime (Style Two), HN 3621
Awakening (Style One), HN 1927
Awakening (Style Two), HN 2837, 2875

B

Baba, HN 1230, 1243-1248
Babette, HN 1423, 1424
Babie, HN 1679, 1842, 2121
Baby, HN 12
Baby Bunting, HN 2108
Bachelor, HN 2319
Balinese Dancer, HN 2808
Ballad Seller, HN 2266
Ballerina (Style One), HN 2116
Ballerina (Style Two), HN 3197
Ballet Class, HN 3134, 3731
Ballet Shoes, HN 3434
Balloon Boy, HN 2934
Balloon Clown, HN 2894
Balloon Girl, HN 2818
Balloon Lady, HN 2935
Balloon Man, HN 1954
Balloon Seller (Style One), HN 479, 486, 548, 583, 697
Balloon Seller, (Style Two), HN 2130
Balloon Woman see Balloon Seller (Style One)
Balloons, HN 3187
Barbara (Style One), HN 1421, 1432, 1461
Barbara (Style Two), HN 2962
Barbara (Style Three), HN 3441
Barliman Butterbur, HN 2923
Basket Weaver, HN 2245
Bather (Style One), HN 597, 687, 781, 782, 1238, 1708
Bather (Style Two), HN 773, 774, 1227
Bathing Beauty, HN 3156
Beachcomber, HN 2487

C

Daisy (Style One), HN 1575, 1961
Daisy (Style Two), HN 3802, 3803, 3804, 3805
Damaris, HN 2079
Dancing Delight, HN 3078
"Dancing Eyes and Sunny Hair" HN 1543
Dancing Figure, HN 311
Dancing Years, HN 2235
Dandy, HN 753
Danielle (Style One), HN 3056
Danielle (Stye Two), HN 3001; Also called Spring Song, HN 3446
Daphne, HN 2268
Dapple Grey, HN 2521
Darby, HN 1427, 2024
Darling (Style One), HN 1, 1319, 1371, 1372
Darling (Style Two), HN 1985, 3613
David Copperfield, M 88
Dawn (Style One), HN 1858, 1858A
Dawn (Style Two), HN 3258
Dawn (Style Three), HN 3600
Daybreak, HN 3107
Daydreams, HN 1731, 1732, 1944
Deauville, HN 2344
Debbie, HN 2385, 2400; Also called Lavender Rose, HN 3481; Moonlight Rose, HN 3483; Old Country Roses, HN 3482
Deborah, HN 2701, 3644
Debut, HN 3046
Debutante (Style One), HN 2210
Debutante (Style Two), HN 3188
December (Style One), HN 2696
December (Style Two), HN 3329
December (Style Three), HN 3412
Deidre, HN 2020
Delicia, HN 1662, 1663, 1681
Delight, HN 1772, 1773
Delphine, HN 2136
Demure, HN 3045
Denise (Style One), M 34, 35
Denise (Style Two), HN 2273
Denise (Style Three), HN 2477; Also called Summer Rose (Style Two), HN 3309
Derrick, HN 1398
Desdemona, HN 3676
Despair, HN 596
Detective, HN 2359
Devotion, HN 3228
Diana (Style One), HN 1716, 1717, 1986
Diana (Style Two), HN 2468, 3266
Diana (Style Three), HN 3310
Diana the Huntress, HN 2829
Diane, HN 3604
Dick Swiveller, M 90
Dick Turpin, HN 3272, 3637
Digger (Australian), HN 322, 353
Digger (New Zealand), HN 321
Diligent Scholar, HN 26
Dimity, HN 2169
Dinky Doo, HN 1678, 2120, 3618
Dinnertime, HN 3726
Discovery, HN 3428
"Do You Wonder...," HN 1544
Doctor, HN 2858
Dolly Vardon, HN 1514, 1515
Dolly (Style One), HN 355
Dolly (Style Two), HN 389, 390, 469. Also called The Little Mother (Style One)
Dominique, HN 3054; Also called Paradise, HN 3074
Donna, HN 2939
Dorcas, HN 1490, 1491, 1558
Doreen, HN 1363, 1389, 1390
Doris Keene as Cavallini (Style One), HN 90, 467

Doris Keene as Cavallini (Style Two), HN 96, 345
Dorothy, HN 3098
Double Jester, HN 365
Double Spooks see Spooks
Dreaming, HN 3133
Dreamland, HN 1473, 1481
Dreamweaver, HN 2283
Dressing Up (Style One), HN 2964
Dressing-Up (Style Two), HN 3300
Drummer Boy, HN 2679
Dryad of the Pines, HN 1869
Duchess of York, HN 3086
Duke of Wellington, HN 3432
Dulcie, HN 2305
Dulcimer, HN 2798
Dulcinea, HN 1343, 1419
Dunce, HN 6, 310, 357

E

Easter Day, HN 1976, 2039
Eastern Grace, HN 3138, 3683
Edith, HN 2957
Elaine (Style One), HN 2791, 3307, 3741
Elaine (Style Two), HN 3214, 3247
Eleanor of Provence, HN 2009
Eleanore, HN 1753, 1754
Elegance, HN 2264
Elfreda, HN 2078
Eliza (Style One), HN 2543, 2543A
Eliza (Style Two), HN 3179
Eliza (Style Three), HN 3798, 3799, 3800, 3801
Eliza Farren, Countess of Derby, HN 3442
Elizabeth (Style One), HN 2946
Elizabeth (Style Two), HN 2465
Elizabeth Fry, HN 2, 2A
Elizabethan Lady, HN 309, also called "A Lady of the Elizabethan Period" (Style Two)
Ellen, HN 3020
Ellen Terry, HN 3826
Ellen Terry as Queen Catherine, HN 379
Elsie Maynard (Style One), HN 639
Elsie Maynard (Style Two), HN 2902
Elyse, HN 2429, 2474
Embroidering, HN 2855
Emily (In Autumn) (Style One), HN 3004
Emily (Style Two), HN 3204
Emily (Style Three), HN 3688, 3806, 3807, 3808, 3809
Emir, HN 1604, 1605; Also called Ibrahim, HN 2095
Emma (Style One), HN 2834
Emma (Style Two), HN 3208
Enchanting Evening, HN 3108
Enchantment, HN 2178
Encore, HN 2751
England, HN 3627
Enigma, HN 3110
Entranced, HN 3186
Ermine Coat, HN 1981
Ermine Muff, HN 54, 332, 671
Erminie, M 40
Esmeralda, HN 2168
Estelle, HN 1566, 1802
Ete (Summer), HN 3067
Eugene, HN 1520, 1521
Europa and the Bull (Style One), HN 95
Europa and the Bull (Style Two), HN 2828
Eve, HN 2466
Evelyn, HN 1622, 1637
Eventide, HN 2814

F

Fagin (Style One), HN 534, M 49
Fagin (Style Two), HN 3752
Fair Lady (Style One), HN 2193, 2832, 2835
Fair Lady (Style Two), HN 3216, 3336
Fair Maiden, HN 2211, 2434
Fairy (Style One), HN 1324
Fairy, (Style Two), HN 1374, 1380, 1532
Fairy, (Style Three), HN 1375, 1395, 1533
Fairy, (Style Four), HN 1376, 1536
Fairy, (Style Five), HN 1377
Fairy, (Style Six), HN 1378, 1396, 1535
Fairy, (Style Seven), HN 1379, 1394, 1534
Fairy, (Style Eight), HN 1393
Fairyspell, HN 2979
Faith, HN 3082
Faithful Friend, HN 3696
Falstaff (Style One), HN 571, 575, 608, 609, 619, 638, 1216, 1606
Falstaff (Style Two), HN 618, 2054
Falstaf (Style Three), HN 3236
Family Album, HN 2321
Family, HN 2720, 2721
Fantasy, HN 3296
Faraway, HN 2133
Farmer, HN 3195
Farmer's Boy, HN 2520
Farmer's Wife (Style One), HN 2069
Farmer's Wife (Style Two), HN 3164
Fat Boy (Style One), HN 530, M44
Fat Boy (Style Two), HN 555, 1893
Fat Boy (Style Three), HN 2096
Father Christmas, HN 3399
Favourite, HN 2249
February (Style One), HN 2703
February (Style Two), HN 3331
February (Style Three), HN 3342
Feeding Time, HN 3373
Female Study, HN 606A, 606B
Fiddler, HN 2171
Field Marshall Montgomery, HN 3405
Fiona (Style One), HN 1924, 1925, 1933
Fiona (Style Two), HN 2694
Fiona (Style Three), HN 3252
Fiona (Style Four), HN 3748; Also called Adrienne, HN 2152, 2304; Joan, HN 3217
First Dance, HN 2803
First Love, HN 2747
First Outing, HN 3377
First Performance, HN 3605
First Recital, HN 3652
First Steps (Style One), HN 2242
First Steps (Style Two), HN 3282
First Steps (Style Three), HN 3361
First Violin, HN 3704
First Waltz, HN 2862
Fisherwomen, HN 80, 349, 359, 631; Also called Waiting for the Boats or Looking for the Boats
Fleur, HN 2368, 2369; Also called Flower of Love, HN 2460
Fleurette, HN 1587
Flirtation, HN 3071
Flora, HN 2349
Florence, HN 2745
Florence Nightingale, HN 3144
Flounced Skirt, HN 57A, 66, 77, 78, 333
Flower Arranging, HN 3040
Flower of Love, HN 2460; Also called Fleur, HN 2368, 2369
Flower Seller, HN 789
Flower Seller's Children, HN 525, 551, 1206, 1342, 1406

Flowergirl (Style One), HN 3479
Flowergirl (Style Two), HN 3602
Flowers for Mother, HN 3454
Flute, HN 2483
Foaming Quart, HN 2162
Folly, HN 1335, 1750
Forget-Me-Not (Style One), HN 1812, 1813
Forget-Me-Not (Style Two), HN 3388
Forget-Me-Nots, HN 3700
Fortune Teller, HN 2159
Forty Winks, HN 1974
For You, HN 3754
Four O'Clock, HN 1760
Fragrance (Style One), HN 2334, 3311
Fragrance (Style Two), HN 3220, 3250
Francine, HN 2422
Francoise, HN 2897
Frangton, HN 1720, 1721
Free As The Wind, HN 3139
Free Spirit (Style One), HN 3157, 3159
Free Spirit (Style Two), HN 3728
French Horn, HN 2795
French Peasant, HN 2075
Friar Tuck, HN 2143
Friendship, HN 3491
Frodo, HN 2912
Fruit Gathering, HN 449, 476, 503, 561, 562, 706, 707

G

Gaffer, HN 2053
Gaiety, HN 3140
Gail (Style One), HN 2937
Gail (Style Two), HN 3321
Gainsborough Hat, HN 46, 46A, 47, 329, 352, 383, 453, 675, 705
Galadriel, HN 2915
Gamekeeper. HN 2879
Gandalf, HN 2911
Gardener, HN 3161
Gardening Time, HN 3401
Gay Morning, HN 2135
Geisha (Style One), HN 354, 376, 376A, 387, 634, 741, 779, 1321, 1322
Geisha (Style Two), HN 1223, 1234, 1292, 1310
Geisha (Style Three), HN 3229
Gemma, HN 3661
General Robert E. Lee, HN 3404
Genevieve, HN 1962
Genie, HN 2989, 2999
Gentleman from Williamsburg, HN 2227
Gentlewoman, HN 1632
Geoffrey Boycott, HN 3890
George Washington at Prayer, HN 2861
Georgiana, HN 2093
Georgina, HN 2377
Geraldine, HN 2348
Gift of Freedom, HN 3443
Gift of Love, HN 3427
Gillian (Style One), HN 1670 1670A
Gillian (Style Two), HN 3042, 3042A
Gillian (Style Three), HN 3742
Gimli, HN 2922
Girl Evacuee, HN 3203
Giselle, HN 2139
Giselle, The Forest Glade, HN 2140
Gladys, HN 1740, 1741
Gleaner, HN 1302
Gloria (Style One), HN 1488, 1700
Gloria (Style Two), HN 3200

Gnome, HN 319, 380, 381
God Bless You, HN 3400
Golden Days, HN 2274
Golfer, HN 2992
Gollum, HN 2913
Gollywog, HN 1979, 2040
Good Catch, HN 2258
Good Companion, HN 3608
Good Day Sir, HN 2896
Good Friends, HN 2783
Good King Wenceslas (Style One), HN 2118
Good King Wenceslas (Style Two), HN 3262
Good Morning, HN 2671
Good Pals, HN 3132
Goody Two Shoes (Style One), HN 1889, 1905, 2037
Goody Two Shoes (Style Two), M 80, 81
Goosegirl (Style One), HN 425, 436, 437, 448, 559, 560
Goose Girl (Style Two), HN 2419
Gossips, HN 1426, 1429, 2025
Grace (Style One), HN 2318
Grace (Style Two), HN 3699
Grace Darling, HN 3089
Grace, W.G., HN 3640
Graduate (female), HN 3016
Graduate (male), HN 3017
Grand Manner, HN 2723
Grandma, HN 2052, 2052A
Granny, HN 1804, 1832
Granny's Heritage, HN 1873, 1874, 2031
Granny's Shawl, HN 1642, 1647
Grandpa's Story, HN 3456
Greta, HN 1485
Gretchen, HN 1397, 1562
Grief, HN 595
Griselda, HN 1993
Grizel, HN 1629
Grossmith's 'Tsang Ihang,' HN 582
Groucho Marx, HN 2777
Guardsman, HN 2784
Gulliver, HN 3750
Guy Fawkes (Style One), HN 98, 347, 445
Guy Fawkes (Style Two), HN 3271
Gwendolen, HN 1494, 1503, 1570
Gwynneth, HN 1980
Gypsy Dance (Style One), HN 2157
Gypsy Dance (Style Two), HN 2230

H

Hannah (Style One), HN 3369, 3655
Hannah (Style Two), HN 3649, 3870
Happy Anniversary (Style One), HN 3097
Happy Anniversary (Style Two), HN 3254
Happy Birthday (Style One),HN 3095
Happy Birthday (Style Two). HN 3660
"Happy Joy, Baby Boy..." HN 1541
Happy Birthday (Style Two), HN 3660
Harlequin (Style One), HN 2186
Harlequin (Style Two), HN 2737, 3287
Harlequinade, HN 585, 635, 711, 780
Harlequinade Masked, HN 768, 769, 1274, 1304
Harmony, HN 2824
Harp, HN 2482
Harriet (Style One), HN 3177
Harriet (Style Two), HN 3794, 3795, 3796, 3797
Harvestime, HN 3084
Hazel (Style One), HN 1796, 1797
Hazel (Style Two), HN 3167
He Loves Me, HN 2046

Heart to Heart, HN 2276
Heather, HN 2956; Also called Marie (Style Three), HN 3357
Heidi, HN 2975
Helen (Style One), HN 1508, 1509, 1572
Helen (Style Two), HN 2994
Helen (Style Three), HN 3601, 3687, 3763; Also called "Miss
    Kay,"HN 3659
Helen of Troy, HN 2387
Hello Daddy, HN 3651
Helmsman, HN 2499
Henley, HN 3367
Henrietta Maria, HN 2005
Henry Irving As Cardinal Wolsey, HN 344
Henry Lytton As Jack Point, HN 610
Henry VIII (Style One), HN 370, 673
Henry VIII (Style Two), HN 1792
Henry VIII (Style Three), HN 3350
Henry Vlll (Style Four), HN 3458
Her Ladyship, HN 1977
"Here A Little Child I Stand..." HN 1546
Herminia, HN 1644, 1646, 1704
Hermione, HN 2058
Hibernia, HN 2932
Highwayman, HN 527, 592, 1257
Hilary, HN 2335
Hinged Parasol, HN 1578, 1579
His Holiness Pope John-Paul II, HN 2888
Hiver (Winter), HN 3069
HM Queen Elizabeth, The Queen Mother (Style One), HN 2882
HM Queen Elizabeth, The Queen Mother (Style Two),
    HN 3189
HM Queen Elizabeth, The Queen Mother As The Duchess
    of York, HN 3230
HM Queen Elizabeth II (Style One), HN 2502
HM Queen Elizabeth II (Style Two), HN 2878
HM Queen Elizabeth II (Style Three), HN 3440
HM Queen Elizabeth II (Style Four), ÿHN 3436
Hold Tight, HN 3298
Holly, HN 3647
Home Again, HN 2167
Home At Last, HN 3697
Homecoming, HN 3295
Hometime, HN 3685
Honourable Frances Duncombe, HN 3009
Honey, HN 1909, 1910, 1963
Hope, HN 3061
Hornpipe, HN 2161
Hostess of Williamsburg, HN 2209
HRH Prince Philip, Duke of Edinburgh, HN 2386
HRH The Prince of Wales (Style One), HN 2883
HRH The Prince of Wales (Style Two), HN 2884
HRH The Princess of Wales, HN 2887
Huckleberry Finn, HN 2927
Hunting Squire, HN 1409: Also called Squire, HN 1814
Hunts Lady, HN 1201
Huntsman (Style One), HN 1226
Huntsman (Style Two), HN 1815: Also called John Peel,
    HN 1408
Huntsman (Style Three), HN 2492
Hurdy Gurdy, HN 2796

I

I'm Nearly Ready, HN 2976
Ibrahim, HN 2095; Also called Emir, HN 1604, 1605
Idle Hours, HN 3115
In Grandma's Days, HN 339, 340 388, 442; Also called Lilac
    Shawl HN 44, 44A and Poke Bonnet HN 362, 612, 765
In The Stocks (Style One), HN 1474, 1475

M

S

T

Tracy, HN 2736, 3291
Tranquility, HN 2426, 2469
Traveller's Tale, HN 3185
Treasure Island, HN 2243
Trotty Veck, M 91
Tulips, HN 466, 488, 672, 747, 1334
Tumbler, HN 3183: Also called "Tumbling," HN 3283, 3289
Tumbling, HN 3283, 3289: Also called "Tumbler," HN 3183
Tuppence a Bag, HN 2320
Twilight, HN 2256
Two-a-Penny, HN 1359
T'zu-hsi, Empress Dowager, HN 2391

U

Uncle Ned, HN 2094
Under the Gooseberry Bush, HN 49
"Upon Her Cheeks She Wept," HN 59, 511, 522
Uriah Heep (Style One), HN 545; M 45
Uriah Heep (Style Two), HN 554, 1892
Uriah Heep (Style Three), HN 2101

V

Valerie, HN 2107, 3620
Vanessa (Style One), HN 1836, 1838
Vanessa (Style Two), HN 3198
Vanity, HN 2475
Veneta, HN 2722
Vera, HN 1729, 1730
Verena, HN 1835, 1854
Veronica (Style One), HN 1517, 1519, 1650, 1943
Veronica (Style Two), M 64, 70
Veronica (Style Three), HN 1915
Veronica (Style Four), HN 3205
Vice Admiral Lord Nelson, HN 3489
Victoria (Style One), HN 2471, 3416
Victoria (Style Two), HN 3735, 3744
Victorian Lady, HN 726, 727, 728, 736, 739, 740, 742, 745, 1208, 1258, 1276, 1277, 1345, 1452, 1529
Victorian Lady (Style Two), M 1, 2, 25
Viking, HN 2375
Viola, HN 3706
Viola d'Amore, HN 2797
Violin, HN 2432
Virginals, HN 2427
Virginia, HN 1693, 1694
Vivienne, HN 2073
Votes For Women, HN 2816

W

Waiting For A Train, HN 3315
Waiting For The Boat; see Fisherwomen
Wales, HN 3630
Wandering Minstrel, HN 1224
Wardrobe Mistress, HN 2145
Water Maiden, HN 3155
Wayfarer, HN 2362
Wedding Day, HN 2748
Wedding Morn (Style One), HN 1866, 1867
Wedding Morn (Style Two), HN 3853
Wedding Vows, HN 2750
Wee Willie Winkie (Style One), HN 2050
Wee Willie Winkie (Style Two), HN 3031
Welcome, HN 3764
Welcome Home, HN 3299

Well Done, HN 3362
Welsh Girl, HN 39, 92, 456, 514, 516, 519, 520, 660, 668, 669, 701, 792. Also called Myfanwy Jones
Wendy, HN 2109
West Indian Dancer, HN 2384
West Wind, HN 1776, 1826
W.G. Grace, HN 3640
What Fun, HN 3364
What's The Matter, HN 3684
When Was I Young, HN 3457
Wigmaker of Williamsburg, HN 2239
Will He, Won't He, HN 3275
Willy-Won't He, HN 1561, 1584, 2150
Wimbledon, HN 3366
Windflower (Style One), HN 1763, 1764, 2029
Windflower (Style Two), HN 1920, 1939
Windflower (Style Three), M 78, 79
Windflower (Style Four), HN 3077
Windmill Lady, HN 1400
Windswept, HN 3027
Winner, HN 1407
Winning Putt, HN 3279
Winsome, HN 2220
Winston S. Churchill (Style One), HN 3057
Winston S. Churchill (Style Two), HN 3433
Winter (Style One), HN 315, 475
Winter (Style Two), HN 2088
Winter Welcome, HN 3611; Also called "Caroline," HN 3170
Winter's Day, HN 3769
Wintertime (Style One), HN 3060
Wintertime (Style Two), HN 3622
Wistful (Style One), HN 2396, 2472
Wistful (Style Two), HN 3664
With Love, HN 3393, 3492
Wizard, HN 2877, 3121
Wizard, The, HN 3722, 3732
Woman of the Time of Henry VI, HN 43
Wood Nymph, HN 2192
Writing, HN 3049

Y

Yearning, HN 2920, 2921
Yeoman of the Guard, HN 688, 2122
Young Dreams, HN 3176
Young Knight, HN 94
Young Love, HN 2735
Young Master, HN 2872
Young Melody, HN 3654
Young Miss Nightingale, HN 2010
Young Mother with Child, HN 1301
Young Widow, HN 1399: Also called Little Mother (Style Two), HN 1418, 1641
Yours Forever, HN 3354: Also called "Kimberley" HN 2969
Yum-Yum (Style One), HN 1268, 1287
Yum-Yum (Style Two), HN 2899
Yvonne, HN 3038

The **Royal Doulton International Collectors Club** publish an informative and beautifully illustrated quarterly magazine, **Gallery,** and offer exclusive pieces each year for "Members Only." Pamela HN3756 is one of the 1996 club exclusives. To obtain more information on the Collectors Club and a Complimentary copy of **Gallery** please contact the Club today.

PAMELA
HN3756
8" (20cm)
Modelled by
Tim Potts

The Royal Doulton International Collectors Club
850 Progress Avenue, Scarborough, Ontario M1H 3C4 (416) 431-4202
Toll Free Canada Wide 1-800 268-4040

20TH CENTURY FAIRS

"Has An Important Announcement"

DOULTON COLLECTORS!   BESWICK COLLECTORS!
WE ARE MOVING TO
"THE POTTERIES"

On June 1, 1997 we will host the Old Stafford Show
at Trentham Gardens, Stoke-on-Trent

For information on the fairs, on Trentham Gardens, on hotels, on things to do
in and around the Potteries, write:

20th CENTURY FAIRS
9 Church Street
London, NW88EE
ENGLAND

The Charlton Press

We ask that collectors having information not included in any of our pricing references to please send it along to our editorial offices in Toronto.

We will consider editorial additions or corrections regarding colourways, varieties, series; issue dates, designs and styles, as well as well as other information that would be of interest to collectors. Photos of models that were unavailable in previous issues are particularly welcome. Black and white, unscreened photos are best, but colour is also suitable.

Your help in providing new or previously unobtainable data on any aspect of Royal Doulton models or collecting will be considered for inclusion in subsequent editions. Those providing information will be acknowledged in the contributor's section in the front of every catalogue

The Charlton Press
Editorial Office
2010 Yonge Street
Toronto, Ontario M4S 1Z9 Fax (416) 488-4656

433

Happy Birthday Bunnykins

Celebrating
20 Years in Business

Write or phone for our monthly newsletter and quarterly Doulton lists
Mail & Phone Orders Accepted

the site of ☘ the green

AMERICAN EXPRESS
DISCOVER
MASTERCARD
VISA

R.R. #1, Dundas, Ontario L9H 5E1
(Highway #5, a half-mile east of
Peter's Corner)

Toll Free in Canada & U.S.A.
1-800-263-4730

Tel: (905) 627-1304
Fax: (905) 627-0511

William Cross
Antiques & Collectibles Inc.

YOUR DOULTON BESWICK SPECIALISTS

LOWEST PRICES WORLDWIDE!!!

We fill want lists! Guaranteed satisfaction!

4631 East Hastings, Burnaby,
British Columbia, Canada V5C 2K3
Tel.: (604) 298 9599
Fax: (604) 298 9563
For orders outside the Vancouver area call:
1 800 639 7771

International orders welcome. We mail anywhere

434

Pirie's Fine Gifts

We buy and sell fine collectibles

Royal Doulton
Royal Crown Derby
Beswick
Beatrix Potter
Brambly Hedge
Hummel & Goebel

(905) 332-9801
(416) 767-1899

Canada

CHARLES & JOANN DOMBECK
- *ROYAL DOULTON SPECIALISTS* -

We Carry Thousands of Discontinued Doulton Figurines, Jugs, Animals, Bunnykins, Beatrix Potter, Etc...
ALL PRICE RANGES

We also offer Current Doulton at Huge Discounts!
Paying Top Prices for Single Pieces or Entire Collections!

CHARLES & JOANN DOMBECK **9552 N.W. 9th Court** **Plantation, Florida** **33324**	In Canada - Call Collect To Order: **305-452-9174** In The U.S.A. Call Toll Free: **1-800-331-0863** Fax 305-452-7854

Colonial House of Collectibles & Santa's North Pole World

ROYAL DOULTON IS OUR SPECIALTY!
We Buy
We Sell
We Appraise

Colonial House Features the Largest Selection of Current and Discontinued Items in the Following Lines:

- OLD & NEW ROYAL DOULTON
- FIGURES AND CHARACTER JUGS
- HUMMELS
- DAVID WINTER COTTAGES
- WALT DISNEY CLASSICS
- DEPT. 56 COTTAGES AND SNOWBABIES
- BELLEEK
- ANRI

- WEE FOREST FOLK
- PRECIOUS MOMENTS
- LILLIPUT LANE
- BOSSONS WALL ORNAMENTS
- SWAROVSKI CRYSTAL
- LLADRO
- DUNCAN ROYALE
- B & G AND R.C.

Send for our latest product catalogue

WE DO MAIL ORDERS

COLONIAL HOUSE ANTIQUES & GIFTS
182 Front Street, Berea, Ohio 44017; 216-826-4169 or 1-800-344-9299; Fax 216-826-0839
Monday to Saturday 10 a.m. to 5 p.m. Or by Appointment

PRECIOUS MEMORIES

Eastern Canada's Largest Doulton Dealer

VISIT OUR STORE WITH OVER 2 000 DOULTON / BESWICK PIECES

Stocking Discontinued, Current, Limited Editions figurines, jugs, animals and Flambé figures. If looking for Limited Editions - give us a call.
Example: "In the Burn" only $895.00

FIGURINES

Royal Doulton
Coalport
Lladro
Precious Moments
Snowman
Bunnykins
Brambly Hedge
Beswick
Winnie the Pooh
Beatrix Potter

TABLEWARE

Portmeirion
Royal Doulton
Wedgwood
Royal Albert
Minton
Royal Crown Derby
Johnson Bros.
Nurseryware

Wedding and Anniversary Gift Centre -FREE Gift Wrapping and Card with Shipment. Insurance Replacement Service. Mail Order our Speciality. Worldwide Guaranteed Safe Delivery.
OPEN: Monday to Saturday 9:00 - 6:00 Year round

GEORGE & NORA BAGNELL
Phone 902 368 1212
Fax   902 368 7321
Orders 1 800 463 5200

PRECIOUS MEMORIES
89 Trans Canada Highway
Charlottetown, PEI
CANADA, C1E 1E8

436

GREAT BRITAIN COLLECTIBLES

FIGURINES
BUNNYKINS
TOBIES · FLAMBÉ
SERIES WARE
BESWICK
KINGSWARE

2235 DUNDAS STREET WEST,
TORONTO, ONTARIO M6R 1X6
TEL: (416) 537-2187
TOLL FREE: 1 (800) 665-4886
FAX: (416) 534-9571

DOULTON SPECIALIST
FREE APPRAISALS
SELLING · BUYING · TRADING
CASH PAID · FREE PRICE LIST

R. PAUL WILLIAMS

*From Maryland through The Virginias and The Carolinas
If You're Looking for Royal Doulton You're Looking for*

Tru-Find Collectibles

"The Dealer in the Derby"

• *Official Royal Doulton International Collectors Club Dealer* •

SHOP LOCATION	SHOP LOCATION	MAIL ORDERS
The Antique Gallery	Mechanicsville Antique Mall	Tru-Find Collectibles
3140 W. Cary Street	Exit 37B Off I-295	P.O. Box 12482
Richmond, Virginia	(Suburban Richmond, VA)	Richmond, VA 23241

WE BUY, SELL & TRADE ALL ROYAL DOULTON

Telephone 804-730-3264

Phillips
LONDON

PHILLIPS, THE WADE, DOULTON & BESWICK SPECIALISTS

*Phillips holds two Wade, Doulton and Beswick wares auctions a year, in
May and October, in England. If you have any items of Wade, Doulton or
Beswick you would like appraised, free of charge, please contact Mark Oliver:
Tel.: (0171) 629-6602, ext. 233 Fax: (0171) 629-8876
101 New Bond Street, London W1Y OAS*

LONDON - PARIS - NEW YORK - GENEVA - BRUSSELS - ZURICH
AMSTERDAM - DUSSELDORF - STOCKHOLM

*Twenty-two salesrooms throughout the United Kingdom.
Members of the Society of Fine Art Auctioneers*

438

MARNALEA ANTIQUES

THE DOULTON SPECIALIST
SERVING COLLECTORS SINCE 1974!

**We carry
One of Canada's Largest Collections of
DISCONTINUED ROYAL DOULTON**

*FIGURINES • JUGS • ANIMALS • PLATES
SERIESWARE • LAMBETH • ROYAL WORCESTER*

MAILING LIST AVAILABLE

*Our Selection's Great - Our Prices Competitive -
and the GST is Always Included!*

**51 MAIN STREET NORTH,
CAMPBELLVILLE ONTARIO L0P 1B0
TEL: 905 854 0287   FAX: 905 854 3117**

We Buy   We Sell

YOURS & MINE LTD.

- **FIGURINES**
- **TOBIES**
- **PLATES**
- **BELLS**

**ROYAL DOULTON, BUNNYKINS
BEATRIX POTTER, HUMMEL
FIGURINES, ETC.**

Box No. 22055
Westmount Post Office
Waterloo, Ontario   (519) 744-8059
Canada N2L 6J7   (519) 836-6757

YESTERDAY'S
Princess & Barry Weiss

Mail order:
P.O. box 296
New City
New York 10956

10 a.m. - 3p.m.
1-800-Toby-Jug
or
212-564-3244
Monday Thro' Friday

After 3p.m. & Week-ends
1-800-Toby-Mug
or
914-634-8456

One of the largest Toby Jug dealers in the United States.
We carry a complete selection of Character Jugs, Figurines,
Animals, Seriesware and Stoneware, etc.,
Highest prices paid for entire collections or single pieces.

SPECIALIZING IN RARE AND DISCONTINUED WADE, ROYAL DOULTON AND BESWICK

The Potteries Antique Centre

DOULTON
Figures, character and tob y
jugs, animals, Bunnykins,
seriesware, stoneware, Flambé
and much more

BESWICK

Animals,jugs,figurines from
Beatrix Potter, Kitty McBride,
Alice in Wonderland, Rupert the
Bear,Disney, David Hand
Animaland & Colin Melbourne

WADE
1930s underglazed and cellulose
figures, animals, Disney, Blow
Ups, Whimsies, Hanna-Barbera,
World of Survival, Connoisseur
Birds and much more

SALESROOM
A large selection of the
following items can be seen in
our showroom 7 days a week

AUCTIONS

We hold two auctions per year, each featuring scarce and rare pieces of Wade, Doulton
and Beswick. Send for your free illustrated auction catalogue, quoting this advertisement, or
contact Mr. W. Buckley to discuss estimates and commission rates.

271 Waterloo Road, Cobridge, Stoke-on-Trent
Staffordshire ST6 3HR, England
Tel.: (01782) 201455 Fax: (01782) 201518

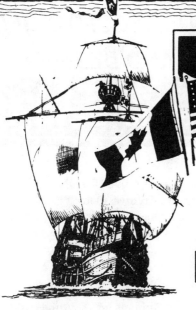

Royal Doulton

Our shop right on the border offers you fine discontinued Royal Doulton from top USA and Canadian collections. Probably the largest selection you have ever seen in ONE STORE!

**— Phone Orders —
NATIONWIDE - 1-800-968-2424**

Seaway China

**COMPANY
MARINE CITY, MI.**

• Jamie & Mary Pole •

We buy and sell new and discontinued ROYAL DOULTON

MICHIGAN - 1-800-968-2424

ONTARIO - 1-800-968-2424

On the St. Clair River at the Canadian Border
102 Broadway, Marine City, MI., USA 48039 (313) 765-9000

YESTERDAY'S SOUTH, INC.

BUY - *YOUR ROYAL DOULTON CONNECTION* - **SELL**

| AUTHORIZED ROYAL DOULTON DEALERS BIG DISCOUNTS | REDEEM COLLECTOR CLUB PIECES THROUGH US | WRITE FOR OUR CURRENT COMPUTER PRINTOUT OF 1000 ITEMS | COLLECTORS OVER 30 YEARS SHOWS & MAIL ORDER |

P.O. BOX 161083
MIAMI, FLORIDA
33116
(IF SHIPPING, CALL FIRST)

1-800-DOU-LTON
1-800-386-5866
IN FLA.: 305-251-1988
FAX: 305-254-5977

ROYAL FIGURINE EXCHANGE

QUALITY, SERVICE & SATISFACTION GUARANTEED

ROYAL DOULTON & BESWICK SPECIALIST

- ANIMALS & BIRDS
- BEATRIX POTTER
- BUNNYKINS FIGURINES
- BUNNYKINS TABLEWARE
- DISNEY CHARACTERS
- FIGURINES & JUGS

(OTHER MAKES AVAILABLE & IN STOCK)

WHEN YOU ARE LOOKING TO —

BUY: ASK ABOUT OUR "FREE" SEARCH N' FIND SERVICE

INSURE: RECEIVE A DETAILED WRITTEN APPRAISAL

REPLACE: UTILIZE OUR UNIQUE PERSONALIZED INSURANCE CLAIM SETTLEMENT PACKAGE

SELL: WE ALWAYS OFFER THE BEST PRICE FOR ENTIRE COLLECTIONS OR SINGLE PIECES

(PURCHASE INSPECT & PACK IN YOUR HOME)

TRADE: YES!!! WE EXCHANGE PIECES

"WE WANT TO WORK FOR YOU"

ROYAL FIGURINE EXCHANGE

95 LAMB AVENUE
TORONTO, ON M4J 4M5

CALL OR FAX (416) 690-1999,
IF BUSY CALL 778-5330

VISA ACCEPTED

❦RITCHIE'S❦
AUCTIONEERS & APPRAISERS
OF ANTIQUES & FINE ART

Canada's Largest Doulton Auction House

RITCHIE'S holds annual Doulton auctions to coincide with Toronto's Fall **Canadian Doulton & Beswick Collectors Fair** and Kitchener's Spring **Canadian Art & Collectible Show & Sale.**

Fall Doulton Auction
Thursday, September 5, 1996

Spring Doulton Auction
Thursday, May 1, 1997

* Each auction offers an extensive selection of discontinued and current Figurines, Character Jugs, Tobies, Seriesware and Art Pottery.

* Catalogues available mid August and mid April, $7.50 (includes GST and PST).

Consignments for our Doulton, Decorative and Fine Art auctions are welcome year-round.

For more information or to be placed on our mailing list please contact us.

288 King Street East, Toronto, Ontario, Canada M5A 1K4
(416) 364-1864 Fax (416) 364-0704
or toll free 1-800-364-3210